S0-BXN-152

ENCYCLOPEDIA OF LIBRARY AND INFORMATION SCIENCE

VOLUME 36

ADVISORY BOARD

ENCYCLOPEDIA OF LIBRARY AND INFORMATION SCIENCE

Executive Editor

ALLEN KENT

SCHOOL OF LIBRARY AND INFORMATION SCIENCE
UNIVERSITY OF PITTSBURGH
PITTSBURGH, PENNSYLVANIA

VOLUME 36

SUPPLEMENT 1

MARCEL DEKKER, INC., New York • Basel

MARCEL DEKKER, INC.
270 Madison Avenue, New York, New York 10016

LIBRARY OF CONGRESS CATALOG CARD NUMBER 68-31232

ISBN 0-8247-2036-9

Current Printing (last digit):
10 9 8 7 6 5 4 3 2 1

PRINTED IN THE UNITED STATES OF AMERICA

CONTENTS OF VOLUME 36

CONTRIBUTORS TO VOLUME 36

B. L. ANDERSON, Chief, Library Documentation Centre, National Library of Canada, Ottawa, Canada: *Canada, Libraries in, 1970-1979*

STEPHANIE C. ARDITO, Project Director, Gerontological Information Program, Syracuse University, Syracuse, New York: *Gerontological Information*

DALE B. BAKER, Director, Chemical Abstracts Service, Columbus, Ohio: *Chemical Abstracts Service*

RAY BOYLAN, Assistant Director, The Center for Research Libraries, Chicago, Illinois: *The Center for Research Libraries*

FRANK KURT CYLKE, Director, National Library Service for the Blind and Physically Handicapped, The Library of Congress, Washington, D.C.: *Bray, Robert S.*

RON COPLEN, Librarian, Harcourt, Brace, Jovanovich, New York, New York: *Publishing Division, Special Libraries Association*

MARTA L. DOSA, Professor, School of Information Studies, Syracuse University, Syracuse, New York: *Gerontological Information*

ROBERT W. FRASE, Executive Director, American National Standards Committee Z39, U.S. Department of Commerce, National Bureau of Standards, Washington, D.C.: *National Commission on New Technological Uses of Copyrighted Works (CONTU)*

CLARA O. JACKSON, Associate Professor, School of Library Science, Kent State University, Kent, Ohio: *Jackson, Sidney Louis*

DAVID KASER, Professor, School of Library and Information Science, Bloomington, Indiana: *Dix, William Shepherd*

FRANZ GEORG MAIER, Director, Swiss National Library, Bern, Switzerland: *Switzerland, Libraries in*

JAMES M. MATARAZZO, Ph.D., Assistant Dean for Student Affairs, School of Library Science, Simmons College, Boston, Massachusetts: *McKenna, F. E.*

JOHN A. MCCROSSAN, Ph.D., Chairperson, Library, Media, and Information Studies, University of South Florida, Tampa, Florida: *Public Library Systems*

ROBERT C. MILLER, Director of Libraries, University of Notre Dame, Notre Dame, Indiana: *Notre Dame. University of Notre Dame Libraries*

LEILA MORAN, Leader, Special Services and Products, National Agricultural Library, U.S. Department of Agriculture, Beltsville, Maryland: *Agricultural Bibliography*

ROBERT B. RIDINGER, Sociology Cluster, Founder Memorial Library, Northern Illinois University, DeKalb, Illinois: *Lesotho, Libraries in*

CONCORDIA SANCHEZ, (Deceased), Ph.D., Director of Libraries, Centro Escolar University, Manila, Philipines: *The Phillipines, Libraries in*

JEFFREY T. SCHWEDES, Ph.D., Association of College and Research Libraries, Chicago, Illinois: *Association of College and Research Libraries*

J. E. SCRIVENER, University Librarian, University of Tasmania, Hobart, Australia: *Australia, Libraries in*

THE STAFF OF THE BRITISH LIBRARY, The British Library, London, England: *The British Library*

DIMITRI R. STEIN, The Gmelin Institute, United States Office, Larchmont, New York: *Pietsch, Erich*

ROY B. STOKES, Director, School of Librarianship, The University of British Columbia, Vancouver, Canada: *Historical Bibliography*

SATORU TAKEUCHI, Ph.D., 4-3-4-206, Tama-shi, Tokyo 192-02, Japan: *Japan, Education for Library and Information Science In*

MARIA A. GARGOTTA TANNENBAUM, Ph.D., 401 East 89th Street, New York, New York: *Italian Bibliography*

GEORGE K. THOMPSON, Special Advisor on Scientific and Technical Information Systems, International Labor Office, Geneva, Switzerland: *International Labor Organization*

LAWRENCE S. THOMPSON, Ph.D., Professor, Department of Classical Languages and Literature, University of Kentucky, Lexington, Kentucky: *Aristophanes of Byzantium; Callimachus; Ebert, Friedrich Adolf; Leibniz, Gottfried Wilhelm; Moslem Libraries (Medieval); Renaissance Libraries*

JULIE A. C. VIRGO, Ph.D., Executive Secretary, Association of College and Research Libraries, Chicago, Illinois: *Association of College and Research Libraries*

HENSLEY C. WOODBRIDGE, Department of Foreign Languages, Southern Illinois University, Carbondale, Illinois: *Latin American National Bibliography; United States and Canadian National Bibliography: Foreign Languages*

PREFACE

We have now completed the production of the ENCYCLOPEDIA OF LIBRARY AND INFORMATION SCIENCE, in 35 volumes, a project that was initiated eighteen years ago in 1965, with the first volume published in 1968.

But the field covered by the ENCYCLOPEDIA is constantly changing, and we find that some articles desperately need to be updated. Some topics have become important which were not even known twenty years ago. Also, following our editorial policy of publishing biographies of prominent figures of the field who are deceased, time has passed and regretfully we must add some at this time. Finally, the alphabetic arrangement of the ENCYCLOPEDIA forced us to omit several topics when authors were hopelessly delinquent and the alphabet and publication scheduled passed them by.

We discussed seriously whether a new edition of the entire ENCYCLOPEDIA should be produced, but decided against it, since such a large proportion of the work still stands the test of time. Rather, we decided to "catch up" in supplemental volumes, starting with this 36th volume. Each volume will be arranged in a separate alphabet. Since the index (volumes 34-35) has just been published, there will be a table of contents in each succeeding volume.

And so we embark on the next phase, which will continue as long as the supplements are considered useful.

Allen Kent
July 1983

AGRICULTURAL BIBLIOGRAPHY

Agriculture is probably the oldest industrial occupation of man, beginning approximately 10,000 years ago with the systematic collection of wild plants for food. Narrowly defined, it is the systematic production of useful plants as food for human consumption. A broader interpretation acknowledges animal husbandry. Spinoffs or byproducts of man's use of plants for food have impacted on the development of fibers, medicine, dyes, and ornaments. As the science of "agriculture" developed, other scientific disciplines supporting research have come to be included in the definition of agriculture in its broadest sense: horticulture, textiles, botany, biology, chemistry, zoology, parasitology, nutrition, rural sociology, hydrology, and engineering. Agricultural research has been a potent factor in transforming human society from a primitive hand-to-mouth level into highly sophisticated civilizations. Research in agriculture and its related sciences has produced an enormous literature ranging from popular trade publications to scholarly scientific works, complex technical reports, and numerous periodicals and journals. The enormity of the literature subsequently created a need to control and provide access to it. In 1769 a country gentleman by the name of Richard Weston published *Tracts on Practical Agriculture and Gardening. In Which the Advantage of Imitating the Garden Culture in the Field is Fully Proved, by a Seven-Years Course of Experiments. Particularly Addressed to the Gentlemen Farmers in Great Britain. With Observations Made in a Late Tour Through Part of France, Flanders, and Holland. Also Several Useful Improvements in Stoves and Green-Houses. To Which is Added, a Complete Chronological Catalogue of English Authors on Agriculture, Gardening, etc. By a country gentleman* (Printed for S. Hooper, London, 1769). An alphabetical list of works running back to 1757 written and edited by members of the Real Società Economica di Firenze Ossia de' Georgofili was published in 1791: *Nota delle Opera Agrarie ed Economiche pubblicate dagli accademici prima della stampa degli Atti* (Atti R. Soc. Econ. Firenze Ossia de' Georgofili, Vol. 1, pp. 44–55, 1791). Bibliographic documentation picked up in the mid-19th century; Karl Ackermann published his *Repertorium der Landes kundlichen Litteratur für den preussischen Regierungsbezirk Kassel in Verein für Naturkunde zu Cassel: Bericht, 26th–31st, 1880–84.* Another early English bibliography, titled "Literature and Bibliography of Agriculture," was published in 1825 in London by John Claudius, in his *An Encyclopaedia of Agriculture; Comprising the Theory and Practice of the Valuation, Transfer, Laying Out, Improvement, and Mangement of Landed Property; and the Cultivation and Economy of the Animal and Vegetable Pro-*

ductions of Agriculture, Including All the Latest Improvements, a General History of Agriculture in all Countries; and a Statistical View of its Present State, With Suggestions for its Future Progress in the British Isles . . . (Longman, Hurst, Rees, Orme, Brown, and Green, London, 1825).

Braulro Anton Ramirez published in 1865 *Diccionario de bibliografia agronomica y de toda clase de escrutes relacionados con la agricultura; Seguido de un indice de autores y traductores, con algunos apuntes biograficos . . .* (Impr. y estereot. de M. Rivadeneyra, Madrid, 1865). The Imperatorskoe Vol'noe Ekonomicheskoe Obshchestvo in Saint Petersburg issued, also in 1865, the *Alfabitno-sistematicheskii katalog biblioteki imperatorskogo bol'nago ekonomicheskago obshchestva 1865* (Tip. R. Golike, Saint Petersburg, 1865), in which each section of Russian works is followed by a section of foreign works in three groups: (*a*) French, Spanish, Italian, and Latin; (*b*) English, Dutch, and Swedish; (*c*) German. By 1869 the U.S. Department of Agriculture had come out with "American Works on Agriculture and Rural Economy," published in its *Report* (Washington, D.C., 1869, pp. 597–607).

Bibliographic efforts have intensified and bibliographic documentation has kept pace with publication of the literature. A selective guide to agricultural and biological reference works was published by J. Richard Blanchard and Harald Ostvold in 1958: *Literature of Agricultural Research* (University of California Press, Berkeley, 1958, 231 pp.). This selective annotated bibliography of reference resources is useful for information on older works not included in Blanchard's later, very comprehensive *Guide to Sources for Agricultural and Biological Research* (University of California Press, Davis, 1981). Complementing the Blanchard work is *Information Sources in Agriculture and Food Sciences*, edited by C.P. Lilley (Butterworths, London, Boston, 1981). This is an evaluative work intended to guide librarians, information scientists, and subject specialists to the worldwide agricultural literature and information resources. Its bias is heavily British and European.

Among general guides to resources in scientific and other general fields supporting agricultural research are *Guide to Reference Books* (compiled by Eugene P. Sheehy, American Library Association, Chicago, 1976) and *Guide to Reference Material* (compiled by A. J. Walford, 3rd ed., The Library Association, London, 1973). While the Sheehy work is strong in the social sciences and humanities, the Walford bibliography is more thorough in its coverage of science, particularly agriculture. Identification of bibliographies is assisted by a type of work known as a bibliography of bibliographies. In this category are placed such titles as: *Agriculture: A Bibliography of Bibliographies* (compiled by Theodore Besterman, Rowman and Littlefield, Totowa, N.J., 1971; compiled by the publisher from the 4th ed. of the author's *A World Bibliography of Bibliographies*); *Survey of Abstracting Services and Current Bibliographical Tools in Agriculture, Fisheries, Nutrition, Veterinary Medicine and Related Subjects* (compiled by Sigmund von Frauendorfer, BLV Verlagsgesellschaft, Munich, [1979]); and "Agricultural Research Literature: A Bibliography of Selected Guides and Periodicals" (compiled by Anthony P. Harvey, *Agricultural Research Index*, Guernsey, British Isles, Vol. 2, pp. 957–1043, 1970). Another guide is *Internationales Handbuch der Bibliographien des Landbaues/World Bibliography of Agricultural Bibliographies* (Bayerischer Landwirtschaftsverlag, Munich, 1957). A classified listing of nonserial bibliographies can be found in *Internationale Bibliographie der Fachbibliographen für Technik, Wissenschaft und Wirtschaft: Ausgabe A: International Bibliography of Bibliographies in Techniques, Science and Economics* (9th ed., Verlag Dokumentation, Munchen-Pullach, 1969). A bibliographic guide to bibliographies of Russian agricultural literature is available in *Bibliograficheskie ukazateli sel'skokhoziaistvennoi' literatury, 1783–1954, gogy* (compiled by Nikolai Mikhailovich Mikheev, Sel'khozgiz, Moscow, 1956). The Landbouwhogeschool, in Wageningen, the Netherlands, has compiled its *Bibliography of Agricultural Bibliographies, 1961–1970* (Inter-Documentation Company, Zug, Switzerland, 1973).

Current Awareness Bibliographies

These tools, issued on a periodic continuing basis, serve to alert the researcher about new publications. They are generally omnivorous in coverage and nonevaluative. A forerunner of today's current awareness tools, no longer published, is *Agricultural Index: Subject Index to a Selected List of Agricultural Periodicals and Bulletins* (H. W. Wilson, New York, Vols. 1–49, 1919–1964). In 1964 this index was retitled *Biological & Agricultural Index* (Vol. 50, No. 1–, October 1964–). A monthly alerting service prepared by the National Agricultural Library is the *Bibliography of Agriculture* (Vol. 1–, 1941–). A nontraditional format is employed by the Institute for Scientific Documentation (Philadelphia) in its *Current Contents: Agriculture, Biology & Environmental Science* (Vol. 4, No. 1–, January 3, 1973–; formerly *Current Contents: Agricultural, Food and Veterinary Sciences*), which reproduces title pages of significant journals in these fields. International alerting services include *FAO Documentation: Current Bibliography* (Food and Agriculture Organization of the United Nations, Documentation Center, Rome, January 1972–), which continues *FAO Documentation: Current Index* and *Inter-American Center of Documentation and Agricultural Information: Bibliografias* (Inter-American Institute of Agricultural Sciences, Turrialba, Costa Rica, No. 1–, 1970–).

Library Catalogs and Lists of Agricultural Library Reference Collections

Printed lists of specialized library collections are an invaluable guide to resources for the scientific investigator and writer; the *Dictionary Catalog of the National Agricultural Library, 1862–1965* (Rowman and Littlefield, New York, 1967–1970, 73 vols.) is probably the largest single index to a worldwide collection of monographic literature dealing with agriculture and related subjects in numerous languages, reproducing, as it does, the author, title, and subject entries in the retrospective card catalogs of the library. The *Dictionary Catalog* is supplemented by the *National Agricultural Library Catalog* (1966–) and updated monthly with annual and quinquennial cumulations; a two-volume index for the period 1971–1975 is also available. Representative examples of other printed catalogs in specific or allied agricultural subject fields are: (*a*) the *Dictionary Catalog of the Giannini Foundation of Agricultural Economics Library, University of California, Berkeley* (G. K. Hall, Boston, 1971, 12 vols.), which covers economic aspects of agricultural labor; land utilization, valuation, and tenure; costs of production, marketing, and transportation of agricultural products; water resources, including water supply, water quality, and desalination of salt water; farm management, agricultural credit, finance, insurance, and taxation; cooperation; rural poverty, population, organizations, and institutions; prices and cost of living; food supply; recreation; conservation of natural resources, including marine and estuarine; and food supply problems of developing nations; (*b*) the *Catalogue of the Library of the Arnold Arboretum of Harvard University* (Cosmos Press, Cambridge, Mass., 1914–1933, 3 vols.), which focuses on books relating to dendrology, general descriptive botany, the cultivation of trees, and the works of travelers in which appear descriptions of trees and of general features of vegetation; (*c*) the *Author Catalogue of the Royal Botanic Gardens Library, Kew, England* (G. K. Hall, Boston, 1974, 5 vols.), particularly rich in early botanical books and in works on plant taxonomy and distribution; (*d*) the *Dictionary Catalogue of the Yale Forestry Library, Henry S. Graves Memorial Library, Yale University* (G. K. Hall, Boston, 1962, 12 vols.), which presents an accumulation of references to forestry literature from the early 18th century up 1962; (*e*) *A Dictionary Catalogue of the Blacker–Wood Library of Zoology and Ornithology* (G. K. Hall, Boston, 1966, 9 vols.), which contains the bulk of the natural history holdings of the McGill University Library; (*f*) *Catalogue of the Library of the Museum of Comparative Zoology, Harvard University* (G. K. Hall, Boston, 1968, 8 vols.), distinguished for its rich holdings of older and often unique materials; and (*g*) the *Dictionary Catalog of the Water Resources Center Archives, University of California, Berkeley* (G. K. Hall, Boston, 1970, 5 vols., updated with supplements), relating to the engineering, economic, social, and legal aspects of water.

Corollary to the printed catalogs are lists of library reference collections, useful to the agricultural researcher as a guide to primary resources of information: *Agriculture and Biology: Selected Reference Sources in Mann Library* (compiled by Barbara Rose, Albert R. Mann Library, Cornell University Libraries, Ithaca, N.Y., 1970) represents a guide to reference publications in an academic library. *Catalogue of Current Bibliographies in the Reference Room of the Central Library of the Agricultural University* (Landbouwhogeschool Bibliotheek, Wageningen, the Netherlands, 1974) is representative of a substantive European library. Particularly useful for Latin American material is *Coleccion de referencia de la Biblioteca Comemorativa Orton* (Instituto Interamericano de Ciencias Agricolas, Turrialba, Costa Rica, 1967).

Periodicals Information Bulletins

A number of periodical publications of professional societies in the agricultural sciences publish lists of new books, book reviews, and recently published papers.

These are particularly valuable to the researcher and librarian seeking to keep informed of advances in specific agricultural disciplines. Some selected examples of such periodicals are: *Agricultural Meteorology, Agricultural History, Ceres, Economic Botany, Experimental Agriculture, Journal of Forestry, Nutrition Reviews*, and *Science*. Some general newsletter-type publications with information about newly published documents are *News Report*, published monthly by the National Academy of Science, Washington, D.C.; *NFAIS Newsletter*, issued bimonthly by the National Federation of Abstracting and Indexing Services; *Information Reports and Bibliographies*, a bimonthly issuance of Science Associated International; *Sci-tech News*, a quarterly publication of the Special Libraries Association; and *Library Journal*, a monthly publication devoted to a review of new books in many fields. In the agricultural field, the *Quarterly Bulletin of the International Association of Agricultural Librarians and Documentalists* contains book reviews, announcements of new publications, and bibliographies. The newsletter of the National Agricultural Library, U.S. Department of Agriculture—*Agricultural Libraries Information Notes*—includes information on selected new publications, bibliographies, and translations. This is by no means a complete list; each scientific discipline embraced by agriculture produces a variety of alerting mechanisms.

Subject Bibliographies

BIOLOGICAL SCIENCES

Bibliographies on natural history, botany, zoology, bacteriology, and entomology are included in this category. The bibliographic literature is extensive and various reference sources should be consulted, such as Blanchard's *Guide to Sources for Agricultural and Biological Research;* the AGRICOLA data files of the National Agricultural Library, U.S. Department of Agriculture; and Sheehy's *Guide to Reference Books*. Primary guides to the whole field of biological sciences are *Biological & Agricultural Index: A Cumulative Subject Index to Periodicals in the Fields of Biology, Agriculture, and Related Sciences* (H. W. Wilson, New York, Vol. 50–, 1964–) and *Biological Abstracts from the World's Biological Research Literature* (Biological Abstracts, Philadelphia, Vol. 1–, 1926–). Important papers in experimental biology, anatomy, biochemistry, pharmacology, immunology, experimental zoology, cytology, genetics, and animal behavior are covered in *International Abstracts of Biological Sciences* (Pergamon, London, Vol. 1–, 1954–).

An indispensable aid to retrospective literature on American natural history is *A Bibliography of American Natural History: The Pioneer Century, 1769–1865*, compiled by M. Meisel (Premier, Brooklyn, 1924–1929, 3 vols.). For botany, a useful guide to the literature can be found in *Botanical Bibliographies: A Guide to Bibliographic Materials Applicable to Botany*, compiled by Lloyd H. Swift (Burgess, Minneapolis, [1979], 804 pp.). The *Plant Science Catalog: Botany Subject Index*, compiled by the U.S. Department of Agriculture Library (G. K. Hall, Boston, 1958, 15 vols.), contains references as published in books and scientific materials from earliest times up to mid-1952, when the catalog was discontinued.

In addition to the Blacker–Wood Library catalog and the catalog of Harvard University's Library of the Museum of Comparative Zoology, the *Bibliographia Zoologica* (Sumptibus Concilii Bibliographici, Zurich, 1896–1934, 43 vols.) represents an international classed bibliography of zoology valuable for its references to the historic or retrospective literature. Another useful source is R. C. Smith's *Guide to the Literature of the Zoological Sciences* (6th ed., Burgess, Minneapolis, 1962). A very specialized index is the *Index-Catalogue of Medical and Veterinary Zoology* (U.S. Bureau of Animal Industry, Washington, D.C., 1932–1952, 18 parts in 7 vols.; Supplements, 1953–), which deals with the literature on cestodes, nematodes, trematodes, and thornheaded worms.

A number of abstracting journals and bibliographic guides are available in the field of economic entomology and pest control. The *Index to the Literature of American Economic Entomology* (Entomological Society of America, College Park, Md., 1905–1915 to 1959, 18 vols.) covers comprehensively the first half of the century for the United States, its territorial possessions, Canada, and Mexico.

PHYSICAL SCIENCES

Applications of the hard sciences to various aspects of agricultural investigation have created interdisciplinary materials and fields of investigation. These fields—agricultural chemistry, soils and fertilizers, agricultural engineering, meteorology—apply the principles of physical sciences to agriculture.

Chemistry is acknowledged as a basic science involving all aspects of human, animal, and plant life sciences. The basic tool for accessing the literature is, of course, *Chemical Abstracts* (American Chemical Society, Columbus, Ohio, Vol. 1–, 1907–). A number of excellent guides to the literature are available, such as *Literature of Chemical Technology* (American Chemical Society, Washington, D.C., 1968) and *A Guide to the Literature of Chemistry*, compiled by E. J. Crane, A. M. Patterson, and E. B. Marr (2nd ed., Wiley, New York, 1957). These and other guides are described in detail by Blanchard in *Guide to Sources for Agricultural and Biological Research*. Access to historical materials is available in Henry Carrington Bottom's *A Select Bibliography of Chemistry* (Smithsonian Institution, Washington, D.C., 1893–1904, 4 vols.) and Denis I. Duveen's *Bibliotheca Alchemica et Chemica: An Annotated Catalogue of Printed Books on Alchemy, Chemistry and Cognate Subjects . . .* (Weil, London, 1949). Bibliographic current awareness tools include *Chemical Titles* (Chemical Abstracts Service, Columbus, Ohio, Vol. 1–, 1960–) and *Current Abstracts of Chemistry and Index Chemicus* (Institute for Scientific Information, Philadelphia, 1960–).

The indexing and abstracting services for chemical literature are useful as a guide to the literature of soils and fertilizers, as is the *Bibliography of Agriculture*. The Commonwealth Agricultural Bureaux (England) have published numerous annotated bibliographies, as have agricultural societies and academic institutions. An authoritative listing is given in Blanchard's *Guide to Sources. . . .* Illustrative of the type of bibliographies produced in this field are *Fertilizers: Applications, Economics, and Production (a Bibliography with Abstracts)*, compiled by R. J. Brown (National Technical Information Service, Springfield, Va., 1977); and *An Anno-*

tated Bibliography of Memoirs and Papers on the Soils of the British Isles, compiled by B. T. Bunting (Geomorphological Abstracts, Department of Geography, London School of Economics, London, 1964), which contains over 1,000 references to the soils of the British Isles. Latin American countries are treated in *Bibliography on Soil and Related Sciences for Latin America* (Food and Agriculture Organization of the United Nations, Rome, 1966, World Soil Resources Report No. 25). Significant publications on tropical soils are listed in *Bibliography of Soils of the Tropics*, compiled by Arnold C. Orvedahl (Agency for International Development, Technical Assistance Branch, Office of Agriculture, Washington, D.C., 1975–1977, 2 vols., Agriculture Technology for Developing Countries: Technical Series Bulletin No. 17). Corollary subject fields are water resources and irrigation, each bibliographically well documented.

Agricultural engineering is another interdisciplinary science drawing upon principles of physical and engineering sciences, with a rich bibliographic literature. An important resource is Carl W. Hall's *Bibliography of Bibliographies on Agriculture and Related Subjects* (American Society of Agricultural Engineers, Saint Joseph, Mich., 1976, ASAE Publication Nos. 9–76). *Agricultural Engineering Abstracts* (Commonwealth Agricultural Bureaux, Farnham Royal, Slough, England, Vol. 1–, 1976–) and *Applied Science and Technology Index* (H. W. Wilson, New York, 1913–) provide a high level of coverage for the English-language literature. Other important indexes are *Bulletin bibliographique international du machinisme agricole* (Centre National d'Eudes et d'Experimentation du Machinisme Agricole, Antony, France, 1966–), *British Technology Index* (The Library Association, London, Vol. 1–, 1962–), *Engineering Index 1906–* (Engineering Index, Inc., New York, Vol. 1–, 1934–), and *Landwirtschaftliches Zentralblatt: Abt. I: Landtechnik* (Akademie–Verlag, Berlin, Vol. 1–, 1955/1956–). Among the significant bibliographies are *A Bibliography of Farm Building Research, 1945–1958* (Agricultural Research Council, London, 1959–1961, 7 vols.), with six supplements for the years 1962–1970; *Classed Subject Catalog of the Engineering Societies Library* (G. K. Hall, Boston, 1963, 12 vols.), with supplements; and *Energy for Agriculture: A Computerized Information Retrieval System* (7th ed., Agricultural Engineering Department, Michigan State University, East Lansing, 1979).

SOCIAL SCIENCES

Generally, the social sciences as applied to agriculture embrace agricultural economics and rural sociology. Social sciences is an inclusive category for disciplines which can be combined with agriculture but belong to neither the physical nor biological sciences, such as agricultural economics, agricultural geography, agricultural history, agricultural biography, agricultural legislation, land reform, agricultural development, rural sociology, and agricultural education. There is a wealth of bibliographies but no one overall guide to the whole complex field. Significant bibliographic resources, however, are to be found in *A London Bibliography of the Social Sciences . . .* (School of Economics and Political Science, London, 1931–1962), the *Public Affairs Information Service Bulletin* (Public Affairs Information Service, Inc., New York, Vol. 1–, 1915–), the *Social Sciences Citation Index*

(Institute for Scientific Information, Philadelphia, 1974–), *World Agricultural Economics and Rural Sociology Abstracts* (Commonwealth Bureau of Agricultural Economics, Oxford, Vol. 1–, 1958–), and *American Bibliography of Agricultural Economics* (prepared by the American Agricultural Economics Documentation Center in cooperation with the U.S. Department of Agriculture, Vols. 1–4, July 1971–November 1974). Current bibliographic data collected at the center are entered in the AGRICOLA system as a distinct subfile.

Selected bibliographies on aspects of agricultural economics are numerous; typical examples are *Latin American Agriculture: A Bibliography on Pioneer Settlement, Agricultural History and Economics, Rural Sociology and Population (Including Immigration and Foreign Minorities)*, and *Agricultural Cooperation and Credit, from the Holdings of the Widener Library, Harvard University* (Martin H. Sable, ed., University of Wisconsin–Milwaukee, Milwaukee, 1970, Latin American Center, Special Publication No. 1). The Council of Planning Librarians issues many bibliographies of agricultural significance in the social sciences field, as for example, *Agribusiness: An Introductory Bibliography* (Monticello, Ill., 1976).

A current series of bibliographies on agricultural labor is issued by the Michigan State University Center for Rural Manpower and Public Affairs. The Texas Agricultural Experiment Station's Department of Agricultural Economics and Sociology has issued two important bibliographies in its Departmental Information Report series: *Bibliography Relating to Agricultural Labor*, by David C. Ruesink and Bruce T. Batson, and *Bibliography Relating to Contemporary American Agricultural Labor*, a supplement compiled by Ruesink and Karen Mergart.

The literature of agricultural geography is covered in several general indexes and bibliographic guides, but of particular significance is *GEO Abstracts* (Geoabstracts Ltd., University of East Anglia, Norwich, England, 1966–), which lists published items in European languages.

General guides, indexes, and abstracts to the historical sciences should be consulted for references to agricultural history. A classified guide to the international agricultural history can be found in *Bibliographia Historiae Rerum Rusticarum Internationalis, 1960–61* (Edidit Museum Rerum Rusticarum Hungariae Budapestini, Magyar Mezogazdasagi Muzeum, Budapest, 1964–). Of interest to American scholars is Everett E. Edward's *A Bibliography of the History of Agriculture in the United States* (U.S. Department of Agriculture, Washington, D.C., 1930, Miscellaneous Publication No. 84). The Agricultural History Center, University of California–Davis is preparing a new comprehensive bibliography; each aspect of American agricultural history is to be published in a separate volume. A related work, compiled by John T. Schlebecker, is *Bibliography of Books and Pamphlets on the History of Agriculture in the United States, 1607–1967* (Clio Press, Santa Barbara, Calif., 1969). Irwin Weintraub directs attention to contributions of Blacks in *Black Agriculturists in the United States, 1865–1973: An Annotated Bibliography* (Pennsylvania State University Libraries, University Park, 1976, Bibliographic Series No. 7). There are also many excellent short bibliographies published in journals or issued separately, which should not be overlooked.

For bibliographic guidance to the literature on agricultural legislation, the general indexing and abstracting services—*Bibliography of Agriculture, Biological and Agricultural Index, AGRINDEX, World Agricultural Economics*, and *Rural Sociology Abstracts*—should be consulted. Additional resources may be found in the dictionary catalogs of two of the most prestigious U.S. law schools: *Dictionary Catalog of the Columbia University Law Library* (G. K. Hall, Boston, 1969, 28 vols. plus the first supplement covering 1967–1972) and *Annual Legal Bibliography: A Selected List of Books and Articles Received by the Harvard Law School Library* (Langdell Hall, Cambridge, Mass., Vol. 1–, 1961–).

The bibliographic literature on land reform is extensive. Not to be overlooked are such publications as *Bibliographie des Schrifttums über Agrarstruktur und Landeskultur (Verbesserung der Agrarstruktur) in der Bundesrepublik Deutschland, 1949–1970* (compiled by Hans-Gunther Rohte, Landschriften-Verlag, Berlin, [1971]), *Bibliography on Land Tenure* (compiled by J. Tchiersch, FAO Rural Institutions Division, Rome, 1972), *Reforma agraria y tenencia de la tierra: Catalog colectivo* (Centro Interamericano de Documentacion e Informacion Agricolas, Turrialba, Costa Rica, 1972, the center's Bibliografias No. 7), and *Land Administration: A Bibliography for Developing Countries* (compiled by H. W. West and O. H. Sawyer, University of Cambridge, Department of Land Economy, Cambridge, 1975). The Land Tenure Center Library at the University of Wisconsin has published a number of useful bibliographies, an example of which is *Bibliography: Agrarian Reform and Tenure, with Special Sections on Agricultural Finance, Taxation and Agriculture, Agricultural Statistics, and Bibliographical Sources* (The Library, Madison, 1964).

Many national governments and international organizations—Commonwealth Agricultural Bureaux, Agricultural Development Center, the Food and Agriculture Organization (FAO), Institute of Commonwealth Studies, the Great Britain Overseas Development Administration, the U.S. Agency for International Development, and the U.S. Library of Congress—have published numerous bibliographies dealing with agriculture and rural development. As a branch of the agricultural sciences, however, the range of studies covered (physical and human resources, government services, planning, policies, economics) precludes citing individual bibliographies beyond drawing the reader's attention to *Rural Development Abstracts* (Vol. 1–, 1978–) published by the Commonwealth Agricultural Bureaux.

Rural sociology as an academic discipline is often coupled with studies in the field of agricultural economics, and many of the abstracting, indexing, and bibliographic services in that discipline should be consulted. Independent bibliographic publication is prolific, but there are also specialized bibliographic series published by the Commonwealth Bureaux of Agricultural Economics, the Council of Planning Librarians, and FAO. Since its inception the U.S. Department of Agriculture has influenced and directed agricultural education through state and federal extension services. The literature can best be located through the indexing and abstracting services referred to throughout this article, which cover the broad field of agricultural research and studies. Attention should be directed to *Education Index* (H. W. Wilson, New York, 1929–) and *Rural Extension, Education and Training Abstracts* (Commonwealth Agricultural Bureaux, Farham Royal, Slough, England, 1978–). A useful selective bibliography for educators is *Agricultural Education in a Technical Society: An Annotated Bibliography of Resources* (compiled by Mary Ruth Brown et al., American Library Association, Chicago, 1973).

Survey of Bibliographic Work in the U.S. Department of Agriculture

RESOURCES OF THE NATIONAL AGRICULTURAL LIBRARY

Since 1862 the library of the U.S. Department of Agriculture (USDA) has made available bibliographic knowledge of world agricultural literature through a variety of publication formats: bulletins, accession lists, newsletters, and special lists. The bibliographic newsletter *Agricultural Library Notes* was issued from 1926 to 1942; it was superseded in July 1942 by the *Bibliography of Agriculture*. The *Bibliography* has been published continuously since 1942 and is basically an index to the journal literature acquired by the National Agricultural Library. In-depth subject coverage includes agricultural economics and rural sociology, agricultural products, animal industry, agricultural engineering and farm equipment, food and human nutrition, forestry, plant science, crop production, pest control, soils and fertilizers, botany, entomology, and chemistry in reference to agricultural production and products. The language coverage is worldwide, provided that a summary, abstract, or title is available in a language in which the indexers have expertise. Currently, the *Bibliography* is divided into ten sections: a main entry section, five main entry subsections, a geographic index, a corporate author index, a personal author index, and a subject index. CCM Information Corporation, a subsidiary of Macmillan Publishing Company, assumed publication with Volume 34, 1970, using computer-processing magnetic tapes supplied by the library and using several vocabulary control mechanisms. The resulting subject and author indexes provide access to the literature in considerably less time than required by traditional indexing practices. Publication was taken over in 1975, with Volume 39, by Oryx Press. At this juncture the contents were expanded, and various sections dropped by Macmillan were reinstated. Separate sections of USDA, FAO, Experiment Station, and Extension Service publications with full bibliographic data were added. The *Bibliography of Agriculture* today is a monthly index to the literature of agricultural and allied sciences, based upon indexing records in AGRICOLA (Agricultural On-Line Access), the computerized bibliographic data files of the National Agricultural Library. AGRICOLA is prepared by the National Agricultural Library, U.S. Department of Agriculture. It is a family of data bases, covering worldwide journal and monographic literature and U.S. government reports in agricultural and related subject fields, which contain bibliographic records from 4,000 serial titles. The coverage is from January 1970 to the present. Subfiles have been incorporated into AGRICOLA which increase accessibility to available documents:

1. AAEDC (American Agricultural Economics Documentation Center): Items are indexed in depth and abstracted cooperatively by USDA, the American Agricultural Economics Association, the Canadian Society for Agricultural Economics, and Agri-

culture Canada. This material is tagged with the letters AGE or AGC in the document locator section. There are more than 10,000 citations.

2. FNC (Food and Nutrition Education and Informational Materials Center): Items selected are indexed, abstracted, and entered into the AGRICOLA Master Tape as separate entities tagged FNC. The primary emphasis is on all aspects of volume feeding targeted to school food service personnel. The scope of the center is expanding to cover all aspects of foods and nutrition. Citations number over 15,000.
3. BRU: Brucellosis file, prepared by Emergency Programs Information Center, Animal Plant Health Inspection Service, USDA. Documents are bibliographically described and indexed in depth for the EPIC program. There are more than 2,000 citations.
4. ENV: Environmental Impact Statements of interest to agricultural researchers covering publications from 1977 on. Each statement is bibliographically described with in-depth indexing. Citations number over 525.

Beginning in January 1884 a list of "Accessions" to the department library was published in various issues of the U.S. Department of Agriculture's Bulletin Series. These lists contained both monographic and serial citations and were at first arranged alphabetically by entry. Later lists were arranged alphabetically under subjects. A new bibliographic publication—*Monthly Bulletin*, 1910–1913—included "Notes" of interest to agricultural librarians and a list of "Accessions" arranged alphabetically under 36 or more subject categories.

Agricultural Library Notes, issued monthly by the library, with the cooperation of the libraries of the land-grant colleges and the state Agricultural Experiment Stations, began publication in January 1926 as a means of communication between the agricultural librarians of the United States. Included in this newsletter were lists of new agricultural periodicals and "changed titles," and a "Selected List of Mimeographed Publications of the U.S. Department of Agriculture." In 1937 "Principal Library Accessions" were listed in the *Notes*. This publication ceased in 1942; a new monthly newsletter was reinstated in 1975 titled *Agricultural Libraries Information Notes*, which continues on an abbreviated scale the tradition of listing "New Serial Titles Received at NAL," "New Publications of Note," "New Bibliographies," and "Agricultural Translations."

As the National Agricultural Library completed its first century of service in 1962, a decision was made to publish the library's card catalog. This had been an unrealized ambition of previous librarians that only then became feasible with modern reproduction techniques and methods. The *Dictionary Catalog of the National Agricultural Library, 1862–1965* (Rowman and Littlefield, New York, 1967, 73 vols.) contains in one alphabetic sequence, author, title, and subject entries for monographs and serials; and subject entries for monographs, serials, and analytics as cataloged for the main collection of the National Agricultural Library and for its Bee Culture and Beltsville Branches. At the end of the *Dictionary Catalog* is a list of translations of foreign journal articles in the library collection. The *Dictionary Catalog* is supplemented by the *National Agricultural Library Catalog, 1966–1970* (12 vols.), the *National Agricultural Library Catalog: Indexes 1971–1975* (2 vols.), and the monthly *National Agricultural Library Catalog* in which all books and new periodicals added to the National Agricultural Library during the previous month are listed.

The *Plant Science Catalog: Botany Subject Index*, compiled by the U.S. Department of Agriculture Library, has been described already. From 1965 to 1969 the library operated a special notification service, by means of the *Pesticides Documentation Bulletin*, as part of the department's expanding research in pesticides and pest control. The *Bulletin* was an index to the literature on pest control and included diseases, pests, and parasites of plants and animals; pest, parasite, and disease control; entomology, in general; biological states of plants and animals as they are affected by chemicals and biologicals; weeds; and residues of poisons wherever found.

Separate bibliographies on topics of current interest have been issued in such series as *Bibliographic Bulletin* (U.S. Department of Agriculture Library, Washington, D.C., 1943–1954) and *Library List* (U.S. National Agricultural Library, Washington, D.C., 1942–1978). Currently, separate bibliographies are published in a newly established departmental series: *Bibliographies and Literature of Agriculture*. This series provides a vehicle within the U.S. Department of Agriculture in which bibliographic information compiled by scientists, researchers, librarians, and other professional personnel from all USDA agencies can be published and made available to interested sections of the public on a national basis. An informal series, *Quick Bibliography Series* (U.S. National Agricultural Library, Beltsville, Md., 1977–), includes bibliographies resulting from automated literature searches in response to customer requests. They are selected for currency of topic and probable value to a large audience.

BIBLIOGRAPHIC ACTIVITIES OF OTHER USDA AGENCIES

Bibliographic activity is carried on in many U.S. Department of Agriculture agencies. The Office of Governmental and Public Affairs (variously, Office of Communications and Office of Information) has compiled various lists and indexes accessing reports, research materials, and technical documents as well as popular publications. The *List of Available Publications of the U.S. Department of Agriculture* (List 11) is issued irregularly every 2 to 3 years. The *Bimonthly List* is a current supplement with brief annotations for the most important titles. An author–subject index to all printed publications of the department—*Index to the Publications of the United States Department of Agriculture, 1901–1925*—was published in 1932; three supplements were issued, for 1926–1930, 1931–1935, and 1936–1940. Retrospective coverage was provided by *List of Titles of Publications of the United States Department of Agriculture from 1840 to June 1901, Inclusive*, published in 1902 by the Office of Information; supplements were issued in 1927, 1932, 1936, 1941, and 1945.

The U.S. Office of Experiment Stations published in 1924 the *List of Bulletins of the Agricultural Experiment Stations in the United States from Their Establishment to the End of 1920*, a useful guide to the agricultural literature of the period covered. These lists were limited primarily to the regular bulletin series of the state Experiment Stations and excluded circulars, annual reports, and ephemeral publications. The *Experimentation Station Record* (Vols. 1–95, 1889–1946) is primarily an abstract record of publication by American Agricultural Experiment Station and department scientists in nonofficial journals. Important foreign publications were also abstracted.

Numerous separate subject bibliographies have been compiled by USDA researchers and published in various departmental and agency series. Access to these may be gained through the *Monthly Catalog of the Superintendent of Documents*, the *Bibliography of Agriculture*, and other subject indexes. Bibliographic serial titles of importance are the *Index-Catalogue of Medical and Veterinary Zoology*, a basic catalog of authors published in 18 volumes in the period 1932–1952, which is kept up to date by supplements; *Agricultural Economics Bibliography* (Vols. 1–97, 1930–1942); and *Agricultural Economics Literature* (Vols. 1–16, 1927–1942).

International Agricultural Bibliographic Activity

Various foreign government agencies and international organizations are making substantial contributions toward the development of agricultural bibliography. The International Association of Agricultural Librarians and Documentalists, founded in 1955, seeks to promote national and international bibliographic documentation. Its *Quarterly Bulletin* contains book reviews and lists new monographic and serial publications.

The Commonwealth Agricultural Bureaux (CAB) publish numerous bibliographic, abstracting, and review publications in the agriculture, animal health, food science and technology, forestry, and nutrition fields. This organization is a cooperative venture established by the Commonwealth governments to provide information and other specialized services to people in agricultural and related fields. This information service is based on 24 abstract journals covering the whole range of the agricultural sciences. Current world literature in many languages is scanned. Since 1973 all references have been made available in machine-readable form. Typical CAB bibliographic products are *Animal Breeding Abstracts, Dairy Science Abstracts, Field Crop Abstracts, Forestry Abstracts, Herbage Abstracts, Horticultural Abstracts, Helminthological Abstracts* (*Series A* and *Series B*), *Index Veterinarius, Nutrition Abstracts and Reviews, Plant Breeding Abstracts, Review of Applied Entomology* (*Series A* and *Series B*), *Review of Medical & Veterinary Mycology, Review of Plant Pathology, Soils & Fertilizers, Veterinary Bulletin, Weed Abstracts, World Agricultural Economics* and *Rural Sociology Abstracts*.

Central government agencies in East European socialist countries and the U.S.S.R. provide agricultural and biological documentation services. Complete information about some of the East European services is difficult to obtain. In the Soviet Union, the All-Union Institute of Scientific and Technical Information publishes the *Referativnyi zhurnal* in 64 sections, most on a monthly basis, which cover comprehensively the world literature of science and technology, with the exception of clinical medicine. Titles of various sections of interest to agriculture are *Biologiia* [Biology], *Lesovedenie i lesovodstvo* [Forestry], *Pochvovedenie i agrokhimiia* [Soil Science and Agricultural Chemistry], *Rastenievodstvo* [Plant Growing and Breeding], *Zhivotnovodstvo i Veterinariia* [Animal Husbandry and Veterinary Medicine], *Traktory i sel'skokhoziaistvennye mashiny i orudiia* [Tractors and Farm

Machinery and Equipment], *Biologisheskaiia khimiia* [Biological Chemistry], and *Khimiia* [Chemistry].

The Food and Agriculture Organization of the United Nations is, as would be expected, a prolific publisher of agricultural documents. UNESCO also issues publications of agricultural and biological interest. Among the guides to documents of these international organizations are *Documents of International Organizations: A Bibliographic Handbook Covering the United Nations and Other Intergovermental Organisations*, compiled by Theodore D. Dimitrov (International University Publications, London, American Library Association, Chicago, 1973); *Publications of the United Nations System: A Reference Guide*, compiled by Harry M. M. Winton (Bowker, New York, 1972); and *International Bibliography, Information, Documentation* (Unipub, New York, Vol. 1–, 1973–, quarterly).

The Food and Agriculture Organization of the United Nations has assumed responsibility for the development of a worldwide system for the dissemination of agricultural information. A tangible demonstration of progress in this direction was the issuance in 1975 of *AGRINDEX*, an international index to world agricultural literature. This bibliography is a monthly computer-produced citation index to worldwide information in all areas of agriculture, including fisheries and forestry. Input is supplied by 92 participating countries. Entries are arranged alphabetically by author under subject categories and commodity codes. If original material cited is not available in a local library or from the contributing center which is indicated in the citation, it may be requested through interlibrary loan services from major agricultural libraries and documentation centers of the Worldwide Network of Agricultural Libraries (AGLINET) coordinated by FAO.

Awards

The Eunice Rockwood Oberly Memorial Award is, perhaps, the only public recognition offered for bibliographic efforts in the field of agriculture or related sciences in the United States. The award is administered by the Science and Technology Section, Association of College and Research Libraries of the American Library Association. Eunice Rockwood Oberly, whom the award honors, spent her professional career with the U.S. Department of Agriculture, serving successively with the Bureau of Animal Industry, the Division of Vegetable Physiology and Pathology, and the Bureau of Plant Industry. Her highly specialized contributions to bibliography were devoted almost entirely to phytopathological subjects. The Oberly Award has been presented in the odd-numbered years since 1925, with the exception of 1943 when it was omitted because of World War II and 1969 when a recipient was not selected.

LEILA MORAN

ARISTOPHANES OF BYZANTIUM

Aristophanes of Byzantium (ca. 257–ca. 180 B.C.) came to Alexandria in early youth. He studied under Callimachus, Eratosthenes, and possibly Zenodotus. He succeeded Eratosthenes as head of the Museion in 195 or 194. He may have retired before his death, and there is a vague rumor (from the *Suda*) that he was forcibly prevented from emigrating to Pergamon, presumably to be a senior scholar in the growing library of the Attalids. His pupil Aristarchus of Samothrace (ca. 217–145) was a successor, although the obscure Apollonius the Eidograph (ὁ εἰδογράφος) appears between Aristophanes and Aristarchus in the list of Alexandrian librarians recorded in Oxyrhyncus papyrus Number 1241.

Aristophanes was a man of great learning and scholarly acumen (sometimes clouded by subjective opinion), but only a few fragments of his original work survive. His editorial work was largely absorbed in that of his successors and thus obfuscated, but we know his major projects and something about his methods. His edition of Homer was probably an improvement on Zenodotus and Rhianus (b. ca. 275). He followed Zenodotus in many respects, but he also restored some with an ὄβελος which Zenodotus had completely omitted. His subjective judgments based on Alexandrian standards of propriety are a legacy of Zenodotus. Aristophanes also edited Hesiod, Alcman, Alcaeus, and Pindar, and it is likely that he produced definitive editions of Euripides and the comedies of Aristophanes. He may have been the source for the rather curious organization of 15 of Plato's dialogues into trilogies. His introductions to some of the plays of Aeschylus, Sophocles, and Euripides have survived in abbreviated form. His adjustments and supplements to Callimachus's *Pinakes* were likely based on solid critical and bibliographic studies. His literary interests approached his own time when he wrote a monograph on Menander. As a grammarian he produced Περὶ ἀναλογίας a polemic against the Περὶ ἀνωμαλίας of the Stoic Chrysippus, setting in motion a controversy that lasted into Quintilian's day and beyond.

Particularly important was Aristophanes' effort to create a system of accentuation and punctuation. He is credited with the acute, grave, and circumflex accents to protect the Greek language from corruption by the non-Hellenic elements who used Greek as a *lingua franca*. The hyphen, comma, colon, full stop, the mark of elision, and the short stroke to indicate division in a word are attributed to him. So too are the indications of quantity: ˘ for short, ¯ for long. For textual work he used the ὄβελος; also an asterisk (*) where sense is incomplete, or where meter is changed in poetry; the κεραύνιον (T) where several consecutive lines seem not to be authentic, instead of repeating the ὄβελος; and the reverse sigma, ἀντίσιγμα (Ɔ), to indicate tautology.

It would be hazardous to rank the Alexandrian librarians in terms of learning, achievement, or influence. While Aristophanes pulled together the best work of his predecessors and often made improvements, he also made substantial original contributions, possibly more than can be identified. It is likely that his tenure of 12 or 15 years was not surpassed in creative literary scholarship by any librarians of the Museion collection during the two and a half centuries of its existence.

BIBLIOGRAPHY

Busch, Wilhelm, *De bibliothecariis Alexandrinis dui feruntur primis*, Fock, Leipzig, 1884 (Rostock diss.).

Lehrs, Karl, *De Aristarchi studiis Homericis*, 3rd ed., Apud S. Hirzelium, Lipsiae, 1882.

Nauck, August, ed., *Aristophanis Byzantini Alexandrini fragmenta*, Collegit et disposuit Augustus Nauck, Accedit R. Schmidtii Comm. de Callistrato Aristophaneo, Sumptibus Lipperti et Schmidtii, Halis, 1848.

Parsons, Edward Alexander, *The Alexandrian Library, Glory of the Hellenic World: Its Rise, Antiquities, and Destructions*, Elsevier, Amsterdam, London, New York, 1952.
As its florid title suggests, this work is to be used with caution, but it does contain suggestive leads for the judicious scholar. It is not a work to be used by a beginner in the fields of library history or classical studies.

Sandys, Sir John Edwin, *A History of Classical Scholarship*, 3rd ed., 1920; Reprinted, Hafner, New York, 1958, Vol. 1, pp. 126–131.

LAWRENCE S. THOMPSON

ASSOCIATION OF COLLEGE AND RESEARCH LIBRARIES

The Association of College and Research Libraries (ACRL), the largest division of the American Library Association (ALA), is a national organization of academic and research libraries and librarians. In 1979 ACRL had 8,904 members. Approximately half of these members worked in university and research libraries, one-third in college libraries, and slightly under one-fifth in 2-year college libraries.

The goals of ACRL are to: (*a*) enhance the quality of service in academic libraries and further the progress of higher education, (*b*) promote the professional growth and career development of academic and research librarians, and (*c*) represent the interests and support the programs of academic and research libraries (*1*).

ACRL advances these goals by serving as a channel of communication among academic librarians and between academic librarians and the larger society. Imagine for a moment how crushing the burden on individual libraries and librarians would be if they were suddenly cut off from all communication with one another. Working in isolation, each institution would have to find its own solution to every problem. No librarian could benefit from the experience of any other librarian. The question of standards would not even arise.

It was to create regular avenues for communication among librarians that ACRL and, indeed, the American Library Association itself were founded. ACRL maintains four principal channels for communication among academic librarians: meetings, committees, publications, and a central office.

Meetings

Since the late 19th century, conferences and meetings of professional groups have been an American institution. They reflect our penchant for association and our passion for professional self-improvement.

In 1853 American librarians held their first convention in New York City. About one-fifth of the 81 librarians who attended the meeting were college librarians (*2*). Not until a generation had passed, however, and the crisis surrounding the Civil War was over, did American librarians hold a second national meeting. Finally, in the spring of 1876, Melvil Dewey and Frederick Leypoldt sent out their famous call for a conference of librarians to promote "efficiency and economy in library work" (*3*). Among the 103 librarians present when the conference convened in Philadelphia in September were about ten college librarians (*4*).

The focal point of the 1876 meeting was the reading of papers on practical library subjects such as cooperative cataloging, indexing, and public relations. The response to the program was apparently positive because the conference participants voted on the final day of the meeting to establish the American Library Association and to hold annual conferences (*5*).

The American Library Association was from the beginning predominantly a public library organization. But the areas of common interest between public and academic libraries are extensive, and for the first dozen years of the association's existence the college librarians attending ALA conferences did not hold separate meetings. Finally, in 1889, a group of 13 college librarians caucused at the annual conference in Saint Louis and recommended that a college library section be formed.

The following year, at the 1890 annual conference in the White Mountains of New Hampshire, 15 librarians representing most of the major colleges of the eastern seaboard—including Harvard, Yale, Columbia, the Massachusetts Institute of Technology, and Brown—held the first meeting of the College Library Section (*6*). The new section was a small, relatively informal discussion group attended for the most part by administrators who could afford long-distance travel. The annual meetings of the section provided a forum for the presentation and discussion of papers on such topics as reference work, cataloging, departmental collections, union lists, and the like (*7*).

In 1897 the section acquired a new name, the College and Reference Library Section (to recognize the participation of reference librarians), and began after the turn of the century to select officers to plan annual meetings. Not until 1923, however, did the section adopt its own bylaws and thereby cross the line that separates a discussion group from a section within ACRL today. The 1923 bylaws regularized the existence of the section by establishing a Board of Management with three officers to conduct the business of the section between conferences and by providing for the levying of annual membership dues of 50 cents (*8*).

In the course of the 1920s attendance at section meetings grew from 90 in 1923 to 240 in 1926 and peaked in 1928 at 800 before dropping off to 600 in 1929. The program meetings of the section during the '20s and '30s consisted of general sessions for the whole section and separate roundtables for college librarians and for reference librarians. The topics discussed at section meetings are familiar and suggest how persistent are the issues that academic libraries face: faculty status and personnel classification, teaching bibliography to students, interlibrary loan, library standards, etc. (*9*).

During its nearly five decades of existence from 1890 to 1938, the College and Reference Section served primarily as a forum for discussion. But, beginning in the 1920s, pressure began to build in the academic library profession for the creation of a stronger professional organization capable of pushing forward a broad range of activities, programs, research, and publications. The occasion for a radical restructuring of the section came in the mid-1930s when ALA roundtables representing teachers college librarians and junior college librarians expressed the desire to affiliate with the College and Reference Section.

In 1936 the chair of the section appointed the Committee on Reorganization to develop plans for restructuring the section. The final report of the committee in 1938 recommended the adoption of new bylaws that would transform the section into an "association of college and reference libraries" with "full autonomy" over its own affairs. The new bylaws provided for the creation of subsections within the association for college libraries, junior college libraries, teachers college libraries, university libraries, and other groups that might wish to affiliate.

The section approved the proposed bylaws in June 1938 and officially became the Association of College and Reference Libraries (ACRL) by the end of the year. The ALA Council responded by ratifying a new ALA constitution that made provision for the creation of self-governing divisions within ALA, entitled to receive a share of ALA dues. ACRL swiftly prepared a new constitution of its own that met the conditions for division status, and the ALA Council recognized ACRL as ALA's first division on May 31, 1940 (*10*).

The Association of College and Reference Libraries started its new life with six newly formed subsections of its own: the University Libraries Section, College Libraries Section, Junior College Libraries Section, Agricultural Libraries Section, Librarians of Teacher Training Institutions Section, and Reference Libraries Section.

In 1956 the Reference Libraries Section departed to join the newly formed Library Reference Services Division. As a result, ACRL substituted "Research" for "Reference" in its name and became the Association of College and Research Libraries (*11*). By 1979 the association had 13 sections: the three "types of libraries" sections plus the Art Section, Asian and African Section, Anthropology Section, Bibliographic Instruction Section, Education and Behavioral Sciences Section (into which the old Teachers Training Section had been incorporated), Law and Political Science Section, Rare Books and Manuscripts Section, Science and Technology Section (with which the Agricultural Section had been merged), Slavic and East European Section, and the Western European Specialists Section.

In the 1970s ACRL added a new type of grouping to its national organization—the discussion group. By 1979 ACRL had discussion groups for Cinema Librarians, Librarians of Library Science Collections, Personnel Officers of Research Libraries, Staff Development in Academic Research Libraries, Undergraduate Libraries, and Alternatives to the Card Catalog. The discussion groups are a reincarnation, in a sense, of the original College Library Section. They provide a relatively informal framework within which librarians with similar interests may gather to exchange ideas and information.

In 1951 ACRL took the first step toward encouraging participation at the local level by recognizing its first local chapter—the Philadelphia Area Chapter. ACRL now has 22 chapters covering 27 states and one Canadian province. The purpose of the chapters is to bring the national organization closer to individual members and to encourage programs beneficial to members at the local level. The national ACRL encourages chapter programs by contributing $1.50 to each chapter for every personal member of ACRL living within the geographic area served by the chapter.

ACRL, with its sections, chapters, and discussion groups, grew rapidly after its beginnings in 1938. ACRL membership jumped from 737 in 1939 to 2,215 in 1941, rose to 4,623 in 1950 (*12*), and stood at 8,904 in 1979. The association offered to its growing membership an ever-widening array of conference programs, preconferences, program meetings, institutes, workshops, and discussion sessions. In 1979, for example, three ACRL sections held preconferences before the ALA national conference. Nine ACRL sections and several section committees sponsored programs at the 1979 ALA annual conference in Dallas. And ACRL's discussion groups held meetings at both the midwinter conference and the annual conference in 1979.

The association as a whole sponsors program meetings for academic librarians at ALA conferences and frequently sponsors or cosponsors preconferences and institutes. In 1979, for example, ACRL cosponsored the Fourth International Conference on Approval Plans at Milwaukee, and in 1980 it sponsored three preconferences before the ALA conference in New York: one on Designing Staff Development Programs, a second for ERIC users, and a third on the Accreditation Process for Academic Libraries.

On its 40th birthday in 1978 ACRL took a giant step forward by convening its first national conference, distinct from ALA, in Boston. The conference featured a 3-day schedule of major addresses and research papers that attracted 2,625 participants. In follow-up surveys, participants rated the conference high for focusing on academic librarianship, for stimulating research on the issues facing academic librarianship, and for bringing together librarians with a common professional interest in academic libraries. Because of the favorable reaction to the conference, the ACRL Board voted in 1979 to hold national conferences of the association every second year.

Committees

As an addition to its traditional program meetings, the old College and Reference Libraries Section opened a second channel for communication among academic librarians around the turn of the 20th century by appointing special committees to coordinate studies and develop projects on special subjects. The early topics of committee inquiry are familiar to librarians today: professional status, library buildings, library statistics, library education, and library standards.

By midcentury ACRL committees were acting as a focus for investigation and action on a wide spectrum of issues facing academic libraries, including library cooperation, the relationship of libraries to academic institutions, library research, book selection, and, of course, academic status, professional education and development, library statistics, and library standards (*13*).

ACRL committees have played a leading role in advancing the cause of academic status for academic librarians. In 1971 the ACRL Committee on Academic Status drew up "Standards for Faculty Status for College and University Libraries." The ACRL Board approved the standards in June 1971, and as a corollary ACRL drafted with the American Association of Colleges (AAC) and the American Association of University Professors (AAUP) the "Joint Statement on Faculty Status of College and University Librarians." ACRL, AAC, AAUP, and a host of other associations endorsed the statement, which laid down a clear definition of the obligations and benefits of academic status and established a benchmark against which to measure progress in achieving academic status.

In the field of professional development, ACRL's most important recent contribution was the Academic Library Internship for Administrators of Black College Libraries. In 1972 the ACRL Internship Committee drew up plans for an internship program for librarians of predominantly Black institutions. The Andrew W. Mellon Foundation agreed in December 1973 to underwrite the program with grants totaling $350,000. During the 4-year period of the program (from 1974 to 1978) 25 librarians from predominantly Black institutions of higher education served as management interns for periods of 3 to 9 months at nationally known academic libraries. The evaluation conducted at the end of the program suggests that the interns carried back to their home institutions a broad understanding of the management techniques and styles employed in large academic libraries.

ACRL's involvement in library statistics goes back to 1906 when James T. Gerould read a paper to the College and Reference Library Section on comparative statistics. Gerould himself started an annual compilation of "Statistics for Academic Libraries." Known in the 1920s as "Princeton Statistics," the compilation later became *ARL Statistics* (*14*).

In 1941 ACRL itself began to collect statistics for college and university libraries and continued to do so until the late 1950s when the service was discontinued in order to avoid duplicating the efforts of the National Center for Educational Statistics. In 1979, however, ACRL's University Library Section, citing the need for up-to-date comparative library statistics in a usable format, proposed that ACRL collect comparative statistics for the university libraries not covered by *ARL Statistics*. Accordingly, ACRL started a pilot project in 1979 to collect statistics for non-ARL libraries and to determine the feasibility of expanding the statistical survey to include college and community college libraries.

It is in the field of standards that ACRL committees have made some of their most important recent contributions to academic librarianship. In 1957 ACRL's Committee on Standards, after 2 years of work, produced the "first real set of 'Standards for College Libraries' to enjoy the consensual support of the profession" (*15*). Since then, ACRL committees have written the revised "Standards for College Libraries" (in 1975), "Evaluative Checklist for Reviewing a College Library Program" (based on the 1975 standards), "Standards for Junior College Libraries" (in 1960), "Guidelines for Two-Year College Learning Resources Programs" (which appeared in 1971 and superseded the 1960 standards), "Statement on Quantitative Standards for Two-Year Learning Resources Programs" (published in 1979 as a supplement to the 1971 guidelines), and "Standards for University Libraries" (produced in 1979 as a joint effort of ACRL and the Association of Research Libraries).

Publications

One of the most powerful motives that led to the establishment of ACRL in 1938 was the desire to stimulate research and publication in academic librarianship. ALA's first Activities Committee, a body appointed in the 1920s to review the activities and structures of ALA, reported in 1928 that the ALA publishing program had neglected scholarly and bibliographic publication, the areas of greatest interest to academic librarians. This neglect, said the committee's report, had been so extensive "as to threaten at times actual withdrawal of the College and Reference Section from A.L.A." (*16*).

A year after its creation in 1938 ACRL established an official journal called *College and Research Libraries* (*C&RL*). The first issue of the new quarterly publication appeared in December 1939. It was at one and the same time a professional journal and an outlet for research, an official organ of ACRL, and a vehicle for the exchange of news about libraries and librarians.

A. F. Kuhlman, the first editor of *College and Research Libraries*, believed that "the absence of a professional journal devoted specifically to the interests of college, university, and reference libraries . . . no doubt accounts to a large extent for the lack of a definitive literature dealing with these institutions" (*17*). Under a series of able editors from Kuhlman in the 1940s to Richard D. Johnson in the 1970s, *C&RL* established itself as a premier scholarly journal for the publication of empirical research in academic librarianship, and it has helped to build up a body of knowledge and intellectual technique for the academic library profession. In 1950 Arthur Hamlin, then ACRL's executive secretary, called *C&RL* "the principal jewel in the Association crown" (*18*).

The ACRL Board of Directors acted in 1951 to make *College and Research Libraries* a perquisite of membership and to send the journal to members without charge. This far-reaching decision made it possible for *C&RL* to play a key unifying role in the association and in the profession. In recognition of the growing quantity and quality of research and writing about academic librarianship, the association decided in 1956 to publish *C&RL* on a bimonthly rather than a quarterly basis. And in 1967, in order to allow the journal to concentrate on its role as a scholarly publication, ACRL took the step of separating the news and "people" sections from the journal and incorporated them into a separate monthly news publication. This new ACRL publication, *College and Research Libraries News*, has served since 1967 as the official newsletter of the association and as a clearinghouse for news about academic libraries and librarians.

To make available works of scholarship on academic librarianship that are too long for inclusion in *C&RL* journal, ACRL began the ACRL Monographs series in 1952. By 1979 the series had grown to 40 titles and had acquired a new name, ACRL Publications in Librarianship. The first volume in the series was Joe W. Kraus's *William Beer and the New Orleans Public Libraries, 1891–1927*. Recent titles include *Libraries for Teaching, Libraries for Research*, edited by Richard D. Johnson; and *Aspects of the Nineteenth-Century British and North American Book Trade*, edited by Richard G. Landon.

ACRL began publishing *Choice*, the monthly book selection journal for college libraries, in 1964. *Choice* lists and carries compact reviews of significant new books and publishes a regular feature on periodicals of interest to college libraries. It seeks to review and evaluate publications both for their place in the literature of the field and for their potential value to an undergraduate college library.

Choice serves to update *Books for College Libraries*, the retrospective list of books for college libraries that ALA first published in 1967 and brought out in a second edition in 1975. Published in Middletown, Connecticut, *Choice* in 1979 had a circulation of approximately 6,000, a budget of $600,000, and a staff of 21.

ACRL also issues ACRL Non-Print Media Publications, a series that includes audiocasettes, videocassettes, and slide–tape programs on such topics as library instruction, personnel management, instructional development, etc. In addition, ACRL prints and makes available a wide variety of guidelines, standards, instruction books, directions, and proceedings produced by ACRL committees and sections. And finally, there are newsletters of the ACRL chapters. All these publications contribute to the ACRL mission of fostering communication among librarians.

Headquarters Office

ACRL and its network of sections and committees grew so rapidly after 1938 that by the end of World War II the association could no longer, as A. F. Kuhlman put it, "be expected to run of its own accord" (*19*). The elected leaders of ACRL were convinced that it was now essential to have a professional executive secretary, working under the direction of the president and Board of Directors, to integrate the activities and services of the association.

As early as 1931 the ALA Council, recognizing that the interests of academic libraries had not always received adequate attention at ALA headquarters, authorized the appointment of the College Library Advisory Board (CLAB) to advise the

ALA Board of Directors on academic library questions. One of the first recommendations of CLAB was that a full-time academic library specialist be employed at ALA headquarters to provide information and advisory services for college librarians. The ALA Council approved this recommendation for a college library specialist in principle, but throughout the rest of the 1930s and the war period, ALA never found the money to fill the position (*20*).

The issue came to a head in 1946 when ACRL, with its growing membership and pressing need for professional staff, made clear that it would seriously consider withdrawal from ALA if the question of funds for a paid executive was not resolved satisfactorily. ALA responded within the year by appropriating funds to finance an ACRL headquarters staff (*21*).

Orwin Rush, the librarian of Clark University, came to ALA headquarters in the spring of 1947 as ACRL's first executive secretary. After launching the new ACRL office and clearing the way for its future, Rush departed for the University of Wyoming in 1949. In his place came Arthur Hamlin, fresh from the University of Pennsylvania. Hamlin described the ACRL office in the early '50s this way: "Physically, the ACRL headquarters office is a second-floor front room, complete with fireplace, in the large, old-fashioned, reconverted mansion which is ALA headquarters at 50 East Huron Street in Chicago. Here an active staff of four, the executive secretary, the publications officer, a secretary and a clerk-typist, with their typewriters, telephones, file cabinets, and visitors hold forth. Like many a library staff area, ACRL headquarters is a noisy, crowded, active place" (*22*).

Although a modern headquarters building replaced the old mansion in 1961, the ACRL office remains still, at the beginning of the 1980s, "a noisy, crowded, active place." The executive secretary oversees a busy staff of six: three program officers, an administrative assistant, an administrative secretary, and a secretary.

It is the responsibility of the executive secretary and the ACRL staff to coordinate the work of ACRL's 22 committees, 13 sections, 81 section committees, 6 discussion groups, 5 editorial boards, and 22 chapters. To make certain this complex structure operates smoothly, the headquarters office keeps a close eye on the myriad details of elections and appointments, meeting times and places, minutes, committee reports, budgets, and so on.

The ACRL office works closely with committees and sections to plan stimulating meetings at ALA conferences, and it carries a large share of the burden for making the arrangements for ACRL preconferences and national conferences. Planning for these conferences begins years in advance; detailed arrangements must be worked out for hotel space, meeting times, exhibits, programs, publicity, and finances.

The ACRL office supports ACRL's publication program by providing assistance to the editors of *College and Research Libraries*, Publications in Librarianship, and Nonprint Media Publications; by working closely with the editor of *Choice*, who reports to the executive secretary; by publishing and distributing the many publications of ACRL committees and sections; and by editing *C&RL News*, the association's monthly news publication.

A key focus of ACRL headquarters activity is professional development for academic librarians. At the request of the ACRL Board the ACRL office initiated in

1980 a long-term effort to build a continuing-education program for ACRL members and to develop models for staff development in academic libraries. *C&RL News* contributes to the association's efforts in this area by publishing a regular column on continuing education and a monthly listing of continuing-education opportunities for librarians. The *News* also carries job listings every month, and as a spin-off from this, the ACRL office operates the Fast Job Listing Service which mails to subscribers special advance listings of the job notices that appear in *C&RL News*.

Finally, the ACRL headquarters office serves as a clearinghouse for information on academic library problems and issues. This role has several aspects. In the first place, the office must handle the questions that come in by mail or telephone. A large proportion of these inquiries seek information about what libraries are doing in a given area of policy or practice. In order to respond to these inquiries with reliable information, the ACRL office began a project in 1979 to survey a sample of 100 academic libraries four times a year about key areas of library policy and practice. The results of the ACRL surveys have helped the headquarters office keep the membership as a whole informed about how different libraries are handling common problems. The ACRL University Libraries Statistics project, mentioned earlier in this article, plays a similar role. This project, which is administered by the ACRL staff, helps the office to answer questions of a quantitative nature about academic libraries.

Second, the ACRL office acts as a clearinghouse for information on ALA activities and services. The office is in daily contact with the staff of other ALA divisions and offices, including the Washington office, and serves in a sense as an ambassador for academic libraries and librarians at ALA headquarters.

Third, the ACRL office, and especially the executive secretary, acts as the ambassador of the association to other library and information associations and to the world of higher education and government. The executive secretary attends meetings and gives talks in many parts of the country in the course of a year. In doing so, he or she constantly tries to open up the lines of communication in the academic library profession and between that profession and the larger society.

Conclusion

The Association of College and Research Libraries has grown from a small discussion group of college librarians to a large national organization with thousands of members and a network of committees, sections, discussion groups, and chapters. The purpose of the association from the beginning has been communication. The first medium of communication provided by the old College Libraries Section was the program meeting. The second was the special committee to investigate library problems. The third was a publications program that began in 1939 when the new association started publication of *College and Research Libraries*. And the fourth principal channel of communication provided by ACRL is its headquarters office.

All these avenues of communication have helped academic librarians to learn from one another, to advance the quality of academic library service, and to promote a better understanding of the role of libraries in academic institutions. Perhaps the single greatest accomplishment of ACRL, however, has been its contribution to the development among academic librarians of the sense of belonging to a worthy and learned profession.

REFERENCES

1. "ACRL Mission and Goals Revision," ACRL Board of Directors Minutes, 1979, Annual Meeting, Dallas, Texas, June 27, 1979.
2. Charles Edward Hale, "The Origin and Development of the Association of College and Research Libraries, 1889–1960," Unpublished doctoral dissertation, Graduate Library School, Indiana University, Bloomington, 1976, p. 12.
3. Dennis Thomison, *A History of the American Library Association, 1876–1972*, American Library Association, Chicago, 1978, p. 6.
4. Hale, Ref. *2*, p. 25.
5. Thomison, Ref. *3*, pp. 8, 9.
6. Hale, Ref. *2*, pp. 33–36.
7. Ref. *2*, pp. 36–37, 49, 52, 69.
8. Ref. *2*, pp. 40–42, 46–48, 66–68.
9. Ref. *2*, pp. 75–76, 82.
10. Ref. *2*, pp. 106–107, 109–112, 119, 121–124, 136–138; "Association of College and Reference Libraries: Report of the Committee on Reorganization," *ALA Bull.*, **32,** 810–815 (October 15, 1938); "Reorganization of the College and Reference Section," *ALA Bull.*, **31,** 591, 593–598 (September 1937).
11. Ref. *2*, pp. 190, 198–199, 235.
12. Ref. *2*, pp. 83, 179.
13. Ref. *2*, pp. 53, 170–173.
14. Ref. *2*, pp. 54–55.
15. David Kaser, "A Century of American Librarianship as Reflected in Its Literature," *College Research Lib.*, **37,** 116 (March 1937).
16. Thomison, Ref. *3*, p. 116.
17. A. F. Kuhlman, "Introducing 'College and Research Libraries'," *College Research Lib.*, **1,** 8 (December 1939).
18. Arthur T. Hamlin, "Annual Report of the ACRL Executive Secretary, 1949–1950," *College Research Lib.*, **11,** 272 (July 1950).
19. A. F. Kuhlman, "Can the Association of College and Reference Libraries Achieve Professional Status?" *College Research Lib.*, **7,** 151 (April 1946).
20. Hale, Ref. *2*, pp. 156–161.
21. Thomison, Ref. *3*, pp. 168–169.
22. *ACRL Organizational Manual,* Association of College and Reference Libraries, Chicago, 1956, pp. 10–11.

JULIE A. C. VIRGO
JEFFREY T. SCHWEDES

AUSTRALIA, LIBRARIES IN

Background

The development of a country's library system, in common with that of its other social and cultural institutions, is in a large measure molded by factors of geography, history, economics, government, and the structure and attitudes of its society. In long-established societies the influences of these factors are interwoven and overlaid, but in one as young as Australia—still to complete its second century—their effects are still evident. It is, therefore, helpful to an understanding of Australian library development to look first at the more significant of these determining factors.

Australia is an island continent with an area of just under 300,000 square miles (7,682,300 square kilometers). It is in the region of Southeast Asia—its immediate neighbors (excepting New Zealand) are Papua–New Guinea, Indonesia, and the Philippines—and lies between latitudes 10°41' and 43°39' south. Because of its location within the southeast trade winds belt and the presence of a highland chain close to the eastern coast, much of the continent is arid. By contrast, the coastal areas in the east, southeast, and southwest and the island of Tasmania are well watered, the latter three areas under the influence of the westerlies. These climatic factors have been a significant determinant of Australia's population distribution.

European habitation dates from 1788 when a British penal settlement was established on the site of present-day Sydney, and the eastern half of the continent, from longitude 135° east, was declared a Crown Colony under the name of New South Wales. Further settlements with predominantly convict populations followed: Hobart Town (1804) and Launceston (1806) in Tasmania (then Van Diemen's Land); Brisbane (1824) in what was later to become Queensland; Melbourne (1837) in Port Phillip District, later to become Victoria. Two "free settler" colonies were established in the same period: Perth (Western Australia) in 1829 and Adelaide (South Australia) in 1836. Transportation of convicts to the eastern colonies had ceased by 1852, but the free colony of Western Australia, because of difficulty in attracting sufficient labor, accepted convicts in 1850 and continued to receive them until 1868.

Throughout their foundation period the Australian colonies were directly ruled from Britain through colonial governors, but with increasing population and wealth came a clamor for self-government. The Australian Colonies Government Act of 1850 provided for each of the colonies to prepare a draft system of government which it would submit to the British Parliament for embodying into legislation. In this way New South Wales in 1855 and Victoria, Tasmania, and South Australia in 1856 became self-governing colonies. Queensland achieved this status in 1859 when it was separated from New South Wales. Western Australia, largely because of its late adoption of convictism, did not become self-governing until 1890. The newly independent colonies, isolated from one another by considerable distances and very conscious of their sovereign powers, each developed their legal, fiscal, and economic structures with little regard for those of the others. This separation was taken to the length of levying customs duty on the passage of goods between colonies and, with the development of rail transport, the adoption of three incompatible track gauges. However, as the colonies grew, the inconveniences of separate development became more obvious and common interests were perceived. This produced a movement toward federation during the 1880s and 1890s which culminated in the creation, in 1901, of the Commonwealth of Australia. Formal union did not, however, end state pride and rivalry, and the Federal Constitution left a large range of powers with the state parliaments.

Despite consciously preserved state differences, there has always been an underlying uniformity of social structures and attitudes. These were originally a direct transplant from Victorian England, and even after the political ties with the mother country were loosened, cultural and economic bonds remained close. Religion, education, law, commerce, and the professions all were patterned on British models and, in their essentials, continue to be to this day. However, since the Second World War three influences have modified at least the surface of Australian society. The first, in chronological order, has been the impact of American attitudes and methods which began with the inundation of U.S. servicemen during the Pacific war and has subsequently been strengthened by close diplomatic and military ties, penetration of the economy by American business ventures, and exposure through the media to American popular culture. The second influence has been that of the European migrants brought to the country in their hundreds of thousands as a matter of government policy. These immigrants came first from Eastern Europe, Germany, and the Netherlands; later they came from the Mediterranean region. Many, particularly of the latter group, have established discrete communities in the major cities, and they have become a significant social and cultural force. Their presence is inevitably making the once homogeneous Australian culture pluralistic. The third influence is Australian society's own growing perception of its identity as an independent nation, living in the ambit of Asia.

Though Australia is almost as large as the continental United States (including Alaska), its population is only around 14.4 million. It is, nevertheless, highly urbanized with 61% of its number living in the five major capital cities. Another six centers, with populations ranging from 141,000 to 380,000, account for a further 9% of the total (see Table 1).

TABLE 1

Populations of Major Centers (June 1979)

Sydney	3,193,000	Newcastle	380,000
Melbourne	2,740,000	Canberra	241,000
Brisbane	1,015,000	Wollongong	224,000
Adelaide	933,000	Hobart	168,000
Perth	884,000	Geelong	141,000
		Gold Coast concentration	143,000

With the exception of Perth in the southwest corner of the continent and Hobart in the island state Tasmania, all of these centers are situated in the east and southeast coastal fringe. The major centers are fairly widely scattered, air distances between them being: Brisbane to Sydney, 480 miles; Sydney to Melbourne, 460 miles; Melbourne to Adelaide, 410 miles; Adelaide to Perth, 1,380 miles. Most of the secondary centers are situated fairly near to one or other of the large capitals. Newcastle and Wollongong are, respectively, 90 miles north and 50 miles south of Sydney; Canberra, the national capital, is 155 miles south of Sydney and 205 miles north of Melbourne; Geelong is 40 miles southwest of Melbourne. Hobart is 390 air miles southeast of Melbourne. Outside the urban concentrations, population is rather thinly distributed.

Historical Survey

While the early Australian settlements consisted mainly of convicts and their keepers, there was little opportunity for the civilized amenities of society to develop. However, by the 1820s Sydney and Hobart Town had a growing number of free men—settlers and officials—who thought of these towns not as places of temporary exile but as their homes for the future, and who wished to establish in them the amenities they had enjoyed in their former homes. It is at this point that the history of Australian libraries begins.

In 1821 a group of the leading citizens of Sydney made a combined catalog of their private collections so that they could more easily borrow books from one another. Two years later these same citizens contributed funds to establish the Australian Subscription Library and Reading Room, from which, through various metamorphoses, eventually grew both the Public (now State) Library of New South Wales and the City of Sydney Public Library. Meanwhile in Hobart Town a reading and newspaper room existed in 1822, and in 1826 the Hobart Town Book Society was founded on a subscription basis. In 1834 the founding settlers of South Australia, prior to their departure from England, established the South Australian Literary Society for the purpose of forming a library collection which would be taken with them to their colony. That library, when eventually set up in Adelaide 3 years later, was operated on a subscription basis but was available for reference to nonsubscribers. After a history of financial difficulties it was eventually merged with the Adelaide Mechanics Institute in 1853 to form the government-subsidized South Australian Institute.

These early subscription libraries and others of their kind which flourished, often briefly, over the next half century were not "public" libraries in the accepted sense because their use was exclusive to those sufficiently affluent to pay the quite substantial (£2–£5) annual subscription rates. Their financial bases were never very sound, and some on occasion received government subsidies, usually in return for making their services available to a broader range of users.

An attempt was made to meet the presumed intellectual needs of the working class by the establishment of "mechanics institutes" and "schools of arts." Modeled on the British institutes originally established by George Birkbeck, these were centers provided by the conscientious middle classes for the education and moral improvement of working men, and they usually incorporated a collection of uplifting books. The first such was the Van Diemen's Land (or Hobart Town) Mechanics Institute, established in 1827. This was followed by the Sydney Mechanics School of Arts (1833), the Newcastle Mechanics Institute (1835), the South Australian Library and Mechanics Institute (1838), and the Melbourne Mechanics Institute (1839). The movement spread rapidly and by the turn of the century there were over 1,000, half of which had been established in the preceding two decades. Most had memberships ranging from 100 to 200 and possessed less than 1,000 books. After the 1850s, the original concept of the institutes as a means of moral uplift gradually declined, and they tended to become social and recreational centers. The associated libraries were given over to the provision of fiction at least as much as serious literature.

Following the establishment of self-government the colonial governments began to interest themselves in the provision of libraries. At first this tended to be limited to the granting of small subsidies in support of mechanics institutes, but, one after the other, the colonies established fully government-supported public libraries in their capital cities. The first such actually predated self-government: In 1853 the Legislative Council in Melbourne voted £13,000 for the establishment of a public library—£10,000 for a building and £3,000 for books—and appointed a board of trustees to run it. The Melbourne Public Library was opened in its new building on February 11, 1856. In 1869 the New South Wales government purchased the collection (and later, the building) of the Australian Library and Literary Institution (the name by which the Australian Subscription Library was then known), and reopened it as the Free Public Library of Sydney. The Tasmanian Public Library, which had previously existed precariously from 1849 to 1867 as a subscription library with some government assistance, was reopened in 1870 with financial endowments from both the colonial government and the Hobart Town Council. This dual funding continued until 1944 when the government assumed full responsibility and changed the name to the State Library of Tasmania. The government of South Australia, in 1884, established by statute a combined Public Library, Museum, and Art Gallery of South Australia. The South Australian Institute was largely absorbed into this body, its more valuable books being transferred to the Public Library while the lighter literature formed the basis of a separately created Adelaide Circulating Library. In Western Australia a commission, appointed in 1886 to advise the Legislative Council on the use of funds voted for the celebration of Queen Victoria's jubilee, recommended that £3,000 be used for the establishment of a free public library. The library was opened in January 1889 with the title Victoria Public Library, which was subsequently changed to Public Library of Western Australia in 1904. Queensland's library had a fitful start. In 1895 the colonial government purchased a private collection to form the nucleus of a public library; in 1896 a board of trustees was appointed and the proposed institution was named the Brisbane Public Library; 2 years later the name was changed to Public Library of Queensland, though the actual library did not become a reality until 1902.

Each of these libraries, when first established, was intended to provide a reference collection for the people of the capital city in which it was located. By the turn of the century three (Sydney, Melbourne, Hobart) had also established lending branches to provide home reading for their local populations, and all but Brisbane and Hobart had an arrangement for providing books to institutions in country centers. With the passage of time they assumed wider responsibilities and developed from city libraries to state libraries. This change in role was acknowledged in some name changes: The Melbourne Public Library was renamed the Public Library of Victoria, and the Free Public Library of Sydney became the Public Library of New South Wales in 1895. The renaming of the Brisbane and Perth libraries has already been noted, and those in Hobart and Adelaide carried the broader designation from their inception. As will be noted later, all eventually adopted the title of State Library.

From the late 1860s the colonial governments made sporadic attempts to stimulate the establishment of free municipal libraries along the lines of those set up in Britain at the time. The New South Wales Municipalities Act passed in 1867 provided for foundation grants of up to £200 to be made to any local government authority willing to establish a free library in its area. Several councils established libraries and received the grant, while others took over libraries of schools of arts and continued them as subscription libraries. Similar legislation was passed by Tasmania in 1867, Victoria in 1869, Queensland in 1878, South Australia in 1887, and Western Australia in 1906. These attempts were virtually foredoomed to failure because local governments did not then have an adequate financial base to maintain the libraries they were responsible for.

The second half of the 19th century saw three other significant steps in the development of Australian libraries: the establishment of parliamentary libraries, the founding of the first four universities, and the promulgation of copyright acts requiring library deposit. The parliamentary libraries, when first established, were in fact legislative council libraries. They became parliamentary libraries when colonial parliaments were set up following adoption of the Australian Colonies Government Act by each of the colonies.

The first legislature to establish a library was that of New South Wales, in 1843. It was followed by Victoria and Tasmania in 1851, South Australia in 1853, Queensland in 1860, and Western Australia in 1891. The primary purpose of these libraries was to provide a collection of reference works, including proceedings and statutes, for use of the legislators. Several, however, also collected literary and general works for members' recreational reading. New South Wales was, again, the first colony to found a university: The act which established the University of Sydney was passed in 1850 and the institution was inaugurated in 1852. Victoria followed with the University of Melbourne Act in 1853, an act of 1874 founded the University of Adelaide, and the University of Tasmania was established by an act of 1890. The founding acts usually provided for the establishment of a library, and the provision was implemented within 2 or 3 years except in the case of the University of Tasmania, which did not have an organized library until more than 20 years later. The copyright acts passed by the colonial Parliaments in this period all made provision for legal deposit in designated libraries of one copy of every work published in the colony. The first of these acts was passed by Victoria in 1869 and required deposit of publications with the Public Library. South Australia followed in 1878 and, as a government-supported library had not as yet been established, the deposit right was vested in the South Australian Institute. The New South Wales act, passed in 1879, vested deposit rights in both the Free Public Library and the University of Sydney Library. Queensland promulgated its copyright act in 1887, 15 years before it had a public library, and nominated the Parliamentary Library and the Museum as depository recipients; the right was not extended to the Public Library until 1949. Western Australia's act, of 1895, designated the institution then called the Victoria Public Library as the depository. Tasmania has never passed a copyright act, but the Library Act of 1943 requires deposit with the State Library. The granting of depository rights to the infant state libraries was an important step both in strengthening their collections and in securing substantially complete holdings of indigenous publications.

A final noteworthy development of the 19th century was the first tentative attempt to form an association of persons concerned with libraries. When the (British) Library Association was founded in 1877, Judge (later Sir Redmond) Barry, president of the Trustees of the Public Library of Victoria, led a small Australian delegation to the inaugural meeting. Barry not only delivered a paper but was also elected a senior vice-president of the new association. This episode, however, did not immediately inspire any emulative action in Australia and almost 20 years were to pass before an Intercolonial Library Conference was convened in Melbourne in 1896. The conference was arranged largely on the initiative of the Trustees of the Public Library of Victoria, and the delegates represented all colonies except Western Australia. Its main achievement was to form the Library Association of Australasia, which was intended to be a focal organization for librarians, library authorities, and interested laymen in Australia and New Zealand (New Zealand's participation proved to be only nominal). The association remained in existence only until 1902 but in its brief life it convened three conferences and, from April 1901 to June 1902, published a journal, *The Library Record of Australia*.

The first 30 years of the 20th century saw an extension and consolidation of initiatives begun in the preceding half century but few new developments. The one important advance was a byproduct of the great political event of the time—Federation. The Parliament of the Commonwealth of Australia was inaugurated on January 1, 1901, and within 4 weeks of its creation it set up a joint library committee to advise on the establishment of a parliamentary library. The committee envisaged a library modeled on the United States Library of Congress which would not only serve the legislature but also become a great library serving the nation. The Commonwealth Parliamentary Library formally came into existence in 1902 and was located, with the Federal Parliament, in Melbourne. The purchasing of materials began immediately, but for the next 25 years, while the library remained in Melbourne, it relied heavily on the resources of the Public Library and Parliamentary Library of that state. In 1909 it was considerably strengthened by the acquisition of a private collection consisting of 10,000 volumes of Australiana, and in 1912 the Commonwealth Copyright Act gave it the depository right to one copy of any book, pamphlet, or periodical published in Australia. The title Commonwealth National Library was given to the Australasian section in 1923 and was later adopted for the whole library. In 1926 the library was transferred to the new federal capital, Canberra.

The Public Libraries of New South Wales and Victoria had achieved preeminent positions among Australian libraries by the turn of the century and both continued to build their collections steadily. In 1910 the Public Library of New South Wales opened its Mitchell Library wing, built to house the remarkably extensive collection of Australiana offered by the collector, David Scott Mitchell, in 1898. A new building to house the Public Library of Victoria was opened in 1913, its centerpiece being an impressive domed octagonal reading room of a size comparable with that of the British Museum. Earlier the Tasmanian Public Library had been given a Carnegie Corporation grant of £7,000 for a new building which it occupied in 1907. The Public Library of South Australia established a children's department in 1915 and an archives section in 1920—each being the first of its kind in the country. In Brisbane the Oxley Memorial Library was founded in 1926 as an Australiana and Queenslandiana collection, and it was for many years the de facto state archives. Though administered by a separate board of trustees, it was housed in the Public Library from 1934 and was incorporated into it in 1946.

Though generally the attempts to develop municipal libraries had foundered, there were two notable exceptions. The Broken Hill (New South Wales) Council Library was opened in 1906, and the Sydney Municipal Library was established in 1909 when the Sydney City Council took over the lending branch of the Public Library. Both have survived as active libraries to the present, the latter now being known as the City of Sydney Public Library. Two further university libraries were established during this period, those of the University of Queensland (1911) and the University of Western Australia (1913). These completed the original group of state universities, and no further universities were founded until after the Second World War though two of the existing universities established undergraduate colleges in rural centers—Canberra University College (University of Melbourne) in 1929 and New England University College (University of Sydney) at Armidale (New South Wales) in 1938.

Toward the end of the 1920s the idea of a national library association was revived, and at a conference in Melbourne in 1928 the Australian Library Association was launched. The initiative came from the Institutes Association of South Australia, and (primarily for this reason) the new body was considered suspect in New South Wales where the continuance of institute libraries was seen as the major impediment to the establishment of government-supported free libraries. In the event, neither New South Wales nor Western Australia joined the association. Ironically, this institute-dominated body sponsored a move which was shortly to bring about its own demise and turn the course of library development firmly away from the institutes. A conference of the association held in 1933 supported a proposal to request the Carnegie Corporation of New York to undertake a survey of Australian libraries. The corporation agreed and nominated Ralph Munn, director of the Carnegie Library of Pittsburgh, to conduct the survey. E. R. Pitt, chief librarian of the Public Library of Victoria, was selected to assist Munn, and the survey was carried out in 1934.

The Munn–Pitt Report, published in 1935 by the Australian Council for Educational Research under the title *Australian Libraries: A Survey of Conditions and Suggestions for Their Improvement,* proved to be a watershed in the development of public libraries and significantly affected most other areas of library activity. It revealed that Australian library organization lagged behind that of most civilized countries, and it was particularly critical of the institute libraries, which were described as "cemeteries of old and forgotten books." The report's main recommendations were:

1. The strengthening and extension of the profession of librarianship with the establishment of a professional association and a system for training librarians
2. Encouragement of the Commonwealth National Library in its aims to act as a great depository library, collect historical records pertaining to Australia as a whole, and provide bibliographic services to all other libraries
3. The combining of the state reference library with a capital city lending library in states other than New South Wales
4. The establishment of rate-supported municipal free libraries outside of the capital cities, with the gradual conversion or elimination of institute libraries
5. The establishment, as a state responsibility, of district or regional library services covering small towns and rural areas

The report had an immediate impact on all who were concerned with library provision. Supporters of institute libraries were particularly offended, and the Australian Library Association, which had been a sponsor of the survey, felt itself unable to support implementation of the report. Thus demoralized, the association thereafter faded out of existence. On the other hand, the supporters of the free library concept and many others concerned about educational and cultural matters set about campaigning for implementation of the report's recommendations. In New South Wales the Free Library Movement was founded and this soon spread to other states. Two executive officers of the Australian Council for Educational Research who had been closely associated with the Munn–Pitt survey from its inception, together with the Commonwealth national librarian and the state librarians, formed a body called the Library Group. The objectives of this body were to work for implementation of the Munn–Pitt recommendations, to keep matters of library development before the public, to advise the Carnegie Corporation of developments, and to seek further support from the corporation. Grants were obtained to assist the Free Library Movement, to stimulate education in librarianship, and to help establish a new association of librarians.

In 1937 a third, and this time successful, attempt was made to found a national library association. John Wallace Metcalfe, then deputy librarian of the Public Library of New South Wales, was the prime mover in founding the Australian Institute of Librarians, which (unlike its predecessors) limited its membership to professional librarians and had as its main objective the raising of standards of librarianship. Branches were formed in all states and in the Australian Capital Territory, and all branches were represented at the institute's first conference in Sydney in 1938.

At the same time, attention was given to rectifying the lack of formal training facilities for librarians. Within the Public Library of New South Wales, J. W. Metcalfe conducted courses for school librarians from 1938 and in the following year offered a fuller program primarily for staff of local public libraries. In 1941 the courses were further developed and placed on a regular footing, thus establishing what was in fact a school of librarianship. The Commonwealth National Library began courses of instruction for its own staff in 1938 and established a training school in 1946. In 1941 the Australian Institute of Librarians set up its Board of Examination and Certification and conducted its first examination in June 1944. The institute's examinations soon became the accepted path to professional qualification, and the schools set up in libraries began to prepare candidates for these examinations. The Public Library of Victoria and the State Library of Tasmania both began offering courses on this basis in 1949.

At governmental level, the Munn–Pitt Report resulted in the passing of a series of Library Acts each of which established a State Library Board and made provision for free public library services supported by local government bodies with a state government subsidy. The New South Wales Library Act was passed in 1939 though not fully implemented until 1944. Tasmania and Queensland both passed Library Acts in 1943. Victoria's Free Library Service Board Act was passed in 1946; and West Australia's Library Board of Western Australia Act, in 1951. South Australia, in 1939, passed the Libraries and Institutes Act setting up the Libraries Board of South Australia, which was charged with control of the Public Library. However, state subsidy to local government libraries did not come until the Libraries (Subsidies) Act of 1955, and it was not required that these libraries should be free.

The outbreak of the Second World War, with the attendant diversion of national attention and priorities to war effort, undoubtedly retarded the impetus toward reform which the Munn–Pitt Report had generated. That so much was achieved under the adverse circumstances of the 1940s indicates the extent to which the need for reform was felt. Soon after the war the Commonwealth government, with financial assistance from the British Council, brought Lionel McColvin, city librarian of Westminster, to Australia to conduct a further survey of public library provisions. This survey, the report of which was published in 1947, was more limited than its predecessor. McColvin agreed with most of the Munn–Pitt recommendations and reemphasized the inadequacies noted in that report and in the publications of the Free Library Movement. He was critical, however, of the policy of gradualism in replacing the institute libraries with free public libraries and considered that much more should have been achieved during the preceding 12 years.

The decade following the war was relatively inactive. Apart from library legislation already noted, the main new developments were in university libraries. Two new universities were established during this period—the Australian National University (Canberra) in 1948 and the New South Wales University of Technology (later the University of New South Wales) in 1949. Both immediately set about creating their libraries. In 1951 the University of Technology established the Newcastle University College, which was to become the University of Newcastle in 1965. The New England University College became the University of New England in 1954, its Dixson Library being already well established if small.

The most important single event of the period, however, was the reconstitution in 1949 of the Australian Institute of Librarians to form the Library Association of Australia. The principal feature of the reconstitution was that membership was broadened to include library authorities and interested lay persons. This move has subsequently been seen by some as a retrograde step but was seen at the time as necessary to ensure continued promotion of the movement for library development, which had ceased to have a focal point with the winding down of the Free Library Movement consequent on the creation of the Library Boards. In other aspects the association explicitly continued the functions and policies of the institute. The association received a further grant from the Carnegie Corporation in 1951 to assist with administrative costs until it became self-supporting, and membership grew rapidly as it engaged in a wider sphere of activities. In 1956 it was decided that the status and authority of the association would be strengthened by incorporation under a royal charter and negotiations to this end were commenced.

More significant than the actual events of the postwar decade was the emerging awareness of the interdependence of libraries, irrespective of type or location, and the need for cooperative development. This awareness led, in 1956, to the establishment of the Australian Advisory Council on Bibliographical Services (AACOBS). As a prelude to that move there had been three conferences of Commonwealth and State Library Authorities, in 1949, 1953, and 1955. These conferences were primarily concerned with library resources and national planning, and the 1953 conference set up a working party to prepare a plan for national bibliographic services. The working party was much influenced by the recommendation of a UNESCO conference on bibliographic services (Paris, 1950) that there should be national planning bodies closely related to national libraries or bibliographic centers. The report of the working party, adopted by the 1955 conference, recommended the setting up of: (*a*) a national planning body consisting of representatives of the national and state libraries and of the governing bodies of those libraries, one representative of the Commonwealth Scientific and Industrial Research Organization, three of the universities, and three of the Library Association; and (*b*) a national bibliographic center attached to the Commonwealth National Library which would provide a secretariat for the planning body (AACOBS), carry out bibliographic projects, and act as a bibliographic information center and clearinghouse. These recommendations were implemented by the following year, and AACOBS has met annually since.

In the immediate postwar period the holdings of the Commonwealth National Library had grown rapidly and its functions had expanded. By the mid-1950s it was felt that a reassessment of the library's role was needed, and in 1956 the federal government appointed a committee of inquiry under the chairmanship of Professor G. W. Paton to advise on future development. The report of this committee, presented in 1957, recommended that the parliamentary library, national library, and national archival functions which the Commonwealth National Library had been performing should be separated, and added that proper effect could not be given to the recommendations without the provision of a new building. The National Library Act of 1960 gave effect to these recommendations and established the National Library of Australia as a body corporate under the control of a council of nine members. Action was also taken on the Paton Committee's final point, and planning of a new National Library building commenced in 1961. The library occupied its new home, a monumental building on the shores of Lake Burley Griffin, in August 1968 and for the first time in three decades had all its collections and operating sections under one roof.

The beginning of the 1960s saw another major library survey. The proposal for a survey "to identify, locate and describe present strengths and weaknesses in resources" originated with AACOBS, and Maurice F. Tauber, Melvil Dewey Professor of Library Service at Columbia University, undertook to conduct it with support from the Fulbright Committee. Assisted by W. D. Thorn, then secretary of AACOBS, he examined 162 libraries in the period February to July 1961. The voluminous report which followed was so specialized, consisting as it did largely of descriptive and statistical data, that it was never formally published. A limited number of copies were reproduced and lodged with the major libraries, and AACOBS published a summary in 1963, giving the essence of Tauber's observations. No specific recommendations resulted from this survey, which was in the nature of a national resource stocktaking; however, it did focus attention on the absence of any overall policy or coordination in collection building. This aspect was addressed by AACOBS in 1963 when it appointed the National Book Resources Development Committee under the chairmanship of C. A. Burmester to prepare an acquisition plan on a national basis and to assess the implications of such a plan as it would affect individual libraries. The committee submitted a preliminary report in June 1964 which suggested principles for a national acquisition plan and defined the roles various types of library would have in such a plan. A final report was presented in October 1965 and led to the establishment the following year of AACOBS Book Resources Committees in each state and the Capital Territory. Initially these committees were concerned with coordination of acquisitions and rationalization of collection development, but gradually the range of their activities broadened and this was acknowledged in 1972 when they were reconstituted as AACOBS Regional Committees with enlarged memberships and terms of reference.

Another, more specialized survey was undertaken 3 years after Tauber's. Both Munn–Pitt and Tauber had found library provisions for children, and particularly school libraries, to be inadequate, and this had been a matter of continuing concern to the Children's Libraries Section of the Library Association of Australia (LAA) since its inception. In 1964 the section invited Professor Sara Fenwick of the University of Chicago Graduate Library School to survey Australian school and children's libraries. Her report, published in 1966, was generally critical of the children's services provided by public libraries; of the gross inadequacy of school library collections, staffing, and services; and of the absence in most state libraries of a vigorous supervisory service for the state or region. Following Professor Fenwick's visit, the Children's Libraries Section prepared standards for school libraries which were approved by the LAA in 1965 and published in the following year. Also in 1966, the School Libraries Section of the LAA was formed, and the association's Registration Examination curriculum was revised to offer a wider range of electives in library work with children. AACOBS, the LAA, and individual librarians and educators began to lobby for federal funding for school libraries.

The area of most notable library growth during the 1960s was in the institutions of tertiary education. In 1935 the Munn–Pitt survey found total holdings of 527,000 volumes in the existing six universities, 22 years later nine universities held 1,619,000 volumes, at the time of the Tauber survey there were ten universities with total holdings of 2,756,000 volumes, and in 1970 the 15 universities held 6,240,000 volumes. This growth of 50% in the number of institutions and 126% in the size of holdings in the decade 1961–1970 was in a large measure due to the Murray Committee Report of 1957. In the postwar period there had been an ever-increasing demand for university places and the Commonwealth government had necessarily become involved in the provision of funds, which had formerly been a state responsibility. In 1956 the government appointed the Committee on Australian Universities, chaired by Sir Keith Murray, to consider the future role and needs of universities and recommend means of providing for the needs. The committee's report recommended immediate and generous federal funding, the establishment of new universities, and the setting up of a grants committee. The government acted swiftly to implement all recommendations and a period of unparalleled development followed. Though the university libraries did not receive "earmarked" funds and most continued to receive about the same proportion of the institution's revenue as previously, the increase in total revenue was such that they were funded at a substantially higher level. The new universities established post-Murray were Monash University (Melbourne), in 1958; Flinders University of South Australia (originally founded as a second campus of the University of Adelaide in 1963 and given autonomy in 1966); and La Trobe University (Melbourne) and Macquarie University (Sydney), both in 1964. In 1961 the Canberra University College was amalgamated with the Australian National University, and in 1965 Newcastle University College became the University of Newcastle. Two new university colleges, subsequently to become autonomous, were also established at this time: Townsville University College (of the University of Queensland) and Wollongong University College (of the University of New South Wales), both in 1961.

In 1961 the federal government appointed yet another committee, the Committee on the Future of Tertiary Education in Australia, under the chairmanship of Sir Leslie Martin. The report of this committee, *Tertiary Education in Australia,* was presented in 1964–1965 and recommended the development of a second, vocationally oriented, avenue of tertiary education in parallel with the universities. The government adopted this concept and in 1965 established the Commonwealth Advisory Committee on Advanced Education (renamed Australian Commission on Advanced Education in 1971) to advise on the development and funding of colleges of advanced education. In some states these colleges were developed from existing institutions such as advanced technical colleges, institutes of technology, and monodisciplinary colleges, but many new colleges were formed also. In 1972 the government decided that teachers' colleges, excluded from consideration in 1965, should also become colleges of advanced education. The libraries of virtually all of the existing colleges were quite inadequate to support a program of tertiary education, and the Advisory Committee established its Library Sub-committee to investigate the situation. In 1972 the commission recommended provision of $5,000,000 for the development of library collections in the 1973–1975 triennium. The vast amounts of money required to develop the advanced education sector inevitably resulted in some lessening of the support accorded to universities, and after 1968 university libraries did not fare quite as well as they had in the preceding 8 or 9 years.

Fundamental changes in the education of librarians were initiated during the 1960s. The University of New South Wales established the first full-time school of librarianship in 1960 with John Metcalfe as its director. The school initially offered only a 1-year postgraduate Diploma of Librarianship but introduced a Master of Librarianship degree from 1964 and subsequently offered a Ph.D. program and a graduate Diploma in Archives Administration. A second school, of very different nature, was established at the Royal Melbourne Institute of Technology in 1963. It initially offered a 2-year undergraduate course leading to the award of the Associate Diploma—Librarianship; a 1-year graduate diploma course was added in 1966, and the Associate Diploma course was extended to 3 years in 1970. The first report of the Commonwealth Advisory Committee on Advanced Education expressed the view that the training of librarians was properly an undertaking of the colleges and, with two exceptions, this has been the pattern of subsequent library school development. The Library Association, whose Board of Examiners had till this time been concerned almost exclusively with administering the Registration Examinations, now became involved in assessing courses offered by outside institutions and determining on the accreditation of those institutions. In September 1964 the association adopted the *Minimum Standards for the Recognition of Courses in Librarianship,* which, with subsequent revisions, form the basis on which accreditation is determined. The association had also, since 1961, espoused the principle of graduate qualification for professional membership, but initial opposition from nongraduate librarians delayed implementation of the policy until 1976.

One other event of the 1960s must be noted. As mentioned earlier, the LAA commenced negotiations in 1956 for incorporation under a royal charter. This proved an inordinately lengthy and complex process but it finally reached fruition when the Letters Patent were signed and passed under the Great Seal on January 29, 1963.

For library development as for most other areas of activity, in Australia as elsewhere, the 1970s began with optimism and ended with resignation if not pessimism. The quickening pace of development which began in the late 1950s carried through into the early 1970s and was given an added boost at the end of 1972 with the election of a reformist federal government which was eager to devote more of the nation's resources to socially desirable objectives. The new initiatives had barely been announced, however, before the Australian economy was affected by the instability which was becoming evident in all industrial economies. By the end of 1975 there was a different government in Canberra, federal spending was being cut back sharply, and unemployment was rising. In this environment, programs for library development were severely curtailed, and most available thought and effort was channeled into holding the ground already gained. Nevertheless, ways were found to make advances here and there.

One of the most significant features of the 1970s was the concern with national information policy and cooperative activities. In 1971 the Council of the National Library appointed a committee to investigate the national need for scientific and technological information services. In the course of its investigation the committee (known as STISEC from its title, Scientific and Technological Information Services Enquiry Committee) conducted two surveys: one of the users of such information, the other of libraries. The STISEC Report, published in 1973, not unexpectedly revealed that resources in this area were inadequate. It also established that users of scientific and technological information were severely disadvantaged by lack of access to information sources and services. It recommended that the Australian government establish a scientific and technological authority to advise on the development of a national information policy and promote the orderly development of information services; to foster coordination and extension of existing Commonwealth, state, and private library and information services; and to provide those organizations with supplementary funding, as needed. It further recommended that the Commonwealth should provide the authority with $3.5 million over the first 3 years. The government decided that the National Library should become the authority and amended the National Library Act accordingly. However, it increased the library's budget for 1973–1974 by only $100,000 for the purpose of implementing the STISEC recommendations.

In 1974 it was decided that the National Library should develop a countrywide network of library-based information services. This project, named ALBIS (Australian Library Based Information Service), did not proceed beyond the early stage of feasibility studies because of staffing and budgetary restrictions imposed on the National Library from 1975. However, the library proceeded to implement whatever it could of the infrastructure of such a system. In 1974–1975 it reorganized its staff and collections into three national subject libraries: Australian National Scientific and Technological Library (ANSTEL), Australian National Social Sciences Library (ANSOL), and Australian National Humanities Library (ANHUL). Each of these libraries actively developed a wide range of SDI (selective dissemination of information) and other bibliographic services. The major bibliographic data bases were acquired to support these information services, and since 1976 on-line access to MEDLINE (and more recently, BIOSIS) has been provided through the Department of Health computer facilities. In 1977 the National Library was instrumental in arranging the establishment of AUSINET, an on-line information network accessing a number of overseas and Australian data bases. This, however, was never a National Library system, being originally operated by a user consortium and later taken over by a commercial organization. A proposed national cataloging data network (BIBDATA) did not proceed beyond the conceptual stage, but in 1979 the library contracted with the Washington (State) Library Network for use of its system (WLN) on an experimental basis and this may enable BIBDATA to be set up. Meanwhile the National Library has, since 1974, operated an Australian MARC record service which provides either catalog cards or machine-readable records on tape.

Two significant developments took place in 1981: The National Library, faced with funding restrictions and staff ceilings, decided to abandon the subject-library structure in favor of a function-based organization of three main divisions—reference, technical services, coordination and management—and a secretariat. In November of that year the National Library inaugurated the Australian Bibliographic Network, following some 18 months of consultations with libraries and a trial-run period. This is an on-line shared cataloging system using the WLN cataloging software.

The STISEC proposals, and to an extent the ALBIS concept, were primarily concerned with the high-level information requirements of researchers, industry, and scholars. However, there was also concern in many quarters that the more mundane information needs of ordinary people were not being adequately met by the public libraries. In 1966 AACOBS prepared a submission to the Commonwealth government entitled *Libraries for the Public: A Statement of Deficiencies in Public Library Services and a Plea for Commonwealth Financial Support*. This document failed to provoke any government action, and in 1968 the statement was revised and strengthened, and once again submitted. Despite subsequent direct representations to ministers by officers of AACOBS and concerned lay people, no action was taken until the change of government. In March 1975 the prime minister appointed the Committee of Inquiry into Public Libraries in Australia under the chairmanship of Allan Horton, librarian of the University of New South Wales, and charged it to inquire into the current role and effectiveness of state, regional, and municipal libraries in serving the information and recreation needs of the community; to report on the desirable future roles for, and development of these libraries; and to recommend measures to give effect to these developments. The committee's report, *Public Libraries in Australia,* was presented in February 1976. Its principal recommendations were that public libraries should be the collective responsibility of Commonwealth, state, and local governments and funded in part by each; that a statutory body should be set up to advise government on national policies for development; and that Commonwealth funding of $20 million per annum be provided over a 10-year period to assist state and local governments to eliminate the serious inadequacies of existing library services and initiate development of more effective services.

Unfortunately, by the time the report was presented the government had again changed and the country was in economic difficulties. The report was referred to an interdepartmental committee and, at the time of writing more than 3½ years later, still had not been presented to Parliament.

There has been greater success in establishing limited cooperative schemes, primarily in the area of technical services. Since 1975 a number of regional projects, most involving computerized services, have been initiated. In Victoria a consortium of university and college libraries and the Library Council of Victoria (the State Library authority) has established CAVAL Limited. The acronym stands for Cooperative Action by Victorian Academic Libraries, and the objective of the company is to provide joint services to, or arrange cooperative activities between, its members. At present its primary activity is the provision of a computer-based cataloging service. A similar venture in New South Wales is CLANN (College Library Activity Network in N.S.W.), established by a group of CAEs to provide a joint computerized cataloging service. The South Australian Department of Education has established SAERIS (South Australian Education Resource Information Service) to maintain a union catalog data base of the holdings of South Australian school libraries and provide microfiche or card catalog service to individual schools. Further developments envisaged are on-line inquiry, circulation control, and an acquisition system. TECHNILIB, a computer-based technical services center, has been set up by a group of regional public library systems in the greater Melbourne area, and in Brisbane the State Library of Queensland has developed a very sophisticated on-line system called ORACLE to provide acquisitions, cataloging, and circulation services to its own departments, and to public libraries in the region with the possibility of later selling services to clients.

The momentum of tertiary education development continued until the middle of the decade. Three new universities were established—Griffith (Brisbane) in 1971, Murdoch (Perth) in 1973, and Deakin (Geelong, Victoria) in 1975—and the remaining two university colleges were upgraded: Townsville University College became James Cook University in 1970, and Wollongong University College became the University of Wollongong in 1975. The economic downturn after 1975, together with a marked decline in the number of persons seeking admission to universities in the same period, has adversely affected the funding of all universities and hence of their libraries. The effect has been particularly serious on libraries of the newest universities, which had not had time to build even basically adequate collections and services before being faced with financial restrictions. Much the same situation has developed in the colleges of advanced education. Of the 68 colleges which provided library statistics for 1980, 47 had collections of under 100,000 volumes, 15 held between 100,000 and 183,000 volumes, and only 6 ranged between 306,000 and 507,000 volumes. Many of the smaller colleges have become barely viable and there seems no possibility of their libraries reaching even minimum levels of adequacy.

The number of library schools grew enormously between 1970 and 1976: 12 were established in colleges of advanced education (four of these offering teacher–librarian courses exclusively or primarily) and two in universities. One university school (in the University of Adelaide) was discontinued at the end of 1978 and some of the colleges' schools are having difficulty in remaining viable. It is a sad turn of events that institutional funding and hence career opportunities were restricted at the very point in time when avenues for professional education were most numerous and varied. The unique feature of library education in the '70s was the introduction of training courses for paraprofessionals. The first of these was established by the Victorian Department of Technical and Further Education, on the initiative of the state branch of the LAA, in 1971. Since then all states have introduced similar courses leading to a library technician certificate or diploma (the actual designations of the awards vary from state to state), and these courses are presently offered in 12 technical and further education institutions.

The Present Pattern

Australian library services are essentially organized along state lines. There is no formal national structure though an active network of informal arrangements exists. The National Library has considerable authority by virtue of its position as the library for the whole of Australia, but it is no more than primus inter pares. Within the states there is a measure of hierarchical structuring insofar as the state libraries, or the authorities which run them, do exercise varying degrees of direction over local public library services and, in some cases, over other groups of libraries as well. The several other types of library, however, operate independently of the formal state structure. As was noted at the end of the preceding section, recent attempts to have the federal government establish an overriding national authority, of one kind or another, have come to nothing.

While the organizational pattern of library services is largely decentralized, the distributional pattern, within states, is centralized. The major resources are concentrated in the six state capitals and Canberra. Beyond these, the only centers with any resource strength are the five cities in which nonmetropolitan universities are located and three other cities with sizable college libraries. The rest of the country—with about 30% of the population—has only rudimentary library provision or none at all. This pattern is an inevitable product of the country's population distribution, but it does pose a problem for library authorities, and ultimately for governments, which is yet to be solved.

The following sections briefly describe the component elements of the Australian library scene as they are at the present. Much information, particularly of a background nature, has already been given in the historical survey; these notes present an overall picture.

NATIONAL INSTITUTIONS

The National Library of Australia

The National Library is an autonomous corporate body governed by a council of 11 members, including the director-general as executive officer, which is responsible to the Ministry for Home Affairs. Its functions, as prescribed in the National Library Act of 1960, are to maintain and develop a national collection of library materials including a comprehensive collection of Australiana; to make these materials available to persons and institutions; to provide bibliographic and other services in the interest of the nation and for the special purposes of Parliament, departments, and authorities of the Commonwealth, and of Commonwealth territories; and to cooperate in library matters with other institutions and persons, both in Australia and elsewhere. In 1979 it held nearly 2 million volumes and received about 95,000 serials and newspapers. In addition it has substantial holdings of microforms, films, sound recordings, scores, graphic art, photographs, and maps. The deposit right it has enjoyed under the Copyright Act since 1912 has ensured that its coverage of Australian publications since that date is almost total, and it is constantly seeking to extend this coverage. It also has an extensive collection of Australian manuscripts. Other significant collection strengths are in Asian-language materials, European literature, and United States materials. In addition it has the country's largest collection of motion picture films, from which it actively lends. Of equal importance with its collections are the bibliographic services which the National Library provides. Foremost of these are the *Australian National Bibli-*

ography (ANB) and *Australian Government Publications*, which between them record all Australian publishing output. It maintains the National Union Catalogue of Monographs (NUCOM) in card form, which it publishes on microfilm, and compiles two other union lists—*Guide to Collections of Manuscripts Relating to Australia* and *Serials in Australian Libraries: Social Sciences and Humanities* (SALSSAH). The former is published in loose-leaf form, while the latter (previously in loose-leaf) is progressively being released on microfiche. In the field of information service it publishes *Australian Public Affairs Information Service* (APAIS) and issues a large number of current awareness bulletins. It also provides searches against a range of the major international data bases and operates the Australian MEDLINE service. The library's central cataloging activities include participation in the U.S. Library of Congress Shared Cataloging Program, operation of the Australian MARC Record Service (AMRS), and a catalog card production service. It also provides the secretariat for AACOBS and assists with bibliographic and investigative projects of that body.

Australian Archives

Established in 1961 (formerly it was a responsibility of the National Library), the Australian Archives is the largest archival institution in the country. Its headquarters are in Canberra and branches are maintained in all capitals, Darwin, and Townsville. Most of its holdings consist of records of the Commonwealth government though there are some colonial governmental records which were transferred to the Commonwealth at federation. One exception to its coverage of Commonwealth records is the archives of wartime fighting units held by the Australian War Memorial. A curious feature of this organization is that it was established, and has since operated, without specific legislative backing. The problem was considered by an interdepartmental committee in 1962 but its report was never submitted to the government. In 1973 a former dominion archivist of Canada was appointed to advise on the future development of the Archives, and his report recommended the enactment of a national archives act. A bill for an archives act, introduced into Parliament in 1978, contained some contentious matters, such as the right of the Archives to collect private documents of individuals associated with the Commonwealth. It was referred to a Senate select committee and, at the time of writing, still had not become law. Despite its lack of legal authority, the Archives surveys government departmental records, houses noncurrent records, arranges disposal, preserves records of permanent value, and controls public access to the records under a "30-year" rule.

CSIRO Library System

Though not officially constituted as such, the library system of the Commonwealth Scientific and Industrial Research Organisation (CSIRO) forms a de facto national library service for scientific and technological material. CSIRO was established by act of Parliament in 1949 though its history extends back through predecessor organizations (Commonwealth Council for Scientific and Industrial Research, Commonwealth Institute for Science and Industry) to 1916. The library had its origin in 1919 and became a system in 1928 when books and journals relevant to the work of individual divisions were transferred from the Head Office collection to those divisions. The present structure of the system consists of the Central Library, located in Melbourne, and 70 divisional libraries and document centers throughout the country, each of which is attached to a division or an individual laboratory or field station. The Central Library maintains a general scientific collection and coordinates the activities of the divisional libraries, whose collections are specialized to the interests of the units they serve. Many of the divisional libraries now hold major collections of national importance—for example, the National Standards Laboratory library in Sydney, which houses a unique collection relating to the maintenance of standards of measurement and to the physical sciences in general. Total holdings of the system exceed 1 million volumes. The library system is part of the organization's Central Information, Library, and Editorial Section (CILES), established in 1973, which maintains an extensive information and publication program. Bibliographic and reference publications include *CSIRO Abstracts, Australian Science Index, Scientific and Technical Research Centres in Australia* (a biennial directory), and *Scientific Serials in Australian Libraries*. This latter is a union catalog, companion to SALSSAH, which in the past was issued in loose-leaf form but is now being progressively issued on microfiche. In addition to its bibliographic publications, CILES operates a very sophisticated computer-based information system drawing on the major scientific and technical data bases to provide SDI and retrospective information retrieval services.

STATE LIBRARIES AND LIBRARY AUTHORITIES

Each state has a central, government-maintained, library located in the capital city. These State Libraries provide reference, interlibrary loan, and, in some instances, direct loan services; and they have responsibility for maintaining state archives except in Victoria and New South Wales where there are now separate archives authorities. Many serve state government departmental libraries; in Tasmania the State Library has, since 1976, been responsible for the complete management of departmental libraries; in addition, it staffs the Parliamentary Library and operates the state's school library services branch. Each receives by law depository copies of material first published in its state, and all but Tasmania and South Australia maintain separately designated libraries of Australiana and state-related material. These collections are: in New South Wales the Mitchell and Dixson Libraries, in Queensland the John Oxley Library, in Victoria the La Trobe Library, and in Western Australia the Battye Library. The State Library of Tasmania has three collections—Tasmanian Collection, W. L. Crowther Library, Allport Library, and Museum of Fine Arts—which could form such a library, but the latter two collections are encumbered by special conditions in the terms of their bequests. The reference holdings of the state libraries vary greatly in size and depth, ranging from about 300,000 volumes for the smallest to over a million for the largest. All have, within the resources available to them, attempted to develop broad collections (including some specialization), to preserve material irrespective of current demand to provide for research, and to support other libraries which maintain current collections only. The state library authorities—variously called Library Board (Queensland, Tasmania, and Western Australia), Libraries Board (South Australia), and Library Council (New South Wales and Victoria)—are responsible for controlling the state library, on the one hand, and administering the state government's support to local public library services, on the other. The way in which this latter function is carried out varies in nature and extent. In Western Australia, South Australia, and Tasmania the bookstock of local libraries is generally provided by the state library authority; whereas in New South Wales, Victoria, and Queensland it is supplemented by the State Library. In addition to the provision of bookstocks, the extension services generally provide advice, planning and promotional assistance, and bibliographic and information service. It is worth noting that in November 1978 the state and public libraries in Tasmania became a single unified system under the control of the Tasmanian Library Board. The State Library now no longer resides solely in Hobart but is spread, in both its reference and lending functions, over the whole state.

PUBLIC LIBRARIES

Local public libraries in Australia, with the exception of those in Tasmania, are generally provided by local government authorities and maintained jointly (but in varying ways and proportions) by those authorities and the respective state governments. The pattern of provision is extremely varied, ranging from single, usually small, council libraries existing in isolation, through relatively large city libraries with satellite branches, to regional library systems supported by several municipalities and involving often quite large numbers of libraries. Joint or regional systems are prevalent partly because they are favored by state library authorities as being the most effective and economical way of ensuring the maximum library provision to all districts, and partly because, with many sparsely populated rural local government areas, joint responsibility is the only means by which any library service could be funded. A survey commissioned by the Committee of Inquiry into Public Libraries (based on 1974–1975 data) revealed that of 883 local government authorities, 655 provided library services under supervision of state library authorities; 265 of these were involved in supporting 46 regional library services, a further 56 supported 27 joint services, and 322 operated individual library services. One hundred and twelve local government authorities did not provide any form of library service —7% of the total population was unserved in any way. The varying ways in which state library authorities are involved in the support of local libraries have been noted in the preceding paragraph. Not surprisingly, the best local library systems are found in the affluent municipalities of the major cities. Many of these have modern, very attractive, and well-equipped buildings, both for their regional headquarters and their branch libraries, and provide access to large and varied bookstocks. At the other end of the scale are individual libraries operated by some poorer metropolitan councils and rural shires, which are staffed on a part-time basis by unqualified staff and have minimal holdings, much of which are of little interest to their users.

UNIVERSITY AND COLLEGE LIBRARIES

University Libraries

There are 19 universities; 14 are located in capital cities (including Canberra) and five in provincial centers. Their libraries together hold some 14 million volumes, and one, the University of Sydney Library, has the largest collection in the country with in excess of 2.7 million volumes. Another six have (at the end of 1980) over 1 million volumes. These collections represent a very significant proportion of the total information resources of the nation, and, though the primary responsibility of the libraries is to students and staff of their parent institutions, they make their holdings available to others through interlibrary loans, intramural use, and a measure of direct lending, particularly to staff and advanced-level students of other tertiary institutions. Close consultative links exist between the administrators of these libraries fostered by the informal Committee of Australian University Librarians (CAUL), which meets at least annually and between meetings maintains a steady flow of communication by means of "round robin" correspondence. All libraries established in the 1960s and '70s, with the exception of Monash University Library, are essentially centralized. Monash, being developed on a scattered campus, established a distributed system consisting of the central library and three subject-specialized branch libraries. The libraries of the older universities (except for New England) are decentralized in varying degrees, ranging from a multitude of branch and departmental libraries as found in the Universities of Sydney, Melbourne, and Queensland to something near the Monash pattern in the University of New South Wales. All have their central libraries housed in excellent buildings erected since 1958, though most are already outgrowing them. Despite their comparative wealth of holdings, none feels that its resources are adequate to the demands placed upon the libraries, and financial restrictions (which have become particularly onerous since 1975) have forced staffing cutbacks, reduced acquisitions, and necessitated wholesale cancellations of serials subscriptions. In an attempt to maximize cost-effectiveness, most university libraries are increasing their effort to automate housekeeping activities—an area in which, though not the first, they were among the pioneers. Some are looking to formalized arrangements of cooperative activity such as the Victorian organization, CAVAL, mentioned in the preceding section.

College Libraries

The colleges of advanced education can be grouped, roughly, into four categories: (*a*) the "Central Institutes of Technology," of which there are three in Melbourne and one in each of the other capitals except Hobart; (*b*) a secondary group of colleges which were either developed from former technical colleges or newly established in the period 1966–1975; (*c*) the former teachers' colleges; and (*d*) monodiscipline colleges. As mentioned in the preceding section, only six have moderately large collections, and it could be claimed that this group of libraries has little to contribute to the nation's bibliographic wealth. Such a view would, however, overlook the fact that because of their vocational and practical emphasis, college libraries have a range of material little represented in, say, the university libraries. Also, the generally very small holdings of the monodiscipline colleges actually represent coverage in reasonable depth of the limited field in which they collect and are therefore quite significant resources. College librarians themselves are very aware of the paucity of their resources and so have been more active than most in seeking ways of mitigating the effects of this deficiency. Many have been very innovative in improving bibliographic access to their collections, in developing information services and reader education programs, and in devising means of cooperative utilization of resources. There have also been a number of research projects, funded by the (former) Commission on Advanced Education, aimed at identifying the library needs of college populations and defining standards of provision. In these aspects the college librarians have been ahead of their university colleagues.

SCHOOL LIBRARIES

Until the beginning of the 1970s school libraries were, with a few exceptions, deplorably inadequate where they existed at all. The provision of Commonwealth funding from 1969 and the establishment of, first, the Commonwealth Secondary Schools Libraries Committee and then, in 1974, the Primary Schools Libraries Committee enabled a notable transformation in a very few years. All states now have a central school library service, directed by a supervisor of school libraries, which is involved in policy planning, supervision and staffing of school libraries, and the provision of central services. In addition, the availability of federal funds enabled an extensive program of library building and stocking to be undertaken in both state and independent schools. This development in turn produced a shortage of teacher–librarians which led to the expansion of existing library schools and the establishment of a number of new ones. At this point in time a majority of Australian schools have some form of library provision, and many, particularly at the secondary level, have well-housed and well-stocked libraries manned by trained staff. There is a degree of cooperation between the school library services of the various states, facilitated through the Australian Council of School Library Supervisors. The South Australian service is in the process of developing a sophisticated computer-based system (SAERIS) to provide, first, cataloging support services and a union catalog facility and, subsequently, other processing support services. This system is now being developed to provide service to other states. A number of joint school–public libraries, sometimes called "community libraries," have been set up on a trial basis in Victoria and South Australia. The success of these libraries is varied, and it is too early to say whether they will become a permanent part of the Australian library pattern.

SPECIAL LIBRARIES

The *Directory of Special Libraries in Australia* (3rd ed., 1972) lists 776 such libraries, of which 254 are in New South Wales and 226 in Victoria. Even allowing for the fact that 70 are university branch and departmental libraries, and a further 48 are libraries of the CSIRO system, the total is considerable. These libraries vary greatly in their nature, size, and importance. They are as diverse in type and subject field as the parent organizations which maintain them. Broadly, they can be categorized as parliamentary libraries, government department and agency libraries, hospital libraries, the libraries of learned societies and professional bodies, and those of industrial and commercial firms. There are parliamentary libraries attached to each State Legislature and the Federal Parliament. Though in their earlier days a number performed the function of club libraries as much as sources of information, nearly all now maintain excellent reference collections and provide a variety of research and information services to parliamentarians. With their well-developed holdings of government documents they contribute significantly to the national bibliographic resources. Some of the libraries of government departments hold significant resources in their specialized fields, but the majority are little more than adequate working collections. There have been moves in recent years by some governments to consolidate and rationalize departmental libraries when possible. Many of the learned society and professional body libraries, some of which had long histories and hence valuable collections of older material, have come under the control of, or been incorporated into state and university libraries. Hospital libraries are almost without exception purely working collections. Those in the major teaching hospitals are either outposts of the university's medical library or are jointly maintained by the hospital and the university; some of this group have built up modest research strengths. In Melbourne the main government-supported medical libraries (including those of the universities) belong to the Central Medical Library organization, located at the University of Melbourne, which has compiled a union catalog of holdings and encourages a cooperative acquisition policy within the group. Few libraries of businesses are in any way distinguished though some of the larger firms, especially those with overseas connections, have invested in information retrieval services. There is, however, nothing like the demand for information officers which exists in Britain and North America.

ASSOCIATIONS

Library Association of Australia

The LAA is the major association of librarians and other persons concerned with library and information activities in Australia. Its Royal Charter of Incorporation states the objects of the association as: "a) to promote, establish and improve libraries and library services; b) to improve the standard of librarianship and the status of the profession; c) to promote the association for the foregoing objects of persons engaged or interested in libraries or library services." It is controlled by its General Council, the executive and members of which are all elected directly by the membership at large. The permanent staff of the association is headed by the executive director and operates from headquarters in Sydney. The association has eight branches covering the six states, the Northern Territory, and the Australian

Capital Territory; and all members resident in Australia belong to one or another of the branches. There are also 10 sections, based on type of library or activity, to which members elect to belong. There is a Board of Education (formerly Board of Examiners) whose principal responsibility in the past was to administer the Registration Examinations. This examination system was discontinued at the end of 1980, and the board is now primarily concerned with accreditation of courses offered by schools of librarianship. The LAA conferences, which are held biennially, are convened in each of the capital cities in rotation. The association publishes *The Australian Library Journal* (quarterly) and a fortnightly newsletter, *Incite*. Four of the sections publish journals related to their fields of interest. Proceedings of the biennial conferences are also published. In 1981 membership of the association totaled 7,615, of whom 5,559 were professional members.

School Library Associations

Associations of school librarians exist in all states and the Northern Territory, and there is a national body, the Australian School Library Association (ASLA), which has a federal relationship to the state bodies. ASLA conducts national conferences and has as its objectives the promotion of research, the establishment of standards, and the fostering of public and government awareness of the needs and importance of school libraries. It publishes *School Libraries in Australia*.

Other Associations

The Australian Society of Archivists, established in 1975 to give archivists a more distinct corporate entity than they felt they had as members of the LAA, holds biennial conferences and publishes *Archives and Manuscripts* twice-yearly. The Library Automated Systems Information Exchange (LASIE), a largely Sydney-based group of systems librarians and others interested in automation, is concerned with standardization, information exchange, and education in the field of library application of computers. It conducts seminars and conferences and publishes the bulletin *Lasie*. The Library Technicians Association of Australia is a body representing paraprofessional library staff. Membership is open to all who have completed or are attending a library technicians course, and its interests at this stage of its development appear to be largely industrial.

Australian Advisory Council on Bibliographical Services

AACOBS is an association of institutions rather than individuals. Its membership consists of a chairman who, to date, has always been a distinguished layman, the director-general of the National Library, a representative of the Council of the National Library, the director-general of the Australian Archives, all state librarians (representing the state libraries), a representative from each state library authority, all university librarians (representing the universities), the chief librarian of the CSIRO (representing that organization), two representatives of the LAA, and varying numbers of representatives for each of the other types of libraries, for archives, and for the library schools. (A full assembly numbers about 67 persons.)

There are Regional Committees of AACOBS in all states but Tasmania and in the Capital Territory. Membership of these committees follows the same principle as that of the council but in a much reduced form. The Advisory Council meets annually, usually for 2 days; the Regional Committees meet four to six times a year. A Standing Committee consisting of nine members is appointed each year. This body meets frequently to deal with business on a continuing basis and acts as a steering committee for the full council meetings. The business of AACOBS is almost anything to do with libraries and information services, but more particularly it is concerned with national policy and coordination, development and bibliographic control of resources, the relationship of the National Library to other libraries and library activities, and the influencing of governments with respect to funding and legislation affecting library and information interests. The major projects undertaken by AACOBS are carried out by working parties which are appointed for each particular task. At the time of writing, AACOBS was in the process of reconstituting itself. Its role as a forum of library representatives will be transferred to the state bodies, which will be renamed State Committees and will have a more active role. The National Council will have a much reduced membership consisting of the chairman, 3 ex officio members, and about 30 members elected by the State Committees. This structure will come into effect in 1982.

LIBRARY EDUCATION

With the phasing out of the Library Association's Registration Examinations in 1980, the education of future librarians became entirely the responsibility of library schools in colleges and universities. There are currently 17 such schools, only three of which are in universities. The association's Board of Education maintains a close surveillance of these schools and the courses they offer. LAA recognition is given to individual courses rather than to institutions and is determined in the light of principles set down in the association's "Statement on Recognition of Courses in Librarianship." Accreditation teams will visit each of the library schools at least once every 3 years and review staffing levels, course content, and assessment method in determining whether to grant or renew accreditation. Basically four types of courses are offered at present: (*a*) a graduate diploma course in either librarianship, teacher–librarianship, or archives administration requiring 1 year of full-time or 2 years of part-time study; (*b*) an undergraduate degree or diploma course requiring 3 years of full-time or equivalent part-time study; (*c*) an undergraduate Bachelor of Education—Librarianship (or similar title) course requiring 4 years of full-time or equivalent part-time study of both education and librarianship; and (*d*) a postgraduate degree (master's) course requiring 1½ to 2 years of full-time or equivalent part-time study. In addition, the University of New South Wales School of Librarianship offers both a Master of Librarianship and a Ph.D. by research. The training of paraprofessionals (library technicians) is undertaken by colleges of technical and further education. The pattern of training varies considerably but involves a large component of work experience. The original course, established in 1971 at Whitehorse Technical College, Melbourne, required 1 year of a "sandwich" course (a week of full-time study followed by a week of full-time employment) and 1 year of part-time study involving work release and/or evening attendance. The relative proportions of study and work experience in courses offered at other institutions vary from this model but not greatly. There are currently 16 institutions offering such courses.

BIBLIOGRAPHY

In addition to the sources listed here, many useful articles are to be found in the following journals: *Australian Academic and Research Libraries* and *Australian Library Journal*.

Australia, Committee of Inquiry into Public Libraries, *Public Libraries in Australia: Report of the Committee* . . . (Horton Report), Australian Government Publishing Service, Canberra, 1976.

Australia, Scientific and Technological Information Service Enquiry Committee, *The STISEC Report: Report to the Council of the National Library . . . May 1973,* National Library of Australia, Canberra, 1973–1975, 2 vols.

Balnaves, John, and Peter Biskup, *Australian Libraries,* 2nd ed., Clive Bingley, London, 1975.

Borchardt, D. H., and J. I. Horacek, *Librarianship in Australia, New Zealand and Oceania,* Pergamon, Sydney, 1975.

Bryan, Harrison, and Gordon Greenwood, eds., *Design for Diversity: Library Services for Higher Education and Research in Australia,* University of Queensland Press, Saint Lucia, 1977.

Bryan, Harrison, and R. M. McGreal, *The Pattern of Library Services in Australia: A Statement for the Australian Advisory Council on Bibliographical Services,* National Library of Australia, Canberra, 1972.

Munn, R., and Ernest R. Pitt, *Australian Libraries: A Survey of Conditions and Suggestions for Their Improvement,* Australian Council for Educational Research, Melbourne, 1935.

McColvin, L. R., *Public Libraries in Australia: Present Conditions and Future Possibilities with Notes on Other Library Services,* Melbourne University Press for the Australian Council for Educational Research, Melbourne, 1947.

Ryan, S. L., *The Development of State Libraries and Their Effect on the Public Library Movement in Australia, 1809–1964,* Library Board of Queensland, Brisbane, 1974.

J. E. SCRIVENER

BRAY, ROBERT S.

Robert S. Bray was named chief of the Division for the Blind of the Library of Congress on May 1, 1957. Previously, he had served as chief of the library's Technical Information Division. His professional career spanned 37 years, 15 of which were devoted to directing library service for blind and physically handicapped individuals.

From the outset, Mr. Bray was dedicated to expansion of library services for handicapped individuals. Whereas division services had remained largely the same since 1931, when the program was established by Congress, significant changes were experienced from 1957 to 1972, when Bray retired.

In 1957, for example, 28 regional libraries served 58,197 blind readers, and 338 new book selections (140 braille, 2 in Moon type, and 196 disk recordings) in 43,114 volumes were added to the collection annually. One braille and one recorded magazine only were offered readers, and the annual budget was slightly more than $1 million. By 1972, 51 regional libraries and 60 subregional libraries were serving about 300,000 readers. A music library was established as part of the division in 1962, which has since become the national source for music scores, instructional materials, and music textbooks in braille and recorded formats; the division's mandate was extended by Congress in 1966 to include service for physically handicapped individuals; 1,149 new selections (300 braille and 849 disk and tape recordings) in 474,605 volumes were added to the collection annually; and the budget had increased to $8.9 million.

During these 15 years, technical improvements were made in sound-reproducing machines, the cost of producing disk recordings was reduced, magazines were produced on flexible disks, and cassette recordings and playback equipment were introduced. In addition, the division initiated experiments in computerization of catalogs, closer cooperation with public libraries and community organizations, and greater utilization of volunteer resources.

Throughout his tenure, Mr. Bray sought to instill the philosophy that special library service for handicapped individuals is a necessary channel to entire nonprint library collections as varied and accessible as public library collections, and not social work or rehabilitation. Under his administration, regularly scheduled national and regional conferences of librarians serving blind and physically handicapped individuals were established. These conferences, together with consultant visits by division staff, helped to prevent the isolation of the national administration from the regional and subregional libraries and volunteer organizations that actually served readers.

By the early 1970s subregional libraries had become an important component of the network distribution system. Most are located in community public libraries and operate under the guidance of regional libraries. Each provides a community-based library service for 200 or more readers. The establishment of deposit collections of braille and recorded books in hospitals, nursing homes, schools, and institutions was also encouraged. Similarly, the multistate center concept for storage and distribution of materials developed in late 1969; implementation, however, was not realized until 1974.

Robert Bray took advantage of early technical advancements to improve service to handicapped individuals. Based on the knowledge that more book selections could be made and more copies provided to readers if costs were reduced, recording speeds were reduced from 33 rpm to 16 rpm and eventually to 8 rpm. This reduction of speed permitted more material to be recorded on each disk. It also meant that users of the recorded material could enjoy more reading with less handling of the books and equipment. To provide current periodicals, the division promoted use of lower-cost flexible disks for magazines. The bimonthly magazine for readers, *Talking Book Topics* (which announces current titles that can be borrowed), was expanded during this period.

To improve reliability and facilitate easier handling and operation, the division's sound-reproducing equipment was redesigned. The weight of the talking-book machine, for example, was reduced from about 30 to 12 pounds. And the first experiments using self-contained tape cartridges for recorded books were conducted in the early 1960s. Ultimately the Philips tape cassette system was developed, and it was piloted in 1969.

Since its inception, library service for handicapped readers has depended largely upon the work of volunteers and volunteer organizations. During Robert Bray's administration, the Telephone Pioneers of America was brought into the program. This organization of active and retired communications workers repairs talking-book and cassette machines, and trains machine agency employees to make minor repairs. Volunteer organizations were also encouraged to do tape recordings and to perform braille transcription services. Simultaneously, the division made a commitment to public education programming, including a national exhibit schedule.

Robert Bray was a native of Cincinnati, Ohio. He graduated from George Washington University in 1941 with an A.B. degree and studied library science at Catholic University. He was with the District of Columbia library system before joining the Library of Congress in 1940. He died of cancer at age 59, 2 years after retiring as chief of the Division for the Blind and Physically Handicapped.

Robert Bray's contributions to library service for blind and physically handicapped individuals have been acknowledged widely. He received:

1. The 1973 Ambrose M. Shotwell Memorial Medal and Scroll from the American Association of Workers for the Blind, Inc.
2. A 1972 honorary degree of Doctor of Humane Letters from Pacific University, Forest Grove, Oregon
3. A 1969 Distinguished Service Award from the Library of Congress
4. The 1968 Migel Medal from the American Foundation for the Blind
5. The 1968 Apollo Award from the American Optometric Association
6. A 1966 Outstanding Achievement Award by the Commission on Standards and Accreditation of Services for the Blind
7. A 1964 citation for "outstanding contribution in providing recordings for the blind" from the National Braille Press, Boston, Massachusetts

Mr. Bray held the following positions:

1. American Foundation for the Blind, Board of Trustees
2. National Braille Association, Board of Directors; President, 1963–1965
3. Recording for the Blind, Inc., Board of Directors
4. President, American Library Association, Association of Hospital and Institution Libraries, 1968–1969
5. Commission on Accreditation of the National Accreditation Council for Agencies Serving the Blind and Visually Handicapped, Board of Directors
6. Chairman, American Library Association Round Table on Library Service for the Blind, 1964–1966

Biographies appear in *Biographical Directory of Librarians in the United States and*

Canada (1970, p. 117), *Current Biography* (February 1966, pp. 3–5), and *Who's Who in America* (Vol. 35, 1968–1969).

FRANK KURT CYLKE

THE BRITISH LIBRARY

Background

The creation of the British Library may well prove to have been the most exciting development of library services in the United Kingdom in the 20th century. It is the culmination of years of effort by librarians, scholars, and government departments to provide the country with a great new national library having comprehensive facilities.

HISTORY AND FORMATION

Before the British Library was created, central reference, lending, and bibliographic services in the United Kingdom were spread between five organizations. These confused and wasteful arrangements hindered the development of services at the national level, and in 1971 the government, as a consequence of the report of the National Libraries Committee, therefore decided to set up a new national library combining the functions, staff, and collections of the library departments of the British Museum (which included the National Reference Library of Science and Invention), the National Central Library, and the National Lending Library for Science and Technology, together with those of the British National Bibliography Ltd. and the government's Office for Scientific and Technical Information, under a new statutory authority to be known as the British Library Board. In 1972 the British Library Act became law, followed by the establishment of the statutory authority on July 1, 1973.

The British Library started with four great advantages. First, the nation had acquired in the library departments of the British Museum one of the most comprehensive and valuable collections of books and manuscripts in the world, not least because the Museum Library was the earliest to require by law that a copy of every book, journal, and newspaper printed in the country should be deposited by publishers. These collections now constitute the Reference Division of the British Library. Second, the library has an interlibrary lending service, based on the National Central Library and the National Lending Library for Science and Technology, which were combined to form the Lending Division of the British Library. Third, the library has acquired the very efficient bibliographic services developed by the British National Bibliography Ltd. This backup link, now forming the Bibliographic Services Division of the library, offers the possibility of providing internal, external, and international information services of the highest quality. Fourth, most of the functions of the government's Office for Scientific and Technical Information were transferred to the library to form the nucleus of its Research and Development Department, which promotes and supports research and development related to library and information operations in all subject fields.

HOW THE BRITISH LIBRARY OPERATES

The British Library is managed by a board comprising a chairman (part-time), a chief executive who is also deputy chairman, the executive heads of three operational divisions, and nine part-time members. The Library Board is corporately responsible for all activities of the library, and although not part of the Government Civil Service, it has the same sort of relationship to the government as the British Broadcasting Corporation and other similar large public corporations. It is accountable to Parliament but has a very large degree of autonomy. To provide expert advice and assistance the board has set up advisory committees covering all major aspects of the library's activities so as to fully reflect the views of users. In this way it hopes to ensure that its policies and operations are broadly acceptable to users and other libraries and information services.

The British Library Act specifies that the library is to consist of a comprehensive collection of books, manuscripts, periodicals, films, and other recorded matter, whether printed or otherwise; therefore the library has to be concerned with the whole range of nonbook materials. The government, in determining the level of resources to be made available to the library, has to bear in mind these broad terms of reference. Second, the library is to be managed as a national center for reference, study, and bibliographic and other information services in relation both to scientific and technological matters and to the humanities: Two important principles are therefore established—the library's activities cover information services of all kinds and cover all subject fields. The third point is that it is within the power of the Library Board to carry out and sponsor research, and to contribute to the expenses of library authorities or others providing library facilities, whether for members of the public or otherwise. It will be seen, therefore, that not only is the British Library well equipped to provide central services for other libraries in the country, but it also has the legal powers to act as an agent of the government in promoting the growth of more effective library and information services throughout the United Kingdom.

The British Library is the principal national depository for British copyright publications, the producer of the national bibliography, the central institution for interlibrary loans, a major developer and operator of computer-based bibliographic and other information services, and the main source of support in Britain for research in library and information science. Given this concentration of central functions and the substantial resources of money, highly skilled staff, and printed and manuscript material of all kinds, the library is being planned to be at the center—the hub, as it were—of the country's library services.

The library's functions have been grouped into three operational divisions—Reference, Lending, and Bibliographic Services—and a Research and Development Department, all of which are described in detail in later sections of this article. Geographically, the library is widely dispersed. The Lending Division is, and will continue to be, at one center in Yorkshire. The Reference Division, Bibliographic Services Division, Board Headquarters, Research and Development Department, and Central Administration are at a number of London addresses, but it is planned to unite them in a single building in London, the first phase of which should be completed in the early 1990s.

FURTHER INFORMATION

General information about the British Library may be obtained from the Press and Public Relations Section, the British Library, 2 Sheraton Street, London W1V 4BH. Specific enquiries should be addressed to the particular division or department concerned, the addresses for which are given at the end of the respective sections of this article.

The Reference Division

The Reference Division was formed from the former library departments of the British Museum. It thus inherited one of the world's largest collections of books and manuscripts, and a scholarly tradition built up over more than two centuries. The division comprises the Departments of Printed Books, Manuscripts, Oriental Manuscripts, and Printed Books, and the Science Reference Library. Since 1973 the constituent parts have come some considerable way toward integration but are still scattered geographically over 15 sites in London, and they are not likely to be physically united until a new building is available. The Reference Division has close links with the Bibliographic Services Division, particularly in the fields of cataloging and automated information services, and the division acts as one of the Lending Division's principal backup libraries, providing photocopies of material for which no lending location can be found. The Reference Division does not make material from its collections available on interlibrary loan.

Because of the division's historical diversity and geographical distribution, it has been felt particularly important to create an administrative unity. The setting up of a divisional office and of divisional bodies to control areas of work common to the constituent departments has worked toward integration. Certain activities which were previously dealt with departmentally are now centralized: These are the photographic services, exhibitions, education, conservation, and publications. There is also a small research office.

The photographic services offer a variety of types of reproduction, to both readers in person and the general public by post, of which the most frequently requested are electrostatic copying (over 3.6 million prints in 1978–1979) and microfilm (nearly 5.5 million frames in 1978–1979). Increasing use is being made of microform for conservation purposes, and the library has reached agreement with commercial microform publishers for the distribution of reproductions of some important collections and series. In particular, the Burney collection of pre-1800 London newspapers and the Civil War tracts collected by George Thomason are being filmed.

An exhibitions officer and his staff arrange, principally in the library's public areas (the King's Library and the Grenville Gallery), both permanent displays of important historical items such as Magna Carta, the Shakespeare first folio, and the Gutenberg Bible, and special exhibitions, of which there are at least 10 a year. These are usually organized to coincide with the commemoration of notable persons or events, or to display particular strengths of the collections. Material is also lent, where possible and under strict safeguards, for inclusion in exhibitions at other institutions.

The Education Service is a recent creation. Daily gallery talks highlight permanent displays and special exhibitions, and visits from educational establishments, mostly schools, are arranged. Leaflets and tape–slide presentations serve to make exhibited material widely available.

The library has a long tradition of publication of catalogs of books and manuscripts as well as special exhibition catalogs, postcards, and slides. There has recently been a considerable expansion in this activity, and an annual list is issued.

Before the creation of the British Library, binding and book conservation work was carried out by a bindery controlled by HMSO (Her Majesty's Stationery Office) on behalf of the Museum departments. Following a report by a consultant in 1975, which painted a gloomy picture of the state of the collections (and, indeed, of library collections in general), a conservation office was set up. It concentrates not only on increasing the volume of work done by the HMSO bindery and outside contractors, but also on the development of new techniques for dealing with the deterioration of paper and binding materials, and on improving the environmental conditions.

Department of Printed Books

The Department of Printed Books is the largest part of the Reference Division. It holds over 8 million volumes, chiefly in the fields of the arts, humanities, and social sciences; and the collections are growing at a rate of 600,000 items (books, serial and newspaper parts, atlases and map sheets, and printed music scores) per year. There are at present 551 staff (110 with academic or professional qualifications) and about 30,000 registered readers.

When the British Museum was opened in 1759, the principal collections of printed books brought together were those of Sir Hans Sloane, the physician (1660–1753), and the old Royal Library of the Kings of England. Some of the more notable subsequent additions were the 17th-century Civil War tracts collected by George Thomason, presented by King George III in 1762; the plays bequeathed by David Garrick in 1779; and the works on natural history left by Sir Joseph Banks in 1820. In 1823 King George IV gave the Museum the library of his father, King George III. The King's Library, designed by Sir Robert Smirke, was built to house the 65,000 volumes. The final large early bequest was received in 1847 from the book collector Thomas Grenville, about 20,000 volumes, many in very fine condition. Important purchases included the French Revolution tracts of John Wilson Croker (acquired in three parts in 1817, 1831, and 1856) and the library of Dr.

Charles Burney (acquired in 1818), which included an invaluable collection of 700 volumes of early newspapers.

The days of such munificent bequests may have passed and most of the library's accessions now come from other sources. Even from the earliest days the library has also obtained material by legal deposit. This has been enforced actively since the mid-19th century when Sir Anthony Panizzi was director and principal librarian. Government-supplied purchase grants also date from this period. One of the greatest library administrators of all time, Panizzi created in 1839 a cataloging code which formed the basis of British Museum cataloging until the late 1960s, as well as being responsible for the building of the famous round Reading Room in 1857.

The present strengths of the collections are very much due to Panizzi's efforts. The library has an outstandingly important collection of rare books, which although comprising only 2% of the stock, accounts for 10% of its use. The archival collection of British publications built up as a result of the operation of the Copyright Act is of immense importance both nationally and internationally in the context of Universal Bibliographic Control. The department also has the national collection of foreign literature. About 250,000 volumes were destroyed by bombing during World War II, and although considerable efforts have been made, it has not yet proved possible to acquire copies of all the lost items and some must be regarded as irreplaceable, except in microform.

Admission to the reading rooms is restricted to those over 21 who wish to consult material which is not readily available elsewhere. Postgraduate students and academic staff form the majority of readers, but the services are also much used by professional research workers, publishers' assistants, journalists, and other members of the general public. The reading areas include the round Reading Room, shown in Figure 1; the North Library, where rare books are consulted; and the Official Publications Library, where government documents are to be seen; as well as a reference collection in the social sciences.

Books in the British Museum building are usually delivered to reading areas in about an hour; but because of shortage of space, about 2 million books are shelved in a store at Woolwich (Southeast London), and these are normally delivered within 24 hours. The shortage of accommodation for books is one of the most pressing problems faced by the department.

Information services are provided at enquiry desks in the reading rooms, and enquiry staff also answer questions from nonusers of the library by letter and by telephone, calling, where necessary, on the specialist knowledge of senior staff. An on-line information service has recently been started in the Reading Room. The selection and indexing of reference books (there are about 30,000 in the reading rooms), mainly bibliographies with some standard texts, is also done by information staff.

Books published in Great Britain and Ireland are received by legal deposit through the Copyright Receipt Office and cataloged at the Bibliographic Services Division before being placed in the library. Foreign acquisition is by purchase of both new and secondhand material, donation, and international exchange. In pur-

FIGURE 1. *The Reading Room of the British Library.*

chasing, the library's aim is to acquire a representative selection of the output of each country, with an emphasis on scholarly works and excluding science and technology, which are dealt with by the Science Reference Library. International exchange agreements, whereby British official publications are supplied through HMSO in exchange for foreign material, are particularly valuable where currency restrictions impede the normal trade channels.

Language specialists maintain links with dealers and suppliers in their respective countries or areas, and the material acquired is also cataloged and indexed in these language and culture groups.

The rare books branch acquires, catalogs, and provides specialist information on noncurrent British books and incunabula wherever printed. The library is still very active in acquiring older material and in filling gaps in the collections. Recently, the nucleus of the library of John Evelyn, mainly books with Evelyn's annotations, was purchased at auction.

Information about the library's holdings was first made generally available when the *General Catalogue of Printed Books* was published between 1881 and 1905. A revised edition was started in the 1930s but abandoned in 1954 at the letter *D*. The third *General Catalogue* was produced by photolithography and published between 1959 and 1966: With its supplements, it now covers material cataloged up to 1975. In that year a new catalog was begun: It includes imprints from 1971, cataloged to machine-readable (UK MARC) standards by the Anglo-American code (AACR) and produced on computer-output-microfilm (COM); fiche is also available. This form of output ensures that catalog records are available in far less time than by the former manual methods. Catalog records from this department will shortly be available on-line through BLAISE (British Library Automated Information Service).

The *General Catalogue* has proved of worldwide value as the closest approximation as yet to a universal bibliography. Two future developments may further increase its usefulness: A commercial publisher is to produce a cumulation of the catalog and its supplements; and it is likely that, in the longer term, as a quite separate project to be undertaken within the library, the *General Catalogue* will be converted to machine-readable form, compatible with other computer-produced catalogs.

The department has published, over the years, a number of other catalogs of more specialized interest, many of which form lasting contributions to scholarship. Such are the British Museum *Catalogue of Books Printed in the Fifteenth Century* and the *Short-Title Catalogues* of early books in various languages. The *Subject Index of Modern Works* was initiated by G. K. Fortescue and volumes printed so far cover the years 1880 to 1960. Further volumes covering to 1975 are in preparation. This is an alphabetical subject catalog. The new catalog from 1975 uses PRECIS (preserved context indexing system), which is designed to be of particular use in computer-based cataloging systems.

The department includes certain special collections which are kept separately from the general library. The Newspaper Library at Colindale in North London houses foreign newspapers (as well as British newspapers except pre-1800 London imprints) and weekly and fortnightly periodicals. There are some 513,000 volumes and parcels of newspapers and 124,000 reels of microfilm, representing in all about 35,000 titles. About 3,000 current titles are received each year. The catalog of the Newspaper Library was published in 1976. Because of the sheer volume of material and the rapid deterioration of poor-quality paper, the microfilming program (which already covers foreign papers) is to be extended to cover many British titles. The originals may be removed to remote storage to be kept for archival purposes only.

Printed music scores are housed in the Music Library (books on music and musicians are, with a few exceptions, in the general library). Among its outstanding collections are the Royal Music Library, which includes important Handel autographs, deposited in 1911 and given in 1957; and the Paul Hirsch collection of scores and books bought in 1946. Part of the Official Publications Libraries is set aside as a Music Reading Area, where the music catalog volumes and reference books are to be found. There is no printed catalog of the entire music collection, but current proposals are likely to lead to publication.

The Map Library houses a uniquely complete set of Ordnance Survey materials and an extensive collection of early maps and topographical material (including some of special importance relating to pre-Revolutionary America), and it also acquires current maps from all parts of the world. The Map Library has its own reading room.

The Philatelic Collection is preeminent among the world's historical collections of postage stamps and other philatelic material. In particular, it houses the valuable collection bequeathed by Thomas Keay Tapling in 1891. There is a permanent display of stamps in the King's Library and occasional special exhibitions are also arranged.

The Library Association Library has been since 1973 part of the Reference Division's Information Branch, and while continuing to provide reference and lending services to members of the Library Association it also functions as a British Library staff library and produces a current awareness bulletin (CABLIS) on librarianship. CABLIS is intended principally for staff but is also available to other libraries and individuals on subscription.

Since 1977 the library has housed an important project, the 18th-century short-title catalog (ESTC), which aims to provide machine-readable records for all works from the English-speaking world printed in the 18th century. This is an immense task, given the expansion of publishing in the 18th century and the degree of comprehensiveness aimed at. The ESTC team has begun by cataloging to the desired standard 18th-century material in the Reference Division, much of which had not been properly described before or was completely uncataloged. Records are also supplied by a growing number of cooperating libraries. It is hoped to make the catalog available eventually in microform (COM).

Further information can be obtained from Public Services, the British Library, Department of Printed Books, Great Russell Street, London WC1B 3DG.

The Department of Manuscripts

The collection of manuscripts in this department is the main British national collection of Western manuscripts and goes back to the foundation of the British Museum in the middle of the 18th century. It then comprised the collection made by Sir Robert Cotton and given to the nation by his grandson, the Harleian collection formed by the first two Harley Earls of Oxford, the manuscripts in the Royal Library (presented by King George II), and the manuscripts of Sir Hans Sloane. Since then a number of important collections have been acquired en bloc. These have included the manuscripts of the Marquess of Lansdowne (acquired 1807), Charles Burney (1818), King George III (1823), the Earl of Bridgewater (donated by the Egerton family, 1829), the Second Earl of Arundel (1830), the Duke of Buckingham and Chandos (Stowe, 1883), and T. J. Wise (Ashley, 1939). Steady accumulation (through purchase, gifts, and bequests) of other material has so swelled the series of "Additional Manuscripts" that in 1978 this series passed 60,000 volumes.

The collections also comprise very large numbers of charters, rolls, papyri (in Greek and Latin), seals, and ostraca. In 1973 the collections, in common with those of the other "library" departments of the British Museum, passed to the British Library on its formation.

The scope of the existing holdings and of the fields in which acquisitions are made is so broad as to defy definition. In some ways it is easier to define the scope of present acquisitions negatively; the material acquired is normally not predominantly of regional or local interest, while historical papers do not normally include business archives (publishing being a prominent exception). There are many large collections of historical and political papers, including those of prime ministers (exemplified by the massive Gladstone papers) and other leading British statesmen and military and intellectual figures. There is much English literary material, going back to the unique manuscript of *Beowulf*, including many medieval manuscripts, and forward to the present day, via autographs of the Romantic poets and the great Victorian novelists and a vast collection of the papers and writings of Bernard Shaw. Drama is particularly well represented, since the department holds the plays submitted for censorship to the lord chamberlain between the years 1824 and 1968, and also the text of plays performed since then, received under the terms of the Theatres Act of 1968 (when the censorship ended). The library's musical material in manuscript is held in the department; a particular strength is the holding of 20th-century British composers, including Elgar, Holst, and Vaughan Williams. Topographical material includes very large holdings of manuscript maps. The collection of illuminated manuscripts, including the Lindisfarne Gospels, is extremely strong in both British and Continental material. The manuscripts of theological significance include two very important early biblical texts, the Codex Sinaiticus and Codex Alexandrinus. In current acquisitions the emphasis is on British material, but there are other fields in which the holdings are very strong—Greek papyri, for instance—and to which additions continue to be made.

The department has its own reading room, to which the delivery of requested manuscripts is very swift. A full range of photographic services is available. There is a large permanent display of illuminated manuscripts (in the "Grenville Library") and of literary and historical manuscript material, including two copies of the 1215 Magna Carta (in the "Manuscripts Saloon"). The department plays a prominent part in the program of special exhibitions. The principal catalogs of the additions to the collections cover quinquennial periods, the most recent (1979) being that of the acquisitions of the period 1946–1950. More recent acquisitions are covered by the less elaborate "registers of additions" published periodically in the Special Series of the List and Index Society. Some specialized catalogs are also published (e.g., for the Gladstone and Lord Chamberlain's Collections), while others are projected for the Blenheim Papers, Holland House Papers, Ashley Collection, and the Yates Thompson illuminated manuscripts. The "amalgamated index" (of the indexes of all published catalogs) is to be published in microfiche.

The department is involved in liaison with much official governmental work; for example, in the Department of Trade's concern with licenses for export (the Keeper of the department being ex officio expert adviser on the export of manuscript material) and in advice on certain fiscal matters to the Inland Revenue authorities and the Treasury.

Current preoccupations, apart from those common to most book collections—problems of space and conservation—include difficult questions of priority in cataloging. The backlog in producing full catalogs of recent acquisitions seems likely to be remedied, but at the cost of postponing much needed new catalogs of the Cottonian and other early collections. Machine readability for the indexes to the catalogs remains to be achieved. The contemporary economic situation may pose great problems concerning acquisitions since taxation is driving much important material onto the market, and at the same time, individuals and institutions have come to see rare and valuable possessions, such as manuscripts, as possible "hedges" against inflation.

Further information can be obtained from the British Library, Department of Manuscripts, Great Russell Street, London WC1B 3DG.

The Department of Oriental Manuscripts and Printed Books

HISTORY

The foundation collections of manuscripts and printed books of the British Museum (1753) contained some Oriental material. This expanded rapidly in the 19th century, and a special Oriental Subdepartment in the Department of Manuscripts was formed in 1867. By taking over the collections of Oriental material in the Department of Printed Books, this was enlarged to become the Department of Oriental Printed Books and Manuscripts in 1892. On the inauguration of the British Library in 1973 it was renamed the Department of Oriental Manuscripts and Printed Books. In 1975 the Oriental Exchange Unit, which acquires government publications from the countries of Asia, was transferred from the Department of Printed Books to this department.

COLLECTIONS

Among the 40,000 manuscripts and 400,000 printed books in the department are represented all the literary languages of Asia and of North and Northeast Africa. They include splendid illustrated manuscripts from Persia and India; Hebrew and Arabic religious texts, many of them of great calligraphic beauty; early block-printed books from the Far East; and much else.

The department currently subscribes to about 4,000 journals, while the Oriental Exchange Unit deals with a further 10,000 titles.

The printed book collections have been developed to provide a representative coverage of the literature of the countries concerned, not only in their classical aspects but also, increasingly, modern literature, as well as official documentary publications and other materials required for the study of contemporary Asia and North Africa in all its aspects.

The character of the collections and specialization of staff make it convenient to consider the department as representing five main linguistic or geographical groups:

1. Hebrew, together with Coptic, Syriac, Georgian, Armenian, and the languages of Ethiopia
2. Islamic; namely Arabic, Persian, Turkish, and the Iranian and Turkic languages of Central Asia
3. South Asian, including Sanskrit, Hindi, Urdu, Bengali, Tamil, Sinhalese, Tibetan, etc.
4. Southeast Asian, including Burmese, Thai, Vietnamese, Malay, Indonesian, and Javanese
5. Far East: Chinese, Japanese, Korean, Mongol, and Manchu

The department has a reference collection of bibliographic works and other studies in Western languages relating to Asia and North Africa, but the main collections in European languages are located in the Department of Printed Books.

SERVICE TO THE PUBLIC

The senior staff, consisting of 12 members in senior grades, nine research assistants, and eight part-time special assistants, are language specialists. Their tasks are to select new material, to conserve the collections, and to make them readily available through catalogs and indexes. Since they are experts in the general culture of the people whose literature is in their care, they are also frequently consulted on the religion, history, sociology, art, politics, and economics connected with that literature, in addition of course to bibliographic and related matters. They are supported by an administrative and clerical staff of 30.

The department has a reading room seating 26, with a reference collection on open shelves. It welcomes visitors from all parts of the world. Books from main collections can be obtained quickly, as the stores for the most heavily used sections are near at hand.

Enquiries from scholars and from the general public are dealt with personally, by telephone, and by correspondence.

PUBLICATIONS

A major feature of the department is the publication of its printed catalogs. Because of the nature of the languages concerned, the catalogs have to be very specialized. Many of them were the first to be published in their field. More than 100 languages are involved, covering an immense variety of scripts.

Separate catalogs for individual languages or language groups are printed and published from time to time, while current cataloging is on cards which are accessible to readers in the reading room.

In addition to the catalogs, monographs on various aspects of the collections, together with postcards and wallets of color slides devoted to the arts of the book in Asia, are produced. A recent publication is a *Guide to the Department*, giving more detailed information on its collections, catalogs, and services.

EXHIBITIONS

The department plays a large part in the British Library's program of exhibitions. Recent major exhibitions have been *The Qur'an* (1976), *The Christian Orient* (1978), and *Safavid Painting* (1979). Numerous smaller exhibitions are also presented from time to time.

ACQUISITIONS

The aim of the department is to acquire all significant materials in the realms of the humanities and social sciences in the languages of Asia and North and Northeast Africa. For historical reasons the strongest part of the collections has hitherto related to the Middle East and the countries of the British Commonwealth, but since 1945 there has been increasingly full coverage of other countries of Asia and North Africa as well.

The bulk of the monographs and academic journals is obtained by direct purchase from booksellers in the country concerned, whereas the acquisition of government publications through the Oriental Exchange Unit is maintained almost wholly through official exchange agreements, in many cases at the governmental level. Senior staff visit their own special language areas from time to time in order to ensure a continuous and reliable supply of material.

CONSERVATION

The conservation of the collection poses particular problems, over and above those connected with books and manuscripts in general. This is because:

1. Many specialized materials are used in the regions covered, such as papyrus, palm leaf, birch bark, silk, wood, bone, ivory, and metal.
2. Illuminations and miniatures, often in fragile condition, are included in many of the manuscripts.
3. Most serious of all, many of the books produced in recent years in the countries of origin have been printed on unstable paper.

The conservation officers of the department are developing new techniques, and rediscovering traditional ones, for dealing with these problems. This benefits not only the department but a wider international clientele which seeks advice from time to time.

BEYOND THE DEPARTMENT

There are other parts of the British Library where collections of Oriental interest, but mostly in Western languages, are maintained. The department is closely linked with these in its day-to-day work, and also with departments of the British Museum, such as Oriental Antiquities and Western Asiatic Antiquities. The department also keeps in touch with other Orientalist libraries in this country—partly through informal contacts and partly through a series of Library Groups concerned with the Middle East, South Asia, Southeast Asia, China, and Japan—and with the British Academy's Oriental Documents Committee, which is concerned with the recording, cataloging, and publishing of archival materials in Oriental languages.

The department participates in the International Congress of Human Sciences in Asia and North Africa (formerly the International Congress of Orientalists) and in a body closely associated with it, the International Association of Orientalist Librarians.

An important feature of the department's policy is to arrange regular visits by its senior staff to universities, libraries, and other academic institutions in Asia and North Africa in order to keep abreast of developments there and to keep foreign scholars informed of the department's work. While abroad, the staff engage in valuable field work to promote research in subjects of concern to the British Library.

The Science Reference Library

The Science Reference Library, known by this title since the creation of the British Library Reference Division in 1974 (*1*), has already been mentioned in the *Encyclopedia of Library and Information Science* (Vol. 3, p. 298) as the National Reference Library of Science and Invention. The Science Reference Library is based on the principles of its main predecessor, the former Patent Office Library founded in 1855 by Bennet Woodcroft (1803–1879), particularly its emphasis on free public access. The original collection in Southampton Buildings, off Chancery Lane, has been claimed to be the first British open-access library freely available to the public (*2*). That tradition continues, and a reader's ticket is not needed for access to this department of the Reference Division. Its own principal reading room closes at 9 P.M. on weekdays.

The Science Reference Library contains one of the largest and most comprehensive reference collections of the world's scientific and technical literature. It is at present in two parts known (from their locations) as the Holborn and Bayswater Branches. The former, housed in three buildings, holds literature in the inventive sciences and related technologies, official industrial property publications, and trade literature; this now includes almost 20 million patent specifications from every country in the world that publishes them. The Bayswater Branch is particularly strong in literature on the life sciences—including medicine and biology—the earth and astronomical sciences and their related technologies (e.g., public health, agriculture), pure and applied mathematics, and material in all the Science Reference Library's subjects—other than intellectual property—written in Oriental and Slavonic languages. The total stock as of 1979 consisted of over 54,000 different serials, 152,200 books, trade literature from over 5,000 companies, and the official patent, trademark, and design publications of about 100 countries. Conventional printed literature is normally held in preference to microforms, but the library has substantial and growing holdings of the latter (about 1,600,000 microforms by 1979, chiefly microfiche and aperture cards). The collections are on open shelves as far as the limited space in several buildings permits, but these will be one of the earliest parts of the British Library to be moved into the new building in the Euston Road, whose first phase is planned for completion in the 1990s.

The library is primarily, though not exclusively, intended for use by science graduates, engineers and technologists, research workers, librarians, and other professional readers. At present the most intensive use of patent specifications is by patent agents and professional patent researchers. The majority of patent agent firms are situated in (or have an office in) central London, but there are one or two firms of patent agents in most major industrial centers. The needs of undergraduate students and laymen are not specifically catered for. However, in fields where there is little academic literature, particularly in the craft technologies, the criterion adopted is that works chosen for the library should be suitable for those already practicing the craft or have a relevance to invention.

To facilitate access to patents and the information they contain, the practice was instituted in the last century of distributing sets of patent documents to libraries outside London which undertook to make them publicly available. Today, 13 public libraries receive sets of U.K. patent specifications (and in some cases foreign ones as well), and a further 13 receive only copies of the officially published U.K. patent journals, indexes, abstracts, etc. The annual cost of providing the documents (now over £750,000) has since 1974 been met by the British Library. In view of the apparently low level of use of some of the collections, changes in European patent practice, and the requirements and consequences of the U.K. Patent Act 1977, the effectiveness of these arrangements is being reviewed in full consultation with interested organizations and individuals.

The Science Reference Library's two main catalog sequences are on cards from 1930 to late 1974, and on microfiche thereafter. The author catalog on cards contains entries under personal authors and sponsoring organizations, and under title in the case of conferences, serials, and similar items more likely to be known by title. For the computer-produced microfiche catalog, the Anglo-American Cataloging Rules have been adopted, and items generally have title entries in addition to the usual entries under persons or organizations. The subject classifications at Holborn and Bayswater differ since the original and still extant Holborn scheme has been modified for use at Bayswater; this modified classification is used in some unified catalogs. The author–title and classified microfiche catalogs are available for purchase as individual sets or on annual subscription.

The Science Reference Library shares with the rest of the British Library a responsibility to act "as a national centre for reference, study and bibliographical and other information services, in relation both to scientific and technological matters and to the humanities," as laid down in the British Library Act 1972 (*3*). Above all the Science Reference Library seeks to serve industry by providing backup facilities for special libraries, particularly where they require access to the full range of scientific/technical literature, and immediate response to the demands of government and its agencies. The library's staff are well versed in the availability of "centres of excellence" in specific subject areas and hope to extend existing publications to other listings of information sources and directories (*4, 5*). The library has a particular concern for data compilation and the comprehensive collection of spectral data publications (*6*).

While remaining a reference library whose stock is not lent, the Science Reference Library's aim is to serve both users who can be present in person and those at a distance—through enquiries received by telephone, Telex, or in writing. Requests for bibliographic data, for selective lists of references on particular topics, and also enquiries for specific data are accepted. The library issues various publications, the majority free of charge. They have two main aims: first, to help anyone using scientific and technological literature, irrespective of whether a visit to the library is possible; and second, to describe in detail the service to readers using the library. The Science Reference Library attracts about 160,000 visits every year, during which time some 2 million documents are consulted.

Unusual among the Science Reference Library's services is linguistic aid. In the course of collection building a number of people have been recruited whose command of one or more foreign languages is of sufficient competence to attempt, with the reader's help, an oral rendering of selected portions of an item into English; a prior appointment is generally necessary. A wide range of languages is handled in this way.

A photocopy service available both to individual users and to organizations currently receives over 100,000 orders a year and supplies over 350,000 items: journal articles, extracts from books, foreign patents, and British patents and patent abridgments. Requests can be made in person at either branch, or by post or Telex; payment can be made by cash or by deposit account.

Both branches have installed computer terminals for searching an increasing number of on-line information retrieval services, and the use of the services, either by enquirers in person or by staff on their behalf, is growing rapidly.

As a part of the British Library Reference Division with special responsibilities for science and technology the SRL has many international links with other libraries and institutions; for example, it is in close touch with developments in the European Patent Office and associated legislation.

Further information can be obtained from the External Relations Section, the British Library, Science Reference Library, 25 Southampton Buildings, Chancery Lane, London WC2A 1AW.

The British Library Lending Division

INTRODUCTION

The British Library Lending Division was formed in July 1973, when the British Library came into being, from the National Lending Library for Science and Technology (NLLST) and the National Central Library (NCL). The National Central Library had been formed in London in 1916 as the Central Library for Students; it was primarily a national switching center for interlibrary loan requests, maintaining the national union catalog, serving as a backstop to the various regional interlending systems, and acting as the center for international requests in both directions. It also operated as the national center for book exchange between libraries, accepted for its own stock books withdrawn from other libraries, and in the 1960s built up by purchase a collection of current American books in the humanities and social sciences, as well as selected journals and foreign-language books in these subjects.

The National Lending Library for Science and Technology, after a short time in London when it was building up its stock, started at Boston Spa, in Yorkshire, in 1961 as a central collection for the supply of scientific literature, using as a foundation the back runs of many journals that it took over from the Science Museum Library. By 1970 it was acquiring a comprehensive collection of journals and report literature in science and technology and the social sciences, as well as books and conference proceedings in science and technology.

When the British government decided, as a consequence of the report of the National Libraries Committee in 1969 (7), to set up the British Library, it was decided to integrate the NCL and NLLST at Boston Spa, and both libraries started to plan for the integration—the NCL by acquiring British and other English-language books in the humanities and social sciences in addition to the American books it already acquired, the NLLST by extending its coverage of journals to the humanities and social sciences. When the NCL moved to Boston Spa with its collection of 800,000 volumes and its union catalog in July 1973, there was therefore a fairly comprehensive current collection and acquisition program, supplemented by union catalogs giving access to the holdings of other British libraries.

The principle on which the NLLST was based and on which the British Library Lending Division operates is that the great majority of interlibrary loan requests in the United Kingdom should be met from a central lending collection. This is radically different from the interlending systems in virtually all other countries, which are in essence cooperative systems—libraries draw on one another's resources by means of union catalogs, which may be held in a central or a public library. The main arguments for centralized supply are:

1. It can achieve a faster supply—especially important in science and technology—because:
   a. the system can be designed specially for fast supply, and
   b. requests can be sent there with a high chance of first-time success.
2. It can achieve a high satisfaction rate because:

   a. items in low demand, not otherwise available in the country, can be readily acquired; and
   b. items in heavy demand, often not supplied by other libraries because they are in use, or recently purchased, or for reference only, can be acquired in as many copies as necessary to meet demand.
3. With a high total demand, systems designed for maximum efficiency, and economies of scale, the total cost of interlending, even if the cost of acquisition is included, is less than with systems depending on union catalogs and the cooperation of other libraries.

That these reasons are valid is suggested by the fact that the British Library Lending Division currently receives about 500,000 interlibrary loan requests a year from foreign libraries—perhaps half of all international interlibrary loan requests. The total demand on the Lending Division grew from 226,000 requests in 1962–1963 (for the NCL and NLLST together) to 2,860,000 in 1978–1979. The Lending Division handles three-quarters of all interlibrary loan requests made by British libraries (*8*).

The staff numbered over 700 full-time-equivalent persons in 1979. The budget for 1979–1980 was around £9 million, of which £2.3 million was for acquisitions. Only about 30% of each budget has been spent on staff. Revenue—from the supply of loans and photocopies, translating fees, sale of publications, and MEDLARS searches—was about £3 million in 1978–1979.

ACQUISITIONS

Since the aim is to meet the bulk of demand from stock, the Lending Division endeavors to acquire as comprehensively as possible those categories of publication most in demand. There is no limitation as to subject, country of publication, or language, except for monographs. The categories are set out in Table 1.

TABLE 1

Stock and Acquisitions of the British Library Lending Division (1979)

Category	Holdings	Annual intake
Serials	140,000 titles	51,500 titles
Monographs	2,100,000 volumes	75,000 volumes (excluding donations)
Reports in microform	1,755,000	110,000
Dissertations	350,000	6,000
Music	37,000	6,500 (including donations)
Conference proceedings[a]	103,000	12,000
Translations[a]	430,000	15,000
Microfilm	Roll microfilm: over 1,070 miles (1,723 km)	
Doctoral dissertions	40 U.K. universities and Council for National Academic Awards supply their doctoral theses for filming	
Total stock	Over 3 million volumes of books and periodicals, and 2.25 million documents in microform	

[a] Figures relate to items indexed: Many of these items are included also in other categories.

These categories are very broad ones, and within each category many items in very low use are acquired, partly because the cost of attempting precise selection might well be more than that of comprehensive purchase, partly because comprehensive acquisition serves as a guarantee to other British libraries. Selection is by scanning notices issued by publishers and booksellers, by blanket orders (in the case of North American monographs), by acquiring packages (such as those offered by the U.S. National Technical Information Service and Her Majesty's Stationery Office), by searching national bibliographies where necessary (e.g., *British National Bibliography*), and by monitoring demand. Failures or weaknesses in the acquisition system are generally quickly indicated by the inability to satisfy demand in particular areas.

The categories listed in Table 1, if coverage were completely comprehensive, would meet well over 95% of demand for recently and currently published material. The main category of material not acquired is foreign-language monographs, apart from Russian monographs in science and technology, which are virtually unobtainable if not bought on publication. Other foreign-language monographs are bought in response to demand where possible. They are not purchased otherwise because the total demand is very low (less than 2% of total demand on the Lending Division), the cost of comprehensive purchase would be very high, and precise selection in advance is not possible. Reliance therefore has to be placed on other sources, as described later.

The same applies to less recent publications, which cannot now generally be acquired. Little effort is spent on secondhand purchase, except of back runs of serials in demand, although a good deal of older material is donated by other libraries which no longer have space or use for it. The repository role of the Lending Division is also described later.

Other categories of material not acquired are fiction and other "popular" works, and nonbook materials. The demand for these is relatively very low and is met mainly through the nine regional systems in the United Kingdom.

If inaccurate and inadequate requests, and requests for items not yet published or received, are discounted, about 83% of all interlending demand is met from the stock of the Lending Division.

THE DIVISION'S SUPPORTING SYSTEM

To gain access to older material and current material—mostly foreign-language monographs—not acquired by the Lending Division, a supporting system is necessary (*9*). This takes two main forms, each accounting for about 5% of demand on the Lending Division. The first form of support consists of selected libraries to which requests are sent directly by the Lending Division, and which do not normally lend to other libraries except through the Lending Division. The Lending Division pays them the full estimated costs of handling the requests.

These are mostly very large general libraries, such as the six legal deposit libraries in the United Kingdom and Ireland, the London Library, and the British Library of Political and Economic Science; or smaller specialized libraries, mostly private libraries, such as the Royal Society of Medicine, the Linnean Society, and the English Folk Dance and Song Society Library. The British Library Reference Division, one of the legal deposit libraries, does not lend but serves as an important source of photocopies of journal articles, particularly older volumes in the humanities and social science. The other legal deposit libraries are particularly valuable in supplying British publications that are out of print. Since many requests are sent to these supporting libraries on a speculative basis, the satisfaction rate is little higher than 50%.

The other part of the supporting system takes the more conventional form of union catalogs providing access to the holdings of other libraries in the United Kingdom, most of them academic and public libraries supported by public funds. The NCL's union catalogs contained entries from a large number and variety of libraries, but since the British Library came into being the intake of the union catalogs has been confined to older English-language monographs and current foreign-language monographs, the main categories of material not held or acquired by the Lending Division. The great majority of material in these categories is acquired by a relatively small number of libraries, mainly in universities, and no more than 70 libraries now contribute to the union catalogs. It is possible to exercise considerable control over this limited number of contributors. These catalogs, filed by the Berghoeffer system (under which initials and forenames of authors are ignored, and variant forms of surnames—e.g., Smith and Smyth—are interfiled), are currently maintained in conventional card form, although automation is being explored; the catalogs also contain records of the stock of the Lending Division. In addition to these, computer-output-microfiche union lists are available of books acquired by libraries that are members of the nine regional systems (mostly public libraries). The books in these lists are recorded solely by International Standard Bibliographic Number (ISBN). Although the great majority of them are acquired also by the Lending Division, the ISBN regional lists serve a valuable purpose in providing an alternative source of supply for books in heavy demand. Requests are not sent by the Lending Division to libraries recorded by union catalogs as holding requested items, but instead the requesting libraries are given a list of locations to which they can apply. About 80% of requests that are given locations in this way are satisfied.

The supporting system as a whole handles about 10% of the demand on the Lending Division, and it satisfies about 7%.

DEMAND AND PERFORMANCE

The growth rate of demand is shown in Table 2 and Figure 2. Figures 3–5 show the sources from which demand comes and the subjects and forms of requested items. The dominance of science and technology among subjects, and of serials among forms of material, may be partly due to the fact that the main precursor of the Lending Division, the NLLST, concentrated on scientific serials, but it is probably a fair reflection of the pattern both of scholarly publication and of scholarly

TABLE 2

Growth of Demand on the British Library Lending Division[a]

Year	Number of requests	Year	Number of requests
1962–1963	229,000	1970–1971	1,215,000
1963–1964	332,000	1971–1972	1,529,000
1964–1965	419,000	1972–1973	1,757,000
1965–1966	578,000	1973–1974	1,912,000
1966–1967	632,000	1974–1975	2,164,000
1967–1968	765,000	1975–1976	2,370,000
1968–1969	950,000	1976–1977	2,540,000
1969–1970	1,141,000	1977–1978	2,645,000
		1978–1979	2,861,000

[a] Figures for 1962–1963 through 1972–1973 are combined figures for the NCL and NLLST.

use. Although industrial libraries account for less than 20% of total demand, they constitute the vast majority of the Lending Division's 5,600 registered U.K. users.

As stated earlier, 83% of valid requests are met from the Lending Division's stock, and a further 7% from other libraries in the United Kingdom. A further 1% of requests are sent abroad. The satisfaction rate varies by form of material, as shown in Figure 6. (The proportion of *satisfied* requests is lower than the proportion of *satisfiable* requests, since libraries are able to opt for a search in Lending Division stock only; many requests which fail at this level could undoubtedly be satisfied elsewhere if this were requested.)

As many requests as possible—about two-thirds—are met by photocopies, within the terms of the United Kingdom Copyright Act 1956.

Any library or other organization in the United Kingdom can register with the Lending Division as a borrower. Many registered borrowers are small industrial firms without libraries or information services. A charge (currently about three-quarters of the cost of supplying an average item) is made for each satisfied request.

OVERSEAS SERVICES

In addition to the nearly 2,400,000 requests received from British libraries, 500,000 a year are received from libraries abroad (*10*). The International Loan and Photocopy Services are descendants of the NCL's International Loan Service and the NLLST's Overseas Photocopy Service.

The large majority of requests received from abroad are for photocopies of journal articles, papers in conference proceedings, or reports. Only about 25,000 foreign loan requests are received each year; by no means all of these are for British

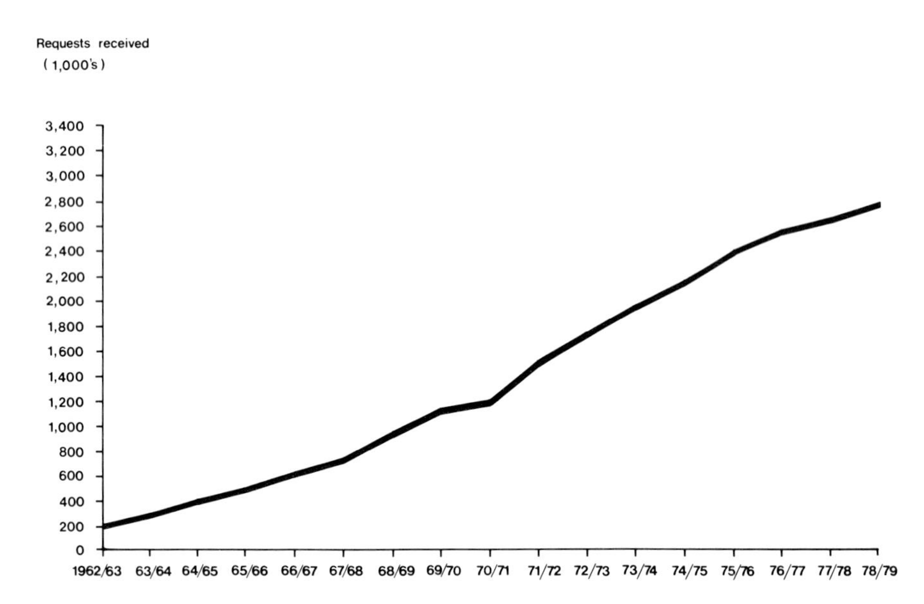

FIGURE 2. *Interlibrary loan demand on the British Library Lending Division, 1962–1963 through 1978–1979.*

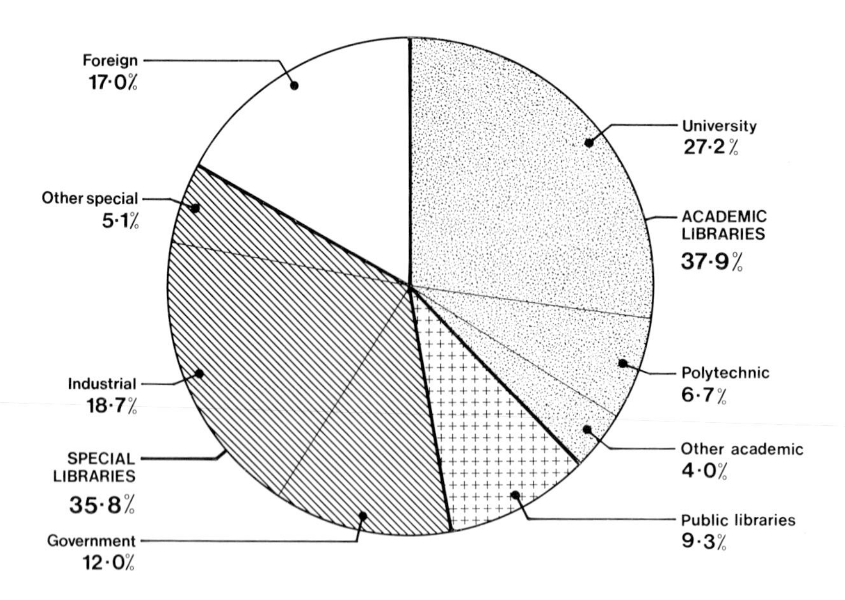

FIGURE 3. *Sources of requests made to the British Library Lending Division.*

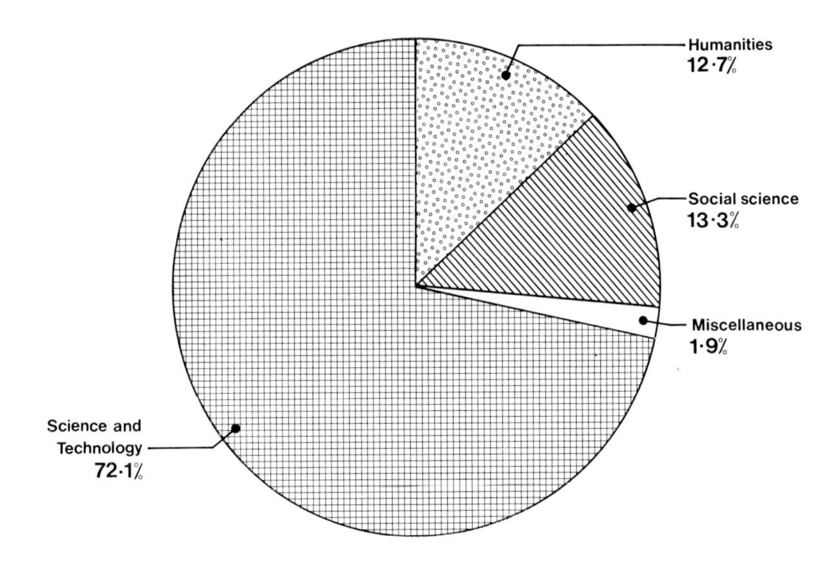

FIGURE 4. *Subjects of requests made to the British Library Lending Division.*

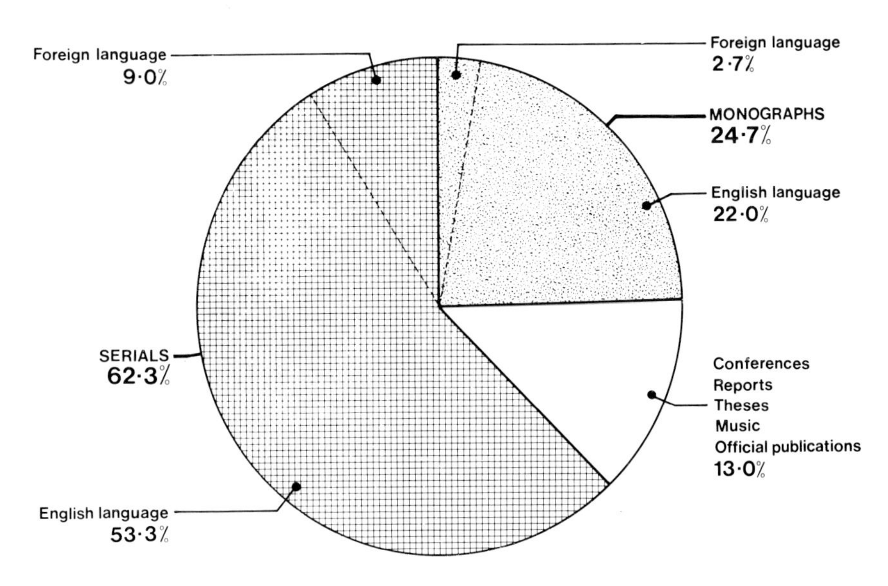

FIGURE 5. *Forms of material requested from the British Library Lending Division.*

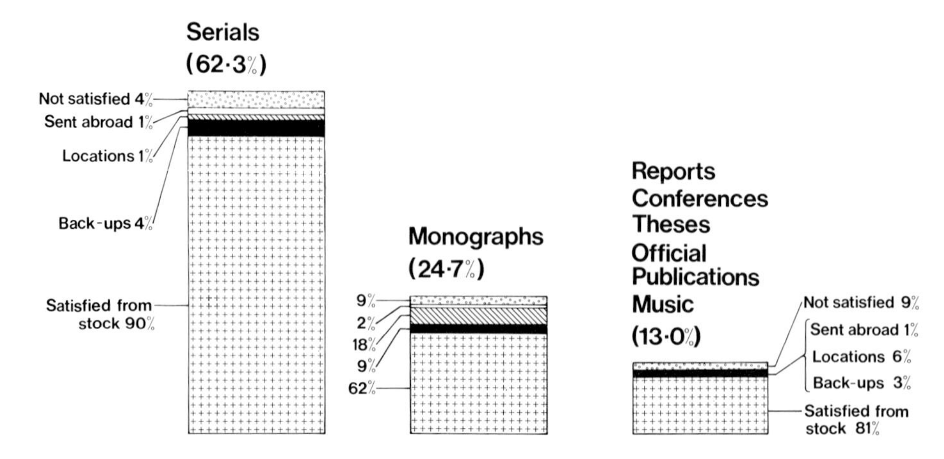

FIGURE 6. *Satisfaction rates for requests made to the British Library Lending Division.*

publications, but a special effort is made to supply British books requested by foreign libraries, and if necessary a search is made for other sources of supply in the United Kingdom (*11*). Loan requests are normally accepted only if they come through recognized national loan centers. The great bulk of loan demand comes from Europe, particularly Western Europe. Airmail is used whenever it is faster, and the average postal costs of transactions are recovered.

By contrast, any organization or individual may register with the Lending Division as a user of the International Photocopy Service, and demand is evenly divided between Europe and the rest of the world. The countries making most use of the service are the United States of America, Spain, France, Japan, and Italy. From its beginning in 1967, the International Photocopy Service has expanded at a phenomenal rate (see Table 3 and Figure 7). Foreign users of the service pay charges that not only recover the whole costs of supplying items but contribute significantly to acquisition costs.

TABLE 3

Overseas Demand on the British Library Lending Division[a]

Year	Number of requests	Year	Number of requests
1967–1968	21,100	1973–1974	173,000
1968–1969	31,800	1974–1975	219,000
1969–1970	55,000	1975–1976	301,000
1970–1971	76,700	1976–1977	377,000
1971–1972	96,400	1977–1978	414,000
1972–1973	126,000	1978–1979	485,000

[a] Figures for 1967–1968 through 1972–1973 are combined figures for the NCL and NLLST.

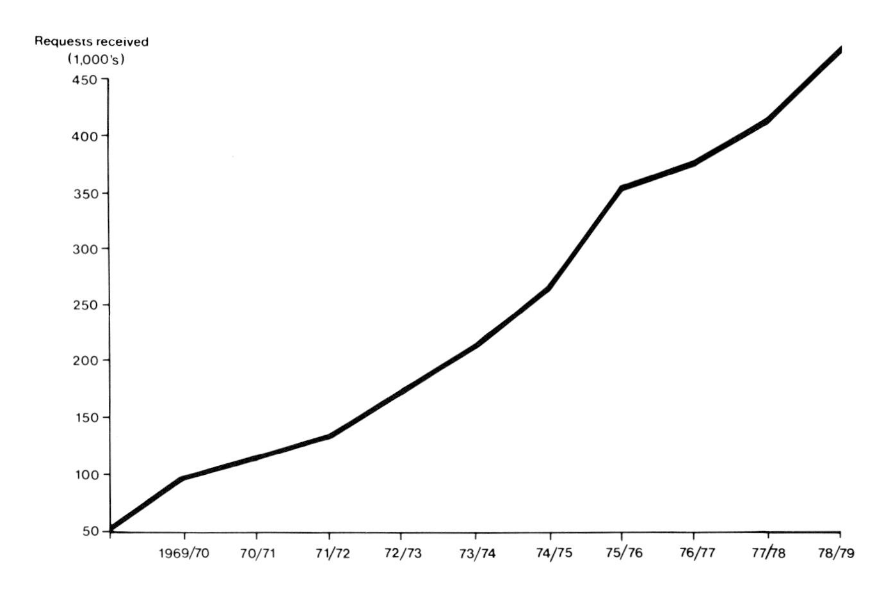

FIGURE 7. *Overseas demand on the British Library Lending Division, 1968–1969 through 1978–1979.*

Because of its major involvement in international lending and photocopying, the International Federation of Library Associations and Institutions established at Boston Spa in February 1975 an IFLA Office for International Lending (*12*). This small office has the responsibility of furthering international lending by the improvement of procedures (including a revised international request form), by publishing guides to international loan centers, by collecting statistical and other information on trends and developments, by giving advice where requested, and by acting as a switching center for exceptionally difficult requests.

SYSTEMS AND PROCEDURES

To handle the very large volume of demand—on average 11,000 requests per working day—systems and procedures must be simple and robust (*13*). Conventional library practices are largely ignored, and the system is designed specifically to perform the single function of lending and photocopying.

Stock is arranged on the shelves in the simplest possible way to ease retrieval, so that access to most items can be obtained without recourse to the catalogs. In the case of journals and recent English-language monographs, arrangement is alphabetically by title; in the case of report literature, report codes are used; and other methods are used as appropriate for other forms of material. This makes it possible for most requests to be directed straight to the shelves; the remainder, and those not found at the shelves, are passed to records sections, where they are searched in internal and other lists. They may at this stage be identified as being in stock; otherwise they are sent on to supporting libraries (as explained earlier) or given locations of other libraries as found in the union catalogs. Libraries are allowed to select between three levels of search: stock only, stock plus other libraries in the United Kingdom, and stock plus other libraries in the United Kingdom plus foreign libraries.

Records of stock, and of the holdings of other libraries, are kept in the minimal form necessary to identify items, and as little cataloging as possible is done by Lending Division staff. For example, many book suppliers send cards with the books, while for specially ordered books the order slip is used as a catalog record on the books' arrival. Where original cataloging is necessary, it is done by low-grade staff under the general supervision of professional staff (*14*).

Requests are accepted only on the Lending Division's own request forms, which are specially designed three-part forms. The form includes a self-addressed adhesive label which is used to dispatch the requested item, and the request form, placed in a transparent plastic folder, is put on the shelves in place of the book to constitute the only record of the transaction. The color of folders is changed each week, and the color coding enables overdues to be identified. Recalls for items, whether overdue or wanted by other libraries, make use of one part of the request form.

Request forms may be sent on by the Lending Division to supporting libraries, which can use them in the same way; or they may be returned to requesting libraries with locations of holding libraries, to which they can then be sent.

A charge is made for each item supplied. The charging system is the simplest possible. A standard unit charge is made, although photocopies over a certain number of pages have to have additional coupons attached. The request form itself acts as currency, and request forms are sold in batches to registered users. There is thus no individual payment or invoicing, nor any problem of claiming payment after transactions have been completed. In the case of foreign libraries, payment is by means of forms in the case of loans and coupons in the case of photocopies. Foreign libraries using Telex establish deposit accounts with the Lending Division.

As little processing as possible is done to incoming stock. For example, items are stamped but not bookplated. Most journals are left unbound; those in heaviest use are bought in more than one copy, of which at least one set is fully bound and another is bound cheaply in individual parts with transparent plastic covers. By this means, photocopying is made easier, and individual issues can be lent much more cheaply when necessary, leaving on the shelves other issues of the same volume for other users.

About 20% of requests are received by Telex. Nearly all of these are now converted by computer to standard three-part request forms. Requests from some foreign institutions are received direct by computer—especially the Center for Research Libraries and the U.S. National Library of Medicine—and from the end of 1978 an Automatic Document Request Service, using the British Library Automated Information Service (BLAISE), has been possible. In this procedure, references retrieved from the data base can be transmitted direct to the Lending Division as interlibrary loan requests. Similar links will be established with other data base operators.

While mail is still used for the majority of requests, increasingly nonpostal transport schemes are being used (*15*). These involve the transmission of loans and photocopies by road and rail to nodes in various parts of the country. Here vans collect them and distribute them to the individual libraries, at the same time picking up returned loans. These nonpostal systems have proved cheaper than mail, at least as fast on average, and more reliable.

To maintain an efficient service, great emphasis is placed on management abilities, and there is relatively little need for professional library skills (*16*). The ability to handle staff and to maintain an efficient service is crucial at all levels. Because tasks have been designed to be as simple as possible, the proportion of professional staff is relatively very small (about one-sixth of the total complement), and senior management is very small in number.

REPOSITORY ROLE

The NCL from its earlier days performed the function of receiving from other libraries books withdrawn from their stock, and adding them to its own stock as required. It also operated as a book exchange and distribution center for the United Kingdom and internationally. The NLLST also encouraged gifts of unwanted material, particularly back runs of serials.

When the British Library Lending Division was established, the two sets of operations were integrated. Items offered by other libraries are added to stock in almost all cases where they are not already held; the remainder are offered first to other British libraries, then to foreign libraries. In this way, very substantial additions have been made to the older stock of the Lending Division. Very few serials that are now offered are not already held, but about 40% of the monographs offered are accepted for stock. Most material is sent direct to the Lending Division, but some is offered on cards and dispatched as required direct to the Lending Division or to other libraries by the offering library. In 1978–1979 about 27,000 monographs and 200 yards of serials (about 3,000 equivalent volumes) were added to stock; about twice these amounts were offered to other libraries. The repository role of the Lending Division is likely to grow more important as libraries increasingly run short of space (*17*).

TRANSLATING SERVICES

The Lending Division collects translations into English from other sources as extensively as possible. The division also publishes, in cooperation with various British research associations, 11 translated journals, mostly cover-to-cover translations of Russian journals.

OTHER ACTIVITIES

From the earliest days of MEDLARS, the NLLST operated as the UK MEDLARS center. With the development of on-line searching, the British Library Bibliographic Services Division now operates this through BLAISE, while the Lending Division is still responsible for indexing many British medical journals and for off-line searches. The Lending Division offers courses for librarians and information officers in the use of the literature of science and technology, the social sciences, and the humanities—the last two in cooperation with York University Library. These courses consist of lectures and guided practical searches (*18*).

In addition to publicity literature, the Lending Division produces several publications (*18*). *Interlending Review* was originally basically a house journal but now deals with all aspects related to interlending throughout the world (*19*). It includes a detailed annual report on the activities of the Lending Division. The *Index of Conference Proceedings* was first produced as a byproduct of the internal keyword list used to help identify requests for conferences, and it has been published since 1963 (*20*). It is a monthly, cumulating into annual and ultimately quinquennial volumes. Each year the list *Current Serials Received* is published (*21*). Apart from the translated journals already mentioned, other publications are mainly occasional.

FURTHER INFORMATION

Enquiries about the division and its services should be sent to the British Library Lending Division, Boston Spa, Wetherby, West Yorkshire LS23 7BQ.

The Bibliographic Services Division

INTRODUCTION

In August 1974 the Bibliographic Services Division (BSD) was established within the British Library. Its function is to provide centralized cataloging and other bibliographic services related to the needs of the national library and the library and information community. After many years of planning it exists as a firm base for the future development of centralized bibliographic services in the United Kingdom.

The basic approach of the division to its bibliographic function is to integrate the internal processing operations of the British Library with external services to the library community so that its cataloging, classification, and indexing activities create records which can be used for any required purpose. To achieve this measure of integration the division has adopted bibliographic standards which will be used throughout the British Library.

On a wider front the BSD is also profoundly concerned to integrate its own cataloging activities with those of other major national centers. To provide comprehensive bibliographic services to the library community at large implies providing access to a vast store of bibliographic records. An international MARC network is being set up to provide the supply of records. It is in the interests of the library communities of all countries to develop international standards for use in this network and thus greatly increase the utility of the system. A significant part of the division's activities is directed toward this objective.

The BSD is organized into two main sections. These are Copyright and English Language Services, which includes the Bibliographic Standards Office and the Subject Systems Office, and BLAISE (British Library Automated Information Service). These are supported by the the Systems Development and Computer Operations Section and the Management Services Section.

COPYRIGHT AND ENGLISH LANGUAGE SERVICES

The section is responsible for processes involving the bibliographic content of records—cataloging, classification, and indexing. It has special responsibility for current publications and also the English-language intake from the Reference Division.

Most of the staff and the resources of the division are devoted to the production of regular internal and external publications and services. The central operations of cataloging, classification, and indexing form the core of these activities. At present these are still closely associated with particular publications, but the general trend is toward specialization according to process rather than publication. As the flexibility of the computer is fully exploited, most records will be held in a common data base and will appear in a variety of publications. Although the division's processing activities now extend far beyond handling the national output, it retains and will always retain a special responsibility for cataloging U.K. publications. These are received through the Copyright Receipt Office.

Under the Copyright Act of 1911 (as amended by the British Library Act 1972) the British Library is entitled to receive within 1 month of publication, a copy of every book, newspaper, or other publication issued in the United Kingdom. The Copyright Receipt Office now handles more than 300,000 items each year. These include:

242,000 newspapers and periodical parts
35,000 monographs
8,500 maps and atlases
3,200 items of music

The *British National Bibliography* (BNB) is based on copyright intake and since the formation of the division much effort has been applied to obtaining as quickly as possible, all material due under the Copyright Act. A continuous monitoring process has been set up to check trade announcements and trade bibliographies. This has already significantly increased the amount of material being deposited under the act. The introduction of the "Cataloguing in Publication" (CIP) system has resulted in further improvements in performance. The Copyright Office is one of the main sources of intake into the descriptive cataloging and subsequent operations within the division. The following operations and offices are included within the Copyright and English Language Services section:

1. Descriptive cataloging
2. Classification and subject indexing
3. "Cataloguing in Publication" Office
4. Nonbook cataloging
5. Serials Office
6. Publications
7. Bibliographic Standards Office
8. Subject Systems Office

Descriptive Cataloging

The descriptive cataloging operations in the division at present cover the English-language intake of the Reference Division plus the very small percentage of copyright intake in other than English. This is the first stage in the very complex operation of integrating the British National Bibliography cataloging systems with those of the Reference Division.

Bibliographic Services Division's cataloging is based on the Anglo-American Cataloging Rules (AACR), which were adopted by the British National Bibliography in 1968. Cataloging done elsewhere in the British Library was also brought into line with AACR when the system was transferred to the computer.

Cataloging is done on MARC record bibliographic forms in what has become almost a traditional technique. The operation differs superficially from cataloging for manual systems in that a fairly detailed tagging system is applied by the cataloger to the record, but there is a more fundamental difference in that the cataloger is preparing a book description which does not conform to any particular output situation.

All records prepared in the Descriptive Cataloguing Section are permanently held on magnetic tape. These can be used to prepare the interim, annual, and multiannual cumulations of the British National Bibliography.

Classification and Subject Indexing

The majority of books processed are classified by both Dewey (DC) and Library of Congress (LC) systems and are given Library of Congress Subject Headings. All books are PRECIS (Preserved Context Indexing System) indexed. Combining these operations into an integrated system is one of the most complex processes within the division.

The processes of classification and indexing begin with the subject analysis of the document. The indexer prepares a PRECIS "string," which is a sequence of terms with syntactic links. This string, which is a highly formalized subject statement, is passed with the document through the Dewey Classification operation and the Library of Congress Subject Heading operation. In each system the task is to assign a number or subject heading which matches the subject analysis contained in the PRECIS string. When these "conversions" are complete the PRECIS string is permanently related in the authority files and in the computer system to its DC and LC equivalents.

Subject information is added to the computer files every evening and checked the following day. Each subject "package" of information is accessible by means of a number which acts as a machine address. Once a package relating to a particular subject has been recorded, later publications on the same topic can pass rapidly through the system simply by quoting this number on the data input sheet.

Once each day's subject information has been checked the cataloging sheets are passed to the keyboarding team, who prepare magnetic tape for the computer bureau. After editing, the corrected magnetic tape output is prepared for computer typesetting machines which produce positive film pages. The final printing is done from the computer-produced film.

"Cataloguing in Publication" Office

The office organizes the provision of professionally compiled information on forthcoming British books. By the middle of 1979 nearly 300 U.K. publishers were participating. Publishers are required to supply front matter (title page, introduction, contents, etc.) at the earliest moment possible. From this information an authoritative catalog record is prepared. The information appears: in BNB about 2 months before publication, on MARC tapes, on the British Library data base, and in the book itself, on the back of the title page as a CIP entry.

The information can be used by the librarian for the purposes of acquisition, cataloging, and classification. It benefits the publisher and the bookseller by stimulating earlier sales.

Once the book is published and deposited in the Copyright Receipt Office, the MARC record is upgraded by the addition of data not available at the earlier stage. The completed entry then appears in the relevant cumulations of BNB.

Nonbook Cataloging

The cataloging activities of the Bibliographic Services Division are traditionally concentrated almost entirely on the recording of printed material, but it is accepted that there is an urgent need for improved bibliographic control and recording of nonbook material. The problems are considerable. There is no general archival collection similar to the printed material collection in the Reference Division, there is no legal deposit requirement, and there is no listing remotely resembling the *British National Bibliography.*

However, the increasing concern has led to work involved in the development and application of "bibliographic" standards for nonbook material. The Learning Materials Recording Study is exploring in practical trials the possibility of a national cataloging and information service for audiovisual materials. It is establishing the technical feasibility of decentralized cataloging with central processing of records.

Format development and bibliographic standards are also being considered in relation to the application of AACR2 and MARC adaptations by other libraries cooperating to form an audiovisual data base.

Serials Office

National Serials Data Centre. The center (NSDC) was established in 1975. It has four main functions: (*a*) to register all new serials published in the United Kingdom and to allocate an ISSN (International Standard Serial Number) to each, (*b*) to liaise with the International Center of the ISDS (International Serials Data System) in Paris and to organize the transmission of machine-readable records between the two centers, (*c*) to respond to demands from U.K. libraries for ISSNs for existing serials and to initiate a regular program for numbering of all existing serials, and (*d*) generally to promote the use of ISSNs within the United Kingdom.

The center is a national node of the International Serials Data System established within the UNISIST program and consisting of a network of national and regional centers coordinated by an international center in Paris. The international file, which will be available to libraries through the NSDC, carries ISSNs which uniquely identify each journal and which will become increasingly important in serials processing.

British Union Catalogue of Periodicals. The Serials Office is also responsible for the preparation of the *British Union Catalogue of Periodicals.* BUCOP, which is published by Butterworths, first appeared in 1955. It records the serial holdings of about 500 British libraries, many of whom contribute on a regular basis. The production system is semimechanized using IBM punch cards. The publication appears quarterly with annual and multiannual cumulations.

Since its first appearance BUCOP has been an important part of the interlending apparatus of the country, but now that the vast majority of all interlending is met directly from the Lending Division, a reappraisal of the form and content of the national serials listing service is necessary.

A serials bibliography based on British Library holdings and a number of other selected libraries is proposed as a substitute for BUCOP. The new bibliography could provide both an on-line service through BLAISE and a published and regularly updated bibliography.

Publications

British National Bibliography. The most important publication of the division is the *British National Bibliography*, which first appeared in 1950 and has been published weekly ever since. The objects of the *British National Bibliography* are to list, with certain exceptions, new books published in Great Britain; to provide an authoritative catalog record and Dewey Classification number; and to index the precise subject of each item listed.

The items excluded from BNB are: publications without a British imprint, periodicals (except first issues and changed titles), music, maps, and certain government publications.

The number of entries in BNB has grown significantly, from about 12,000 in 1950 to 40,600 in 1978. This roughly represents the increase in British monograph publishing between these dates. Throughout its publication history, BNB has tended to set rather than follow bibliographic fashion:

1. The successful use of chain indexing made its impact through its use in BNB.
2. Reliable cataloging standards were introduced, particularly with the adoption of AACR in 1968.
3. In 1971 the 18th edition of the Dewey Classification was accepted without modifications.
4. The PRECIS system of indexing was introduced in 1971.

5. "Cataloging in Publication" records were introduced in BNB in 1977.
6. Entries appear in BNB 2 months before the publication of the book itself.

AACR2 and the 19th edition of Dewey are in the process of adoption, from January 1, 1981.

Mention should also be made of the BNB catalog card service established in 1956. Since 1974 demand has declined, but during the 1960s and early '70s the BNB card service was a significant feature of British library systems.

British Education Index. The first issues of the *British Education Index* (BEI) were published by the librarians of the institutes and schools of education as a small private-circulation journal. Between 1962 and 1969 it was published by the Library Association and from 1970 onward by the British National Bibliography Ltd. In 1978 over 195 journals were indexed for periodical articles covering all education and related topics such as child psychology and delinquency. In addition to journals, BEI has since 1972 indexed papers from the more important conference proceedings, books, and pamphlets listed in the *British National Bibliography*.

The preparation and production of BEI was transferred to the BSD computer system in 1976. To achieve this a special "subject heading" version of the PRECIS system was developed so that citations could be arranged under an alphabetic sequence of headings derived from PRECIS strings. The index appears quarterly with annual cumulations.

British Catalogue of Music. The *British Catalogue of Music* (BCM) is a record of new music—with the exception of certain types of popular music—published in Great Britain. In addition it records foreign music available in this country through a sole agent. Entries for books about music which have appeared in the *British National Bibliography* are also listed. BCM has been published since 1957. The catalog appears in two interim issues and an annual volume.

The catalog is presented in three sections: classified section, composer and title index section, and subject index. The classified section is arranged by the E. J. Coates Music Classification, using alphabetic notation and a faceted construction. This has proved to be eminently suitable as a basis for the arrangement of a music catalog, but the use of special schemes is now in conflict with the general policy of the Bibliographic Services Division—which is to adopt standard systems and codes wherever possible. Acceptance has been given to the "phoenix schedules" based on Dewey: ISBD (Printed Music) will be available shortly and a MARC format for music has been approved. In addition, preparation work is in hand for a 1957–1976 cumulation of BCM.

Books in English. This publication is the largest and most up-to-date current bibliography in the English language; it appears on ultrafiche which has a packing density of 2,380 frames per 6-inch by 4-inch transparency. An annual edition in this physical form consists of about nine transparencies with over 100,000 entries.

The source of *Books in English* (BIE) is the British Library and Library of Congress MARC files. These files are merged every 2 months, and the complete file (less foreign-language material) is processed into BIE master tape which is subsequently converted first into 35-mm microfilm using computer-output-microfilm (COM) technique, and then to a microfilm of the microfilm. Bimonthly progressive cumulations then result, with an author–title arrangement. Therefore, by fully utilizing computer technology to handle massive files and COM technology to obtain reduction ratios of 150:1, it is possible to achieve a currency, coverage, and economy that cannot be matched by traditional print services.

Bibliographic Standards Office

A major responsibility of the Bibliographic Services Division is to distribute cataloging information to the U.K. library community. This responsibility cannot be met in isolation. The BSD must necessarily collect catalog data from other national centers and distribute this information. It is a basic policy of the British Library to promote the development of an international system which facilitates this. This is the responsibility of the Bibliographic Standards Office, whose activities are very largely devoted to British participation in the development of the international bibliographic system known as Universal Bibliographic Control (UBC).

The office acts as a focus, within the British Library, for the development and application of standards for: (*a*) cataloging rules, (*b*), filing rules, (*c*), transliteration, and (*d*) machine formats.

Work is carried out at the international, national, and internal levels. At the international level, this involves revision of AACR, formulation of ISBD(G)—General International Standard Bibliographic Description—and development of UNIMARC exchange formats. National functions reflect the central position occupied by the British Library in the creation of MARC records in areas where standardization is lacking but necessary. These concern filing rules, serials format, materials terminology, UK MARC format for music, and nonbook materials. Work at the internal level ensures a common internal approach to cataloging practice, through implementation of AACR2 (from January 1, 1981) and the MERLIN authority files.

Subject Systems Office

The main functions of the office are to:

1. Design and test indexing systems for use in the British Library and in the bibliographic services produced by the Bibliographic Services Division
2. Carry out research related to the general problems of indexing and to specify indexing techniques which might be developed for use in the multilingual MARC network

Most of the work of the office is closely related to the development of PRECIS (Preserved Context Indexing System) as a universal indexing system. An early version of PRECIS was adopted for use in BNB in 1971; and an extensively revised version (PRECIS II), in 1974. In 1976 the system was extended to cover the requirements of the *British Education Index*.

PRECIS was planned from the outset with computer production in mind, to provide indexing data for MARC records and to generate subject indexes to the BNB. The original research in the system had the following objectives:

1. The computer, not the indexer, would generate all the index entries. The task of the

indexer was to prepare an input string containing the terms which were the components of the index entries plus certain codes which would serve as computer instructions during entry generation.

2. The system should incorporate an open-ended vocabulary: That is to say, new terms were to be freely admitted as they occurred in the literature.
3. The terms in the index should be supported by an adequate system of references ("See" and "See also") from semantically related terms. These too would be generated by the computer from a machine-held thesaurus.

PRECIS research was concentrated on an examination of the relationship between terms: first, the syntactical relationships between terms in index entries and, second, the semantic relationships betweens terms in a thesaurus which would serve as a source for "See" and "See also" references. In PRECIS II the objectives of the research and development begun in 1968 have been largely achieved. The next stage of development is testing the multilingual capacity of the system; that is, the use of PRECIS in translingual switching systems from a source to a target language (e.g., switching from English into French or German, or switching from French or German into English). This investigation is seen as a basic contribution toward the long-term objective of designing a common indexing system for use in MARC and UNISIST networks.

AUTOMATED INFORMATION SERVICE

The name BLAISE (British Library Automated Information Service) has been adopted for all the BSD's computer-based services as well as for the on-line facility. It has been operational since April 1977. All services are derived from a data base stored on an IBM 360/370 computer provided by a commercial computer bureau. The bibliographic files that are available are the UK MARC current file (BNB), 1974–; UK MARC retrospective file (BNB), 1950–1973; LC MARC current file, 1974–; and LC MARC retrospective file, 1968–1973.

These files now total over 1 million records for books and some serials cataloged by the British Library and the U.S. Library of Congress. UK MARC contains records from the *British National Bibliography* and the U.K. "Cataloguing in Publication" program; that is, information received from the publisher in advance of publication. LC MARC contains material in English and an increasing number of foreign languages and CIP data.

BLAISE Services

Three types of service are supplied from the data bases: (*a*) complete tape service, (*b*) selective record service (SRS), and (*c*) local catalog service (LOCAS). The complete tape service and selective record service are designed for those libraries that have established their own computer-based services and are using the central system as a source of data. Tapes comprising all new BNB MARC records and converted LC MARC records are dispatched weekly to libraries with in-house computer systems. Tapes are available in versions suitable for most computers.

The selective record service (SRS) permits libraries to submit requests for individual records on file; each library then receives a monthly tape of matched requests as well as a statement of its unmatched requests.

For libraries not having or not wishing to use local computer facilities, the local catalog service (LOCAS) provides computer-produced catalogs derived from the British Library data base. These catalogs are tailored to the requirements of the individual libraries. Records selected from the data base may be amended and local material may be added. Local records may also be added. The output, which is normally on microfiche or microfilm, is locally defined. Entries may be full or brief; the sequence may be alphabetical or classified; updating is at the discretion of the user, but usually monthly. Flexibility made possible by the use of the computer is the keynote. The significance of the MARC local catalog service is that it is a comprehensive attempt to produce customer-specific services through a central system. The potential for such services is very considerable. In future they will probably coexist with on-line catalogs.

For on-line information retrieval, BLAISE offers the following uses:

1. Reader services—finding out what has been published in any subject field.
2. Acquisitions—allows the identification of items for potential acquisition.
3. Cataloging—provides a source of authoritative catalog records.
4. Interlibrary loans—on-line document request service from the Lending Division for photocopies or loan of items.
5. The EDITOR subsystem is a program written for on-line cataloging. The system allows:
    a. Records to be transferred from the MARC files to a subfile unique to each user, where they can be edited.
    b. New records to be created and added to the main data base.
    c. Local information to be added.
    d. Output of on-line/off-line prints or magnetic tape.
    e. Transmission of records to LOCAS for COM catalog production.

Further Developments

The establishment of EURONET (the European Community's data transmission network for scientific and technical information) is likely to make significant changes in the pattern of information provision in the United Kingdom.

BLAISE is part of the United Kingdom's contribution to EURONET DIANE (Direct Information Access Network for Europe), which represents the ensemble of information services that European hosts will offer via the EURONET telecommunications network. When fully operational the network will provide access to about 100 data bases on 29 host computers; entry points in all the Community countries; fast, reliable, and low-cost transmission; and tariffs based only on volume and time, not distance.

Apart from the data bases at present offered, BLAISE hopes to add the British Education Index, the Conference Proceedings Index, ISDS, and RBUPC (Research in British Universities, Polytechnics, and Colleges).

SUPPORT SECTIONS

Systems Development and Computer Operations

This section is responsible for management of computer operations associated with bibliographic services and the extension of the computer system to provide new services.

Management Services

This section is responsible for the financial control of the BSD's operations and services. It also acts as a focus for the coordination of systems development and operational services.

FURTHER INFORMATION

Enquiries about the division and its services should be sent to the British Library, Bibliographic Services Division, 2 Sheraton Street, London W1V 4BH.

The Research and Development Department

INTRODUCTION

The Research and Development Department was originally the Office for Scientific and Technical Information, which formed a part of the government's Department of Education and Science. In 1974, however, it became part of the newly formed British Library.

The department stimulates and supports library and information research, including the development and experimental operation of systems, and promotes the application of the results of this research to the benefit of library and information services as a whole. For these purposes it may award grants and contracts to institutions wishing to undertake projects of wide or general interest that can influence the effectiveness of:

1. Primary (including preliminary) publications
2. The informal flow of information
3. The classification, cataloging, indexing, storage, retrieval, and translation of information
4. The operation and use of libraries and other information services
5. The education and training of librarians, information specialists, and end users

Grants are normally given for research done in the United Kingdom. However, the department supports short study visits to other countries, either as part of larger projects or as projects in their own right. It also supports short-term visiting fellowships for both United Kingdom and overseas residents.

HOW THE R&D DEPARTMENT OPERATES

The broad lines of policy governing the Research and Development Department's operation are laid down by the British Library Board (see under History and Formation in the Background section of this article), while advice is given by a formally constituted advisory committee and by various more informal committees related to specific projects, programs, or areas of research.

In dealing with unsolicited proposals, the department works in a manner similar to research councils in the United Kingdom, using a refereeing and sometimes a committee procedure in order to assess the soundness and potential value of the proposed research. However, being small, it strives to be as informal as possible, making personal contact with applicants and maintaining close contact with project staff. Its terms and conditions of grant are also similar to those of the research councils.

A proportion of its funds are allocated to projects identified, with external advice, as being of national importance. These may be commissioned from suitable institutions or taken over by interested institutions and supported by grants, after refereeing. Many of these projects—for example, a 1978 study of the transport of interlibrary loans—contribute to thinking and decisions about national policy issues.

In 1978–1979 the department had a staff of 31 (18 professional), and its funds amounted to £1.2 million.

The department obliges all project heads to submit reports on their work, usually for publication, and encourages them to publish independently in accordance with normal research practice. It stimulates leading national organizations to make use of research material in meetings and conferences, and also stimulates educationalists to incorporate the results in their courses. Where results are likely to prove of particular value or interest, it disseminates more extensively or intensively, choosing from among the following methods: (*a*) publications and conferences; (*b*) seminars, courses, and workshops; (*c*) demonstrations; (*d*) provision of on-line teaching facilities in library/information schools; and (*e*) participation in projects, especially by research workers and practitioners.

In subjects where there is much information/library research, development, and advanced practice to report, in the United Kingdom or abroad, the department supports special information officers in suitable institutions. They collect and analyze a large amount of information, disseminate it through newsletters and other methods, and answer individual inquiries. Where a research center is created with the department's support, it undertakes similar information functions. A list of existing centers and information offices is given at the end of this section.

PUBLICATIONS

The *British Library R&D Newsletter*, published three times a year, is available free of charge on request. It announces new projects, reports from time to time on the more significant ones, and lists all formal reports resulting from the projects. These reports are normally in a numbered series, and a complete list of them is available and updated regularly. Details of reports and how to obtain them are set out in a special leaflet obtainable from the department. Papers incorporating the results of research are often published in the *Journal of Documentation*, the *Journal of Information Science*, the *Journal of Librarianship, Program*, and other journals.

FURTHER INFORMATION

Enquiries about the department and its operations should be sent to the R&D Department, British Library, 2 Sheraton Street, London W1V 4BH—unless they relate specifically to centers and information offices created with support from the department. The addresses of the latter are as follows:

Aslib Research and Consultancy Division, 36 Bedford Row, London WC1R 4JH (Telex: 23667)

Centre for Research on User Studies, Sheffield University, Western Bank, Sheffield S1O 2TN (Telex: 54348)

Library Management Research Unit, Loughborough University of Technology, Loughborough, Leicestershire LE11 3TU (Telex: 34319)

National Reprographic Centre for Documentation, Hatfield Polytechnic, Endymion Road Annex, Hatfield, Hertfordshire AL1O 8AU

Primary Communications Research Centre, Leicester University, Leicester LE1 7RH (Telex: 341198)

Note Added in Proof: The information in this article was correct when supplied (May 1979); addresses have been updated where necessary. The British Library now has responsibility for the India Office Library and Records. This was transferred from the Foreign and Commonwealth Office to the British Library on April 1, 1982.

REFERENCES

1. M. W. Hill, "The Science Reference Library within the British Library Reference Division," in *British Librarianship Today* (W. L. Saunders, ed.), The Library Association, London, 1977, pp. 73–83.
2. *Bennet Woodcroft and the Heritage of British Patents: Text of a Centenary Exhibition*, Department of Trade, London, 1979.
3. Great Britain, *Statutes, British Library Act 1972*, Sec. 1(2).
4. The British Library, Reference Division, Science Reference Library, *List of Publications* (irregular).
5. The British Library, Science Reference Library, *Guide to Government Department and Other Libraries and Information Bureaux*, 23rd ed., J. Burchell, London, 1978.
6. R. Coman, *A Guide to the Published Collections of Special Data Held by the SRL*, The British Library, Science Reference Library, London, 1977.
7. Great Britain, *National Libraries Committee: Report*, HM Stationery Office, London, 1969 (Cmnd. 4028).
8. M. B. Line and R. B. Steemson, "Interlibrary Lending in the United Kingdom," *Interlend. Rev.*, **6**(2), 31–38 (April 1978).
9. J. S. Davey, "The Back-up System to the British Library Lending Division," *Interlend. Rev.*, **6**(2), 54–55 (April 1978).
10. J. S. Davey and E. S. Smith, "The Overseas Services of the British Library Lending Division," *UNESCO Bull. Lib.*, **19**(5), 259–267 (September–October 1975).

11. M. B. Line and A. Seal, "The Ability of the British Library Lending Division to Supply British Publications on Loan to Other Countries," *BLL Rev.*, **5**(4), 119–126 (October 1977).
12. M. B. Line, "The Functions of an IFLA Office for International Lending," *IFLA J.*, **2**(1), 34–38 (1976).
13. K. P. Barr, "Systems and Procedures at the BLLD," *BLL Rev.*, **4**(3), 71–78 (July 1976).
14. M. M. Barwick and A. Sheldon, "Cataloguing of Monographs at the British Library Lending Division," *Interlend. Rev.*, **7**(3), 102–103 (July 1979).
15. D. Russon, "Transport Schemes for Interlibrary Loans," *Interlend. Rev.*, **6**(4), 115–177 (October 1978).
16. M. B. Line, "Policy, Management and Communications at the British Library Lending Division," *Interlend. Rev.*, **6**(4), 118–124 (October 1978).
17. A. Allardyce and M. B. Line, "The Repository Role of the British Library Lending Division," in *The Future of Library Collections* (J. W. Blackwood, ed.), LMRU Report No. 7, Loughborough University of Technology, Loughborough, Leicestershire, 1977, pp. 64–69.
18. A. G. Myatt, "Promoting the Use of Literature at Boston Spa," *College Research Lib.*, **38**(6), 477–486 (November 1977).
19. *Interlending Review*, British Library Lending Division, Boston Spa, England (quarterly; formerly *BLL Review*).
20. *Index of Conference Proceedings Received*, British Library Lending Division, Boston Spa, England (monthly, with annual and 5-year cumulations).
21. *Current Serials Received*, British Library Lending Division, Boston Spa, England (annual).

BIBLIOGRAPHY

Annual Report of the British Library, The Library, London, 1973/1974–.

The British Library, *Bibliographic Services Division Newsletter*, No. 1, 1976–.

"The British Library Lending Division in 1976/77," *BLL Rev.*, **5**(3), 87–95 (July 1977).

"The British Library Lending Division in 1977/78," *Interlend. Rev.*, **6**(3), 75–83 (July 1978).

"The British Library Lending Division in 1978/79," *Interlend. Rev.*, **7**(3), 69–80 (July 1979).

Coward, R. E., "The British Library Bibliographic Services Division," in *British Librarianship Today* (W. L. Saunders, ed.), The Library Association, London, 1976, pp. 109–135.

Esdaile, Arundel, *The British Museum Library*, Allen and Unwin, London, 1947.

Goodacre, H. J., and A. P. Pritchard, comp., *Guide to the Department of Oriental Manuscripts and Printed Books*, British Museum Publications Ltd. for the British Library, London, 1977.

Green, S. P., "The British Library," in *Manual of Library Economy: A Conspectus of Professional Librarianship for Students and Practitioners* (R. Northwood Lock, ed.), C. Bingley, London, 1977.

Line, M.B., "BLLD Progress Report 1974/75," *BLL Rev.*, **3**(3), 65–73 (July 1975).

Line, M. B., "BLLD Progress Report 1975/76," *BLL Rev.*, **4**(3), 63–70 (July 1976).

Line, M. B., "The British Library Lending Division," in *British Librarianship Today* (W. L. Saunders, ed.), The Library Association, London, 1976, pp. 86–108.

Miller, Edward J., *Prince of Librarians: The Life and Times of Antonio Panizzi*, A. Deutsch, London, 1967.

Miller, Edward J., *That Noble Cabinet: A History of the British Museum*, A. Deutsch, London, 1973.

Nickson, M. A. E., *The British Library: Guide to the Catalogues and Indexes of the Department of Manuscripts*, The British Library, London, 1978.

Richnell, Donovan T., "The British Library Reference Division," in *British Librarianship Today* (W. L. Saunders, ed.), The Library Association, London, 1976, pp. 45–85.

Saunders, W. L., ed., *British Librarianship Today*, The Library Association, London, 1976.

Taylor, L. J., *A Librarian's Handbook*, The Library Association, London, 1976. (This book brings together the texts of authoritative statements that are difficult of access or available only in pamphlet form—e.g., the British Library "White Paper" and the *British Library Act 1972.*)

Urquhart, D. J., "[BLLD] Progress Report, 1973/74," *BLL Rev.*, **2**(3), 79–83 (July 1974).

THE STAFF OF THE BRITISH LIBRARY

CALLIMACHUS

Callimachus (ca. 310–ca. 240) of Cyrene was the most famous and popular of all Hellenistic poets. There are more papyri of his work than of that of Euripides, and Homer alone is quoted more frequently. Our interest in Callimachus is primarily for his association with the Alexandrian Library, and his literary career must be noted here only briefly. He is credited with some 800 titles in prose and in verse. We have his hymns (to Zeus, Apollo, Artemis, etc.) in hexameters and elegiacs; 64 epigrams; fragments of his longest and most famous poem, Αἴτια (causes, or origins, of local tradition, mainly religious); fragments of the *Hecale*, the most famous epyllion in Greek literature, some 1,000 lines on Theseus's destruction of the bull of Marathon; and scraps of his lyrics. Celebrated is "The Lock of Berenice," of which only a few lines of the original survive; but it was translated by Catullus (Poem 66) and ultimately reflected in Pope's "Rape of the Lock." The literary feud with Apollonius of Rhodes (q.v.), who may have been his superior at the Museion, has been noted.

It is generally agreed that Callimachus was never the head (*prostates*) of the Alexandrian Library, particularly in view of the omission of his name from Oxyrhynchus papyrus Number 1241, listing the librarians. However, he was the most industrious bibliographer and literary historian of antiquity, and his Πίνακες τῶν ἐν πάσῃ παιδείᾳ διαλαμψάντων καὶ ὧν συνέγραψαν in 120 volumes, a monumental biobibliographical work, was based on the collections of the Museion. The *Pinakes* was divided into six classes of poetry and five of prose, although there may well have been more of the latter. There was also a section of miscellaneous works (παντοδαπὰ συγγράμματα). Within each group, authors were arranged alphabetically. Under each author, the various works were arranged alphabetically under the key word in the title. For the drama, dates of production were provided. In the case of disputed authorship all pertinent facts were cited. The number of rolls for each title was noted, and the opening words and total of the lines (στίχοι) were also recorded. The same information was on the label (σίλλυβος) attached to the roll itself.

The *Pinakes* resembles strongly the modern *catalogue raisonné*, and, indeed, it was the prototype for antiquity, even though the method had to be rediscovered in the 16th century. There is no work of comparable scope, but other catalogs in the Greco-Roman world, of which we have traces, reflect the influence of Callimachus. There was Περγαμηνοὶ πίνακες (probably not the exact title) for the great library of the Attalids in Pergamon, and it is reasonable to suggest that it resembled the great work of Callimachus. Still, it must not be assumed that the *Pinakes* was Callimachus's totally independent creation. Wendel has identified a similar method used in Ashurbanipal's archive of clay tablets in Nineveh three centuries earlier. Yet most basic discoveries have primitive models (printing is an egregious example), and the genius of a Callimachus or a Gutenberg is necessary to convert them to maximum utility.

BIBLIOGRAPHY

Blum, Rudolf, "Kallimachos und die Literaturzeichnung bei den Griechen," Archiv für Geschichte des Buchwesens, **18,** 1–360 (1977), also published as a Sondrabdruck by Buchhändler-Vereinigung GmbH, Frankfurt am Main, 1977.

Callimachus, *Callimachea*, edited by Otto Hermann Eduard Schneider, In aedibus B. G. Teubneri, Leipzig, 1870–1873, 2 vols.

Herter, Hans, "Kallimachos aus Kyrene," in Paulys *Realencyclopädie der classischen Altertumswissenschaft*, 1931, Supplement Vol. 5, Cols. 386–452.

Wendel, Carl, *Die griechisch-römische Buchbeschreibung, verglichen mit der des Vorderen Orients*, Hallische Monographien No. 3, Halle, 1941.

Wendel, Carl, "Das griechische Buchwesen unter babylonischem Einfluss," *Forschungen und Fortschritte*, **25,** 173–176 (1949); reprinted in his *Kleine Schriften zum antiken Buch- und Bibliothekswesen*, Greven Verlag, Cologne, 1974, pp. 200–209.

LAWRENCE S. THOMPSON

CANADA, LIBRARIES IN, 1970 TO 1979

Introduction

Dr. Morton's article in Volume 4 of this Encyclopedia traced the history of Canadian libraries from their 17th-century beginnings to 1969. Since libraries in Canada come under provincial jurisdiction, she treated each province and the territories as separate units and discussed all aspects of library development within them. With that groundwork laid, however, it becomes possible to take a national perspective and try to identify trends. For this purpose, a type-of-library approach is suitable, and, accordingly, this account of developments from 1970 to 1979 is organized in that way. The types are academic libraries (college, university, and school), public libraries (including provincial and regional libraries), and special libraries (company, government, institution, and association libraries). The three major libraries which received individual treatment in the initial volume are not dealt with, except in passing, in this supplement; they are the National Library of Canada, the Canada Institute for Scientific and Technical Information (which also has national responsibilities), and the Library of Parliament.

SOURCES

It would be encouraging to be able to report that since Dr. Morton wrote, the sources of information on Canadian libraries had ceased to be fragmented and inchoate, that cumulating research had broadened our understanding in all areas, and that national histories and syntheses were appearing. The contrary is unfortunately true. Although substantial individual studies of specialized areas have been made, the one major attempt to deal with library developments in the country as a whole remains *Canadian Libraries in Their Changing Environment*, edited by Loraine and Carl Garry, which appeared in 1977 (*1*). Consequently, the record still has to be pieced together from many sources, with no guarantee that the pieces available will form a coherent whole. The chief resource for this piecing has been the files of the Library Documentation Centre of the National Library of Canada. Since 1970 the center's staff has been indexing all material, whether published or unpublished, that it has been able to discover on Canadian library developments. While the center would not claim complete coverage, its files do provide a unique record of the 1970s, and they have therefore been used extensively.

PROCEDURE

In general, developments in each type of library are described under such headings as legislation, standards, statistics, finance, resources, special services, automation, and cooperation and networking. Certain related topics—education, research, associations, publications—are briefly discussed in the final section.

Academic Libraries

COLLEGE LIBRARIES

In this context "college libraries" does not denote the degree-granting independent or university-affiliated colleges, but the community colleges, institutes, and other kinds of postsecondary educational institutions established in response to the need for technical and vocational training. In the period covered by this survey, they included: in Ontario, the 22 Colleges of Applied Arts and Technology (CAATs) as well as a number of other colleges (agricultural, etc.); in Quebec, more than 40 Collèges d'enseignement général et professionnel (Cégeps) plus some private colleges (e.g., business, music, or theology); in New Brunswick, the single New Brunswick Community College with its multiple campuses around the province. In Saskatchewan, in addition to the more formal institutions, they included 12 community colleges which operated largely without fixed locations and relied on the provincial and regional libraries for their resources.

Legislation and Governance

The colleges themselves most frequently (though not invariably) fell under a department of education, or a variant of it: the Ministry of Universities, Science, and Communications in British Columbia; the Department of Continuing Education in Saskatchewan; and the Department of Advanced Education and Manpower in Alberta. These three provinces and Quebec had specific acts dealing with colleges; the others did not. College libraries felt the effects of government policies and directives at one remove, through their impact on the parent institution; guidelines specifically for libraries were not the general rule. As a result, development even within one province could be very unequal.

Special Problems

The college library's problems arose from its relative newness (a great many were products of the '60s); from the need to provide multiple campuses (each with adequate staff, collections, and services) and to decide on the proper degree of centralization; from the nature of their user populations, in which part-time students often far outnumbered full-time registrants; and from the need to coordinate highly specialized collections in some areas (e.g., in schools of nursing, many of which had been taken over by colleges) with the central library (if there was one) or other campus libraries. There were few guidelines or models to help the libraries find solutions.

Standards

The Canadian Association of College and University Libraries (CACUL) published *Standards Recommended for Canadian Community College Libraries* in 1973 (*2*). The standards were stated mainly in qualitative terms, and the quantitative norms proposed had not in general been reached by libraries by 1976–1977, the date of the latest statistics available.

The coordinators of Quebec's Cégeps approved somewhat similar standards in 1973 (*3*), and these were followed with a detailed quantitative statement, published in 1975 (*4*). Statistics Canada figures for Quebec for 1976–1977 included both Cégeps and private colleges, so it was impossible to say definitely whether the Cégeps at least were reaching those standards; certainly Quebec college libraries as a whole did not, except in the number of volumes per student.

An initiative in British Columbia held considerable promise. The Ministry of Education, in cooperation with the College Principals' Group and the Council of Post-Secondary Library Directors, approved 11 role statements for library resource centers, and an experienced college librarian was assigned to develop qualitative/quantitative statements to match them. It was expected that if the results were accepted, the ministry would provide funds for upgrading substandard operations.

Reliable statistics for college library growth were impossible to obtain, partly because of nonresponse, partly because the institutions eligible for inclusion in surveys varied, partly also because the college libraries were surveyed along with university libraries and the results were sometimes inadequate to describe the college library situation fully. Moreover, the latest complete statistics available pertained only to 1976–1977 (*5*) and therefore did not reflect the increasing economic restraints of the last years of the decade. (Preliminary results for 1978–1979 [*6*], made available to the writer by Statistics Canada, were taken into account, however, when appropriate.) These caveats must be borne in mind while reading what follows.

Statistics Canada figures for 1970–1971 (*7*) indicated that the operating expenditures of college libraries as a percentage of total institutional operating expenditures ranged from 0.6 to 9.8% among the libraries reporting, with roughly 63% of respondents accounting for less than 5%, and 37% accounting for 5% or more of their institutions' totals. Only three libraries reported percentages reaching the 8% recommended in the CACUL and Fédération des cégeps standards. Volumes per full-time student ranged from 17 (Ontario CAATs) to 120 (Quebec colleges other than the Cégeps, which averaged 28 per student). Library operating expenditures per full-time student ranged from $40.46 (Ontario colleges other than the CAATs) to $139.69 (Prince Edward Island).

TABLE 1

Selected Statistics of Canadian College Libraries, 1970–1971, 1976–1977, and 1978–1979[a]

	Region[b]					
Ratios	Atlantic	Quebec (Cégep & other)	Ontario (CAATs & other)	Central	British Columbia	Canada
Volumes per FT student[c]						
1970–1971	37	40	18	25	25	31
1976–1977	65	30	21	35	39	29
1978–1979	60	—	19	28	45	—
Library operating expenditures per FT student						
1970–1971	$ 90.84	$ 65.90	$ 67.42	$ 86.39	$133.31	$ 73.89
1976–1977	$185.74	$ 80.36	$132.70	$204.29	$293.07	$122.39
1978–1979	$208.51	$104.12	$130.20	$227.85	$436.01	$150.74
Number of FT students per FT staff member						
1970–1971	129	148	190	134	138	156
1976–1977	138	202	147	95	74	152
1978–1979	132	216	174	111	59	157

[a] Saskatchewan's 12 community colleges, which rely mainly on the provincial and regional libraries for resources, are not included in the figures.

[b] Atlantic Provinces: Newfoundland, Prince Edward Island, Nova Scotia, and New Brunswick; Central Provinces: Manitoba, Saskatchewan, and Alberta.

[c] FT, full time.

The number of students per full-time staff member ranged from 78 in Quebec colleges other than the Cégeps (which averaged 171) to 269 in Ontario colleges other than the CAATs. These ratios were all higher than the 63 students per staff member envisaged by the CACUL standards, although in one case the ratio was lower than the 1:100 called for by the Cégeps standards. (These were the ratios for colleges with fewer than 1,000 full-time students, which constituted 65% of those reporting.)

Table 1 gives figures for 1970–1971 regrouped into regions and compared with figures for 1976–1977 and preliminary figures for 1978–1979. Because of problems of nonresponse (total operating expenditures for British Columbia and Quebec in 1976–1977 were not available), comparisons are indicative, not precise. These figures indicate that there were some improvements during the first 6 years of the decade: Except in Quebec, print holdings per student increased (though the national figure was down slightly); except in Ontario, which showed a slight drop in 1978–1979, expenditures per student increased, in some cases substantially; except in Quebec and the Atlantic region, the staff to student ratio had improved by 1976–1977, though only British Columbia was showing major improvement by 1978–1979. While quantity cannot be equated with quality, it is very difficult to attain the latter if holdings are poor and staff too few for the work load to be carried. It seems reasonable to conclude that up to 1976–1977 the situation was improving. The economic restraints of the later years of the decade, however, may have been partly responsible for the generally less favorable volumes per student and students per full-time staff ratios in 1978–1979, although the national average of operating expenditure per student (in current and in constant 1971 dollars) had continued to rise.

Finance

With the possible exception of Quebec, the college libraries seemed to have either held their own or improved their financial position slightly during the first part of the decade. Total reported operating expenditures more than doubled, from $10,485,005 in 1970–1971 to $25,857,969 in 1976–1977, and grew to $33,418,264 in 1978–1979. National expenditures per student of $73.89 in 1970–1971 rose to $122.39 in 1976–1977, about a 65% increase, in current dollars. In 1978–1979 there was a further 23% increase to $150.74.

Resources: Collections

In 1970–1971 college library holdings totaled over 4 million volumes—a 16% increase over 1969–1970. The national average was 31 volumes per full-time student. Acquisitions reported for that academic year were 668,031 volumes, and 38.3% of total expenditures was devoted to materials and binding costs. In 1976–1977 the situation was very different: 20.5% of operating expenditures went for purchase of materials and binding; new acquisitions were down to 443,091 volumes. Total volumes held had increased to 6,110,316 in 1976–1977, but holdings per full-time student had dropped slightly to 29. Because of nonresponse from Quebec, comparable figures for 1978–1979 were not available. Reports of nonprint and microform materials holdings showed considerable increases (from 450,558 items in 1970–1971 to 2,252,354 items in 1976–1977), reflecting the emphasis on such materials characteristic of the college libraries. (In a survey of 44 Quebec college libraries in the mid-1970s, for example [*8*], an audiovisual collection was a library service in 31 of the 44.) A change in the method of counting slides made 1978–1979 figures noncomparable, but even so they indicated continued growth in holdings of these types of material.

Two provinces had special projects under way to assist college libraries. In October 1978 the Alberta government announced that colleges there would share $9 million with the universities over a 3-year period to enable them to improve their collections. Moreover, the grant contained a provision that current levels of support must not be reduced because of this extra funding. In British Columbia the government funded the College Library Collections Development Project, of which Phase I, compilation of a bibliography identifying the basic collections needed to support college courses, was completed in 1978, and the next step, upgrading of collections, was under consideration.

Two factors to be remembered when looking at figures for collection growth are that college libraries contained large proportions of technical material which had to be constantly updated, and that they had no commitment to support research. Consequently, weeding to get rid of out-of-date material had to be frequent—the more so since many libraries were reaching the limits of their space. Growth was thus likely to reflect larger numbers of students or more courses, rather than the building of collections per se.

Resources: Personnel

Figures for numbers of students per full-time staff member appear in Table 1, showing an improvement in three regions. The totals of staff increased in all regions, the increases ranging from 8% in the Atlantic area to 165% in British Columbia. Unfortunately there were no data to indicate whether the level of professional staffing had improved; in 1976–1977, however, librarians constituted about 25% of the total except in the Atlantic region (41%). The ratio of professionals to nonprofessionals recommended by CACUL (1:3) was achieved in all regions but the Atlantic, where it was 1:1½. The proportion of the library budget devoted to salaries increased substantially by 1976–1977, to 71.2% from the 55.6% of 1970–1971.

These ratios conceal the fact that the college libraries' strong emphasis on audiovisual (AV) materials, sometimes on their production as well as their use, required a substantial proportion of skilled AV technicians or other professionals among their staffs. They also do not reveal the effect on staffing of resources spread over multiple locations, whether in one city or in a number of them. Staff resources in such circumstances may be spread very thin, especially if there is no major library in the group able to coordinate effort, offer centralized services, etc.

In 1978 CACUL adopted *Guidelines for Academic Status for Professional Li-*

brarians in Community and Technical Colleges (9). It is still too soon to know what effect these may have. Meanwhile, unionization made advances among college as well as other libraries, and in some cases provisions applied to a whole group. Librarians in the Ontario CAATs, for example, were members of the Ontario Public Service Employees Union–Academic; support staff belonged to the Support Section of the same union. Professional staff of the Cégeps belonged to the Fédération des professionnels salariés et des cadres du Québec of the Confédération des syndicats nationaux [Confederation of National Trade Unions].

Resources: Buildings

In general, college librarians, like special librarians, often had to make do with whatever space was available, much of it not built for library use. Quebec Cégeps apparently fared somewhat better than others; 24 college libraries had been built since 1968, six of them in 1975 alone.

An interesting innovation in the use of space was started in the early '70s by Mount Royal College in Calgary. The college tried the experiment of an open concept-learning library containing closed teaching areas with faculty offices adjacent and "resource islands" of essential materials nearby. Backup collections and technical services areas were grouped at one end of the library space. A formal evaluation of the success of the experiment was scheduled in 1979. Meanwhile other colleges (e.g., the Cornwall Campus of the Saint Lawrence CAAT) adopted Mount Royal's system.

Special Services and Programs

The presence of large numbers of part-time and short-term students meant that college libraries had to give a great deal of attention to making access to their resources as efficient as possible, either through improved organization or through user orientation programs. To give a few examples: Sheridan College Library put its slide collection on colored microfiche so that users could browse easily; in addition, it provided an extensive series of aids for users, from bookmarks containing basic data on the library (hours, etc.) to guides to major topics and "how to" guides (e.g., how to compile a bibliography). The library of the Canadian Coast Guard College supplied packages of books on navigation for the ships used in the sea training of officer-cadets. Saint Lawrence College linked its Brockville and Kingston campuses to facilitate reference service. Other examples of college library responses to user needs could be added.

College libraries in British Columbia were involved in an unusual experiment in teaching on-line searching techniques to librarians in remote areas. Librarians taking the course met at designated colleges in the interior which had facilities for receiving the audio and video signals transmitted via satellite from Simon Fraser University, and also facilities for sending audio signals back. The B.C. Institute of Technology participated in the transmissions. In spite of technical difficulties, the experiment was felt to be a success.

Automation

College libraries in British Columbia were more involved in automated systems than some of their colleagues elsewhere because of the provincial government's funding of their participation in the B.C. Union Catalogue (BCUC) Project. Current college library holdings appeared in the COM (computer output on microfiche) catalog that was produced; in addition, many of the colleges were enabled to complete a retrospective conversion of their holdings. The bibliography produced as Phase I of the College Library Collections Development Project was also being put on tape for easier access.

In Ontario, the College Library Bibliocentre, which handled cataloging and processing for most of Ontario's CAATs, had an automated batch Acquisitions/-Accounting System from 1971 and used the University of Toronto's UTLAS facilities to obtain catalog copy from 1974. As the decade closed, the Bibliocentre was supporting a test of IBM's DOBIS/LIBIS on-line circulation module, and there were plans to test the acquisition module shortly.

These were major projects involving numbers of college libraries; other examples of automation tended to be individual. Red River Community College (Manitoba) was planning to switch from batch to a fully integrated on-line system for its acquisition, cataloging, and reference services. A number of libraries offered computer-based reference service to their users. Some libraries tapped computerized facilities through neighboring libraries; for example, two Alberta colleges received printed MARC catalog records by arrangement with the University of Calgary. The Saskatchewan Technical Institute had a computer-based retrieval system for its audiovisual materials. Though examples might be multiplied, very few of the college libraries listed in *Canadian Library Directory, 2* in 1976 (*10*) reported automated systems, and on the whole, college libraries were less involved than university libraries in automated systems.

Cooperation and Networking

The common forms of cooperation among Canadian libraries in general have been formation of consultative groups; cooperative acquisitions, cataloging, and processing; and improvements in access to resources, whether these were the actual materials (through borrowing agreements, extension of interlibrary loan [ILL] service, deposit collections, and the like), the means of identifying and locating them (through union catalogs and lists), or the means of getting them (through Telex, courier services, etc.). Examples of all these may be found among college libraries, but the main emphasis has been on cataloging and interlibrary loan.

Consultative groups could be informal or formal, meeting to share experience, take common action, etc. Examples were B.C.'s Council of Post-Secondary Library Directors, Ontario's Committee of Librarians of Ontario CAATs, Quebec's Commission des directeurs de bibliothèque of the Fédération des cégeps, and Alberta's Council of College Librarians.

The most advanced programs for development of a bibliographic network which would include college libraries were in British Columbia. Some aspects of the program have already been mentioned—the Collections Development Project and the participation of college libraries in the B.C. Union Catalogue. Through the latter the college libraries benefited from access to cataloging data, and they will ultimately also benefit from the name authorities file being developed by the central office of the project.

British Columbia's college libraries also enjoyed a highly developed provincial interlibrary loan system in which government funding both improved facilities and also helped the universities meet the burden of servicing the heavy loan demand. (Requests jumped over 60% in one university library when the funding scheme became operational.) Government grants made possible the deposit of the COM catalogs of the three university libraries in each of the colleges, along with reading equipment. Telexes were installed; a manual of cost-reducing, standardized routines was drawn up; and existing courier services, where feasible, were modified to improve delivery time. Loans of films did not come under the basic ILL system, but they were coordinated voluntarily through the Media Exchange Cooperative. Access to films from the United States was coordinated through Fraser Valley College, which arranged for a U.S. Post Office box and a courier service.

In Edmonton, three colleges were members of the Federated Inter-Library Loan Service (FILLS), which was granted government funding to hire a technician to work in the University of Alberta Libraries to retrieve materials to fill the colleges' interlibrary loan requests and thus take part of the burden from the university. The experiment was to be evaluated at the end of 1979.

Reciprocal borrowing privileges were offered by all B.C. college libraries to one another and to local public libraries. Arrangements that were similar, but narrower in scope, could be found in other provinces; between nearby college libraries and the University of Calgary, for example.

College libraries cooperated to improve access through union catalogs and lists, and the B.C. example has been described. Alberta college libraries compiled a list of serials held by members of the Alberta Council of College Librarians, and council members agreed on the extent of access they would allow. Ontario college libraries participated individually with other types of libraries in joint union lists or catalogs.

In summary, then, college libraries in Canada were to some extent still unknown quantities at the end of the decade. More, probably, than any other type of library they had to grapple directly with the burgeoning demand for practical, career-oriented education, with retraining and continuing-education needs, and with the demands of newly retired people looking for intellectual stimulation or pursuing studies not possible during their working lives. Consequently their role in their parent institutions was still fluid and developing, and national trends were just becoming discernible.

UNIVERSITY LIBRARIES

During the late 1950s and throughout the '60s Canadian university libraries went through a halcyon period. Budgets increased, new buildings were erected, and faculty, administration, library directors, and governments seemed agreed on the desirability of upgrading university libraries. It was necessary to make good the stagnation of the Depression and World War II years, to build collections large enough to serve the growing numbers of students, and to support the graduate programs which began to proliferate. Generally speaking, money to achieve these aims was forthcoming, and Canadian university libraries grew enormously. A combination of inflation, economic recession, and the prospect of declining enrollments made the situation in the '70s a very different one, however, and many university libraries began to fear that the gains of the '60s would be eroded.

Legislation and Governance

Canadian universities operate under legislation of various kinds—a Universities Act (British Columbia, Prince Edward Island, and Alberta), a Universities Commission Act (Saskatchewan), a University Assistance Act (Nova Scotia), and so on. The need for presenting a common response to government initiatives has fostered interuniversity cooperation, and the resulting councils or associations frequently have committees whose concerns are library oriented. Many started in the 1960s; for example, the Librarians' Council of the Association of Atlantic Universities (1964), the Subcommittee on Libraries of the Conference of Rectors and Principals of Quebec Universities (1968), and the Ontario Council of University Libraries (1966). Others were added in the '70s; for example, Manitoba's Council of Academic Libraries (1973) and the Library Committee of the Association of Universities and Colleges of Canada (1974). These groups provided a forum for consultation, for deciding on common action, for sponsoring needed studies, etc. This trend to cooperation among university libraries was not new to the '70s, though the strength of the trend was perhaps greater.

Standards and Statistics

The Canadian Association of College and University Libraries developed a set of standards for university libraries, called *Trends for the Seventies*, in 1971 (*11*). Though widely discussed, they were not approved by the membership, and nothing to replace them has been published by the Canadian Association of Research Libraries (CARL), the group of larger university libraries which broke away from CACUL and the Canadian Library Association (CLA) to become an independent association in 1976.

Statistics on Canadian university libraries have been gathered by Statistics Canada, by CARL and its predecessor, and (on financial matters) by the Canadian Association of University Business Officers (CAUBO). Except for those produced by CAUBO, the statistics are generally slow to appear and thus of limited current use. Statistics Canada figures were used to prepare Table 2 because they permitted comparisons. Moreover, by courtesy of the Cultural Analysis Section of the Education, Science, and Culture Division, some preliminary figures for 1978–1979 were made available (*12*).

TABLE 2

Selected Ratios of Canadian University Libraries, 1970–1971, 1976–1977, and 1978–1979[a]

	Region					
Ratios	Atlantic	Quebec	Ontario	Central	British Columbia	Canada
Volumes per FT student						
1970–1971	70	84	86	64	77	78
1976–1977	112	106	100	94	109	102
1978–1979	121	111	115	108	123	114
Expenditures per FT student						
1970–1971	$229.04	$235.34	$288.29	$223.60	$296.32	$259.18
1976–1977	$386.30	$402.96	$366.80	$358.74	$520.57	$387.60
1978–1979	$443.21	$600.30	$426.62	$415.63	$628.97	$447.20
Students per FT staff member						
1970–1971	58	42	41	56	42	45
1976–1977	54	52	58	57	47	55
1978–1979	54	58	55	54	45	54
Volumes						
1970–1971						24,093,460
1976–1977						37,490,416
1978–1979						40,732,314
Expenditures						
1970–1971						$ 79,686,319
1976–1977						$142,568,366
1978–1979						$170,104,698
Enrollment						
1970–1971						307,459
1976–1977						367,821
1978–1979						356,462

[a] Sources: Statistics Canada surveys.

The volumes per student ratio improved, notably in the Atlantic and Central regions, in all three periods, but the increases in the staff to student ratio in 1976–1977 hinted at a decline in staffing which figures for 1978–1979 did not confirm, probably because the decline in staffing was paralleled by a decline in enrollment.

Finance

Table 2 indicates substantial increases in amounts spent by university libraries per full-time student, particularly in Quebec and British Columbia, in the years between 1970–1971 and 1978–1979. The *Five-Year Trend Analysis of University Fi-*

nancial Statistics (*13*) published by CAUBO in 1979 revealed, however, that a decreasing proportion of university budgets was being spent for library functions. While individual university libraries may have attained the 10% of the university budget advocated by CACUL, Statistics Canada's figures for 1970–1971 (7) showed that, by province, the highest percentage was a little over 9% (Prince Edward Island and British Columbia), and the rest ranged down to little over 6% (Manitoba). CAUBO figures for 1976–1977, based on all institutions reporting, showed libraries accounting for 5.6% of the universities' operating expenditures. In 1977–1978 the percentage dropped slightly to 5.5%. Therefore, even though the dollar amounts expended rose, libraries became relatively worse off in terms of the proportion of the total institutional budget devoted to them.

Resources: Collections

Canadian university libraries in the 1960s were chiefly concerned with trying to make up for past deficiencies and build up collections to meet the demands of new and expanded programs. By 1970–1971, according to Statistics Canada's figures, six Canadian university libraries had achieved holdings of at least 1 million volumes; among them, the University of Toronto was (as it remains) the largest, with over 3 million volumes at that time. During the '70s collections continued to grow —15 more libraries reached their one-millionth volume—but the libraries' major problem had changed from developing collections to maintaining their quality as budget increases ceased to keep pace with inflation.

Several factors contributed to this change from growth to static or even declining rates of acquisition. Costs of books and journals (especially the latter, in the later years of the decade) rose at rates higher than library budgets did. The amount of money available for acquisitions decreased as the proportion of budget needed for salaries increased. In 1970–1971 library materials and binding were 37.3% of Canadian university libraries' total operating expenditures. In 1976–1977 the proportion was 28.2%; in 1978–1979 it was up slightly at 29.5%. In terms of university expenditure as a whole, CAUBO figures indicated that this was a drop from 2.1% in 1971–1972 to 1.6% in 1976–1977. Translated into dollars, the decrease meant that in 1976–1977 libraries had about $10 million less to spend on books and periodicals than they would have had if the 2.1% proportion had been maintained. While total acquisitions were still over 2 million volumes a year, the total in 1976–1977 was almost 15% lower than in 1970–1971.

Because of the very great increases in periodicals costs, many libraries held major reviews of their subscription lists, usually in conjunction with faculty. The Universities of Alberta and Manitoba and Université de Moncton are examples. Other libraries, such as the University of British Columbia, tried to arrange that an old subscription be dropped before a new one was started. To ensure that unique titles remained within their area, the Universities of Guelph, Waterloo, and Wilfrid Laurier agreed that they would not all cancel the same title. They hoped that by cooperating on retention decisions they could keep serials costs down, yet still be certain of efficient access to a wide spectrum of titles. York University Library shared certain expensive subscriptions with Trent University and cooperated in the acquisition and sharing of legal materials with other Canadian libraries. The University of New Brunswick and Queen's University Libraries exchanged microfilms of their respective holdings of C. G. D. Roberts's manuscripts, so that both would have access to complete collections. Other examples of attempts to compensate for lack of purchasing power by sharing resources could be cited. One interesting variant was the division among B.C. university libraries of responsibility for certain areas of specialization: for Eastern Studies material, the University of British Columbia; African Studies material, Simon Fraser University; Pacific Rim materials in English, University of Victoria.

Rationalization of collections along lines such as these presupposes willingness by the parent universities to rationalize their course offerings. A 1973 study sponsored by the Association of Universities and Colleges of Canada (AUCC) (*14*) called for more consultation with libraries before new programs were established, in order to ensure that library resources would be adequate. Moreover, it is possible that, as funds decrease and enrollments drop, the universities' freedom to decide on the courses they give may become less. If that happens (there are already some restraints on new graduate programs in Ontario), university libraries may find themselves able to drop certain areas of collecting, and even able to transfer collections no longer needed to institutions where the courses are being continued, in order to strengthen the collections there. A series of collection surveys was carried out by the National Library as one aid to rationalization. None were currently under way at the end of the decade, but it was hoped that means might be found to encourage similar efforts.

It would be unfair to paint a picture of unrelieved gloom. The Alberta universities and colleges, as noted in the preceding section, shared the $9-million Heritage Savings and Trust Fund grant to improve collections. At the federal level, the Canada Council's $2-million special grant to support university collections was, by consent of the universities, put into a major project for the microfilming of pre-1900 Canadian titles and the deposit of fully cataloged microfiche sets in university libraries. Some libraries were able, by various special means, to obtain major collections; for example, in 1978 McMaster finally received the Bertrand Russell papers which it had bought 10 years earlier, and the University of Calgary housed, and later (April 1979) incorporated, the collection of the Arctic Institute of North America. This same university added considerably to its holdings of the papers of Canadian authors during the decade. The 1977 Cultural Property Export and Import Act provided for federal assistance, through financing or authorization of tax credits, for approved libraries trying to obtain, or retain within the country, works important to Canada. Mount Allison, Dalhousie, and Memorial University Libraries, for example, benefited from the act's provisions.

Resources: Buildings

A concomitant of the growth of libraries in the 1960s was the growth in the number of new university library buildings. Construction extended into the '70s but tended to be more a matter of extensions and modifications than of major new construction. Yet one of the most striking library buildings in Canada was built during the decade—the new John P. Robarts Library of the University of Toronto. Its size, its facilities, and its position as the center of a complex which includes a rare book library and a library school made it outstanding. The concept behind it was unique as well; it was intended to be a research center for Ontario universities, and provision was made for visiting researchers. Though overshadowed by Robarts, other major libraries or library extensions were constructed: Killam Memorial Library opened in October 1970 at Dalhousie and McGill's Redpath Library was renovated the same year; the University of Prince Edward Island's Robertson Library opened in 1975; Rutherford North Library at the University of Alberta, in 1973; the D. B. Weldon Library, in 1972 at Western Ontario; the Asian Studies Library and Law Library, in 1976 at British Columbia; Saskatchewan's Murray Memorial Library, in 1974; and York University's Scott Library, in 1970.

Even with the new construction, libraries at the end of the '70s were facing the threat of serious space shortages. The possibilities of storage libraries or joint storage centers were being studied (e.g., in the Atlantic Provinces), and individual libraries were considering what portions of the collection could be relegated to less expensive storage. Many libraries turned to microforms, especially of serial publications, to save space as well as to supplement their print collections; microform holdings increased from 8 million in 1970–1971 to over 18 million in 1976–1977 and more than 22 million in 1978–1979.

Resources: Personnel

Total personnel reported for university libraries dropped a little between 1970–1971 (6,776 full-time staff) and 1976–1977 (6,688), and between 1976–1977 and 1978–1979 (6,569). The proportion of professionals (approximately 24%) and the ratio of professionals to nonprofessionals (1:3) remained about the same for the country as a whole. The proportion of operating budget required for salaries increased from 54.4% in 1970–1971 to 63.5% (including fringe benefits) in 1976–1977 and to 64% in 1978–1979. In dollar amounts the change was from $43.4 to $108.9 million in 1978–1979. Faced with rising salary and materials costs not adequately met by budget increases, university libraries tried to deal with the situation by cutting staff (e.g., fewer student assistants), cutting hours of service, eliminating or reducing services, or automating in order to handle the work load without adding to staff.

For their part, library staff became increasingly organized. Support staff frequently joined unions such as the Canadian Union of Public Employees (CUPE), while professionals tended to join faculty associations, many of which belonged to the Canadian Association of University Teachers (CAUT). Examples include the Universities of Moncton, Carleton, Ottawa, Saskatchewan, and Manitoba. Occasionally professionals and support staff were both members of the same union, as at the Université de Montréal. Sometimes support staff were unionized but professionals were not.

Within individual libraries there were demands by professional staff for a greater share in the management of the library, and efforts were made to break out of a rigidly hierarchical or autocratic structure. Sometimes changes were introduced as a result of staff forming unions or joining faculty associations for purposes of collective bargaining; York set up a library council as the result of a union contract. Professionals gained representation on policy and other committees; at the University of British Columbia, for example, librarians elected a member to the Senate of the university. At Carleton University, promotion was by peer evaluation. The means of participation varied, but they were being found.

The situation for the universities as well as the colleges was still fluid, and like the colleges, universities too had their share of strikes, disputes as to whether professionals should organize and, if they did, in what type of bargaining unit, and so on. Occasionally, as at Saint Mary's University, there were conflicting potential bargaining agents involved. One major right gained by some of the library associations was for staff to be granted sabbatical leave or study leave. A number of librarians were able to avail themselves of sabbaticals to pursue special research.

The question of faculty status for academic librarians seems to have been less hotly debated in the '70s, perhaps because more had achieved it, with or without an impetus from collective bargaining. The *Guidelines on Academic Status for University Librarians* (*15*) received final approval from CAUT and CACUL in 1976; in the guidelines the sponsoring associations made the point that what was being requested was that procedures for librarians' appointments, conditions of work, etc., should be analogous to those for faculty, so far as was appropriate. Some libraries (e.g., McGill) instituted a system of ranking staff on their qualifications and achievements instead of on position held.

Services

One area of library service which saw a number of changes in the decade was access to collections. Open stacks in university libraries were no longer news in the '70s, but rising book losses became so, and various electronic or other security systems had to be introduced. Loan regulations used to favor faculty and sometimes graduate students; in this decade some libraries (e.g., the Universities of British Columbia and Manitoba) introduced common rules for all. Undergraduates had not been allowed to request interlibrary loans; at the urging of Atlantic area librarians, CACUL agreed to a trial year and found the experiment satisfactory enough to continue.

In addition to easing access to actual materials, libraries such as Toronto and Guelph, using COM fiche catalogs, put bibliographic information on the library's total holdings into many areas of the campus which earlier would have had only information on local specialized resources. With the aid of government funding British Columbia's three university libraries (Notre-Dame University was closed in 1977) were able to go beyond this and to place COM catalogs of their holdings in all B.C. college libraries. This facilitated the interlibrary loan service which further government funding then enabled the universities to provide.

Besides improving access for their primary users, university libraries tended to ease somewhat their restrictions on use by other institutions or by the public. Ontario and Quebec libraries supported the Inter-University Borrowing Project, which allowed faculty and graduate students of one institution in the group to borrow from any of the others; libraries within these provinces might make other special arrangements as well. For example, University of Waterloo borrowing regulations allowed for borrowing by faculty and by students (if approved) of Conestoga College, by adult residents of the Regional Municipality, and even by secondary school students presenting letters of introduction. As noted earlier, such university–college arrangements were not uncommon; access by the general public was less so. The University of Manitoba Library, however, issued a Citizen's Borrower Card to Manitobans with a legitimate need for access.

Professional schools, especially in law and medicine, have a tradition of service to practitioners in their fields; the new development was the extension of this service on a formal basis to wider areas. For example, at Memorial University, Dalhousie, and the University of Manitoba, the libraries tried to improve information services to medical practitioners provincewide. Other special groups might also be served. The University of British Columbia's Crane Library served visually handicapped students beyond the university, thanks to special funding arrangements made by the B.C. government. Saint Mary's University in Halifax operated its Community Tape Resource Library with government funding from 1975 to 1977, and then continued it independently in order to provide material for blind students in local universities and for the public. University extension libraries run as a service to the general public declined in number as public library facilities improved; for example, McGill's McLennan Travelling Library was absorbed into the public library system. Manitoba's and Alberta's services continued into the 1970s; the former was transferred to the provincial library service, but the latter still functioned at the end of the decade and was heavily used.

Some libraries, anxious to make their resources more widely available but unable to bear the extra cost, devised various schemes for offering service on a full or partial cost-recovery basis. Interlibrary loan charges are discussed in the next paragraph. Charges for on-line retrieval service and for photocopying were common. Some libraries began charging for reference service; the Industrial Relations Library of the University of Toronto for one, preparatory to instituting a subscription program. The University of British Columbia Library received authority to charge for reference service if it seemed desirable.

The service in which charging raised the greatest controversy was interlibrary loans. The large university libraries such as Toronto, McGill, and the University of British Columbia found that they were lending far more than they borrowed, and that they could no longer absorb the costs. In 1976 Toronto—followed by the University of British Columbia, Victoria, and Guelph—started to charge for lending; their example was followed by others, although some that originally charged have stopped, and certain libraries charged only the libraries which charged them. There were usually exemptions from the charges; in Quebec and Ontario, local agreements allowed free service to provincially funded universities; in British Columbia the provincial government reimbursed the universities for the cost of serving the province's colleges, and the University of British Columbia Library was also provided with funds to offset costs of interlibrary loans to Lower Mainland public libraries. University librarians and library associations called upon the federal government to reimburse net lenders for out-of-province loans; they also endorsed the national librarian's concept of a national serials-lending center for the humanities and social sciences. (One for science already exists, de facto if not de jure, in the collections of the Canada Institute for Scientific and Technical Information [CISTI].) Funding for these proposals had not been assured as of 1979; if it becomes available, the National Library's plans for such a center can be implemented and a lending collection of first resort developed.

In the 1970s university libraries gave more attention to orientation programs for students. These included full-credit courses (Acadia, Wilfrid Laurier); library skills components in departmental-credit courses; instructional presentations worked out in conjunction with faculty (Calgary, Concordia, McGill, Memorial, Winnipeg, Western Ontario, York, to name a few); special library programs (Laval); "self-service" slide–tape presentations and walking tours; and the distribution of various printed guides, handbooks, bibliographic finding aids, etc.

Finally, university libraries were active in both preserving Canadian material and ensuring its dissemination. The Canada Council-sponsored Canadian Institute for Historical Microreproductions was the major project under way at the end of the decade, but local programs for microfilming newspapers (Memorial in Newfoundland and university libraries in cooperation in New Brunswick) continued through the decade and should not be forgotten. An interest in the subject of conservation appeared to be developing as the needs in this area became more generally recognized. The National Library was active in the compilation of a retrospective bibliography of early Canadiana, in facilitating the microfilming of newspapers, and, in conjunction with the Public Archives, in supporting a mass deacidification program.

Automation

Canadian university libraries were in the forefront in attempting to use automated systems to improve operations, and the '70s saw their efforts continued, particularly in the area of bibliographic services. The major achievement of the decade was the successful automation of the main library catalog of the University of Toronto and the development of its Library Automation System (UTLAS) into a bibliographic utility whose 500 users made it second in size only to the Ohio College Library Center. The university formally opened its automated facilities for the use of others in 1973, and by the end of the decade UTLAS, now officially an ancillary enterprise of the university, numbered libraries of all types, not just university libraries, among its users. One important user consortium was UNICAT/TELECAT, which consisted of libraries in Quebec as well as Ontario and was the first expansion of UTLAS outside Ontario. (It disbanded, however, in 1980.) UTLAS users by 1979 spanned the country, from Memorial University in Newfoundland to the Union Catalogue Project in British Columbia.

Not all of the early users of UTLAS stayed with the system, finding the cost too high. One which withdrew was the University of Guelph Library, an early advocate of library automation and the library which developed CODOC (Cooperative Documents), an automated system for handling government documents. This library changed to a system based on its own minicomputers, an example which may prove an augury for the future.

Libraries in the Atlantic region turned first to the Blackwell North America system for their bibliographic data, both university and public libraries joining in the project, which started in 1976. Three of the university libraries found that the system did not meet their needs and withdrew. By 1979 the fate of the whole project was, therefore, uncertain.

The Université du Québec had its own system, BADADUQ, developed by 1972; this served the widely scattered campuses of the university and interfaced with local systems where they had been developed.

The B.C. Union Catalogue Project used UTLAS facilities while it decided whether to replicate the Washington Library Network system in British Columbia. (The decision will affect the college as well as the university libraries.) Meanwhile, the first published union catalog, on COM fiche, was produced, to join the growing number of single library microform catalogs (e.g., those of York, Laval, and Guelph) which were developed during the 1970s.

Computer-based reference services could be found in most university libraries by the end of the decade. Where other means of access to data bases did not exist, as in Newfoundland, the university library served the general public as well as its university clientele. Where individual libraries could not initially afford the cost, as in Halifax and Calgary, facilities made available by a larger university enabled a cost-sharing scheme to be worked out, allowing libraries to share a service until able to pay for it independently. University medical libraries which became MEDLINE centers appear to have been equally generous in facilitating access to the service by hospitals and even individual (and perhaps isolated) practitioners.

A number of university libraries automated their circulation systems. Guelph used a locally developed GEAC system, and users were able to access circulation information through a public terminal. Dalhousie bought the CLSI system; Laval used an on-line system; Carleton had a bar-code system. No single system predominated.

Production of serials lists and some acquisition processes were automated in a few libraries. Alberta put the data for its Task Analysis Data Project on tape, and other types of use occurred. Libraries (e.g., the library of the Université du Québec à Trois-Rivières) continued to produce—or use—their own local cataloging systems, although the trend was toward adoption of the more widely used systems.

To date few research reports have appeared on the results of automation for the libraries automated, though such reports may exist as internal documents. Some hard facts, widely disseminated, on gains and losses would be exceedingly helpful to have.

Cooperation

Some instances of university library cooperation have been mentioned in other contexts; for example, consultative groups of chief librarians and cooperative automation projects. One of the most productive consultative groups was TRIUL (Tri-University Libraries), formed in 1970 by the Universities of British Columbia and

Victoria, and Simon Fraser University. Many of the cooperative ventures started informally by this group (e.g., more generous ILL arrangements, service to colleges, reciprocal borrowing for undergraduates) later became, in effect, province-wide policy. The Subcommittee on Libraries of the Conference of Rectors and Principals of Quebec Universities (CREPUQ) sponsored attempts at rationalization and standardization in that province; one of its achievements was to obtain consensus on a method of gathering statistics on library operations. The Ontario Universities Library Cooperative System (OULCS) had some half dozen cooperative ventures to its credit, all still in existence in the '70s. CREPUQ and OULCS members as well as Atlantic area librarians all studied the possibility of storage facilities for less-used materials, but no concrete steps had been taken by the end of the decade.

Cooperation in acquisition and cataloging occurred by means of large automated systems such as BCUC and UNICAT/TELECAT, which allowed members to benefit from one another's cataloging, as well as by bilateral agreements to share each other's UTLAS files such as the Universities of Brandon and Manitoba had. The Laval Library cooperated with the Université de Montréal, the Bibliothèque nationale du Québec, and the National Library of Canada, to develop U.S. Library of Congress–style subject headings in French, which the National Library of Canada publishes for the benefit of libraries in Canada and abroad. The CODOC system for handling government publications, mentioned earlier, was being further developed cooperatively. Another useful cooperative cataloging project was proposed by the University of Regina; namely, that libraries which hold microfiche of the items in Peel's bibliography of Western Canadiana should each agree to catalog a certain portion of the items and make that cataloging available to other contributors. Unfortunately, Regina's proposal did not gain acceptance.

Not surprisingly, cooperative schemes to improve physical and bibliographic access to resources were the most numerous. University libraries in the Halifax area had reciprocal borrowing arrangements; B.C. libraries, the same. The major development of this type was the joint arrangement between Ontario and Quebec universities. Since 1976, faculty, graduate students, and library staff of one university could borrow from others in the two provinces on presentation of suitable identification.

Loan service by university medical libraries to practitioners in their regions has already been noted. The University of New Brunswick provided the interlibrary loan service for seven local institutions. Within Quebec, university libraries agreed not to charge one another for photocopies sent on interlibrary loan.

Improving transport of materials has become more urgent as mail service has slowed down. A noteworthy initiative (September 1979) was a pilot project under which CISTI sent Calgary—by air cargo, twice a week—all interlibrary loans and photocopies for that area. On their arrival, the university saw to their local delivery by truck or mail. The two provincial courier services established in the '60s, Ontario's Inter-University Transit Service (IUTS) and the Quebec Interlibrary Loan Service (PEBUQUILL), continued to speed delivery within the provinces and between them as well, through their transfer points at the National Library and CISTI. A new courier service was started for Halifax–Dartmouth libraries, and established services in British Columbia were modified, as noted earlier.

Bibliographic access through union catalogs and union lists was improved through those cataloging schemes which permitted access to other libraries' holdings; through development of union lists of serials such as the one for Ontario coordinated by York; and through new listings, such as the one of Prairie newspapers, sponsored by the Council of Prairie University Libraries.

The foregoing only skims the surface of the various types of interlibrary cooperation in existence. It does not mention schemes for registers of expensive purchases, which a library could check before ordering a costly item already available in the region, nor a number of intertype schemes. The University of Waterloo, for example, and Kitchener Public Library had agreements which allowed the general public access to the university library, and the public library provided facilities for one of the university's off-campus courses. It does not record rumbles of discontent beginning to be heard in some quarters as the costs of cooperation seemed to outweigh the benefits. It does document some attempts at interprovincial agreement but still lets the essentially provincial nature of most systems appear. This is perhaps inevitable, given the legal jurisdiction of the provinces in the field of education and provincial control of funding for universities. These legal and financial circumstances are potential barriers to more far-reaching cooperation or networking, but they should not be insuperable if genuine benefits will result.

The most immediate problems of university libraries as they entered the 1980s were the maintenance of hard-won quality collections and actual or imminent lack of space to house those collections. Weeding, relegation to storage, and agreement on specializations were some of the solutions proposed. Problems looming ahead were the effects on universities and their libraries of a drop in the birthrate and therefore in enrollment, since funding formulas often have a per capita basis; physical deterioration of large parts of the collection; and the possibility that further advances in communication might make the educational system as we now know it obsolete. University libraries have traditionally had a responsibility to help preserve man's heritage of knowledge and of wisdom; technological advance will not make that less necessary but may change the means by which they must do it.

SCHOOL LIBRARIES

While it may be difficult to obtain information on college and university library developments, there are sources such as annual reports, library newsletters, specialized journals, etc., which will yield information. Such resources for school libraries are fewer; in particular, these libraries do not ordinarily issue independently published annual reports. These data appear, for the most part, in school district or department of education reports, which may be less easy to access or contain only brief summaries. Moreover, there has never been a directory of Canadian school libraries—their probable number alone (about 10,000) would be a barrier to an attempt. Fortunately Statistics Canada has begun a series of surveys of centralized school libraries (*16*), but a starting date in the mid-1970s (1974–1975) means there are no comparative data for the early years of the decade, and, in addition, Quebec data have not always been available for inclusion.

Legislation and Governance

Various provincial and territorial education acts provide for the establishment and funding of schools, but they do not always explicitly authorize schools to set up school libraries or hire staff for them. They may state that the minister has the power to recommend and approve books for schools, and regulations under the acts may contain specific instructions concerning book grants or possibly the number of library staff that may be hired. By 1970 all provinces did offer some sort of grant, often per student, for establishing libraries or for the purchase of instructional materials; but the grants were often unconditional (as in Saskatchewan or New Brunswick, for example), and there was no requirement that the money be spent on library materials or, if it were, that all parts of the school system should benefit. In fact, elementary school libraries for some time tended to be disregarded, and the emphasis was placed on developing libraries in secondary schools. These conditions, by and large, still prevailed at the end of the decade, although more attention was being given to elementary school libraries.

In Canada there has not been strong coordination of school libraries at the provincial level. British Columbia as of 1979 was still without a provincial coordinator for school libraries, but the other provinces had school library supervisors or consultants in the provincial library service (as in New Brunswick) who could advise, assist with book selection, gather statistics of operations, and so on. Some individual school districts had well-coordinated library systems for their districts (a good example was Vernon, B.C.), but at the close of the decade provincewide systems were still embryonic or nonexistent. Since school librarians were, in general, responsible to the principals of their schools, lack of a system has meant that the credit—and discredit—for individual situations must often be traced to the extent of the principals' appreciation of the role of school libraries in supporting modern methods of teaching.

Standards and Statistics

To a large extent it was the change from the old textbook-centered style of teaching that brought the lack or inadequacy of school libraries to the fore and sparked an interest in establishing school libraries, while the trend to consolidated schools serving larger areas made establishment of new libraries feasible. To take Nova Scotia as an example: In early 1970 there were four school libraries in the Halifax area; by 1975–1976 there were 46. There used to be few libraries outside the larger centers, but a 1979 survey (*17*) showed that the province had 263 schools out of some 600 with a library which was used as such (and not as a spare classroom, for example) for 100% of the time.

The Statistics Canada survey of centralized school libraries mentioned earlier (*16*) gives a picture of provincial conditions at the halfway point in the decade except for Quebec, for which there was no report. The survey produced data on 7,665 centralized school libraries in nine provinces, indicating that about 63% of the more than 12,000 schools surveyed had a centralized library, not just classroom or corridor collections. The highest proportion of libraries was found among secondary schools (about 77%); the lowest, among combined elementary and secondary schools (about 53%). The proportion of elementary schools with libraries was just under 63%.

In terms of pupils with access to a centralized library, secondary school students again came off best, over 89% being served. Proportions for the other two categories were slightly over 69% and 80%, respectively.

Interestingly enough, in book holdings per student and in student to staff ratios, the elementary schools were apparently the best served (14 books per student; 905 pupils per full-time librarian). Secondary schools had fewest books per student (11); combined elementary and secondary schools, the highest student to staff ratio (1,744:1). Per pupil expenditures (print and nonprint materials combined) were $6.17 (elementary), $5.96 (elementary/secondary), and $6.90 (secondary), with the highest print expenditure in the secondary school libraries and the highest nonprint expenditure in the elementary schools.

Table 3 displays school library data by region (figures rounded to whole numbers) from this 1974–1975 survey and from preliminary figures for 1978–79 (*18*) made available through the courtesy of Statistics Canada.

Some provincial figures were available for Quebec for 1973–1974 (*19*); though not comparable, they did provide an idea of the school library situation in that province. The number of volumes per student was 11 in elementary and about 12 in secondary school libraries. Acquisitions per student cost $3.44 in elementary

TABLE 3

Selected Ratios of Canadian School Libraries, 1974–1975 and 1978–1979[a]

	Region					
Ratios	Atlantic	Quebec	Ontario	Central	British Columbia	Canada (exclusive of Quebec)
Volumes per FT student						
1974–1975	7	—	13	16	13	13
1978–1979	8	—	16	19	18	16
Expenditures per student for print materials						
1974–1975	$ 2.92	—	$ 5.15	$ 5.86	$ 6.62	$ 5.30
1978–1979	$ 4.04	—	$ 5.76	$ 7.58	$ 9.72	$ 6.58
Number of students per FT staff member						
1974–1975	2,269	—	865	1,379	854	1,007
1978–1979	782	—	650	484	597	607
Number of schools reporting libraries						
1974–1975	771	—	3,745	1,973	1,176	7,665
1978–1979	965	—	3,681	2,196	1,259	8,201

[a] Sources: Statistics Canada surveys.

and $6.14 in secondary school libraries. The number of students per full-time professional was 9,645 and 1,976 in the two groups of libraries, respectively; the number per library staff member (i.e., including support staff) was 1,791 and 467, respectively. Combining the two to obtain a figure more comparable to those in Table 3 gives a ratio of 765 students per full-time staff member.

Standards and guidelines developed for school libraries in the '70s or for certain aspects of school library management existed for British Columbia (*Sources and Resources*, 1978 [*20*]), New Brunswick (in *Planning Guide for School Buildings and Facilities*, 1978 [*21*]), Quebec (*Guide d'aménagement des bibliothèques-centres documentaires des écoles élémentaires*, 1976 [*22*], and *Guide d'aménagement des bibliothèques des écoles secondaires*, 1975 [*23*]), Ontario (*Resource Centre Guidelines*, 1972 [*24*]), and Newfoundland (*Library Manual for Schools in Newfoundland and Labrador*, revised 1977 [*25*]). Many of these contained suggested guidelines only; the British Columbia handbook contained some prescriptive standards. For example, there were standards on space (800 square feet minimum for an elementary school library), staff (1.5–2 teacher–librarians for 701–1,000 students), and collections (1,500 volumes the minimum; 15 books per student). It also set out criteria for evaluating school libraries and specified the responsibility toward the library of the different groups or individuals involved, from the Ministry of Education to the teacher–librarian running the library.

Proposed national standards for school libraries were edited by Branscombe and Newsom for the Canadian School Library Association and the Association for Media and Technology in Education in Canada, and published in 1977 as *Resource Services for Canadian Schools* (*26*). Their approach stressed principles and functions, rather than prescriptions, in this way seeking to accommodate both the provincial differences, which would render national quantitative standards impracticable, and the variations in needs of schools of different sizes. They emphasized the importance of integrating media and print in the services the school libraries (now often called resource centers) give, thus recognizing the continuing trend toward the use of many media of instruction in modern schools. These standards also placed strong emphasis on cooperation, even interprovincial or national—although in this they were ahead of their time. As noted earlier, provinces have yet to achieve the fully coordinated provincial systems which might facilitate interprovincial cooperation if jurisdictional differences could be overcome.

Perhaps the most striking development of the last years of the decade was the surge of interest in preparing guidelines and standards for school libraries. The publication of *Resource Services for Canadian Schools* may have helped—Newfoundland school librarians working on "School Library Policy and Practice for the Schools of Newfoundland" were taking it into account. The growth in numbers and activity of associations of school librarians may have been another factor; eight of the 18 such associations listed in the fifth edition of *Directory of Library Associations in Canada* (*27*) were established in 1971 or later, the most recent being the Yukon School Librarians' Association (1977). They, as well as the longer-established associations, were actively concerned with standards. Whatever the reasons, in addition to those projects already noted, at the end of the decade work was in progress on guidelines or handbooks in Nova Scotia (by the Task Force on

Libraries), Ontario ("a support document"), and Alberta ("Guidelines for Alberta School Libraries," published in 1981). Whether the provisions of such documents will be accepted and implemented will largely depend on their acceptance by the education departments concerned and the departments' willingness to provide support to enable schools to meet the guidelines.

Finance

School library funding has already been touched upon. To recapitulate: It was not always specifically provided for in the provincial legislation or regulations, except perhaps in the form of grants for buying instructional materials, generally calculated on a per capita basis and considered merely a supplement to what the local board would allot. The grants might be nondiscretionary, so that school libraries—or even classroom collections—might not necessarily benefit to the extent possible. In addition, regulations did not always recognize the teacher–librarian as a specialist, even though in most provinces (Nova Scotia and Quebec were exceptions) he or she had to have both a graduate degree or other training in library science and teaching qualifications. Therefore both the man-years and the money for school librarians often had to be found in the general allotments, which already had many claims against them. Figures for total salary costs were not available, but the 1974–1975 Statistics Canada survey (*16*) did indicate that the school libraries surveyed were spending close to $21 million on print and nonprint materials. The 1973–1974 Quebec survey (*19*) indicated that another $10 million at least could probably be added to the Statistics Canada figures to obtain a rough total for Canada. Figures for 1978–1979—also lacking any returns from Quebec—showed increases in all the reporting provinces in amounts spent per student for print materials, and a total expenditure for materials of over $26 million, or roughly $37 per student.

Resources: Collections

School library collections are, naturally, curriculum oriented; they probably tend to be small, but there are no data on which to base an estimate. The Nova Scotia survey mentioned earlier found 81 libraries with fewer than 1,000 books and 14 with over 10,000; how much of an improvement over earlier conditions this represented cannot be ascertained. A directory of superior school library services (*Canadian School Library Programmes of Interest to Visitors* [*28*]) included libraries whose collections ranged from 3,000 to 33,000 volumes, whose space allotments ranged from 768 square feet to 11,000, and whose staff numbered 4.5 at most and in one library consisted only of volunteers. The range and variety among these libraries, chosen for their excellence, indicates clearly how difficult and even misleading generalizations may be.

During the decade various provinces made special efforts to improve school library collections, frequently in conjunction with a program of building or renovating schools that allowed space for a library to be included in the plans. In Prince Edward Island, for example, provision for school libraries was included in the capital costs of the new schools built in the early '70s, while a 3-year Special Resource Centre Grant Program was instituted to help existing libraries upgrade their collections. Quebec regulations allowed for establishment grants as well as book grants. In Alberta in the early '70s a Special Renovation Program of the School Buildings Board resulted in improved library facilities in nearly 100 schools; then in 1975 the province allotted a one-time grant of $15 per pupil to improve school libraries and instructional materials services. In 1977 it further announced an $8-million program to develop and distribute learning resource materials, including many especially prepared on Alberta, to schools in the province. In the mid-1970s British Columbia made available a book entitlement fund of $6.5 million to help bring school library holdings up to a minimum of 10 titles per student in elementary and 15 in secondary schools. Larger book grants to school districts in Newfoundland began in 1970–1971 and at first reportedly could not be utilized effectively because of lack of trained personnel—a situation since remedied. The New Brunswick act of 1967 envisaged a gradual building up of school resources to the point where bookmobile services could be dispensed with, but the grants had not enabled libraries to reach that objective by the target date of 1972. In Quebec, Opération "Fonds de bibliothèque" in 1976 provided a way of having libraries ready and classified by the opening of a school, the province paying at least 70% of the costs of acquiring books, processing and binding them, and buying catalog card sets for them from the Centrale des bibliothèques.

Two trends in connection with school library collections in this period should be noted. The first was the increasing emphasis placed on Canadian content in the library's collections, an emphasis parallelling teachers' and parents' discontent with the lack of Canadian content in school textbooks. The Work Group of the Toronto Board of Education, for example, studied the availability of Canadian books in schools in Toronto; the board also made a one-time grant to allow purchase of Canadian books. Toward the end of the decade British Columbia instituted its School Library Book Purchase Plan which set aside $100,000 to buy the books of provincial publishers and place them in 1,700 school libraries.

The second trend was an emphasis on the need for school libraries to develop sound and explicit book selection policies. One such statement, "Selection of Learning Resources" (*29*), by Haycock, was adopted by the Vancouver School Board in 1978—a first, it was thought, for a Canadian school board. In part the emphasis on selection policies was a response to an increasing number of incidents of censorship or attempted censorship of school library materials. In part it was also a response to the need to clarify priorities in the face of book budgets that were not keeping pace with inflation.

Also to be mentioned—more a fact of life than a trend—was the problem of book losses. School libraries, like others, had to install electronic detection systems to try to protect their collections.

Resources: Personnel

As noted previously, most provinces required both teaching and library qualifications of school library professional staff, and in Canadian usage the term *teacher–librarian* tended to mean one who did possess both, not a teacher with a few or no library courses, as had been the usage. The term *learning resource teacher* for someone with these qualifications, promulgated in *Resource Services for Canadian Schools* (*26*), had not been adopted to any extent, although it had been accepted in "Qualifications for School Librarians" (*30*), approved by the Canadian School Library Association in June 1979. The organization of that document, by areas of competence, was an innovative approach for arriving at statements not conditioned by a specific system, but it left unanswered the question of a practical and consistent method of rating staff on these competencies.

The lack of comparable data from the earlier and later parts of the decade is felt particularly in a discussion of staffing. School libraries have had a long history of inadequate staffing, whether from the point of view of the qualifications of the staff or of the number of staff. Alberta reports from the first half of the decade noted a trend toward replacing teacher–librarians with clericals or library technicians and reducing the amount of library time for those teacher–librarians who remained. Saskatchewan in 1975 was reporting libraries in 70% of its 1,000 schools but had only 100 full-time trained librarians in them. In Ontario in the middle of the decade some boards were cutting back on the amount of professional time allotted to school libraries; a school with fewer than 200 students, for example, might get only 30% of a librarian's time. One survey in 1973–1974 (*31*) found that almost 5% of the people in charge of libraries full time had had no library training whatsoever. The Statistics Canada figures for 1974–1975 (*16*) indicated that 6% of the full-time staff reported were librarians, and 36% had training in school librarianship—42% in all. (It must be remembered that Quebec figures were not included in this result.)

Another facet of school library staffing (again statistics were not available) was the lack of clerical assistance for school librarians and the high use of volunteers, usually unpaid. In extenuation of the first, it must be noted that there may be less need for clerical help where school boards provide centralized technical services for the schools under their jurisdiction. (In Quebec, the Centrale des bibliothèques gives provincewide service.) As for volunteers, it is not too much to say that without them many students would have lacked library service almost entirely.

A 1978 survey by the Ontario School Library Association (*32*) found that staffing had not improved in the second half of the decade, partly as a result of declining school enrollment. Teacher–librarians were being asked to take on two or more libraries; if left in change of just one, they were being asked to give subject instruction as well; libraries in schools with smaller enrollments (fewer than 500 pupils) were not getting full-time staff; and boards were using library technicians, secretaries, or volunteers in place of professionals. The surveyors stressed that their sample might not have been representative, but their conclusions were echoed in comments from many diverse sources.

Special Services

The integration of print and audiovisual materials, and realia into a functional school library collection can no longer be considered a new service of school libraries, and if funds were forthcoming, computer-based reference services would no doubt be accommodated too. (As it happens, these were already available through centralized services provided by school boards in some school districts, notably in British Columbia and Ontario.) Nor is instruction in use of libraries new. What was new in the '70s was a growing emphasis on working more closely with teachers to develop programs that would make the best use of resources that were diminishing as costs rose and budgets did not.

Many school libraries opened before and after regular class hours to allow students more access to the collections; some experimented with special evening hours during examination weeks; there were also suggestions for summer opening. In an attempt to improve access to AV materials, Prince Edward Island put an Audio-Visual Mobile into operation in one of its school units, to serve smaller schools. Instances of special services in individual libraries or in a school district could be multiplied; the special services offered by the Vancouver School Board's library service would be good examples.

School/Public Libraries

Any mention of access brings up one of the main areas of controversy in the school library field—the question of the school-housed public library. Fortunately Amey's *The Canadian School-Housed Public Library*, 1979 (*33*), provides an in-depth treatment of the subject. Amey found that 79% of the joint libraries identified had started in the latter part of the decade, the majority being in Alberta. Assessments of their value ranged from enthusiasm to rejection. Newfoundland's provincial library service officially decided not to establish any more; Alberta library associations advised strongly against their establishment. The two Quebec ministries concerned agreed in 1974 that two cooperating but separate systems for school and public libraries would be developed in the province; but they also agreed that under certain conditions, where there was no likelihood of a public library's being established, a school library might give service to the public and receive grants from the Ministère des affaires culturelles for doing so. In British Columbia the decision to give such service was a matter for the school and the local council; library boards did not have to be consulted. As in Manitoba, there were in British Columbia some successful examples of such an operation, sometimes in new community complexes housing schools and recreational and other facilities in a single area. New Brunswick's regionals had a responsibility for assisting school libraries but not necessarily for establishing joint services. At the end of the decade the tide of opinion seemed to be running against school-housed public libraries, but there were still areas of the country where they meant the difference between no library service at all and at least some service, and for that reason were likely to continue to exist for some time yet.

Automation

To 1979 there had been very little automation activity among school libraries, although Aurora (Ont.) High School Library was making use of UTLAS facilities for a PRECIS indexing experiment, and other Ontario school boards were using its catalog support facilities.

Cooperation and Networking

Here, too, there was little change to report in the 1970s; sporadic examples of school/public library or school/college cooperation occurred but not enough to constitute a trend. Ontario school librarians set up a network of representatives in Ontario's school regions, with communication and consultation as well as joint projects being major objectives. B.C. librarians had begun to discuss the possibility of a provincial network but considered that realization was still far in the future.

For school libraries, then, the '70s were a period of fluctuation, of initial advances slowed by a period of economic stringency in which libraries were easy targets for cutbacks, of budgets eroded by the impact of declining enrollments and even more by inflation, of improvements in staffing slowing under the influence of worsening economic conditions and declining enrollments. There was a great deal of activity by school library associations, particularly in the area of standards and of publications and projects that would help school librarians in their day-to-day work. School libraries were criticized for not having enough Canadian materials and were attacked by censors because of some that they did have. The catalog is depressing, but the fact remains that school libraries and their role were being actively discussed and studied as never before. That was the achievement of the '70s.

Public Libraries

While academic libraries operate within a framework of provincial laws and regulations, the impact of these laws is felt, for the most part, at second hand. Public libraries, on the contrary, because they are tax supported, feel the impact of provincial library legislation directly. For example, it governs whether and under what structure they shall exist and how well they may be supported. No two provincial systems are the same, and for this reason the pattern used in earlier sections on legislation and governance is varied to allow a province-by-province summary of changes during the decade.

LEGISLATION AND GOVERNANCE

Although in a few areas, association-type public libraries still existed (i.e., libraries supported largely by membership fees, not tax supported), the libraries discussed here are the tax-supported public libraries. They may serve one political jurisdiction, or a number; be urban, serving a center with 10,000 or more population; or be rural, serving a municipality with under 10,000 population (Statistics Canada definitions). Regional libraries usually serve two or more municipalities, counties, or districts, but "regional" does not have precisely the same connotation in all provinces. Ordinarily it would describe a system in which a central (regional) library and its branches in various localities provide service to a wide area which affords a reasonable tax base for the system. In Manitoba a "regional" denotes the pooling of resources by two or more political units in order to set up a joint library service for themselves. (One "regional" in the first sense has been operating in the province as a demonstration, as well.) In Ontario the regionals are (except for Metro Toronto) provincially funded coordinating bodies set up to help public libraries improve their services to the public, not to serve the public directly themselves. The Ontario County Library (serving a county, as the name indicates) is closer to the first meaning of "regional" than the Ontario regional libraries are.

"Provincial library" is another term which covers varied types of institutions. Fortunately the decade saw the end of its use in British Columbia and Alberta as a name for their legislative libraries, so that it now refers to a public library which provides central direction and support to the provincial system and also may offer loan services directly as well as through the libraries of the system. Territorial library services are similar, although they operate on grants rather than from a tax base.

With the preceding as a review, developments in each province are considered separately, in geographic order from east to west.

Newfoundland

The Newfoundland Public Library Services began the decade under the Department of Education, but it was transferred in 1972 to the Department of Tourism, Recreation, and Culture. It also began with a change in grant regulations which meant an increase in grants. In 1975 the old act was repealed and a new Public Libraries Act passed, consolidating and updating previous legislation and placing boards operating local and regional libraries under the Public Libraries Board. Previously separate corporations, these boards now have their constitutions set by the central board, which was also named the holder and administrator of local assets. The Public Libraries Board retained its autonomy as a crown corporation under the new act. The director of public library services changed title to chief provincial librarian.

The total library service was funded by the provincial government; municipal taxes devoted to libraries were extra. Prior to the 1970s one regional library had been organized; by the end of the decade three more had been added.

The Public Library Services provided centralized technical processing, reference services, and certain administrative (chiefly financial) services for the libraries under it, and had improved communications by a Telex link to the regions. These central services allowed local librarians to concentrate their efforts on service to the public. It was estimated that through local libraries and books by mail services, at least 80% of the population was being served by the end of the '70s.

Prince Edward Island

The Prince Edward Island Provincial Library did not operate under a library act but as a branch of the Department of Education. The first director of libraries was appointed in 1971; in 1972 budgets for the Confederation Centre Library (which served both public and legislature), the Prince Edward Island Libraries (the public library service), and the Planning Library (a special library which gave much service to the legislature) were combined, and the services were reorganized into Public Library Services, Education Media Services, and Technical Services. In 1973 a special grant allowed a bookmobile service to be started, while the move of provincial headquarters into a new building permitted improved functioning and made allowance for expansion.

An innovation probably unique in Canada was the cooperation of the Provincial Library Film Library and the National Film Board in a Media Centre.

The total number of branches in the system was 20 by 1979, the latest addition being a planned public/school library facility in the province's new French-language school in Unit No. 5.

Nova Scotia

Nova Scotia's Provincial Library was the center of much activity during the decade. The library continued under the Department of Education, but the 1977 amendment to the Libraries Act made a number of other changes in accordance with recommendations made by the Minister of Education's Task Force on Libraries (*34*). Chief among them was the establishment of the Provincial Library Council whose duty was to review the budgets presented by the regional library boards and to make recommendations concerning them to the minister.

By the end of the decade the 11th and last regional library had been established, and only one municipality still remained outside the system in 1979 (it joined in 1981). Estimates were that more than 99% of the population was being reached by the province's 55 branches and 22 bookmobiles.

New Brunswick

The legislation under which the New Brunswick Library Service operated underwent a few amendments during the decade; in 1975 the provisions governing representation on regional library boards were changed, and the regional librarian's position as both member and secretary of the board was confirmed. The ministry responsible for libraries was changed from Education to the Department of Youth, Recreation, and Cultural Resources in 1976.

The number of regional libraries in the province stood at five by the end of the decade, and it was estimated that about 77% of the population was within reach of library service. A new system adopted by the service for reporting on library activities facilitated comparison of the patterns of service in the different regions; it was very easy to see, for example, that Saint John in 1978–1979 showed the highest proportion of adult loans and the lowest of loans to children; that Chaleur and Haut Saint-Jean showed the opposite emphasis; that in all regions, services to young people were virtually nonexistent. From future reports it should be easy to pinpoint changes in service. This type of annual report appeared to be unique to New Brunswick as the decade closed; however, New Brunswick may merely be in the forefront of more meaningful statistical reporting. (Statistics Canada's 1977 survey of public libraries, it should be added, showed a similar recognition of the need to demonstrate service to users more clearly.)

Quebec

Quebec's Service des bibliothèques publiques [Public Library Service] and the Commission des bibliothèques publiques [Public Library Commission] together guided the development of public library service in the province in accordance with the 1959 law. Changes in regulations under the law occurred during the decade; most dealt with specific areas and have been noted in those contexts. A farseeing plan of development proposed by the minister of cultural affairs, Mr. Vaugeois, in 1978 had not been funded as the decade closed.

Other legislation also affecting Quebec public libraries was that which requires them to buy through Quebec booksellers. In general this has meant a further erosion of book-buying power because of lower discounts; libraries also complained of poor service.

The last of the proposed Bibliothèques centrales de prêt [Central Lending Libraries] were completed within the decade, bringing the total to nine from the two with which the decade started. By the end of 1978 over 72% of the population was being served, although mainly in the urban areas. In areas with less than 5,000 population, about 68% were still without library service.

Ontario

The most notable change for Ontario's public library service occurred at the very end of the decade. In 1970 there were changes to the grants regulations, leading to a simplification of the grant structure and an essentially per capita basis for funding. In 1972 the sections on certification of librarians were deleted from the regulations under the act. In 1978 Bill 80 to amend the Ontario Municipal Act caused some problems for the library boards operating under the Public Libraries Act. Under the latter, board members received only expenses; Bill 80 allowed municipal councils to go farther and, in addition, pay council members who sat on library boards. The library board might also remunerate non–council members, but it had to be willing to take money from the library budget to do so.

The Ontario Provincial Library Service operated under the Ministry of Education, then in 1972 came under the Ministry of Colleges and Universities, then was transferred in 1975 to the Ministry of Culture and Recreation. At the end of 1979 a major change in responsibilities was announced. The Provincial Library Service became the Libraries and Community Information Branch of the Information Access Division in the Ministry of Culture and Recreation. In addition to responsibility for public library service, the responsibility for community information centers (sometimes called information and referral centers) was transferred to this new branch—a first in Canada.

Ontario has generally been in the forefront of public library development in Canada, so it was not surprising that it was claimed that 99% of the population had access to public library service.

Manitoba

Manitoba's Public Library Services Branch was established in 1973 in the Department of Tourism, Recreation, and Cultural Affairs, a successor to the service previously organized by the Legislative Library (then called the Provincial Library). The department's name was later changed to Department of Tourism and Cultural Affairs, while developments at the close of the decade placed Public Library Services within the Department of Cultural Affairs and Historical Resources.

Amendments to the Public Libraries Act in 1972 removed the 1-mill ceiling on municipal levies to be allocated to municipal or regional library services and also the requirement that a ratepayer vote must precede establishment of a library. Amendments to the regulations in 1975 provided for increased grants. Even with these changes, the system of grants did not encourage the formation of larger units of service, and in the view of many Manitoba librarians, the legislation as it stood hindered, rather than promoted, library development. The fact that 20% of the province's population in 1979 still had no access to library service tended to support the librarians' view. Librarians also pointed out the need to reestablish the provincial Library Advisory Board. (Substantial improvements in both funding and the regulations governing it were announced for 1980.)

Saskatchewan

Saskatchewan's Public Libraries Act of 1969 remained in force, but studies (one completed, one under way) preliminary to new legislation indicated that a serious revision would probably occur in the 1980s. A proposal for legislation to make library service mandatory in the province failed to obtain support—evidence of centrifugal tendencies in a province where a genuine system of public libraries has been developing. Further evidence—if needed—could be found in the rejection of the moderately centralist recommendations of the Bewley Report (*35*) and in the announced decisions (some later rescinded) by certain regional members to withdraw in favor of independent existence. Amendments to the regulations in 1970 and 1974 provided for grants to city libraries and for capital grants, respectively.

The last two of Saskatchewan's seven regional libraries were formed in 1972 and 1973; with the coverage provided by the city libraries of Regina and Saskatoon, and the direct lending services of the Provincial Library, 85% of the population had access to libraries by the end of the decade.

It is perhaps worth adding a reminder that Saskatchewan has a specifically designated minister in charge of libraries—a unique distinction.

Alberta

The Library Services Branch of Alberta Culture operated within the terms of the 1956 Libraries Act, but the Libraries Amendment Act of 1976 made changes in the section on financial assistance to libraries which have supported the branch's efforts to improve library service in the province. It also included a potentially important provision, that the minister might prescribe standards of service a library must meet to be eligible for grants. New regulations in 1977 provided that Edmonton and Calgary public libraries would furnish backup service for rural libraries, and that grants to encourage regional library development would be available. Perhaps partly as a result of the prospect of funding, the new Marigold Co-operative Library System was in process of formation at the end of the decade, and other areas were considering regional development too.

The earlier Library Advisory Board dissolved in frustration at its impotence in 1971, but the new Alberta Library Board was appointed in 1978 and does not seem likely to suffer the same fate. The new one as originally constituted was a lay board and had responsibility for advising the minister.

An experiment in library governance at the local level was started late in the decade by Calgary Public Library, which established Branch Advisory Committees with members from the local communities for two of its branches. The outcome will be watched with interest by other libraries.

British Columbia

British Columbia's public library service began the decade as the Library Development Commission responsible to the minister of education, then to the provincial secretary, and then to the minister of recreation and conservation. In 1978 it became the Library Services Branch, and at the end of the decade it was responsible to the Ministry of Provincial Secretary and Government Services. The amendments to the Public Libraries Act which changed the commission to the Library Services Branch also contained a provision that a library advisory council might be appointed, but this had not been done by the end of 1979. (Some appointments were announced in 1980.)

In addition to changes in the act, the situation in British Columbia was further complicated by the fact that two new library systems created during the 1970s did not come under the Public Libraries Act: The Cariboo–Thompson–Nicola integrated service experiment was set up under the Societies Act, and the Greater Vancouver Library Federation (a cooperative venture of Lower Mainland libraries) was created by Order-in-Council.

One early amendment to the library act should perhaps be noted, inasmuch as it was invoked during the decade and may be again—namely, that if a municipality or school district withdraws from a regional library, it has no title or right in the assets (including books) of the regional board.

Yukon Territory

While libraries in the provinces have problems of scattered populations and long distances to deal with, those problems are compounded for librarians seeking to provide library service to the sparse populations of the Yukon and Northwest Territories. Add to sparseness of population the current disagreements between the White and Indian and Inuit populations over land claims; add differences in culture and in levels of education; add some resentment of things southern and of the degree of control still maintained over the territories' governments by Ottawa—and the librarian's task becomes more difficult. Modern library service in the Yukon was only 10 years old in 1971 when the Yukon Regional Library, as it was called, became the Library Services Branch, a division of the Government of the Yukon Territory, with responsibility for public library service, school library service, and archives. It was then under the Department of Tourism, Conservation, and Information Services. In 1974 the branch was restructured into Administration, Yukon Archives, Technical Services, Library Services, and Media Services. In 1979 a further restructuring emphasized the parallel archives and library services components of the branch, by then officially part of the Department of Information Resources.

In the early '70s the branch served 23 permanent outlets in various communities, plus a number of changing service points. In 1979 it served seven branches (including Whitehorse), 16 schools, 13 book stations, and 13 other institutions (e.g., a hospital medical library, the Indian Resource Centre, and correctional institutions).

There was still no territorial library legislation in force in the Yukon in the 1970s.

Northwest Territories

The success of the Yukon Regional Library roused interest in a similar service for the Northwest Territories, and in 1966 the Territories Council passed the ordinance under which the N.W.T. Public Library Services from its headquarters at Hay River provided a free public library service to the mixed, very scattered population of the territory. In the mid-1970s the service came under the Department of Natural and Cultural Affairs; it had earlier reported to the Office of the Assistant Commissioner, Programs. Since the mid-1970s the service has been empowered to make grants toward the salaries of local librarians; unfortunately, the service has not had the funding to allow it actively to encourage new communities to join the system. But in spite of lack of staff and lack of funds, member libraries grew from 12 in 1970 to 27 in 1979; and deposit collection stations, from 9 to 21, giving access to libraries to about 73% of the population.

Establishment of a Northwest Territories library board was forecast in the commissioner's speech in January 1979; it had not taken place by the end of that year.

Surveys

One aspect of public library activity during the decade which has been touched on only in passing is the number of surveys and studies which occurred. They covered single libraries, single systems, regions, or whole provinces. Among provincial surveys, Nova Scotia had its Minister's Task Force (*34*); Bowron surveyed the Ontario library scene (*36*); Newsom suggested guidelines for Manitoba public library development (*37*) and then, with Richeson and Gill, studied rural libraries in Alberta (*38*). That province also received the controversial Downey Report (*39*), with its proposal for a network of libraries. The Saskatchewan Library Development Board surveyed libraries in its province (*40*); the B.C. Library Development Commission brought in the last of a series of 5-year development plans for the province in 1971 (*41*). A new survey, this time national in scope, got under way at the end of the decade—Project: Progress. It was sponsored by the Canadian Library Association and funded with money pledged by library boards across the country. The final research design was a modification of one (*42*) worked out by the Centre for Research in Librarianship, Faculty of Library Science, University of Toronto. Emphasis was to be on social, economic, and other factors which could be expected to affect public library decision making in the 1980s.

Another welcome set of initiatives in the decade was the beginning of sample surveys of reading interests and library use by Statistics Canada—a time series of data on these subjects has never existed. It should at last become possible to discern trends.

STANDARDS AND STATISTICS

There was little national activity on public library standards during the decade, although British Columbia (*43*), Saskatchewan (*44*), and Quebec (*45*) published quantitative standards during the period. The B.C. standards were particularly interesting because municipal public libraries and public library associations had to be able to meet certain designated standards in order to qualify for grants after April 1980. Publication in 1978 allowed 2 years' lead time to enable libraries to catch up.

The Quebec standards, published in the middle of the decade, were not prescriptive. A 1979 study (*46*) was made of the extent to which Quebec libraries had achieved the ministry's suggested norms. The author of the study found that only 20% of the communities receiving library grants met the standards for books per capita, that about the same percentage spent more than 25% of the library budget on books, and that libraries in three communities bettered the recommended 1:6,000 ratio of librarians to population. On the plus side, 62% of the libraries had three or more circulations per capita, and 58% received more than a suggested minimum of $5 per capita for their operations.

Statistics Canada's published surveys for 1970 (*47*) and 1976 (*48*) provided data for a study of changes during the decade. In addition, figures for 1977 were also made available to the author through the courtesy of the staff of the Cultural Analysis Section of Statistics Canada. Selected ratios and totals for all three years are given in Table 4.

Changes in definitions of certain categories and in data items collected made precise comparisons between 1970 and 1976–1977 impossible, but the trends were clear. (Figures for 1976–1977 were taken from 5-year comparative tables in the preliminary report of the 1977 survey whenever feasible, and the reader is referred to this report for historical series which cannot be included here.) Holdings of print materials per capita rose very slightly; per capita expenditures more than doubled, in most cases. A look at the actual purchasing power of the 1977 dollar amounts, however, showed real rises of approximately 54% to 80% over the 7 years. The ra-

TABLE 4

Selected Ratios of Canadian Public Libraries, 1970, 1976, and 1977[a]

Ratios	Region						
	Atlantic	Quebec	Ontario	Central	British Columbia	Territories[b]	Canada
Volumes per capita							
1970	0.9	0.6	1.7	1.2	1.4	(2.1)	1.2
1976	1.2	0.9	2.3	1.7	1.7	(3.1)	1.6
1977	1.2	1.0	2.4	1.7	1.7	(3.4)	1.7
Expenditures per capita							
1970	$ 1.60	$ 1.06	$ 4.73	$ 2.65	$ 3.28	($ 7.37)	$ 2.91
1976	$ 4.09	$ 2.75	$10.29	$ 6.18	$ 8.63	($14.29)	$ 6.81
1977	$ 4.27	$ 2.63	$11.64	$ 6.82	$ 9.52	($13.72)	$ 7.48
In constant (1971) dollars	$ 2.66	$ 1.63	$ 7.24	$ 4.24	$ 5.92	($ 8.52)	$ 4.65
Population per FT librarian							
1970	26,917	51,836	11,635	30,111	15,156	(9,800)	18,985
1976	20,981	51,521	8,773	18,713	10,634	(13,000)	14,316
1977[c]	20,426	33,572[d]	8,675	19,214	11,084	(10,667)	13,762

[a] Sources: Statistics Canada surveys.

[b] Calculated by author from Statistics Canada data.

[c] Does not include librarians in municipal libraries serving fewer than 10,000 people.

[d] Part of the increase in FT professionals was due to redefinition of the category.

tio of trained librarians to population improved over the period but was beginning to slip again in the western regions.

User populations, service points, and sources of funding among academic libraries have a degree of homogeneity and definition that public libraries do not enjoy. Does the public library serve children? Young people? Adults? What adults? Well-educated middle-class users, the disadvantaged, the aged, ethnic groups, business and professional people, laborers and union men or women, housewives? The variety is endless. A series of surveys on reading habits and use of leisure time by Statistics Canada (*49*) may produce some answers, along with local library surveys and, it is anticipated, the results of Project: Progress. For funding, most public libraries have to deal with two levels of government, local and provincial, on terms that vary from province to province and within provinces over time. Service points are another problem. For the academic library they must obviously be somewhere in the academic complex. The public library has no such easy basis for decision, and complications of politics, costs, and prior occupancies may militate against what may seem the ideal placement. Table 5 sets out, to the extent feasible, the contrast between 1970 and 1977 on some of these points.

TABLE 5

Facilities, Users, Staff, and Funding of Canadian Public Libraries, 1970 and 1977[a]
(Figures in parentheses indicate the number of service points)

	Region						
Aspect	Atlantic	Quebec	Ontario	Central	British Columbia	Territories	Canada
No. of libraries by type							
Provincial							
1970	4	—	—	1	1	2	8
1977	4(85)	1(2)	—	1(1)	1(4)	2(27)	7(119)
Regional							
1970	15	2	28[b]	21	3	—	69
1977	18(165)	5(284)	30[b](296)	29(430)	4(150)	—	86(1,325)
Urban							
1970	—	69	73	22	15	—	179
1977	1(5)	65(132)	99(360)	22(87)	20(65)	—	207(649)
Rural							
1970	—	37	244	146	49	—	476
1977	—	29(29)	236(279)	154(154)	39(39)	—	458(501)
Total							
1970	19	108	345	190	68	2	732
1977	23(255)	100(447)	365(935)	206(672)	64(258)	2(27)	760(2,594)
Users							
Population							
1970	2,018,000	6,013,000	7,637,000	3,523,000	2,137,000	49,000	21,377,000
1977	2,206,000	6,278,000	8,354,000	3,862,000	2,494,000	64,000	23,258,000
Estimated adult users							
1970	—	—	—	—	—	—	—
1977	534,000	1,247,000	3,432,000	1,274,000	1,106,000	—	7,593,000
Percentage of population	24.2	19.9	41.1	33.0	44.3	—	32.6
Staff							
Librarians							
1970	75	116	672	117	141	5	1,126
1977	108	187	963	201	225	6	1,690
Other							
1970	291	359	2,025	668	383	15	3,741
1977	403	575	2,919	901	634	16	5,448
Total							
1970	366	475	2,697	785	524	20	4,867
1977	511	762	3,882	1,102	859	22	7,138

(continued)

TABLE 5 (continued)

	Region						
Aspect	Atlantic	Quebec	Ontario	Central	British Columbia	Territories	Canada
Population per staff member							
1970	5,514	12,659	2,832	4,488	4,078	2,450	4,392
1977	4,317	8,239	2,152	3,505	2,903	2,909	3,258
Operating income sources (%)							
Local taxes							
1970	29.6	66.1	69.9	75.3	83.6	—	69.4
1977	17.2	70.0	70.8	70.1	79.8	—	68.7
Provincial grants							
1970	66.2	21.5	19.7	13.8	10.7	99.9	20.8
1977	80.8	25.2	21.8	24.6	15.9	99.9	25.2
Other							
1970	4.2	12.4	10.4	10.9	5.6	0.1	9.8
1977	2.0	4.8	7.4	5.3	4.3	0.1	6.1
Total income[c]							
1970	$ 3,313,627	$ 6,225,221	$ 38,251,297	$ 9,814,291	$ 7,133,844	$361,175	$ 65,099,455
1977	$ 10,063,514	$17,566,904	$114,506,363	$33,119,059	$24,517,355	$912,125	$200,685,320

[a] Sources: Statistics Canada surveys.

[b] Includes county libraries.

[c] Does not include surpluses carried over from previous year.

Since figures for number of service points in 1970 were not published, the growth in their number since then cannot be calculated. There were 2,288 in 1972, however; a growth of 13% in 5 years. This would seem to indicate that service points were increasing at least enough to keep pace with population growth overall, a conclusion supported by figures showing a decline in population per service point between 1972 and 1977, except in the central provinces. (See Text Table III in the 1977 Statistics Canada survey.) The estimated proportions of adult users were highest in British Columbia and Ontario, which have long histories of public library support, and lowest in Quebec, which did not start development of its system until about the 1960s.

FINANCE

The low percentage of income from local taxation in the Atlantic region shown in Table 5 reflected the centralization into provincial systems of the public libraries in those four provinces, while the absence of any local funding in the territories reflected both centralization and the political situation of those areas. The proportion of local support rose negligibly in Quebec and Ontario and dropped in the central provinces and British Columbia, while outside sources of funds dropped sharply in all areas except the territories. The rise in provincial grants in Quebec is shown by the rise in the percentage, but the overall drop in the central region disguises the tremendous increase in Alberta, where grants jumped from $400,000 to over $2 million in 1977, and where it was further announced in 1979 that the grants would be indexed to the cost of living.

In current dollars, income tripled over the 7 years; in constant (1971) dollars, however, the amount (approximately $125,000,000) was less than double. Reports from most regions indicated that increases in 1979 grant allotments were likely to be small, so that public libraries, like academic libraries, were caught in the dilemma of budgets which did not meet increases in inflation. Cuts in services in some areas were reported.

One type of supplementary funding which became available to some libraries during this period was grants from provincial lottery funds. The most comprehensive and best-established program was the Ontario grants from the Wintario lottery; they could be used for building, for improving collections, for special programs and services, etc. Manitoba in 1979 set aside $250,000 from lottery funds to improve physical facilities of libraries in rural municipalities and a further $¼ million went to the city of Winnipeg to improve its collection. Saskatchewan libraries were pressing for similar access to such funds in that province. In British Columbia libraries were taking advantage, not of lottery funds but of special programs in other provincial departments to obtain financing for specific projects. In Toronto the public library was cooperating with two other city departments to develop a new branch library.

One source of funds conspicuous by its absence was the federal government. Since libraries are a provincial matter, federal funds, if any, have generally been tapped through the special programs of the various departments—programs offering assistance in hiring students for summer jobs are an example. In addition, services offered by the National Library of Canada and the Canada Institute for Scientific and Technical Information constitute indirect subsidies to public (and other) libraries.

Public libraries, through the Canadian Library Association, have long agitated for federal involvement; their last brief ("CLA Brief to Special Joint Committee on Constitution of Canada," August 30, 1978) recommended adding to the constitution a paragraph which would assign to the Canadian Parliament responsibility for developing and coordinating libraries and library-related information services for the national benefit. Other briefs have advocated specific changes in the National Library's role to make it a vehicle for direct federal assistance; for example, addition of authority to make grants in support of special projects or equalization.

Examples of National Library services new in the 1970s were the Multilingual Biblioservice (described later), which was for public libraries only, and the Canadian Book Exchange Centre, which accepted surplus books and serials from donor libraries and redistributed them to others which needed the material. Compilation of the national bibliography, *Canadiana*, was automated, and because of that, various new fiche products could be made available to Canadian libraries. Moreover, automation of the Canadian Union Catalogue had begun, ensuring that it would continue its contribution to a Canadian bibliographic network.

RESOURCES: COLLECTIONS

Unlike university libraries, Canadian public libraries do not have a strong mandate for building resource collections whose virtue is their depth and completeness. Rather, their mandate is to meet the current needs of their communities—which may require depth and breadth, but not necessarily so. The one exception to this is in the area of local history, and the '70s saw increased efforts by public libraries large and small to find and preserve the record of their communities.

Table 4 indicates that the number of volumes per capita rose slightly in the 7 years for which there were data. While an average of fewer than two books per capita seems low, and no doubt does indicate limited resources in many areas, it must be remembered that public libraries have to weed their collections regularly. A growth statistic of this sort does not show that turnover, which is a more important factor in ensuring the quality of the collection for its purpose than mere accumulation of volumes. It should also be noted that between 1972 and 1977 the rate of acquisitions (as a percentage of print volumes held) rose in Ontario, the central region, and British Columbia, and dropped slightly in the Atlantic region. (No figures were available for Quebec.) Further, the number of volumes held rose in all regions (including Quebec) between 1976 and 1977, the average national increase being 5.4%. Unfortunately the growth rate between 1969 and 1970, at the start of the decade, which was 10.5%, was not comparable because there were no figures for Quebec; it was therefore impossible to be sure of whether there had been a decline or not.

One trend noticed in regard to other libraries was not found in collections data supplied by public libraries: There had not been a strong swing to audiovisual materials or microforms away from print. This is not to say that music and microform collections, for example, did not increase, nor that more exotic collections (videodisks and talking books, not to mention toys, puzzles, patterns, and postcards) did not find their way into public libraries. However, in 1970 such materials were 2.9% of combined print and nonprint holdings recorded; in 1977, about 4.1% (some figures for Quebec were missing)—scarcely a major change.

The proportion of operating expenditure spent on materials and binding in 1970 ranged from 19% in Quebec to 30% in the territories; the national average was 20%. In 1976 the proportions ranged from just under 16% in Ontario to a little over 20% in the Atlantic region, the national average being just under 17%. Comparable figures for 1977 were over 17% for the national average, a low of 16.5% in Quebec and British Columbia, and a high of 21% in the territories. The same trend toward spending a lower proportion of the budget on materials was thus affecting public libraries too, but in them the change was much less pronounced than in university libraries.

One special collection found in many public libraries was almost lost to them as a result of federal government cutbacks. Many public libraries have the right to select certain government documents to be deposited free in the library. Funds for the government agency responsible for distribution were drastically reduced in 1977, and the agency proposed in 1978 to cut off about half of the depository libraries. (Cuts affected university and government libraries as well.) Librarians, already inconvenienced by the closing, a few years earlier, of the Information Canada bookstores, raised a storm of protest through local and national associations that brought home to the agency the importance of this service to libraries and, through them, to citizens. The proposed cuts were canceled.

As in other types of library, deterioration of collections through overuse, mutilation, and theft increased during the period; there were also some serious losses through fires. One important type of conservation undertaken was the microfilming of local newspapers. Of a different type, but also important for Canadian studies, was the filming of Metro Toronto's Canadian Catalogue, a rich source of bibliographic data on early Canadiana.

RESOURCES: PERSONNEL

As the statistics show, the total number of library staff increased between 1970 and 1977 and so did the number of professionals (the former by 47%; the latter by 50%). Whether the upward trend held for the last years of the decade was uncertain; news of cutbacks seemed more frequent and job openings fewer. The ratio of population to full-time librarians also dropped (Table 4), as did the ratio of population to total staff (Table 5)—indications of increased staffing in some areas at least. Individual libraries may not have fared so well. Metro Toronto Library, for example, had to cut back service 20% over summer 1979; its staff could no longer cope with a 300% increase in use. It was not unique; the 1977 Statistics Canada survey found a drop in the average number of full-time librarians in urban service points.

In 1970 salaries took 60% of public library operating expenditures. The lowest percentage was 51%, in the territories; the highest, 63%, in British Columbia. In 1976 the average for Canada was 62%, the lowest proportion (57%) being spent by the territories and Quebec, and the highest (66%) again being in British Columbia. In 1977 comparable figures were 64% for Canada and a low of 63% in Quebec and a high of 67% in the Atlantic region—a much narrower range than before.

Unionization made strides in public libraries, too, during the decade. A major organizing body was CUPE (Canadian Union of Public Employees), and the predominant pattern seemed to be for professionals and support staff to join the same bargaining unit. Occasionally there were independent units, as in Nepean (Ont.) Public Library. Hamilton (Ont.) Public Library professionals for a time had their own union but became part of CUPE. As in academic libraries, strikes were not unknown; one of the earliest library staff strikes in North America was in Ontario, in the London Public Library.

In other areas, the bringing of librarians in the provincial service under provincial employment regulations (e.g., in Newfoundland and Nova Scotia) was in itself an achievement, as were Yukon's grants to aid in paying branch library staff, starting in 1970. Public librarians did not have the equivalent of the academic librarian's sabbatical, but Saskatchewan and Alberta had bursary and research fellowship programs administered by the Provincial Library and Alberta Culture, respectively, and some union contracts contained provision for study leave.

RESOURCES: BUILDINGS

There was a fair amount of building activity during the decade, and surveys in Alberta and Ontario in 1979 showed little diminution there—in Alberta, 33 libraries had built, were building, or were planning to build in 1979; in Ontario, nearly 130 had renovations or new buildings planned. A few scattered examples may be mentioned: the extension to Halifax City Regional Library, a new library at Portage La Prairie (Man.), new headquarters for the Yukon library service, and libraries opened in new community center complexes in British Columbia. Three major buildings opened in 1977; they were the Saint Catharines Centennial Library, the Winnipeg Centennial Library, and the Metropolitan Toronto Library, the latter a spectacular design by Raymond Moriyama.

More attention was paid during the decade to the adequacy of library buildings, not just for collections and service (a perennial problem) but for access by the handicapped. A survey of 24 new or renovated buildings in Ontario (*50*) turned up only four without special facilities for the handicapped, while Toronto used a special grant to add facilities to some of its older libraries. Doubtless similar projects could be found in other areas.

SPECIAL SERVICES

It would be impossible to detail the many special services begun by public libraries for their users during this period. In many cases the service was not entirely new, but its expansion was. One interesting attempt to improve service to regular users should be noted as well: New Brunswick's experiment with giving bookmobile service at night as well as during the day.

Services to shut-ins, to nursing homes, clinics, penitentiaries, etc., increased. Services to shut-ins were offered by libraries from Saint John's, Newfoundland, to Victoria, British Columbia; Halifax City and Scarborough (Ont.), to name two, delivered books to homes. Saskatoon Public Library put paperback deposits in hospitals and halfway houses; Calgary bought specially selected materials to start collections in two local jails (to give two examples of many). Standards for institution libraries in the federal Canadian Corrections Service were adopted in 1977 (*51*). Provincial library services in Manitoba, Saskatchewan, British Columbia, and Newfoundland offered books by mail as a service to readers in remote areas; the Northwest Territories service did likewise but was prevented by lack of staff from expanding the service as it would have liked. Alberta funded special services, based on Edmonton and Calgary Public Libraries, for the less well-served northern and southern regions of the province; deposits of books, backup reference and technical processing services at headquarters, and Zenith lines to eight resource libraries were among the services offered during the experiment, which ended in 1980. (The experiment became an established program.)

The installation of improved facilities for the physically handicapped in many libraries has been noted. Oakville Public Library pioneered in 1978 a special radio service for the blind, available to them on special reading equipment. The Mid-western Regional Library System videotaped book reviews which, with captions replacing the sound, were made available to cable television outlets for the benefit of deaf viewers. Newfoundland prepared an audiocatalog of records and cassettes available in the province, with locations; Saskatoon's talking-books catalog in 1978 was also on tape. Many libraries increased their holdings or began a talking-book service; Saint John Public Library and the Greater Vancouver Library Federation, to give but two examples. Manitoba was developing plans to improve service out-side Winnipeg by circulating blocks of talking books. A major report on Canadian library service to the handicapped was sponsored by the National Library (*52*), which also for a time supported a Division for the Visually and Physically Handi-capped to act as a clearinghouse and base for coordination of the national efforts. Unfortunately, because of economic restraints, funding for the division was not forthcoming and it was dissolved. (Adequate support was obtained in 1982.)

A very special group of handicapped users began to receive more attention dur-ing the decade—namely, the illiterate or near-illiterate. Regina Public Library was in the forefront of public library–sponsored literacy programs. Examples of other programs were those of North York (Ont.) and Halifax City; the Saint John Li-brary housed the literacy collection of a local group. A service to all concerned in such programs was Metro Toronto's funding of compilation of the *Directory of Adult Basic Education Programs in Canada*, 1978 (*53*). Going beyond a literacy program, Vancouver's Britannia Library sponsored a Learning Centre with Van-couver Community College in order to provide tutorial assistance in basic educa-tion for adults.

Two other groups of services developed during the decade were services to eth-nic groups and to native peoples. Metro Toronto through its Languages Centre had been an early proponent of service to those who speak languages other than En-glish or French, but the federal government's policy of multiculturalism and the es-tablishment of the National Library's Multilingual Biblioservice, partly as a result of it, gave additional impetus to the movement. The Biblioservice supplied on re-quest blocks of cataloged books in 26 languages to provincial library services or agencies, and they in turn circulated them among local libraries which needed the books. In some libraries these books were the major source of foreign-language material; in others, such as Edmonton, which had a special provincial responsibili-ty, the Biblioservice materials supplemented the local collections. While it is invi-dious to single out a few libraries when so many deserve mention, only specific ex-amples can give an idea of the range. Toronto had strong Italian and Chinese collections; York, a West Indian collection. Victoria (B.C.) undertook to serve a growing East Indian population, Manitoba's Evergreen Regional became a center for Icelandic materials, and so on.

Services to Indian bands began or improved during the decade, whether under public library sponsorship (as often in the case of Saskatchewan regionals) or de-veloped by the bands themselves (as occurred to a considerable extent in Ontario). A majority of the public library acts contained provisions for aid for service to In-dians, and native peoples themselves began to take more responsibility for seeing that the provisions were acted upon. In addition, bands were often aided by workshops sponsored by nearby public library services. Formation of the Original Peoples Library Association was a further advance.

Libraries during the period sponsored many cultural activities, from puppet shows for children to author's readings. One unusual program was Regina Public Library's Writer in Residence Program, cosponsored with the Canada Council—a first of its type. The writer selected gave writing workshops and readings of his own work; he also had time free for his own writing.

Some new developments in service to children should also be mentioned. York Public Library and others experimented with combining adult and children's collections instead of separating them—though Scarborough, in contrast, started to separate theirs during this period. The development of toy libraries has been mentioned; there were also efforts to involve children in art, in writing, and even in library orientation for their peers. (A Montreal library had children narrating the tape for a slide–tape presentation on how to use the library.) Story hours were not new—though charging for them was, and a few Ontario libraries had to do that in order to continue their programs. Burnaby sent a "Storybus" to day-care centers in its area. Oakville again pioneered in Canada; it offered a pre–reading readiness computer program to a pilot group of 160 youngsters.

Movements toward more publication of children's own writing, toward producing more Canadian children's books (including books for children in native languages), and toward publicizing Canadian children's books all influenced library service to children during the period. A center for much of this activity was the Children's Book Centre, established in 1976 for the purpose of promoting the reading, writing, publishing, and selling of Canadian children's books. Its preparation of publicity and informational materials—to name just one activity—has been a very useful aid to libraries. In addition, the hiring of a children's literature consultant by the National Library provided a focus for information on Canadian children's books past and present, in both official languages, that has been very helpful to school and public libraries alike.

Canadian public libraries were also involved in the development of community information centers during the decade—sometimes directly, as in London Public Library's Crouch Neighbourhood Resource Centre; sometimes indirectly, through the publication of directories of community resources (e.g., by Halifax City, Frontenac County [Ont.], and Burnaby Public Library [B.C.]). The change of Ontario's Provincial Library Service into a branch responsible for both public libraries and information centers has already been noted.

RELATIONSHIP TO OTHER SERVICES

The question of school-housed public libraries has been discussed in the section on schools; the public library's relationship to community information centers (separate but supportive) has been touched on in the preceding section. One other relationship should be mentioned because of the considerable heat it generated at the time. That was the federal government's short-lived Information Canada experiment. This was a program for making information on federal government programs and publications more widely available by establishing Information Canada centers and bookstores across the country. A series of misunderstandings on both sides initially led to considerable hostility toward the program on the part of some public libraries, while others welcomed the initiative and housed the service within the library (e.g., Newfoundland Public Library Service). The service had just begun to prove its value and to produce a number of publications very helpful to libraries when it too fell victim to the restraint program. Its demise and the demise of the bookstores were as vigorously protested as its inception had been, but to no avail.

AUTOMATION

Interest in automation increased during the period 1970–1979 and, more to the point, money to implement automated projects began to be available. In general, public libraries were concerned with automating their circulation systems, automating cataloging (and acquisitions when possible), and providing access to computer-based information retrieval services.

Computerized circulation systems were installed in a branch of Calgary Public Library and in Edmonton, Lethbridge, Red Deer, London, and Oakville Public Libraries. Toronto Public Library monitored its overdues and sent notices by computer. Ottawa Public Library was selected to be the test library for an automated circulation system in its region; Vancouver Public was well into planning to automate circulation. Computer-based reference services were provided free by some libraries (e.g., Saskatchewan and Nova Scotia Provincial Libraries, and Hamilton and Kitchener Public Libraries) and at a fee by others (Calgary, Edmonton, and Metro Toronto). North York, one of the pioneers in offering such service, subsequently dropped it but hoped to reinstate the service in the 1980s.

A fair number of libraries used UTLAS facilities for computerized catalog support: for example, Burnaby and Richmond, in British Columbia; East York, Etobicoke, Hamilton, Metro Toronto, Midwestern Regional Library System (off-line use only), Mississauga, Niagara Regional Library System's processing center (until it closed), North Central Regional Library System (Tri-Regional Catalogue), North York, Ottawa, Scarborough, and York, in Ontario. The Saskatchewan Provincial Library and the Regina and Saskatoon Public Libraries agreed to join as of 1980. Alberta Culture used UTLAS to obtain copy, when possible, for its collection of foreign-language books. Many of the Ontario libraries used UTLAS as members of the UNICAT/TELECAT consortium, thus gaining access to a file of cataloging for French books through sharing the files of the Quebec library members. Other libraries developed their own systems (Fraser Valley and Vancouver Island Regionals [B.C.], Dartmouth Regional [N.S.], and Wheatland Regional [Sask.]). A number of libraries switched to COM fiche or film catalogs once their catalogs were on tape (e.g., Etobicoke and Scarborough).

Other public libraries maintained files (often union files) for serials and films on computer. Saskatchewan Technical Institute had a computer-based retrieval system for its AV materials; Metro Toronto operated an on-line film-booking system. In an even newer development, Scarborough agreed to house two TELIDON terminals during field trials of this videotex system. The terminals were to be available to the public and carry mostly community and consumer information and data on library acquisitions.

COOPERATION AND NETWORKING

Consultative groups formed in the '70s varied from the Ontario Public Librarians Advisory Committee, formed of representatives from four other groups, to the informal meetings of British Columbia's Area 5–North Shore Library Administrators, who met to discuss problems, share experience, etc. The Interlibrary Council of Grande Prairie (Alta.) brought together librarians of all types; the Council of Administrators of Large Urban Public Libraries was confined to librarians from cities of 100,000 or more population. The formation of the Provincial and Territorial Library Directors Council enabled directors from all parts of the country to meet and discuss both common and unique needs and developments.

Cooperative acquisition, cataloging, and processing systems were developed by the Comité interrégional des bibliothèques publiques of Quebec; the several Bibliothèques centrales de prêt and a public library which comprised it cooperated not only in cataloging but also in buying furniture and developing public relations materials. Parkland Library and Northwest Library in Manitoba started an agreement in 1976 to share books and cataloging services.

Examples of improved access to collections through reciprocal borrowing or interchangeable borrowers' cards could be found in agreements among libraries in the Owen Sound area, in the Niagara Regional Library System, among members of the Greater Vancouver Library Federation (who shared reference service as well), among three Montreal area libraries, between Ottawa and Hull, and between Greater Victoria Public Library and Camosun College. (There were a number of such public/college library agreements.) An interprovincial agreement between the two Parkland Regionals, the one in Manitoba and the other in Saskatchewan, was a less usual type.

Deposit or exchange of collections, or just housing collections, was another common type of cooperation. Examples were the Ontario Joint Fiction Reserve, begun in 1972; the cooperating libraries divided the alphabet among themselves and agreed to accept, house, and service works by authors in their alphabet group. The Saskatchewan Provincial Library also arranged to house last copies of fiction. Kirkland Lake and Parry Sound Public Libraries served Laurentian University's continuing-education students; Port Colborne offered facilities for Niagara CAAT's extension course on law; the Haney (B.C.) library provided space for a collection of books and AV material and equipment for Douglas College; Medicine Hat Public Library provided Medicine Hat College with a rotating fiction deposit collection; Kitchener Public Library borrowers could use University of Waterloo materials, and the public library had a direct computer link to the university to enable it to check on the status of any volume requested. Unusual was the international agreement in 1973 between the Brockville, Ontario, and Ogdensburg, New York, libraries to exchange blocks of large print books.

A noteworthy ILL agreement of the decade was that between the provinces of

Alberta and Saskatchewan to facilitate loans between them of materials difficult to obtain.

Cooperation through improved communication links was provided by the installation of a Telex system linking the Provincial Library and resource and regional libraries in Saskatchewan, a similar Telex link among Montreal public libraries, and the installation of Zenith lines in Alberta. Development of courier services—for example, among libraries of the Windsor–Sarnia area in Ontario and the Lower Mainland area of British Columbia—also contributed to speedier communication.

The occasional union list of serials or films has been mentioned in other contexts. With regard to union catalog developments, it should be noted that there was, up to the end of 1979, no provision for British Columbia public libraries to join the B.C. Union Catalogue Project. Entry of the libraries of the Greater Vancouver Library Federation was assured for 1980, however, by a special grant of $3,000,000. Another development was the possibility that the Nova Scotia Union Catalogue might have to restrict itself to being a union catalog of the collections of provincially funded libraries only, but fortunately this did not happen.

A step toward networking was taken by Ontario public libraries when the regionals agreed in 1977 to pool a special grant from the province and fund a Network Development Office Project, to run from June 1978 to May 1980. Drawing on the expertise of the Metro Toronto Library Systems Office, and with the advice of various interested groups, the Network Office staff was charged with studying and recommending plans for public library networking in Ontario.

The problems facing public libraries at the end of the decade included those other libraries have met, plus some peculiar to them: diminishing resources; theft and vandalism; attacks by would-be censors; and complaints by Canadian authors that Canadian libraries did not stock their books, and by Canadian publishers that Canadian librarians "buy around." Added to these was a renewed demand by authors for Public Lending Right payments. Through the Canadian Library Association the libraries made clear their sympathy with the authors' plight, but equally stated their belief that such payments from library funds would be, in principle, unjustified.

Problems for libraries in Ontario were the prospect of deconditionalization of grants (i.e., grants for libraries would no longer be so specified) and the possibility of independent library boards being replaced by committees of local councils. Up to 1979 these did not seem to be active concerns in other areas, though they were serious for the future of Ontario libraries.

In an attempt to make their case known and to tap grass-roots user support, public librarians, chiefly through their associations, mounted strong lobbying efforts when particularly threatened (as was the case during the Manitoba "Libraries in Crisis" campaign and the protest against heavy budget cuts in Nova Scotia) or when anxious for change (as in Alberta during the debates that led to the major improvements in service that finally occurred). The examples given were single efforts, but most librarians appreciated that communication was an ongoing process, and that their efforts should be continuous. Funds for staffing such continued efforts were not generally available, however.

Another source of grass-roots support which has sometimes been neglected is the library trustee. Often their goodwill is frustrated by lack of information, and librarians (and trustees' associations) toward the end of the decade started to give attention to informing new—and old—trustees of their duties and responsibilities. The Joint Regional Library Boards Association of Nova Scotia was formed in 1976 to provide a forum for ideas, a means of cooperation among boards, and a vehicle for making their views known to the bodies responsible for public library service. The New Brunswick Library Council along with the Library Service sponsored its first workshop for trustees in 1979; the Yukon library service likewise held its first one in this period. The Ontario regionals prepared useful trustees' handbooks, and the Canadian Library Trustees' Association started work on kits of informational materials.

Taking their message directly to the public, libraries in all parts of the country participated in local events, sponsored information booths and presentations at meetings such as those of mayors and reeves of municipalities, used TV and radio spots to advertise service, made surveys of their communities' needs, and so on. The public library is the one type of library which requires no secondary qualifications as a condition of access, and as such it is uniquely valuable. The value is not, however, self-evident, and Canadian libraries have begun to appreciate that their potential users may have to be educated in the use of this resource.

Special Libraries

Perhaps the least understood and certainly the worst-documented group of libraries in Canada is that of special libraries. There is no agreement even on a definition of the type. As described here, they are the libraries which are working tools of an organization or institution, set up to assist the employees or members of the organization to do their jobs better—in other words, the objectives of special libraries are to promote the objectives of their parent organizations. The latter may be government departments or agencies (the largest group in Canada), companies, or associations or institutions. Specialized subject departments of university or public libraries are not included.

The name *special library* is used here, but the term *information center* is gaining ground and is a more accurate description of the service, the basic components of which are provision of working space, materials, citations, and answers, with an emphasis on the last two. Information analysis centers, whose concern is almost exclusively with assessed and evaluated answers, are not discussed. The growing number of information services, whose concerns are primarily citations and answers (and, to a lesser extent, the provision of materials), are referred to as appropriate.

There is little that can be said, in the present state of our knowledge, about the governance of most Canadian special libraries. They were variously placed in their organizations, and even where there was a common parent organization (as in the case of government libraries), there was little uniformity of library service among departments. However, one of the trends of the 1970s was the growth in the number of government libraries and the beginning of efforts at self-imposed coordination. Ontario led the way with its Ontario Government Librarians' Council (1970); then came the Alberta Government Libraries' Council (1974); the Association of Saskatchewan-Government Libraries (1975); the Comité de coordination des bibliothèques gouvernementales du Québec, the Council of Federal Libraries, and the Government Libraries Association of British Columbia (all in 1976); and finally, the Nova Scotia Government Libraries Council (1978).

Among the government libraries the legislative libraries probably experienced the greatest changes. In British Columbia the functions of the legislative librarian and the provincial archivist were separated in the early '70s. In 1974 the Alberta Provincial Library became the Legislature Library under a legislature librarian; one part of it, the Library Services Section, was given official responsibility for advising and assisting Alberta government libraries. The Manitoba Legislative Library for a time functioned as a provincial library but reverted to its proper name and style when the Public Library Service was set up. The Ontario Legislative Library became officially the Legislative Library, Research, and Information Services in 1978, reporting to the Speaker and being formally required to table an annual report in the Assembly. In 1979 the 128-year-old Nova Scotia Legislative Library was by ordinance removed from the jurisdiction of the Provincial Library and became answerable to the chairman of the Legislature Internal Economy Board, who is also the Speaker of the House.

In addition to these structural changes, a new development was the formation of research units staffed by subject specialists in the legislative libraries of Quebec and Ontario—a service on the model of that of the Library of Parliament. Alberta was also considering introduction of such a service.

A few other experiments in organization should be noted. In Quebec a Bibliothèque administrative was formed in 1972 by combining the libraries of nine departments housed in Buildings G and H of the complex of Quebec government buildings. The intention was to improve both economy and efficiency by centralizing collections and services. The idea, though appealing, runs contrary to the well-attested principle that if an information service is to be used to the full, it has to be close to its users. A recent article on the library (*54*) noted the development of small documentation units in many of the departments in the complex, so the experiment would seem to have been only partly successful.

Planning for another experiment, in British Columbia, had just been completed at the end of the decade. Under the plan the University of British Columbia would coordinate, and be a resource for, a network of all the teaching hospital libraries in the Vancouver area. Funding was obtained to begin the network in 1982.

A third development during the period was the organization in Alberta, Ontario, and British Columbia of law society library systems, and the attempts in Quebec and New Brunswick to do likewise. In Saskatchewan efforts were being directed toward upgrading the courthouse libraries.

STANDARDS AND STATISTICS

Since special libraries are, by definition, all different, general standards do not exist. Canadian hospital library standards had been developed by 1975 (*55*) and seemed to be having some influence with hospital accreditation bodies. Alberta government libraries developed standards for their operations in 1975 (*56*). One of the objectives of the new Nova Scotia Government Libraries Council was to do the same for Nova Scotia. The report, *Basic Readers' Services* (*57*), put out by the Readers' Services Committee of the Council of Federal Libraries in 1979, documented service norms in federal libraries.

There has been no Statistics Canada survey of special libraries since 1964, so that the only national figures published have been those derived by Anderson from her first two directories (*58*), from the first two parts of the *Canadian Library Directory* (*59*) compiled in the Library Documentation Centre, and from the records of new libraries noted for the center's files. The results can only be considered indicative, but they were at least compiled with a defined group of libraries in mind.

Figures for volumes per user were not available and would be largely meaningless if they were, for the special library's emphasis is on getting what contains the needed information, not on building collections as such. Volume counts bear little relationship to number of potential users, who ranged from five per library staff member in, for example, a consulting or legal firm, to 5,000 or more when the library served clientele across the country and even abroad, as some bank libraries did. Even less was it possible to obtain data on budgets. Some libraries were simply forbidden to release the information; others existed amid such complicated financial arrangements that it would be difficult to isolate the total or to ascertain what proportion the library total was of the amounts that the parent organization spent on information.

Some data on these topics may be gleaned for special libraries included in surveys of law, art, and music libraries (*60*) carried out by the Resources Survey Division of the National Library before it was disbanded. Some data were also available for federal government libraries as the result of a survey in the early '70s (*61*). But for the country as a whole data were lacking.

The data available did permit the documenting of a trend which illustrates the relationship between special library development and the state of the economy. The '50s and the '60s were the periods of greatest special library growth in Ontario and Quebec. The '70s, however, saw growth shifting westward, especially to Alberta and Saskatchewan, as oil, gas, potash, and other resource development brought both prosperity and a greater need for up-to-date, relevant information. Petroleum and gas company libraries mushroomed in Calgary, for example, while government libraries and law firm libraries increased greatly in Edmonton.

If special libraries flourish during periods of economic growth, they tend to shrink or disappear in times of economic stringency. During the 1970s federal libraries, for example, experienced staff cuts; some libraries were closed and others merged in order to reduce costs. Similar retrenchment took place among business and industrial libraries, and among libraries in associations dependent on members' dues for their funding. About 50 closures or mergers were documented for the years 1976 to 1978 alone. Yet between the publication of *Canadian Library Directory, 2* in 1976 (*10*) and the end of the decade, the Library Documentation Centre added reports of more than 500 new special libraries to its files. Even allowing for the fact that some libraries may have been in existence but not listed in the

TABLE 6

Numbers of Special Libraries in Canada, by Region, 1975–1976, and Additions to 1979[a]

Region	Number 1975–1976	Percentage 1975–1976	Libraries noted 1977–1979[b]	Total	Percentage
Atlantic	68	6.2	37	105	6.5
Quebec	273	24.9	76	349	21.7
Ontario	472	43.0	180	652	40.6
Central	206	18.8	184	390	24.3
British Columbia	75	6.8	31	106	6.6
Territories	4	0.4	—	4	0.2
Canada	1,098	100.0	508	1,606	100.0

[a] Sources: Files of the author and of the Library Documentation Centre.

[b] Since these libraries have never been surveyed, these figures are likely to be higher than a proper survey would show.

Directory, and that many might not have met its staffing criterion, such growth attested the vitality and value of this type of library.

Table 6 gives numbers of special libraries, including additional libraries noted in the years 1977 to 1979; Table 7 gives a breakdown by broad subject areas. It must be stressed that libraries identified in 1977 through 1979 have *not* been surveyed, and that a proper survey might lower the numbers appreciably.

FINANCE

As already noted, special library budget information was not available, but comments in the library press made it clear that, like other types of library, special libraries too faced budget cuts or staff freezes during the 1970s. In response, a few curtailed service or adopted a policy of charging for service given to users outside the library's parent organization. The Council of Federal Libraries set up a working group to study the problem as it affected federal libraries and to try to develop a charging policy for this group.

RESOURCES: COLLECTIONS

The extent of the holdings of Canadian special libraries can only be guessed at. With a few exceptions, notably the legislative and some other government libraries, Canadian special libraries remained small, the majority probably holding 5,000 or fewer items. The value of these collections lay not in their extent but in their depth within narrow, highly specialized subject fields, from astrophysics to ticks. Sometimes a group of libraries in a particular field were concentrated in one region, together forming a potential local resource; for example, pharmaceutical libraries in Montreal, insurance and bank libraries in Toronto, petroleum libraries

TABLE 7

Canadian Special Libraries by Subject Specialization, 1975–1976, and Additions to 1979[a]

Subject area	Number 1975–1976	Percentage 1975–1976	Libraries noted 1977–1979[b]	Total	Percentage
Arts and humanities	54	4.9	72	126	7.8
Sciences and technology	546	49.7	245	791	49.3
Social sciences	498	45.4	191	689	42.9
Total	1,098	100.0	508	1,606	100.0

[a] Sources: Files of the author and of the Library Documentation Centre.

[b] Since these libraries have never been surveyed, these figures are likely to be higher than a proper survey would show.

in Calgary, and marine biology libraries on the east and west coasts. Proximity sometimes facilitated collection rationalization, as in the case of the agreement on serials retention policies among Toronto bank libraries.

Federal library collections constituted some of the most valuable resources in the country on subjects such as geology, anthropology, statistics, Canadian art, and agriculture, to name a few. The libraries were de facto national resource collections, but they had no mandate to serve users beyond their departments, and certainly no special funding or staffing to enable them to do so. The Council of Federal Libraries set up a group to study the problem; and meanwhile, to make the collections better known, it sponsored publication of two directories of the most important collections—one covering the sciences (*62*); and the other, for the social sciences (*63*).

RESOURCES: PERSONNEL

Analyses of personnel data made by Anderson (*64*) indicated that staffing may have improved slightly over the period, but that there still remained a good many one-person libraries or libraries not professionally staffed. The ratio of professional to nonprofessional varied; on the average it appeared to be around 1:1.5 or 1:2.

For the most part special libraries in organizations were too few to be organized, but some government librarians (e.g., federal librarians) were unionized. One major change in the decade was the switch by federal librarians from the Professional Institute of the Public Service to the Public Service Alliance of Canada (PSAC), a move which brought both professional and support staff in government libraries under the same bargaining agent. A further development was the launching of a case by PSAC before the Canadian Human Rights Commission, on the ground that the federal government had shown sexual discrimination in setting librarians' salary scales. Members of the Library Science Group (65% female) were paid about a third less than Historical Researchers (75% male), and yet, the union claimed, they were doing work comparable to that of the librarians. The decision (in 1980) was in favor of the librarians.

RESOURCES: SPACE

Probably a few more special libraries than before went into quarters specifically planned for them during this decade—the Canadian Imperial Bank of Commerce, the Bank of Canada, and the federal Department of Finance, for example—but, in general, special libraries continued to do the best they could with the space they were allotted, and tried by vigorous weeding to keep expansion to a minimum.

SERVICES

The *raison d'être* of the special library is the services it gives; these are varied, but within one government libraries group, the federal libraries, a survey sponsored by the Council of Federal Libraries (*65*) revealed a remarkable degree of consensus on basic services for users (those given by 90% or more of the libraries reporting) and demonstrated as well the effect of increased staffing on service. Specialized services for hospital staff, such as provision of customized literature kits or the presence on rounds of a clinical librarian, appeared during the decade. Occasionally indexes or data compilations developed for in-house use proved of wider interest, and the special libraries made them available to others. A good example was the exchange and publicizing of indexes to the current status of bills by legislative libraries and the Library of Parliament. In addition, legislative libraries often provided a public service by indexing the journals of the legislature or issuing lists of provincial government publications.

RELATIONSHIP TO OTHER LIBRARIES

Special libraries of necessity have to draw upon the resources of other libraries to supplement their more limited collections, and unless the service can be bought, they must rely on the goodwill of other libraries to obtain what they need. Medical and law libraries, however, frequently enjoyed a considerable degree of support from nearby medical or law school libraries, and examples of assistance of this type have been described in the university libraries section. Other special relationships of this kind existed between faculties of management and local business libraries (e.g., at McGill).

AUTOMATION

Computer-based reference service appeared in special libraries before the 1970s, but the decade saw an increase in the number of special libraries with their own on-line searching facilities. One notable expansion of such services was the installation of MEDLINE terminals in hospitals; the Medical Library at McGill's Royal Victoria Hospital was the first to obtain one, and eight other libraries promptly followed suit. As a concomitant of this extended use, on-line users groups were formed; for example, in Halifax, Edmonton, and Vancouver.

Special libraries also used computers to build their own data bases; for example, the index to the *Ottawa Journal*, a reports index for the National Parks Documentation Centre, an information file for the Sports Information Resource Centre, and so on.

A consortium of education libraries in Toronto used UTLAS facilities to build a union file preliminary to producing a catalog that could be placed in multiple locations; Ontario government libraries started a series of seminars to try to decide on an automated system that would meet their cataloging needs. Four federal libraries arranged to join the National Library's DOBIS system starting in 1980. Some small special libraries in British Columbia were able to take advantage of UTLAS facilities for catalog assistance by using a local company which joined the B.C. Union Catalogue Project and searched UTLAS files on their behalf. A number of the larger federal libraries either joined UNICAT/TELECAT or used UTLAS as individual customers, while the Environment Canada Library developed its own system, ELIAS. The International Development Research Centre replaced its ISIS system by a modification, MINISIS. In Alberta, Schick, a library consultant, devised innovative uses of computers and word processors for the library systems she set up.

COOPERATION AND NETWORKING

Automation facilitated many of the cooperative projects undertaken by special libraries during this period: the Alberta government libraries' union catalog and union list of serials; the Quebec government libraries' union catalog—first on cards, then on fiche through participation by the Bibliothèque administrative in UNICAT/TELECAT; the revised union list of serials compiled by the Eastern Canada Chapter of the Special Libraries Association (SLA); and the union list of medical library journals produced for Montreal hospital libraries.

But the chief vehicles for special library cooperation were the specialized associations, which helped special librarians compensate for the isolation in which many of them must work. The two Canadian SLA chapters (in Montreal and Toronto) continued their work, and the Canadian Association of Special Libraries and Information Services (CASLIS), formed in 1969, established chapters in Ottawa, Toronto, Calgary, and Edmonton during the 1970s. These chapters were particularly active sponsors of continuing-education programs for their members. CASLIS also instituted a national award for service to special librarianship; the first recipient, in 1979, was Dr. Jack Brown, retiring director of CISTI. The specialized health libraries group of CASLIS broke away to form the Canadian Health Libraries Association, to which a number of local health library groups adhered as chapters. This association was, among other activities, concerned with promoting the use of the hospital library standards developed earlier. Many special librarians with interests in automation, information theory, etc., became members of the Canadian Association for Information Science, which was established in 1970 to promote an interest in information science.

The government library associations have been described earlier; in addition, the Association of Parliamentary Librarians in Canada was formed in 1975. Informal and formal local associations and groups of law librarians appeared during the decade, supplementing the support given by the (national) Canadian Association of Law Libraries established earlier. Music librarians broke from CLA to set up their own association; art libraries as of 1979 remained under the aegis of CASLIS.

Special libraries associations were also at times a vehicle for cooperation with general associations; for example, the Edmonton Chapter of CASLIS affiliated informally with the Library Association of Alberta. Joint programs and workshops with other library and information science groups were common.

Special libraries flourished as a type during the '70s, although individual libraries and groups of libraries felt the results of economic conditions in mergers and closures, restricted budgets, and losses of staff. Perhaps more than other libraries during the period, special libraries had to be concerned with evaluation of service, performance measurement, and justification of their existence. One outgrowth of that concern was an interest in application of marketing techniques in libraries. Numerous seminars on evaluation and performance measurement were held: The Council of Federal Libraries sponsored the preparation of a handbook on performance measurement (*66*) by the Federal Libraries Liaison Office, the office of the National Library which acted as secretariat for the council. There was probably an increase in the number of information/documentation services established in parallel with or supplementary to libraries, while the free-lance librarian passed from being a phenomenon to a fact of library life. Special libraries both availed themselves of the services of the free-lancers and were used by them in the course of their work.

General Topics

Subjects such as associations, research, education, and publications have been touched on throughout the preceding discussions, and the sections which follow supplement what has been written.

ASSOCIATIONS

The work of associations of special libraries has been described, but association activity and the proliferation of associations among libraries of all types marked the whole decade. In 1971 there were 43 library associations in Canada; by 1979 there were 158. They represented national, regional, provincial, local, and special interests, and the number would be even higher if staff associations of individual institutions were counted. The Canadian Library Association continued its work as the national English-language association; the French-language association, Association des bibliothécaires de langue française (ACBLF), in 1973 became ASTED (Association pour l'avancement des sciences et des techniques de la documentation). A new special-interest association was the Indexing and Abstracting Society of Canada, established in 1977. Its members were concerned with both traditional and automated indexing methods.

Certain trends were noteworthy. One was the interest in forming "friends of the library" groups displayed by public libraries and some university libraries. At least six public library "friends" groups were established between 1977 and 1979 alone. A second was the formation of what may be called "ethnic associations"; for example, the Polish-Canadian and Chinese-Canadian Librarians' Associations. A third—again a phenomenon of the last 3 years of the decade—was the formation of on-line users' groups in many parts of the country. The CLA On-Line Users Interest Group was set up to try to provide some coordination for them. Finally, library technicians' associations were organized in five provinces in the '70s and proved very active and vocal in support of their members.

The associations provided forums for members' problems, lobbied in their interests, produced publications important to members, and fostered professional development through continuing-education opportunities. Associations were also responsible for encouraging the two Ontario library schools to give courses in Ottawa.

LIBRARY EDUCATION

By the end of the 1970s there were seven Canadian library schools; the eighth, at the University of Ottawa, had closed in 1972. All seven had dropped the 1-year accredited B.L.S. program and were giving the 2-year accredited master's degree as the first professional degree. In addition, two schools—the Faculty of Library Science, University of Toronto; and the School of Library and Information Science, University of Western Ontario—began Ph.D. programs in the early 1970s, and each had graduated its first doctoral student before 1979. The Toronto Faculty had moved into a new building of its own adjoining the Robarts Library at the beginning of the decade. These spacious, well-designed quarters were among the best library school facilities on the continent.

The major new development in formal education was the degree courses given in Ottawa by the two Ontario schools for those wishing to upgrade a B.L.S. or start the M.L.S. Faculty commuted to Ottawa, where local universities provided meeting and library facilities. Students were also able to use the files of the Library Documentation Centre and the National Library's book and serial collections. In addition to the degree programs, these schools, like the others, were deeply involved in continuing-education programs, a major educational trend of the 1970s.

Another innovation was the "librarian in residence" program, which was most closely associated with the Dalhousie school. That school also added a "writer in residence" program toward the end of the decade.

At least nine library technician training programs started or restarted during the '70s, one of them (at the Sheridan CAAT) including an option in health science library procedures. More than half the new programs outside Quebec were for 2 years; in Quebec, where the courses were given by the Cégeps, programs lasted 3 years. After 1975 the Cégep programs became documentation rather than library technology programs, marking an increased emphasis on preparation for work in records management centers, bookstores, etc., as well as libraries and AV centers. Directors outside Quebec tended to look to CLA's "Guidelines for the Training of Library Technicians," 1977 (*67*), for initial guidance; Cégep programs (including courses and number of entrants permitted) were more controlled and uniform, and followed the Quebec college guidelines for documentation technology programs.

In addition to the technicians' programs, New Brunswick and Nova Scotia both conducted formal correspondence courses for library assistants.

Quebec regulations allowed entry of 205 new technician students a year; the number of graduates would presumably be the same or nearly so. The 15 other Canadian programs in 1979 graduated about 380 library technicians. Librarians graduated in 1979 numbered 538, an increase of 21 (roughly 4%) over 1978. Women graduates still outnumbered men by better than three to one.

LIBRARY RESEARCH

Interest in library research increased during the 1970s, although in the last 5 years of the period only about 100 projects were registered by the Library Documentation Centre for notification to UNESCO's International Information System on Research in Documentation (ISORID) program. The inclusion of provision for sabbaticals and study leave in academic library contracts, however, began to show results as the decade ended, and the creation of the Centre for Research in Librarianship at the Faculty of Library Science, University of Toronto, with its facilities for visiting researchers, provided a focus for research efforts. The Toronto Centre, like the Library Documentation Centre, was interested in improving the recording and dissemination of information on Canadian library research, but neither had found a formula for overcoming what seems to be the ingrained reluctance of Canadian researchers to report what they are doing.

LIBRARY PUBLICATIONS

Canada does not as yet have a strong library press, although a number of improvements occurred during the decade, such as the appearance of the *Canadian Journal of Information Science* (*68*), the strengthening of existing library association newsletters and bulletins, the appearance of many new regional library bulletins in Ontario, regular publication of the proceedings of the conferences of the Western Canada Chapter of ASIS (*69*) and Canadian Association for Information Science (*70*), and the successful launching of *Canadian Materials* (*71*), a review periodical covering Canadian educational books, kits, films, etc. Some important studies and surveys appeared: Jarvi's survey (*72*) of government publications practices, Amey's study of Canadian school-housed public libraries (*33*), Laidlaw's survey of library orientation practices (*73*), the Garry volume (*1*) noted earlier, the surveys of the Resources Survey Division of the National Library of Canada (*60*), the *Mélanges* in honor of Father Edmond Desrochers (*74*), Lamonde's *Bibliothèques de collectivités* (*75*), and the various public library surveys mentioned earlier. There is a great need for research in Canada, but perhaps a greater need for well-documented syntheses of information on Canadian library history, development, and current status which can provide a firm base of knowledge as an infrastructure for research.

Summary

Any attempt to identify major trends in or characteristics of Canadian libraries during the period of the 1970s is a certain invitation to controversy. But the attempt must be made.

For college libraries, the outstanding features were the strong involvement of the libraries with audiovisual materials as well as with books and the very heterogeneous nature of their clientele, ranging from students just out of school to the retired, from factory workers in retraining courses to university graduates seeking technical expertise they lacked.

For university libraries, on the other hand, the main concerns were collections and automation. Concern over collections involved problems of how to maintain them in the face of inflation, how to use microforms to best advantage, and how to improve resources in support of Canadian studies. Concern with automation stressed its use in bibliographic control and the possibilities of sharing information through networking on a national and even international basis.

School libraries similarly gave much attention to raising the Canadian content of their collections. Like college libraries, they were also concerned with integrating media of many types with books as resources for instruction. Possibly their chief problem during the decade was staffing, however; not only number of staff but also their qualifications, with the question of the relative value of teacher versus library training still to the fore.

Public libraries were best characterized during this period by the range, variety, and depth of their outreach services—to the handicapped, to prisoners, to native peoples, to ethnic groups, to the illiterate. Concern for Canadian content was for most of them nothing new; however, there was much greater attention paid to preserving local community history during this period. Another trend was the emphasis on community information services, provided either as part of the library's regular operations or through special facilities.

Special libraries in the '70s were perhaps mainly concerned over coming to terms with the proliferating numbers of data bases, computerized indexes, etc., which were becoming necessary to their work, whether produced within the parent organization or commercially. They were also concerned over their relationship to developing networks from which they—by reason of size, procedures, or governance—seemed likely to be excluded.

All libraries faced the problems of budgets which were not keeping pace with inflation; of defining the best mix of librarians, subject or technical experts, technicians, and support staff to maintain or improve service; and of ensuring a true understanding of the needs of current users and finding ways of reaching nonusers.

But perhaps more harmful in the long run than the economic problems was the continued fragmentation of libraries and librarians into ever smaller and more specialized interest groups. Cooperation there was and networking there was, but usually within fairly narrowly defined subsets of the total library community. Admittedly this was convenient and doubtless more efficient, and certainly it was in line with the trend to specialization that has characterized the 20th century. Yet Canadian libraries in 1979 were still comparatively few in number and, in their present state, unable to speak with a strong, united voice that could be heard among other conflicting voices. Recapturing a sense of community and interdependence may be one of the most important tasks for Canadian librarians in the 1980s as they seek to exploit the new technologies of information transfer that are developing.

Note Added in Proof. Preliminary data from the 1979 Statistics Canada survey of public libraries became available after this article was completed. They showed an increase to 959 in number of libraries responding, and to 2,854 in number of service points. Income reported was $249 million; expenditures, $243 million. Number of books held and circulation per capita had increased slightly to 1.8 and 5.1, respectively, and both the average number of direct circulations and of interlibrary loans had risen. There was also evidence of a better ratio of professional staff to population served. In short, the new data presented a fairly encouraging picture of this important group of libraries at the end of the decade (*76*).

ACKNOWLEDGMENT

The author was assisted in the preparation of this article by the staff of the Library Documentation Centre of the National Library of Canada.

A NOTE ON FURTHER READING

Information on Canadian libraries has to be culled from many and varied sources. Three annual surveys are published, however. That in the *Bowker Annual of Library & Booktrade Information* appears sporadically and tends to be topical. Those done by Brian Land for the *ALA Yearbook* since 1976 (covering events of 1975 on) touch on the year's highlights in all areas relative to librarianship. The *Annual Review of Canadian Libraries* prepared by Professor S.D. Neill since 1973 (covering 1972 on) appeared at first in the now defunct *Canadian Library Progress* and is being continued in the *Journal of the Canadian Library Science Society* (No. 3 appeared in 1980). The reviews deal with trends and issues of current concern rather than with events. The *Canadian Library Handbook 1979–1980* (Micromedia Limited, Toronto) contains a number of articles describing the state of Canadian librarianship in 1979, but such articles will be excluded from future issues.

Journals useful for keeping up with Canadian developments include the major association journals (*Canadian Library Journal, Documentation et bibliothèques*, and *Canadian Journal of Information Science*) and the information bulletins of the provincial or regional library associations or library agencies. Broad coverage of current news may be found in *Feliciter, Nouvelles de l'ASTED*, and *Quill & Quire*.

There is no index to Canadian library journals as a whole, but selected titles are covered by the regular library science indexes. Monographic publications which appear on the tapes of the national bibliography, *Canadiana*, may be searched on-line on the CAN/OLE system.

REFERENCES

1. L. S. Garry and Carl Garry, eds., *Canadian Libraries in Their Changing Environment*, York University, Centre for Continuing Education, Downsview, Ont., 1977.
2. Canadian Association of College and University Libraries, *Standards Recommended for Canadian Community College Libraries*, CACUL, n.p., 1973.

3. Fédération des Cégep [*sic*], Commission des coordonnateurs de bibliothèque, *Normes des bibliothèques de Cégep,* The Federation, Montréal, 1974.
4. Fédération des Cégeps, Commission des directeurs de bibliothèque, *Normes des bibliothèques de Cégep, Doc. no 2: Quantification*, The Federation, Montréal, 1975.
5. Statistics Canada, Education, Science, and Culture Division, *Culture Statistics: University and College Libraries in Canada 1976–77*, Statistics Canada, Ottawa, 1979.
6. Photocopied tables supplied to the author by Statistics Canada (Table 2 of its *Service Bull.: Culture Statistics*, 3[3], 5 [May 1980]).
7. Statistics Canada, Education, Science, and Culture Division, *University and College Libraries in Canada 1970–71*, Information Canada, Ottawa, 1973.
8. J.-M. B. Léveillé, "Les Bibliothèques de CEGEP face au regroupement des ressources éducatives," *Information CB*, **10,** 10–11 (May 1976).
9. Canadian Association of College and University Libraries, Community and Technical College Libraries Section, *Guidelines for Academic Status for Professional Librarians in Community and Technical Colleges*, CACUL, n.p., 1978.
10. *Canadian Library Directory, 2: University, College and Special Libraries*, National Library of Canada, Ottawa, 1976.
11. Canadian Association of College and University Libraries, Second University Library Standards Committee, *Trends for the Seventies: Guidelines for Canadian University Libraries*, CACUL, Montreal and Toronto, 1971.
12. Photocopied tables supplied to the author by Statistics Canada (Table 1 of its *Service Bull.: Culture Statistics*, 3[3], 6 [May 1980]).
13. Canadian Association of University Business Officers, *Five-Year Trend Analysis of University Financial Statistics*, CAUBO, Ottawa, 1979.
14. L.-P. Bonneau and J. A. Corry, *Quest for the Optimum: Research Policy in the Universities of Canada*, Association of Universities and Colleges of Canada, Ottawa, 1973, Vol. 2, pp. 1–17.
15. *Guidelines on Academic Status for University Librarians,* Canadian Library Association, Ottawa, 1979.
16. Statistics Canada, Education, Science, and Culture Division, *Culture Statistics: Centralized School Libraries in Canada, 1974–75*, 1st issue, Statistics Canada, Ottawa, 1977.
17. J. G. Reade, *The Nova Scotia School Library Survey 1979*, Nova Scotia School Library Association, Halifax, 1979.
18. Photocopied tables supplied to the author by Statistics Canada (Table 3 of its *Service Bull.: Culture Statistics*, 3[3], 6 [May 1980]).
19. G. Legendre and J.-M. B. Léveillé, "Relevé des bibliothèques au juin 1974," *CB Information,* **8,** 19–26 (April 1975).
20. British Columbia, Ministry of Education, *Sources and Resources: A Handbook for Teacher-Librarians in British Columbia*, The Ministry, Victoria, 1978.
21. New Brunswick, Department of Education, *Planning Guide for School Buildings and Facilities*, The Department, Fredericton, 1978 (?).
22. Québec, Ministère de l'Éducation, *Guide d'aménagement des bibliothèques–centres documentaires des écoles élémentaires*, The Ministry, Québec, 1976.
23. Québec, Ministère de l'Éducation, *Guide d'aménagement des bibliothèques des écoles secondaires*, The Ministry, Québec, 1975.
24. Ontario Teachers' Federation, *Resource Centre Guidelines,* The Federation, Toronto, 1972.
25. Newfoundland and Labrador, Department of Education, Division of Instruction, *Library Manual for Schools in Newfoundland and Labrador*, 3rd ed., The Department, Saint John's, 1977.
26. F. R. Branscombe and H. E. Newsom, *Resource Services for Canadian Schools*, McGraw-Hill Ryerson, Toronto, 1977.
27. *Directory of Library Associations in Canada*, 5th ed., prepared in the Library Documentation Centre, National Library of Canada, Ottawa, 1979.
28. Canadian School Library Association, *Canadian School Library Programmes of Interest to Visitors*, The Association, Ottawa, 1979.
29. K. Haycock, "Selection of Learning Resources: A Policy Statement," *Bookmark*, **20**(1), 27–30 (September 1978).

30. "CSLA Report: The Qualifications for School Librarians," *Moccasin Telegraph*, **22,** 12–15 (Fall 1979).
31. D. Fennell, "Education for School Librarians: The Ministry of Education," *IPLO Quart.*, **16,** 156–167 (April 1975).
32. "Declining Enrolment: A Blow for School Library Services: Results from a Survey of the Members of the Canadian School Library Association," *Moccasin Telegraph*, **21,** 35–38, 42 (Fall–Winter 1978).
33. L.J. Amey, ed., *The Canadian School-Housed Public Library*, Occasional Paper No. 24, Dalhousie University Libraries and Dalhousie School of Library Service, Halifax, 1979.
34. Nova Scotia, Department of Education, *Report on the Minister's Task Force on Libraries*, The Department, n.p., 1978.
35. L. M. Bewley, *Public Library Legislation in Saskatchewan: Analysis and Recommendations*, n.p., Vancouver (?), 1978.
36. A. Bowron, *The Ontario Public Library: Review and Reorganization*, Information, Media, and Library Planners, Toronto, 1975.
37. H. E. Newsom, *Guidelines for the Development of Public Library Services in Manitoba*, University of Alberta, Edmonton, 1974.
38. H. E. Newsom, M. E. Richeson, and D. Gill, *Alberta Rural Libraries Project*, Report prepared for Alberta Culture, Youth, and Recreation, n.p., 1974, 3 vols.
39. M. E. Manley-Casimir, *The Right to Know: Policies, Structures and Plans for the Development of Library Services in Alberta*, A Report to the Department of Culture, Youth, and Recreation, L. W. Downey Research Associates, Edmonton, 1974.
40. Keith Turnbull, "The One-System Approach to Libraries," Unpublished working paper on libraries and library development in Saskatchewan, 1975.
41. British Columbia, Library Development Commission, Committee on Library Development, *Proposal for Province-Wide Organization of Library Services in British Columbia*, The Commission, Victoria, 1971.
42. University of Toronto, Centre for Research in Librarianship, *Project: Progress: The Future of Public Libraries in Canada, a Research Design*, Centre for Research in Librarianship, University of Toronto for the Canadian Association of Public Libraries of the Canadian Library Association, Toronto, 1976.
43. British Columbia, Library Services Branch, *Quantitative Standards for Public Libraries in British Columbia,* The Branch, Victoria, 1978.
44. Saskatchewan Library Association, Task Force on Standards, *Standards for Libraries within Regional Library Systems in Saskatchewan*, 2nd ed., rev., The Association, Regina, 1979.
45. Québec, Service des bibliothèques publiques, *Normes pour les bibliothèques municipales*, The Service, Québec, 1974.
46. Y.-A. Lacroix, "Présent et futur du réseau des bibliothèques publiques au Québec," *Documentation et bibliothèques*, **25,** 177–188 (December 1979).
47. Statistics Canada, Education, Science, and Culture Division, *Survey of Libraries Part I: Public Libraries 1970*, Information Canada, Ottawa, 1973.
48. Statistics Canada, Education, Science, and Culture Division, *Culture Statistics: Public Libraries in Canada 1976,* Statistics Canada, Ottawa, 1978.
49. Statistics Canada, Education, Science, and Culture Division, *Users and Resources of Public Libraries in Canada*, by N. Verma, Statistics Canada, Ottawa, 1979; and "Selected Leisure Time Activities, February 1978," *Service Bull.: Culture Statistics*, **1,** 1–6 (January 1979).
50. G. Buller, "New Public Library Buildings in Ontario," *Ontario Lib. Rev.*, **63,** 299–320 (December 1979).
51. F. White, *Standards for Correctional Institution Libraries of the Canadian Corrections Service*, n.p., 1977(?).
52. National Library of Canada, Task Group on Library Service to the Handicapped, *Report*, The Library, Ottawa, 1976.
53. *Directory of Adult Basic Education Programs in Canada,* Movement for Canadian Literacy, Toronto, 1978.
54. O. Blouin-Cliche, "Le Partage des ressources et des coûts à la Bibliothèque administrative du gou-

vernement du Québec," in *Proceedings of the 7th Canadian Conference on Information Science, Banff, Alta., 1979*, Canadian Association for Information Science, Ottawa, 1979, pp. 43–49.
55. "Canadian Standards for Hospital Libraries," *Canadian Med. Assoc. J.*, **112,** 1272–1274 (May 17, 1975).
56. Alberta Government Libraries' Council, Standards and Specifications Committee, *Standards and Specifications for Alberta Government Special Libraries*, Queen's Printer, Province of Alberta, Edmonton, 1975.
57. Council of Federal Libraries, Readers' Services Committee, *Basic Readers' Services*, National Library of Canada, Ottawa, 1979.
58. B. L. Anderson, comp., *Special Libraries in Canada: A Directory*, 2nd ed., CLA Occasional Paper No. 73, Canadian Library Association, Ottawa, 1968; *Special Libraries and Information Centres in Canada: A Directory*, Canadian Library Association, Ottawa, 1970.
59. *Canadian Library Directory 1: Federal Government Libraries*, National Library of Canada, Ottawa, 1974; cf. also Ref. *10.*
60. National Library of Canada, Resources Survey Division, *Research Collections in Canadian Libraries: II: Special Studies–3. Law Library Resources in Canada*, by Viola Bird (1975); *6. Fine Arts Library Resources in Canada* (1978); *7. Music Library Resources*, (1980), The Library, Ottawa, 1975–1980.
61. *Summary of the Federal Government Library Survey Report,* National Library of Canada, Ottawa, 1974.
62. J. Parkkari, ed., *Science and Technology Collections in Canadian Government Libraries: A Guide*, NRC No. 16220, Canada Institute for Scientific and Technical Information, National Research Council of Canada, Ottawa, 1977.
63. Council of Federal Libraries, Collection Rationalization Committee, *Social Science and Humanities Collections in Canadian Government Libraries: A Guide*, Publications Series, National Library of Canada, Ottawa, 1978.
64. B. L. Anderson, "Special Library Statistics," *Feliciter*, **23,** 4 –5 (September 1977).
65. Council of Federal Libraries, Working Group on Charging for Library Services, *Charging Practices in Federally-Supported Libraries: Results of the 1977 Survey*, The Council, Ottawa, 1979.
66. Council of Federal Libraries, Working Group on Performance Measurement, *Performance Measurement in Federal Libraries: A Handbook*, Publication Series, National Library of Canada, Ottawa, 1979.
67. "Guidelines for the Training of Library Technicians," pp. 50–51, 53 of M. R. Angel and G. R. Brown, "Survey of Library Technician Programs in Canada," *Canadian Lib. J.*, **34,** 41, 43, 45–51, 53–55 (February 1977). (Revision published by CLA in 1982.)
68. *Canadian Journal of Information Science*, Canadian Association for Information Science, Ottawa, Vol. 1, No. 1 –, May 1976–.
69. American Society for Information Science, Western Canada Chapter, *Proceedings*, First Conference –, 1969 –.
70. Canadian Association for Information Science, *Proceedings*, First Conference –, 1973 –.
71. *Canadian Materials*, Canadian Library Association, Ottawa, 1971 –.
72. E. T. Jarvi, *Access to Canadian Government Publications in Canadian Academic and Public Libraries*, Canadian Library Association, Ottawa, 1976.
73. S.M. Laidlaw, "Progress and Recent Developments in Canadian Libraries," in J. Lubans Jr., ed., *Progress in Educating the Library User*, Bowker, New York, 1978, pp. 125–209.
74. *Livre, bibliothèque et culture québécoise: mélanges offerts à Edmond Desrochers, s.j.*, ASTED, Montréal, 1977, 2 vols.
75. Y. Lamonde, *Bibliothèques de collectivités à Montréal (17e–19e siècle): Sources et problèmes*, Bibliothèque nationale du Québec, Montréal, 1979.
76. Statistics Canada, "Public Libraries in Canada, 1979," *Service Bull.: Culture Statistics,* **4,** 1–6 (August 1981).

B. L. Anderson

THE CENTER FOR RESEARCH LIBRARIES

The Center for Research Libraries (CRL) is a cooperatively supported library for libraries. Its basic purpose is to make accessible to its members more library materials than they can afford to acquire for their own individual collections. The center collects and provides access to, through interlibrary loans, material that, while essential for research, is apt to be so infrequently used at any one institution that it can be shared by the major research libraries of North America. In 1979 the center's membership consisted of 110 major research libraries located throughout the United States and Canada. As of that date there were also 70 associate members. Most of the full members were universities, but some large public libraries and two state libraries also belonged. Associate members included colleges, public libraries, governmental research institutes, and business corporations.

To understand the nature of the material collected by the CRL, it must be kept in mind that most of the material in the large university and other research libraries of the world is infrequently used. This is the result of three factors: specialization, language, and timeliness. As the world's knowledge (and the publications containing it) has grown, researchers have had to become more specialized in order to master it. This has meant that large research libraries serving a community of scholars have had to be able to provide materials that will meet the potential needs of a wide variety of specialists. As a result, most large research libraries regularly collect materials that will not be needed at their institution for many years, and must do so if they are to be prepared to meet the future potential need of specialized research. It is not only the highly specialized new materials, however, that are apt to be infrequently used. Many materials in foreign languages are infrequently used simply because relatively few persons among the library's patrons have the ability to read them.

With the passage of time, most publications become less frequently consulted. Partially, this is because most of the patrons' reading time is taken up trying to keep current with new publications, partially because the essential information in them gets distilled and the essence concentrated in new treatments of the subject, and sometimes because the information in them becomes outdated for current use. While the rapidity with which materials decline in frequency of use, and the extent of the decline, varies from field to field, most materials printed in any given year become less frequently used with time. But, though infrequently used, they remain essential sources of information, not only for historical research but also for research in some current special problems, and must remain accessible.

These factors have been exacerbated in recent years by the exponential increase in the number of new publications being issued each year. As a result of these factors, research libraries that wish to continue to meet the wide variety of needs of the researchers they serve must add to their resources at an ever-increasing rate, while at the same time maintaining access to the materials they have collected in the past. It has long been obvious that this is a task that not even the richest institution could ever hope to meet acting alone.

Libraries have tried to meet this challenge through cooperative endeavors. The Center for Research Libraries is one of the more ambitious and successful of these endeavors. The center provides a facility to which members can send infrequently used materials that had been acquired for their own collections but now are infrequently used due to their age. The center retains one copy of all items sent by the members, and these form a common pool upon which all members can draw. The center's facility has been designed for the most economical storage of materials, and thus, the membership is paying for the housing of one copy of each title in inexpensive storage rather than each paying to store the infrequently used item in the more expensive space in its own stacks.

The CRL also acquires through direct acquisitions those items that it can be anticipated will be infrequently used at any one member institution. This allows the members to have access to these materials without each having to acquire them at a cost which the use will not justify. Money saved through these shared acquisitions can then be used to purchase material that is apt to have greater use at the individual institution.

As an institution dedicated to serving other libraries through interlibrary loans, the center is able to organize its collections and procedures to provide more rapid service than usually exists through interlibrary lending. This, coupled with the fact that material is available to the members by right rather than courtesy, creates for the members a significant advantage over normal interlibrary borrowing.

What was to become the Center for Research Libraries began operations as the Midwest Inter-Library Center. It was originally incorporated on March 4, 1949, as a not for profit corporation by 10 midwestern universities. Its origins really should be traced back to 1939 when John Fall of the New York Public Library and Keyes D. Metcalf of the Harvard University Library were asked by a group of presidents of midwestern universities to study the feasibility of establishing a deposit library in the Midwest. This study concentrated on the idea of constructing a cooperative warehouse in which the members might rent space. The lack of interest in this program by some librarians prevented its immediate realization, and then World War II postponed whatever action might otherwise have resulted.

When the war ended, however, interest in a cooperative endeavor among midwestern libraries was revived and resulted in a report prepared by E. W. McDiarmid, then the librarian at the University of Minnesota, entitled *A Midwest Inter-Library Program.* The principal recommendation of this report was that there be established a Midwest Inter-Library Corporation, one of whose functions would be to "establish and maintain a central deposit library, known as the Midwest Inter-Library Center for the cooperative ownership, housing and servicing of 'little-used' research materials" (*1*). Perhaps the most important factor that distinguished the proposed center from other cooperatively maintained depository libraries, and has in turn led to its later growth, was the fact that the material was to be cooperatively owned. McDiarmid noted that "it should be made clear that all books in the Center are the joint property of all member institutions. An institution which places material there (other than in storage for itself) should understand that it is no longer free to recall that material" (*2*). This principle meant that once material was given to the center, every member had the assurance of continued access to it whether it had ever been in their own library or came from another institution. Members might therefore feel free to discard from their own collections infrequently used titles which were held by the center, with the assurance that they jointly owned the copy at the center. Perhaps more significantly, this principle was later to facilitate the development of direct acquisitions by the center of materials whose use could be anticipated to be infrequent.

McDiarmid's report concluded with this note:

> It should be reiterated that the proposal for the *Inter-Library Center* involves a major change in present library thinking. In place of the goal of bigger and better libraries on every campus, the *Center* poses the goal of more efficient and more complete service to scholarship and society. If faculty members and Librarians are willing to accept this viewpoint, the *Inter-Library Center* can be made a success (*3*).

It was thus with this warning of the revolutionary nature of what they were doing that the 10 midwestern universities launched the Midwest Inter-Library Center in 1949. The site for the proposed building was donated by the University of Chicago, while the Carnegie Corporation and the Rockefeller Foundation provided grants totaling a million dollars for the construction. Mr. Ralph T. Esterquest became the director on October 1, 1949. The building was completed in August 1951, with the official dedication being held on October 5 of that year. However, due to delays in the installation of the stacks, full operations did not get underway until 1952.

During the early years of the Midwest Inter-Library Center the major emphasis was upon the deposit of materials withdrawn from the collections of the members. Deposits were divided into two classes designated as being part of the "Planned Program" and the "Miscellaneous Program." The Planned Program consisted of a number of well-defined types of material such as college catalogs, doctoral dissertations, and state documents. It was felt that these types of material lent themselves to rapid identification in the collections of the member libraries, thus avoiding the expensive and time-consuming weeding process. It was decided that the center itself would make no attempt to provide conventional cataloging for materials of this type, but that they would be shelf-cataloged; that is, they would be systematically arranged on the shelves in a manner that would make them easily accessible when requests were received. This procedure would allow a large quantity of material to be processed and made accessible at a fraction of the cost of conventional cataloging and in a much shorter time. The Miscellaneous Program was to include any materials that members wished to deposit that did not fall in the scope of one of the planned programs. These materials would be given full conventional descriptive cataloging under their main entries.

An attempt was also made to establish a "Fragmentary Sets Program" through which the center would actively solicit broken files of serial publications from member institutions in order to combine these into more complete files at the center. Due to the difficulties of coordinating such a program, it was soon dropped; though in fact, fragmentary sets were brought together at the center over the years, although in an unsystematic manner.

From its beginning the center had a program for the direct acquisition of materials that could be expected to be infrequently used, though initially the budget for this program was very modest. Except for a few "preferred classes" of material, all direct acquisitions had to be approved by an Advisory Committee consisting, for the first 2 years, of five of the chief librarians from member libraries, and thereafter of all of the chief librarians at member libraries.

The growth of the center's collection was extremely rapid. By 1955 close to 1,000,000 volumes had been deposited in the center, and by 1964 the total had reached around 2,000,000 volumes. Through direct acquisitions, either by gift or purchase, the collection of newspapers, state documents, foreign government documents, and the publications of university bureaus of business research grew rapidly. In the mid-1950s the center began to acquire some of the major microform projects, such as those devoted to English literary periodicals and French drama. In some instances these projects were acquired with funds outside of the regular budget, with interested members paying a special assessment to purchase the particular project.

Another major development in the center's acquisitions program occurred with the purchase of an extensive collection of publications of the Russian Academy of Sciences from its founding in 1723 through 1956. An arrangement was made for the center to acquire all future publications of the academy, from 1957 forward, as they were published. While the members of the center would continue to purchase academy publications selectively according to their interests, the knowledge that the center had all publications would assure them of access to those publications they decided not to purchase. This was one of the first instances when it was decided that a blanket purchase by the center, which was bound to result in some duplication with the holdings of individual members, was justified in that it would allow all members greater selectivity.

The center also began to maintain a number of programs that served institutions outside of the regular membership. These programs were made possible from various sources of special funding and were not limited to the Midwest. In 1955 the center began to operate the Association of Research Libraries' Foreign Newspaper Microfilming Project (FNMP). This project acquires, either through the purchase of positive copies or through original filming, selected foreign newspapers from around the world. It is supported by the subscriptions of the institutions that wish to participate, and these institutions have the right to borrow the films or purchase positive copies of those newspapers filmed by the project for the cost of printing.

Also in 1955, a project funded by the National Science Foundation was begun to subscribe to those titles abstracted by *Chemical Abstracts* or listed in *Biological Sciences Serial Publications: A World List* that were not held by any of the center's members. This project eventually led to over 4,000 subscriptions being entered, mostly to foreign journals, and these were maintained out of the center's budget when the National Science Foundation funding came to an end.

By the end of the decade the center's membership had increased to 19 institutions. In 1959 Mr. Gordon R. Williams became the second director of the center, Mr. Esterquest having resigned in 1958 to take a position at Harvard University.

The early 1960s were a period of reevaluation and change. It had already become obvious that the available stack space would soon be exhausted, while center programs were continuing to expand. As previously noted, some of these programs already had an impact outside of the Midwest region. In fact, in 1961 all geographic restrictions on membership were removed, making research libraries throughout North America eligible to join. Several factors were behind this move. First, it had been discovered that the geographical distance from the center made no significant difference in a library's ability to use the center effectively. The fact that the center was a facility dedicated to interlibrary lending had made it possible for it to fill requests much more rapidly than the normal library could, and this tended to more than offset the effect of distance. It also had become clear that the nature of the material deposited in the center and acquired directly by the center was such that conflicts in use were extremely infrequent. It was judged that these conflicts were so rare that the membership could safely be expanded to include many more libraries. Finally, it had also become apparent that even a 10- or 12-state region provided too small a base to acquire all the materials to which the libraries in the region needed to have access. Expanding the membership, and thus the financial base, would make more funds available for acquisitions without a corresponding increase in membership fees. It was on the basis of these factors that it was decided to drop the geographical restrictions on membership.

This decision, coupled with an impending space problem, led the center's Board of Directors to feel that the time had come to reconsider the center's long-term goals. In order to do this the Board of Directors called for a study to review and evaluate basic premises and present operations, as well as looking for ways in which to make the center more broadly useful nationally (*4*). To do this, they invited Dr. Stephen McCarthy, director of libraries at Cornell University, and Dr. Raymond Swank, dean of the School of Librarianship at the University of California at Berkeley, to conduct an exhaustive survey. This survey was conducted in the period between May 1963 and June 1964, and considered all phases of the operations and the impact that these had upon the membership.

While the surveyors in their report noted a number of problems related to the center's rapid growth and the sometimes unclear ideas among the members as to what its ultimate function should be, they began the summary of their conclusions and recommendations by stating, "It may be observed first that, with the possible exception of the Farmington Plan, the Midwest Inter-Library Center has been the most ambitious, imaginative and successful cooperative venture yet undertaken by American research libraries" (*5*). Besides pointing to a number of accomplishments in support of this statement, the surveyors made a number of recommendations. Two of the most significant of these were that the center should stress the cooperative acquisition program and that it "should formally cease to be a regional agency and should become a national institution" (*6*).

Soon after the report was issued several steps were taken to carry out the latter recommendation. In January 1965 the name was changed to the Center for Research Libraries to eliminate any connotation of regionalism. The governance structure was also changed in order that it might function effectively with a much larger number of institutions participating.

As the highest governing body the Council was created, to consist of two representatives from each member institution. One of these representatives would be the head librarian of the member institution; and the other, a nonlibrarian appointed by the chief administrative officer of the institution. It was expected that the nonlibrarian would normally be an administrative officer who would be aware of the long-range goals of the institution and not just the problems of the library. The Council was given responsibility for approving the center's budget, determining the criteria for membership, electing the Board of Directors, and serving as an advisory group to the board. The Board of Directors was to manage the affairs of the center. This body would consist of 16 persons, 15 to be elected by the Council from among its members, plus the director of the center, who would serve ex officio. Of the elected directors, not less than six nor more than nine were to be librarians (7).

Even prior to these steps, the center's membership had spread outside the Midwest region with the University of Toronto becoming the 22nd member in 1963. By 1968 the membership had reached 33 institutions and extended from Harvard University and Princeton University on the East Coast to the University of British Columbia and the University of California at Los Angeles on the West Coast. In 1968 the scope of the center's membership was further expanded, when provision was made for smaller institutions to join as associate members. Prior to this, membership was limited to institutions with broad programs of advanced research that maintained large research libraries. The class of associate membership was established so that smaller institutions might take part in the center's programs. However, in order that the programs might continue to be focused on the needs of the large research libraries, associate members were given no voice in the governance of the center. The growth in membership accelerated during the 1970s, and by mid-1979 there were 110 full members and 70 associate members.

The emphasis upon direct acquisitions, either through gifts or purchase, continued to grow, partially as a result of the McCarthy–Swank report, though the deposited materials still form a significant portion of the center's holdings. The CRL has several methods for determining what is to be acquired. As is the case in most libraries, continuing commitments take up a major portion of the center's acquisitions budget. These commitments arise in a number of ways, some of which are described later.

Large one-time purchases are made upon the recommendation of a member library and the affirmative vote of the majority of the membership. Any responsible staff member of a member institution may recommend a title or collection to be acquired by the center. The center's staff then prepares a full description of the material and sends this with a ballot to the directors of all member libraries or to a person designated by the director to receive such proposals. While in the early years these ballots went almost exclusively to directors, they now go primarily to staff members at member institutions with responsibility for the local collection development program.

For certain categories of material there exists what is referred to as the "demand purchase program." This program is designed to make available to researchers materials that are neither in the local library nor in the CRL but that are needed for ongoing research. Requests come as normal interlibrary loan requests, and once it is determined that the material is not available at the center, an order is placed for the item, and it is sent immediately to the requesting institution when it is received.

The categories of material covered by this program are foreign doctoral dissertations, newspapers in microform, archival materials in microform, and U.S. state documents published from 1953 to date. As would be expected, this program has certain budget limitations.

Through the combination of deposits and direct acquisitions, the CRL has developed a rich and diversified collection of material to supplement the resources of the members. Some of the areas of particular strength should be noted.

Several of the planned classes of material have developed into the strongest such collections in the nation or the world. The collection of foreign doctoral dissertations is the largest in the world, numbering approximately 600,000 titles. The bulk of this collection has come from the deposits of the members and the transfer in 1956 of 250,000 dissertations from the Library of Congress's uncataloged collection. The CRL receives on a continuing basis all printed doctoral dissertations from 43 Western European universities. In fact, any foreign doctoral dissertation is potentially available from the center, whether it was printed or produced only in typescript, under the demand purchase program described earlier.

The official publications of U.S. states and territories form another important class of material held by the center. Through gifts and deposits well over 100,000 volumes of state publications printed prior to 1952 have been acquired, and these are continually being added to. Since 1952 the CRL has been acquiring directly from the states and territories and their various departments and agencies all their printed publications, with the exception of a few specified classes of material. These materials are augmented by the Library of Congress's Early State Records microfilm project and the State Censuses microfiche project produced by KTO Microform.

The collection of U.S. and foreign college and university catalogs numbered over 125,000 volumes in 1979. Again the bulk of this collection was formed through the deposits of members and gifts from other institutions, but for U.S. institutions the center has continued to acquire the catalogs and administrative reports for approximately 2,000 colleges and universities. Gifts and deposits of foreign college and university catalogs continue to be received.

Newspapers are another type of material of which the CRL has an outstanding collection. Either through deposits of newspapers in original format or through acquiring microfilm editions, the center has built a collection containing the back files of over 3,600 titles. These include unique files of a large number of foreign-language newspapers published in the United States. Subscriptions to the microfilm editions of several hundred titles from both the United States and abroad are maintained. Many members will subscribe to a newspaper but then discard the newsprint after a specified period and depend on the center for the back file. Access to titles not yet in the collection is provided through the demand purchase program.

The collection of foreign government documents represents a diversified collecting effort on the part of the center. The base for the collection was formed through the deposits of members. Statistical publications issued by demographic, agricultural, economic, and similar offices are especially well represented among the deposited material. During the 1950s subscriptions were entered to a number of publications, either because a member wanted to cancel a particular title or because the titles came from countries in which there was little interest at the time and so no library was collecting them. In 1958 the center began receiving as a gift from the U.S. government, under the Wheat Loan program, most of the government documents issued in India, and it has continued to receive these under the Public Law 480 program and more recently the Library of Congress's Special Foreign Currency Program. At various dates the center began participating in the other PL-480 and National Program for Acquisitions and Cataloging (NPAC) projects for South and Southeast Asia and currently receives government documents extensively from these areas of the world. As a result of purchase proposals voted on by the members, the center has further enhanced its holdings of foreign government documents by purchasing various microform and reprint editions.

There are a number of types of material that are collected exclusively through gifts and deposits. The most significant of these are the large collections of U.S. primary and secondary textbooks and the collection of U.S. children's literature.

An important type of material that has been collected exclusively through direct acquisitions is archival material in microform. Many large archival collections in microform have been acquired as the result of purchase proposals voted on by the members. When the advantage of the CRL collecting this type of material became clear, it was decided to make it eligible for demand purchase to fill current research needs at member institutions. This program has become one of the primary means by which researchers at member institutions can gain access to the microfilmed holdings of the U.S. National Archives and the Public Records Office in Great Britain as well as other archival collections around the world.

By 1979 the number of current journal subscriptions came to approximately 14,000 titles. The scientific and technical journals whose subscriptions had begun under the National Science Foundation grant and journals published by the Russian Academy of Sciences continue to be received. Around 1970 the CRL began to receive all journal titles, except those in the fields of clinical medicine and agriculture, acquired through the Public Law 480 program for South Asia and all journals acquired under NPAC for Southeast Asia. In the period 1973–1978 a grant from the Carnegie Corporation of New York enabled the center to enter approximately 2,000 new subscriptions. These subscriptions entered under the Carnegie grant were based upon the recommendations from members of titles they wished to cancel or newly begun titles in which they were interested but did not want to acquire themselves. All subscriptions begun under this program were continued when the Carnegie grant expired.

A major portion of the CRL's total collection consists of materials that do not fall into any of the planned classes and are distinguished only by the fact that they are apt to be infrequently used at any one research library. Miscellaneous deposited materials are primarily 19th- and early 20th-century imprints, though some older imprints are also found. While publications related to most subject fields will be found among these deposited materials, the natural sciences, technology, medicine, and religion are particularly well represented.

Miscellaneous materials acquired in microform and reprint editions cover a wide range of dates, parts of the world, and subject disciplines. The amount of research material in microform editions that has been produced in recent years through the efforts of various commercial publishers and libraries has greatly increased the resources available to researchers. A great deal of this material had previously existed only in the older and larger institutions. Microfilming has made it potentially available to all libraries. However, due to the cost, libraries have had to restrict their purchases of this material to those microform collections that are most apt to be needed at their institution. CRL purchases have allowed institutions that will only occasionally need to use the material in a particular project to have easy and assured access to it and to spend their scarce funds on other publications needed more frequently. This thus has a direct effect upon the ongoing collection development programs at the member institutions. With these large microform and reprint sets in mind, a bibliographer at one of the center members wrote: "Traditionally, we have taken into account the holdings of nearby universities as one of many considerations in the review process for expensive purchases. Now we also formally consider the holdings at CRL. In this way, we add another level of justification for purchase or non-purchase of those items reflecting primary or secondary needs. Whatever the local decision is, we are able to provide some means of access to the materials"(*8*).

In its general deposit and acquisition policies, the center has attempted to avoid, as much as possible, emphasis on particular geographical areas or subject disciplines. This has been necessary in order to support the broad range of interests common to all large research libraries and to avoid offering greater service to some with particular interests. However, in order to provide an effective means for cooperation in fields in which only a part of the membership has a significant and present research interest, the center operates several cooperative microform projects in international studies. These are supported by special subscriptions by those institutions that wish to participate.

These projects are the Cooperative Africana Microform Project (CAMP), begun in 1963; the South Asia Microform Project (SAMP), begun in 1969; the Southeast Asia Microform Project (SEAM), begun in 1970; and the Latin American Microform Project (LAMP), begun in 1975. Each project was initiated at the instigation of committees composed of area-study bibliographers and scholars connected with the various area-study associations. These committees approached the Center for Research Libraries as the institution uniquely organized and situated to best provide shared access to cooperatively acquired library materials. Besides purchasing microform copies of material to which the members of the project have shared access, each area-study microform project carries out a good deal of original filming of rare and deteriorating material related to the particular area of the world. Decisions as to what to film or purchase are made by committees composed of area-study bibliographers from the participating institutions. These committees have offered a unique opportunity for some of the leading area-study bibliographers in the nation to come together on a regular basis and make decisions concerning resources that should be acquired to best meet the research needs of scholars interested in particular areas of the world.

The founding of the Midwest Inter-Library Center in 1949 was a clear indication that many librarians and university administrators were firmly convinced that the days were gone when research libraries could hope to be self-sufficient. In the years since then the continued growth in the number of publications available, coupled with the increasing stringency of funds available to libraries, has made it clear to most librarians that cooperation and resource sharing are necessities if research libraries are to continue to meet the demands placed upon them. This has led to a number of cooperative ventures aimed at sharing resources.

The success of the Center for Research Libraries, as evidenced by the growth in its membership and its expanded programs, points to one significant approach to resource sharing among libraries. While other approaches, such as the sharing of bibliographic information through on-line systems and more efficient methods of handling interlibrary loans, are important, the experience of the Center for Research Libraries indicates that it, or some centralized library like it, will continue to have an important role to play as research libraries become more dependent on resources outside their own collections. Several factors can be noted in support of this conclusion.

1. Experience has shown that a great deal of library material is used so infrequently that one copy, if it is readily available when needed, can serve the needs of the nation. Whole classes of material, such as older issues of college catalogs and doctoral dissertations, can be easily identified as material that is apt to be so infrequently used that one collection in the nation is sufficient to meet research needs. Titles that do not fall into such classes may be more difficult to identify, but their existence is clearly indicated by the experience of the CRL and a number of use studies done at individual libraries (*9*). While serving 180 libraries, the center has found that less than 4% of the material sent out on loan needs to be recalled and that these recalls tend to involve only a few titles. In only a very few instances has the CRL found it necessary to acquire duplicate copies in order to meet the needs of patrons.

2. The growth of the Center for Research Libraries and the development of the British Library Lending Division at Boston Spa both point to the advantages of the existence of a centralized lending library. While local library programs may have to change due to such factors as shifts in the academic programs of their institution, library space problems, and fluctuations in the funds available for libraries, a centralized lending library offers the assurance that certain materials will remain available even if they can no longer be acquired or retained in the local collection. With the CRL's strong South Asian collection in mind, one South Asia bibliographer has stated: "In terms of the South Asia programs, we have become accustomed to believing that if we (at a particular library) do not retain a particular periodical title, we (as a member of CRL) will have assured access to that title because we know it will be at CRL. . . . As space problems increase at university libraries, and indeed as financial problems develop at LC's field offices, it has been comforting to feel that cutting back on a number of lesser used journals or government documents does not mean those titles are totally unavailable to researchers; with only relatively short delay they are available on loan from the Center. We have learned to rely on CRL. Its collections have been assumed to be one of the few knowns among many unknowns in the formulation of a national network of South Asian collections" (*10*). As indicated by this statement, librarians are becoming aware of

the fact that a centralized and easily accessible collection provides greater flexibility in shaping local collections.

3. The pooled resources of a number of institutions make it possible to accomplish things that simply would not be affordable for institutions acting alone. In some instances a few libraries acting together might be able to justify expending the funds needed for a particular project, but in others, the combined resources of a very large number of institutions are needed. The activities of the study-area microform projects administered by the CRL are particularly noteworthy in this respect. By combining the resources of most of the institutions interested in a particular area of the world, it has been possible to microfilm important research materials that would not have been available otherwise.

4. The efficiency involved in handling interlibrary loan requests through a centralized facility exclusively dedicated to lending materials to distant libraries should not be underestimated. Because there are no local patrons that must be served first, the CRL's entire operation is organized for handling interlibrary loan requests. This means that requests can usually be processed much more rapidly than in a local library whose first responsibility is to local patrons. In an age of instantaneous electronic communications and jet planes, the speed with which the request can be handled at the lending library has increasingly become the important factor in terms of the time it takes to fill a request and get the material to the patron. The distance between the lending library and the requesting library has become less important and will continue to become even less important as new technologies in communications are developed.

In the first 30 years of its existence the Center for Research Libraries demonstrated the advantages of a centralized lending library for providing access to infrequently used research materials. It is also an example of how libraries can cooperate in a very concrete manner to solve their mutual problems. As resource sharing and cooperation become more important in the thinking of librarians in the years ahead, the CRL will undoubtedly continue to play an important role in their planning.

REFERENCES

1. E. W. McDiarmid, *A Midwest Inter-Library Program,* Chicago, 1949, p. 6 (mimeographed).
2. Ref. *1*, p. 9.
3. Ref. *1*, "Summary," p. 8.
4. Midwest Inter-Library Corporation, Board of Directors, *Minutes of the Semi-Annual Meeting, January 4, 1963,* p. 4 (mimeographed).
5. Stephen A. McCarthy and Raymond C. Swank, *The Midwest Inter-Library Center: Report of a Survey, May 1963–June 1964*, p. 125 (mimeographed).
6. Ref. *5*, pp. 126–127.
7. Center for Research Libraries, *The Report of a Survey with an Outline of Programs and Policies*, Center for Research Libraries, Chicago, 1965, pp. 5–6.
8. John Shipman, "Signifying Renewal as Well as Change: One Library's Experience with the Center for Research Libraries," *Lib. Acquisitions: Practice Theory*, **1,** 247 (1978).
9. Gordon Williams, "Inter-Library Loans: The Experience of the Center for Research Libraries," *UNESCO Bull. Lib.*, **28,** 76–77 (March–April 1974).
10. Maureen L. P. Patterson, "Library Support for South Asian Studies: A Review and Outlook for

the Next Decade," Paper delivered at the South Asia Council Workshop, Ann Arbor, Michigan, November 10–12, 1978, p. 10.

BIBLIOGRAPHY

Boylan, Ray, "Serial Publications in the Center for Research Libraries," *Serials Rev.*, **5**, 79–82 (1979).

Center for Research Libraries, *Annual Report*, 16th–, 1964/1965–.

Center for Research Libraries, *Handbook*, 1969–.

Center for Research Libraries, *Newsletter*, No. 103–, March 30, 1966–.

Center for Research Libraries, *The Report of a Survey with an Outline of Programs and Policies*, Center for Research Libraries, Chicago, 1965.

Ellsworth, Ralph E., "Tasks of the Immediate Future," *Lib. Quart.*, **22**, 18–20 (1952).

Esterquest, Ralph T., "Cataloging and Classification Plans of the Midwest Inter-Library Center," *J. Cataloging Classification*, **7**, 3–6 (Winter 1951).

Esterquest, Ralph T., "Treatment of Serials at the Midwest Inter-Library Center," *Lib. Resources Tech. Serv.*, **2**, 121–126 (1958).

McCarthy, Stephen A., and Raymond C. Swank, *The Midwest Inter-Library Center: Report of a Survey, May 1963 to June 1964*, n.p., n.d. (mimeographed).

McDiarmid, E. W., *A Midwest Inter-Library Program*, Chicago, 1948 (mimeographed).

Metcalf, Keyes D., "University Libraries Face the Future," *Lib. Quart.*, **22**, 5–12 (1952).

Midwest Inter-Library Center, *Newsletter*, No. 1–102, October 31, 1949–October 1, 1964.

Midwest Inter-Library Corporation and Midwest Inter-Library Center, *Annual Report*, 1st–15th, 1949/1950–1963/1964.

Shipman, John, "Signifying Renewal as Well as Change: One Library's Experience with the Center for Research Libraries," *Lib. Acquisitions: Practice Theory*, **1**, 243–248 (1978).

Williams, Gordon, "The Center for Research Libraries: Its New Organization and Programs," *Lib. J.*, **90**, 2947–2951 (1965).

Williams, Gordon, "Inter-Library Loans: The Experience of the Center for Research Libraries," *UNESCO Bull. Lib.*, **28**, 73–78 (March–April 1974).

RAY BOYLAN

CHEMICAL ABSTRACTS SERVICE

A common feature of most science libraries is shelves lined with tall, thick volumes of *Chemical Abstracts* (CA). A complete set of this digest of the world's chemical literature and its indexes from 1907 to the present fills more than 200 feet of shelf space and grows steadily at the rate of about 9 feet per year.

Huge as these figures are, however, they are insignificant beside the acres of shelf space that would be required to house the journals, books, and reports containing the more than 9 million documents in over 50 languages referenced and abstracted in CA. More important yet, the information of interest to any particular

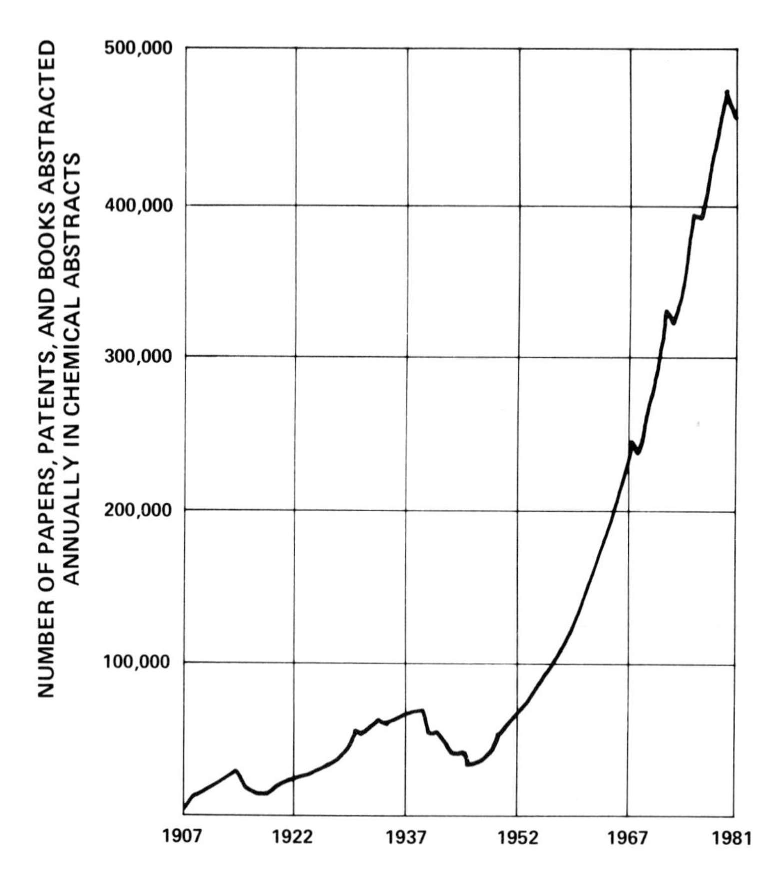

FIGURE 1. *Growth of* Chemical Abstracts *since 1907.*

researcher for any particular research project would be effectively buried without the thorough and precise CA indexes or their computer-searchable counterparts to serve as guides.

When the American Chemical Society launched *Chemical Abstracts* in 1907, the year's issues contained just under 12,000 abstracts of scientific papers and patents, almost half of them reporting on work done in Germany. Today, Chemical Abstracts Service (CAS) abstracts and indexes almost half a million scientific papers, patents, books, and other documents annually (Fig. 1). What began as virtually a one-man enterprise has grown into the largest staff division of the American Chemical Society with more than 1,150 employees housed in a multi-million-dollar complex of buildings adjacent to the Ohio State University campus in Columbus (Fig. 2).

From 1907 through 1955, publication of *Chemical Abstracts* was subsidized in whole or in part from American Chemical Society member dues. Since 1956, however, CAS has met its operating budget, which now amounts to more than $45 mil-

FIGURE 2. *Chemical Abstracts Service headquarters in Columbus, Ohio.*

lion annually, entirely through revenue from the sale of its publications and services with the exception of occasional aid for specific research and development projects provided by the National Science Foundation and other federal agencies.

Moreover, *Chemical Abstracts* is no longer the only information service provided by the Chemical Abstracts Service. Automated processing systems developed during the late 1960s and early 1970s not only improved the currency of abstracts and facilitated the production of indexes but have also made possible new and varied services for individuals and industry; computer files and search services permitting on-line, interactive retrieval of relevant chemical structure diagrams, abstract numbers, and bibliographic references; and an array of specialty handbooks and guides.

It All Comes Through Columbus

All CAS information services are derived from an initial intellectual analysis of the literature made by over 300 technical and language specialists based in Columbus, assisted by about 800 volunteer abstractors around the world. This core of experts includes chemists, engineers, metallurgists, pharmacologists, and medical doctors who speak among them such languages as Urdu, Belorussian, and Azerbaijani as well as the more frequently required Russian, Japanese, and German.

The process begins with acquisition: Over 14,000 journals published in over 150 nations (Fig. 3) and the patents issued by 26 countries and two international agencies, as well as reports, conference proceedings, and other technical documents,

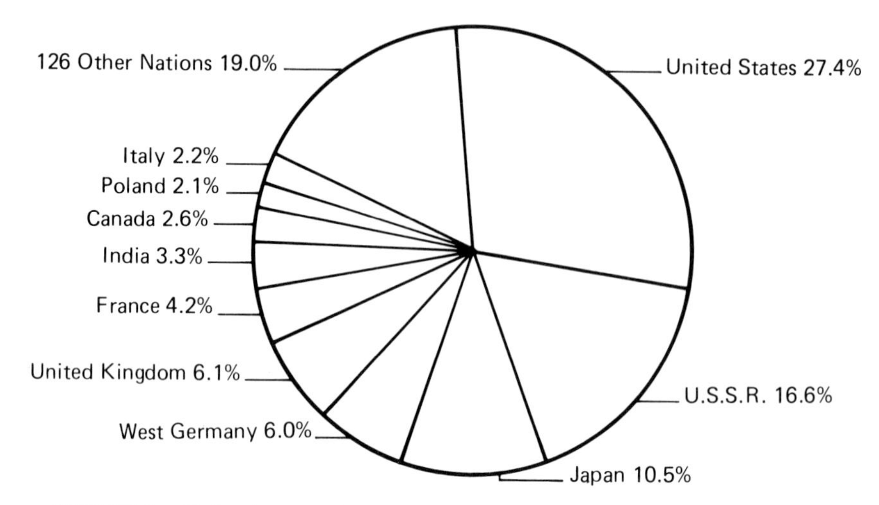

FIGURE 3. *National origin of journal articles abstracted in* Chemical Abstracts (*1981*).

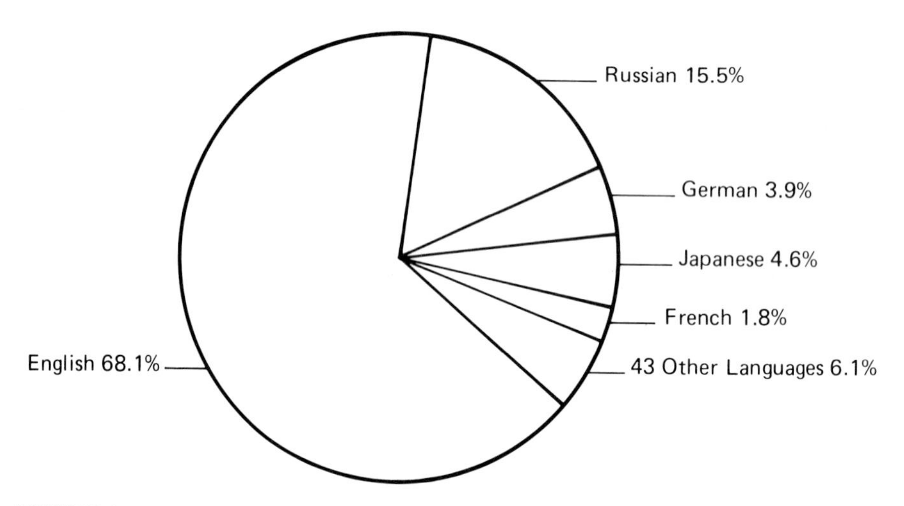

FIGURE 4. *Language of publication of journal articles abstracted in* Chemical Abstracts (*1981*).

are scanned to select those containing new information on chemistry or chemical engineering. While two-thirds of the literature selected comes from overseas, more than 65% is originally published in English (Fig. 4). When a document is found to be both new and of chemical interest, it is assigned to one of CA's 80 sections on the basis of its principal subject and directed to the particular document analyst with the language skills and technical background to analyze, abstract, and index it.

The informative abstract favored by CAS (Fig. 5) is a brief summary of the major findings or disclosures contained in the document and may include information on new reactions, compounds, materials, techniques, procedures, apparatus, and properties, as well as new theories or applications reported. Indicative abstracts, which describe the contents of a document rather than summarize the information

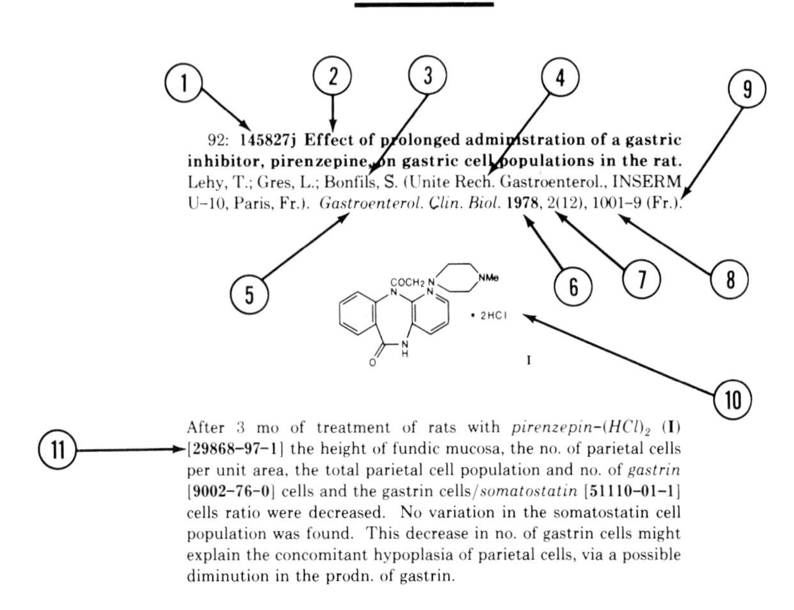
CA ABSTRACT

92: **145827j Effect of prolonged administration of a gastric inhibitor, pirenzepine, on gastric cell populations in the rat.** Lehy, T.; Gres, L.; Bonfils, S. (Unite Rech. Gastroenterol., INSERM U-10, Paris, Fr.). *Gastroenterol. Clin. Biol.* **1978**, 2(12), 1001–9 (Fr.).

• 2HCl

I

After 3 mo of treatment of rats with *pirenzepin-*$(HCl)_2$ (**I**) [**29868-97-1**] the height of fundic mucosa, the no. of parietal cells per unit area, the total parietal cell population and no. of *gastrin* [**9002-76-0**] cells and the gastrin cells/*somatostatin* [**51110-01-1**] cells ratio were decreased. No variation in the somatostatin cell population was found. This decrease in no. of gastrin cells might explain the concomitant hypoplasia of parietal cells, via a possible diminution in the prodn. of gastrin.

1. The abstract number. The CA Volume number is set off by a colon from the abstract number, while the letter following is a check-letter by which each reference is computer-validated.
2. The document title in boldface type.
3. The complete author names given in inverted style.
4. The address where the reported work was performed, or where correspondence regarding the work is to be sent.
5. The journal title in abbreviated form, in italic type.
6. The year of publication.
7. The volume number of the publication followed by the issue number in parentheses.
8. The page numbers the article occupies within the journal.
9. The language of the original document.
10. Structural formulas, identified by boldface Roman numerals.
11. CAS Registry Numbers, which follow the chemical substance names for all abstracts which are also available in the computer-readable files.

FIGURE 5. *An abstract of a journal article as it appears in* Chemical Abstracts.

contained in it, are published to call attention to books, reviews, biographies and obituaries of chemists, and papers on chemical education and the history of chemistry. The purpose of these abstracts is to provide access to the primary literature, not to replace it.

Each abstract is preceded by a heading, which for journal articles includes such information as the title, authors, location of work, journal title, year of publication, volume and issue numbers, pagination, and language of the original document. For patents, the heading includes names of inventors and assignees, country and patent number, date of publication, classification, and data on patent application. The heading is designed to identify the original completely.

In addition to preparing the abstract, document analysts also index each document thoroughly so that scientists or engineers interested in finding the document for different reasons can all be led to the abstract, and through it to the original document. The average abstract receives at least 16 different index entries, and some are assigned more than 1,000.

More than 8,000 abstracts—over 1 million words—are published in CA every week. To provide access within the issue itself, Keyword Indexes are included in the back of each weekly issue. The keywords are selected from the abstracts and represent the terminology favored by the author of the document. Also included with each issue are an Author Index and a Patent Index that links families of patents on the same invention.

Six months—26 issues of CA—constitute a single volume. Comprehensive Volume Indexes are published and mailed within 6 months after the close of this period. Subjects in the Volume Index are grouped according to a controlled terminology designed to ensure that documents on the same subject can be retrieved, regardless of the terms chosen by the authors to describe it. For instance, papers which would appear in the Keyword Index at such scattered locations as "cancer," "tumor," and "neoplasm" will appear together in the Volume Index under "carcinogens."

Particular pains are taken to ensure consistency in the indexing of chemical substances. A group of specialists spend full time deriving systematic index names for the chemical substances mentioned in the documents analyzed by others. CAS policy is to index all substances described in a paper for which information is given on actual preparation or on properties, uses, or applications.

The CA index name is based on nomenclature rules developed by the International Union of Pure and Applied Chemists (IUPAC) which have been extended to types of substances for which IUPAC has not yet derived rules. The name is then inverted so that families of related substances appear near each other in the alphabetically arranged Chemical Substance Index. Since many chemical substances have several names—often including trade names as cryptic and unhelpful as Red No. 5 and MON 097—an invariant index name is essential to prevent scattering of references.

The CA index name is tightly based on the substance's molecular structure. Each name is built around a central structural feature called the "parent," with additional chemical groups indicated by tacking their names onto the parent under carefully defined conventions. As an example, the dihydroxy derivatives of benzoic acid are known to chemists by such names as gentisic acid, protocatechuic acid, and β-resorcylic acid, but they are grouped together in the Chemical Substance Index as:

Benzoic acid, 2,4-dihydroxy-
__________, 2,5-dihydroxy-
etc.

Cross-references from names and subject categories favored by researchers to the controlled terminology employed in the CA Volume Indexes are listed in the CA Index Guide.

Help from Computers

As bits of information are culled from the chemical literature, they are recorded in a computer-readable data base to form a largely undifferentiated pool (Fig. 6). Bits of information can be entered into the pool of data as they are prepared, in any sequence. Then when a particular service is produced from the pool, information can be selected, sorted, and arranged rapidly for that service and still remain available to appear (perhaps in very different order and format) in subsequent publications or computer files.

The computer also checks for accuracy all information that can be precisely characterized—structure diagrams, systematic index names of chemical substances, numbers, journal titles, and controlled index terms. In the abstract text itself, the computer abbreviates some words automatically and flags possible misspellings for human correction before publication.

The results of this computer processing are then displayed on the screen of an on-line terminal for review by a document analyst (Fig. 7). There, the analyst can add or delete words and sentences, alter order, and correct errors, entering these changes directly into the computer without introducing an additional keyboarding and subsequent reediting step. Once the material is corrected and released by the analyst, the computer selects the appropriate pieces of information for a particular publication or file, converts it into the proper form for publication, sorts and alphabetizes index entries, justifies and hyphenates text, makes up pages, inserts structure diagrams in the text where appropriate, and composes the material on film, paper, or tape from which offset printing plates are produced.

Indexing of chemical substances is supported by a special group of computer files known collectively as the CAS Chemical Registry System. Before the system was introduced in 1965, every substance selected for indexing had to be assigned an index name by a chemist. Only then could it be determined whether the substance had been indexed, and therefore named, previously.

The foundation of the Chemical Registry is a structure file, which contains a unique and unambiguous computer-language description of each substance's molecular structure. A separate name file contains more than 8.5 million names on record to describe the more than 5.8 million substances in the structure file. The

FIGURE 6. *Information processed for CAS publications and services is recorded in a computer-readable data base.*

two files are linked by a three-part hyphenated number called the CAS Registry Number, which is assigned to each unique substance.

The Chemical Registry System supports the indexing effort by retrieving the CA index name when presented with either a common name or a computer-readable form of the substance's two-dimensional structure diagram. If the substance is not retrieved from the file, then it is new to the system and must be named by a nomenclature specialist. Thereafter, the substance is added to the file, and its index name can be retrieved should the substance be mentioned in the literature again.

The computer processing was introduced in a rudimentary form in 1965, when CA indexes were running 22 months behind the close of a volume period. The exponential growth of the literature, which has been occasionally characterized as "explosive" in the years after World War II, put severe strains on the highly redundant and labor-intensive manual system that had been employed by CAS since 1907. In the late 1950s, doubts were expressed concerning whether it would be possible to hire the number of skilled people necessary, or integrate them into the la-

FIGURE 7. *Abstracts and index entries are edited on the screen of an on-line terminal before being released to the computer data base for publication.*

bor stream fast enough, to handle the continued growth expected. The shift to computer processing immediately improved currency of both abstracts and indexes, and allowed CAS to keep up with the increase in the chemical literature, as hoped. Through its additional virtue of flexibility, it has made possible new and more individually tailored information services which reduce the enormous scale of the chemical literature, allowing specific companies, government agencies, or even individual researchers to focus on that small portion of the literature which interests them. Yet another byproduct of the data base created through the switch to computer processing is an array of computer-searchable files permitting speedy retrieval of relevant chemical structure diagrams, abstract numbers, and bibliographic information.

Services Large and Small

CHEMICAL ABSTRACTS

Only the comprehensive and well-established *Chemical Abstracts* currently approaches full use of all the information contained in the CAS data base. The full text of abstracts in all subject areas, all bibliographic information, all index entries, and some material from the Registry files appear in CA and its accompanying indexes. The abstracts are organized into 80 subject-related sections according to the principal subject of the paper or patent abstracted. The sections, in turn, are organized into five broad groupings labeled Biochemistry (Sections 1–20), Organic Chemistry (21–34), Macromolecular Chemistry (35–46), Applied Chemistry and Chemical Engineering (47–64), and Physical, Inorganic, and Analytical Chemistry (65–80). Sections 1 through 34 are published one week; Sections 35 through 80 appear the following week.

Each weekly issue is indexed by author and patent number, and includes an alphabetical listing of keywords and phrases selected from the abstracts and the titles of the documents.

Comprehensive indexes are published for each volume (26 weekly issues) of CA. These indexes, which usually fill about half as many pages as the abstracts themselves, include:

1. A Chemical Substance Index, which indexes by systematic name the chemical substances mentioned in each document, including substances that may not have been referred to in the abstract.
2. A General Subject Index, which contains controlled index entries for classes of substances, applications, uses, properties, reactions, apparatus, processes, and biochemical and biological terms. (Prior to 1972, the Chemical Substance and General Subject Indexes were combined as a single Subject Index.)
3. A Molecular Formula Index, which lists under the molecular formula the index name and Registry Number for each indexed substance corresponding to the formula as well as the abstract numbers for documents that contain information about them.
4. An Index of Ring Systems, which lists the index names for specific ring systems indexed during the period according to the number, size, and elemental composition of the component rings.
5. An Author Index, which lists all individual and corporate authors of publications, inventors, and patent assignees.
6. A Patent Index, which links families of patents on the same invention.

An Index Guide explains the organization and use of the indexes and contains cross-references from common substance names to the index names used in the Chemical Substance Index, cross-references from authors' subject terminology to the preferred terms used in the General Subject Index, and policy notes that can aid in finding references in the indexes. Figures 8 and 9 illustrate how the Volume Indexes and the Index Guide can be searched to locate abstracts in CA.

Every 5 years (every 10 years prior to 1957) the Volume Indexes are merged and republished as a massive Collective Index to the period's chemical and chemical engineering literature. The most recently published Collective Index (1977–1981) contains more than 25 million index entries for more than 2.2 million papers, patents, and other documents, and occupies more than 125,000 pages.

Weekly issues of CA and the Collective Indexes also are published on 16-mm microfilm and microfiche.

INDEX GUIDE

Flame
burners for—see *Burners*
coating by—see *Coating process*
extinguishing of—see *Fire*
luminescence in
see
Luminescence
cando-
Luminescence, chemi-
photometers—see *Photometers*
retardants
see
Fireproofing
Fireproofing agents
Fire resistant materials
spectrometers—see *Spectrometers*
spectrum of—see *Spectra* and related headings
torch—see *Torches*
FLAME 3
See *Computer program*
Flameproof MC 36
See *Polyphosphoric acids, amides*
Flammability
redn. of
see
Fireproofing
Fireproofing agents
Flammable substances
See *Combustibles*
Flammex 5AE
See *Benzene, pentabromo(2-propenyloxy)-* *[3555-11-1]*

GENERAL SUBJECT INDEX

Fireproofing agents
acrylic polymer alkyl bromide alkyl phosphorus chlorine compd. mixts., for corrugated paperboards, P 70096f
acrylic polymer metal salts, for cotton and cotton polyester fabrics, P 24743s
alkali aluminum oxalates, for polyester fibers, P 86278c

•
•
•

melamine
for polyamide, for elec. connectors, P 24405h
for poly(dimethylphenylene oxide)-butadiene styrene copolymer blends, P 6988w
melamine hydrohalide derivs., for polyolefins, P 85831r
melamine phosphorus pentachloride ammonia reaction products, for cotton and cotton-polyester textiles, P 7446e
melamine tetrakis(hydroxymethyl)phosphonium chloride-urea copolymer, for cotton and cotton-polyester fabrics, P 153372u
metal compds. contg. quinacridone or phthalocyanine compds., for thermoplastic resins, P 85834u

CHEMICAL ABSTRACTS

[50-00-0], had 410 h as time to reach 94% absorbence at 5.8 μ, compared with 50 h for a sample contg. no **I** and 130 h for a sample contg. 2,2'-methylenebis(6-*tert*-butyl-4-methylphenol) instead of **I**.

87: **85831r Flame-retardant polymeric compositions containing melamine hydrohalides**. Lindvay, Michael W. (Velsicol Chemical Corp.) **U.S. 4,028,333** (Cl. 260-45.8NT; C08K5/34), 07 Jun 1977, Appl. 642,012, 18 Dec 1975; 6 pp. Melamine hydrohalide derivs. are thermally stable fireproofing agents for polyolefins. Thus, *polypropylene* (**I**) **[9003-07-0]** contg. 20% *melamine dihydrobromide* (**II**) **[63556-96-7]** and 5% Sb_2O_3 had an O index 28.0 compared with 17.0 for **I** alone. Thermogravimetric anal. of **II** showed a 10% wt. loss at 293° compared with 200° for trichloromelamine.

87: **85832s Oligomeric polyesters from long-chain dicarboxylic acids as plasticizers for vinyl polymers**. Chang, Shu-Pei; Ridgway, Robert W. (United States Dept. of Agriculture) **U.S. 4,029,627** (Cl. 260-31.6; C08K5/10), 14 Jun 1977, Appl. 611,374, 08 Sep 1975; 4 pp. Oligomeric polyesters were prepd. from long-chain dicarboxylic acids, *propylene glycol* (**I**) **[57-55-6]** and a monocarboxylic acid or monoalc. terminator,

FIGURE 8. *General subject search for references on fireproofing polyolefins.*

INDEX GUIDE

Melaleuca leucadendron
See *Cajuput*
Melalit
See *1,3,5-Triazine-2,4,6-triamine, polymers, polymer with formaldehyde [9003-08-1]*
Melamine
See *1,3,5-Triazine-2,4,6-triamine [108-78-1]*
Melamine resins
See *1,3,5-Triazine-2,4,6-triamine, polymers*
Melampodin
See *Oxireno[7,8]cyclodeca[1,2-b]furan-3-= carboxylic acid, 5-[[(2,3-dimethyloxirany= l)carbonyl]oxy]-1a,4,5,5a,6,7,8a,10a-= octahydro-4-hydroxy-10-methyl-6-= methylene-7-oxo-, methyl ester, [1aR-[1aR*,2E,4S*,5S*(2R*,3R*),5aS*,= 8aR*,9E,10aS*]]- [35852-26-7]*

CHEMICAL SUBSTANCE INDEX

1,3,5-Triazine-2,4,6-triamine *[108-78-1]*,
compounds
butoxymethyl derivs., acrylic polymer coatings contg., electrophoretic, P 54616v
reaction products
properties of fluid concrete in relation to delayed addn. of, 140222v
with formaldehyde, polyethylenimine and urea, primers, for photosensitive printing plates, P 169379n

•
•
•

compd. with 1,3,5-triazine-2,4,6(1*H*,3*H*,5*H*)-= trione (1:1) *[37640-57-6]*, fireproofing of automobile covers with, 86266x
dihydrobromide *[63556-96-7]*, fireproofing agents, for polypropylene, P 85831r
mixt. contg. *[62927-88-2]*, methylolated, creaseproofing agents, for dyed polyester-cotton blends, 24650j

FORMULA INDEX

$C_3H_6N_6$
Guanidine, 1*H*-1,2,4-triazol-3-yl- monohydriodide *[62877-75-2]*, 5871r
1,3,5-Triazine-2,4,6-triamine *[108-78-1]*. See Chemical Substance Index
borate *[54649-97-7]*, P 119419e, P 153551b
compd. with 1,3,5-triazine-2,4,6(1*H*,3*H*,5*H*)-= trione (1:1) *[37640-57-6]*, 86266x
dihydrobromide *[63556-96-7]*, P 85831r
homopolymer *[25778-04-5]*, P 10499e, P 69421b, P 109417p, P 121931j, P 140787h, P 155630a, P 188226b. For general derivs. see Chemical Substance Index
mixt. contg. *[62927-88-2]*. For general derivs. see Chemical Substance Index

REGISTRY HANDBOOK-NUMBER SECTION

63556-96-7 1,3,5-Triazine-2,4,6-triamine, dihydrobromide $C_3H_6N_6.2BrH$
63556-97-8 5-Benzoxazolecarboxylic acid, 2-(4-methylphenyl)-, methyl ester $C_{16}H_{13}NO_3$
63556-98-9 5-Benzoxazolecarboxylic acid, 2-(4-methylphenyl)- $C_{15}H_{11}NO_3$

CHEMICAL ABSTRACTS

[50-00-0], had 410 h as time to reach 94% absorbence at 5.8 μ, compared with 50 h for a sample contg. no **I** and 130 h for a sample contg. 2,2'-methylenebis(6-*tert*-butyl-4-methylphenol) instead of **I**.

87: **85831r Flame-retardant polymeric compositions containing melamine hydrohalides**. Lindvay, Michael W. (Velsicol Chemical Corp.) **U.S. 4,028,333** (Cl. 260-45.8NT; C08K5/34), 07 Jun 1977, Appl. 642,012, 18 Dec 1975; 6 pp. Melamine hydrohalide derivs. are thermally stable fireproofing agents for polyolefins. Thus, *polypropylene* (**I**) **[9003-07-0]** contg. 20% *melamine dihydrobromide* (**II**) **[63556-96-7]** and 5% Sb_2O_3 had an O index 28.0 compared with 17.0 for **I** alone. Thermogravimetric anal. of **II** showed a 10% wt. loss at 293° compared with 200° for trichloromelamine.

87: **85832s Oligomeric polyesters from long-chain dicarboxylic acids as plasticizers for vinyl polymers**. Chang, Shu-Pei; Ridgway, Robert W. (United States Dept. of Agriculture) **U.S. 4,029,627** (Cl. 260-31.6; C08K5/10), 14 Jun 1977, Appl. 611,374, 08 Sep 1975; 4 pp. Oligomeric polyesters were prepd. from long-chain dicarboxylic acids, *propylene glycol* (**I**) **[57-55-6]** and a monocarboxylic acid or monoalc. terminator,

FIGURE 9. *Chemical substance search starting with a common name, a molecular formula, or a Registry Number.*

COMPUTER SEARCH SERVICES AND COMPUTER-READABLE FILES

The CAS ONLINE chemical substance search and display system provides on-line access to the CAS Chemical Registry computer file, which contains information on the molecular structures of over 5.8 million chemical substances reported in the world's chemical literature since 1965. CAS ONLINE enables scientists around the world to search this file for substances that share structural features of interest. This ability, called "substructure searching," is important to scientists and researchers because substances that share particular combinations of atoms and bonds may share properties of interest as well.

Access to CAS ONLINE is through remote terminals connected to host computers at CAS through international telecommunications networks. Queries are entered in the form of a chemical structure diagram—a two-dimensional picture of a substance's molecular structure (Fig. 10). Structure diagrams of substances that include the specified structural features are displayed as answers to the search, along with the systematic name and up to 10 other names for each substance and the substances' CAS Registry Numbers. The searcher also has the option of receiving full

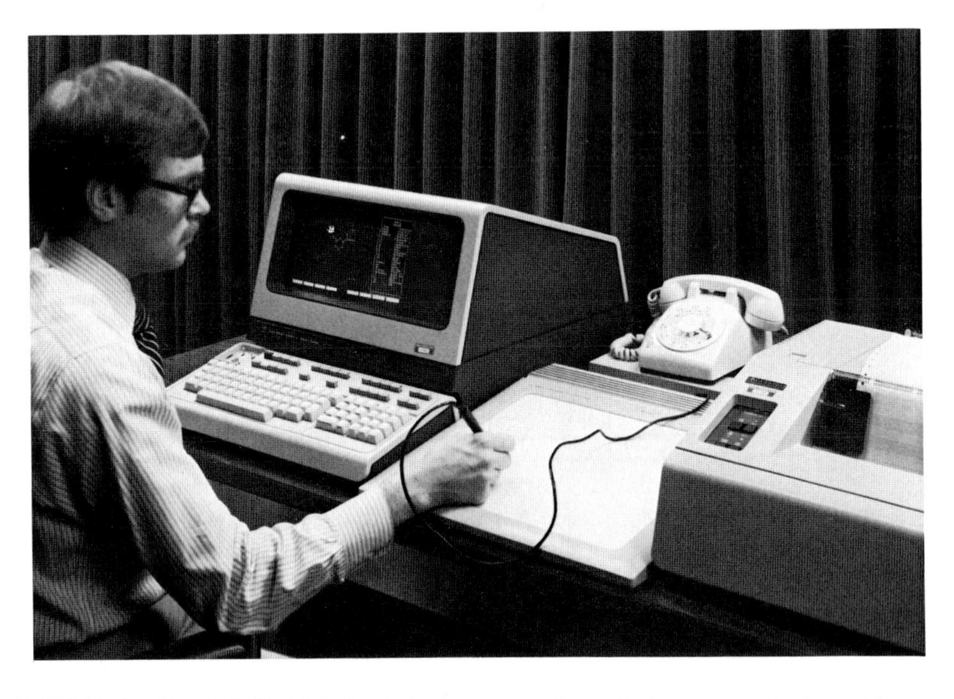

FIGURE 10. *The CAS ONLINE chemical substance search and display system makes it possible to search millions of records in the Chemical Registry System for substances that share particular arrangements of atoms and bonds.*

bibliographic information for the 10 most recent references about each substance in the literature.

Much of the bibliographic information in the CAS data base also is available in computer-searchable form. The most comprehensive of the computer-readable bibliographic files is CA SEARCH, which contains the complete heading information (the CA abstract number, names of authors or patentees, the full title of the paper or patent, and the complete bibliographic citation for all documents abstracted in *Chemical Abstracts*) along with the Keyword Index terms and General Subject Index and Chemical Substance Index entries for the document. A number of organizations in the United States and abroad currently offer public search services based on the CA SEARCH file under licensing arrangements. CAS will offer access to this file through the CAS ONLINE service in the near future.

Computer-readable versions of the *Chemical Abstracts* Index Guide, *Chemical Industry Notes*, and the *CAS Source Index* also are available. (*Chemical Industry Notes* and the *Source Index* are described later in this article.)

SERVICES FOR INDIVIDUALS

CAS also produces publications and services designed to help individual scientists and engineers keep up with the latest developments in their fields of interest.

To alert chemists and chemical engineers to current papers in the world's leading chemical journals, CAS produces *Chemical Titles,* a biweekly listing of and index to the titles of papers published in 700 journals.

Abstracts appearing in weekly issues of *Chemical Abstracts* are available in five separate Section Groupings: Biochemistry Sections, Organic Chemistry Sections, Macromolecular Sections, Applied Chemistry and Chemical Engineering Sections, and Physical, Inorganic, and Analytical Chemistry Sections.

The newer *CA Selects* service provides current-awareness publications that cut across the traditional topical boundaries of the *Chemical Abstracts* subject sections. In this service, search profiles defining highly specific chemical or chemical engineering topics are processed against the CAS data base every 2 weeks to produce inexpensive bulletins containing the CA abstracts and citations for recent publications and patents on those topics. *CA Selects* bulletins are offered on more than 100 topics, including corrosion, organic reaction mechanisms, antitumor agents, solar energy, pollution monitoring, and Raman spectroscopy.

For chemists, chemical engineers, and others engaged in management, production, or marketing, CAS produces *Chemical Industry Notes*, a weekly compilation of brief, informative extracts from more than 80 key trade, industrial, and business periodicals published in nine nations.

HANDBOOKS AND AIDS FOR SEARCHING

CAS also produces a variety of handbooks, reference works, and aids for searching the data base.

The *Parent Compound Handbook* contains structure diagrams, index names, molecular formulas, and other data for more than 50,000 cyclic, acyclic, and cage structures whose names provide the parent headings under which related substances and their derivatives are grouped in the CA Chemical Substance Index.

To help searchers locate copies of journals, patents, and other documents cited in its publications and services, CAS compiles the *Chemical Abstracts Service Source Index*, which identifies all scientific and technical publications cited in *Chemical Abstracts* since 1907, as well as publications covered by several other major abstracting and indexing services, and indicates which of 400 major libraries hold copies of them.

CAS also conducts instructional workshops and publishes workbooks on effective searching of its publications and computer-readable files.

USER-DESIGNED SERVICES

In recent years, CAS has been endeavoring to broaden access to its data base by providing services defined by and tailored to the needs of specific users of chemical and chemical engineering information. In one such service, CAS produces specialized abstract bulletins for the exclusive use of staff members of research and manufacturing organizations. In another, CAS helps scientists and engineers keep abreast of new developments by searching the computer files of information being processed for current issues of *Chemical Abstracts* and selecting from them abstracts of interest to particular individuals.

An International Enterprise

While CAS began as an information service for American chemists, it has become a truly international one. Today CAS is the only comprehensive abstracting and indexing service in chemistry outside of the Soviet Union, and most of the world depends on its publications and services for access to the literature of chemical science and technology. More than three-quarters of the material abstracted and indexed comes from outside of the United States, and two-thirds of the circulation of *Chemical Abstracts* is overseas.

Until 1960 CAS produced a limited range of publications and information services by traditional methods. The introduction of highly automated information-processing and publishing methods has made it possible to produce a wide range of new information services for the scientific and industrial communities. CAS now is actively seeking new ways to serve the changing information needs of individual scientists and engineers, industry, government, and universities, worldwide.

BIBLIOGRAPHY

General

CAS Today, Facts and Figures About Chemical Abstracts Service, Chemical Abstracts Service, Columbus, Ohio, 1980.

History

Skolnik, H., and K. M. Reese (eds.), *A Century of Chemistry,* American Chemical Society, Washington, D.C., 1976.

Coverage

Baker, D. B., "Recent Trends in Chemical Literature Growth," *Chem. Eng. News*, Vol. 59, June 1, 1981.

Langstaff, E. M., and G. K. Ostrum, "Access to Polymer Information in *Chemical Abstracts*," *J. Chem. Inf. Comput. Sci.*, **19,** 60 (1979).

Moody, R. L., and B. C. Zahm, "*Chemical Abstracts* as a Resource for Health and Safety-Related Chemical Information," *J. Chem. Inf. Comput. Sci.*, **20,** 12 (1980).

Moulton, C. W., "Fossil Fuels in *Chemical Abstracts*," *J. Chem. Inf. Comput. Sci.*, **19,** 83 (1979).

Rowlett, R. J., Jr., "Gleaning Patents with *Chemical Abstracts*," *Chemtech*, **9,** 348 (1979).

Computer-Based Processing System

O'Dette, R. E., "The CAS Data Base Concept," *J. Chem. Inf. Comput. Sci.*, **16,** 165 (1975).

Rowlett, R. J., Jr., "A Total Publication System for Scientific Information," *IEEE Trans. Prof. Commun.*, **PC-18,** 229 (1975).

"Towards a Modern Secondary Information System for Chemistry and Chemical Engineering," *Chem. Eng. News*, **53,** 30 (June 16, 1975).

Specialized Information Services

Blake, J. E., V. J. Mathias, and J. Patton, "*CA Selects*—A Specialized Current Awareness Service," *J. Chem. Inf. Comput. Sci.*, **18,** 187 (1978).

Blower, P. E., L. G. Wade, and R. R. Peercy, "Design Your Own Information Service," *CAS Rep.*, No. 9, May 1980.

Chemical Registry System and CAS ONLINE

Dittmar, P. G., R. E. Stobaugh, and C. E. Watson, "The Chemical Abstracts Service Chemical Registry System: I. General Design," *J. Chem. Inf. Comput. Sci.*, **16,** 111 (1976).

Farmer, N. A., and M. P. O'Hara, "CAS ONLINE: A New Source of Substance Information from Chemical Abstracts Service," *Database*, **3,** 10 (1980).

Morgan, H. L., "The Generation of a Unique Machine Description for Chemical Structure," *J. Chem. Doc.,* **5,** 107 (1965).

CAS Source Index

Dayton, D. L., J. R. Larson, G. E. Reisz, M. C. Steensland, and R. S. Tannehill, Jr., "CASSI, File for Document Access," *Special Lib.*, **69**(9), 337 (1978).

DALE B. BAKER

DIX, WILLIAM SHEPHERD

William Shepherd Dix was born in Berryville, near Winchester, Virginia, on November 19, 1910. The only child of William S. Dix, a local merchant, and Loula

(Henson) Dix, he early manifested a strong interest in books and reading that presaged his illustrious later career as a librarian. After graduating from Hagerstown High School in Maryland, some 50 miles north of Berryville, young Dix returned to his native state in 1927 to matriculate at the University of Virginia. Majoring in English literature, he took the baccalaureate degree with honors 4 years later. He was elected to Phi Beta Kappa, and he also managed the track team. Staying on at Charlottesville after graduation, he earned the M.A. degree in 1932.

Dix then moved south to Rome, Georgia, where he spent the balance of the Depression years as master of Darlington School for Boys. Family life began for him during this period. On June 6, 1935, he married Jane Allison Griffin, of a local family, who came later to be seen almost as often at library conclaves as he did. The Dixes had three children: daughter Martha and sons William, Jr., and Griffin.

Beginning in 1940 Dix served for 2 years as director of a Carnegie-funded project in adult education known as the Committee on Private Research, and as instructor of English at Western Reserve University. From 1942 to 1944 he taught English at Williams College, and then in the latter year he went to Harvard as research associate and assistant personnel director in the Radio Research Laboratory, a wartime creature of the Office of Scientific Research and Development. When the laboratory was disbanded in 1946, he stayed on at Harvard for a year as instructor of English. Also in 1946 he took the Ph.D. degree in American literature at the University of Chicago, submitting a dissertation on "The Theatre in Cleveland, Ohio, 1854–1875."

In 1947 Dix was appointed assistant professor of English at Rice Institute in Houston, Texas, and in the following year he was asked by the president if he would also assume the directorship of the institution's library. Exemplifying the strong sense of duty that pervaded his life, Dix accepted the assignment, even though at the time he was unenthusiastic about it. His lack of enthusiasm, however, did not deter him from working effectively, and his 5 years in the post were marked by a number of significant accomplishments.

Few people in the last half-century have succeeded as library administrators without library training, although many have tried. Dix, however, was eminently successful, perhaps in part because of his great respect for the library profession. He frequently expressed his regret that he had not himself been able to attend a library school. By studying hard and working long, he overcame the deficiency and moved on into roles of rapidly increasing leadership in the library community. The American Library Association (ALA) put him to work from 1951 to 1953 as chairman of its Intellectual Freedom Committee, then much beleaguered by the sweep of McCarthyism. Dix had already been active in support of academic freedom through the American Association of University Professors, so this proved to be an especially felicitous assignment for him. He was the chief drafter of the committee's landmark statement "On Freedom to Read," which in 1953 gained the joint imprimatur of the ALA and the American Book Publishers Council. In 1952 he was elected first vice-president and president-elect of the Texas Library Association.

In 1952 Princeton University librarian Julian P. Boyd resigned to dedicate his time to editing the papers of Thomas Jefferson, and President Harold W. Dodds offered the post to William S. Dix. He accepted the offer effective February 1, 1953, beginning a task that would extend until his retirement in 1975. The balance of his life exhibits a remarkable progression of professional and social service activities as one of the nation's most effective educational statesmen.

Dix's activities in the library community were heavily in the service of the American Library Association and of the Association of Research Libraries (ARL). Following his tenure on the Intellectual Freedom Committee, the ALA made him chairman of its important and influential International Relations Committee from 1955 to 1960, and he served on the ALA Council in 1958 and on the Directors Board of the Association of College and Reference Libraries from 1955 to 1958. His service to ALA was capped by his election to its presidency, which he filled with distinction in 1969–1970. He was executive secretary of the Association of Research Libraries from 1957 to 1960 and was elected to its chairmanship in 1962. Perhaps most important among his other ARL activities was his chairmanship of its Shared Cataloging Committee from 1964 to 1968, an assignment which culminated in the establishment of the National Program of Acquisitions and Cataloging in the Library of Congress under the Higher Education Act of 1965. A frequent consultant on library management problems, Dix also was a member of the advisory committees of the New Jersey State Library, the Rutgers University library school, the Duke University Library, and the Harvard University Library.

Dix's counsel was sought far beyond the strict confines of the library community. In 1955 he was appointed to the United States National Commission for UNESCO, which he then chaired during the last 2 years of his 6-year term. He was a member of the U.S. Department of State's Advisory Commission on International Book and Library Programs and of the U.S. Office of Education's Advisory Council on Graduate Education. He was a director of Franklin Book Programs, the H. W. Wilson Company, the Rockefeller Archive Center, and the Council on Library Resources; and he was a member of the National Commission on New Technological Uses of Copyrighted Works.

In the last two decades of his life Dix was also very active on the international scene. In 1958 he advised the Ford Foundation on a university development project in Baghdad. Also in that year and again in 1960 he attended UNESCO general conferences in Paris, in the latter year as vice-chairman of the American delegation. He was a delegate to the Conference of Asian National Commissions for UNESCO in Manila in 1961, and he was a member of the Asian–American Assembly in Kuala Lumpur in 1963. Thereafter he was seen frequently on diverse library missions ranging from Tokyo to Copenhagen to Dhahran.

Despite all of his responsibilities at the national and international levels, however, Dix never slighted his obligations to the Princeton community. During his tenure as librarian there, the general holdings of the University Library more than doubled from 1,220,000 to 2,715,000 volumes, and many fine rare books and manuscripts were acquired as well. Additional library space was constructed, including a 400,000-volume storage annex in 1968 and a new mathematics–physics library in the same year. He also undertook numerous extra–library service activities for the university, including the presidency of the local chapter of the American Association of University Professors and the chairmanship of the Judicial Committee of the University Council during the tumultuous times of the late 1960s and early 1970s. He was an elder in the First Presbyterian Church of Princeton, and he chaired the church's social action committee during its successful efforts to gain open-occupancy housing in the community.

Although not a prolific author, Dix contributed significantly to the professional press. His only book, aside from his dissertation, was entitled *The Amateur Spirit in Scholarship*. Published by the Western Reserve University Press in 1942, before he entertained the notion of becoming a librarian, the volume reported the current status and future prospects of scholarly inquiry being carried on by persons not trained in research, summarizing his work in Cleveland with the Committee on Private Research. Author also of a score of substantive articles ranging over such various subjects as library budgeting, collection building, leadership, and cataloging, Dix enjoyed a reputation for not picking up his pen until he had something to write, and as a result he was widely read.

It is worth noting that Dix's most influential writings tended to be done for very specific purposes. Cases in point are his drafting of the "Freedom to Read" statement in 1953 and his articulate discussion paper presented for the ARL to the National Commission on the Financing of Postsecondary Education in 1973. Doubtless the most influential statement of his life, however, was his inaugural speech as ALA president in 1969. In a seeming universe of strident voices clamoring for attention at that raucous historic conference in Atlantic City, Dix's low-key appeal for understanding and a return to rational discourse stood almost alone in its tone of measured moderation. His great mediating skills were tested and proved during that presidential year when, under his leadership, the American library profession began its long, slow recovery of civility.

It was his ability to empathize, his ability always to view himself in another person's stead, that made him so effective a statesman, not only in large general assemblies but also in small work groups and committees, as well as one-on-one in simple conversation. He always listened before he spoke. It was these important humane qualities, perhaps more so than his professional knowledge, that gained him many awards and recognitions, including honorary doctoral degrees from the University of Florida (1967) and Washington College (1971), and the coveted Melvil Dewey Award (1969) and the prestigious Joseph W. Lippincott Award (1971) from the ALA.

Dix had a certain military bearing about him. Tall (6 feet) and of spare frame (150 pounds), his erect stance and purposeful stride bespoke always self-assurance and a large reserve of latent energy waiting to be tapped. His close-cropped sandy hair, glinty but merry blue eyes, ruddy complexion, and ever-present briar pipe, which he flourished like a swagger stick, completed the image of a fashion-plate Ivy League gentleman. He was as comfortable in his clubs—the Cosmos, Century, Princeton of New York, and Grolier—as he was in his home on McCosh Circle in Princeton, New Jersey, where he died of a heart condition on the night of February 21, 1978.

BIBLIOGRAPHY

Bryant, Douglas W., "A Tribute to Bill Dix, 1910–1978," *Wilson Lib. Bull.*, **52,** 614–615 (April 1978).

Current Biography Yearbook 1969, H. W. Wilson, New York, 1969, pp. 126–128.

McGaw, Howard F., "William S. Dix," *College Research Lib.,* **14,** 200 (April 1953).

Rogers, Rutherford D., "First Vice-President/President-Elect," *ALA Bull.*, **62,** 880–882 (July 1968).

Who's Who in America, 1978–79, Marquis, Chicago, 1978, p. 852.

DAVID KASER

EBERT, FRIEDRICH ADOLF

Friedrich Ebert (1791–1834), son of a Lutheran minister, was educated in philological and theological studies at Leipzig and Wittenberg, and took his degree at the latter institution in 1812. Early in his scholarly career he was attracted to librarianship, and in 1813 he accepted a position in the University of Leipzig Library. In 1814 he went to the Royal Library in Dresden and was associated with this institution until his death at the early age of 43. In the years 1823–1825 he worked in the Herzog August Library in Wolfenbüttel, then returned to Dresden as *Oberbibliothekar*.

In the few years remaining to him, before a fatal accident on a ladder in the bookstacks, he had a singularly productive bibliographic career. His *Allgemeines bibliographisches Lexikon* (1821–1830, 2 vols.), with significant annotations in the style of Brunet earlier and of Graesse later, is a work of enduring value, still useful. His sensitivity for the bibliographically significant books made this work an indispensable reference tool immediately. There was an English edition by Arthur Browne, *A General Bibliographical Dictionary* (Oxford, 1837, 4 vols.).

Ebert's notions on library education were advanced for his day. *Die Bildung des Bibliothekars* (1820, 2 eds.), to which Brunet referred as "Le portrait du bibliothécaire," is still important for the study of the history of education for librarianship. His *Geschichte und Beschreibung der Königlichen Öffentlichen Bibliothek zu Dresden* (1821) remains a basic work for the history of a great library almost destroyed by the United States Air Force in 1945. *Zur Handschriftenkunde* (1825–1827) contains notions on paleography that are viable today.

In his short life Ebert assembled a valuable personal collection, above all his correspondence with other scholars. It went to the Dresden library at his death.

BIBLIOGRAPHY

Leyh, Georg, "F. A. Ebert," *Zentralblatt für Bibliothekswesen*, **51,** 599 (1934).

Schnorr von Carolsfeld, Franz, "Ebert, Friedrich Adolf," in *Allgemeine deutsche Biographie*, Duncker, Leipzig, 1875–1912, 56 vols., Vol. 5, p. 585.

LAWRENCE S. THOMPSON

GERONTOLOGICAL INFORMATION

Conceptual and Historical Background

The development of concepts and definitions, in a rapidly growing interdisciplinary field, is usually influenced by the disciplines that bear upon its study. In recent decades work in gerontology has significantly accelerated. Approaches to research cut across the physical and life sciences, the social sciences, and the humanities, as well as most professional fields.

Although conceptual frameworks and terminology in gerontology are still unsettled, several major efforts undertaken over the years to organize and synthesize theories that had emerged from different disciplines have brought structure and clarity into the field. While European countries focused on biomedical issues of aging, social gerontology emerged in the United States as a new interdisciplinary area of study side by side with biological and physiological research into the aging process. In one of the early works aimed at the identification of research themes, Korenchevsky discussed the problems of aging and strategies needed to initiate and carry out investigations (*1*). In the late 1950s integrating efforts in gerontology culminated in the organization and interpretation of concepts and research findings in the *Handbook of Aging and the Individual: Psychological and Biological Aspects* (*2*) and the *Handbook of Social Gerontology: Societal Aspects of Aging* (*3*). In his chapter in the latter volume, Tibbitts identified the necessary relationship between decision making and applied research by stating that "in social gerontology the need for sound bases for social action may be said to have demanded the appearance of the field itself" (*4*, p. 23). A third volume, *Aging in Western Societies* (*5*), synthesized the multicultural aspects of social gerontology in the United States.

Almost two decades later a set of new handbooks provided a state-of-the-art assessment and integration of gerontological research that had been undertaken in the interim years. Publication of the *Handbook of Aging and the Social Sciences* (*6*), the *Handbook of the Biology of Aging* (*7*), and the *Handbook of the Psychology of Aging* (*8*) was welcomed by the field as the creation of a knowledge base for further research, policy making, and practice. Further consolidation, explication of concepts, and dissemination of information in the diverse areas of gerontology are taking place at the conferences and symposia of the various professional associations: the American Association of Retired Persons, the American Geriatrics Society, the Association for Gerontology in Higher Education, the Gerontological Society, and others.

Gerontology has been described as a branch of knowledge dealing with individual human aging and the aging of societies. Human aging is the process of cumulative changes that occur during the life cycle of the human individual; the aging of societies refers to demographic and sociocultural changes in a population. Although there is no specific determination of when age-related changes take place in the individual—and thus, gerontology in its broadest sense may be defined as the science of life-span changes—gerontologists study mainly the phenomena during the last third of the life-span. Theoretical contributions to social gerontological research have been reviewed in the historical perspective by Maddox and Wiley in their paper "Scope, Concepts and Methods in the Study of Aging" (*9*). The literature of social gerontology may include such themes as demography of aging, behavior and personality, cultural and environmental aspects, aging and social organization, aging and the economy, and government and politics.

Some theorists argue that gerontology may be thought of as encompassing two fields: social gerontology and clinical gerontology, including geriatrics. Social gerontology was characterized by one of its founders as "an organized field of knowledge concerned with the behavioral aspects of aging in the individual, with aging as a societal phenomenon and with the interrelationships between the two" (*4*, p. 22). Social gerontology is particularly interested in the ways a society treats its older members. Clinical gerontology has been discussed as an emerging specialty in medicine that grew out of geriatric practice. Its clinical branch deals with issues of patient care; preventive, diagnostic, and curative measures; and the team approach to geriatric practice. Research activity is aimed at the study of cumulative anatomic and physiological changes in later adulthood. In recent years clinical gerontology and geriatrics have often surfaced in the literature in conjunction with medical education and training (*10–13*). Akpom and Mayer surveyed American medical schools and found that fairly low priority is accorded to geriatrics in educational programs (*14*).

Aging, a universal phenomenon, attracted the creative thought of philosophers, statesmen, writers, and artists for centuries before gerontology as an area of systematic study emerged. Yet, geriatrics and gerontology have their roots in the late 19th century, and only the 1940s brought about the scientific and social trend that has created the complex structure of research investigations, policies, legal measures, governmental interventions, and services that we call today the gerontological, or "aging," sector. Philibert traced this trend and its humanistic implications in his paper "Philosophical Approach to Gerontology," considering the "rejection and ignorance of pre-scientific literature on aging as ruinous to the study of aging" (*15*). Achenbaum provided a historical analysis of changes in the images of the old in the United States (*16*).

Bailey attributed the intellectual parentage of gerontological studies to Carl Jung, Charlotte Bühler, and Erik Erikson (*17*). He viewed gerontology as a discipline focusing on the interrelatedness of all life-span changes. This existential life-span vision, however, was not the underlying motivation of most age-related studies that represented the forerunners of current social gerontological investigations. From the 1920s to the '40s, inventories of the social and economic aspects of aging were undertaken in several countries. Tibbitts offered an overview of the social trends that accounted for this interest: scientific and technological progress, increase of the average life expectancy, growing visibility of the aged and their changing position in society, shifts in the role of the family, new value orientations, and the need for more systematic knowledge to undergird social policies (*4*).

In the 1940s, age-related studies advanced along parallel lines in several fields. This period marked the institutionalization of discipline-based gerontological research in the United States. Biologists established the American Research Club on Aging, the American Psychological Association initiated its Division of Later Maturity and Old Age, and the Committee on Social Adjustment in Old Age of the

Social Science Research Council began its work. With the establishment of the Gerontological Society in 1945, the launching of the *Journal of Gerontology* the next year, and the First International Congress in Gerontology in Liege, the process of integrating the work in various disciplines and countries began. However, separate disciplinary orientations remained strong, as symbolized by the inception of two divisions—the Division of Psychology and Social Science and the Division of Biomedical Science—in the Gerontological Society in 1952. As specialties continue to multiply and diversify, the bridging of gaps between the orientations of various subbranches within gerontology remains a difficult process.

The formal definition of what we mean by "old" has attracted the attention of researchers, policy makers, and legal experts. Gerontologists in developmental psychology drew on the work of Erik Erikson, who identified the crucial turning points in human development during adulthood. Recent theorists, however, established different developmental stages. Research has identified age groups such as the "young-old" and the "old-old" (*18*). In addition, concepts of "functional age" and "social age" have been introduced (*19*). For legal purposes, it was deemed necessary to construct a chronological parameter, "legal age," for the last segment of human life. However, a chronological definition of aging as a static life-phase is arbitrary. Today, aging is considered a process that proceeds throughout the life cycle rather than a rigidly definable stage.

In the literature, scientific studies, policy analyses, and factual descriptions of interventions are tightly interwoven with expressions of the broad social movement. During the rise of social movements, language and definitions often change to reflect value orientations and attitudes. In recent years "ageism," a term used with behavioral and political implications, has come to connote a negative social attitude toward the process of aging at any stage of the life cycle.

The meaning of history in gerontology has been interpreted and institutionalized in two different ways. The records of gerontology, the papers of pioneer gerontologists, and the administrative archives of organizations constitute a wealth of resources for historical research. Moreover, the memory of the aged and accounts of life reviews represent invaluable depositories of creative thinking and experience. Oral historians have been striving to develop methods for the recording and preserving of this heritage.

Under the auspices of the Gerontological Society, the All-University Gerontology Center at Syracuse University, the Institute of Gerontology at the University of Michigan, and other gerontology centers are engaged in the cooperative planning of a national gerontological archives program. The need to establish such a program was first addressed at the annual meeting of the Gerontological Society in Louisville, Kentucky, in 1975, and again at the society's meeting in San Francisco, California, in 1977. A committee on history and archives was formed, and it is now initiating the planning stages of a program that would identify, inventory, and preserve gerontological manuscript collections, administrative papers, and other records of historical value. It is foreseen that multiple sites at institutions and agencies will serve as repositories of materials within their own areas of interest and expertise.

Following its beginning in 1948, the most important development in the practice of oral history was the establishment of the Oral History Association in November 1967, a year after the first national colloquium was held at Lake Arrowhead, California. Largely through the association, the profession is making tremendous inroads in the study of diverse modern movements and peoples. The association has contributed to the maturing of the profession with remarkable successes, including acceptance by bibliographers, sponsorship of workshops, numerous ongoing research programs listed in the association's *Directory*, and an increasing number of Pulitzer Prize books emanating from oral history research (*20, 21*).

Research Dissemination and Utilization

The literature of social gerontology indicates that the role of information exchange during the research process—from the identification of problems to the dissemination and utilization of findings—has been readily acknowledged. According to Philibert, "the strongest motivation for studying aging has been throughout history the will to make the best out of it. Intervention has been, and still is, the ultimate goal of research in aging" (*15*, p. 38). In 1946 the first issue of the *Journal of Gerontology* gave an account of social and economic concerns that needed research attention. The question of the lack of systematized theoretical knowledge was raised. In the ensuing decades investigations proceeded at several universities and research centers. As indicated before, during the 1950s, the massive effort to generate and integrate gerontological knowledge commenced.

Riley and Johnson published a fundamental set of essays on research implementation in various service professions working with the elderly (*22*). Simultaneously, the Committee on Research and Development Goals of the Gerontological Society recommended that "it will be necessary . . . to accumulate vast amounts of information about the elderly themselves and about those approaching old age" (*23*, p. 7). The need for scientific documentation was also identified. The First International Course in Social Gerontology in Lisbon stressed the importance of communicating research through gerontological excerpta and abstracts, bulletins, university-based information centers, and national information banks. The International Center of Social Gerontology proposed an agenda for the development of an information system making international research information in gerontology available to researchers anywhere (*24*). This recommendation is still awaiting implementation.

Before the dissemination of gerontological research in the United States could be realistically discussed, the federal government had to act on the widely felt need for a national research policy. In 1974 the Research on Aging Act authorized creation of the National Institute on Aging (NIA) within the National Institutes of Health, for the "conduct and support of biomedical, social and behavioral research and training related to the aging process and the diseases and other special problems and needs of the aged." By enacting funding for the NIA, Congress placed confidence in new research efforts that would alleviate "problems of old age by extending the healthy middle years of life." The institute supports research on many levels. The Extramural and Collaborative Research Program encourages investigations at universities, hospitals, medical centers, and nonprofit institutions, and provides support to train scientists for research careers in aging. Biological and medical studies range from molecular and cellular research and clinical investigations to psychological and social aspects of aging. Policy statements and research agendas indicating the direction and priorities of the NIA's national research plan have been issued (*25, 26*). The reports of the various panels of the institute and the *Special Report on Aging* reflect research accomplishments and findings. Recently, emphasis has shifted from the institute's disease orientation toward a more unifying approach to research on the normal physiological changes of advanced age and the behavioral, social, cultural, and economic aspects of aging.

Research in gerontology is carried out by a variety of institutions across the country. Biological and medical studies have been conducted at the basic science departments of medical colleges and centers, hospital research facilities, and university departments. Several public sector institutions, including the National Academy of Sciences and the Institute of Medicine, are participating in coordinated research planning. Research in social gerontology, often using the interdisciplinary team approach, has centered in academic institutions, research centers, and gerontological organizations and agencies. A large portion of studies in the human service sector is focusing on need assessment and evaluation research. Multidisciplinary Centers of Gerontology, authorized by the Older Americans Act of 1965 as amended, have been established at universities and colleges across the nation through grants made available by the United States Administration on Aging. The centers are responsible for coordinating the gerontological research and teaching activities of faculty in different departments and for providing consultation to community organizations. Special emphasis has been placed by the grants on the use of information on aging in academic curricula. The 1973 Older Americans Act amendments specified that each center, among other responsibilities, "serve as a repository of information and knowledge with respect to the areas for which it conducts basic and applied research" (*27*).

Research on aging has also been conducted under the Public Health Services Act, which provides grants and contracts for the study of biomedical, psychological, and social aspects of aging. The Comprehensive Employment and Training Act, the Social Security Act, and other federal statutes have also funded various studies. Several investigations with policy implications have been supported by the Center for Studies of the Mental Health of the Aging in the National Institute of Mental Health. In addition, numerous private foundations provide grants for aging research, as indicated in *Funding in Aging: Public, Private and Voluntary* (*28*).

In respect to research dissemination, two directions may be distinguished: (*a*) the diffusion of research findings to policy makers, practitioners, and advocates in order to provide general awareness of advances in knowledge; and (*b*) planned policy research and evaluation research directly applicable to social problems (*29–31*). Several programs have been initiated to identify modes of bridging the gap between gerontological research findings and their use by those who develop policies and services. Examples are the Research Dissemination and Utilization

Program of the Social Policy Laboratory of the Andrus Gerontology Center at the University of Southern California, and the Knowledge Utilization Program at the Denver Research Institute, University of Denver. At the latter institution, video packages have been prepared and tested for public libraries on topics such as barrier-free access to buildings, services for the home-bound, and health and legal issues. Project SHARE—a Clearinghouse for Improving the Management of Human Services, funded by the United States Department of Health and Human Services (formerly Department of Health, Education, and Welfare)—serves as a source of information on these and similar programs. Such efforts are expected to ameliorate the "translation" of the results of research, a problem Beattie saw as a "major barrier to the use of research by those providing services" (*32*).

There are themes underlying research in social gerontology, especially on human longevity, that are of universal concern. Ethical and philosophical issues involving death and self-determination, the potential extension of the life-span, the quality of life in old age, the multiple jeopardy of minority elderly, research on older subjects, and patients' rights are examples. A series of value-oriented papers resulted from a conference held at the University of Chicago with the support of the National Science Foundation. Biogerontologists, ethicists, philosophers, and physicians spoke to the ethical aspects of policy decisions (*33*). Of the several research-related concerns that emerge from the gerontological literature, one needing special emphasis is the necessity of a two-way information flow between the older population, on the one hand, and scientists, policy makers, and service deliverers, on the other, in order to avoid stereotyping the elderly as passive "problems."

The quality of data and their lack of availability for research in aging present serious problems. Systematic evaluation of complex federal programs for the elderly has become a necessity, but it is difficult to obtain data about service recipients. To demonstrate the need for a national information system to provide data for the measurement of conditions and problems of older people, the United States General Accounting Office conducted a study of the noninstitutionalized elderly in Cleveland, Ohio (*34*). Concepts and survey instruments were designed by the Older Americans Resources and Services (OARS) program of the Duke Center for the Study of Aging and Human Development. The United States General Accounting Office stated that "to design and plan for the delivery of services to older persons, society, the Congress, and the executive branch need information on their lives, and the impact of services on them. Currently, this information is spread piecemeal through Federal, State, local and private agencies" (*35*, p. ii). The report recommended establishment of a national information system on services to the aged.

With the growing capability of designing and searching computerized social science data files, some of these problems might soon be removed. Data files are often generated by survey research projects and can be used for secondary analysis by other researchers. Granick and Kleban have described a file of data, derived from a longitudinal study of the biological and behavioral functioning of individuals, supported by the National Institute of Mental Health (*36*). The utilization of data files has been greatly enhanced by the creation of the National Archive of

Computerized Data on Aging with support from the Administration on Aging. The program, jointly administered by the Institute of Gerontology and the Inter-University Consortium for Political and Social Research at the University of Michigan, collects aging-related data, makes them available, and seeks to improve their utilization through training seminars. The Research Instrument Bank in Aging (RIBA), maintained by the Midwest Council for Social Research on Aging under contract with the Administration on Aging, includes scales, indices, batteries of questions or items, and single questions or items which have been tested by researchers.

Not only researchers but also service deliverers and policy makers have a need for demographic data and for the combination of these data with various indicators on the quality of health, social conditions, and environmental conditions of the elderly. The United States Bureau of the Census issued a volume on the demographic aspects of aging in the Current Population Reports (*37*). The complexity of using census data in relation to aging was documented by Kindig and Warren (*38*). Theoretical and developmental work on social indicators relevant to aging is underway at the Institute for Interdisciplinary Studies in Minneapolis (*39*), at the University of Iowa (*40*), and several other places.

Public Policy and Services to the Aging

Because of the increasing role of governments at various levels in the planning, financing, and regulating of health care, social services, nutritional and educational programs, and other aspects of contemporary life, public policy alternatives are crucial issues for the elderly, their families, and those who develop and operate human services. From a few basic data, we can make inferences for the growth of the "aging enterprise." Since the turn of the century the population 65 years and older has increased nearly eight times. The total population during the same time increased only about four times. In 1900 persons 65 and over represented about 4% of the total. In the same year, 63% of the elderly lived in families, 30% lived alone, and about 6% were institutionalized. In 1977 about 14% of the older population lived in poor families or as unrelated individuals in other homes with incomes below the poverty level. About 27% of the elderly not living in families were poor in 1977 (*41*, pp. 1–2). Gold identified six roles of the federal government that were focused on improving the life of the elderly: assuring an adequate income, noncash benefits, the protection of individual rights, research, social services, and the coordination of intergovernmental programs (*42*). Views of the soundness of age-segregated programs vary, but there is agreement that the complexity of program structures and eligibility requirements calls for more effective information dissemination about their availability and nature. Problems in service delivery to the minority elderly were identified in a Rand Corporation study (*43*), and a critical picture of the "bewildering maze of bureaucracy" was given by testimony at congressional hearings on the "Fragmentation of Services for the Elderly" (*44*).

At the White House Conference on Aging in 1961, recommendations were made by the gerontological community concerning income, health, nutrition, housing, transportation, employment and retirement, education, roles and activities, and spiritual well-being. A decade later, at the White House Conference of 1971, physical fitness; the role of governmental and nongovernmental organizations; planning; research and demonstration; and facilities, programs, and services were added to the former national agenda of concerns. Special sessions dealt with the multiple jeopardy of the minority aged.

The 1981 White House Conference on Aging, authorized on October 18, 1978, was designed to draw national attention to the increasing population of older Americans and the policies necessary to meet their needs. Major issues confronting the delegates were: improving the economic well-being of the elderly, making quality health care more readily available, establishing a more comprehensive social service delivery system, expanding availability of appropriate housing, long-term care and retirement policies, greater employment opportunities, overcoming stereotypes of the aging, and encouraging further biomedical research into the aging process. Seven technical committees were formed to handle these issues. The conference was attended by a total of 1,800 delegates, selected to reflect the number of older persons in each state, minorities, and national organizations. Selection of one-half of the delegates was determined by each state (*45*).

The idea for a federal agency to serve the needs of the elderly was an outgrowth of the 1961 White House Conference on Aging. The Older Americans Act of 1965 set forth 10 objectives for assisting older Americans and established the United States Administration on Aging as a focal agency. It also authorized grants for community social service projects through the states, research and demonstration projects, and training for service roles. The act has been amended several times. The 1969 amendments added a program of areawide model projects for testing new approaches to social service delivery and provided for the Foster Grandparent and Retired Senior Volunteer programs. The National Nutrition Program was created in 1972.

To increase the planning and administrative capacity of state governments and their units on aging which had been in existence since the late 1940s, the Older Americans Act amendments of 1973 mandated state planning and service areas, and more coordinated social service systems at the local level through the designation of area agencies on aging. The same legislation authorized the multidisciplinary centers of gerontology, thus initiating the now well-known national network with linkages between academic research and the system of state offices and area agencies (*46*). In order to give more support and flexibility to this network, the National Information and Resource Clearing House was created, as well as multipurpose senior centers, the Community Service Employment Program for Older Americans, and the Federal Council on the Aging.

Programs in transportation, home service, legal counseling, and assistance in home maintenance were identified as priorities in 1975. The second part of the decade saw the intensification of the consumer and political roles of the aged. The mere availability of services was seen as unsatisfactory without the facilitating role of advocacy. The Comprehensive Older Americans Act Amendments of 1978, therefore, made federal, state, and local agencies responsible for assisting the elderly population by active advocacy techniques (*47, 48*). At the same time, the Federal Council on the Aging—already engaged in policy review and advising the president, the Congress, and the Administration on Aging—was authorized to serve as a spokesman on behalf of older Americans by commissioning and publishing studies, making recommendations with respect to federal policies, and collecting and disseminating information to the public.

Under the 1978 Amendments, two new areas received emphasis: development and implementation of a national manpower policy by the Administration on Aging, and a demonstration program designed to identify new ways to organize, finance, and deliver long-term care services. In addition, a national center and five regional centers will provide training, technical assistance, and legal services to state and area agencies and other community organizations in support of their advocacy function.

Specific titles in a long series of congressional laws added to the development of the current legal status and rights of older people. In most cases, chronological age served as a determinant of eligibility for some services and privileges as well as a basis for restrictions such as mandatory retirement. For example, the Age Discrimination Act of 1975 prohibited discrimination and provided for judicial review, while Title III of the Discrimination Study Act, "Study of Racial and Ethnic Discrimination in Programs for Older Americans," authorized the Commission on Civil Rights to undertake a comprehensive study and to gather data and information through public hearings. The Domestic Volunteer Service Act of 1973 mandated grants and contracts for the Foster Grandparents and Older American Community Service programs and other volunteer service projects. The Congregate Housing Services Act of 1978 opened the way to low-rent housing for the elderly and also to affiliated support services. In addition, the Library Services and Construction Act was amended to authorize grants to states for public library services for older persons.

Vocational rehabilitation programs and comprehensive services for independent living for "older blind individuals" were mandated by the Rehabilitation Act of 1973, and grants to states for medical assistance programs as well as various services were made possible under Titles XIX and XX of the Social Security Act as amended. The enactment of the Social Security Act of 1935 provided entitlement to family benefits in the program of old age, survivors, and disability insurance. The act has made a difference in the retirement patterns of working Americans by establishing 65 as the standard age for retirement and then, with changed regulations, by influencing a strong downward movement in typical retirement age. In 1947 the Social Security Act authorized the social services program, which has been liberalized over the years by various amendments. In 1974 Title XX replaced Titles IV-A and VI, and with the enactment of this new law greater power was given to the states to design their own social service programs. The current Title XX program encourages each state to provide services that would reduce, prevent, or eliminate dependency, and that would reduce inappropriate institutional care by providing for community-based care, home-based care, or other forms of less intensive care. One significant aspect of this legislation is the provision for accountability to citizens. A required state plan, besides ensuring citizen participation, is intended to help a state coordinate all social programs and build a new social services strategy. The Program of Health Insurance for the Aged and Disabled (Medicare), Title XVIII of the Social Security Act, provides benefits to most people age 65 and over. Health insurance protection under this program is available to eligible persons without regard to their income or assets. Medicare consists of two parts: the Hospital Insurance Program (HI) and the Supplementary Medical Insurance Program. The Medical Assistance Program (Medicaid), Title XIX of the Social Security Act, appropriates grants to states, enabling them to furnish medical assistance on behalf of families with dependent children, the elderly and blind, or disabled individuals whose income and resources are insufficient to meet the cost of necessary medical services. Rehabilitation and other services help such families and individuals attain or retain capability for independence or self-care (*48*).

Together with the Older Americans Act and its amendments and federal and state regulations, these laws have built a complex world of legal provisions around the elderly. It would be difficult not to recognize the critical need for information that can cut across this maze and assist older individuals and their families and advocates in the realization of elderly rights. All legislation originated in a number of committees of the House and the Senate, adding to the fragmentation of legal provisions and relevant information. The Senate's Special Committee on Aging and the House's Select Committee on Aging serve as sources of studies, reports, and information, although these committees have investigative and oversight responsibility rather than legislative authority.

The influence of voluntary associations, special interest groups, and political organizations has dramatically increased in recent years (*49*). These organizations have adopted information utilization and dissemination techniques and, in numerous cases, active lobbying methods which can marshal both data and public opinion on behalf of their membership or constituencies. The American Association of Retired Persons (AARP) and the National Retired Teachers Association (NRTA) have a strong impact nationally. The Gray Panthers organization is known for its advocacy work, its efforts to change public images of the aging, and its impact on national-level policies. The rights of the minority elderly have been represented by a range of organizations. The National Association of Spanish Speaking Elderly, the National Caucus of the Black Aged, the National Center on the Black Aged, and the National Indian Council on Aging are examples of a growing sector with policy, research, and public education orientation. Information concerning the legal rights of the elderly and relevant legislative, regulatory, and judicial actions is available from the Legal Research Services for the Elderly, the National Senior Citizens' Law Center, and numerous others.

In addition to these national efforts in advocacy, service delivery agencies, senior centers, community organizations, and various types of institutions began to integrate advocacy techniques with their work. The Older Americans Act of 1965 as amended includes several provisions for the participation of older persons in the policy process; for example, representation on the Federal Council on Aging that has responsibility for policy review, evaluation, and recommendations to the president, the Congress, and appropriate federal officials, and for the provision of a public forum for discussion.

The Comprehensive Older Americans Act Amendments of 1978 made federal, state, and local agencies on aging responsible for advocacy for the elderly within their levels of government. Thus, consumer participation of the elderly may take several forms: awareness of the role of public agencies and the use of their information, participation in public hearings and the expression of needs thereby, representation on boards of state and local agencies, and active advocacy on behalf of other older people (*50–53*). Demone has synthesized recent theories and practices in introducing change in human service policy and delivery (*54*), and Cohen gave an overview of the citizen consumer's role in the development of integrated services and case management (*55*). Publication of a large number of guides and manuals has assisted the consumer to function in this essentially political climate. The growing literature of policy analysis and citizen participation provides insights through research reports, case studies, and state-of-the-art reviews.

Information for Gerontologists and Others Working with the Elderly

The potential users of gerontological information include policy makers, researchers, educators, advocates, students, members of voluntary organizations, and the wide variety of specialized workers who staff the extensive and complex health care and other human service delivery systems. Miller and Cutler were among the first to address the problems of information services and resources in the field of aging (*56*). They observed that the field "is affected by the multidisciplinary nature of the subject and the dispersion of relevant bibliographic materials" (p. 198). Beall and Mulak pointed out the need to improve access to foreign-language and foreign-source materials (*57*). Hicks spoke of the elderly as a new group of potential computer users or clients of information search services (*58*). Other voices of concern and suggestions for new information systems and services could be heard at meetings and panel discussions of professional associations.

The problem of gerontological information services lies in the enormous heterogeneity of both resources and user needs. An attempt to identify and summarize some of the characteristics of gerontological information was made by Brindle, Dosa, and Gee (*59*); their major points are:

1. Social, economic, legal, political, and other problems are sometimes perceived and described from the perspective of one discipline or policy direction only, without indicating their relationships with other issues.
2. The literature of aging-issue areas is scattered in a large number of fields.
3. Cultural perceptions and value judgments sometimes influence the information that is available.
4. Because of the diversified interests of various groups, advocacy organizations, and professional fields, it is difficult to identify a unified professional outlook.
5. There is a lack of tested and evaluated models of information systems for various user groups because the field is relatively new.
6. There are no established standards and measurements to assess the value of information for users in the same discipline or other disciplines and professions.

7. There are mainly impressions rather than research findings on what kinds of data are needed by policy makers and service deliverers and in what form or package.
8. There is a question of who should evaluate, synthesize, and disseminate research information for use by policy makers and practitioners.
9. It is hard to find information about reliable and tested programs designed to disseminate information to the elderly and to involve the elderly in program planning and evaluation.

In respect to bibliographic control of the gerontological literature, the bibliography compiled by Dr. Nathan Shock and his associates in the *Journal of Gerontology* has represented the key resource since 1961. The Shock bibliography lists, under broad subject categories, journal articles, scientific papers, conference proceedings, monographs, research reports, government documents, and other publications in gerontology. University Information Services, Inc., located in Ann Arbor, Michigan, commenced publication of *Gerontological Abstracts* in 1976. Available to subscribers in journal or card format, this service provides abstracts of publications from international scholarly journals, as well as news items and editorial notes. Abstracts cover three subject areas: social, clinical, and biological aspects of gerontology. Social aspects encompass psychology, women, quality of life, crime, politics, and myths and stereotypes, among others. The clinical abstracts include topics such as the heart, respiratory system, alcoholism, and hospital care; the biological section is further broken down into such areas as biochemistry, endocrinology, and genetics. The Institute of Gerontology, at the University of Michigan, published *A Core List of Significant Works in 1978;* 1,000 entries, selected with the assistance of nationally known experts in diverse fields, aid libraries in the development of collections in aging. Basic books in social gerontology are highlighted, but the list also includes reference materials (*60*). To supplement bibliographic services, libraries have developed informal cooperation with each other. The National Gerontology Resource Center, at the National Retired Teachers Association and American Association of Retired Persons, provides information and research assistance to these and other aging-related organizations and their libraries. The Resource Center includes a collection of approximately 6,000 volumes in the subject areas of social gerontology and retirement, and offers computerized literature searches.

The focal point for information about aging policies and service programs, the National Clearinghouse on Aging (NCA; originally the National Information and Resource Clearing House), was created in the Administration on Aging by the Older Americans Act amendments of 1973. The clearinghouse is responsible for collecting, analyzing, organizing, and disseminating information for and about the older population, including publication of the periodical *Aging*. Coordination of federal information and referral programs and fostering of the development of information and referral services in communities across the country are additional important functions.

In 1976 the NCA published the first edition of the *Thesaurus* of aging terms, based on the document and report collection located at the clearinghouse, and a revised edition was issued the following year (*61*). In 1978 the first of a series of contracts for the Service Center for Aging Information (SCAN) system was awarded to Norman Hodges and Associates in Rockville, Maryland, for the development and operation of the Central Control Facility. The following major products and services of SCAN have been announced: (*a*) a comprehensive bibliographic data base including abstracts of gerontological literature in computer-readable format, (*b*) custom searches of the data base carried out at resource centers to be operated under contracts from the Administration on Aging, (*c*) national online access to the data base through a commercial organization, (*d*) a monthly journal containing bibliographic references with abstracts of gerontological literature, and (*e*) microfiche and paper copies of all documents in the data base except those protected by copyright (*62*). Contracts for two of the three projected resource centers have been awarded to the Franklin Research Center. The Social–Behavioral Science Resource Center is located in Philadelphia and encompasses information on research and the theory of gerontology. The Social Practice Resource Center in Silver Spring, Maryland, collects and disseminates information on the practice and application of gerontology.

Two printed indexing publications, available through SCAN, contain a wealth of information not normally found in the published literature. *A Comprehensive Inventory and Analysis of Federally Supported Research in Aging* was initially prepared by Documentation Associates, under contract with the National Clearinghouse on Aging. Coverage includes research in aging funded by all federal agencies since 1966. In addition, original papers, prepared by nationally known experts, describe critical aspects of gerontological research (*63*). The *Cumulative Index of AoA Discretionary Projects* is a listing of nearly 3,000 documents, originated between 1965 and 1978, on 240 sets of microfiche. In addition to projects funded by the Administration on Aging, the microfiche collection includes the holdings of the National Clearinghouse on Aging. This index and the microfiche collection have been distributed to all regional and state offices on aging and most university gerontology centers around the country (*48*). Several current awareness newsletters produced by SCAN announce titles and corresponding microfiche numbers of documents on selected topics such as income and aging, preretirement planning, continuing adult education, and health care.

With the emergence of the National Aging Network for service planning and delivery, information support to service providers, planners, educators, and others became a major issue. A variety of prototype information programs have been funded by the Administration on Aging since the mid-1970s. The scope of this article permits the mention of some examples only. The Ethel Percy Andrus Gerontology Center, at the University of Southern California in Los Angeles, has been operating a computerized search and retrieval system called Andrus Gerontology Exchange (AGEX) since 1978. AGEX offers: (*a*) computer tapes of bibliographic citations on special topics based on the center's Research Library holdings, (*b*) custom bibliographies based on user request in hard-copy format, (*c*) lists of the center's publications on selected topics, and (*d*) a reprint request service of literature authored by center faculty, staff, and researchers (*64*). In 1976 Duke University received funding for the design and implementation of an information service to assist educators. KWIC (Keyword Indexed Collection of the Training Resources in Aging Project) developed an information bank of training materials relevant to the field of aging, which is dependent on the cooperation and contributions of persons producing training materials (*65*). Another Duke University program, ASTRA (Analysis and Selection of Training Resources in Aging), in conjunction with the Educational Products Information Exchange (EPIE) in New York, developed a detailed format for reviewing gerontological training materials (*66*). In 1979, AoA's Service Center for Aging Information assumed the activities of the KWIC/ASTRA Training and Educational Resources Program.

From 1974 to 1978, the Texas Department of Public Welfare offered a free computerized search service in the field of aging. Developed as part of a Title IV Research Utilization grant from the Administration on Aging, the Aging Research Information System (ARIS) included approximately 12,000 individual abstracts of research reports. The basic purpose of the experimental service was "to make it possible for the user to select—from the thousands of pages of research abstracts—the few pages of material that are directly relevant to the client's particular problem" (*67*). At the University of California, PROJECT IDEA was funded by AoA for 3 years to "develop a model of data acquisition, compilation, and dissemination" for state and area offices of aging. In 1977 a directory was published which classified into nine broad subject groupings, and indexed summaries of, innovative service programs in aging. The project also compiled information about innovations by area agencies on aging (*68*).

Syracuse University's All-University Gerontology Center and School of Information Studies have been operating the Gerontological Information Program (GRIP). Between 1976 and 1979 the prototype GRIP I used an integrated approach to research, systems development, and education in gerontological information. Based on a need assessment study on the kinds of information needed by individuals in human service delivery and older persons' organizations, GRIP I provided two kinds of information services: current awareness in the form of a periodic newsletter and on-demand information searches using computerized retrieval systems, area libraries, and special collections. An empirical evaluation of GRIP I was conducted in 1979 (*69*). With the award of two new grants from the Administration on Aging in 1979, GRIP II continues to provide information support to organizations and service agencies working with the elderly and to Syracuse University programs involved in gerontological education and research. Special attention is being focused on the generation of state-of-the-art papers and bibliographies on special topic areas relevant to curriculum development and long-term care policies.

In keeping with the suggestion of Miller and Cutler for a permanent committee of information specialists within the Gerontological Society (*56*), gerontological librarians formed an advisory committee in the society's Education Section in 1977. At the 1978 annual meeting the goals of this library–information specialist committee were outlined as: (*a*) the provision of a forum for information exchange; (*b*) the promotion of comprehensive, timely, and accurate information in the field of gerontology; and (*c*) the encouragement of the growth and quality of gerontological librarianship. Gerontological information professionals represent a wide range of activities in academic libraries, educational resource centers of multidisciplinary gerontology centers, medical colleges and hospital geriatric programs, nursing homes and long-term care facilities, government agencies, professional organizations, archival programs, institutional libraries, and large human service agencies. Owens suggested in the preliminary draft of a "Directory of Gerontological Libraries and Resource Centers in the United States" that "there is a need for the creation of communication channels between gerontological libraries to promote the building of collections, referral services and inter-library loans" (*70*). In view of the intensive development and growth of gerontology and the educational efforts in other professions, there also is a critical need for educational programs in gerontological information resource management and library services. As of 1978 only four schools in the United States with master's programs in Library Science—North Texas State University, Syracuse University, Wayne State University, and the University of Wisconsin—offered courses in gerontological information and librarianship (*71*). In 1980 Rutgers University was in the process of designing courses in this area. The next few years will present a challenge to gerontological library–information professionals to go beyond the preliminary steps in cooperation to the institutionalization of this branch of the profession by: (*a*) identifying the parameters of the field, (*b*) developing objectives and professional standards, (*c*) organizing programs where policy needs may be identified and advances in the field are reported, (*d*) initiating research, (*e*) making recommendations for curriculum development, and (*f*) disseminating information about gerontological information to other information groups and other professions.

Education and Training in Gerontology

The twin processes of education and information transfer are closely interwoven at both the conceptual and practical levels. Formal educational programs, as well as library and information services, provide individuals with knowledge resources. The traditional differences between the two processes are the direction that educational institutions give the learner and the influence they exert on the objectives, modes, and applications of learning. But as more and more adult learners engage in independent study and take responsibility for their own educational planning and direction, the differences between "educating" and "informing" tend to diminish. Thus, the inclusion of educational gerontology in the present article is probably more justified than the inclusion of any other subfield in gerontology would be.

Educational gerontology has developed from two relatively new fields—adult education and social gerontology—and is described in different terms by various observers. Peterson outlined three major aspects (*72*): (*a*) educational endeavors designed for persons who are middle-aged and older; (*b*) education about aging for a general or specific public; and (*c*) educational preparation of persons who are, or intend to be, employed in serving older people in a professional capacity. Ehrlich and Ehrlich, on the other hand, described a four-part educational framework in which higher learning institutions have responsibilities to (*73*): (*a*) provide appropriate learning opportunities for middle-aged and elderly consumers in order to broaden living options in late life; (*b*) integrate education about the life cycle and the meaning of aging into all levels of the educational system; (*c*) offer continuing education for service practitioners to upgrade their potential as well as to entice new workers into the field; and (*d*) develop new knowledge, test new services, and raise standards within the service community through research and demonstration projects

Educational gerontology received national attention at the 1971 White House Conference on Aging. The Education Section, with 269 delegates, produced 23 recommendations, responding to such questions as "what basis should be used in allocating financial and manpower resources for education and aging; what populations among the aged should receive special attention; what types of educational services should be developed; what are some ways of effectively providing these services" (*74*).

The need for gerontological education at several levels has increasingly been felt. In 1969 there were a third of a million professional and technical workers serving primarily or exclusively older persons, but only 10–20% of them had any formal training in age-related subjects. In a survey of future educational requisites and interests of professional personnel and volunteers serving senior citizens in Hartford, Connecticut, Dickstein found that there was interest among practitioners in pursuing studies, but not in developing specific careers in gerontology (*75*). He recommended the establishment of accredited, college-level courses to meet the need for in-service training. In 1976 it was found that most persons working with the elderly still had no formal training in gerontology except through summer institutes and short-term training sessions (*76*).

Response to these needs came from the Congress, the National Institute on Aging, and the Administration on Aging, as well as from the academic and professional sectors. Butler and Speith projected that by 1982 the National Institute on Aging would have a budget "in the neighborhood of $90 million" (*77*, p. 112). They envisioned NIA as "providing support for several thousand senior researchers, research associates, and graduate-student assistants." In addition, NIA hoped to support 500 trainees and postdoctoral fellows per year within a few years. Trainees were recruited from, and many of them returned to, universities and colleges in order to strengthen or initiate integrated programs of gerontological research, education, and community service. The Multidisciplinary Centers of Gerontology Program was authorized by the 1973 Older Americans Act amendments and was officially instituted in 1976 when appropriations became available. Title IV-A was designed to fulfill the education and training needs of personnel in the organizations and programs that have sprung up since the early 1970s. In 1977 specific criteria were established to ensure that educational institutions increase the number of minorities in their programs and that they develop curricula on minority issues.

When the 1978 Amendments to the Older Americans Act were enacted to strengthen the development and implementation of comprehensive community-based service systems, with special emphasis on advancing the well-being of the frail elderly, the Title IV-A Training Program and the Multidisciplinary Centers of Gerontology Program moved to the forefront of structuring gerontological education at academic institutions. The Long Term Care Gerontology Center Program and the Geriatric Fellowship Program have been designed to improve services to the chronically impaired elderly. The Minority Research Associate Program, together with the Minority Recruitment Program, is directed at improving the quality of services for minority elderly. A special study is investigating manpower requirements, and other projects are addressing the need for policy studies and technical assistance. Consequently, the Administration on Aging began to foster a more coordinated approach to education and training on a regional level (*78*).

Gerontology has become one of the fastest growing subjects of interest in academic institutions. In 1978, 1,000 colleges and universities in the United States—triple the number of 5 years earlier—offered at least one course in gerontology, and perhaps 30 or 40 had programs for career education and training in gerontology (*79*). Abraham Monk outlined four basic propositions for gerontological curriculum planning in higher education (*80*): (*a*) study of policy adjustments to the "leisure as life-style" mentality of our society, (*b*) reappraisal of an extended individual life cycle and its implications for education throughout the life-span, (*c*) social policy reform, and (*d*) gerontological social planning, with an emerging concern for generating alternatives to institutionalization of the aged. Monk expressed a need for a "dual educational policy that encompasses the immediate market demands for training of workers in gerontology, as well as the learning needs of the middle aged and older adults" (*80*).

The unusual growth of academic programs during the 1960s and '70s generated a national concern about standards and quality. A joint research project of the Association for Gerontology in Higher Education and the Gerontological Society, "Foundations for Establishing Educational Program Standards in Gerontology," found that a core of essential multidisciplinary knowledge for all people working in the field of aging indeed exists and should be offered through a variety of programs. The Foundation Project also attempted to identify a "core" literature and develop lists of references. Data were collected by the following question: "What books or articles are, in your view, essential reading for gerontology students (List up to five in your own field and up to five in other fields)." This attempt was not successful. Responses revealed no agreement about what literature is essential or for what field particular information resources are useful. Consequently, the research team acknowledged "the need to provide guidance regarding printed literature and other educational resource material that can assist most effectively in building the basic gerontological curricula" (*81*).

The literature suggests that, in addition to formal curricula, there is a demand for short-term training related to specific jobs people perform in services and programs. Monk referred to this kind of program as providing problem-solving, issue-oriented, and multidisciplinary training rather than conceptual or theoretical education (*80*). As one of the early models of in-service training for gerontological service providers, a program at the University of Pennsylvania focused efforts on determining the impact of in-service training on the quality of services to the elderly. Recommendations were made for close cooperation between service providers and training programs in developing training objectives and processes (*82*).

Originated in Europe, the concept of lifelong learning has been defined as education for all ages any time the learner needs the competencies being taught or benefits from the educational process in other ways. Gerontologists strongly advocate education during every stage of the life cycle. Havighurst suggested that effective adult education should focus on two aspects: the instrumental and the expressive (*83*). As cochairman of the Education Section of the 1971 White House Conference on Aging, McClusky observed that, in any random sample of the population, the oldest are the most poorly educated (*74*). Although research presents no evidence that as a healthy person ages the ability to learn declines, older persons usually do not perceive education as being particularly relevant to their needs, because they regard educational services as being separate from other service programs. Education, McClusky concluded, should be regarded as a principal component of all the services designed to meet the necessities of living.

There has been a trend in the United States for organizations to provide two kinds of educational programs to the elderly: lifelong learning and preretirement planning. Lifelong learning may occur formally—through private and public schools, colleges and universities, and radio and television programs—or informally, through local organizations. Community colleges in recent years have provided older persons with adult education and a link to community services (*84*). Community schools offer services in terms of needs, often involving adult learners in program development and participation. Universities see a growing responsibility to channel information to older persons to update their knowledge and thus assist them in coping with a changing society. The Institute for Retired Professionals enables retirees to find creative activities and assume new roles on university campuses. Preretirement education, conveying planning skills and strengthening the capacity to adjust to changing conditions, is usually provided through informal programs by older persons' organizations, churches and synagogues, labor unions, industry, farm and business organizations, civic associations, libraries, and community centers.

Three examples will illustrate the availability of information resources on educational gerontology. Data for the National Gerontology Education Data System were collected by Bolton (*85*), who surveyed 400 postsecondary educational institutions offering credit instruction in gerontology. The report, "Gerontology in Higher Education—The State of the Field," includes information on structure, curricula, and degrees pertaining to the programs; and on faculty profiles, with indication of gerontological teaching experience, educational background, professional affiliations, and publications. Seltzer, Sterns, and Hickey discussed the major conceptual and academic issues in higher educational gerontology (*86*). The *National Directory of Educational Programs in Gerontology*, compiled by Betsy Sprouse (*87*), was designed "to inform educators, professionals, and students of the nature and location of gerontology-related courses, degree programs, educational services and training programs. . . . Information has been collected on the gerontological activities of 1,275 colleges and universities in the United States" (p. ii).

Information for Older Persons

The creativity of the aged is a human resource that needs to be stimulated and fostered. An understanding of psychological concepts helped gerontological educators to gain a new perspective on the older learner (*88*). Similarly, an awareness of research into the information acquisition and communication patterns of the elderly is a necessary background for the development of relevant information services. Beattie saw the role of information planners as interventive and positive: "Those responsible for the development and utilization of information and the design of communication technology will be instrumental in building new identities and new opportunities for older persons" (*89*, p. 23). This notion puts information professionals into an interdisciplinary field where they work with sociologists, social workers, communication researchers, managers, and other professionals on gerontological team research as well as program development. Although this trend is in its beginnings, interdisciplinary team projects have been carried out in both academic and community settings.

Information services for older persons need to be designed both in public libraries and in other community or private settings. The goal is to bring the information to the elderly if handicapping, physical, or psychological conditions or lack of transportation present problems. Activities may include information support to senior centers and older persons' organizations in planning and designing programs; ombudsman service to nursing homes and forming links between the frail elderly and the outside world; ongoing dissemination of information to the homes of older persons in the form of newsletters or radio and television programs; information about the availability of services, programs, and activities; or reading guidance and delivery of materials to the home-bound. Such information activities may be developed by advocacy groups, older persons' organizations, intergenerational community groups, religious and civic organizations, the area agency on aging, public libraries, and many other types of agencies.

Research has found that communication barriers in disseminating information to the aged may include stereotyped images of older persons and lack of opportunity for natural intergenerational exchange. Obler and Albert brought together, in an interdisciplinary collection, essays on the relationship between language and communication in the elderly (*90*). Both clinical and experimental studies concluded that linguistic strategy rather than deterioration of ability is responsible for changes in the elderly's language use. A number of research papers, emanating from communication science, deal with the images of aging in the mass media. Other disciplines—particularly political science, public administration, policy science, and sociology—became concerned with the political implications of the misconceptions about the aged. Cutler noted that policy formulation tends to be influenced by the preferences of the decision maker (*91*). The same stereotypes might negatively influence the development of information systems for older persons, including information needs perceived by the designers, the kinds of information resources incorporated into the system, and the channels selected to reach the elderly. Works that synthesize the issues involved in aging politics and insights generated by research on ways the elderly seek and obtain information are fundamental to the planning of information services (*92–94*).

Informal support networks of the elderly represent another dimension in the literature that contributes to the conceptualization of formal information systems. A support network may be described as an interactive group of people on whom an individual depends for morale, emotional support, assistance, and coping information. The importance of the informal network in the life of the older person increases with the complexity of the social environment. Research has found that such natural helping networks are often primary resources for the elderly (*95*). The existence and role of informal support networks need to be considered in planning formal information activities for older persons in any situation, but especially in cases of the ethnic, racial minority, rural, isolated, and institutionalized elderly. Sussman provided a state-of-the-art review of family systems and kin networks (*96*). The use of the informal network model was studied by Ruffini and Todd in connection with the Senior Block Information Service in San Francisco (*97*). O'Brien and Wagner conducted an empirical study of the ways frail older persons seek help through their support network and recommended further research into the problems that informal networks may create in blocking the way to formal services (*98*). Findings of such research may have significant implications for information system planning.

Information and referral (I&R) services constitute one of the most important modes of information delivery to the elderly. The main functions of these services are: (*a*) linking people in need of services with the appropriate agency or program and (*b*) collecting and making available data about human services, and thus assisting in the community planning process by discovering duplications or gaps in programs. The Administration on Aging sponsored a number of landmark studies on, and facilitated the development of, information and referral. Under contract to AoA, Long studied their design and evaluation (*99*). An especially valuable feature of this study focuses on the involvement of community residents in service planning and assessment. Alternative techniques applicable to the evaluation of I&R services were reviewed by Burkhardt (*100*). Six substantive issues guiding evaluation were identified and discussed, and recommendations were made for more rigorous benefit-cost analyses than those used to date. Schmandt, Bach, and Radin concentrated on I&R services for the elderly poor in reference to the Supplemental Security Income Program (*101*). Their study of I&R at federal, state, and local levels, conducted in four states and 16 localities, concluded that local initiatives were the most important factors determining the quality of services. Two guidelines on referral were made available in recent years by the United Nations Educational, Scientific, and Cultural Organization (*102*) and by the United States Administration on Aging (*103*). These represent basic sources for public librarians and others who are evolving cooperative arrangements with professional workers in the human service field. The increasing need for such cooperation was demonstrated by the action of the United States National Commission on Libraries and Information Science, establishing a Task Force on Community Information and Referral Service (*104*). In announcing the new working group, the commission stated in its news release: "If the library is to become the first place in the community to which people turn when seeking information on services, it must provide the library user at all socio-economic and cultural levels information and, where appropriate, referral to sources that can provide answers and assistance to meet their needs."

Public Library and Related Programs

The recent history of public library services to the aging in this country was described and documented by Javelin (*105*); thus, only a brief outline is warranted here. Javelin traced the development of these services to 1941, when the Cleveland Public Library established its Adult Education Department and began to offer, first, recreational, and then, educational programs for the elderly. Other libraries, including the Boston Public Library, followed suit. Several authors of this pioneering era, marked by enthusiasm and dedication, acknowledged librarianship's debt to the influence of gerontological research in sociology and to the initiative of social workers serving the aged. Grants from the Fund for Adult Education of the Ford Foundation supported several studies and experimental programs. In the late 1940s, however, a period of decline in policy-level interest and professional activity set in. The 1950s saw the spectacular rise of information science research and development in all areas of scientific and technological information. Paralleling this trend, interest in management information systems (MISs) was transmitted from the national defense and industrial sectors to urban communities and was catapulted into widespread applications to urban information systems during the 1960s and early 1970s. The social turmoil of this period drew the attention of public libraries to much needed service to disadvantaged populations, especially minority groups.

A renewed surge in gerontological activities in librarianship could be witnessed in the early 1970s. Generally, three achievements in this period are given credit in the literature for an overall effort to inventory public library activities in relation to the elderly and to synthesize research, policy direction, and program development. The two-phase *National Survey of Library Services to the Aging* was carried out under contract to the United States Office of Education (*106, 107*). Using survey research techniques, the firm of Booz, Allen, and Hamilton, Inc., in conjunction with the Cleveland Public Library, surveyed 1,300 public libraries in communities with a population of 25,000 or more. The study predicted an increase in library interest among the elderly due to the rise of the educational level of this population. It is noteworthy that the survey research team emphasized the need for direct information service to the elderly, as well as information needs of gerontologists. Recommendation was made for the establishment of a central reference facility for all types of information concerning the aging.

Simultaneously with the second phase of the national survey, Kanner completed his widely cited dissertation "The Impact of Gerontological Concepts on Principles of Librarianship" at the University of Wisconsin (*108*). The study identified five fields in social gerontology with direct relevance for public library objectives and functions: (*a*) perspectives on the societal context of aging, (*b*) social life space, (*c*) physical life space, (*d*) aging and public policy, and (*e*) education for later maturity. The third work of synthesizing impact, an issue of *Library Trends* edited by Phinney, encompassed a partial, if not comprehensive, state-of-the-art review of library services to the aging (*109*). Focusing on public libraries, papers covered historical aspects; the reading interests and needs of older people; programs and activities in libraries; staffing requirements and problems; research in gerontology and implications for the public library, as well as some examples of research in librarianship; and library implications of the 1971 White House Conference on Aging.

Public libraries have a long tradition of serving the handicapped, the homebound, and the institutionalized. According to Jordan, "a few public libraries experimented with home delivery around the turn of the century" (*110*), but these efforts have gradually disappeared. Presumably, the well elderly have used these services along with the sick and the disabled. In 1931 the Pratt–Smoot Act established the Division for the Blind (now the Division for the Blind and Physically Handicapped) in the Library of Congress, which subsequently developed a network of regional libraries for the blind. In 1964 the American Library Association's Committee on Library Service to an Aging Population made a statement of responsibility for assuring that the institutionalized aged "continue to get the library service they have a right to expect" (*111*). Title II-B of the Higher Education Act of 1965 made available funding to train librarians to work with the institutionalized elderly. Has the rest of the elderly population been reached? Genevieve Casey noted that about 80% of the libraries which responded to the National Survey of Library Services to the Aging operate some special service for older persons: "Most of this service (61.7 percent) is to the handicapped, homebound, or institutionalized—a group who constitute about 25 percent of the aging" (*112*, p. 166).

The professional commitment of librarians serving these special-problem groups in the gerontological sector has been institutionalized by the formation of the Library Service to the Impaired Elderly Section (LSIES) within the American Library Association's Association for Specialized and Cooperative Agencies. This section will act as an information clearinghouse, develop standards and innovative techniques of service, encourage library schools and continuing-education programs to design relevant courses, and cooperate with other pertinent organizations (*113*).

Influenced by public awareness of the increasing number of older people and the impact of the White House Conferences, the library has become concerned with programs for the elderly, generally, and with education on aging. The Library Services and Construction Act, as amended, authorized support for public library programs for the elderly. Wayne State University's week-long Institute on Public Library Service to the Aging developed a 17-point statement defining principles of public library service to older persons (*114*). The strongest impetus for such service and public policy supporting it was generated by the 1971 White House Conference. The final report, *Toward a National Policy on Aging*, outlined the needs of older Americans and, together with other recommendations, affirmed the important role of the public library as a primary community resource, because "older adults are increasingly advocating and participating in lifetime education . . ." (*74*,

p. 7). In 1975 the American Library Association's Reference and Adult Services Division published its "Guidelines for Library Services to an Aging Population." Potential library involvement was outlined as: (*a*) knowledge and information collection, (*b*) knowledge and information dissemination, and (*c*) creative action by which new services are initiated in libraries (*115*).

The public library's role in serving the older population in the community has been a controversial issue. Some librarians argue that while special services to the home-bound, the handicapped, and the institutionalized elderly are justified, other older members of the community should be encouraged to participate in regular library programs. Others feel that the aging process, during the last third of the lifespan, creates common physiological and psychological problems for people. Thus, a common need for library programs for all elderly exists. Although relatively little of this controversy is reflected in the literature, the issue is a recurring one at conferences and professional meetings. The current trend is moving toward a division between: (*a*) recreational reading and adult learning materials made available to the community, including the elderly; and (*b*) information services designed to meet the special needs of the older population. Casey made a concise assessment of these needs and their relationships as well as strategies for varied services (*112*). Hameister described the library as a source of "information to the elderly" and "information about the elderly" (*116*). The library has a responsibility to give community support to local area agencies on aging, senior clubs and centers, and other organizations of older persons. Both Casey and Hameister stressed the library's role in dispelling the myths and stereotypes of aging.

There are many effective library programs which carry out the educational, cultural, recreational, and informational goals of the White House Conferences; the legislative mandates of the Congress; and the professional guidelines of the American Library Association in a variety of ways. Public libraries have demonstrated particular interest in two areas: information and referral services (*117*), and adult independent learning. I&R services have a particular meaning and usefulness for the elderly who face a growing complexity of service structures and regulations. The Administration on Aging supports study and development of I&R for the elderly. Formal involvement in adult independent learning is a fairly new experience for public libraries. The Office of Library Independent Study and Guidance Projects was established in the College Entrance Examination Board in 1972. The office developed and tested a 3-year pilot project on learners advisory services and information support services in selected public libraries and in a statewide project. Findings and implications of the pilot study were reported by Mavor, Toro, and DeProspo (*118*).

Other innovative programs reported in the literature include a case where young adults interact with senior citizens in locating and preserving primary source material of local history. A statewide Right-to-Read Project was responsible for a local newspaper column in large print. A "Symphony for Seniors" brings free classical performances of quality to older persons. In another community, librarians offer reading materials on all subjects to persons attending a nutrition center. Music, physical exercise, and education for retirement planning and budgeting represent other program models (*119*). For further review of the principles and patterns of public library service for the elderly, Eisman's "Public Library Programs" may be consulted (*120*). New trends in library approaches to aging services have been described in the literature in terms of more direct advocacy by librarians on behalf of older persons (*121*), a change since library policies for advocacy were reviewed (*122*); more joint ventures between libraries and colleges in providing high-quality and low-cost continuing education (*123*); and increased use of cable communications to disseminate information not at present provided by most public libraries (*124*).

Library services to nursing homes, extended care facilities, retirement centers, boarding houses, and senior centers are included in many public library outreach programs. The oldest and best-developed model, the nursing home library service, appears to have been first developed by Genevieve Casey at the Detroit Public Library in 1948. In some communities, institutionalized or home-bound elderly persons are bussed to the library for book review sessions, craft demonstrations, and other types of activities. Those who are unable to leave their rooms in nursing homes and other institutional settings need services providing book carts stocked with recreational and informational reading, including large-print publications and other special devices for those with impaired sight. Nursing home and retirement home residents often serve as volunteers to maintain and circulate collections and to organize book talks, newspaper clubs, and reading sessions for those who are unable to read.

A complex and growing area, where librarians have been cooperating with other professionals, encompasses the concepts and activities related to oral history, the life review, music therapy, art therapy, writing therapy, and others. Although these activities are usually operated by the institution's administration rather than by the public library, one of them, bibliotherapy, has a long history associated with librarianship as well as with psychology. Parkes discussed the development, diversification, and concerns of "institution libraries" in state and federal institutions for the developmentally disabled, the mentally ill, and the physically handicapped (*125*). Services, not only to the staff but also to the residents, are described, and thus, this work contributes to the understanding of the situation of the elderly in these settings. The role of the library is seen in relation to the human aspects of the institutional environment.

International Issues

From a historical perspective, the role of international information played a decisive role in the development of both the popular perceptions of aging and trends in age-related studies. Historians distinguish several waves of social and scientific influences that have flowed back and forth between Europe and the United States. For example, they point out the impact of the medical and biological research of Europe on American medical studies and, subsequently, on the negative image of the aged in popular science magazines and encyclopedias around the turn of the century (*16*). The 1920s are described as the era of an outpouring of American literature about how to combat old age and the influence of this wave on European thinking (*126*). Since its beginnings, the study of aging has developed strong ties among scientists around the world. In the United States, gerontology was said to be born out of international contacts. In the 1930s Vladimir Korenchevsky, a member of the British Branch of the International Club for Research on Aging, came to the United States to explore contacts with his colleagues and eventually was influential with the founding of the American Research Club on Aging. This alliance became a historical symbol of the prevailing theme of international exchange in the field of aging. The long tradition of scholars seeking out each other across political and geographic boundaries encompasses goals such as organizing international meetings and symposia in order to identify mutual philosophies and objectives; integrating research efforts into cross-national and cross-cultural projects; exploring new research concepts and methodologies; opening new channels for making research findings known; studying policy models and programs, and their transferability; and developing educational exchanges and cooperation. All these patterns were present in the cross-continental contacts of gerontologists and geriatrists, all of them residing in the more industrialized countries where the policy implications of the growing numbers of old people were first recognized. The exchange of ideas was the most intensive among researchers who formed the first international organizations in gerontology, with policy analysts, demographers, professional practitioners of various backgrounds, historians, and educators gradually joining in the international dialogue.

The evolution of cross-national ties in gerontology may be traced through the activities of professional societies, intergovernmental organizations, and international conferences. In the professional domain, the International Association of Gerontology was established in 1950 to promote research in several scientific fields. Its Committee on Social Science Research was formed 6 years later, demonstrating the need for demographic and socioeconomic data on all aspects of societal and individual aging. The association organizes an International Congress of Gerontology every 3 years to provide a forum for communication among scientists, practitioners, and educators. In the 1960s, the International Center of Social Gerontology took the lead in promoting coordination of research and the standardization of methodologies (*24*). The International Federation on Ageing publishes the quarterly *Ageing International*, and information on national organizations of senior citizens is available from the International Senior Citizens Association. These nongovernmental organizations (NGOs) are active in mobilizing international leadership, promoting research, and publishing.

Intergovernmental organizations began to move into the gerontological field in the early 1960s. Concerned with the situation of older workers, income maintenance, and social security, the International Labor Organization published *Older People: Work and Retirement* in 1962. The Food and Agriculture Organization and the World Health Organization have been conducting studies in nutrition of the elderly. The 1974 World Health Organization report, *The Planning and Organizing of Geriatric Services*, represented this organization's first attempt to deal with the health issues of the elderly in developing countries.

In 1974–1975 the secretary-general of the United Nations prepared a major report on the conditions and needs of the elderly, and proposed a framework for national policies (*127*). The report, together with recommendations of an Expert Group, constituted a basic overview of international issues. A brief discussion of the role of information systems was included. As a result of the General Assembly's resolution, in 1975, the Information Exchange System on Aging was initiated as a three-phased program to collect and coordinate information obtained from national correspondents and other sources.

In 1978 an International Conference on Aging, sponsored by the French Institut de la Vie under the auspices of the United Nations Fund for Population Activities, took place in New York. The theme, "Aging: A Framework of Characteristics and Considerations for Cooperative Efforts Between the Developing and Developed Regions of the World," included such concerns as: (*a*) the transmittal of awareness of issues in the field of aging to the developing countries, (*b*) transmittal of scientific knowledge and technology in gerontology to the Third World, and (*c*) transmittal of Third World traditions and experiences in this field to the developing world. As Beattie observed in his report, the meeting stressed the need to "distinguish between information exchange in the areas of scientific methods and technology and research findings from solutions to the societal and individual problems and issues related to aging" (*128*, p. 13).

Research in the 1950s and 1960s was concentrated in two broad areas: the social aspects of aging and the biomedical processes of aging. In both fields, researchers were seeking to form international teams for simultaneous investigations in several countries. In social gerontology, considerable attention was devoted to the social and cultural status of the aged in various societies. The orientation was characterized by Western anthropological and sociological approaches, one of the pioneering works being a sociocultural study of aging in some 71 societies by Simmons (*129*). As Press and McKool stated, "much of our knowledge about aging is based upon observation and inference from western industrial society" (*130*, p. 297). Even the truly cross-cultural projects, targeted on populations in non-Western countries, were conceptualized, organized, and conducted by Western researchers (*131*).

As these so-called non-Western societies gradually made their way into the center of world politics as "developing countries," the various degrees of industrialization and modernization they underwent began to change their social institutions and, at least in the urban areas, the life-style of large segments of their populations. Similarly, cultural traditions, such as the position of the elderly in society, began to show the impact of change. As a report of the World Health Organization observed: "The problems of the aged in the developing countries have not yet assumed the same importance as in the developed countries, nor have they attracted much attention. . . . The situation is, however, changing rapidly as a result of urbanization, industrialization, and a shift from a subsistence to a market economy" (*132*). At the same time, the political orientation of the educated leadership in most developing countries calls for more endogenous research as the basis of national policy making and development. The trend in many countries is toward government-directed research vested in small-scale, but locally staffed, projects—with technical aid in planning, research design, and evaluation coming from the large international donor agencies (*133*). Although the concepts of social gerontology have not yet spread to many developing countries, the trend toward endogenous research seems to signal a new era of international cooperation. If researchers in the developing areas of the world become engaged in studying the cultural and social impact of urbanization, the situation of the older members of society might become a more important research area for them than it is at the present. Then, the sharing of gerontological research information would become truly worldwide.

The second, and considerably less developed, field of gerontological information exchange encompasses national policies, legislation, economic measures, and social programs for the elderly. European countries, where the populations aged during the last quarter of the 19th century, have a more in-depth experience in this field than the United States (*134*). Most of the experiences of gerontologists in exchanging policy- and program-related information took place at conferences where the participants were mainly from Europe, the United States, and other industrialized countries. In spite of their differences in approach to the government's role in health care, income maintenance, and social welfare programs, industrialized countries share societal characteristics which make the exchange of social gerontological information relevant to them. Some of these social phenomena—for example, improved health care, advanced technology, increased leisure time, women in the work force, complex structure of institutional arrangements for the care of the elderly—generated an extensive volume of literature in recent years. This documentation is assumed to be accessible through bibliographic channels, although Beall reported that his study found weaknesses in the availability and utilization of such materials (*135*). The problem in gerontological information exchange among industrialized nations lies in the lack of adequate information mechanisms that would organize and repackage research findings originating in different countries for easy access by policy makers, planners, and practitioners.

Cooperation between developing countries and industrialized countries in exchanging social program–related information is practically restricted to information about social security systems. The regional conferences and publications of the International Social Security Association represent resources in this area. One of the problems of international collaboration regarding culturally determined issues, such as attitudes toward the aging, is the assumption that information about how policy models or social programs work in economically and technologically advanced countries will always be relevant to developing countries. This assumption is central to many information dissemination programs including technical consultation, conferences, newsletters, audiovisual packages, and other information products. There is a need to supplement the formal information activities of international organizations in gerontology by conferences and workshops that would bring together Third World policy makers and professionals who are concerned with the aging with their colleagues in industrialized countries for the informal discussion of needs and experiences in policy and program development.

Note Added in Proof. Several programs described in this article are no longer current; however, they have established valuable models of various gerontological information systems and services. The bibliography by Dr. Nathan Shock in the *Journal of Gerontology* was discontinued after the November 1980 issue. The Service Center for Aging Information (SCAN) is presently comprised of the following components: the Central Control Facility (CCF), contracted to InterAmerica Research Associates, Inc. (Rosslyn, Va.), and the Social Gerontology Resource Center (SGRC), under contract with the Franklin Research Center (Silver Spring, Md.). The latter component includes both the Social–Behavioral Sciences Resource Center and the Social Practice Resource Center. The newsletter *Information Exchange* provides current information on services.

REFERENCES

1. Vladimir Korenchevsky, "The Problem of Aging and the Ways and Means of Achieving the Rapid Progress of Gerontological Research," in *The Social and Biological Challenge of Our Aging Population*, Columbia University Press, New York, 1950, pp. 7–24.
2. J. E. Birren, ed., *Handbook of Aging and the Individual: Psychological and Biological Aspects*, University of Chicago Press, Chicago, 1959.
3. Clark Tibbitts, ed., *Handbook of Social Gerontology: Societal Aspects of Aging*, University of Chicago Press, Chicago, 1960.
4. Clark Tibbitts, "Origin, Scope, and Fields of Social Gerontology," Ref. *3*, pp. 3–26.
5. E. W. Burgess, ed., *Aging in Western Societies: A Survey of Social Gerontology*, University of Chicago Press, Chicago, 1960.
6. Robert H. Binstock and Ethel Shanas, *Handbook of Aging and the Social Sciences*, Van Nostrand, New York, 1976.
7. C. E. Finch and Leonard Hayflick, eds., *Handbook of the Biology of Aging*, Van Nostrand, New York, 1977.
8. J. E. Birren and K. W. Schaie, eds., *Handbook of the Psychology of Aging*, Van Nostrand, New York, 1977.
9. George L. Maddox and James Wiley, "Scope, Concepts and Methods in the Study of Aging," in *Handbook of Aging and the Social Sciences* (R. H. Binstock and E. Shanas, eds.), Van Nostrand, New York, 1976, pp. 3–34.
10. Ralph Goldman, "Geriatrics as a Specialty: Problems and Prospects," *Gerontologist*, **14**(6), 468–471 (December 1974).
11. Raymond Harris, "Model for a Graduate Geriatric Program at a University Medical School," *Gerontologist*, **15**(4), 304–307 (1975).
12. J. J. Pattee, "Training Objectives of a Well Developed Geriatrics Program," *J. Geriatrics Soc.*, **26**(4), 167–169 (1978).
13. United States, National Institute on Aging, *Aging and Medical Education*, Bethesda, Md., 1979.
14. C. Amechi Akpom and Suzanne Mayer, "Survey of Geriatric Education in U.S. Medical Schools," *J. Med. Educ.*, **53**(1), 66–68 (January 1978).
15. Michel Philibert, "Philosophical Approach to Gerontology," in *Dimensions of Aging: Readings* (J. Hendricks and C. Davis Hendricks, eds.), Winthrop Publishers, Cambridge, Mass., 1979, pp. 379–394.
16. W. A. Achenbaum, *Old Age in the New Land: The American Experience Since 1790*, Johns Hopkins Press, Baltimore, Md., 1978.
17. Stephen Bailey, "The Several Ages of Learning," *Change*, **8**(4), 35–39 (May 1976).
18. Bernice L. Neugarten, "Age Groups in American Society and the Rise of the Young-Old," *Ann. Am. Acad. Political Social Sci.*, **415**, 187–198 (September 1974).
19. Leonard D. Cain, "Aging and the Law," in *Handbook of Aging and the Social Sciences* (R. H. Binstock and E. Shanas, eds.), Van Nostrand, New York, 1976, pp. 342–368.
20. Charles W. Crawford, "Oral History: The State of the Profession," *Oral Hist. Rev.*, 1974, pp. 1–9.
21. Amelia R. Fry and Willa Baum, "A Janus Look at History," *Am. Archivist*, **32**(4), 319–326 (1969).
22. Matilda W. Riley and M. E. Johnson, *Aging and Society: Aging and the Professions*, Vol. 2, Russell Sage Foundation, New York, 1969.

23. Robert J. Havighurst, "The Status of Research in Applied Social Gerontology," *Gerontologist*, **9**(4), Part II (Winter 1969).
24. S. Bergman, "Coordination of Research Policies in Social Gerontology," in *First International Course in Social Gerontology*, International Center of Social Gerontology, Lisbon, Portugal, 1970, pp. 101–110.
25. Robert N. Butler, "Research Programs of the National Institute on Aging," *Public Health Rep.*, **92**(1), 3–8 (January–February 1977).
26. United States, National Institute on Aging, *Our Future Selves: A Research Plan on Aging,* Prepared by the National Advisory Council on Aging, Bethesda, Md., 1979.
27. United States, Administration on Aging, *Older Americans Act of 1965, as Amended: History and Related Acts*, Department of Health, Education, and Welfare, Washington, D.C., July 1979.
28. Lilly Cohen, Marie Oppedisano-Reich, and Kathleen Hamilton Gerardi, comps. and eds., *Funding in Aging: Public, Private and Voluntary*, 2nd ed., Adelphi University Press, Garden City, N.Y., 1979, © 1977.
29. M. S. Goldstein, A. C. Marcus, and N. P. Rausch, "The Nonutilization of Evaluation Research," *Pacific Sociol. Rev.*, **21**(1), 21–44 (June 1978).
30. C. H. Weiss, ed., *Using Social Research for Public Policy-making*, Columbia University, New York, 1976.
31. C. H. Weiss, ed., "Research for Policy's Sake: The Enlightenment Function of Social Research," *Policy Anal.*, Fall 1977, pp. 531–545.
32. Walter M. Beattie, Jr., "Aging and the Social Services," in *Handbook of Aging and the Social Sciences* (R. H. Binstock and E. Shanas, eds.), Van Nostrand, New York, 1976, pp. 619–642.
33. United States, National Science Foundation, *Extending the Human Life Span: Social Policy and Social Ethics* (Bernice L. Neugarten and Robert J. Havighurst, eds.), Government Printing Office, Washington, D.C., 1977.
34. United States, General Accounting Office, *Report to the Congress on the Well-being of Older People in Cleveland, Ohio,* Washington, D.C., 1977 (HRD-77-70).
35. United States, General Accounting Office, *Conditions of Older People: National Information System Needed,* Washington, D.C., 1979 (HRD-79-95).
36. Samuel Granick and Morton H. Kleban, "Data File of NIMH Study of Healthy Aged Males," *Gerontologist*, **17**(6), 531–536 (December 1977).
37. United States, Bureau of the Census, *Demographic Aspects of Aging and the Older Population in the United States*, Government Printing Office, Washington, D.C., 1976 (Current Population Reports, Ser. P-23, No. 59; ERIC, ED 124 476**).
38. H. I. Kindig and Robert Warren, "Adequacy of Census Data in Planning and Advocacy for the Elderly," *Gerontologist,* **16**(5), 392–396 (1976).
39. Institute for Interdisciplinary Studies, *Indicators of the Status of the Elderly in the United States*, Minneapolis, Minn., 1974.
40. F. C. Pampel, *Social Change and the Aged: Recent Trends in the United States*, University of Iowa, Iowa City, 1980.
41. United States, Bureau of the Census, *Social and Economic Characteristics of the Older Population: 1978*, Government Printing Office, Washington, D.C., 1979 (Current Population Reports, Special Studies, Ser. P-23, No. 85).
42. B. D. Gold, "The Role of the Federal Government in the Provision of Social Services to Older Persons," in *Political Consequences of Aging*, Annals of the American Academy of Political and Social Science, Vol. 415, AAPSS, September 1974, pp. 55–69.
43. Duran Bell et al., *Delivering Services to Elderly Members of Minority Groups: A Critical Review of the Literature*, Rand Corporation, Santa Monica, Calif., 1976.
44. United States, Congress, House, Select Committee on Aging, *Fragmentation of Services for the Elderly, Hearings . . . , 94th Congress, 1st Session, April 4, 1977*, Government Printing Office, Washington, D.C., 1977.
45. New York State, Office for the Aging, *News* (Albany), **6**(2), 2–3 (1980).
46. United States, Congress, House, Select Committee on Aging, *The Emerging Aging Network: A Directory of State and Area Agencies on Aging*, Government Printing Office, Washington, D.C., 1978 (95th Congress, 2nd Session, Committee Print 166).

47. C. L. Estes, *The Aging Enterprise: A Critical Examination of Social Policies and Services for the Aged*, Jossey-Bass, San Francisco, 1979.
48. United States, Administration on Aging, National Clearinghouse on Aging, *Cumulative Index of AoA Discretionary Projects, 1965–1978*, Department of Health, Education, and Welfare, Washington, D.C., 1979.
49. H. J. Pratt, *The Gray Lobby*, University of Chicago Press, Chicago, 1976.
50. L. A. Baumhover and J. D. Jones, eds., *Handbook of American Aging Programs,* Greenwood Press, Westport, Conn., 1977.
51. J. Dancy, Jr., *The Black Elderly: A Guide for Practitioners*, University of Michigan, Institute of Gerontology, Ann Arbor, Mich., 1977.
52. Linda Horn and Elma Griesel, *Nursing Homes: A Citizen's Action Guide*, Beacon Press, Boston, Mass., 1977.
53. Barbara Thomas et al., *Citizen Participation in Identifying and Prioritizing the Needs of Older Adults and Retired Persons*, Multidisciplinary Gerontology Center of Iowa, Iowa City, 1977.
54. H. W. Demone, Jr., *Stimulating Human Services Reform*, United States Department of Health, Education, and Welfare, Project SHARE, Rockville, Md., 1978 (Human Services Monograph Ser. No. 8).
55. A. C. Cohen, *The Citizen as the Integrating Agent: Productivity in the Human Services*, United States Department of Health, Education, and Welfare, Project SHARE, Rockville, Md., 1978 (Monograph Ser. 3).
56. Emily H. Miller and Neal E. Cutler, "Toward a Comprehensive Information System in Gerontology: A Survey of Problems, Resources, and Potential Solutions," *Gerontologist*, **16**(1), 198–206 (June 1976).
57. George Thomas Beall and Susan Mulak, "Perspectives on the Availability and Utilization of Foreign-source Informational Materials in Gerontology," *Gerontologist*, **17**(6), 537–543 (December 1977).
58. Bruce Hicks, *Computer Outreach*, University of Illinois, Department of Secondary Education, Urbana, Ill., September 1976 (ERIC, ED 138 293).
59. Elizabeth A. Brindle, Marta L. Dosa, and Gerald M. Gee, "A Prototype Gerontological Information Program," in American Society for Information Science, *Information Management in the 1980's*, Proceedings of the 40th Annual Meeting, Chicago, Illinois, 1977, Vol. 14, Knowledge Industry Publications, Inc., White Plains, N.Y., 1977, p. 7 (abstract and microfiche text).
60. Willie M. Edwards and Frances Flynn, *Gerontology: A Core List of Significant Works*, University of Michigan, Institute of Gerontology, Ann Arbor, Mich., 1978.
61. United States, Administration on Aging, National Clearinghouse on Aging, *Thesaurus,* 2nd ed., Department of Health, Education, and Welfare, Washington, D.C., 1977, © 1976.
62. United States, Administration on Aging, "Guide to AoA Programs: Research and Demonstration, Education and Training," Prepared for the Gerontological Society, 31st Annual Scientific Meeting, Dallas, Texas, November 16–20, 1978, Department of Health, Education, and Welfare, Washington, D.C., 1978.
63. United States, Administration on Aging, National Clearinghouse on Aging, *A Comprehensive Inventory and Analysis of Federally Supported Research in Aging, 1966–1975*, Department of Health, Education, and Welfare, Washington, D.C., 1976.
64. Ethel Percy Andrus Gerontology Center, "The Gerontological Information Center Invites *You* to Interactively Search Its Database," University of Southern California, Los Angeles, 1978.
65. Carol L. Van Steenberg and Robin B. Karasik, "Get KWIC Help: An Information Service to Assist Trainers in Aging," Paper presented at the Annual Meeting of the Gerontological Society, New York, New York, October 29, 1976 (ERIC, ED 143 912).
66. Lockie Jayne McGekee and Susan Gaylord, eds., *Analysis and Selection of Training Resources in Aging*, Duke University, Center for the Study of Aging and Human Development, KWIC Training Resources in Aging Project, Durham, N.C., 1978.
67. Texas State Department of Public Welfare, *Aging Research Utilization Report* (Research Utilization Project, The Generation Connection, Austin, Texas), **3**(4), 14 (Winter 1976–1977).
68. University of California, *Innovative Developments in Aging Directory*, Second printing, PROJECT IDEA, San Francisco, May 1978, © 1977.

69. Marta L. Dosa, Elizabeth A. Brindle, and Gerald M. Gee, *Gerontological Information Systems and Services*, Syracuse University, School of Information Studies, Syracuse, N.Y., 1980.
70. H. Jean Owens, "Directory of Gerontological Libraries and Resource Centers in the United States: A Preliminary Draft," Wayne State University, Institute of Gerontology, Learning Resources Center, Detroit, Mich., n.d.
71. Patrick Wash, "Librarians Serving Older People," *Occupational Outlook Quart.*, **22**(1), 48–52 (Spring 1978).
72. David A. Peterson, "Educational Gerontology: The State of the Art," *Educ. Gerontol.*, **1**(1), 61–68 (January–March 1976).
73. Ira F. Ehrlich and Phyllis D. Ehrlich, "A Four-part Framework to Meet the Responsibilities of Higher Education to Gerontology," *Educ. Gerontol.*, **1**, 251–260 (1976).
74. White House Conference on Aging, *Toward a National Policy on Aging, Final Report*, Vol. 2, Government Printing Office, Washington, D.C., 1973 (ERIC, ED 072 346).
75. Howard W. Dickstein, "Survey of Needs for Services to the Elderly: Final Report," Manchester Community College, Hartford, Conn., June 1, 1972, 82 pp.
76. "Working with Older People," *Occupational Outlook Quart.*, **20**(3), (Fall 1976).
77. Robert N. Butler and Walter Spieth, "Trends in Training in Research Gerontology," *Educ. Gerontol.*, **2**(2), 111–113 (1977).
78. Sean M. Sweeney, "New Directions for the Administration on Aging Education and Training Program," *Educ. Gerontol.*, **5**(1), 1–15 (January–March 1980).
79. Robert Lindsay, "Gerontology Comes of Age," *New York Times*, Sect. 13, Col. 5, 11, January 8, 1978.
80. Abraham Monk, "Gerontological Education: Propositions for Curriculum Planning in Higher Education," *Educ. Gerontol.*, **3**(3), 265–275 (July–September 1978).
81. Harold R. Johnson et al., eds., "Foundations for Gerontological Education," *Gerontologist*, **20**(3), Part II (June 1980).
82. Virginia M. Gilliland and Tom Hickey, "Curriculum Design for the In-service Training Context," Paper presented at the 101st Annual Meeting of the American Public Health Association, San Francisco, California, November 8, 1973; Symposium on Training Models for Delivery of Health Care to the Elderly, Pennsylvania State University, College of Human Development, University Park, Pennsylvania, June 1975, 17 pp.
83. Robert J. Havighurst, "Education Through the Adult Life Span," *Educ. Gerontol.*, **1**(1), 41–51 (January–March 1976).
84. R. E. Patterson et al., *Lifelong Learning in America*, Jossey-Bass, San Francisco, 1979.
85. C. Bolton, "Gerontology in Higher Education: The State of the Field," Paper presented at the Gerontological Society, 30th Annual Scientific Meeting, San Francisco, Calif., 1977 (ERIC, ED 154 300**).
86. M. Seltzer, H. Sterns, and T. Hickey, eds., *Gerontology in Higher Education: Perspectives and Issues*, Wadsworth Publications, Belmont, Calif., 1978.
87. Betsy M. Sprouse, ed., *National Directory of Educational Programs in Gerontology*, Association for Gerontology in Higher Education, Washington, D.C., 1978, © 1976 (ERIC, ED 140 015**).
88. Patricia K. Alpaugh et al., "Age and Creativity: Implications for Education and Teachers," *Educ. Gerontol.*, **1**(1), 17–37 (January–March 1976).
89. Walter M. Beattie, Jr., "Our Aging Population: Implications for Information and Communication Sciences," Paper presented at a Research Conference on Communication and Aging, Michigan State University, East Lansing, Mich., March 6, 1975.
90. L. K. Obler and M. L. Albert, eds., *Language and Communication in the Elderly: Clinical, Therapeutic, and Experimental Issues*, Boston University Medical School and Boston Veterans Administration Medical Center, Boston, Mass., 1980.
91. N. Cutler, "Demographic, Social-psychological and Political Factors in the Politics of Aging," *Am. Political Sci. Rev.*, **71**(3), 10–13 (September 1977).
92. J. W. Dimmick, T. A. McCain, and W. T. Bolton, "Media Use and the Life Span: Notes on Theory and Method," *Am. Behav. Scientist*, **23**(1), 7–32 (September–October 1979).
93. Jon Hendricks and C. Davis Hendricks, *Aging in Mass Society: Myths and Realities*, Winthrop Publishers, Cambridge, Mass., 1977.

94. T. J. Young, "Use of the Media by Older Adults," *Am. Behav. Scientist*, **23**(1), 119–136 (September–October 1979).
95. Beatrice Ferleger, "Natural Helping Networks for the Elderly: Improving Service Delivery Through the Informal System," in Community Council of Greater New York, Research Utilization Unit, *Research Utilization Briefs*, 1979.
96. Marvin B. Sussman, *Family Systems in the 1970's: Analysis, Policies and Programs*, Case Western Reserve University, Department of Sociology, Cleveland, Ohio, 1971.
97. J. L. Ruffini and H. F. Todd, Jr., "A Network Model for Leadership Development among the Elderly," *Gerontologist,* **19**(2), 158–162 (April 1979).
98. J. E. O'Brien and D. L. Wagner, "Help Seeking by the Frail Elderly: Problems in Network Analysis," *Gerontologist*, **20**(1), 78–83 (February 1980).
99. Nicholas Long, *Information and Referral Services: Research Findings*, Vol. 1 and Appendix, United States Department of Health, Education, and Welfare, Office of Human Development, Administration on Aging, Washington, D.C., 1977 (ERIC, ED 154 282; for 1975 edition, Appendix 1, see ERIC, ED 154 281**).
100. J. E. Burkhardt, "Evaluating Information and Referral Services," *Gerontologist*, **19**(1), 28–33 (February 1979).
101. Jurgen Schmandt, Victor Bach, and B. A. Radin, "Information and Referral Services for Elderly Welfare Recipients," *Gerontologist*, **19**(1), 21–28 (February 1979).
102. United Nations, Educational, Scientific, and Cultural Organization, *Guidelines on Referral Centers*, Paris, 1979.
103. United States, Administration on Aging, National Clearinghouse on Aging, *Information and Referral: How to Do It,* Vol. 1, Parts 1–4, Government Printing Office, Washington, D.C., 1977.
104. United States, National Commission on Libraries and Information Science, "Community Information and Referral Service," News Release, April 29, 1980.
105. M. C. Javelin, "How Library Service to the Aging Has Developed," *Lib. Trends*, **21**(3), 367–389 (January 1973).
106. *National Survey of Library Services to the Aging,* by Booz, Allen, and Hamilton, Inc., for United States Office of Education, Cleveland Public Library, Cleveland, Ohio, 1971.
107. *National Survey of Library Services to the Aging (Second Phase)*, by Booz, Allen, and Hamilton, Inc., for United States Office of Education, Cleveland Public Library, Cleveland, Ohio, 1972.
108. E. E. Kanner, "The Impact of Gerontological Concepts on Principles of Librarianship," Ph.D. Dissertation, University of Wisconsin, Madison, 1972.
109. Eleanor Phinney, "Library Services to the Aging," *Lib. Trends*, **21**(3), 359–458 (January 1973).
110. R. T. Jordan, *Tomorrow's Library: Direct Access and Delivery*, Bowker, New York, 1970.
111. Dorothy Romani, "Guidelines for Library Service to the Institutionalized Aging," *Am. Lib.*, **1**(3), 286–289 (March 1970).
112. Genevieve M. Casey, "Library and Information Needs of Aging Americans," in *Library and Information Needs of the Nation: Proceedings of a Conference on the Needs of Occupational, Ethnic, and Other Groups in the United States*, Government Printing Office, Washington, D.C., 1974, pp. 162–170 (ERIC, ED 101 716).
113. "Service to the Impaired Elderly," *Am. Lib.*, **10**(4), 211 (April 1979).
114. Genevieve M. Casey, "Public Library Service to the Aging," *Am. Lib.*, October 1971, pp. 999–1004.
115. American Library Association, Reference and Adult Services Division, "Guidelines for Library Services to an Aging Population," *RQ*, **4,** 237–239 (Spring 1975).
116. Dennis R. Hameister, "Conceptual Model for the Library's Service to the Elderly," *Educ. Gerontol.*, **1**(3), 279–284 (July 1976).
117. Leigh Estabrook, "Emerging Trends in Community Library Services," *Lib. Trends*, Fall 1979, pp. 151–164.
118. A. S. Mavor, J. O. Toro, and E. R. DeProspo, *The Role of Public Libraries in Adult Independent Learning*, Parts 1–2, College Entrance Examination Board, New York, 1976.
119. Ann Erteschik, *Library Programs Worth Knowing About*, United States Office of Education and Chief Officers of State Library Agencies, Washington, D.C., September 1977 (ERIC, ED 145 858).

120. Harriet L. Eisman, "Public Library Programs," *Wilson Lib. Bull.*, **53**(8), 564–569 (April 1979).
121. Stephanie Ardito, "Advocacy and Information: Research Issues and Practice," Paper presented at the 32nd Annual Scientific Meeting of the Gerontological Society, Washington, D.C., November 27, 1979.
122. Jane Robbins, *Citizen Participation and Public Library Policy*, Scarecrow Press, Metuchen, N.J., 1975.
123. Paul J. Little and J. Richard Gilliland, "OASES in Oklahoma," *Lib. J.*, **102**(13), 1458–1461 (July 1977).
124. Bissy Genova, "Video and Cable: Emerging Forms of Library Service," *Lib. Trends*, **28**(2), 297–310 (1979).
125. Lethene Parkes, "The Library in the Institution," *Lib. Trends*, **26**(3), 319–340 (Winter 1978).
126. P. N. Stearns, *Old Age in European Society: The Case of France*, Holmes and Meier, New York, 1976.
127. United Nations, Department of Economic and Social Affairs, *The Aging: Trends and Policies*, New York, 1975 (ST/ESA/22).
128. Walter M. Beattie, Jr., "Aging: The Developed and Developing World," A Report on Recommendations of the International Meeting on Aging Sponsored by the Institut de la Vie under the Auspices of the United Nations Fund for Population Activities, United Nations, New York, April 3–5, 1978.
129. L. W. Simmons, *The Role of the Aged in Primitive Societies*, Yale University Press, New Haven, Conn., 1945.
130. Irwin Press and Mike McKool, Jr., "Social Structure and Status of the Aged: Toward Some Valid Cross-cultural Generalizations," *Int. J. Aging Human Devel.*, **3**(4), 297–306 (1972).
131. D. H. Lowell, "Trends in Anthropological Gerontology: From Simmons to the Seventies," *Int. J. Aging Human Devel.*, **7**(3), 211–220 (1976).
132. World Health Organization, *Planning and Organization of Geriatric Services*, Geneva, 1974 (Technical Report Ser. 548).
133. Uma J. Lele, *The Design of Rural Development: Lessons from Africa*, Johns Hopkins University Press for the World Bank, Baltimore, Md., 1975.
134. Gerald Musgrave, *Social Security Worldwide: A Classified Bibliography*, VANCE Bibliographies, Monticello, Ill., 1978 (Public Administration Ser. 1).
135. George Thomas Beall, "Emergence of an Information System in Aging: The International Context," Remarks prepared for presentation at the Symposium on Emergence of an Information System in Aging, Gerontological Society Annual Meeting, New York, 1976.

STEPHANIE C. ARDITO
MARTA L. DOSA

HISTORICAL BIBLIOGRAPHY

Bibliography is the study of books as material objects. Historical bibliography, consequently, is the history of every aspect of that study. It is an integral part of the whole field of bibliographic studies and can only be removed or ignored at the risk of great loss to bibliography in general. In spite of this, many discussions on the nature of bibliography either down-play its role or ignore it completely. Two reasons above all may have contributed to this situation.

Historical bibliography must exist as a part of historical studies as a whole. It comprises activities of the human mind which cannot be divorced from man's other activities and accomplishments. The physical objects which are the subject of historical bibliography are themselves both cause and effect of human change and development. It is not too uncouth a generalization to say that a book was the root cause of many of the world's great revolutions. It is equally true that great books have grown out of revolutions. Hitler's *Mein Kampf* is as true for the first statement as Clarendon's *History of the Rebellion* is of the second. It is obviously impossible to disassociate "the book" from history itself. This is quite apart from the status of books which are primarily, or perhaps solely, the record and interpretation of historical events. Instances also abound in which not only is the text of the book of historical significance, but also the circumstances of its authorship and publication are of historical concern. The *Marprelate Tracts* are important even when the text is viewed in isolation, but when the tracts are explained in terms of their authorship and the particular methods of production and distribution, their additional impact on an understanding of their times is very marked. Aspects of the development of the book trade are, however, rarely considered as part of the web and woof of history by professional historians. It is difficult to see how they can be so largely disregarded in those chambers of history where they seem to be most relevant; namely, the social, cultural, and economic. In the introduction to his *English Social History*, G. M. Trevelyan wrote:

> Social history might be defined negatively as the history of a people with the politics left out. It is perhaps difficult to leave out the politics from the history of any people, particularly the English people. But as so many history books have consisted of political annals with little reference to their social environment, a reversal of that method may have its uses to redress the balance. During my own lifetime a third very flourishing sort of history has come into existence, the economic, which greatly assists the serious study of social history. For the social scene grows out of economic conditions, to much the same extent that political events in their turn grow out of social conditions. Without social history, economic history is barren and political history is unintelligible.
>
> But social history does not merely provide the required link between economic and political history. It has also its own positive value and peculiar concern. Its scope may be defined as the daily life of the inhabitants of the land in past ages: this includes the human as well as the economic relation of different classes to one another, the character of family and household life, the conditions of labour and of leisure, the attitude of man to nature, the culture of each age as it arose out of these general conditions of life, and took ever-changing forms in religion, literature and music, architecture, learning and thought (*1*).

This delimitation covers the particular interests and concerns of historical bibliography in the wider historical field. In the same introduction, Trevelyan wrote, "Our imagination craves to behold our ancestors as they really were, going about their daily business and daily pleasure." In general historical terms this is similar to the attitude expressed by McKerrow throughout his *Introduction to Bibliography* (*2*). His stress was on the importance in bibliographic studies of a complete understanding of what went on in a printing office. Only by the exercise of the imagination, based upon a firm knowledge of the methods of the printing processes, can reasonable deductions be made to explain the bibliographic problems encountered in a book. Historical bibliography is, without doubt or shadow of contradiction, an aspect of historical studies in general and of social, cultural, and economic history in particular (*3*).

Unfortunately, the chief places in which studies similar to this have been taught for the past many decades have been schools of librarianship. The term "unfortunate" is applicable because in many cases such courses have been labeled "history of the book," or something similar, and have exhibited many of the restrictions which are suggested by the title. They have tended all too often to be divorced from other courses of bibliographic study and have not frequently been associated with historical courses. The result has been, in divers instances, the development of a course which exists in isolation from other areas of study to which it is, by nature, closely allied. It has often, but not invariably, been developed as a course which exhibited an apron-string attachment to the "dame-school" theory of history, reminiscent of the days when the learning of history was associated with the parrotlike memorization and regurgitation of dates. Historical bibliography, along the same lines, consisted of a succession of names of printers and their major works, with little understanding of the forces which created the printing situation and the effect caused by the publication. The final indignity has often been that such a course has been regarded as, and frequently openly so described, an "enrichment course," with the implication that it is available if anyone is interested but that it is not really fundamental to any area of librarianship. Bibliography needs continuous redefinition and, because it exists primarily to serve other disciplines, has to be evaluated in terms of its relationship to those associated fields, but the core of the matter must always be the light which historical understanding can shed upon bibliographic problems. This can be demonstrated with reference to certain specific areas.

The history of the development and use of the varied materials which have been used to convey ideas over the centuries is of basic importance. Clay, papyrus, prepared skins, and paper have been the main materials over the centuries. The sequence of use of these substances provides the broad background to the study, but of equal importance is the pattern of use of each category of material. The skins which were used as, primarily, writing materials would be those which were largely native to the area of their writing. Unprepared skins could not travel distantly; prepared skins were costly to transport, and the need did not arise so long as some type of skin was locally available. It also depended upon the total economy of an area because, naturally, since skins do not regrow on animals, the local customs had also to support the disposal of the flesh. It is often necessary in certain areas of bibliographic examination to establish some basic facts about the membranes which have been used in a particular instance, especially so far as date and nature of the skins is concerned. Following the discovery of the Dead Sea Scrolls, this area of investigation was among the earliest pursued. Dating was by means of the jars in which the scrolls were stored, the linen wrappings around the scrolls, and the leather of the scrolls themselves. Fragments of blank samples of the skins were tested in a laboratory of leather technology and shown, by their nature and the grouping of the hair follicles, to be of young goats and lambs. In the examination of paper, dating can be by watermarks or by an analysis of the constituent fibers in the paper. The former can, in theory, provide reasonably specific dating for paper, and as our methodology improves and our repository of dated watermark designs becomes larger, it should enable much more precise dating to be accomplished.

The work which Allan Stevenson did on the *Constance Missal* (*4*) and the Netherlandish block books (*5*) provides excellent examples of the application of the method. The paper analysis as conducted in the Carter–Pollard investigation of the T. J. Wise forgeries provided an example of the second category (*6*). The fourth chapter of their *Enquiry*, in which the paper was discussed, was a brief survey of the history of papermaking materials in the 19th century. This perspective indicated quite clearly that the three categories of paper which they isolated—(*a*) pamphlets containing esparto, (*b*) esparto papers with minute traces of chemical wood, (*c*) chemical wood papers—were all wrong historically for the dates which the pamphlets bore.

The history of papermaking, technically and economically considered, has made great strides in the post–World War II years, as can be seen by studying the publications of the Paper Publications Society (*7*). Paper evidence has contributed significantly to bibliographic studies during the last generation and it has largely been of a historical nature. In spite of this, there is still much that we do not know and which we need to know if we are to have sufficient historical background to enable us to view bibliographic problems in their right setting. For many periods we know little about the economic aspects of the paper trade, including such ancillary but important matters as tariff duties. We do not have sufficient and accurate information regarding the location and production of paper mills. Following closely upon this, there is only sporadic access to the question of supply of paper from the mill or supplier to the printing house. This entails linking this study with the development of trade routes in general and all the well-developed lines which corresponded throughout the ages to the journeyings of Chaucer's shipman, "twixt Middleburgh and Orwell."

The history of type design and typefounding is another clearly established area. In the early days of modern bibliographic studies—that is, in the last quarter of the 19th century and the early years of the 20th century—this was the most clearly defined area of bibliographic studies, and it was approached almost entirely from the historical standpoint. This was due to a circumstance which was itself of historical significance. Paleography is very properly a part of bibliographic studies since it deals with the one feature of manuscripts which allows them to be placed for provenance and period more accurately than any other bibliographic feature. The handwriting of manuscripts provides evidence as to period and place of writing to a remarkable degree of accuracy. Even the idiosyncrasies of an individual scribe can be noticed and recorded, making later recognition in another manuscript a matter of reasonable possibility. The ability to know handwriting styles and individual peculiarities must obviously depend upon a minute and painstaking study of the various hands. This was the area of expertise possessed by many of the early bibliographers before they turned their attentions to the printed book and, in many instances, to the early printed book in particular. As was only natural, they viewed typography as the natural historical successor of paleography, as indeed it was. When they turned their attentions to typography as evidence in early printed books, they found very similar sets of circumstances. Types were designed and founded to meet local demands and frequently to suit the individual needs of a particular printer. The more experimentally minded the printer and the earlier on in the very fluid history of early typography, the more likely it is that there will have been successive redesigning and recutting of the type. Some types were much more admired by other type designers and printers than were other styles, and so they became designs which influenced later developments. It will be readily apparent from the writings of the early bibliographers how much this affected their outlook and dictated the kind of problem to which they addressed themselves. Recent events give several examples of the strengths and the weaknesses of historical studies in type design as contributions to bibliographic analysis.

When the so-called Cracow Fragments came up for reconsideration shortly after World War II, much of the argument was based on the very early development of a type. The Weisbaden Fragment had for a long time been tentatively dated as being of 1447, mainly on the nonbibliographic evidence that the work itself was a calendar for 1448. It was not regarded as reasonable that such a work should have been printed any later than the year before its use. On typographic grounds, however, this solution was open to doubt. In the very early years of movable type, printing designs changed with very great rapidity, and the probable date of a type can frequently be narrowed down to a brief period of time. On this basis the date of the Weisbaden Fragment was much more satisfactorily placed about 10 years later than the 1447 date suggested by informal evidence. On reexamination, it became clear that the work was not a calendar which would, as supposed, have been valid for the following year only but rather an "astrological ephemeris" for popular rather than "scientific" use and so had a life expectancy of 2 to 12 years. In this case typographic evidence related to the development of type proved to be decisive.

That this is not always so can be seen in the studies related to the *Constance Missal*, to which reference has already been made. In much of the discussion which took place regarding the typographic evidence of the missal, an early date was advanced (*8*). The evidence of the paper is now generally regarded as more conclusive, and the historians of typography are, therefore, now faced with the task of explaining the apparently early date of typographic design at a considerably later date than that which they had hitherto advanced.

Another area of typographic history is that of the relation of type design to other arts, including some which are basically nonbibliographic. In the early days of movable type printing, the important relationship was between type design and manuscript letter forms. Indeed the relationship is so close at all periods that Stanley Morison, one of the greatest of typographic historians, normally spoke in general of "letter design," of which some aspects might be calligraphic and some typographic. In the experimental years of printing there was, naturally, one model only for the printer or typographer to use—the manuscript book. In general, that model would be a manuscript book of the area in which the printer worked and a book of the same kind. Thus the type of a Mainz-printed Bible of 1455 would have a type whose design was as close as possible to the book hand which would be used in a Bible written in Mainz at the same period. Similarly a printed book of tales of romance and chivalry of Paris in 1475 would have a type similar to the hand used in a contemporary Parisian book of the same kind. When the manuscript book ceased to be of general importance there was no cessation of outside influences on type design. The increased interest in engraving in the 18th century had a decided influence on the development of modern-faced type designs, and it is of particular interest that Baskerville was, at an early stage in his career, one who lettered on stone. Similarly the emergence of sans-serif type in the third decade of the 20th century is a part of the same artistic expression which produced *art deco* and the Bauhaus movement in architecture.

Much bibliographic work of an analytical nature must still be largely based on typographic evidence. The principle, but not the practice, of this is easy to establish in areas such as incunabula where change was rapid and where the whole structure of the typefounding industry and the use of its products by printers make it possible to attribute certain type styles to particular printers with a reasonable chance of success. As the typefoundries grew and their types were available for widespread and general sale, the close relationship between foundry and printer begins to disappear. A large part of the problem of using typographic evidence more effectively than can at present be done is the lack of a body of evidence as to the trade practices of the foundries. With which countries in general and with which printers in particular did individual foundries trade? What was the range of type designs and sizes available from a particular foundry at a particular time? There are extremely few type specimen sheets extant, and, of those, an even smaller number have been reproduced to make comparisons possible.

It is a logical step to move from a consideration of type to think of the problems related to ink. The comparatively few references made to ink, until a very short time ago, were limited to aspects of production standards and technique. Two certain allusions were to the great care which, for example, John Baskerville and William Morris took over the manufacture and the storage of their inks. But these were usually designed to emphasize their qualities as printers and bore more on the aesthetic qualities of their work than something which was innately bibliographic. Special cases, however, tend to bring about reevaluations, and this is what has happened with ink. Because few bibliographic investigations depended upon the analysis of ink, there was little cause to study the history and development of ink manufacture. This is not to say that there had been no studies at all, but simply that they frequently did not have bibliographic motivation and, naturally, did not stress those aspects. Recent investigations have, however, used the evidence of the ink in certain cases with important results. One of the most important was in relation to the Vinland Map. During the investigations which were carried out in order to test the authenticity of the map, the ink was subjected to analysis. The presence of anatase titanium dioxide in the ink was sufficient to suggest that it was a modern forgery because this anatase was not produced commercially until around 1920. On the other hand, its presence in the ink could have come from a source that acted on the map since its original writing. Whatever the final outcome, it does not lessen the importance of a knowledge of the constitution and manufacture of the ink used. It is clear that over the centuries of writing and printing with ink a variety of formulas were used in its manufacture, yet certain knowledge related to its historical development is still not well documented. There is only one major work dealing with the history of ink and it dates from very early in this century (*9*).

Another area of historical development within the book trade to which attention has been given for some years is that of printing house practice. Some work in the late 19th century was very much along these lines and led to some important developments at a crucial point in the early growth of modern bibliographic studies. It was a matter of considerable influence that men like William Blades wrote and talked so much and so knowledgeably about the work of the printer and his shop at a time when the importance of these activities within the history of the book was being appreciated almost for the first time. It may well be that his initial interest was primarily antiquarian. The establishment of the Saint Bride's Museum at the same time is a further token of that same attitude. Any original limitations relating to this, however, did not last very long. Bibliographers were following rapidly in the wake of Blades who followed the trail further and applied the knowledge more specifically to bibliographic studies. Of the great triumvirate at the beginning of the 20th century, it was McKerrow who went the furthest in this direction with the greatest speed. He opened up to modern view for the first time the intricate operations of the Elizabethan printing press. The incunabulists had, for the most part, not paid great attention to the operation of the press and the running of the office which was responsible for the books which they were studying. Since McKerrow, it is difficult to the point of impossibility for the bibliographer of any period to imagine that the press methods of any town at a particular time are not important as the bedrock of much of the work. Studies have been conducted which attempt to understand the operations of one particular press and even more so in relation to one particular work. The modern studies on the characteristics of individual compositors take this theme a step further and encourage us to seek more detail regarding the real individuals behind such tentative ascriptions. It has always been difficult to establish the true identity of many of the people working within the book trade, and increasingly the search has been directed into the archives of printing establishments and organizations. The measure of success which can follow this approach, and which should encourage further investigation on similar lines, can be judged by such recent publications as McKenzie's works on the Stationers' Company apprentices throughout the 17th and 18th centuries (*10*).

Solid biographical information is also lacking, and much needed, in the field of book illustration. There is a reasonably firm background of information regarding the development of the various processes of illustration over the years. This is, no doubt partially, due to the fact that the study impinges upon and is closely related to art history in general. This is an important relationship and one which needs to be stressed. For many periods in many countries, the artists who engaged in book illustration were also engaged in other artistic pursuits. We are, consequently, seeking for the comparatively few book illustrators amid a much wider body of artists rather than looking for an isolated group of practitioners. Throughout the majority of the years of the book we are not looking at the work of the original artist when we come to examine the book itself. We are seeing the original design through the eyes and the techniques of an intermediary. We are accustomed to the usual phrases in lists and bibliographies of "*by* A *after* B"; or at the foot of an engraving, "*pinxit* X, *sculpsit* Y." The original artists can frequently be identified with some ease, although it should never be assumed that identification will be automatic. The secondary artists—the engravers of an original design—are, however, notoriously difficult to unmask. In many periods of the book's history they were insignificant individuals in the art world and not, normally, the stuff of which biographical dictionaries are made. Much research needs to be undertaken in order to lay bare the basic facts of the career of many artists of this nature; much of that research will, as will be indicated later in other areas also, need to be conducted as local and regional history.

Binding is also very much regionalized in that some binding traditions have clearly defined areas of influence. Nevertheless, it is important not to expect that every binding design will fit into a clearly marked style. Although there is enough unity to speak of a Canterbury style of binding or to recognize common features in Spanish bindings of the 11th to the 15th centuries, such conveniences are not always possible. A description of a book as a "Parisian binding," while it does nothing to set it apart from hundreds of thousands of other books for which this would equally be true, is enough to begin to place it in some kind of sequence. This is equally true of ascriptions to an individual binder, to a general style of decoration, or to associated binding features such as gauffered edges, fore-edge paintings, or marbled end papers. The history of binding involves many factors in addition to the aesthetic treatment of a design on the boards and the spine. The types of leather and their localized methods of tanning and dressing, the differing methods of forwarding from time to time and place to place, the introduction of new materials such as book cloth for casing in the 19th century; these are all aspects which were subject to development and change and, therefore, can be viewed in a historical context. Peripheral to the main concerns of bookbinding history is another feature which is often of great interest and importance. The master bookbinder was, naturally (in common with other artists), anxious that the work should be known and acknowledged as his. It was, therefore, a common practice for the binder to sign the work in some manner or another. In many instances the name can be found lettered in gold along the doublure of the front or back board. In many other instances the name is recorded on a small binder's ticket, usually affixed to the inside of the front board. These frequently have an additional interest and importance in that they record addresses and sometimes ancillary occupations as well. Many such items have hitherto been ignored when the books have been recorded, although they provide important information regarding certain aspects of the trade.

So far the concern has been with matters which are, in one sense, internal to the books themselves, but a book is much more than a collection of paper, print, and binding. It is, at its most important level, the product of a society designed for the uses of that society. It is only a tiny percentage of books which have been produced simply as displays of technical competency and artistic achievement. For the most part books are initially the creation of writers who, in addition to having a message or a story or emotion to convey, also hope to make money. Because the author is the true instigator of whatever appears finally as a published work, it follows that the history of authorship is a fundamental area of study in historical bibliography. The rewards of authorship—whether seen as aspects of patronage, the results of copyright legislation and protection, influenced by the attitudes of booksellers and publishers to matters such as advertising and promotion, the results of literary agents, or the effect of the rise and fall of reviewing and reviewers—are all matters which, in one way or another, have some kind of influence. Surprisingly, because it is a matter which has both literary and historical importance, the history of authorship is not well researched nor adequately documented. References can be found to many aspects of authorship in the letters, diaries, and autobiographies of writers, but these are not numerous and those which are available in reliably edited editions are very few indeed. There are available a comparatively small number which survey a particular period, such as those of Phoebe Sheavyn or Arthur Collins (*11*), and a few which deal with the background of a particular author (*12*).

An obvious extension of our need for more information regarding the economic aspects of authorship is an interest in the actual "methods" of authorship. The problems which arise in textual studies which have a relationship to bibliographic analysis are frequently rooted in an author's work habits. Authorial habits vary from those which pass from pen to printer at white-hot speed, a condition which is found in much pamphleteering and many 19th-century novels which were published in serial or part form, to instances of agonized rewriting and redrafting. An author who is inclined to the latter course is also likely to be one who regularly rewrites between printings of the work. Many of these attitudes of an author are shaped not only by personal traits and idiosyncrasies but also by the requirements of the trade itself at any one period for a particular kind of material. Similar habits will be found to apply at widely separated periods; for example, the early drafts of Elizabethan and Jacobean drama which Greg christened "foul papers" are precisely similar in intent to, say, the many rewritings and amended versions of Malcolm Lowry. Authorship always has had one clear basic function, to create a work and then to hand the creation over to whatever organization is in control of the means of multiplication of the text and its wider distribution.

It follows, then, that the history of the book trade, in the most all-embracing sense of the term, is in a very real sense the basis of historical bibliography. It is under that umbrella that all the various specialized activities which have been mentioned come together to present a unified picture. It is a whole picture of the trade at all periods which alone can provide the background and also the detail which will permit bibliographic judgments to be made. In spite of this, our knowledge is but fragmentary. The detailed histories of publishing, printing, authorship, trade practices, papermaking, binding, illustration, typography, reading taste, government control, and much more beside of similar character, all provide the kaleidoscope which is the history of the material means for the transmission of texts. To write even a small part of it is a formidable task and has been, and still proves to be, a daunting exercise. It seems likely that, in common with some other areas of research, there may be one important solution.

In the preface to the original edition of his *Tudor Cornwall*, A. L. Rowse wrote, "I am convinced that the time has come in our historical writing for a synthesis of local and national history. (One may go further to see the history of one's own parish as part of the history of Europe, a moment in the movement of the human spirit.) . . . It is in this direction, I feel, that great progress may be made next in our historical studies: perhaps more than in any other field" (*13*). If this is true of history as a whole, it is assuredly true of historical bibliography. Much of the research which needs to be done can very profitably be conducted at a local rather than the national level. Printing tended to be a localized industry and binding was very much so; although publishing had clear national and international implications, the bookselling which provided the actual outlet of the trade was very much tied to a specific locality. Reading taste, which, in one sense, is the final judgment on all the preceding technical and trade processes, is best assessed regionally. Booksellers' advertisements in local journals, recorded borrowings from every kind of library, sale catalogs recording the disposal of collections; these are examples of the kind of evidence which provides a background to the study of reading interests and tastes.

There are already indications that some work has begun in this general direction. Studies of the book trade in certain areas are already revealing new information regarding previously shadowy figures. The analysis of subscription lists is revealing valuable information as to reading taste. The catalogs of libraries and the records of borrowings from such collections by individuals of more than average interest have opened up new avenues of investigations on both the general and the personal level. It is information of this kind which, when placed appropriately in the whole jigsaw puzzle of historical bibliography, will give us our best hopes for a wider study of the book in all its aspects.

REFERENCES AND NOTES

1. G. M. Trevelyan, *English Social History*, Longmans Green, London, 1942.

2. R. B. McKerrow, *An Introduction to Bibliography for Literary Students*, Clarendon Press, Oxford, 1927.

3. One of the first books which began to pay attention to this aspect was: Lucien Febvre and Henri-Jean Martin, *L'Apparition du livre*, 1958; English translation, by David Gerard, *The Coming of the Book*, N.L.B., London, 1976. The historical perspective of the "book" is particularly apparent in the final chapter, "Le livre, ce ferment" [The Book as a Force for Change]. A more detailed, and more recent, study on the same lines is: Elizabeth L. Eisenstein, *The Printing Press as an Agent of Change*, University Press, Cambridge, 1979, 2 vols.

4. Allan Stevenson, *The Problem of the "Missale Speciale*," Bibliographical Society, London, 1967.

5. *British Museum Quarterly*, **31,** 83–87 (1966–1967).

6. John Carter and Graham Pollard, *An Enquiry into the Nature of Certain Nineteenth Century Pamphlets*, Constable, London; Scribner, New York, 1934.

7. Paper Publications Society, *Monumenta chartae papyraceae historiam illustrantia, or, Collection of Works and Documents Illustrating the History of Paper* (E. J. Labarre, general ed.), The Society, Hilversum, 1950–.

8. The most important recent journal articles on the *Missal*, to be read in sequence, are: (*a*) Victor Scholderer, "Missale speciale Constantiense," *Book Collector*, 1955, pp. 8–15; (*b*) Curt F. Bühler, "Who Printed the *Missale speciale Constantiense*?" *Book Collector*, 1957, pp. 253–258; (*c*) Curt F. Bühler, "The Constance Missal and Two Documents from the Constance Diocese," *Papers of the Bibliographical Society of America*, **50,** 370–375 (1957); (*d*) Irvine Masson, "The Dating of the *Missale speciale Constantiense*," *Transactions of the Bibliographical Society*, 1958, pp. 81–101; (*e*) Curt F. Bühler "Another View on the Dating of the *Missale speciale Constantiense*," *Transactions of the Bibliographical Society*, 1959, pp. 1–10; and (*f*) Curt F. Bühler, "The 'Missale Speciale' and the Feast of the Presentation of Blessed Virgin Mary," *Papers of the Bibliographical Society of America*, **66,** 1–11 (1972).

9. David Nunes Carvalho, *Forty Centuries of Ink, or a Chronological Narrative Concerning Ink and Its Background,* Banks Law Publications, New York, 1904.

10. D. F. McKenzie, *Stationers' Company Apprentices 1605–1640*, Bibliographical Society of the University of Virginia, Charlottesville, 1961; and *Stationers' Company Apprentices 1641–1700*, and *Stationers' Company Apprentices, 1701–1800*, Oxford Bibliographical Society, Oxford, 1974–1978.

11. Phoebe Sheavyn, *The Literary Profession in the Elizabethan Age*, 2nd ed., University Press, Manchester, 1967; Arthur S. Collins, *Authorship in the Days of Johnson*, Routledge, London, 1927; and Arthur S. Collins, *The Profession of Letters, 1780–1832*, Routledge, London, 1927.
12. Few of these give anything more than a very general account. Examples of the type of work of which more are needed are such studies in relation to one author as: John Butt and Kathleen Tillotson, *Dickens at Work*, Methuen, London, 1957; and Robert L. Patten, *Charles Dickens and His Publishers*, Clarendon Press, Oxford, 1978.
13. A. L. Rowse, *Tudor Cornwall: Portrait of a Society*, 1941.

ROY B. STOKES

INTERNATIONAL LABOR ORGANIZATION

The Treaty of Versailles created the International Labor Organization (ILO) in 1919. Article 396 of the treaty stipulated that one of the most important functions of this organization would be the centralization and distribution of information concerning the conditions of workers and the development of labor laws. The ILO, in fact, outlived the League of Nations (which had been created at the same time) and became the first specialized agency associated with the United Nations in 1946.

The ILO engages in such activities as:

1. The formulation of international policies and programs to help improve working and living conditions, enhance employment opportunities, and promote basic human rights
2. The creation of international labor standards to serve as a basis for national authorities in putting these policies into action
3. An extensive program of international technical cooperation to help governments in making these policies effective in practice
4. Training, education, research, publishing, and information dissemination activities to help advance these efforts

Its original membership of 45 nations had grown to 144 by 1980. Between 1919 and 1980 dozens of international labor standards were promulgated, in the form of 153 Conventions and 162 Recommendations. These standards are set by the annual tripartite International Labor Conference at which governments, employers, and workers are represented. Over 5,000 international commitments have so far been made in regard to these Conventions, which cover many areas, including certain basic human rights (such as freedom of association, abolition of forced labor, elimination of discrimination in employment), labor conditions, social security, occupational safety and health, and employment of women, children, and special categories such as migrant workers and seafarers.

The ILO has established supervisory procedures to ensure their application. They involve objective evaluation by independent experts and tripartite review at the International Labor Conference of the manner in which obligations are complied with. There is a special procedure to investigate complaints of infringements of trade union rights.

In 1901 the International Association for Labor Legislation had set up at Basel an International Labor Office, which published a periodical compilation of texts of laws and regulations concerning conditions of work in all countries. These were published in the *Bulletin of the International Labour Office* during the period 1906–1919. Following the end of World War I, the newly created International Labor Office in Geneva (the secretariat of the International Labor Organization) took over this function, and it continues to publish this compilation as the Legislative Series.

The Legislative Series contains translations of texts of major new laws enacted. In addition, an annual supplement contains a chronological listing by country of other important new labor legislation. A consolidated index to the texts published in the Legislative Series for the years 1919–1978 was issued in 1980 (*1*).

In addition to disseminating information about labor legislation, the ILO also reported on recent developments in the social and labor field in the weekly bulletin *Industrial and Labour Information* (1922–1940) and in the annual *I.L.O. Year-Book* (1930–1939/1940). Beginning in 1935, the latter contained a statistical supplement which later became a publication in its own right; this continues to this day as the *Year Book of Labour Statistics*.

A detailed guide to serial and monographic publications of the ILO covering the period between the two world wars was issued in 1951 (*2*).

Two purchases of important labor libraries helped constitute the ILO Library. The Basel library of the former ILO was purchased in 1920; and the Ghent library of the International Association for the Fight against Unemployment, in 1928. The library also built up a prodigious collection of Soviet newspapers and periodicals which attracts scholars from many countries.

In the early 1920s close collaboration was maintained between the libraries of the ILO and the League of Nations. The first librarian of the League, Miss Florence Wilson, had been the librarian of the American Peace Delegation Library in Paris, and her counterpart in the ILO, Miss H. A. Lake, was the former librarian of the British Ministry of Labour. Together they proposed that the Universal Decimal Classification should be applied in both libraries.

At the end of 1923 Andre de Maday, a well-known sociologist and labor specialist, was appointed new chief of the library. With his encouragement, Mr. Albert Thomas, the director-general of the ILO, expressed a desire in his annual report for 1928 that governments and other institutions adopt the principle of international legal desposit in respect to all libraries such as the ILO. He stated that the ILO Library in particular should receive all publications concerning labor, its history, and laws.

In the spring of 1926 the ILO moved its offices to a new building overlooking Lake Geneva, within 10 minutes' walking distance of the League of Nations. The ILO had formerly been housed in a number of old hotels. At the time of its move, the library consisted of 150,000 volumes. Ten years later Mr. de Maday estimated the size of the library to be 400,000 volumes in approximately 50 languages. He retired in 1937 and was succeeded by Joseph Wilson Haden. Printed Library of Congress cards were introduced during Mr. Haden's term as librarian (*3*).

During World War II the ILO transferred operations to Montreal, returning to Geneva in the spring of 1948. One member of the library staff did, however, remain in Geneva to receive and forward to Montreal those publications which managed to come in from various sources. It was in this way that the ILO Library was one of the few outside Germany which continued to receive Nazi periodicals published in Germany during the war.

In January 1975 the ILO moved its headquarters to a new building in Grand-Saconnex, a suburb of Geneva. Modern facilities were provided for the library. Its collections have actually declined in size over the past few years, an indication of the vast amount of weeding being carried out. Some esoteric materials have been sold or given to other research libraries in Switzerland, or deposited in the British Library Lending Division. Following its reinstallation in the new building, the library contained approximately 350,000 books and received 10,000 serials. During the period 1967–1980, George K. Thompson was the chief librarian.

Beginning in the early 1960s information collection and dissemination activities were reassessed as the ILO grew in size, in membership, and in complexity, owing to the increasingly interdisciplinary nature of its work. A number of external management consultants surveyed the library and documentation facilities of the ILO and recommended the creation, in 1965, of a new Central Library and Documentation Branch. With the advent of computer technology and its application in information storage and retrieval work, the latter set out to design a completely integrated library automation and retrieval software package, known as ISIS (Integrated Set of Information Systems). Originally a punch-card system, ISIS went on-line in 1969, a year which both marked the ILO's 50th anniversary and brought the ILO the Nobel Peace Prize for having succeeded in its goals of introducing labor reforms that have removed some of the most flagrant social injustices in numerous countries.

ISIS was widely used within the ILO for a number of bibliographic and nonbibliographic applications. During the period 1970–1975 several dozen institutions in 15 countries obtained the software from the ILO. The ISIS software is currently marketed by UNESCO, and by 1980 the latter had made 58 further installations of the system. An offshoot of ISIS, called MINISIS, has been produced by the International Development Research Centre in Ottawa. MINISIS makes use of modern data base management techniques and is intended for use on minicomputers. Together ISIS and MINISIS have been installed in more than 100 locations on every continent around the world.

Within the ILO, the software is being used to maintain two major bibliographic data bases, one prepared by the library and another by the International Occupational Safety and Health Information Center (CIS). A range of information products are produced from the files, in the case of the former: a monthly printed abstracts journal, *International Labour Documentation;* COM (computer output in microform) microfiche indexes; and a data base, LABORDOC, available for on-line searching in many countries. All input is prepared centrally in Geneva. Abstracts are written in English, but the data base can be searched using the trilingual *ILO Thesaurus* in French and Spanish as well (*4*).

CIS produces eight times a year a journal of technical abstracts in separate English and French versions, *CIS Abstracts*, and *Bulletin CIS*. The *Abstracts* are indexed using terms in the *CIS Thesaurus*. These files are also available for on-line searching under the names CIS-ILO and CIS-BIT. Document delivery of items contained in the data base is available in microfiche form or photocopies, either from CIS itself or from some of its national centers.

The pre–World War II publications of the ILO which reported on recent developments in the social and labor field are being revived in a new form. A quarterly *Social and Labour Bulletin* has been issued since 1974, and a biennial *World Labour Report* is planned for the early 1980s. A number of other information services are also operated by the ILO. Detailed information about these is contained in a directory issued at irregular intervals (*5*).

Following the withdrawal of the United States from the ILO in 1977, information services and staff were seriously curtailed. Even following the return of the United States in 1980, the ILO program and budget were maintained at reduced levels. The library staff, for example, declined from 55 officials in 1974 to 25 in 1980. In spite of present budgetary constraints, plans are being made for the gradual implementation of an "International Labor Information System" (ILIS) over the period 1982–1991.

The considerable experience gained since the mid-1960s with the use of computerized information systems, coupled with great strides made in telecommunications and computer technologies, makes it possible to believe that some new or existing services might be further developed in the next decade:

1. Expansion of systems and services into nonbibliographic information, including legislation, statistics, learning materials, research in progress, directories, and full-text materials
2. Linkage of ILO regional offices, field projects, and institutions in member states via telecommunications networks
3. Implementation of personal documentation systems for researchers on microcomputers
4. Preparation of self-contained, inexpensive small computer system and training packages

It is hoped that the global system of information networks on labor problems comprising ILIS will result in a series of interconnected worldwide sectoral information systems on a variety of topics in the social and labor field.

REFERENCES

1. *Legislative Series: Chronological Index of Legislation 1919–78*, ILO, Geneva, 1980, 238 pp.

2. *Catalogue of Publications in English of the ILO, 1919–1950*, ILO Library Bibliographic Contribution No. 5, ILO, Geneva, 1951, 379 pp.

3. "The International Labour Organisation Library in Geneva," by Linda S. Kropf (Stoddart) and George K. Thompson, *Lib. History*, **4**(6), 173–182 (Autumn 1978).

4. *ILO Thesaurus: Labour, Employment and Training Terminology*, ILO, Geneva, 1978, 223 pp.

5. *Directory of United Nations Information Systems*, Vol. 1: *Information Systems and Data Bases*, Inter-Organization Board for Information Systems, Geneva, 1980, 465 pp.

G. K. THOMPSON

ITALIAN BIBLIOGRAPHY

The first Italian example of a bibliography of bibliographies was the *Mare magnum* of Francesco Marucelli (1625–1703), who collected thousands of books from which he compiled his work dealing with all subjects (about 6,000) of all times. The *Mare magnum*, in 111 manuscript volumes, was started in 1670 and was continued, after the author's death, by his nephew Alessandro and by Angelo Maria Bandini. It is still unpublished and is held by the Marucelliana Library in Florence, which was founded after Marucelli ordered in his will that his books be brought to Florence and that a public library be built next to his family palace. The library was opened in 1752. Guido Biagi, who was the director of the Marucelliana, published an index to the work, *Indice del Mare magnum*, in Florence in 1888 (Indici e cataloghi delle biblioteche italiane, Vol. 9, published by the Istituto Poligrafico dello Stato, Rome).

Anton Francesco Doni compiled the *Libraria prima* (Venice, 1550) and *La seconda libraria* (Venice, 1551). These were published together as *La libraria prima e seconda* in 1557–1558 in two volumes, the first dedicated to authors and printed books, and the second to manuscripts. He attempted a bibliographic survey and literary criticism of contemporary works.

Il giornale dei letterati, a scientific magazine started in 1668, included bibliographic information. It was published in Rome by Francesco Nazzari and surveyed books published in Italy and abroad. Nazzari reviewed French books, and others reviewed scientific books in other sections of the publication. It was continued up to 1679 and was succeeded by a magazine of the same name published by Benedetto Bacchini, first in Parma (1686–1690) and then in Modena (1692–1695).

From 1696 to 1717 the *Galleria di Minerva* informed its readers about "what had been written by the scholars of Europe not only in the present century but also in the past in any subject either sacred or profane."

The *Giornale dei letterati d'Italia*, founded in 1710 in Venice by Apostolo Zeno, Scipione Maffei, and Antonio Vallisnieri, included the most famous scientists and scholars of that time among its editors and contained book reviews. It lasted until 1740.

Two bibliological studies of the last century were: Volume 1 of G. Montarolo's *Biblioteca Bibliografica italiana*, published in Modena in 1885 (this work is unfinished), and the *Catalogo di opere biografiche e bibliografiche raccolte da D. Bonamici*, published in Lucca in 1893.

The major Italian bibliographic work, the *Bibliotheca bibliographica italica* compiled by Giuseppe Ottino and Giuseppe Fumagalli, was published in two volumes in Rome–Turin in the period 1889–1895. Two annual supplements for the years 1895–1896 were published by Giuseppe Ottino in Turin in 1896–1897, and the third and fourth supplements (expanding coverage to 1900, with general indexes of the six volumes) were published by Emilio Calvi in Rome–Turin in 1901 and 1902. The subtitle of the work is *Catalogo degli scritti di bibliologia, bibliografia e biblioteconomia pubblicati in Italia e di quelli riguardanti l'Italia pubblicati all'estero*. In its second part it contains a list of the Italian literary, historical, and scientific bibliographies from the 16th century to 1900. An anastatic reprint of the work was published in Graz in 1957 by Akademische Druck- und Verlagsanstalt.

A partial supplement for the years 1900–1920 is Giuseppe Fumagalli's *La bibliografia*, Numbers 11 and 12 of Guide bibliografiche della Fondazione Leonardo per la cultura italiana (Fondazione Leonardo, Rome, 1923). Fumagalli also compiled the *Vocabolario bibliografico*, which was posthumously published by G. Boffito and G. De Bernard (Olschki, Florence, 1940). For the years 1921–1946, G. Avanzi published the *Bibliografia italiana*, second edition (Istituto nazionale per le relazioni culturali con l'estero, Rome, 1946). He also published other supplements in the periodical *L'Italia che scrive*. Since 1952 the work has been continued annually as the *Italia bibliografica* of Giuseppe Sergio Martini. Olga Pinto's *Le bibliografie nazionali*, originally published in Milan in 1935, was republished in the second revised edition in 1951 (Olschki, Florence, reprinted 1969). Two supplements to the work were published in *La bibliofilia*, Volume 59, 1957, pages 35–54 (for the years 1950–1955), and Volume 65, 1963, pages 55–80 (for the years 1955–1959) (Olschki, Florence).

After 1847 the major Italian catalog of works published in Italy and abroad in Italian is Attilio Pagliaini's *Catalogo generale della libreria italiana*, sponsored by the Associazione Editori of Milan. It was published as follows: *Catalogo generale della libreria italiana dall'anno 1847 a tutto il 1899*, in three volumes, by author; *Catalogo generale della libreria italiana dall'anno 1847 a tutto il 1899: Indice per materie*, in three volumes, by subject (Associazione Tipografica Italiana, Milan, 1901–1905); *Primo supplemento dal 1900 al 1910*, in two volumes, by author (Milan, 1912–1914); and *Secondo supplemento dal 1911 al 1920*, in two volumes, by author (Milan, 1901–1928). Pagliaini's son, Arrigo Plinio Pagliaini, published six volumes of supplements in Milan, between 1932 and 1940: *Terzo supplemento dal 1921 al 1930*, in two volumes, by author; and *Indice per materie dal 1900 al 1920*, in four volumes, by subject. Between 1956 and 1958 he added a two-volume index, by author, covering the years 1931 to 1940 (Supplement 4, Milan). Under the sponsorship of Società Italiana Autori e Editori, Rome, the work was reprinted in 1964 by Kraus Reprint of Vaduz, Liechtenstein, and the United States, by permission of the Società Italiana Editori of Milan.

The *Bibliografia italiana: Giornale dell' Associazione libraria italiana, compilato sui documenti*, published in 19 volumes (Florence–Milan, 1867–1885), was the forerunner of the *Bibliografia nazionale italiana*. Until 1957 all publications were listed in the monthly *Bollettino* regarding Italian publications received according to the publishing law by the Biblioteca Nazionale Centrale of Florence (founded in 1886), which thus recorded all books published in Italy between 1886 and 1957. The complete sets later became practically unobtainable, and (instead of reprinting the monthly editions) the Centro Nazionale per il Catalogo Unico and the Biblioteca Nazionale Centrale of Florence, with the support of Kraus Reprint, produced a computerized cumulation of the approximately 700,000 entries contained in the 72 volumes of the *Bollettino*. This is the *Bibliografia nazionale italiana: Catalogo cumulativo 1886–1957 del Bollettino delle pubblicazioni italiane ricevute per diritto di stampa dalla Biblioteca Nazionale Centrale di Firenze*, in 41 volumes (Nendeln,

Liechtenstein, 1968–1969, published by arrangement with the Centro Nazionale per il Catalogo Unico delle Biblioteche Italiane e per le Informazioni Bibliografiche, Rome). The forerunner of the center was the Centro Nazionale di Informazioni Bibliografiche, at the Biblioteca Nazionale Centrale Vittorio Emanuele of Rome, founded in 1931 according to the goals of the International Commission for Intellectual Cooperation of the League of Nations. It was reorganized in 1951 with the present name and has the purpose of helping Italian and foreign scholars in their research, in particular by indicating libraries and collections where they can find publications, manuscripts, or documents of interest to them. Since 1958 the center has been compiling and distributing the current index cards of Italian book production. The *Bibliografia nazionale italiana: Catalogo alfabetico annuale* has been edited and published monthly since 1958 by the Biblioteca Nazionale Centrale of Florence under the sponsorship of the Centro Nazionale per il Catalogo Unico.

Some special bibliographies are worth mentioning: The *Dizionario di opere anonime e pseudonime di scrittori italiani o come che sia aventi relazione all' Italia*, by Gaetano Melzi (Milan, 1848–1859), was continued by Giambattista Passano with the *Dizionario di opere anonime e pseudonime in supplemento a quello di Gaetano Melzi* (Ancona, 1887). Giuseppe Fumagalli's *Lexicon typographicum Italiae: Dictionnaire géographique d'Italie pour servir à l'histoire de l'imprimerie dans ce pays* (Olschki, Florence, 1905) is fundamental for the beginnings of and developments in printing in Italy. An addition to it is Fumagalli's *Giunte e correzioni al Lexicon typographicum Italiae* (Olschki, Florence, 1939). L. Ferrari's *Onomasticon: Repertorio bibliografico degli scrittori d'Italia dal 1501 al 1850* (Hoepli, Milan, 1947) includes Italian writers from 1501 to 1850.

Bibliographic sources are the catalogs of the Italian libraries: The *Primo catalogo collettivo delle biblioteche italiane*, edited and published by the Centro Nazionale per il Catalogo Unico delle Biblioteche Italiane, Rome, is a union catalog of Italian libraries and reflects the holdings of books published between 1501 and 1957 at the four national libraries (Florence, Milan, Naples, and Rome) and at seven other state libraries in Rome (A-Barq., Rome, 1961–1979, Vols. 1–9). A special volume was dedicated to Dante as a memorial of the 700th anniversary of the poet's birth, *Dante Alighieri 1265–1965*, which adds to the list of Dante items under "Alighieri" of the *Primo catalogo* a list of incunabula, the works acquired since 1957, and 66 facsimiles.

The series Indici e cataloghi delle biblioteche italiane, published by the Istituto Poligrafico dello Stato, Rome, and supervised by the National Commission of Indexes and Catalogs, is dedicated to the treasures of the Italian libraries, both manuscripts and printed works; for example, the *Indice generale degli incunaboli delle biblioteche d'Italia*, compiled by T. M. Guarnaschelli, E. Valenziani, and E. Cerulli (Vols. 1–4, 1943–1965); by E. Valenziani, E. Cerulli, P. Veneziani, and A. Tinto (Vol. 5, 1972); and by E. Valenziani and P. Veneziani (Vol. 6, 1980). Publisher Leo Olschki, besides publishing the *Inventari dei manoscritti delle biblioteche d'Italia* (which started in 1890 and went up to Volume 100 in 1981), continues issuing bibliographic works in the series Biblioteca di bibliografia italiana.

Partial bibliographies are: (*a*) Clementina Rotondi, *Bibliografia dei periodici toscani* (*1847–1852*) (Olschki, Florence, 1952), *Bibliografia dei periodici toscani* (*1852–1864*) (Olschki, Florence, 1960), and *Bibliografia dei periodici toscani* (*1864–1871*) (Olschki, Florence, 1972); (*b*) Benvenuto Righini, *I periodici fiorentini (1597–1950): Catalogo ragionato*, two volumes (Sansoni Antiquariato, Florence, 1955); (*c*) *Bibliografia filosofica italiana 1850–1900* (Istituto di Studi Filosofici, Rome, 1969); (*d*) *Bibliografia filosofica italiana dal 1900 al 1950*, compiled by the Istituto di Studi Filosofici and Centro Nazionale per le Informazioni Bibliografiche with the cooperation of the Centro di Studi Filosofici Cristiani, Gallarate, four volumes (Edizioni Delfino, Rome, 1950–1956); (*e*) *Bibliografia filosofica italiana*, compiled by the Centro di Studi Filosofici Cristiani, Gallarate (annual, 1949–); (*f*) *Dizionario bibliografico delle riviste giuridiche italiane con i sommari analitici*, compiled by Vincenzo Napoletano (Giuffré, Milan, 1865–); (*g*) Giuseppe Pitré, *Bibliografia delle tradizioni popolari d'Italia* (Turin, 1894), which covers publications on Italian folklore up to 1894 (the second volume, up to 1916, the year of the author's death, is still unpublished); (*h*) Paolo Toschi, *Bibliografia delle tradizioni popolari d'Italia dal 1916 al 1940* (Barbera, Florence, 1946), which continues Pitré's work; (*i*) *Bollettino di bibliografia e di storia delle scienze matematiche e fisiche*, founded by Baldassarre Boncompagni, Volumes 1–20 and general index in the last volume (Rome, 1868–1887); (*j*) *Bibliografia matematica italiana*, Volumes 1–23 and two series indexes (to Vols. 1–9 and 10–20) (Cremonese, Rome, 1950–1972); (*k*) Giuseppe Boffito, *Biblioteca aeronautica italiana illustrata* (Olschki, Florence, 1929), and *Biblioteca aeronautica italiana illustrata: Primo supplemento decennale*, 1927–1936 (Olschki, Florence, 1937); (*l*) L. Cicognara, *Catalogo ragionato dei libro d'arte di L. Cicognara*, two volumes (Pisa, 1821); (*m*) Fabia Borroni, *"Il Cicognara": Bibliografia dell' archeologia classica e dell' arte italiana*, Volume 1 (Parts I and II) and Volume 2 (Parts I–VII; Part IV in four sections) (Sansoni Antiquariato, Florence, 1954–1967); (*n*) Claudio Bonacini, *Bibliografia delle arti scrittorie e della calligrafia* (Sansoni Antiquariato, Florence, 1953); (*o*) Claudio Sartori, *Bibliografia della musica strumentale italiana stampata in Italia fino al 1700*, Volume 1 and Volume 2 (Olschki, Florence, 1952–1968); (*p*) Giuseppe Prezzolini, *Repertorio bibliografico della storia e della critica della letteratura italiana dal 1902 al 1932*, two volumes (Rome, 1937–1939), and *Repertorio bibliografico della storia e della critica della letteratura italiana dal 1933 al 1942*, two volumes (New York, 1946–1948), with a second edition (1902–1942) in four volumes (Rome, 1948); (*q*) *Indici del Giornale storico della letteratura italiana*, Volumes 1–100 and supplements, 1883–1932, compiled by C. Dionisotti (Turin, 1948); (*r*) Emilio Calvi, *Biblioteca di bibliografia storica italiana: Catalogo tripartito delle bibliografie finora pubblicate sulla storia generale e particolare d'Italia* (E. Loescher, Rome, [1903]; the first supplement, 1905–1906, was published in *Rivista delle biblioteche* [Florence], Vol., 16, 1908, pp. 129–143); (*s*) *Bibliografia storica nazionale*, a classified record of books and periodical articles published in Italy and about Italy, from 1939 (Laterza, Bari, 1942–); (*t*) *Bibliografia dell' età del Risorgimento in onore di Alberto Maria Ghisalberti* (Olschki, Florence, 1971–1977), in four volumes; (*u*) *Bibliografia del Socialismo e del Movimento operaio italiano*, Volume 1: *Periodici*, in two parts (Olschki, Florence, 1956); Volume 2: *Libri, opuscoli, articoli, almanacchi, numeri unici*, in four parts (Olschki, Florence,

1962–1968); and *Supplemento 1953–1967: Libri, opuscoli, articoli, almanacchi, numeri unici*, in three parts (Olschki, Florence, 1975–1980); and (*v*) *Bibliografia della stampa periodica operaia e socialista italiana* (*1860–1926*), edited by Franco Della Peruta, three volumes (Feltrinelli, Milan, 1961).

Since 1975 the Società Editrice Il Mulino of Bologna has published *L'informazione bibliografica: Rivista trimestrale di analisi per autore, titolo e parole chiave dei libri pubblicati in Italia*. This quarterly originated from the bibliographic service of the Consorzio Provinciale per la Pubblica Lettura di Bologna [Society for Public Reading of the Province of Bologna], which also issued the *Dizionario bibliografico 1967–1971*, edited by Pasquale Petrucci, in five volumes (Società Editrice Il Mulino, Bologna, 1972). The *Dizionario* was an annual record of all the books published in Italy with the exception of textbooks for primary and secondary schools and juvenile literature. *L'informazione bibliografica*, on the other hand, analyzes only the publications of publishers who have committed themselves to submit their books, but in practice it includes the most qualified publications through four indexes: keyword (or subject), author, and title indexes, and the bibliographic index (which contains, besides the bibliographic information, a summary of the book). The first three indexes refer to the bibliographic index.

Other bibliographic periodicals are: *Giornale della libreria: Rivista bibliografica e d'informazione dell' editoria italiana*, monthly, published since 1888 by the Associazione Italiana Editori, Milan (after 1887 it superseded the *Cronaca* and *Avvisi* published until 1887 as Parts 2 and 3 of the *Bibliografia italiana*); and *Libri e riviste d'Italia: Rassegna mensile di informazione culturale e bibliografica*, monthly (1950–), sponsored by the Ministero dei Beni Culturali e Ambientali, Rome.

A bibliography of books in print is: *Catalogo dei libri in commercio*, published by Editrice Bibliografica, Milan, in cooperation with the Associazione Italiana Editori, Milan. The 1979 and 1981 editions, in three volumes arranged by author, title, and subject, are distributed by Bowker, New York. The previous editions (1970, 1975, and 1976) are one-volume works.

MARIA A. GARGOTTA TANNENBAUM

JACKSON, SIDNEY LOUIS

Sidney Louis Jackson was born on September 13, 1914, to Julia Goldberg Jackson, trained as a teacher, and Walter Jackson, graduate of Cooper Union, an engineer, writer, and later a transportation consultant. He spent his early years in Brooklyn, after which the family moved to Mount Vernon, New York, where he attended the local public schools through high school. He traveled to Europe with his family in 1928 and 1932, and to Palestine in 1934.

In 1931 he entered Columbia College, from which he graduated with an A.B. in history in 1935. His paper "The Desirability of Nationalization of the Railroads" won the Bennet Prize. After receiving his M.A. in 1936 in the teaching of history, he continued his study in Teachers College, from which his Ph.D. in the history of American education was awarded in 1941. One of a group of studies developed under Dr. Merle Curti, his dissertation (*America's Struggle for Free Schools*) was published by the Public Affairs Press in 1942 (reprinted in 1965).

Prior to his service in the U.S. Army from 1941 to 1946, Dr. Jackson did substitute teaching and free-lance research and writing. He served in the Signal Corps as a captain, writing the story of the Alcan Highway. After the conclusion of World War II, he spent 6 months in the Philippines. On his return Dr. Jackson worked for the American Red Cross in Washington, D.C., as an associate historian, and for the Anti-Defamation League in Buffalo. He also handled research assignments for the United Nations, helped catalog the library of the late Benjamin Sonnenberg, and served under Paul Ross in New York City's LaGuardia administration. During 1949–1950 he attended Columbia University School of Library Service and simultaneously took a job as cataloger in the Brooklyn Public Library during Francis St. John's administration—to stay for 9 years.

In 1959 he accepted a position in the Department of Library Science at Kent State University (KSU). The department was then in the College of Education, but it was separated as an independent school on achieving accreditation in 1963. In 1965 Dr. Jackson was promoted to the rank of professor.

Courses he normally taught included: Cataloging (at various levels), Adult Guidance and Services, Historical Foundations of Libraries and Librarianship, Historical Development of Reading Materials, History of Scientific Literature, Public Library Service, intermediate and advanced Reference and Bibliography, Research Methods, and Social Science Literature. In 1977 he developed a seminar, "The Library and the Black Community," in conjunction with KSU's Pan African Studies and Cleveland figures. He also taught two courses in the Honors College: History of Science (a guided reading course) and Sources of Marxism.

During the summers from 1964 to 1978 Dr. Jackson traveled to most of Europe, East and West, visiting libraries, library schools, museums, and bookshops—and many individuals associated with them. He attended the conferences of the International Federation of Library Associations in Budapest, Lausanne, and Brussels, where his knowledge of languages and wide library and societal interests brought him into contact with many individuals.

Among his notable writings—which related to cataloging, library history, reading materials, and user interests and needs—is the pioneer *Catalog Use Study*, published by the American Library Association (ALA) in 1958. From 1964 to 1968 he edited "Review of Current Research" for the *Journal of Education for Librarianship*, and "In Review" from 1968 to 1971. He wrote numerous articles for library periodicals (his objective was to have at least one article in each significant library journal), for the *Encyclopedia of Library and Information Science*, and for the *ALA World Encyclopedia of Library and Information Services*.

History remained embedded in his functioning, and he considered his *Libraries and Librarianship in the West: A Brief History* (McGraw-Hill, New York, 1974) the product of his combined training and his central interest in society, past and present. For ALA's centennial he developed *A Century of Service* (ALA, 1976), with the cooperation of E. J. Josey and Eleanor Herling.

Prior to his death on May 8, 1979, he was at work on a history of the encyclopedia. The first installment appeared in the *Journal of Library History* (Vol. 12, 1977, pp. 342–358); and the second, in the *International Library Review* (Vol. 13, 1981, pp. 3–16).

Dr. Jackson participated in local, state, and national professional groups related to his teaching, suggesting research and sharing findings. Among them were: Northern Ohio Technical Services Librarians, of which he was vice-president in 1965–1966, and Ohio Library Association, in which he served as chairman of the Intellectual Freedom Committee in 1964–1965. As a member of the Library History Round Table of ALA, he participated in several library history seminars. He was also a charter member of ALA's SRRT.

His papers, including his unfinished history of the United States ("America's Promise"), are collected in the archives of the Kent State University Library. His remaining family includes his wife Clara, son Joseph, daughter Miriam, brother Gabriel, and mother.

CLARA O. JACKSON

JAPAN, EDUCATION FOR LIBRARY AND INFORMATION SCIENCE IN

Libraries in Japan

PEOPLE AND BOOKS

The area of Japan encompasses 143,737 square miles, and as of 1978 the population was 115,174,000. The people form a close-knit ethnic group and speak a single language. The literacy rate in the 1960s was 98% (*1*). The total number of publishers was 4,092, with 11,741 bookstores in operation as of 1980 (*2*). It is as if an area smaller than the State of California included 53% of the U.S. population and 77.4% of the bookstores on the North American continent (*3*). In 1979, 27,177 titles were published; their average price was 2,483 yen (¥) (equivalent to $11.04 in U.S. currency as of July 1980) (*4*). In the same year, the number of monthly magazines sent from publishers to bookstores was estimated as 1,397,230,000; and of weekly magazines, 1,163,120,000 (*5*). Annual sales of books, magazines, newspapers, and textbooks amounted to ¥1,476,189,000,000 (U.S. $6,560,840,000), or ¥12,817.03 per capita (U.S. $56.96) (*6*). The total annual purchase of books and periodicals by Japanese libraries as of 1978 was estimated at ¥50,700,000,000 (U.S. $225,330,000), only 5% of the annual sales of books and magazines (*7*). It has been suggested that the Japanese general public prefers to buy books and to keep them in their own homes rather than to use public libraries. On the other hand, the number of books circulated to the general public from public libraries has increased year by year since the 1960s, reaching 117,813,000 volumes in 1979 (*8*). General data on libraries in Japan are given in Table 1.

TABLE 1

Libraries in Japan: Number (by Type of Library), Holdings, and Staff Members[a]

Libraries	Main	Branch	Bookmobiles	Holdings	Staff members[b]	
National Diet Library	1	33	0	3,970,932	847	
Public libraries						
Prefectural	73		81	15,210,000	2,039	(44)
Municipal	846		284	43,802,000	6,262	(379)
Town and village	320		45	4,435,000	376	(423)
Private	31		0	1,916,000	134	(28)
Total	1,270		410	65,363,000	8,811	(874)
College and university						
National	87	232		46,228,000	2,666	(221)
Municipal	33	19		5,505,000	358	(45)
Private	313	158		47,523,000	4,183	(509)
Junior: 13–14th grade	377	8		9,992,000	805	(427)
10–14th grade	61	0		2,238,000	187	(53)
Total	871	417		111,486,000	8,199	(1,255)
School libraries[c]						
Primary (1–6th grade)	23,365					
Junior high	10,509					
Senior high	4,998					
Total	38,872					
Special[d]						
Governmental	33					
Ministerial research institutes	155					
Public cooperation	62					
Local authorities	471					
Research institutes (in universities)	250					
Learned societies	235					
Private enterprise	655					
Foreign organizations	24					
Others	135					
Total	2,020					

[a] Compiled from data in *Libraries in Japan, 1979*, Japan Library Association, Tokyo, 1979.

[b] The numbers in parentheses are for part-time workers; these are not included in totals for full-time workers.

[c] The data are drawn from unpublished sources of the Japan School Library Association.

[d] *Library White Paper, 1979*, Japan Library Association, Tokyo, 1979, p. 35.

LIBRARIES

National Diet Library

The sole national library in Japan is the National Diet Library in Tokyo, established in 1948. This collection acquires 110,000 volumes annually, and the library has been functioning as the center of bibliographic control, library cooperation, and reference service. It has also been instrumental in developing the Japan MARC system, using Chinese characters and Japanese syllabaries for both input and output.

Public Libraries

There are 47 prefectures in Japan, and all these have prefectural libraries. In these prefectures—which include 3,278 cities, wards, towns, and villages—only 845 localities have their own libraries (*9*). Municipal libraries have been a driving force behind the public library movement since 1970. In 1977 the number of books circulated from the municipal libraries was four times as many as the number for 1970; in 1978 the number surpassed the number for the total population in Japan. Children's books circulated in 1978 amounted to 54% of the total circulation (*9*). Further development of a network of public libraries has been planned in order to extend public library services into localities in remote areas.

College and University Libraries

The total number of holdings, 93,530,000 volumes in Japanese college and university libraries, ranks third among college and university libraries worldwide (*10*); however, the number of books circulated yearly accounts for only 11.4% of the total holdings because the main function of these libraries has been regarded as service to faculty members and some students who are especially eager to read. This means that functions of academic libraries other than acquisition and preservation have not been much emphasized. Recent statistics show that the total number of reference librarians is only 426 (including 53 part-time workers) to provide service for a student enrollment of 1,952,392 (*11*). Enthusiastic librarians have devoted themselves to developing services for the users and to encouraging students' use of the library in each institution. Cooperation has been advocated by enthusiastic librarians and faculty members. The Ministry of Education has intended to develop a system of library cooperation among national university libraries, but the administrative staff of bigger libraries have hesitated to bring an interlibrary loan system into operation because of concern that the interlibrary loan system could be a heavy burden for their staff members (who have been overwhelmed by their routine work), and that their libraries might gain no reciprocal advantage from smaller libraries.

School Libraries

The Japan School Library Association has estimated that 96% of the primary, 98% of the junior high, and 99.4% of the senior high schools have libraries (*12*). Although school libraries exist throughout Japan, their services cannot always be very active. Elementary and secondary education in Japan has not been free from the strong pressure surrounding entrance examinations for higher institutions, and teachers at these levels have little interest in using school libraries as a vital part of their educational goals. Moreover, there is a trend for high school students themselves to demonstrate little interest in reading books other than texts and drillbooks because of the intense pressure of the entrance examination; in leisure moments they prefer to seek gratification in music, easy comic books, or other types of recreation.

Special Libraries

It has been said that there are 4,000 special libraries in Japan, but only 2,020 libraries are specifically known to the Special Library Association of Japan (*13*). Most of them have only one or two library staff members. The size of each collection is not big, but the libraries tend to be well organized. Library cooperation and interlibrary loan are active. After the "oil shock" of 1973, the economic growth of Japan was halted, and the special libraries suffered because of reduction of budgets and personnel. On the other hand, users' demands on library services have not only increased but have also advanced to higher levels. Librarians are forced to develop effective methods of library service and to reduce the costs of their library operations.

ATTITUDE OF THE GOVERNMENT: "A JOB THAT CAN BE DONE BY ANYONE"

One of the peculiar features of Japanese libraries, common to all five types of libraries mentioned, is lack of regard for professionality. From the beginning of modern libraries in 1872 up to the present, national and local governments in Japan have been reluctant to regard librarians as professionals. All personnel in libraries, except for persons hired after 1964 in national university libraries (successful candidates for the civil service examination in the library field), can be replaced by any government employee. The government authorities have felt that library positions can be held by anyone who has a higher education—and not necessarily of a professional nature. This attitude has hindered the development of education for librarianship in Japan. It can be said that most of the efforts of Japanese library leaders have been concentrated on establishing the professionality of librarians in the minds of national and local government officials.

THE PUBLIC LIBRARY: "A GOVERNMENT AGENCY OF MINOR IMPORTANCE"

The Japanese government does not regard the public library as a significant agency for the development of individual citizens but regards it rather as an agency to serve the particular purpose of the government: that is, controlling the political attitudes of the citizenry. Japanese laws relating to education and public libraries do describe individual development as an objective, and central and local governments are assigned to develop educational institutions to carry out this objective; but, in reality, centralization of the administrative power has been strengthened to the point that educational institutions have become government agencies: Public libraries have not been an exception to this rule.

The public library itself, however, cannot work to control the political attitudes of the citizenry, and its effectiveness for this purpose has been questioned by the government. In the post-1945 period a system of new institutions, called citizens' public halls, was developed. The citizens' public hall is a center for social education where citizens are expected by the government to get together, to discuss, to read, to obtain advice on their daily living, and to develop friendships. Building of these halls was initiated beginning in 1946 by local boards of education, with the strong financial backing of the Ministry of Education (*14*). A comparison of public libraries and citizens' public halls is given in Table 2. Social education is planned for the development of people outside of schools. In Japan, the citizens' public hall, the public library, and the museum have been regarded by the Social Education Law of 1949 as government agencies for social education.

The Ministry of Education has placed much more emphasis on the citizens' public hall and its supervisor, the manager of social education, than on the public library and the professional librarian; however, the level of professional education for managers of social education is far lower than that for professional librarians. This seeming paradox suggests that the Ministry of Education does not place much emphasis on professional preparation in the field of social education, but does emphasize the career of manager of social education as a government employee. In other words, the Ministry of Education aims to supervise the citizens' public hall in

TABLE 2

Public Libraries and Citizens' Public Halls

	Number of institutions			Number of staff members			State subsidy (in million yen)
	Main	Branch	Total	Full-time	Part-time	Total	
Public libraries	995	223	1,218	8,554	1,201	9,755	1,116
Citizens' public halls	9,470	6,926	16,326	13,276	25,879	39,155[a]	9,357[b]

[a] Ref. *15*.

[b] Ref. *16*.

each locality through the government official designated as manager of social education, not through a well-trained social education specialist. Given this philosophy on the part of official policy makers, the public library, which is ranked lower in importance by the Ministry of Education, would have no reason to be supervised by professional library personnel.

Education for Librarianship

PRE-1945 PERIOD

Inagi Tanaka

The first modern library in Japan was Tokyo Library, established in 1872. The first librarian trained in a foreign country was Inagi Tanaka (1855–1925), then a staff member of Tokyo Library. He was trained at the Harvard University Library in 1888 and 1889 under the directorship of Justin Winsor. After leaving the United States, Tanaka visited European libraries and returned to Japan in 1890. Soon he was appointed as director of the Tokyo Library. It was he who promoted the establishment of the Japan Library Association in 1892, and he devoted himself to the dissemination of methods of library administration which had not been known to the Japanese library field. He was also the first to advocate a view of librarians as professionals, insisting that his staff members at Tokyo Library (later, the Imperial Library) were "scholar–librarians with technical skills in cataloging Chinese, Japanese, and foreign books," and that such librarians should be given rank and salary comparable to those of college professors (*17*). Despite his zeal in advocating this viewpoint, the Japanese government took no steps to indicate recognition of librarians' professional status or to improve librarians' salaries. Though Tanaka did not devise any method for educating such scholar–librarians—or, indeed, show any interest in education for librarianship—his expression "library administration belongs to a kind of profession" has been adopted by his followers whenever they have insisted on the professional nature of library work.

Mankichi Wada

It was Mankichi Wada (1865–1934), the director of Tokyo Imperial University Library, who for the first time in Japan, in 1898, pointed out the importance of education for librarianship. He emphasized that education for librarianship and the activities of the American Library Association had been important factors in the development of American libraries (*18*). From that time until his death, he was a leading Japanese library educator and a proponent of education for librarianship. His efforts were aimed in every direction to establish education for librarianship in Japan; for example, advocating the establishment of a national library school, opening a short training institute for librarians, seeking to establish a system of apprenticeship, giving lectures on library administration and library history at Tokyo

Imperial University (as well as at some other universities and at Ueno Library School), and planning a certificate system for professional librarians (*19*).

Among his various efforts, his plan for establishing a national library school was partially fulfilled by the foundation of Ueno Library School (though it was not included in the educational system of Japan until 1964) and by the enforcement of the certificate system for professional librarians from 1937 to 1943. Encouraged by his continuing efforts, many library proponents advocated a system combining formal education and a certificate examination as an ideal method of education for librarianship.

Short Training Institutes

In 1899 the first Library Ordinance in Japan was promulgated. This measure indicated that local governments might establish local public libraries, that a private person also might establish a private library for the use of the general public, and that libraries could be attached to public or private schools. In 1900 the Ministry of Education published Tanaka's *Library Administration*, which was soon regarded as a textbook for establishing libraries. Motivated by these factors, 55 libraries were established throughout Japan from 1900 to 1903. In the Kyoto and Osaka area, a local library association was organized in 1900, and its journal began publication in the same year. Library activities began to attract the attention of the general public.

Reflecting these changes, the Japan Library Association (JLA) planned its first short training institute in 1903. Heizo Itoh (1856–1929), then the associate librarian of the Ohashi Library, assumed responsibility for its planning. Itoh, a scholar of the Italian language, was a professor of Italian at the Tokyo Foreign Language College. It is thought that he studied library services in Italy during his stay there in the 1880s (*20*).

The curriculum of the short training institute was: establishing libraries, library administration, cataloging, classification, library history, critical bibliography, and practicum. Lectures were also delivered on such subjects as statistics, academic libraries, history of Japanese literature, governmental libraries, and European and American libraries. This curriculum has been regarded as a prototype of the short training institute of later days. Instructors were Tanaka, Wada, Itoh, and other library leaders. It was held for 2 weeks, 3 hours each night; 37 participants received the diploma. Most of them joined the Japan Library Association, utilized their newly acquired library techniques for the establishment and development of their local libraries, and worked as influential local members of the JLA.

Based on the success of this short training institute, library leaders asked the Ministry of Education to sponsor a short training institute for librarians and urged the view that educating librarians was one of the necessary duties of the Ministry of Education. Because of the continued efforts of librarians in this direction, the Ministry of Education sponsored short training institutes in 1908, 1912, and 1919, while the JLA itself sponsored another in 1916. From the late 1920s to 1945, in accordance with the increasing tension in the economic, political, and military situation, the Ministry of Education sponsored short training institutes many times in order to disseminate the policy of the government to the general public through library services and activities of librarians. Local library associations and local chapters of the JLA also sponsored local short training institutes of one day or two, and encouraged local librarians to participate in them.

Ueno Library Training Institute

In addition to their efforts to open short training institutes in various places, Japanese library leaders emphasized the need for establishing a national library school. In 1907 the periodical of the JLA, [*Japanese*] *Library Journal*, began publication, and education for librarianship and the establishment of a national library school were stressed in almost every issue. Emphasis was placed on the necessity for technical skills in processing books in Japanese, Chinese, and Western languages. These efforts, however, failed to produce any positive result.

On the other hand, the Japanese government and the Diet had to cope with the economic and political changes produced by World War I. The head of the Social Education Section of the Ministry of Education, Kazu Norisugi, conceptualized the public library as an effective agency of the government in molding the thought of the general public. This idea struck him when he saw a wartime poster of the American Library Association, "Read to Win!" during his stay in the United States in 1918. Norisugi planned to establish a school for librarians, but the high officials of the Ministry of Education did not accept his viewpoint—suspecting, rather, that he planned to increase his own administrative power by establishing a formal school. Finally, he decided to maintain a short training institute on a permanent basis as one of the projects of his own section (*21*). For this reason the institute, although unofficially designated Ueno Library School, was not included in the school system of Japan until it was "upgraded" to the status of the National Library Junior College in 1964; formerly, its graduates were not given any privilege similar to those accorded graduates of any formal school. Wada and other library leaders were asked to cooperate with Norisugi in planning the curriculum of the institute, which opened in June 1921; it offered a 1-year course for secondary school graduates lasting 40 weeks a year, with 30 hours of classes per week. Instructors were drawn from the faculty members of Tokyo Imperial University and from the staff of the Imperial Library. Although there was no full-time faculty member until 1947, the faculty members of this new training institute were as outstanding as those of Tokyo Imperial University.

The curriculum was: library administration, cataloging, classification, critical bibliography, library history, practicum, English, French, German, humanities, and natural sciences. From 1922 to 1944 this institute produced 541 graduates, finally ceasing its activities because of the crisis of manpower during the war. Among the graduates are many librarians outstanding for their library activities and their learned products on librarianship: They became the library leaders of the post-1945 period.

Certificate Examination

The Library Ordinance of 1899 was revised in 1933 in order to place all the public libraries in Japan under the direct control of the Ministry of Education through the central library system. In this revision, it was stated that a library *should* have a director and a certain number of "keepers of books" and clerks. The previous version had provided that a library *may* have a director, a keeper of books, and clerks. By the terms of the revision, all libraries were required to have a keeper of books as a professional staff member. In order to produce a certain number of keepers of books, the provisions for the certificate examination were set forth in the Revised Ordinance of Public Library Personnel. This marked the first time in Japanese library history that the status of librarians was clearly defined and provided for in library legislation. From 1937 to 1943 the examination was given once a year in Tokyo, and 113 out of 170 applicants passed it and were given the Certificate of Keeper of Books by the Ministry of Education. The test consisted of a 4-day written examination (two subjects a day) and a 1-day oral examination. By passing this examination, Ueno graduates earned the official certificate, and their status was consequently expected to be improved in the government system; however, this system fell into disuse in 1943 before it was fully developed (*22*).

Other Plans

Besides these efforts toward education for librarianship, library proponents publicized their hopes for establishing a formal school of librarianship or a course of librarianship in a formal school; for example, a major course of library science at a university, a course of librarianship in a teachers' college, a course of librarianship as one of the minor electives in a normal school, local library schools in the large cities, a central library college in Tokyo, etc. None of these plans materialized except for a short-term experiment in a normal school carried on by an enthusiastic instructor of the school.

Library Associations

Besides the local library associations and the local chapters of the JLA, many organizations of librarians were formed and their activities encouraged librarians to study librarianship. Among them, the most outstanding ones were the Alumni Association of Ueno Library School [Unsokai] and the League of Young Librarians (LYL), Osaka. Both organizations had their own periodicals and published articles written by members. The members of the Alumni Association of Ueno Library School gradually became a driving force within the JLA and the Japanese library movement. The members of the League of Young Librarians published *Nippon* [Japan] *Decimal Classification*, *Nippon Cataloging Rules*, and the *List of Nippon Subject Headings* as the fundamental tools for processing books. Without the continued activities of the LYL, these three fundamental tools might not have come into being, and library leaders before, during, and after World War II would not have developed as they did. The educational function of the Alumni Association of Ueno Library School and the LYL should thus be rated highly.

POST-1945 PERIOD

The Library Laws

World War II brought Japanese libraries disaster on a scale which their librarians had not experienced in the previous library history of Japan. It was estimated that half of Japan's book resources were wiped out (*23*). The end of the war brought an end to military disaster and to cultural seclusion from foreign countries. The general public began to show a keen interest in reading books and acquiring new knowledge, and librarians anticipated that the ideal situation which librarians had been hoping for was approaching.

As a guideline for library services and librarianship in the new era, library leaders (active librarians in the previous period) asked the Ministry of Education to promulgate the Library Law. The ministry was not eager to promulgate the Library Law prior to promulgation of the Social Education Law, which, from the viewpoint of the Ministry of Education authorities, was to regulate the function of library services under the leadership of the Ministry of Education. After 4 years of continued efforts by librarians, the law was finally promulgated in April 1950, 1 year after promulgation of the Social Education Law. Because of the different standpoints of the General Headquarters, the Allied Forces, and the Ministries of Education, of Finance, and of Home Affairs—as well as because of the severe financial situation in the late 1940s—the provisions of the law fell far short of the ideal hoped for by Japanese librarians. It was said that substance had been sacrificed for shadow.

The law did provide for free public library services and recognition of professional staff members and of methods of education for librarianship, but recognition of the professionality of librarians remained nominal.

Another contribution to library legislation is the School Library Law of 1953. In other words, only public and school libraries in Japan have been the subject of library legislation, and only these have reared a structure of education for librarianship on a legal foundation. College and university libraries and special libraries have neither library laws nor legislation on education for librarianship. In these fields, education for librarianship for public libraries has been regarded unofficially by librarians as a minimum qualification. Opinions and plans on education for different types of librarians have appeared since the 1960s, but none of them have been officially approved as yet.

The National Diet Library has its own legislation, the National Diet Library Law of 1948 and the Regulations of the Organization of the National Diet Library of 1970. The library educates its staff members by its own program, to which the provisions of the Library Law of 1950 are not applied.

Library Legislation on Education for Librarianship

The Library Law of 1950 provides for professional staffing of public libraries as follows:

> [The Keeper of Books and the Assistant Keeper of Books]
> Article 4: The professional personnel of libraries shall be called the Keeper of Books [*Shisho* in Japanese] and the Assistant Keeper of Books [*Shisho-ho*].
> 2. The Keeper of Books shall be engaged in the professional operation of the libraries.
> 3. The Assistant Keeper of Books shall assist Keepers of Books in their duties.
>
> [Qualifications of the Keeper of Books and of the Assistant Keeper of Books]
> Article 5: Those who are covered by any one of the following shall be qualified as Keeper of Books.
> (1) Graduates of universities or colleges [13th–16th grade or 13th–14th grade] who have completed the training institute under the provision of Article 6.
> (2) Graduates of universities or colleges who have studied subjects on libraries.
> (3) Those who have three years or more of experience as Assistant Keeper of Books . . . and who have completed the training institute under the provision of Article 6.
> 2. Those who are covered by any one of the following shall be qualified as Assistant Keeper of Books.
> (1) Those with the qualifications for the position of Keeper of Books.
> (2) Graduates of upper secondary schools who have completed the training institute for the position of Assistant Keeper of Books under the provision of Article 6.
>
> [Short training institutes for Keeper of Books and for Assistant Keeper of Books]
> Article 6: Short training institutes for Keeper of Books and for Assistant Keeper of Books shall be conducted at the request of the Minister of Education by universities or colleges which have a department of education or of teacher training.
> 2. The contents of the course of study, credits and other necessary matters concerning the successful completion of short training institutes for Keeper of Books and Assistant Keeper of Books shall be set by Ministry of Education ordinances; the number of credits to be acquired shall not be less than fifteen.

The curriculum and the number of credits provided for in the Enforcement Regulations of the Library Law (September 6, 1950) were as given in Table 3.

The School Library Law of 1953 provides for school library services as a compulsory duty of each school; it also mandates placement of a teacher–librarian at each school and education for teacher–librarianship. As for the teacher–librarian, the law reads:

> [Teacher–Librarian]
> Article 5: The teacher–librarian [*Shisho-kyoyu*] shall be placed at each school in order to perform the professional duty of the school library.
> 2. The post of teacher–librarian prescribed above shall be filled by a teacher. This teacher shall be one who has completed the short training institute for teacher–librarians.
> 3. The short training institute prescribed above shall be conducted by colleges or universities at the request of the Minister of Education.
> 4. Besides those items prescribed above, the curriculum, number of credits and other necessary items concerning the short training institute for teacher librarianship shall be provided for by Order of the Minister of Education.

TABLE 3

Curriculum of the Short Training Institutes

For keeper of books[a]		For assistant keeper of books	
Course	Credits	Course	Credits
	Required Subjects		
Group A[b]			
Introduction to Libraries	2	Outline of Libraries	1
Library Resources	2	Processing of Books	2
Reference Work	2	Cataloging and Classification	3
Practicum	1	Circulation	2
Cataloging	2	Annotation of Reference Books	1
Practicum	1	Bookbinding and Mending	1
Classification	2	Audiovisual Materials	1
Practicum	1	Library Statistics	1
Library Activities	2	Reprography	1
	Elective Subjects		
Group B[c]		*Group A*[c]	
Reading of Books and Books for Young Adults	1	History of Libraries	
History of Books and Libraries		Library Architecture and Equipment	
Library Architecture and Equipment	1		
Special Problems in Processing	1		
Information Retrieval	1		
Group C[c]		*Group B*[c]	
Social Education	1	Social Education	
Social Research	1	Journalism	
Humanities and Social Science Bibliography	1	Stenography	
Science and Technology Bibliography	1		
Mass Communication	1		
Audiovisual Education	1		
Number of credits required:			
Keeper of Books	19[a]		
Assistant Keeper of Books	15		

[a] Revised in 1968.

[b] All credits required.

[c] Two credits required.

The curriculum and the number of credits provided for in the Regulation of the Short Training Institute for Teacher–Librarian are listed in Table 4.

TABLE 4

Teacher–Librarian Curriculum

Subjects[a]	Credits
Outline of School Libraries	1
Management and Operation of School Libraries	1
Book Selection	1
Processing Techniques	2
Use of Nonbook Materials	1
Children's Reading Activities	1
Instruction in the Use of School Libraries	1

[a] For all seven subjects, eight credits are required.

Levels of Education

Based on the provisions of the Library Law of 1950 and the School Library Law of 1953, education for librarianship in Japan has been carried on in the colleges (4-year and 2-year) and universities. Table 5 gives the number of institutions by level and type of training.

TABLE 5

Librarianship Training, by Level of Education[a]

	Number of institutions offering each diploma		
Level of education	Keeper of books	Assistant keeper of books	Teacher–librarian
Undergraduate (major)	2		2
Junior college (major)	1		1
Undergraduate (minor)	68		76
Junior college (minor)	72		67
Correspondence course	2		3
Short training institutes	10	6	10
Graduate program major in:			
Library and information science	1		
Education	2		
Literature	1		
Home economics	1		
Totals	160	6	159

[a] Ref. *24*.

The Diploma to Be Keeper of Books is granted when a student graduates from any of the programs noted in Table 4, regardless of the level of education, length of study, or quality of education in library science. In other words, the Diploma to Be Keeper of Books granted at a junior college level and the one granted at a graduate school are treated equally as far as determining the qualification of a keeper of books. Of course, the rank and salary of employees of specific institutions differ according to the circumstances of each academic career. Some have felt that qualification as a librarian should allow for gradations based on individual levels of education in the field of library science. In 1972 the Division of Education for Librarianship, JLA, advocated a plan to introduce a four-rank grade system based on the academic qualification of each librarian. On the other hand, strong opposition was voiced against this grade system on the grounds that rank and salary of employees of specific institutions already differ according to one's academic career, and that it was not necessary to classify librarians by a grade system in library science. The grade system has not materialized as yet.

Curriculum

Most of the programs offering a minor in library science feature a curriculum similar to that of the short training institute provided in the Enforcement Regulations of the Library Law of 1950. This curriculum for the short training institute has been severely criticized because of its low requirement (only 19 credits toward the diploma), brevity of education (a 2-month summer course in the case of the short training institute), lack of academic discipline, and concentration on technical instruction. The Ministry of Education advocated in 1968 that the present 19-credit curriculum should be regarded as a primary level or introduction to library science, with an advanced level of an additional 19 credits to be developed in each institution offering library science programs; however, the Ministry of Education did not attempt to revise the provisions of the Library Law of 1950. Without revising the law, establishment of new advanced courses is almost impossible in most private institutions, because of the difficulty of gaining approval from the financial officers of the institutions. If the law is revised, there is a strong possibility that revision of the present curriculum in each institution would follow because the school authorities would be required to observe the provisions of the law.

Recruiting Problem

Data on institutions offering library science programs, students who received the diploma, and students who were employed in libraries in 1977 are given in Table 6.

The number of students in three correspondence schools and of keepers of books produced by the short training institutes is unknown; however, it can be estimated that at least 10,000 students a year will receive the Diploma of Keeper of Books, and that less than 5% of them are employed in libraries. As for the education of teacher–librarians, only 2.21% of the total graduates were employed in

TABLE 6

Library Science Programs and Graduates[a]

Level of institution	Number of institutions	Number of students who: Received the diploma	Were employed in libraries
Keeper of Books			
Four-year schools			
National	3	2	1
Municipal	4	83	8
Private	61	2,715	134
Totals	68	2,800	143
Two-year schools			
National	1	149	111
Municipal	2	79	6
Private	66	4,535	186
Totals	69	4,763	303
Totals for keeper of books	137	7,563	446
Teacher–Librarian			
Four-year schools			
National	15	376	—
Municipal	3	66	1
Private	58	1,888	68
Totals	76	2,330	69
Two-year schools			
National	—	—	—
Municipal	2	36	—
Private	62	2,555	42
Totals	64	2,591	42
Totals for teacher–librarian	140	4,921	111

[a] Ref. *25*.

1977. This excessive supply of diploma holders has been questioned, but no solution has been found as yet.

Eminent Library Schools in Japan

Courses composing a major in library science or library and information sciences total 60 or more credits. The Department of Library and Information Sciences at

Keio University was originally established in 1951 as the Japan Library School in Keio University, under the auspices of American librarians. Keio's was the first undergraduate-level library school in Japan. In the first 5-year period, the courses were taught by American professors. Since 1956 instruction has been carried out by Japanese faculty members and occasional visiting professors from the United States. In order to meet the demands of an information-oriented society, a master's program was established in 1967 with an emphasis on the handling of information—the first program of its kind in Japan. It may safely be said that only this program can be interpreted as a "professional school" in the American sense of the term.

From 1951 to 1978 a total of 1,007 students were graduated from the undergraduate course of library science, and many are working in the fields of academic and special libraries. It should be noted that establishing a new department of library science in a Japanese university is very difficult, because the Japanese academic domain has not recognized library science as an academic subject, considering it rather as a mere technique. Despite various difficulties, the school at Keio was developed and established graduate programs. The reputation of the school has not always been favorable. A graduate of the school who has been eminent in public libraries said, "the school has been working in a different world which is at some distance from libraries in Japan . . . " (*26*). This may be true, but the efforts of faculty members, students, and Keio University at large to maintain and develop the school deserve considerable credit.

Two other graduate programs in departments of education (Tokyo and Kyoto Universities) have emphasized development of research activities by each student, but they have not demonstrated much interest in producing practitioners, in order to avoid duplicating the functions of the Keio programs.

Institutions offering a major course of librarianship at the undergraduate level are Keio University and Toyo University. Despite the strong impetus given to Keio by American librarians, Toyo's course of librarianship originated from the keen and persistent interest in education for librarianship on the part of two librarians of the university, Miss Iwamoto and Mr. Wada. Toyo maintained the short training institute from 1950 to 1973 and produced 7,999 keepers and assistant keepers of books (*27*). The efforts of Iwamoto and Wada rate special recognition.

The major school at the junior-college level is the National Library Junior College, formerly the Ueno Library School. Though the level is that of a junior college, the institution has a 1-year training course for graduates from other colleges and universities. This program, which has been regarded as the center of education for librarianship in Japan, concluded its 60-year history in March 1981 in conjunction with the beginning phase of the University of Library and Information Science opened in April 1980.

Eminent among the minor courses are: Dokkyo, Kanto Gakuin, Kokugakuin, Nihon, Rikkyo, Senshu, and Tsurumi Universities in the Tokyo area; Aichigakuin in Nagoya; and Doshisha, Mukogawa, and Notre-Dame Universities in the Kyoto and Osaka area.

Training for Practitioners

Besides the education for librarianship prescribed in the library laws, the Ministry of Education and various library associations have sponsored primary- and secondary-level training institutes.

The Ministry of Education has sponsored a short training institute for keepers of books in public libraries, held in Tokyo for 3 weeks every year since 1959. The Japan Library Association has sponsored local training institutes of primary and secondary courses in cooperation with the local library associations; these have been offered every year since 1968 in smaller cities. The Japan Institute for Library Science, Osaka, has sponsored its primary and secondary courses on processing techniques since 1965. The Society for the Study of Problems of Librarians has offered its training institute once a year since 1972, not only for local library workers but also for local people interested in the private library movement for local library services in general and children's services in particular. This society has also published several books on library services, and these books have contributed to the dissemination of ideas regarding contemporary library services among the general public.

In the academic library field, training institutes for academic library workers have been sponsored by the Ministry of Education, the Private University Library Association, the League of Private University Associations, and the Association of Junior College Libraries. Reflecting the increased demands of an information-oriented society, the divisional meeting of the All-Japan Library Conference of 1958 declared that professional librarians should have knowledge of, and training in, a particular field of study and that they should not be all-purpose librarians. The short training institute on documentation sponsored by the Ministry of Education, that on information retrieval sponsored by the Japan Information Center of Science and Technology, and the Seminar on Library and Information Sciences sponsored by Tokyo University have been held every year for experienced librarians.

The Japan School Library Association (JSLA) has sponsored, once every 2 years, the short training institute for local leaders of school libraries. The JSLA has cosponsored, with local boards of education, the short training institutes of advanced course work for teacher–librarians and keepers of books for schools every year in almost all the prefectures. The JSLA has also sponsored occasional workshops for library science instructors in order to provide a forum for discussion of effective teaching methods and to promote improvements in the curriculum. Local boards of education also sponsor workshops or short training institutes in various cities. The Ministry of Education has sponsored the School Library Study Conference every year since 1955, inviting teachers' consultants from local boards of education as well as teacher–librarians.

These trends can be interpreted as evidence that the short training institute and the minor courses for librarianship have begun to be regarded as basic education, and that these specialized training institutes have developed by implication into advanced courses.

Besides these advanced courses, Kinki Area (Osaka, Kyoto, and their vicinity)

School Library Association has sponsored its short training institute once a year since 1979, in order to give training for school library workers who have had no professional preparation.

OBSTACLES TO DEVELOPMENT

A Loophole in the Laws

It was the great forward step in Japan when public libraries and school libraries became the object of legislation and when education for librarianship began to be offered at colleges and universities; however, every law has a loophole, and these provisions were not as effective as public and school librarians had anticipated.

The Library Law of 1950 does allude to professional staff, but it simply prescribes that "professional personnel of libraries shall be called Keeper of Books and Assistant Keeper of Books"—it does not say that professional librarians *shall be placed* in each library (*28*). While the School Library Law of 1953 does provide that a teacher–librarian shall be placed in each library (*29*), it has an additional provision stipulating that "despite the provision . . . a school may delay appointment of a teacher–librarian for a certain period of time."

Originally, these provisions reflected the concern felt in the early 1950s about the financial burden that would be imposed on localities required to place professional staff members in every library. At that time, local (as the national) governments labored under sharp fiscal constraints. Despite continued efforts of public and school librarians and despite an improvement in the economic situation, these provisions have not been deleted from the law as yet; moreover, they have been used as a pretext by local and school authorities who attach no importance to public or school library services and therefore do not intend to allocate funds to these services.

Lingering Views on the Nature of Librarianship

Along with such loopholes in the library laws, actual government policy has set a negative pattern for recognition of librarians as professionals. Although the Ministry of Education has occasionally emphasized the role of librarians, it has made no effort to establish the professional status of librarians in the government system; similarly, local governments have made no move to improve the status of librarians.

As for the qualifications of a library director, the Library Law prescribes:

> Article 13, Item 3: The directors of libraries that are established by local public bodies which receive promotional subsidies [for developing public library services] from the State . . . shall be individuals who possess the qualifications of Keeper of Books. . . .

This single provision on the qualification of library directors has failed to bring about the appointment of professional librarians to library director positions because it is interpreted by local authorities in this fashion: A local government may not want to receive the state subsidy; therefore, the director need not be a keeper of books. A local government which has no plans to promote public library services can thus easily disregard the provision and appoint government officials or schoolteachers to important library positions. As of 1978 there were 1,096 public library directors, and their qualifications were as follows: Of the 676 full-time library directors, 218 held the Diploma to Be Keeper of Books, and 458 had no diploma. Of the 420 part-time library directors, 15 held the Diploma to Be Keeper of Books, and 405 had no diploma (*30*). This means that only 20% of the library directors hold the Diploma to Be Keeper of Books. It is hardly remarkable, under these circumstances, that every meeting of library directors provides an occasion for overriding of views put forward by diploma-holding keepers of books, who are outnumbered by individuals transferred from various government posts. In accordance with the increase in local bodies which do receive the government's promotional subsidies, the number of library directors holding the Diploma to Be Keeper of Books is increasing, but the political and financial situation of local governments and their policy toward public libraries do not warrant any great optimism.

A lack of regard for the professional nature of their work also extends to young library staff members. According to a survey conducted in 1977, only 0.6% of local governments (4 out of 684) responded that librarians in the locality were promoted as librarians (i.e., specialist in library matters) and that this promotion had a legal basis in each locality; 4% (25 local governments) replied that librarians were promoted as librarians not on a legal basis but by tradition. The remaining 95.4% (655 local governments) treated librarians as similar to other local government employees; 61% (417 local governments) responded that librarians could be transferred to other positions without the agreement of the transferred employee, and the remaining 39% (267 local governments) said that such transfers would not be done "in principle" (i.e., it would be done at any time if the local authorities thought it necessary) (*31*). In other words, most of the young, enthusiastic librarians face uncertain career prospects. However keen his interest in library service may be, such an employee must realize that he could readily be transferred to a clerical job unrelated to librarianship.

The "loophole" in the School Library Law of 1953 has reinforced the tendency of boards of education and school personnel to view the status of the teacher–librarian in a negative light. As of 1980 a few prefectural boards of education have stationed full-time teacher–librarians in several high schools in their localities, but full-time teacher–librarians are seldom found in junior high or primary schools. In these schools, one teacher or several may be asked to take care of the school library on a part-time basis. In lieu of a full-time teacher–librarian, the keeper of books for schools will be hired to process all library business. Most of the keepers of books for schools are young women: Some are high school graduates who have received a diploma as assistant keeper of books at a short training institute, while others are junior college graduates who have earned the keeper of books diploma in a college program or at a short training institute. Many, however, have no credentials in library science. None of these employees are classified as professional staff or as faculty members (including one who held a teacher certificate); all are classified as members of the clerical staff of the school administrative office. Their status is precarious and their rank and salary remain low, with no prospects of promotion in sight. A major concern of the school library field in Japan has been the need to provide a legal underpinning for improved status of school librarians and to hold out realistic hopes for better salary scales and promotion possibilities (*32*).

Colleges and universities have not been the subject of legislation on their libraries and library personnel. The library director is elected from the faculty members, but other library staff members have usually been regarded as clerical workers who can be transferred to any office position in the college or university. One exception is the library personnel of national universities. The requirement for a government employee examination has been extended to library personnel in the national colleges, universities, and research institutions. This examination has been given every year since 1964 by the National Personnel Authority of the Cabinet. The number of successful candidates is not high (12 in 1978), and this system has not served to enhance the general situation of library personnel in colleges and universities in Japan as yet.

Workers in the special library field and their education are not covered by existing library legislation. Some of the larger special libraries have employed competent young librarians who were educated in graduate schools in Japan or in the United States. These libraries have also emphasized the necessity of subject expertise on the part of librarians. On the other hand, most of the other special libraries are managed by one or two staff members who are not always required to hold a diploma as keeper of books and who are not always regarded as professionals. These employees are subject to transfer to another position without advance agreement.

Efforts Toward Better Education

EFFORTS IN PUBLIC LIBRARY PRACTICE

Expectations of Librarians' Professionality on the Part of the General Public

After 1965 a strong movement spearheaded local reading clubs for children. Where local public library services were not developed as yet, individuals opened private libraries in their homes, at local community centers, and at nursery schools. The total number of such groups as of 1976 was 2,064 (*33*). These private libraries attracted the interest of local children, of whom an unexpectedly large number joined their rolls. The active members of local reading clubs were forced to find a solution to problems of selection, acquisition, and circulation of books. They concluded that the only person who could offer reliable advice and friendly suggestions on their activities was the professional librarian. Thus, a high level of expectation of professional librarians and urgent demands for appointment of professional librarians in public libraries have become apparent. Expectations of the qualifications of a professional librarian can be summarized as follows:

A librarian
a) is familiar with the demands of library users;
b) knows library resources;
c) responds to the demands of library users by making library resources available (*34*).

These expectations were not formulated by library users until the activities of local reading clubs for children had developed. The foregoing statement of expectations has been emphasized by Japanese librarians and is included in the Statement of Professional Ethics of Librarians (1980) among the objects to be achieved.

Keeper of Books System

The library policy of the Tokyo Municipality added momentum to the growing interest of the general public in public library services—not only in Tokyo but also in other cities in Japan. However, the statement that "every library should have Keepers of Books" in the Library Policy of 1970 and 1972 has not been carried out by the Tokyo Municipality itself. Motivated by this statement and by support from the general public, a group of enthusiastic librarians, the Society for Study of Problems of Librarians, advocated a plan for a Keeper of Books System and submitted their recommendations to the Tokyo Municipality in 1979 (*35*). The plan includes the following proposals:

a) Library staff members, except for a few clerical workers, should be selected from candidates who hold the diploma of Keeper of Books.
b) Candidates who pass the examination should be given the title "Keeper of Books"; they should not be transferred to other clerical positions, and should be promoted within the library system.
c) In-service training should be carefully planned and conducted in order to develop the ability of Keepers of Books both individually and collectively as a professional group.
d) The status, promotion, and salary scales of Keepers of Books should follow the criteria for other clerical staff.

At the time of writing, the Tokyo Municipality was examining this proposal, and predictions as to outcome were premature. It was clear, however, that adoption of the plan would result in an increase of the number of keepers of books recruited in the Tokyo area, an improvement in the unstable conditions surrounding library employment, and an eventual upgrading of library service. Possible influence of this system on libraries of other municipalities and on education for librarianship could be most significant.

It should be noted that this Keeper of Books System has been advocated by public librarians. They do not insist that keepers of books be given higher salary and status than other clerical employees but that they be promoted in the same way as other clerical staff members. They do not regard professional status as a privilege ensuring superior treatment but as a factor that would allow them to plan a permanent career in the library field. This attitude does not always find support among the librarians in academic and special libraries.

An Advocate of a Certificate Examination System

In order to improve the present situation of education for librarianship, the JLA's Research Committee on the Problems of Librarians has pointed to the need for establishing a certificate examination for professional librarians.

The plan of this committee includes: (*a*) regarding the present 19-credit minor courses as a primary step toward professional library education in the future and (*b*) establishing through the JLA a certificate examination based on higher professional standards. As for the issue of professionality, the committee identifies as fundamental the qualifications of a professional librarian expected by the members of local reading clubs for children. This committee is convinced that meeting the needs of the public, at present and in the future, is the cornerstone of the professional status of librarians (*34*).

A detailed plan for education for librarianship and for a certificate examination through JLA has not been completed by this committee. At the time of writing, the plan for establishing a certificate examination through the association was not welcomed by the JLA's Division of Education for Librarianship.

EFFORTS IN SCHOOL LIBRARY PRACTICE

School librarians have been eager to revise the School Library Law of 1953. Specifically, they wish to delete the alternative provision that "a school may delay appointment of a teacher–librarian for a certain period of time" and to add a section conveying the professional responsibility of keepers of books for schools. They also have attempted to revise the Rules of the Short Training Institute for Teacher–Librarians, to raise the level of education for teacher–librarians, and to add provisions concerning the education for keeper of books for schools comparable to those applied to teacher training. Recently, the Japan Teachers' Union and other teachers' unions have begun to pay considerable attention to this problem from the viewpoint of the standard of living of keepers of books for schools. These teachers' unions and the Japan School Library Association have cooperated to revise the School Library Law. The present plan includes the following points:

A. Each school should have a teacher–librarian.
B. Bigger schools should have a teacher–librarian and one or more Keepers of Books for Schools.
C. The qualification of a teacher–librarian requires:
   a. A teacher certificate.
   b. Professional education of twenty-four credits or more.
   c. At least six years of experience as a teacher.
D. The qualification of Keeper of Books for Schools requires:
   a. Two years of college education with a total of sixty-two or more credits.
   b. Professional education of twenty-four credits or more.
   c. Ten credits or more in a teacher training course (*32*).

If this plan were to become a reality, each of 38,872 schools would have at least one teacher–librarian, and many schools in the bigger cities would have one or more keepers of books for schools. Despite the continued efforts of the Japan School Library Association and other teachers' unions, however, the draft bill had not been discussed in the Diet at the time of writing, because of recent political changes within the government.

EFFORTS IN EDUCATION FOR LIBRARIANSHIP

Standards for Education for Library and Information Science

The Association of University Standards promulgated the Standards for Education for Library Science in 1954 and revised them in 1977. The new version adopted the new term "Library and Information Science" (note that "science" is used in the singular). The document explained that the new term denotes a new concept of unifying library science and information science in order to meet the demands of society upon all types of libraries; it does not, however, imply a simple addition of both sciences. "Library and Information Science" is described as having its theoretical roots in fields as diverse as mathematics, linguistics, logic, physiology, and psychology; and, from the applied sciences, the results of computer technology, printing techniques, telecommunication, and business administration. The new standards are as follows:

Standards for Education for Library and Information Science

Approved by the
Board of Trustees,
Association of University Standards,
Feb. 15, 1977

1. *The Object*: Education for library and information science is intended to teach the theory and practice of library and information science and also to develop students' ability in practical application.
2. *The Curriculum and the Number of Credits*: Professional education subjects are divided into Major Subjects of Study and Related Subjects.
   - A. *Major Subjects of Study*
     - (1) Major subjects of study are subdivided into the following four divisions;
       - a. *Fundamentals*: (six credits or more) A practicum is offered if necessary. (Outline of library and information science, Philosophical history of libraries, Development of scholarship and libraries, Survey on the needs for information, etc.)
       - b. *The Media and Their Use*: (eight credits or more) Experiment or practicum is required. (Information media, Resources for reference work, Practicum in reference work, etc.)
       - c. *Processing of Information*: (eight credits or more) Experiment or practicum is required. (Information retrieval, Techniques of circulation, Seminar in information retrieval, etc.)
       - d. *Administration of Information Systems*: (eight credits or more) Experiment or practicum is required. (Information systems, Seminar in information systems, Administration of information systems, Seminar in administration of information systems, Library mechanization, etc.)
     - (2) Besides the above mentioned, the Practicum in library and information science (two credits or more) is required.
     - (3) The total number of credits for the Major Subject of Study should total a minimum of thirty-eight, including all four divisions and the practicum.
   - B. *Related Subjects*
     - (1) Related subjects should be selected and offered from the wide range of hu-

manities, social sciences, natural sciences, and applied sciences.

(2) Because of the interdisciplinary nature of Library and information science, the following kinds of subjects should be offered relating to the Major Subject of Study: Philosophy, logic, linguistics, history of literature, pedagogy, sociology, business administration, mathematics, outline of natural science, physiology, psychology, and information engineering.

3. *Other Requirements*: Other essentials are identified in the University Standards and Standard for Establishing a University.

Remarks: 1. These standards are a revised version of the Standards for Education for Library Science (settled on April 27, 1954, by the Association of University Standards).

2. These standards are intended to apply to a Department of Library and Information Science, but they can also be applied to a major course in Library and information science offered by a department of a college or university.

When the plan for the new standards was publicized in August 1976, it was criticized severely by library science instructors. Critics asserted that this plan pertained only to the training of special librarians and did not provide for the training of other types of librarians; and further, that it failed to take into account the demands, the situation, and the viewpoints of library users. Under these criticisms, the planning committee added selected humanities areas to the Related Subjects, but the main theme of the plan itself was not altered.

After the new standards were publicized in 1977, a school for librarianship was established by the Japanese government. The new institution's educational philosophy and interdisciplinary curriculum bear a close resemblance to the standards just described.

University of Library and Information Science

This national university was established at Tsukuba City, Ibaraki Prefecture, some 60 miles northeast of Tokyo, on October 1, 1979, and admitted its first students in April 1980 (see Fig. 1). The aim of this university is "to produce future professional staff of outstanding ability for libraries and information centers and to pursue theoretical and practical studies on library and information science" (*36*). In April 1981 it opened its 1-year special course of professional training for graduates from other 4-year colleges and universities. In April 1984 it is expected to add its master's program. The freshman class enrollment was 120, and the total number of students was projected to be 610 in 1985, with a projected faculty of 60 members. With the establishment of this new institution, the National Library Junior College ceased its operation in March 1981.

As the center of study and research for the library and information science in Japan, the institution's first project was installation of the Information Processing Center and Media Equipment Center. A public library was also in the planning stage, to offer service to the local community surrounding the university and to provide facilities for a practicum of public library services to students enrolled in the program. Because of the international nature of library and information science, the university's Foreign Language Center is regarded as a central feature of

FIGURE 11. *The University of Library and Information Science (architect's plan).*

the curriculum. A Health and Physical Education Center will also be established to meet the health care needs of students, faculty, and clerical staff.

The curriculum was planned on the basis of the new standards. One difference is the adoption of five major subjects of study, instead of the four set forth in the standards. The courses are listed in Table 7.

TABLE 7

Curriculum of the University of Library and Information Science[a]

Subjects	Number of credits offered[b]
Foundations A	24r
Humanities	
Outline of Humanities	2e
Logic	2e
Japanese Language and Literature	3e
Philosophy	2e
History of Cultural Exchange	3e
Art; Currents of Thought	3e
Social Sciences	
Outline of Social Sciences	2e

(continued)

TABLE 7 (continued)

Subjects	Number of credits offered[b]
Jurisprudence	3e
Political Science and Public Administration	3e
Sociology	3e
Economics	3e
Business Administration	3e
Natural Sciences	
Outline of Natural Sciences	2e
Mathematics	3e
Statistics	3e
Physics	3e
Chemistry	3e
Life Science	3e
Comprehensive Subjects	—
Foreign Languages	12r
English	8e
German	8e
French	8e
Russian	4e
Chinese	4e
Health and Physical Education	
Lecture	2r
Exercise	2r
Major Subjects of Study	
Library and Information Science	
Outline of Library and Information Science	4r
History of Library and Information Science	2e
Foundation of Information Science	2r
Organization and Administration of Information	2e
Metricbibliography	2e
Cultural History of Libraries I	3e
Cultural History of Libraries II	3e
Critical Bibliography I	3e
Critical Bibliography II	3e
Methodology of Library and Information Science	2e
Library and Information Science Literature in Original Languages	3e
Library and the Society	
Environment of Library and Information Center	3r
Distribution of Academic Information	2e
Use of Information Systems	2e

(continued)

TABLE 7 (continued)

Subjects	Number of credits offered[b]
Library and Information Systems	3e
Communication	3e
Distribution of Information	2e
Psycholinguistics	2e
Publishing Techniques	3e
Distribution of Publications	3e
Copyright: Legal Background and Current Issues	2e
History of Scholarship and Art	2e
Library Architecture	2e
Library Architecture; Seminar	1e
Relation between Information and Society; Readings	3e
Information Media	
Outline of Information Media	2r
Comparison of Information Media	2e
Organization of Information Media	2e
Organization of Information Media; Seminar	2e
Reference Service	2r
Reference Service; Seminar	2e
Resources in Subject Fields I	3e
Resources in Subject Fields I; Seminar	1e
Resources in Subject Fields II	3e
Resources in Subject Fields II; Seminar	1e
Resources in Subject Fields III	3e
Resources in Subject Fields III; Seminar	1e
Resources in Subject Fields IV	2e
Resources in Subject Fields IV; Seminar	1e
Resources in Subject Fields V	2e
Resources in Subject Fields V; Seminar	1e
Organization of Information	
Organization of Information	2r
Information Retrieval I	2r
Information Retrieval II	2r
Information Retrieval III	2e
Cataloging and Classification I	2r
Cataloging and Classification I; Seminar	2r
Cataloging and Classification II	2e
Cataloging and Classification II; Seminar	1e
Cataloging and Classification II; Practicum	1e
Organization of Serial Publications	1e
Organization of New Media	2e

(continued)

TABLE 7 (continued)

Subjects	Number of credits offered[b]
Processing of Rare Books	2e
Processing of Archival Materials	3e
Indexing and Abstracting	2e
Indexing and Abstracting; Seminar	2e
Language of Information Retrieval	3e
Production of Bibliographic Information	2e
Production of Bibliographic Information; Seminar	2e
Data Structure	2e
File Construction	2e
Data Base Construction	2e
Administration of Data Base	2e
Information System	
Information System	2r
Systems Analysis	1r
Administration of Library and Information Center I	3e
Administration of Library and Information Center II	3e
Administration of Library and Information Center III	3e
Administration of Children's Libraries	3e
Computer System	1r
Natural-Language Processing	1r
Pattern Processing	2e
Programming Language	3e
Programming Language; Practicum	2e
Library Automation	2e
Library Automation; Seminar	2e
Library Cooperation	3e
Computer Network	2e
Input and Output	2e
Intelligent Functions	2e
Reprography I	2e
Reprography II	2e
Microform System	1e
Microform System; Seminar	2e
Preservation of Library Materials	2e
Museum Science	3e
Museum Science; Seminar	2e
Library and Information Science; Practicum	3r
Thesis	3r
Foundation B	
Linguistics	3e
Reading Classics; Japanese	3e

(continued)

TABLE 7 (continued)

Subjects	Number of credits offered[b]
Reading Classics; Chinese	3e
Latin and Greek	3e
Comparative Philosophy	3e
Comparative Literature	3e
Reading Science	2e
Comparative Sociology	3e
Business Information	3e
Comparative History of Economics	2e
Business Engineering	3e
Outline of Social Education	3e
International Relations	3e
Environment Planning	3e
Information Mathematics	4e
Applied Physics	3e
Electronics	2e
Information Engineering	3e
History of Science and Technology	3e
Reading in Original Language; English	1e
Reading in Original Language; German	1e
Reading in Original Language; French	1e
Total credits offered	40r; 302e
Minimum requirement for graduation	
Foundation A	24
Foreign Languages	12
Health and Physical Education	4
Major Subjects of Study and Foundation B	104
Total	144

[a] Ref. *37*.

[b] r, required; e, elective.

Though it is too early to predict the future of this university, it should be noted that the new institution represents the first venture of the Japanese government in backing a school of librarianship on a higher academic level. With the largest number of faculty members specializing in the various major subjects and with the highest budget and best facilities as yet made available for library education and research, it stands a good chance of becoming an excellent school of librarianship. Japanese librarians and library users are watching the development of the university with mingled hope and anxiety. Hope centers on the preparation of competent, imaginative, and service-oriented librarians and research workers for an unknown future; fear is expressed that excessive tilting of the curricular balance could result in the production of ever-increasing numbers of technicians processing information for ever-larger and more impersonal companies. In miniature, these hopes and fears mirror the world we live in.

Toward Japanese Education for Library and Information Science

The current status of education for library and information science might be considered chaotic because it is a complex of opinions and practices. On more specific scrutiny, there appear to be at least four factors making for improvement in the present situation. They are: (*a*) the Code of Ethics as a philosophical factor; (*b*) the public's expectation of professional librarians as a practical factor; (*c*) the development of library and information science as an academic factor; and (*d*) the growing consensus on libraries and librarians as a social factor.

The Code of Ethics. The Code of Ethics for Librarianship was approved at the Japan Library Association Annual Conference of 1980, after 6 years of continued effort and discussion. This statement prescribes the roles and responsibilities of librarians with reference to: (*a*) library users, (*b*) library materials, (*c*) self- and group study, (*d*) professional performance, (*e*) library cooperation, and (*f*) contributions to cultural development (*38*). Before this, there was no single statement on the philosophy of librarianship which could be held in common by all types of librarians in Japan except for the Statement on the Freedom of Libraries. The absence of this type of statement might have been related to the existing diversity of opinion; however, this does not mean that the Code of Ethics offers certain solution to the present problems of education for library and information science. In order to address these problems, the Code of Ethics should be taken up as a serious topic of discussion by librarians working in various types of libraries and by library science instructors. Without such discussion, the Code of Ethics itself might remain ineffective in terms of influence on education for library and information science. A focus of discussion should be the point that the Code of Ethics offers a different view of professionality than do traditional ways of thinking. From the beginning of the Japan Library Association in 1892 to the present, Japanese librarians have directed their efforts toward compelling recognition of their professionality from the government and toward establishing the status of librarians within the government system. Contrary to this approach, the Code of Ethics insists that the professionality of librarians must first be established in the minds of library users, and then, on this firm foundation, that recognition on the part of the government is likely to follow (*39*). Whether or not each Japanese librarian and information science instructor accepts this point of view, it offers foci of discussion about what the librarian is, how he should carry out his work, what he should learn, and how professional status may be achieved.

Expectations on the Part of Library Users. Expectations of professional librarians on the part of library users are summarized in a previous section, "Efforts in Public Library Practice." It has been proposed that a librarian:

a) is familiar with the demands of library users;
b) knows library resources;
c) responds to the demands of library users by making library resources available (*34*).

This premise, adopted as a main theme of the Code of Ethics, need not be discussed here in detail; however, it still has practical merit and will be used as a criterion for librarians at each library in order to examine whether or not they are meeting the needs of users. The feedback of information from librarians in practice to library and information science instructors, based on this examination, will contribute much to the reexamination of education for library and information science and will help prevent an ivory-tower atmosphere in library and information science.

The Development of Library and Information Science. The development of library and information science as an academic discipline will be promoted by the research activities of the new national University of Library and Information Science. Its faculty, drawn from such academic fields as library science, information science, mathematics, chemistry, linguistics, history, economics, geography, literature, architecture, and philosophy, and from special and university libraries, will not only undertake to teach various subjects but will also explore the interdisciplinary nature of library and information science for the future. Moreover, cooperation with this institution and Keio or other institutions will be helpful to all concerned.

Establishment of this university will exert considerable influence on the status of librarians in the future because: (*a*) it demonstrates the concern of the Japanese government for the education of librarians; (*b*) it will help to produce a climate of positive opinion for establishing a Keeper of Books System; (*c*) it permits the raising of the basic requirement to be keeper of books from completion of 2 years of college to graduation from a 4-year college or university; and finally (*d*), it may lead to consensus in the library field as to the revision of the present library laws and—based on the provisions of the new law—to the reorganization of the entire structure of education for library and information science.

A Growing Consensus. Reflecting the increased demands of the general public for library services and the efforts of librarians to meet these demands, national and local newspapers have begun to report news on libraries and opinions about the potential of libraries and librarians. Periodicals have also begun to present libraries as a topic of feature articles. Among these trends, one change is to be found in the policy of a government department which had formerly been concerned only with economic development, disregarding cultural facilities. The Land Development Agency, a department of the Prime Minister's Office, has recently begun to take into account the advantages of public library services for Japanese communities. In order to discourage the gravitation of population toward larger cities, the agency had focused on economic and industrial considerations only; however, the officers of the agency recently realized that a lack of cultural facilities has been one cause for the decreased population in some communities and the influx of people to cities having better cultural facilities. Among the latter, good public library services tend to attract new residents to live in a community. As a consequence of this realization, the Land Development Agency and the Ministry of Education joined forces in fiscal year 1979 to pursue research on a library network for local communities (*40*).

These activities, which had not been apparent before 1970, are expected to be of great help in forming a favorable consensus on libraries and librarians and, in turn, on education for library and information science.

These four factors are those which touch directly on the development of education for library and information science in Japan. Other factors, less direct, include the high literacy rate of the general public, the tremendous volume of annual book production, the increased trend toward undertaking higher education, continuing criticism of the present system of entrance examinations, and persisting ambivalence regarding tradition and new knowledge. In order to improve education for library and information science in Japan, both direct and indirect influences should be carefully considered, and a genuine Japanese system—not a copy of another method—should be planned. Though no one can predict the future, at least it can be said that Japanese education for library and information science has begun to take forward steps.

REFERENCES

1. *Unesco Statistical Yearbook, 1968*, UNESCO, Paris, 1969, pp. 30–31.
2. *Shuppan Nenkan* [Publication Yearbook 1980], Shuppan Nyususha, Tokyo, 1980, p. 1926.
3. *Bowkers Annual of Library and Book Trade Information*, 25th ed., Bowker, New York, 1980, p. 476.
4. Ref. *2*, p. 1289.
5. *Minryoku 1979* [National Strength 1979], Asahi Shinbunsha, Tokyo, 1979, p. 139.
6. Ref. *2*.
7. *Toshokan Hakusho 1979* [Library White Paper 1979], Nihon Toshokan Kyokai [Japan Library Association], Tokyo, 1979, p. 16.
8. *Nihon no Toshokan 1979* [Libraries in Japan 1979], JLA, Tokyo, 1979, p. 16.
9. Ref. *8*, p. 12.
10. Ref. *7*, p. 23.
11. Japan, Monbusho [Ministry of Education], *Daigaku Toshokan Jittai Chosa Kekka* [The Investigation of the Actual State of College and University Libraries in Japan], Ministry of Education, Tokyo, 1980, pp. 3, 426
12. Ref. *7*, p. 32.
13. Ref. *7*, p. 35.
14. Japan, *Shakai Kyoiku-ho* [Social Education Law], July 10, 1949, Law 207, Article 5.
15. *Shakai Kyoiku Handobukku* [Social Education Handbook] (Shakai Kyoiku Suishin Zenkoku Kyogikai, comp.), Sogo Rodo Kenkyujo, Tokyo, 1979, pp. 806–807.
16. *Kuni no Yosan 1979* [State Budget 1979] (Zaisei Chosakai, comp.), Doyu Shobo, Tokyo, 1979, p. 202: Revised Budget for the Fiscal Year of 1978.
17. Tanaka, Inagi, "Tokyo Toshokan Keihi Setsugen ni kansuru Iken Yoko" [A Recommendation on the Retrenchment of Expenditure of Tokyo Library], January 1981; Reprinted in "Tanaka Inagi Chosakushu," by Kumahiko Takebayashi, *JLJ*, **36,** 517 (July 1942).
18. "Nihon Toshokan Kyokai Enkaku Ryaku" [An Outline History of the JLA], *JLJ*, No. 30, April 1917, p. 6.
19. Takeuchi, Satoru, "Wagakuni no Shosho Kentei Seido ni tsuite" [The State Certification Examination System in Japan], in *Toshokan to Shuppan Bunka*, Yayoshi Mitsunaka Sensei Kiju Kinankai, Tokyo, 1977, pp. 336–333 [*sic*].
20. Takeuchi, Satoru, "Itoh Heizo," *JLJ*, **74,** 317 (July 1980).
21. Norisugi, Kazu, "Toshokan Koshujo Soritsu Toji o shinobite" [A Reminiscence of the Establishment of Ueno Library Training Institute], *JLJ*, **25,** 201 (June 1931).
22. Takeuchi, Satoru, Ref. *19*, pp. 328–323 [*sic*].
23. Keeney, Philip O., "Reorganization of the Japanese Public Library System—I, Jan. 28, 1948," in

Toshokan Ho Seiritsushi Shiryo (Takeo Urata and Takeshi Ogawa, comp.), JLA, Tokyo, 1968, p. 421.
24. Compiled from the data in *Toshokangaku Kyoiku Tantosha Meibo 1977* [Directory of Library Science Instructors 1977], JLA, Tokyo, 1978.
25. Ref. *24*, p. 134.
26. Kubo, Terumi, "Kokyo Toshokan o torimaku Jokyo no Shoso" [The Environment of Japanese Public Libraries], *JLJ*, **61**, 318 (August 1967).
27. Toyo Daigaku, Toshokangaku Koza, *Toyo Daigaku Toshokangaku Kozashi* [A History of the Course of Librarianship, Toyo University], Tokyo, 1975, p. 19.
28. Japan, *Toshokan Ho* [Library Law], April 30, 1950, Law 118, Article 4.
29. Japan, *Gakko Toshokan Ho* [School Library Law], August 8, 1953, Law 185, Article 5.
30. Compiled from the data in *Japanese Libraries 1978*.
31. JLA, Toshokan-in no Mondai Chosa Kenkyu Iinkai [Research Committee on the Problems of Librarians], "Shishoshoku Seido ni tsuite no Chosa Hokoku" [Survey on the Keeper of Books System], *JLJ*, **72**, 24–25 (January 1978).
32. *Gakko Toshokan, Sokuho-ban* [School Libraries, Announcement], Japan School Library Association, Tokyo, January 25, 1980.
33. *Nenpo Kodomo no Toshokan 1975* [Children's Library Annual 1975], JLA, Tokyo, 1976, p. 36.
34. JLA, Research Committee on the Problems of Librarians, "Toshokan'in no Senmonsei to wa Nani ka?" [What Is the Professional Qualification of Librarians?], *JLJ*, **68**, 107–108 (March 1974).
35. Toshokan Mondai Kenkyukai [Society for the Study of the Problems of Librarians], "Kurashi ni yakudatsu Toshokan o sasaeru Chikara, Tokyo 23-ku ni Shishoshoku Seido o tsukuro!" [Let's Establish the Keeper of Books System in Tokyo Municipality, as an Effective Institution to Develop Our Own Lives], Tokyo, 1979.
36. Toshokan Joho Daigaku [University of Library and Information Science], *Annai* [Catalog], Tokyo, 1979, p. 1.
37. [University of Library and Information Science], *Gakusei Manyual* [Manual for Students], Tsukuba, 1980, pp. 19–22.
38. JLA, "Toshokan-in no Rinri Koryo" [The Code of Ethics for Librarianship], *JLJ*, **74**, 194–195, (May 1980).
39. Ref. *38*, Comment 3 of the Preamble to the Code of Ethics.
40. Japan, [Ministry of Education], *Kokyo Toshokan Sabisu no Netto Waku no Seibi ni kansuru Chosa Kenkyu Hokokusho* [A Report on the Development of a Public Library Service Network], Tokyo, 1980.

SATORU TAKEUCHI

LATIN AMERICAN NATIONAL BIBLIOGRAPHY

The term *Latin American* is used here to refer to all territories south of Miami and the Rio Grande, whether independent or colonial, for which there exist bibliographies of imprints within their area. It is used here as a geographical rather than a linguistic term. It includes the Spanish-, French-, and Portuguese-speaking countries as well as Puerto Rico (a U.S. Commonwealth) and the former British and Dutch colonies in the area that have recently become independent.

The term *national bibliography* is a much discussed one and authorities have reached no agreement concerning it. Frank M. McGowan, "National Bibliography" (this Encyclopedia, Vol. 19, 1976, pp. 50–60), and Richard H. A. Cheffins, *A*

Survey of the Contents of Existing National Bibliographies (UNESCO, Paris, 1977, 45 pp.), have been consulted. McGowan cites several definitions, while Cheffins notes that the scope of a national bibliography could reach from monographs to the listing of records and even postage stamps. All authorities are agreed that government documents are part of a country's national bibliography. In view of the fact that James Bennett Childs, long the outstanding world authority on them, contributed the article "Government Publications (Documents)" to Volume 10 of this Encyclopedia (1973, pp. 36–140), there seems to be no reason to discuss this phase of national bibliography in this article.

Ideally a national bibliography should include data on everything published within the boundaries of the particular area being discussed, regardless of the language in which it is written. This means that such bibliographies should provide data on books, pamphlets, newspapers, periodicals, and government documents. Musical scores, maps, recordings, postage stamps, patents, and dissertations (unless published) seem to be systematically ignored in most national bibliographies. This article notes that most national bibliographies appear to list material only if it is in the official language(s) of the country (Peru recently made Quechua an official language). Many national bibliographies list only separately published books and pamphlets. Others such as the *Anuario bibliográfico peruano* list not only books and pamphlets but newspapers, periodicals, and government documents. There is no consensus among those who compile current bibliographies as to what to include nor as to the arrangement. Those for Mexico, Cuba, Peru, and Brazil, for example, use a classified listing with an author–title index.

This article discusses on a country-by-country basis the pertinent retrospective and current national bibliographies that exist. The section on multinational bibliographies is presented first, and the sections on individual countries are arranged alphabetically. The discussion for each country usually has four parts: (*a*) if a bibliography of bibliographies for the area exists, it is noted, for a good argument could be made that a country's national bibliography could consist of all pertinent sources that provide access to its publications; (*b*) bibliographies of books and pamphlets; (*c*) bibliographies of newspapers and periodicals; and (*d*) bibliographies of material published in any nonofficial language of that country. Parts (*b*) and (*c*) are arranged so that at a glance one can determine what exists for the colonial period and for the 19th and 20th centuries. Part (*d*) is arranged by language.

Current national bibliographies have been published irregularly in most countries. As of 1979 some were published by the country's national library (Venezuela, Peru, Chile, and Mexico are examples); some, as in Costa Rica, were published by a librarians' association; others might be the work of a bookdealer (Werner Guttentag in Bolivia; also, several U.S. current bibliographies published in the 19th century were the work of bookdealers) or might reflect the interest of some bibliographer in his country's bibliographic production (Jorge Eduardo Arellano and his annual list in *La Prensa*). Some of the countries have had excellent, almost uninterrupted coverage, both retrospectively and currently; others have had such poor coverage that their national bibliography can be said to be almost nonexistent.

Geographical, economic, cultural, and political considerations may either hinder or help develop national bibliographies. The rise of the book trade in a given country or an extremely capable librarian at the head of the country's national library may help in the development and continuation of national bibliography.

The introduction to many a national bibliography bemoans the lack of financial support which prevents it from having the necessary staff to compile it; the fact that several so-called *anuarios* cover a 2- or 3-year period is an indication of the difficulties involved in producing a current bibliography of this type. The compilers of many national bibliographies also have complained that the printers and publishers violate various copyright and deposit laws, so that copies of published works are not deposited in the deposit libraries as required by law.

This article shows where and for what periods national bibliographies exist, and it also shows where and for what periods there would seem to be a void in our knowledge of bibliographic production: Where the bibliography provides data on maps, musical scores, postage stamps, recordings, dissertations, and other types of material, this fact is noted, but no attempt has been made to provide either a retrospective or current bibliography of such material.

This article was planned to deal with the state of both retrospective and current national bibliography as of the middle of 1979.

The Scarecrow Press of Metuchen, New Jersey, has published Arthur E. Gropp's *A Bibliography of Latin American Bibliographies* (1968, ix, 515 pp.), its supplement (1971, xiii, 277 pp.), *A Bibliography of Latin-American Bibliographies Published in Periodicals* (1976, 2 vols.), and Daniel Raposo Cordeiro (ed.), *A Bibliography of Latin American Bibliographies: Social Sciences and Humanities* (1979, viii, 272 pp.). These titles contain sections on national bibliographies, printing, periodicals, and journalism. They are indispensable even though, when scrutinized with care, various types of omissions and errors can be found. The student of current national bibliography should consult the various issues of *Bibliography, Documentation, Terminology* (Vol. 1–, 1961–). Almost every volume of the Working Papers of the Seminar on the Acquisition of Latin American Library Materials (SALALM) contains a bibliography of bibliographies. These are invaluable and include data on current national bibliographies. The most recent book-length study on Latin American national bibliographies is that of Irene Zimmerman, *Current National Bibliographies of Latin America: A State of the Art Study* (University of Florida, Center for Latin American Studies, Gainesville, 1971, x, 139 pp.). Useful, though slightly dated, data will be found in Abel Rodolfo Geoghegan, *Obras de referencia de América latina* (Imprenta Crisol, Buenos Aires, 1965, 280 pp.). Jannice Monte-Móral and H. E. Gomes's "ISBD Application to Latin American National Bibliographies" (*UNESCO Bull. Lib.*, Vol. 31, 1977, pp. 233–239, 254) contains much valuable data.

Valerie Bloomfield presented "The Bibliography of the English-Speaking Caribbean Islands" (Working Paper No. B-7) at the UCLA 1979 SALALM meeting. This 24-page paper "is concerned with . . . Antigua, Bahamas, Barbados, Bermuda, British Virgin Islands, Cayman Islands, Dominica, Grenada, Jamaica, Montserrat, St. Kitts–Nevis–Anguilla, St. Luca, St. Vincent, Trinidad and Tobago, Turks and Caicos Islands and the United States Virgin Islands" (p. 1). It is divided into nine parts: national bibliography, retrospective bibliography, subject bibliographies, government publications, periodicals, newspapers, research, maps and atlases, and audiovisual material, sound recordings, and a brief note on films. Pages 14–24 contain "Appendix: Bibliography of the English-Speaking Caribbean Islands."

Multinational Bibliographies

The largest bibliography of material in the Spanish language regardless of the place of publication is the *Manual del librero hispano-americano*, subtitled Bibliografía general española e hispano-americana desde la invención de la imprenta hasta nuestros tiempos con el valor comercial de los impresos descritos por Antonio Palau y Dulcet (2nd ed., Librería Palau and other publishers, Barcelona, 1948–1977, 28 vols. and 381,827 entries). Antonio Palau worked on this monumental work from 1897 to 1954; his sons, Miguel (1923–1927, 1942–1952), Enrique (1949–1954), and Agustín (1954–1977), and Amalia Isabel Asensio de Farreras worked on it from 1955 to 1977. Material about the Spanish-speaking world is included regardless of its language. Reprints of articles are sometimes listed. Much material from Spanish America is included.

The *Catálogo general de la librería española e hispanoamericana años 1901–1930* (Camaras oficiales del libro and other publishers, Madrid and Barcelona, 1932–1951, 5 vols.) attempts to provide pertinent bibliographic data on books published in Spain and Spanish America. Its continuation for 1931–1950 has omitted *hispanoamericano* from its title.

The development of current Western Hemisphere multinational bibliographies seems to have begun in the 1960s. Important are *Fichero bibliográfico hispanoamericano* (Vol. 1–, October 1961–), *Libros en venta en Hispanoamérica y España*, and the *Boletín bibliográfico* of the Centro regional para el fomento del libro en América latina y el Caribe (Vol. 1, No. 1–, July 1974–).

The *Fichero* has been edited since its inception by Mary C. Turner and was a quarterly through Volume 3 (July 1964); with Volume 4, Number 1 (October 1964) it became a monthly. The first three volumes were published in New York by R. R. Bowker; with Volume 4 it began to be published by Bowker Editores Argentina and later by Turner Ediciones SRL. The arrangement is that of a slightly modified Dewey Decimal Classification system. The editor provides as much bibliographic data as are available; prices of the books are often given. Publishers and their addresses are found at the end of each bibliographic listing, and often following this section there are short articles or reviews concerning the book trade or bibliographic matters.

Libros en venta (Bowker, New York, 1964, 1,891 pp.) has had the following supplements: for 1964–1966 (1967, 683 pp.), for 1967–1968 (1969, 565 pp.), for 1969–1970 (1972, 524 pp.), for 1975 (1977, 304 pp.), and for 1976–1977 (1978, 539 pp.). A second edition in two volumes appeared in 1974. The supplements and the second edition were all published in Buenos Aires by Bowker Editores Argentina. Each of these volumes is divided into three parts: authors, titles, and subjects, with a list of publishers and their addresses at the end of each volume. Pertinent bibliographic data are given and often the book's price appears.

The *Boletín bibliográfico* is published in Bogotá and appears at irregular intervals. Thus, Volume 5, Number 1 was dated March 1978, and the combined issue Volume 5, Numbers 2–4 was dated April–December 1978. The arrangement is that of a slightly modified Dewey Decimal Classification system. Books are listed by title, with data then provided on author, translator, place of publication, publisher, date, edition, pagination, series, and price, through Volume 5, in the currency of the publisher's country; with Volume 6 the price in dollars was added. There are title and author indexes to each issue as well as a listing of publishers and their addresses. With Volume 6 Brazilian publications began to be listed, through the cooperation of the Sindicato nacional.

The *CARICOM Bibliography* (subtitled A Cumulated Subject List of Current National Imprints of the Caribbean Community Member Countries . . .), *Current Caribbean Bibliography*, and *Notes bibliographiques caraïbes* are three important multinational bibliographies in the Caribbean area.

The *CARICOM Bibliography* is published in Georgetown by the Caribbean Community Secretariat Library. Volumes 1 and 2, for 1977 and 1978, were annuals. It is planned that from 1979 on the bibliography will appear semiannually and be cumulated. According to Bloomfield, "it incorporates material from the national bibliographies of Barbados, Guyana, Jamaica and Trinidad and Tobago, together with the entries from territories not yet producing national bibliographies submitted to the CARICOM secretariat. The form of entry and arrangement is similar to that adopted by the national bibliographies. . . . Although more of the English-speaking countries are covered by the *CARICOM bibliography*, Bermuda, the British Virgin Islands, Cayman Islands, Turks and Caicos and the U.S. Virgin Islands remain outside its scope" (Working Paper No. B-7, 1979 SALALM Meeting, p. 3).

The *Current Caribbean Bibliography* began publication in 1951. Volumes 1–7 were published in Port-of-Spain, Trinidad. Volumes 8–15 and 17–23 were published in Puerto Rico, and Volume 16 by the New York Public Library. Volumes 1–8 were issued by the Caribbean Commission and Volumes 9–11, Part 1, by the Caribbean Organization. Volumes 9–11, Parts 2–14, and Volume 16– have been issued by the Institute of Caribbean Studies, University of Puerto Rico, and published by CODECA. Volume 15 was issued by the Caribbean Economic Development Corporation (Hato Rey).

According to a "News Item," *Notes bibliographiques caraïbes* (NBC) was begun in October 1977 as a monthly bibliography. It is published in Guadeloupe and is edited by B. Grelle and M. Durand-Barthes. The NBC attempts to provide full information (addresses and prices included) on publications on the Caribbean as an aid to acquisitions for public libraries in the Francophone region. Although heavily biased toward French-language material and sources, the bibliography is intended to include such foreign-language items as come to the editors' attention. Arrangement is by UDC broad classes, and some two dozen journals are scanned for entries. The NBC includes data on and from the French Antilles, which as departments of France have no independent national bibliographies but are included in French national bibliographic sources.

A study of Numbers 15–19 would show that Number 15 (March 1979) contains no bibliography but is an issue entitled *Guides des archives bibliothèques et centres de documentation de la Guadeloupe*, and that Numbers 16–18 (May–July 1979) constitute a triple number in one issue, while Number 19 (August 1979) reverts to being a monthly. The NBC includes films and records.

G. K. Hall in Boston has reproduced the catalogs of several Latin American collections of libraries of the United States. Among these are: *Catalog of the Latin American Collection of the University of Texas Library (Austin)* (1969, 31 vols.; and four supplements in 17 vols., 1971–1977); the New York Public Library, Reference Department, *Dictionary Catalog of the History of the Americas* (1961, 28 vols.; 1st supplement, 9 vols., 1973); *Catalog of the Latin American Library of the Tulane University Library*, New Orleans (1970, 9 vols.; two supplements of 4 vols. each, 1973–1975); *Catalog of the Cuban and Caribbean Library*, University of Miami, Coral Gables, Florida (1977, 6 vols.); and *Catalog of the Latin American Collection*, University of Florida Libraries, Gainesville, Florida (1973, 13 vols.).

The KTO Press in 1979 published the *Catalogue of the West Indian Reference Library of Jamaica*, edited by Robert A. Hill (1979, 10 vols.).

These catalogs, because of their size and comprehensiveness, could serve, *faute de mieux*, as retrospective multinational bibliographies.

John A. Lent, "Oldest Existing Commonwealth Caribbean Newspapers" (*Caribbean Q.*, Vol. 22, 1976, p. 90) and "List of Known Newspapers in Commonwealth Caribbean" (ibid., 1976, pp. 91–106) are of particular value for the list of newspapers published in Bahamas, Barbados, Bermuda, British Virgin Islands, Cayman Islands, Turks Islands, Jamaica, Anguilla, Antigua, Montserrat, Nevis, Saint Christopher (Saint Kitts), Trinidad and Tobago, Dominica, Grenada, Saint Lucia, and Saint Vincent. Data provided are date, title of newspaper, frequency, and year of last known issue.

Beginning with January 1967 the Public Library of Barbados has issued *List of Additions to the West Indian Collection*. It is published quarterly and, at least through 1979, has been circulated gratis.

There are no good lists, either retrospective or current, of Spanish and Portuguese newspapers and periodicals of the area. There are union lists that show the availability of certain titles in certain geographical areas.

Little seems to exist on the English-language press in French-, Spanish-, and Portuguese-speaking Latin America. Of use are: Dennis L. Wilcox, "A Directory of English Language Daily Newspapers in Countries Where English Is a Minority Language" (M.A. thesis, University of Iowa, 1966, xi, 256 pp.; published as *English Language Newspapers Abroad: A Guide to Daily Newspapers in 56 Non-English-Speaking Countries*, Gale Research Company, Detroit, 1967, 243 pp.); and John Lee, "The Expatriate Press: A Survey of English Language Newspapers Around the World" (M.A. thesis, West Virginia University, 1965, vii, 253 leaves).

Karl J. R. Arndt and May E. Olson, *The German Language Press of the Americas 1732–1968: History and Bibliography*, Volume 2 (Verlag Dokumentation, Pullach/Munich, 1973), would seem to be an extraordinarily thorough listing and description of the German-language press in Argentina, Bolivia, Brazil, Canada, Chile, Colombia, Costa Rica, Cuba, Dominican Republic, Ecuador, Guatemala, Guyana, Mexico, Paraguay, Peru, the United States (supplement), Uruguay, and Venezuela. It is referred to in this article as *Arndt–Olson*.

Also of value is Lieselotte Maas, *Handbuch der deutschen Exilpresse 1933–1954* (Carl Hanser Verlag, Munich and Vienna, 1976–1978, 2 vols.). It is arranged alphabetically by title. The preface states that its aim "is to provide a survey of the German exile press in its totality. It will give as detailed a breakdown as possible, in terms of names and data, of all publications that could be traced; it will give concise biographical profiles of their publishers, editors, and key contributors; and finally, it will describe each individual publication and each group of publications in a way that makes readily apparent the aims they set themselves, the job they actually did, and their area of influence" (p. 27). It is a pity that no geographical and proper name indexes were provided.

Jan Kovalik, *World Index of Polish Periodicals Published Outside of Poland since September 1939* (American Polish Documentation Studio, Sunnyvale, Calif., 1972–1974, 4 vols.) provides pertinent data on periodicals in Polish that are or have been published in this area since 1939.

Antigua

Very little has been written about the history of printing in Antigua and of the island's imprints. Wilberforce Eames, "The Antigua Press and Benjamin Mecon, 1748–1765" (*Proc. Am. Antiquarian Soc.*, Vol. 38, October 1928, pp. 303–348) lists six early works printed in Antigua (pp. 323–325).

Antiguan newspapers are listed in E. C. Baker, *A Guide to Records in the Leeward Islands* (Basil Blackwell, Oxford, 1965, pp. 22–23, 101).

Argentina

The Viceroyalty of the Río de la Plata included all or parts of what are now Argentina, Uruguay, Paraguay, and (at one time) Bolivia.

The chief bibliographies of Argentine bibliographies and studies of Argentine national bibliography are: Narciso Binayan; "Bibliografía de bibliografías argentinas" (*Rev. Univ. Buenos Aires*, Vol. 48, 1919, pp. 114–149), Roberto Couture de Troismonts, "The Present State of Argentine National Bibliography" (16th SALALM, 1965, Working Paper No. 12, 14 pp.), Abel Rodolfo Geoghegan, *Bibliografía de bibliografías argentinas* (Casa Pardo, Buenos Aires, 1970, 130 pp.), Hans Gravenhorst, "El panorama bibliográfico documental en la Argentina" (14th SALALM, 1963, Working Paper No. 20, 8 pp.), Josefa E. Sabor, "La bibliografía general argentina en curso de publicación" (*Handbook of Latin Studies*, Vol. 25, 1963, pp. 373–381), and Sabor and Lydia H. Revello, "Bibliografía básica de obras de referencia de artes y letras para la Argentina" (*Bibliografía argentina de artes y letras*, No. 26, 1969?, pp. 1–76).

Argentine Bibliography: A Union Bibliography of Argentinian Holdings in the

Libraries of the University of Buenos Aires (G. K. Hall, Boston, 1980, 6 vols.) contains "an estimated 105,000 cards," and it "lists all works written by Argentine authors or about Argentina, published anywhere in the world through 1977" (G. K. Hall advertisement).

Manuel Selva, Fortunata Mendilharzu, and Lorenzo J. Rosso compiled *Bibliografía general argentina*, subtitled Inventario analítico–crítico de todas las publicaciones argentinas desde el origen de la primera imprenta en el Río de la Plata, hasta el presente (Talleres gráficos argentinos de L. J. Rosso, Buenos Aires, 1931–1933, 2 vols.). This attempt at a retrospective bibliography of Argentina publications reached the letter *C*.

Guillermo Furlong Cardiff, *Historia y bibliografía de las primeras imprentas rioplatenses, 1700–1850* (4 vols.: Vol. 1, Editorial Guaranía; Vols. 2–3, Librería del Plata; and Vol. 4, Librería Huemul, Buenos Aires, 1953–1976) is slightly misnamed, for it reaches only the year 1815. It provides bibliographic descriptions of more than 3,398 items. If copies are not located, references are made to the work of other bibliographers who have described the item. For certain entries, the work is completely reproduced. The "Indice de personas, materias y primeras palabras de publicaciones rioplatenses" in each volume is extremely useful.

This set completely replaces earlier attempts to study the imprints of this period. Few presses have been more thoroughly studied than that of the Imprenta de los Niños Expositos in Buenos Aires. Furlong Cardiff in his notes refers to the most important of these. As this set is now the standard work in this field, the 30 or more studies that it replaces are not listed in this article.

The portions of this set that deal directly with what is now Argentina are: "La imprenta en Córdoba, 1765–1767" (Vol. 1, pp. 101–113) and the bibliography of Córdoba imprints for the period (Vol. 1, pp. 420–452); "La imprenta en Buenos Aires, 1780–1784" (Vol. 1, pp. 115–271) and the bibliography of Buenos Aires imprints (Vol. 1, pp. 452–579); "La imprenta en Buenos Aires, 1785–1807" (Vol. 2, pp. 7–596); "La imprenta en Buenos Aires, 1808–1810" (Vol. 3, pp. 55–390); and "La imprenta en Buenos Aires, 1810–1815" (Vol. 4, pp. 51–735). Other sections deal with colonial printing in Paraguay and Montevideo.

Mention, however, should be made of José Toribio Medina, *Historia y bibliografía de la imprenta en el antiguo Virreinato de la Plata* (Talleres de publicaciones del museo, La Plata, 1892; reprinted N. Israel, Amsterdam, 1965). Part 2 is *Historia y bibliografía de la imprenta en Córdoba (1766)* (xiii, 12 pp.), and Part 3 is *Historia y bibliografía de la imprenta en Buenos Aires, 1780–1810* (xliii, 452 pp.). This was the standard study of printing in this area for more than 60 years.

Juan María Gutiérrez compiled "Catálogo de los libros didácticos que se han publicado o escrito en Buenos Aires desde el año 1790 hasta el de 1867 inclusive . . ." in *Noticias históricas sobre el oríjen y desarrollo de la enseñanza superior en Buenos Aires* . . . (Imprenta del Siglo—de J. M. Cantilo, Buenos Aires, 1868, pp. 573–618). This bibliography also appears in the second edition of this work (La cultura argentina, Buenos Aires, 1915, pp. 385–418).

Juan E. Pivel and Guillermo Furlong Cardiff, "La imprenta del Ejército Republicano, 1826–1828" (*Bol. Instituto de investigaciones históricas*, Vol. 11, No. 45, July–September 1930, pp. 166–175) describes 29 imprints of this press.

Half of the works listed in Antonio Zinny, *Bibliografía histórica de las Provincias Unidas del Río de la Plata desde el año 1780 hasta el de 1821 . . .* (Imprenta americana, Buenos Aires, 1875, 476, xiii, v pp.) were published in 1820 and 1821.

According to Binayan, the first attempt at a current Argentine bibliography would seem to be that of Acislo M. Cabot, *Bibliografía de 1866* (Imprenta española, Buenos Aires, 1867, 16 pp.).

The *Anuario bibliográfico de la República Argentina* for 1879–1887 (publisher varies, Buenos Aires, 1880–1888, 9 vols.) provides data on 7,131 titles. The volume for 1880 includes the section "Diarios y periódicos de la República Argentina." The last volume lists 413 newspapers and magazines. A list of publishers, presses with their addresses, and the number of works published by each appears in the volumes for 1885–1887.

The Instituto bibliográfico of the Universidad nacional (La Plata) published an *Anuario bibliográfico: Letras, historia, educación y filosofía* for the period 1926–1929 (La Plata, 1927–1930, 4 vols. in 6). It lists not only books but material published in slightly more than 100 newspapers and magazines.

The Biblioteca y archivo section of the Ministerio de relaciones exteriores y culto published Numbers 1–18 of the *Boletín internacional de bibliografía argentina* (Imprenta de la H. Camara de diputados, November 1930–December 1932). This series lists 663 works with contents notes.

The Ministerio de justicia y instrucción pública issued a *Registro nacional de la propiedad intelectual, catálogo año de 1934–[1938]* (Buenos Aires, 1936–1939?).

Argentina's Biblioteca nacional issued from 1932 through 1936 a *Lista de las últimas obras argentinas ingresadas en la Biblioteca nacional.* In 1937 it started publication of *Boletín bibliográfico argentino* (Nos. 1–26, 1937–1951), which appeared at irregular intervals and covered the period 1937–1949. The title then was changed to *Boletín bibliográfico nacional* (Nos. 27–33, 1952–1963), and this covered the period 1950–1956.

The *Guía del libro, 1935–1942* (1943, 373, lxviii pp.) and *Guía del libro* ([1959], 133 pp.) both were published in Buenos Aires by the Cámara argentina de editoriales técnicas.

For recent years the best guides to recent Argentine publications are probably the classified lists issued for sale purposes by Fernando García Cambeiro and the Librería del Plata. Buenos Aires is one of the largest centers for publications in Spanish, and it is to be hoped that a current bibliography can be begun and continued for Argentina.

No one has done any study concerning the comprehensiveness of Argentine bibliographies. However, it would seem that a thorough picture of Argentine imprints cannot be had until many more studies are made concerning printing in the provinces. The next part of this section discusses some of these regional bibliographies.

Nicolás Matijevic lists 531 imprints from Bahia Blanca in his *Imprenta bahiense* (Universidad nacional del Sur, Departamento de ciencias sociales, Bahia Blanca, 1978, 91 pp.). The first part of this book is a brief history of printing and of the various presses of this city. The imprint bibliography is arranged by printer. It includes books and city, state, and federal documents as well as periodicals printed in this city.

Ramón Rosa Olmos, *Bibliografía catamarqueña* (Talleres tipográficos del diario "La Union," Catamarca, 1945, 59 pp.) lists 807 publications issued between 1858 and 1945 by writers from Catamarca or about it.

Manuel V. Figuerero, *Bibliografía de la Imprenta del Estado en Corrientes*, subtitled Desde sus origenes en 1826 hasta su desaparición en 1896: Con prólogo de David Pena (Imprenta y casa editora Coni, Buenos Aires, 1919, xxxiv, 323 pp.), lists 166 imprints for this period.

Pabla Cabrera, *La segunda imprenta en la Universidad de Córdoba*, subtitled Adquirida por suscripción popular en 1823 bajo el gobierno del general D. Juan Bautista Bustos (Imprenta de la universidad de Córdoba, [Córdoba], 1930, ii, 197 pp.), provides data on 171 imprints (books, pamphlets, broadsides, newspapers, and periodicals) published between 1822 and 1842.

Fernando Morales Guinazu, "Bibliografía," in his *Historia de la cultura mendocina* (Best hermanos, Mendoza, 1943, pp. 493–610), lists 1,416 publications printed in Mendoza, by Mendozan authors, or about Mendoza which appeared between 1820 and 1940.

The three most important histories of Argentine periodicals would appear to be Oscar R. Beltrán, *Historia del periodismo argentino: Pensamiento y obra de los forjadores de la patria* (Editorial Sopena Argentina, Buenos Aires, 1943, 355 pp.), Juan Romulo Fernández, *Historia del periodismo argentino* (Librería Perlado, Buenos Aires, 1943, 405 pp.), and C. Galván Moreno, *El periodismo argentino: Amplia y documentada historia desde sus origenes hasta el presente* (Claridad, Buenos Aires, 1944, 520 pp.).

The volume by Beltrán provides data on title, date, and place of publication of many newspapers, but the lack of an index to this material makes this information much less easy to locate than in Galván Moreno.

The volume by Fernández not only appears to be the fullest, but it contains a variety of tables that would help in the compilation of a national bibliography of Argentine newspapers and periodicals. "El periodismo en 1892" (pp. 99–105) lists periodicals published in this year. "El periodismo argentino en el siglo xix" (pp. 219–264) is a chronological list of newspapers and periodicals which provides data on dates of publication, title, and city of publication. "El periodismo argentino en 1942: Diarios, periodismo y revistas de la capital federal e interior" (pp. 267–395) is an alphabetically arranged list, first of newspapers and then of periodicals, in which data are given concerning the title, date of first issue, type of publication, director, and place of publication. This listing omits official government bulletins.

The Galván volume is well indexed and would seem to provide much more data on publications outside of the capital than does Fernández. Pages 297–453 deal with the provincial press, alphabetically by province, while pages 477–483 provide a bibliography of 137 items on Argentine journalism.

The earliest scholarly attempt at a listing of Argentine periodicals would seem to be that of Antonio Zinny, *Efermidografía argirometropolitana hasta la caída del gobierno de Rosas,* subtitled Contiene el título, fecha de su aparición y cesación, formato, imprenta, número que se compone cada colección, nombre de los redactores que se conocen, observaciones y noticias biográficas sobre cado uno de éstos, y la biblioteca pública o particular donde se encuentra el periódico (Imprenta del

Plata, Buenos Aires, 1869, xvii, xix, ix, 545 pp.); this is reprinted from *Revista de Buenos Aires* (Vols. 9–13, 1866–1867), where it appeared as "Bibliografía periodística de Buenos Aires hasta la caída del gobierno de Rosas." Zinny provides data on 325 newspapers published in Buenos Aires between 1801 and February 3, 1852. Pages 319–412 list guides, almanacs, and bulletins; while pages 405–406 list newspapers published after February 3, 1852. Zinny also compiled *Efemeridográfia argiroparquiótica o sea de las provincias argentinas* (Imprenta y librería de Mayo, Buenos Aires, 1868, xix, ii, 300 pp.), reprinted from *Revista de Buenos Aires* (Vols. 16–24, 1868–1871). This volume is arranged by province and then alphabetically by title. It describes 129 newspapers published between 1817 and 1852 in Santa Fé, Entre Ríos, Corrientes, Córdoba, La Rioja, San Juan, Mendoza, Tucumán, and Salta. He annotates (pp. 50–57) 23 broadsides published in Entre Ríos and 61 imprints from San Juan (pp. 208–222). Both volumes are well indexed.

The Biblioteca nacional issued *Un siglo de periódicos en la Biblioteca nacional (políticos): Catálogo por fechas, 1800–1899* (Buenos Aires, 1935, 74 pp.). It provides data on 609 Argentine newspapers and 276 from other countries. Holdings and call numbers are given.

R. J. Payró, "La prensa socialista," in *Anuario de la prensa argentina, 1896* (Imprenta de P. E. Coni e hijos, Buenos Aires, 1897, pp. 51–70), is part of a volume (vii, 428 pp.) that lists 610 newspapers including 51 in foreign languages. Pertinent data are provided for each title.

Gabriel Carrasco, "El periodismo en la República Argentina" (*Bol. demógrafico argentino*, Vol. 2, No. 5, 1901, pp. 1–33) provides data on newspapers and periodicals published in 1899.

Avelina M. Ibáñez, "Sinopsis tabular de las publicaciones de caracter periodístico aparecidas en Buenos Aires hasta 1830" (*Segundo congreso internacional de historia de América*, Buenos Aires, 1938, Vol. 5, pp. 45–187) provides data on date, title, press, editor, character, duration, and location.

Other items are:

Alberto B. Martínez, "Censo de los diarios, periódicos y revistas de 1895 y de 1914" (*Tercer censo nacional*, Buenos Aires, 1917, Vol. 9, pp. 271–319).

Ernesto Quesada, "El movimiento intelectual argentino: Revistas y periódicos," in *Reseñas y críticos* (F. Lajouane, Buenos Aires, 1893, pp. 119–141).

The Biblioteca nacional's *Catálogo de las revistas y periódicos existentes en la Biblioteca nacional (con exclusión de los diarios políticos)*, published in three editions (1901, 48 pp.; 1904, 76 pp.; and 1923, 94 pp.).

Guía periódistica argentina, for 1913 (Buenos Aires, n.d., 301 pp.).

For Argentine scientific and technical journals, one can consult: Consejo nacional de investigaciones científicas y técnicas, *Guía de publicaciones periódicas y técnicas que se editan en la República Argentina* (2nd ed., Buenos Aires, 1964, 133, 8 pp.), and Asociación de la prensa técnica Argentina, *Primera guía de las publicaciones especializadas y técnicas argentinas* (Buenos Aires, [1959], 64 pp.).

Two hundred and thirteen agricultural magazines are listed in Roberto Millan, "Catálogo de las publicaciones periódicos de la Argentina sobre agricultura" (*Bol. Ministerio de agricultura de la nación*, Vol. 30, 1931, pp. 227–306).

The chief sources for the study of Argentina's literary journals are: Héctor René

Lafleur, Sergio D. Provenzano, et al., *Las revistas literarias argentinas, 1893–1960* Biblioteca del sesquicentenario, Serie cuadernos culturales, Ediciones Culturales Argentinas, Ministerio de educación y justicia, Dirección general de cultura, [Buenos Aires], [1962], 282 pp.); Nélida Salvador, *Revistas argentinas de vanguardia (1920–1930)* (Publicación de la Facultad de filosofía y letras, Instituto de literatura argentina "Ricardo Rojas," Critica, Tomo 6, No. 1, Facultad de filosofía y letras, Universidad de Buenos Aires, Buenos Aires, [1962]), 108 pp.); and "Revistas literarias argentinas (1893–1940); Aporte para una bibliografía" (*Bibliografía argentina de artes y letras*, No. 9, Sec. 2, January–March 1961, pp. 47–116; a reprint dated [1962] exists).

Ramón Rosa Olmos, "El periodismo catamarqueño en su centenario . . ." (*La Union*, July 18, 1957, pp. 1–2, 4) lists 121 periodicals and newspapers in chronological order and provides data on their dates, frequency, publishers, issues published, etc.

Manuel Florencio Mantilla, *Bibliografía periodística de la provincia de Corrientes* (Imprenta y librería de Mayo, Buenos Aires, 1887, 167 pp.) provides data on 112 newspapers and specialized periodicals. Emilio Mendez Paz, *Periódicos correntinos, 1825–1900* (Talleres tipográficos NISSA, Buenos Aires, 1953, 123 pp.) has a chronological arrangement and provides data on 232 titles. There is a title index as well as one of editors, directors, publishers, and owners.

Unfortunately, the posthumous work by Anibal S. Vasquez, *Periódicos y periodistas de Entre Rios* (Gobierno de la provincia de Entre Rios, Ministerio de bienestar social y educación, Dirección de cultura de Entre Rios, Paraná, 1970, 220 pp.), was published in an incomplete form, as the published work indicates no sources for the data given.

Rogelio Díaz L., "Sintesis histórico–cronólogico del periodismo de la provincia de San Juan 1825 a 1937" (*Anal. Congreso de historia de Cuyo*, Vol. 2, 1937, pp. 375–401) provides data on dates, frequency, political orientation, publishers, affiliations, etc., of 125 newspapers and 23 magazines.

Rosario's Dirección general de estadística del municipio has issued in mimeographed form *Publicaciones periódicas editadas en al año 1939 en la ciudad de Rosario* ([1940], 8 pp.). It provides data on about 130 titles.

Miguel Sola, *La imprenta en Salta: Cien años de prensa (1824–1924) y bibliografía de la imprenta salteña* (Talleres gráficos Porter hermanos, Buenos Aires, 1924, 131 pp.) and his "Adición a la imprenta en Salta" (*Bol. Instituto de investigaciones históricos*, Vol. 25, Nos. 85–88, 1940–1941, pp. 1–20) provide data on slightly more than 300 books, periodicals, newspapers, and government documents.

Luis A. Ledesma Medina, "Reseña de la bibliografía general de Santiago del Estero" (*Rev. Junta de estudios históricos de Santiago del Estero*, Vol. 2, Nos. 5–6, July–December 1944, pp. 156–168) provides a classified approach to publications of this province with the barest bibliographic details (usually only author, title, and date). It is divided into Ciencias sociales, Ciencias puras, Ciencias literarias, Ciencias aplicadas, and Ciencias históricas y geográficos.

José F. L. Castiglione, *El periodismo en Santiago del Estero* (Editorial Yussem, Santiago del Estero, 1941, 60 pp.) is of value for its "Periódicos editados en la ciudad de Santiago del Estero" (pp. 31–51), which lists by date of publication slightly over 100 periodicals. Castiglione provides the date of publication, title, length of publication when he can establish it, editor's name, name of organization that published it, and often type of journal (i.e., political, religious, etc.).

José P. Barrientos, *Historia del periodismo de Tandi* ([Talleres Grafitan, Tandil, 1975], 261 pp.) provides much valuable data on the periodicals of this city in Buenos Aires province. The titles are arranged chronologically for the period 1854 to 1974. A discussion of a title may run from several pages to several lines. Pages 253–257 list the various libraries and private collections that contain the journals discussed in the text, while pages 257–259 list the contents of the Barrientos collection of such material.

The national library and various university libraries have issued periodical lists. However, these almost always list their periodical holdings as a whole, rather than listing only periodicals published in Argentina.

The Argentine German-language press is described in *Arndt–Olson* (Vol. 2, pp. 32–88).

Vojtěch N. Duben, *Czech and Slovak Press Outside Czechoslovakia: Its Status in 1978* (SVU Publications, Occasional Paper No. 4, Czechoslovak Society of Arts and Sciences in America, Washington, D.C., 1978, pp. 33, 37) provides incomplete data on two Slovak periodicals published in Buenos Aires in the 1970s.

Barbados

Douglas C. McMurtrie, *Early Printing in Barbados* (Privately printed, London, 1933, 15 pp.; reprinted from the Autumn 1933 issue of *Paper & Printer*) provides data on the establishment of a printing press on this island in 1730 by two Philadelphia printers, Daird Harry and Samuel Keuner. This study discusses works printed by Keuner and William Beeby and mentions other 18th-century printers.

The earliest discussion of the island's newspapers would appear to be that of Robert Hermann Schomburgk's *The History of Barbados* (Longman, Brown, Green, and Longmans, London, 1848, pp. 124–127), which provides a history of newspapers on Barbados as well as a history of government printing.

A recent study is that of E. M. Shilstone, "Some Notes on Early Printing Presses and Newspapers in Barbados" (*J. Barbados Museum Historical Soc.*, Vol. 26, No. 1, November 1958, pp. 19–33).

The Public Library in Bridgetown began in 1975 to issue the *National Bibliography of Barbados*. This subject list of books received in the Public Library in compliance with legal deposit laws, and of books of Barbadian authorship printed abroad, is a quarterly with annual cumulations. It is classified by subject, with author, title, and series index.

Many Barbados imprints are listed with their locations in Jerome S. Handler, *A Guide to Source Materials for the Study of Barbados History, 1627–1834* (Southern Illinois University Press, Carbondale, 1971, xvi, 205 pp.).

Belize

Roderick Cave, "Printing in Nineteenth Century Belize" (*Lib. Q.*, Vol. 46, 1976, pp. 20–37) is one of the few studies of any kind on this country's printing and journalism. Its two appendixes are particularly valuable for the purposes of this article: They are "A List of Printers in Belize in the Nineteenth Century" (pp. 32–33) and "A Handlist of Belize Newspapers Published before 1900" (pp. 33–36). This article also provides brief data on printing in Bay Islands and the Mosquito Coast.

Bermuda

There would appear to be no retrospective or current bibliography of Bermudian imprints. A few of them will be found listed in Bermuda Book Store, *Guide to Books about Bermuda* (The Store, Hamilton, 1972, 14 pp.) and *Bermudiana: Bibliography* (The Bermuda Library, Hamilton, 1971, 27 pp.).

Douglas C. McMurtrie, "The Printing Press in Burmuda" (*Am. Collector,* Vol. 4, 1927, pp. 62–63) would seem to be one of the few studies on printing in Bermuda.

The most recent history of Bermuda newspapers appears to be that of Waldo Lincoln found in the "Report of the Council" (*Proc. Am. Antiquarian Soc.*, n.s., Vol. 34, 1924, pp. 136–145), to which is appended "Check List of Bermuda Newspapers" (pp. 145–147). Lincoln is also the compiler of "List of Newspapers of the West Indies and Bermuda in the Library of the American Antiquarian Society" (ibid., n.s., Vol. 36, 1927, pp. 130–155).

Bolivia

In colonial times, what is now Bolivia was referred to as "Alto Perú." It was a part of the Viceroyalty of Peru until August 8, 1776, when it was transferred to the jurisdiction of the Viceroyalty of La Plata. In 1612 a press was established by the Jesuits in Juli, on the shores of Lake Titicaca. It lasted but a short time. Printing was reintroduced into this area in 1808 with the publication in La Paz of a proclamation from Governor Tadeo Dávila.

The student interested in the history of printing and of bibliography, both national and otherwise, in Bolivia would be wise to consult Arturo Costa de la Torre, "Historia de la bibliografía boliviana," in *Catálogo de la bibliografía boliviana . . .* (La Paz, 1969, Vol. 1, pp. 23–177).

The greatest of the 19th-century Bolivian bibliographers was Gabriel René Moreno (1836–1908), who compiled *Biblioteca boliviana: Catálogo de la sección de libros i folletos* (Imprenta Gutenberg, Santiago, 1879, 980 pp.), *Primer suplemento a la . . .: Epítome de un catálogo de libros y folletos, 1879–1899* (Imprenta . . . Barcelona, Santiago, 1900, 349 pp.), and *Segundo suplemento a la . . .: Libros y folletos, 1900–1908* (Imprenta . . . Universitaria, Santiago, 1905, 349 pp.).

The first contains 3,529 entries in alphabetical order, with indexes of authors, translators, and editors. The first supplement includes material published before 1879 (items 3530–3617), items published since 1879 (items 3618–4641c), and American books and pamphlets (items 4642–5176). Moreno died on April 28, 1908, and the second supplement was completed by E. Barrenechea and E. O'Ryan G. Items 5177–6031 list Bolivian publications; 6032–6815 list American books and pamphlets published outside of Bolivia.

The *Biblioteca boliviana* has been supplemented by Valentín Abecía in his *Adiciones a la . . . con un apendice del editor, 1602–1879* (Imprenta . . ., Barcelona, Santiago, 1899, 442 pp.). Items 1–350 are the work of Abecía, and items 351–571 are that of E. Barrenechea.

José Rosendo Gutiérrez is important for his *Bibliografía boliviana en 1878* (Imprenta de la Unión americana, [La Paz, 1879], 16 pp.), which would seem to be the first attempt at a current bibliography of Bolivian publications; and for *Datos para la bibliografía boliviana: Primera sección* (Imprenta de "La Libertad," de Esequiel Arzaduru, La Paz, 1874, 255 pp.) and *Segundo suplemento: Últimas adiciones y correcciones a la primera sección* (Imprenta de la Unión americana, La Paz, 1880, 126 pp.). The second supplement includes books and pamphlets printed in Bolivia from 1825 through 1875, Bolivian authors published elsewhere, and books on Bolivia published by foreign authors and printed outside of Bolivia.

Of Arturo Costa de la Torre's *Catálogo de la bibliografía boliviana: Libros y folletos, 1900–1963* (La Paz, 1969–), two of a proposed three volumes have been published. The first volume of 1,255 pages appears to be an extraordinarily complete listing of Bolivian books and pamphlets for the period covered. The arrangement is by author, for whom biographical sketches are often provided. Each author's works are then listed in chronological order.

The second volume adds 2,920 items not found in the second supplement to Gabriel René Moreno's *Biblioteca boliviana, 1900–1908*; it also has a bibliography of 4,160 items that lists works by foreign authors on Bolivia published between 1908 and 1963, and its last two sections are a bibliography of Lake Titicaca and one on Bolivian cartography.

Werner Guttentag Tichauer (1920–) was born in Brelau, Germany, and has lived in Bolivia since 1939. In 1945 he established Los Amigos del libro bookstore in Cochabamba and later founded the Canata publishing house, the name of which was changed to Editorial "Los Amigos del libro." He has been the compiler and driving force as well as the publisher of *Bibliografía boliviana, 1962–1974* (Los Amigos del libro, Cochabamba and La Paz, 1963–1975). With the volume for 1975 its title was changed to *Bio-bibliografía boliviana*.

These volumes provide an excellent picture of Bolivian imprints since 1962. Each volume contains the bibliography of the books printed in Bolivia or by Bolivians published during the year, arranged by authors, and each contains a supplement that lists material published since 1962 that was omitted from the preceding volumes. Some of the issues contain a bibliography of material about Bolivia published outside of this country, and each volume contains indexes by title, subject, publisher, and printer, both for the main body of the work and for the supplement. The data for each entry are extremely full, though it might be helpful to have an indication as to the book's price. The dates and profession of each author are given, and sometimes a brief (several lines) biographical sketch is provided. Important works have their table of contents reproduced; belles-lettres are identified as to literary genre. In the case that a book is a reprint, Guttentag notes, by date and place of publication, earlier editions. All material, regardless of language, is listed. The introductory essays may deal with the status of Bolivian publishing or a brief discussion of what he considers to be the most important works published during the year, or some authority may contribute a bibliography on some phase of Bolivian culture. The *Bibliografía boliviana* includes government publications. Many of the volumes list works by Bolivians translated into other languages. He often includes a section of maps published in Bolivia during the year. The *Bio-bibliografía boliviana* is an annual that appears on a regular basis. It is also an example of a national bibliography compiled by a single individual against sometimes overwhelming odds. Many publishers still make little attempt to obey the laws concerning the information that should appear on the title page, or they do not follow those that regulate the legal deposit of books in La Paz, Cochabamba, Chuquisaca, Potosí, and Tarija.

Regional bibliographies do not seem to be plentiful. Attention can be called to the *Catálogo del libro potosino* (Universidad boliviana mayor "Tomás Frías," Potosí, 1973, 42 pp.).

There are rather large gaps in our knowledge of newspapers and periodicals of the 19th and 20th centuries. Gabriel René Moreno, *Ensayo de una bibliografía general de los periódicos de Bolivia, 1825–1905* (Sociedad "Imprenta y litografía universo," Santiago de Chile, 1905, 334 pp.) and *Ensayo de una bibliografía general de los periódicos: Suplemento (1905–1907)* (published as an appendix to the *Segundo suplemento a la Biblioteca boliviana*) cover the period through 1907. These titles were reprinted as a combined volume in Buenos Aires in 1974 by the Editorial Monserrat (343, xvii pp.). These works present data on 1,435 periodicals.

Werne Golde, *Bibliographie der bolivianischen Zeitschriften, 1953–1954* (Deutsche Schule, La Paz, 1955, 66 pp.) is a mimeographed list of Bolivian newspapers for these years. Its title also appears in Spanish.

Agricultural journals are listed in Armando Cardoso Gonzalo, *Revistas agrícolas: Cronología y clasificación* (Sociedad's boletín bibliográfico, No. 2, Sociedad de ingenieros agrónomos de Bolivia, La Paz, 1962, 75 pp.), and Aliga de Viscarra, *Guía de publicaciones periódicas agrícolas y conexas de Bolivia* (Sociedad's boletín bibliográfico, No. 8, Sociedad de ingenieros agrónomos de Bolivia, La Paz, 1968, 16 pp.).

With the publication of *Bio-bibliografía boliviana* for 1976, it would seem that Guttentag has decided to include data on currently published Bolivian magazines, but not newspapers. This volume and that for 1977 contain an "Ensayo de una bibliografía de revistas." This section not only contains data on the Bolivian magazines but includes journals published outside of Bolivia if they contain material by Bolivians.

Periodicals published in La Paz have been recorded by Nicolás Acosta, *Apuntes para bibliografía: Periodística de la Ciudad de La Paz* (Imprenta de la Unión americana de César Sevilla, La Paz, 1876, 57 pp.).

The country's German press has been studied in *Arndt–Olson* (Vol. 2, pp. 89–90).

Brazil

Antônio Simoēs dos Reis, *Bibliografia das bibliografias brasileiras* (Ministerio da educação e saude, Instituto nacional do livro, Rio de Janeiro, 1942, 186 pp.; Colecão Bl) provides data on 712 items. It is arranged chronologically, with subject and author indexes. Bruno Basseches, *Bibliography of Brazilian Bibliographies* (Blaine Ethridge Books, Detroit, 1978, viii, 185 pp.) contains 2,488 entries. Unfortunately, it is deficient in many ways. The index includes both compilers of bibliographies and subjects.

Laurence Hallewell, "The Development of National Bibliography in Brazil" (*Libri*, Vol. 23, 1973, pp. 291–297), Edson N. da Fonseca, "Panorama de bibliografia brasileira corrente" (in *Handbook of Latin American Studies*, No. 23, pp. 401–404, University of Florida Press, Gainesville, 1961), and da Fonseca's "Desenvolvimento da biblioteconomia e da bibliografia no Brasil" (*Rev. livro*, Vol. 5, March 1957, pp. 95–124) are most useful studies on Brazilian national bibliography.

Augusto Victorino Alves do Sacramento Blake, *Diccionario bibliographico brazileiro* (Typ. nacional, Rio de Janeiro, 1883–1902; reprint Kraus Nendeln, Liechtenstein, 1969) is a seven-volume work (with Index in Vol. 7). It has been separately indexed as *Indice alphabetico do Diccionario bibliographico de Sacramento Blake* (Rio de Janeiro, 1937, 127 pp.). This work is arranged alphabetically by the authors' first names.

The Biblioteca nacional published a national bibliography in its *Boletím bibliográfico*. That published in the period 1886–1888 was classified according to the Brunet system; that published from 1918 to 1921, according to the UDC; that in 1939 was arranged alphabetically by subject; and that issued in 1947, according to the Dewey system. For brief discussions of this bibliographic journal, see the article by Maria Antonieta de Mesquita Barros, "O Boletin bibliográfico da Biblioteca nacional do Rio de Janeiro" (*A Biblioteca*, Vol. 3, 1954, pp. 2–5; reprinted in *Bol. bibliográfico*, Vol. 5, No. 7, 1955, pp. 1–3).

The Instituto nacional do livro in Rio de Janeiro has published the following volumes of *Bibliografia brasileira*: 1938–1939 (1941), 1940 (1954), 1941 (1952), 1942–1945 (1953, 2 vols.), 1946 (1947), 1947–1952 (1957, 2 vols.), 1953 (1954), 1954 (1956), 1955 (1959), 1963, 1964, 1965 (all 1966), and 1966 (1967). The arrangement is that of an author, title, subject dictionary catalog. This set includes government documents. Most contain lists of "Editoras e livrarias" with their addresses. Later volumes have a variety of indexes.

Antônio Simoēs dos Reis compiled *Bibliografia nacional*, for 1942 and 1943 (Z. Valverde, Rio de Janeiro, 1942–1943, 14 vols.).

The Instituto nacional do livro began the publication of "Bibliografia brasileira corrente" in 1956 in *Revista do livro*. In November 1967 it began the publication of the *Bibliografia brasileira mensal*.

The Sindicato nacional dos editôres de livros in Rio de Janeiro published *Edicoēs brasileiras: Catalogo trimestral de livros publicados no Brasil, 1 janeiro* (1963, 132 pp.) and *Edicoēs brasileiras: Catalogo coletivo das editôras, livros saídos de novembro-64 a marco-65* (1966, 128 pp.).

The Sindicato nacional dos editôres de livros also has been responsible for the publication of the following: *Resenha bibliográfica* (Rio de Janeiro, Nos. 1–47, 1968–1972), *Resumo bibliográfico* (1973–March 1976), and *Informativo bibliográfico* (Vol. 1, No. 1–, April 1976–). *Resumo bibliográfico* was a monthly in which the items were arranged according to the 18th edition of the Dewey Decimal Classification system. Author, title, translator, place of publication, publisher, date, pagination, and series data are provided for each entry. The same arrangement is found in *Informativo bibliográfico*. Statistical tables that precede each issue of *Resumo bibliográfico* and *Informativo bibliográfico* are of interest. Publishers' addresses appear in each issue as well as the number of titles of each publisher listed in the month's bibliography.

It appears that Brazilian newspapers and periodicals are best studied on the state level. The following would seem to be the few such lists to cover the country as a whole: Alberto Bessa, *100 annos de vida: A expansão da imprensa brasileira no primeiro seculo da sua existência* (Gomes de Carvalho, Lisboa, 1929, 313 pp.); Brazil's Departamento de imprensa e propaganda, *Relação das publicações periodicas brasileiras anotadas na Secretaria do Conselho Nacional de Imprensa até fev. de 1944* (Impr. nacional, Rio de Janeiro, 1945, 257 pp.) and its Departamento nacional de estatística, *Estatística da imprensa periodica no Brasil (1929–1930)* (Typ. do Dept. nacional de estatística, Rio de Janeiro, 1931, 144 pp.); and *Catálogo de jornais brasileiros, 1808–1889* (Série instrumentos de trabalho—Arquivo nacional, No. 12, Ministério da justiça, Arquivo nacional, Divisão de publicações, Biblioteca, Rio de Janeiro, A Biblioteca, 1979, 36 pp.).

Bessa is chronologically arranged, 1808–1905, with descriptive and historical notes. The *Estatística* has two sections: Periódicos existentes no Brasil and Estatística da imprensa periodica. The material is arranged by states.

In 1908 the Instituto histórico e geográfico brasileiro issued in two volumes its *Annaes da imprensa periódica brazileira, 1808–1908* (Imprensa nacional, Rio de Janeiro).

The *Anuário brasileiro de imprensa* (Vols. 1–17, 1940–1956/1957) has been continued as *Anuário de imprensa, radio & televisão* (Vol. 18–, 1958–).

Brazil's Serviço de estatística da educação e cultura, *Imprensa periódica, 1967* (Rio de Janeiro, 1968, 109 leaves) would appear to be the most recent list of current Brazilian periodicals.

Renato Berbert de Castro, *A primeira imprensa da Bahia e suas publicações: Tipografia de Manuel Antonio da Silva Serva, 1811–1818* (Secretaria de educação e cultura, Salvador, 1969, 167 pp.) is most useful for the publications of this period.

The press of Bahia has also been studied in João N. Torres, *Annaes da imprensa da Bahia: 1° centenário, 1811–1911*, subtitled Catálogo organizado pelos Sócios do Instituto histórico João N. Torres e Alfredo de Carvalho Ferreira (Typ. bahiana de Cincinato Melchiades, Bahia, 1911, 302 pp.).

The following list periodicals of Ceará: João Batista Perdigao de Oliveira,

Catalogo dos jornaes, revistas e outras publicações periodicas do Ceará, 1824–1904 (Typ. "Guarany" de J.G.D.S., [Fortaleza], 1905, 60 pp.), and Guilherme Studart, *Catalogo dos jornaes de pequeno e grande formato publicados em Ceará* (Typ. Studart, Fortaleza, 1896, 32 pp.; 1898, 47 pp.) and a second volume with the same title (Typ. Minerva de Assis Bezerra, Fortaleza, 1904, 93 pp.; reprinted from *Rev. Instituto do Ceará*).

For Espirito Santo, consult Heraclito Amancio Pereira, "A imprensa no Espirito Santo" (*Rev. Instituto histórico e geográfico do Espirito Santo*, Vol. 2, No. 3, 1922, pp. 28–49; Vol. 4, No. 4, 1925, pp. 107–168; and Vol. 5, No. 5, 1926, pp. 41–90).

Remijio de Bellido, *Catálogo dos jornaes paraenses, 1822–1908* (Imprensa official, Pará, 1908, 163 pp.) has three parts: Catálogo alphabetico e descriptivo, Catálogo chronologico, and Catálogo segundo as localidades.

Romairo Martins, *Catálogo dos jornaes publicados no Paraná de 1854–1907* (Typ. e lith. a vapor Impressora paranaense, Curytiba, 1908, 155 pp.) lists the newspapers and periodicals of Paraná.

Alfredo Ferreira de Carvalho, *Annaes da imprensa periódica pernambucana de 1821–1908: Dados históricos e bibliographicos* (Typ. do Jornal do Recife, Recife, 1908, 640 pp.) and "Jornaes pernambucanos de 1821–1889 (simples catálogo)" (*Rev. Instituto archeológico e geográfico pernambucano*, Vol. 52, 1899, pp. 197–232) deal with the periodicals of Pernambuco.

For Rio de Janeiro, the most recent study would seem to be I. O. R. Monteiro, "Catálogo de jornais e revistas do Rio de Janeiro (1808–1889) existentes na Biblioteca Nacional" (*An. Biblioteca nacional*, Vol. 85, 1965, pp. 1–208).

For São Paulo, one can consult two publications of São Paulo, Departamento de estatística, *Imprensa periódica no Estado de São Paulo: Revistas, cadastro por município em 31 dez. 1961* (1962, 21 pp.) and *Imprensa periódica no Estado de São Paulo* (1964, 46 pp.). In addition, there are Lafayette de Toledo, "Imprensa paulista: Memória histórica, 1827–1896" (*Rev. Instituto histórico e geográfico de São Paulo*, Vol. 3, 1898, pp. 301–521), which lists 1,536 newspapers and journals published in this state; and Affonso A. de Freitas, "A imprensa periódica de São Paulo" (*Rev. Instituto histórico e geográfico de São Paulo*, Vol. 19, 1915, pp. 321–1136), which provides a history and bibliography of the periodical press in São Paulo from the establishment of *O Paulista* in 1823 until 1901. The bibliography by Freitas contains 1,496 entries.

The German press in Brazil has been studied by Hans Gehse, *Die deutsche Presse in Brasilien von 1852 bis zur Gegenwart*, subtitled Ein Beitrag zur Geschichte und zum Aufgabenkreis auslanddeutschen Zeitungswesen (Deutschtum und Ausland: Studien zum Auslanddeutschtum und zur Auslandkultur, Heft 43, Aschendorffsche Verlagsbuchhandlung, Münster in Westfalen, 1931, xi, 174 pp.). *Arndt–Olson* (Vol. 2, pp. 91–221) also covers German materials.

Robert J. Smith, Hiroshi Saito, John B. Cornell, and Takashi Maeyama, *The Japanese and Their Descendants in Brazil: An Annotated Bibliography* (Centro de estudos nipo-brasileiros, São Paulo, 1967) is an extremely useful bibliography concerning the Japanese in Brazil. Many of these items were published in Japanese in Brazil. "Japanese-Language Periodicals of Special Interest" (pp. 103–108) provides data on almost a dozen Brazilian–Japanese newspapers and periodicals.

The Yiddish press in Brazil has been studied in Itzhak Z. Raizman, *A fertl yorkhundert Yidishe prese in Brazil, 1915–1940* (the verso of the title page provides an English translation of the title: A quarter of a century Yiddish press in Brazil) (Museum of Printing Art, Safed, 1968, 216 pp.).

Canal Zone

No retrospective or current bibliographies exist that list books, periodicals, and newspapers in the Canal Zone. The student interested in all phases of the Canal Zone should examine the *Subject Catalog of the Special Panama Collection of the Canal Zone Library–Museum* (G. K. Hall, Boston, 1964, 341 pp.). Although this is not a bibliography, it would be possible to make a list of all publications having a Canal Zone imprint.

Chile

J. R. Freudenthal has studied Chilean national bibliography in "Development and Current Status of Bibliographic Organization in Chile" (Ph.D. dissertation, University of Michigan, 1972, 377 pp.; *Diss. Abstr. Int.*, Vol. 33, [1972], p. 2401) and in "Chilean National Bibliography: Origins and Progress" (*Libri*, Vol. 22, 1972, pp. 273–290).

For Chile, the most important bibliographies of bibliography are: Relávila Silva, "Lista de algunas bibliografías publicadas en Chile" (*Bull. Bibliographical Soc. America*, Vol. 3, 1911, pp. 35–37); Ramón A. Laval, *Bibliografía de bibliografías chilenas* (Imprenta universitaria, Santiago, 1915, 71 pp.; reprinted from *Rev. bibliografía chilena y extranjera*, Vol. 3, 1915, pp. 1–25, 49–83, and reprinted by Emilio Vaisse in his *Bibliografía general de Chile* [Imprenta universitaria, Santiago, 1915, pp. v–lxix]); Herminia Elgueta de Ochsenius, *Suplemento y adiciones a la Bibliografía de bibliografías chilenas que publicó en 1915 en Ramón A. Laval* (Imprenta Cervantes, Santiago, 1930, 71 pp.; reprinted from *Rev. bibliografía chilena*, Vol. 3, 1929, pp. 115–176); and Anguita Blanca Matas, "Bibliografía de bibliografías chilenas, 1963–1971" (16th SALALM, *Final Report and Working Papers*, OAS, Washington, D.C., 1973, Vol. 2, pp. 313–324).

No country in this area has a more detailed discussion of its bibliographic activities than Chile. Guillermo Feliú Cruz, *Historia de las fuentes de la bibliografía chilena: Ensayo crítico* ([Editorial universidad católica], Santiago, 1966–1968, 3 vols.) is a work of great value and scholarship, indispensable for the study of Chilean bibliography, whether national or subject.

Emilio Vaisse, *Bibliografía general de Chile: Primera parte*, subtitled Diccionario de autores y obras (bibliografía y bibliografía) . . . (Imprenta universitaria, Santiago, 1915, lxix, 331, x pp.), apparently hoped to be one alphabetical list by author of works published in Chile. Unfortunately it covers only Abalos through Barros Arana.

The earliest attempt at a retrospective bibliography of early Chilean imprints was the anonymous "Catálogo de los libros y folletos impresos en Chile desde que se introdujo la imprenta" (*Rev. ciencias y letras*, Santiago, Vol. 1, 1858, pp. 739–768).

The works of Medina, Montt, and the Biblioteca nacional should be consulted for the pre-Independence period.

José Toribio Medina, *Bibliografía de la imprenta en Santiago de Chile desde sus orígenes hasta febrero de 1817* (Impreso en casa del autor, Santiago, 1891; reprint N. Israel, Amsterdam, 1966, xli, 179 pp.) should be supplemented by its *Adiciones y amplificaciones*, subtitled Obra póstuma, la pública con una introducción Guillermo Feliú Cruz (Universidad de Chile, Santiago, 1939) and by the facsimile edition, *Seguida de las adiciones y ampliaciones del mismo autor*, subtitled Ed. facsimilar: Introducción de Guillermo Feliú Cruz (Fondo histórico y bibliográfico José Toribio Medina, Santiago, 1961, xxxviii, xli, 179, xiv, 131 pp.).

Luis Montt, *Bibliografía chilena [1780–1818]* (Imprenta universitaria, Santiago, 1904–1921, 3 vols.) has had a varied printing history. Volume 2 was published first in 1904, at which time Volumes 1, 3, and 4 were announced as forthcoming. Of Volume 1, 264 pages were printed, and the compiler intended to revise them. In the meantime, what had been printed was sold as waste paper. The 103 pages of Volume 3 that were printed were destroyed by fire at the University Press in 1909. Volumes 1 and 3 were reprinted in 1921 from surviving copies.

In 1963 the Biblioteca nacional published *Impresos chilenos, 1776–1818* in two volumes. The first volume's contents are: Bibliografía histórica de la imprenta en Santiago de Chile; Impresos chilenos, 1776–1818, textos; and Indice cronológico de los impresos que posee la Biblioteca nacional, 1776–1818. The second volume contains: Descripciones bibliográficas de los impresos chilenos, 1776–1818; Textos manuscritos: Actas, bandos, proclamas, ordenes, decretos, pastorales, manifiestos, etc.; Indice cronológico de los impresos chilenos, 1776–1818; and Indice cronológico de los textos manuscritos.

Guillermo Feliú Cruz, "La imprenta federal de William P. Griswold and John Sharpe, 1818–1820" (*Rev. chilena de historia y geografía*, Vol. 40, No. 44, 1921, pp. 405–457, and Vol. 41, No. 45, 1922, pp. 145–172) discusses the history and production of this press.

Santiago Lindsay, in *Catálogo de las obras publicadas en Chile desde el año 1812 hasta el de 1858* (Anuario estadístico de la República de Chile, Entrega 2, Imprenta nacional, Santiago, 1861, pp. 144–156), provides neither place nor publisher for the 961 books and pamphlets and 278 periodicals that are listed.

The period 1812–1876 can best be studied through Ramón Briseño, *Estadística bibliográfica de la literature chilena, 1812–1876*, subtitled Impresos chilenos, publicaciones periódicas; Bibliografía chilena en el extranjero, escritores chilenos publicados en el extranjero o cuyas obras permancen inéditos; Apéndice; Estudio preliminar de Guillermo Feliú Cruz; Edición facsimilar de la Príncipe de 1862 . . . (Biblioteca nacional, Santiago, 1965–1966, 4 vols.). The first two volumes are the facsimile edition of a work first published in two volumes in the period 1862–1879. The third volume contains additions and more detailed data on certain items. The fourth volume is an index compiled by Guillermo Fuenzalida M. and Leonardo Muzzei de G.

David Toro Melo, *Catálogo de los impresos que vieron la luz pública en Chile desde 1877 hasta 1885 inclusives* (Imprenta Gutenberg, Santiago, 1893, 504 pp.) catalogs 2,453 books and pamphlets. It should be supplemented by the Biblioteca nacional's *Anuario de la prensa chilena, 1877–1885: I. Libros, folletos y hojas sueltas* (Imprenta universitaria, Santiago, 1952, 621 pp.), which contains 4,170 entries.

The Chilean Biblioteca nacional has compiled and either published or had published the following volumes of the *Anuario de la prensa chilena:* 1877–1885 (1952), with an introduction by its compiler, Raúl Silva Castro; 1886–1891 (1887–1892); 1892 (1894); 1893 (1895); 1894, 1895 (1897); 1896 (1899); 1897 (1900); 1898, 1899, 1900 (1903); 1901 (1904); 1902, 1903 (1905); 1904, 1905, 1906 (1911); 1907, 1908, 1909 (1912); 1910, 1911, 1912 (1913); 1913 (1914); 1914 (1924); 1915 (1925); 1917–1921 (1963); 1922–1926, 1927–1931 (1963); 1932–1936, published in two parts for 1932–1934 and 1935–1936; 1937–1941, published in two parts for 1937–1939 and 1940–1941; 1942–1946, 1947–1951, 1952–1956 (1964); 1957–1961, 1962 (1963); 1963 (1964); 1964, 1965 (1965); 1966 (1966); 1967 (1969); and 1968 (1970). There is also a supplementary volume for 1877–1964 (1966).

The volume for 1877–1885 includes only books, pamphlets, and broadsides. Those for the years 1886–1890, 1903–1913, and 1915 include books, pamphlets, broadsides, newspapers and periodicals, and other types of copyright registrations. That for 1891 includes all that the prior volumes contain, with a section on the clandestine press of the Revolution of 1891 and publications by Chileans or relating to Chile published outside of Chile. The volumes for the years 1892–1894 and 1896–1902 add a section that is an appendix listing publications omitted from earlier volumes. The volume for 1895 drops the appendix. Only those for 1896 through 1900 add a section that lists musical compositions printed in Chile and those by Chilean composers published outside of Chile. The volume for 1914 lists only books and pamphlets. The volumes for 1916, 1917–1921, 1922–1926, 1927–1931, 1932–1936, 1937–1941, 1942–1946, 1947–1951, 1952–1956, 1957–1961, and 1962 provide data only on books and pamphlets. The volume for 1963 has been expanded to include books, pamphlets, periodical publications, copyright registrations, and books by Chilean authors published outside of Chile. That for 1964 includes the type of material found in the volume for 1963 as well as a section that supplements the periodical list and a section on official publications, which with this volume becomes a feature of succeeding volumes. The volume for 1965 includes, besides the usual sections, an appendix to the *Anuario* volumes for 1962–1964, publications by Chileans or about Chile published outside of Chile from 1935 to 1965, a supplement to the "Anuario de publicaciones periódicas chilenas" for 1932 to 1964, and a supplement on Chilean magazines for the period 1915 to 1964. The volume for 1966 has an appendix to the editions of the *Anuario* for 1932 to 1965, publications by Chileans or about Chile published outside of Chile from 1920 to 1966, and a supplement to the "Anuario de publicaciones periódicas chilenas" for 1908 through 1965. The volume for 1967 includes an appendix to the *Anuario* volumes published from 1960 to 1966, material by Chileans published outside of Chile, and material about Chile for the years 1944 to 1967.

For a listing of this bibliography, see Guillermo Feliú Cruz, *Reseña histórica del Anuario de la prensa chilena de la Biblioteca nacional, 1886–1966* (Dirección de bibliotecas, archivos y museos, Santiago, 1966, 60 pp.).

Until the volumes of the *Anuario* appear for the Allende years, use should be made of Lee H. Williams, Jr., *The Allende Years*, subtitled "a union list of Chilean imprints, 1970–1973, in selected North American libraries, with a supplemental holdings list of books published elsewhere for the same period by Chileans or about Chile or Chileans" (G. K. Hall, Boston, 1977, vii, 339 pp.). Besides books, Chilean serials are listed. Williams lists 2,731 items.

The *Servicio bibliográfico chileno* (Nos. 1–269, September 1940–October/December 1970) served as an ongoing current classified bibliography issued by the firm Zamorano y Caperan for commercial purposes.

Raúl Silva Castro, *Prensa y periodismo en Chile (1812–1956)* (Ediciones de la Universidad de Chile, Santiago, 1958, xv, 413 pp.) must be considered the standard history of journalism (newspapers) in Chile. Only the introduction deals with the history of printing; the rest of the volume is a history of its press. There is an index of personal names, but there is no title or geographical index nor is there any bibliography, though much data can be gleaned from the footnotes.

The literary magazines of the 19th century have been studied in Romulo Ahumada Maturana, "Revista de revistas" (*Rev. artes y letras*, Vol. 5, 1886, pp. 357–368, 439, and Vol. 6, 1886, pp. 131–143), which provides data on 26 literary and scientific magazines published prior to 1882, and in Roberto Vilches, "Las revistas literarias chilenas del siglo xix" (*Rev. chilena de historia y geografía*, Vol. 9, No. 99, July–December 1941, pp. 324–355, and Vol. 9, No. 100, January–June 1942, pp. 117–159). Santiago's Imprenta universitaria reprinted it as a 78-page separate item.

Nicolás Anrique Reyes, "Bibliografía de las principales revistas i periódicos de Chile" (*An. Universidad de Chile*, Vol. 115, 1904, pp. 121–162; reprinted Imprenta Cervantes, Santiago, 1904, 44 pp.) provides data on 35 periodicals.

The *Revista de bibliografía chilena y extranjera* has published E. Vaisse, "Las principales revistas chilenas de índole general desde 1842 a 1878" (Vol. 2, 1914, pp. 172–174, 246–247), and Enrique Sanfuentes Correa, "Los periódicos chilenos olvidados" (Vol. 2, 1914, pp. 383–402, 433–453, and Vol. 3, 1915, pp. 185–195, 291–302).

Lists of periodicals and newspapers can be found in the *Anuario de la prensa chilena* for the years 1886–1915. The *Lista de las publicaciones periódicas chilenas* appeared in 1915, 1916, 1917, 1918, 1921, 1923, 1924, 1925, 1926, 1927, and 1928. None were published for 1919 and 1922. That for 1920 appeared as an appendix (pp. 17–30) to a report that the Biblioteca nacional presented to the Ministry of Education. The volume covering 1929 is entitled *Revistas, diarios y periódicos chilenos;* that for 1930, *Anuario de la publicaciones periódicas chilenas*. Those for 1931, 1932, 1933, 1934, 1935–1936, and 1937–1938 became *Publicaciones periódicas chilenas*. None were published from 1939 to 1951. It resumed publication as an annual in 1952, and material on this type of publication continued to be published separately through the volume for 1962 (1963), after which, in the volume for 1963 of the *Anuario de la prensa chilena*, this title once again began to cover Chilean periodicals. All of these were issued by the Biblioteca nacional with a variety of publishers.

The *Boletín de la Biblioteca nacional* has published "Publicaciones periódicas chilenas: Anuario 1931" (Vol. 2, No. 10, April 1932, pp. 62–72, and Vol. 2, No. 11, May 1932, pp. 91–106), and "Publicaciones periódicas chilenas: Anuario 1933" (Vol. 5, No. 4, April 1934, p. 66; Vol. 5, No. 5, May 1934, pp. 75–82; Vol. 5, No. 6, June 1934, pp. 96–98; and Vol. 5, No. 7, July 1934, pp. 106–114).

This country's German press is discussed in *Arndt–Olson* (Vol. 2, pp. 263–288).

Jean-Pierre Blancpain, *Les allemands au Chile (1816–1945)*, in the series Lateinamerikanische Forschungen (Bohlau Verlag, Cologne and Vienna, 1974), provides useful data on English (p. 1021), French (pp. 1022–1023), and Yugoslav (p. 1023) newspapers published in Chile. It also provides data on German-language periodicals with a short bibliography of the German press in Chile (p. 1038), a discussion of the German press of Santiago and Valparaiso (pp. 1039–1040), the provincial press of Southern Chile (Valdivia, Llanquihue, Frontera, and Magallán) (pp. 1040–1042), almanacs and magazines published by religious groups and German schools as well as specialized journals in German (pp. 1042–1044), and the periodical publications, chiefly newspapers of the Deutsch-Chilenischer Bund (pp. 1044–1045) and the Nazi and anti-Nazi German press in Chile (pp. 1045–1046).

Colombia

Though it is slightly dated, the student of Colombian imprints is advised to consult Gabriel Giraldo Jaramillo, *Bibliografía de bibliografías colombinas* (Publicaciones del Instituto Caro y Cuervo, Serie bibliográfica, 1, 2nd ed., corrected and updated by Rubén Pérez Ortiz, [Imp. patriótica del Instituto Caro y Cuervo], Bogotá, 1960, xvi, 208 pp.). This has a classified arrangement. The author is also indebted to the Instituto Caro y Cuervo for calling to his attention items that he would otherwise not have known about.

Gustavo Otero Múñoz, "Ensayo sobre una bio-bibliografía colombiana" (*Bol. historia y antigüedades*, Vol. 23, 1936, pp. 169–176, 303–315, 418–427, 497–507, 678) reached only part way through the letter *A*.

The following would seem to be the most important retrospective bibliographies of colonial Bogotá imprints: Biblioteca "Luis-Angel Arango" (Bogotá), *Incunables bogotanos—siglo xviii* (Imprenta del Banco de la República, Bogotá, 1959, 240 pp.), Luis Augusto Cuervo, "El primer año de la imprenta en Santafé" (*Bol. historia y antigüedades*, Vol. 30, 1943, pp. 874–877), Aníbal Currea Restrepo, "La imprenta en Santafé de Bogotá" (*Bol. historia y antigüedades,* Vol. 24, 1937, pp. 197–213), Manuel José Forero, *Incunables bogotanos* (Edit. Minerva, Bogotá, 1946, 47 pp.), José Toribio Medina, *La imprenta en Bogotá (1740–1821): Notas bibliográficas* (Imprenta Elzeviriana, Santiago, 1904; N. Israel, Amsterdam, 1964, 101 pp.), and Eduardo Posada, *La imprenta en Santafé en el siglo xviii* (V. Suarez, Madrid, 1917, xii, 153 pp.).

Of particular value in *Incunables bogotanos* are two studies: "La imprenta en Santa Fe de Bogotá, siglo xviii," by Mario Germán Romero, and "Fichas bibliográficas," by Rubén Pérez Ortiz.

The article by Cuervo discusses the only two works published in Bogotá in 1738. Currea's article is more of a history than a bibliography of printing; it covers developments through the mid-19th century, with a discussion of 19th-century Colombian journalism. The study of Forero describes 14 publications published between 1738 and 1812. Medina studies 85 imprints that appeared between 1739 and 1821. Posada describes 88 imprints published between 1739 and 1800.

Bogotá imprints from 1738 through 1834 have been listed by Eduardo Posada, *Bibliografía bogotana* (Imprenta de Arboleda and Valencia, and Imprenta nacional, Bogotá, 1925–1927, 2 vols.; reprinted from *Bol. historia y antigüedades*, Vols. 9–10, 12–13, and 15), and by Gustavo Otero Múñoz and Eduardo Posada, "Bibliografía bogotana" (*Bol. historia y antigüedades,* Vol. 37, 1950, pp. 125–149, 338–374, 505–529, 659–681, and Vol. 38, 1951, pp. 133–157). The second volume of this set contains Tabla cronológica de autores y de impresos anonimos, Tabla cronológica de materias, Tabla alfabética de autores, and Tabla alfabética de materias.

The set by Posada covers the period 1738–1831 and contains 1,410 entries. As Posada died in 1942, it would seem that Otero Múñoz had access to Posada's notes and continued the work with both their names. The series lists 695 works published between 1831 and 1834.

The colonial imprints of Cartagena de Indias have been recorded by José Toribio Medina, *La imprenta en Cartagena de las Indias (1809–1820): Notas bibliográficas* (Imprenta Elzeviriana, Santiago, 1904, 70 pp.), by Andrés Mesanza, "Apuntes sobre publicaciones hechas en Cartagena en el siglo xviii" (*Bol. historial* [Cartagena], Vol. 2, No. 21, 1917, pp. 349–353), and by E. de Saldanha, "Orígenes de la imprenta en Cartagena" (*Bol. historial*, Vol. 2, No. 20, 1916, pp. 319–336).

José Toribio Medina studies the imprints of Popayán, Santa Maria, and Tunja in his *Notas bibliográficas referentes a las primeras produciones de la imprenta en algunas ciudades de la América española . . . (1754–1823)* (Imprenta Elzeviriana, Santiago, 1904, 116 pp.).

Nineteenth-century Colombian imprints should be studied in much greater depth. The following would seem to be among the most important studies on the imprints of this century: Areizipa (pseudonym of J. M. Vergara y Vergara), "Bibliografía neo-granadina: Catálogo de obras literarias originales publicadas en la Nueva Granada" (*El Mosaico*, Vol. 1, No. 47, November 1859, p. 377, and Vol. 1, No. 49, December 1859, pp. 391–392), Gustavo Arboleda, *Apuntes sobre la imprenta y el periodismo en Popayán, 1813–1899* (Talleres poligráficos de El Grito del Pueblo, Guayaquil, 1905, 56 pp.), and Sergio Elías Ortiz, *Noticias sobre la imprenta y las publicaciones del Sur de Colombia durante el siglo xix* (Imprenta del Departamento, Pasto, 1935, iii, 276 pp. [Supplement No. 2 of Vol. 6, Nos. 66–67 of *Bol. estudios históricos*, in which journal it was serially published as "Imprenta y bibliografía del Sur de Colombia"]).

Areizipa lists 84 lyrical and dramatic works of the leading Colombian authors that appeared between 1822 and 1859. It is one of the first attempts at a bibliography published in Colombia. Ortiz studies the imprints of Pasto, Barbacoas, Ipiales, Tuquerres, and Tumaco published between 1838 and 1899. Arboleda studies both books and periodicals published in Popayán in the 19th century.

Data on Colombian 20th-century imprints before 1951 have been sporadic.

Luis Eduardo Nieto Caballero, *Libros colombianos publicados en 1924* was published in three series and three volumes. The first series was published by Imprenta de El Espectador (1925) and Series 2 and 3 by Editorial Minerva (1928). The material in these three volumes reprint Caballero's reviews of Colombian works.

Guillermo Manrique Terán, "Libros del Centenario" (*El Tiempo*, December 31, 1938) discusses the publications issued to celebrate the fourth centennial of the founding of Bogotá (1938).

Raúl d'Eça, *A General Bibliography of Colombian Publications for 1938* (Bibliographical Series, No. 7, Inter-American Book Exchange, Washington, D.C., 1940, 20 pp.) would appear to be the only current bibliography of Colombian imprints issued in the 1930s.

Guillermo Manrique Terán contributed these articles to *El Tiempo:* "El año literario" (December 31, 1939), "Los libros colombianos en 1940" (December 31, 1940), and "Múltiple y amplia fue la producción bibliográfica en el año que termina" (December 31, 1941). These articles discuss in a condensed fashion works on sociology, history, belles-lettres, and other fields.

Ricardo Ortiz McCormick contributed this series of articles to *El Tiempo:* "Panorama de la cultura: El año literario de 1946" (December 31, 1946); "El año literario de 1947" (December 31, 1947); "Balance de la cultura: El año literario de 1951," in its *Suplemento literario* (December 30, 1951; reprinted in *An. bibliográfico colombiano 1951*, pp. 183–188); "La producción bibliográfica en 1952: Aspectos y perspectivas del año literario" (December 31, 1952); "El año literario de 1953" (December 31, 1953); "El año bibliográfico de 1958" (December 31, 1958); "El año bibliográfico de 1959" (January 2, 1960); "Balance de la cultura: El año bibliográfico de 1961" (December 31, 1961, pp. 5, 12); "Balance de la cultura: El año bibliográfico de 1963" (December 31, 1963, pp. 16–17); "El año bibliográfico nacional de 1965," in its *Lecturas dominicales* (January 16, 1966, pp. 2–3, and January 23, 1966, pp. 2–3); "Balance de la cultura: El año bibliográfico de 1964" (December 31, 1964, pp. 24–26); and "El año bibliográfico: Libros y escritores de 1966," in its *Lecturas dominicales* (January 8, 1967, pp. 6–8).

Cali's Biblioteca "Jorge Garcés B." can be said to have begun a genuine revival in current Colombian bibliography with its *Anuario bibliográfico colombiano, 1951* (Imprenta J. G. B., Cali, 1952 [i.e., 1953], 247 pp.). This compilation and the annotations were supervised by Pedro R. Carmona ("estuvieron a cargo de . . ."). It lists many books and articles published in Colombia in 1951. Besides the article by Ricardo Ortiz McCormick already mentioned, it contains an "Informe sobre los problemas bibliográficos de Colombia" by Rubén Pérez Ortiz.

The current national bibliography of Colombia, *Anuario bibliográfico colombiano* (Instituto Caro y Cuervo, Bogotá, Departamento de bibliografía), began in 1958 with the publication of the volume that covered the years 1951–1956. This volume was compiled by Rubén Pérez Ortiz, who also compiled the volumes for 1957–1958 (1960), 1959–1960 (1961), 1961 (1963), and 1962 (1964). With the death of Pérez Ortiz, the title of the annual was changed to *Anuario bibliográfico colombiano "Rubén Pérez Ortiz,"* and Francisco José Rojas became the new compiler. He has edited the following volumes: 1963 (1966), 1964–1965 (1967), 1966 (1968), 1967–1968 (1969), 1969 (1971), 1970–1971 (1972), 1972 (1974), 1973–1974 (1976), 1975–1976 (1978), 1977–1978 (1979), and 1979 (1981).

The *Anuario bibliográfico colombiano* is a classified bibliography of works published in Colombia in Spanish, works translated by Colombians into other languages, and works of Colombian authors translated into other languages. With the 1961 volume, two other sections were added: new periodicals and addresses of bookstores and publishers.

Fermín Peraza Sarausa started publication of his semiannual *Fichas para el Anuario bibliográfico colombiano* in 1961; after a short time its place of publication was changed to Gainesville, Florida, and its title changed to *Bibliografía colombiana.* Its last issue was dated 1970. It was numbered as Volumes 61–62, 67–68, and 71–72 of the series Biblioteca del bibliotecario. It is not as complete as the *Anuario bibliográfico colombiano.*

Antonio Cacua Prada, *Historia del periodismo colombiano* ([Talleres de la editorial "Fondo Rotatovio Policía nacional"], Bogotá, 1968, 448 pp.) is the fullest history of Colombian newspapers and magazines. Besides an index of personal names, it contains all of the titles mentioned in the text and a bibliography.

There are no bibliographies of Colombian periodicals and newspapers as a whole, nor does any current bibliography published in Colombia list them.

Fanny López and Daisy Sanabria have compiled *Publicaciones periódicas colombianas existentes en el Departamento de bibliotecas de la Universidad del Valle* (Cali, 1965, 54 pp.).

David Bushnell, "The Development of the Press in Great Colombia" (*Hispanic American Historical Rev.*, Vol. 30, 1950, pp. 432–452), and Gustavo Otero Múñoz, "Descripción bibliográfica de los periódicos de la época de la Gran Colombia pertenecientes al Fondo Quijano Otero de la Biblioteca nacional," in *Catálogo del "Fondo José María Quijano Otero"* (Edit. "El Gráfico," Bogotá, 1935, pp. 258–318) deal with the early publications of Great Colombia. Bushnell provides such data as title, political affiliation, contents, duration of publication, etc., of newspapers published in Colombia and Venezuela between 1818 and 1828. Otero Múñoz is also the author of "Primeros periódicos colombianos" (*Senderos*, Vol. 1, 1934, pp. 31–36).

"Periódicos que salen actualmente en Bogotá" (*El Mosaico* [Bogotá], Vol. 3, No. 24, 1864, p. 192) provides the titles for 15 newspapers and magazines.

Isidoro Laverde Amaya, "Movimiento periodístico de Bogotá . . . en 1891" (*Colombia ilustrada*, Vol. 1, No. 22, August 7, 1891, pp. 348–350), and his two articles in *Revista literaria*, "Movimiento periodístico de Colombia en 1892" (Vol. 3, No. 25, 1892, pp. 72–74) and "Movimiento periodístico de Colombia en 1893" (Vol. 3, No. 35, 1893, pp. 609–612), are newspaper lists that deal with those of Bogotá and the country as a whole.

Diego Monsalve, "Hermeroteca nacional" (*Colombia cafetera*, Barcelona, [1927], pp. 911–922) is a list of newspapers and periodicals, arranged by department, that were published in Colombia in 1927.

Armando Moreno Mattos has compiled *Publicaciones periódicas en Colombia 1964* (1965, ii, 52 pp.) and *Publicaciones periódicas en Colombia, 1965* (1967, ii, 62 pp.). Both were published by Colombia's Departamento administrativo nacional de estatística. The volume for 1965 lists 408 serial publications.

The Instituto colombiano para el fomento de la educación superior in Bogotá has published the *Directorio de publicaciones periódicas colombianas* (1975, 199 pp.).

The serials issued by the Centro de información económica are listed in Angela Hernández de Caldas and Inés Alvarez de Cruz, *Publicaciones periódicas del CIEB* (Edición preliminar, Cámara de comercio de Bogotá, Bogotá, 1974, 107, 6 pp.).

Angela Hernández Arango, "Revistas agropecuarias editadas en Colombia desde 1906" (*Agricultura tropical*, Vol. 11, No. 1, January 1955, pp. 37–40), and Marian Forero Nougués, "Revistas médicas [de Colombia]" (*Bol. Asociación colombiana de bibliotecarios*, Vol. 1, No. 1, pp. 29–33, which gives pertinent bibliographic data [title, editor, addresses, and issues published in 1956] concerning 31 medical journals), are examples of periodical lists in specialized fields.

Luis Eduardo Puerta, "El periodismo en Manizales" (*Bol. historia y antiqüedades*, Vol. 26, Nos. 301–302, November–December 1939, pp. 863–878) is one of the few studies on the press of Manizales.

The following are useful for the study of the newspapers and periodicals of Medellín: Luis Latorre Mendoza, "Prensa," in *Historia e historias de Medellín* (Imprenta departamental, Medellín, 1934, pp. 241–258); Bernardo G. Puerta, "Los primeros cincuenta años del periodismo en Medellín," in *Repertorio histórico* (Medellín), which ran serially in Volume 1, Numbers 9–12 (1913); and Elena Vérez de Peraza, *Directorio de revistas y periódicos de Medellín* (Biblioteca del Bibliotecario, No. 64, Ediciones Anuario bibliográfico cubano, Medellín, 1962, vi, 21 leaves).

For the study of journalism in Santander, see Horacio Rodríguez Plata, "Apuntes para una historia del periodismo en Santander," in *Conferencias dictadas en el Centro de historia de Santander* (Biblioteca Santander, No. 14, Imprenta del departamento, Bucaramanga, 1942, pp. 11–39).

Pablo Enrique Cárdenas Acosta, "La imprenta en Tunja: Las Publicaciones periódicas de la localidad en una centuria," in Ramón C. Correa (ed.), *Historia de Tunja* (Imprenta departamental, Tunja, 1948, Vol. 3, pp. 7–25), and Ramón C. Correa, "Periodismo tunjano" (ibid., Vol. 3, pp. 26–50) list the newspapers published between 1825 and 1948 in Tunja.

The German-language press is described in *Arndt–Olson* (Vol. 2, pp. 289–290).

Costa Rica

The format and coverage of Luis Dobles Segreda, *Indice bibliográfico de Costa Rica* (Lehmann, Asociación costarricense de bibliotecarios, San José, 1927–1968, 11 vols. in 10) hardly qualify it as Costa Rica's retrospective bibliography. It is essentially a classified, annotated bibliography of material by Costa Ricans and that published outside of Costa Rica about it. The annotations are extremely long. This set is mentioned because various bibliographers have listed it when dealing with Costa Rican national bibliography.

The Universidad de Costa Rica's Facultad de letras y filosofia was responsible for the publication of Jorge A. Lines, *Libros y folletos publicados en Costa Rica durante los años 1830–1849* (San José, 1944, xxv, 151 pp.).

There would seem to be a gap in our knowledge of Costa Rican imprints for the period 1850–1934.

Costa Rican current bibliography for the 20th century would seem to be as follows: Margarita Obregón Loria, *Lista de algunas publicados en los años 1935, 36, 37 y lo que va del 38* (Biblioteca nacional, San José, 1944, 15 pp.), *Publicaciones nacionales, 1943* (Biblioteca nacional, San José, 1944, 28 pp.), and "Publicaciones nacionales, 1944" (*Rev. Archivo nacional de Costa Rica*, Vol. 10, Nos. 1–2, 1946, pp. 58–72); the Biblioteca nacional's *Boletín bibliográfico: Publicaciones nacionales correspondientes al año . . .*, for 1946 through 1955 (1948–1956); and the *Anuario bibliográfico costarricense, 1956–* (1958–).

Most volumes of the *Anuario* are the work of the Asociación costarricense de bibliotecarios, Comité nacional de bibliografía "Adolfo Blen." In view of the fact that some volumes deal with the production of more than one year, the year(s) covered and the date of its publication follow: 1956 (1958), 1957 (1959), 1958 (1961), 1959–1960 (1961), 1961 (1963), 1962 (1964), 1963 (1964), 1964–1965 (1966), 1966 (1967), 1967 (1968), 1968 (1969), 1969 (1971), 1970–1971 (1974), and 1972–1974 (1976).

Bernabe Quiros, "Bibliografía de periódicos costarricense" (*Mem. Secretaría de instrucción pública*, 1897, pp. 145–156) is the earliest listing of Costa Rican newspapers.

Costa Rica's German press is listed in *Arndt–Olson* (Vol. 2, p. 291).

Cuba

There are three important bibliographies of Cuban bibliographies. Fermín Peraza Sarausa, *Bibliografías cubanas* (U.S. Government Printing Office, Washington, D.C., 1945, xiv, 58 pp.) lists, with a classified arrangement, 485 items. Tomás Fernández Robaina, *Bibliografía de bibliografía cubanas (1859–1972)* (Biblioteca nacional "José Martí," Havana, 1973 [i.e., 1974], 340 pp.) is based primarily on the Cuban National Library's collection. The Peraza work is based on that of the Library of Congress, and it includes data on more than 1,300 items. Fernández Robaina includes material published through 1972.

Though printing was not introduced into Cuba until early in the 18th century, Carlos Trelles y Govín begins his retrospective bibliography with the 17th century. His *Bibliografía cubana de los siglos XVII y XVIII* (Imprenta del ejercito, Havana, 1927; Kraus Reprints, Vaduz, 1965, xix, 463 pp.) contains 2,100 entries and is considered as the second edition of his *Ensayo de bibliografía cubana de los siglos XVII y XVIII . . .* (Matanzas, 1907) and of its supplement published in 1908. Trelles y Govín lists material of those born in Cuba who published in Mexico and other parts of the Spanish Empire so that it is both a retrospective bibliography of

Cuban imprints and a bibliography of publications by Cubans regardless of place of publication. It has been corrected and supplemented by Julio J. Le Riverend Busone, "Notas para una bibliografía cubana de los siglos XVII y XVIII" (*Univ. Habana*, Nos. 88–89, January–June 1950, pp. 128–231).

José Toribio Medina, *La imprenta en La Habana (1707–1810)* (Santiago de Chile, 1904; reprint N. Israel, Amsterdam, 1964, xxxii, 199 pp.) provides bibliographic descriptions of 271 imprints for this period. Havana is also included in his *Notas bibliográficas referentes a los primeras producciónes de la imprenta en algunas ciudades de la América española* (1904).

The standard bibliography for the 19th century is Carlos Trelles y Govín, *Bibliografía cubana del siglo xix* (Imprenta de Quirós y Estrada, Matanzas, 1911–1915, 8 vols.; Kraus Reprint, Vaduz, 1965, 8 vols. in 4). It too includes material printed in Cuba as well as works published outside of Cuba that deal with it. Additions to the first volume of this set appear in Luis Marino Pérez, "Labor bibliográfico" (*Rev. bimestre cubana*, Vol. 6, May–June, July–August, September–October 1911, pp. 239–248, 362–372, 429–439). This reviewer faults Trelles y Govín for not taking advantage of recent advances in bibliographic description and for his frequent failure to locate copies.

Carlos Trelles y Govín, *Bibliografía cubana del siglo XX (1900–1916)* (Imprenta de la vda. de Quirós y Estrada, Matanzas, 1916–1917, 2 vols.; Kraus Reprints, Vaduz, 1965, 2 vols. in 1) includes the same type of material as the preceding title.

León Primelles is the author of two volumes published in Havana by Lex. They are *Crónica cubana, 1915–1918 . . .* (1955) and *Crónica cubana, 1919–1922 . . .* (1957). On page 7 of the first volume, the author notes that "Como complememto importante se ha agregado . . . la relación de los libros, folletos y periódicos en cada año en Cuba . . . en secciones intercaladas en los lugares del texto con que guardan mayor relación. Estas secciones . . . forman en conjunto la bibliografía cubana del año."

It would seem that for a period of almost two decades, no attempt was made at a listing of Cuban publications. Lorenzo Rodrígues Fuentes, "Bibliografía cubana" (*Rev. bibliográfica cubana*, Nos. 1–18, May–June 1936 through September–December 1938) provides a current bibliography for this period.

The Biblioteca Nacional José Martí and Editorial Orbe published *Bibliografía cubana* for the following periods: 1917–1920 (issued in the 1970s), 1921–1924 (1978), 1925–1928 (1977), 1929–1932 (1979), and 1933–1936 (1979). With the publication of these volumes, Cuba now has a retrospective and current bibliography that extends from the beginning of printing on the island through the present.

In 1937 Fermin Peraza Sarausa began the compilation of the *Anuario bibliográfico cubano*. It kept this title through 1952. In 1953 it was changed to *Bibliografía cubana*. The volumes in this set were published in Havana through 1959. That for 1960 was published in Medellín, Colombia, and those for 1961 through 1965 in Gainesville, Florida. The volumes for 1966–1968 (Coral Gables, 1967–1970) are entitled *Revolutionary Cuba: A Bibliographical Guide*. This set includes both material published in Cuba and material published outside of Cuba concerning it. Peraza also compiled *Bibliografía cubana: Complementos: 1937–1961* (University of Florida Libraries, Gainesville, 1966, 233 pp.).

For political reasons, Cuba is one of the few countries that had two competing, often complimentary, national bibliographies. This situation lasted for more than a decade. The Departamento colección cubana issued, for the Biblioteca nacional "José Martí," the *Bibliografía cubana*, covering 1959–1962 through 1963–1964. In 1965 this bibliography began to be issued by the Biblioteca nacional "José Martí" on an annual basis. The following volumes exist: 1959–1962 (1968), 1963–1964 (1967), 1965 (1967), 1966 (1968), 1967 (1969), 1968 (1970), 1969 (1971), 1970 (1972), 1971 (1973), 1972 (1974), 1973 (1975), 1974 (1976), 1975 (1977), 1976 (1978), 1977 (1979), and 1978 (1979). The majority of the early volumes, in addition to providing bibliographic data on separately published Cuban imprints, also listed new journals that began to be published during the year covered; biobibliographies were included, as were title and analytical indexes. Over the years the biobibliographies have been dropped. The contents of the volume for 1971 are typical of those that were published in the 1970s. This volume has the following sections: books and pamphlets; periodicals; prints, posters, expositions, and cinema; discography; and postage stamps. Part one includes works by Cuban authors published outside of Cuba. Subject, title, and name indexes are provided. The volume for 1965 has 165 pages, while that for 1975 has 391 pages, an indication both of a greater number of imprints and of a wider scope.

Teresita Bastista Villarreal, Josefina Garcia Carranza, and Miguelina Ponte, *Catálogo de publicaciones periódicas cubanas de los siglos xviii y xix* (Biblioteca nacional "José Martí," Havana, 1965, 246 pp.) lists 283 periodicals and 433 newspapers.

Carlos Manuel Trelles y Govín, "Bibliografía de la prensa cubana (de 1704 a 1900) y de los periódicos publicados por cubanos en el extranjero" (*Rev. bibliográfica cubana*, Vol. 2, 1938, pp. 7–40, 81–114, 145–168, 209–268, and Vol. 3, 1939, pp. 5–34, 67–100, 155–172, 191–196) stops with data on *Las noticias*.

The *Boletín del Archivo nacional* ran "Contribución a la historia de la prensa periódica" from Volume 22 to Volume 35 (1923–1936).

The Ministerio de communicaciones published "Relación de las publicaciones que disfrutan de la franquicia postal e inscripción como correspondencia de segunda clase y que en la actualidad circulan" (*Bol. comunicaciones*, Vol. 42, Nos. 1–6, January 15–March 30, 1943, pp. 83–94) as well as "Circular sobre publicaciones periódicas" (ibid., edición extraordinaria, April 1947, pp. 55–91).

Fermín Peraza S. compiled the *Directorio de revistas y periódicos de Cuba*, for 1942–1948 and 1950–1953 (Anuario bibliográfico cubano, Havana); the volume for 1949 was never published. It was suspended from 1954 to 1962, and the annual volumes for 1963–1965 and 1967 were published in Gainesville, Florida. That for 1966 was not published. The final volume, for 1968, was published in Coral Gables, Florida.

The Biblioteca nacional published in its *Revista*, "Relación de las nuevas revistas cubanas publicadas desde 1950 hasta 1955, existentes en la Biblioteca nacional" (2nd ser., Vol. 9, No. 1, October–December 1958, pp. 297–302).

Nelson P. Valdes and Edwin Lieuwen, *The Cuban Revolution: A Research-Study Guide (1959–1969)* (University of New Mexico Press, Albuquerque, 1971, pp. 10–18) provides a list of newspapers and periodicals for the period.

Israel Echevarria, "Revistas corrientes cubanas: Una lista anotada" (*Caribbean Stud.,* Vol. 4, No. 3, October 1964, pp. 50–65) is a useful list for the period and provides data on 95 titles.

The Cuban Instituto cubano del libro published in 1977 a selective, descriptive, and classified list of Cuban periodicals entitled *Revistas y periódicos cubanos* (79 pp.).

Regional lists of Cuban newspapers and periodicals would include: Maria A. Chapelli, "Periódicos publicados en Camagüey en la era republicana" (*Antorcha,* Vol. 5, No. 1, January 1947, pp. 17, 32); Ateneo de Cienfuegos, *Periódicos y revistas de Cienfuegos, 1845–1940* (Cuaderno de cultura popular, No. 1, Cienfuegos, 1940, 17 pp.), which lists 253 titles; Francisco Fina García, *Bibliografía de la prensa del término municipal de Santiago de Las Vegas* (Asociación de corresponsales y prensa local, Santiago de Las Vegas, 1941, 4 pp.); and Israel M. Moliner, *Indice cronológico de la prensa en Matanzas* (Ateneas de Cuba, [Matanzas], 1955, 18 pp.).

Cuban Studies Newsletter has published "Cuban Periodicals, 1959–1970" (Vol. 1, No. 2, May 1971, pp. 2–12) and "Cuban Periodicals" (Vol. 2, No. 3, November 1971, pp. 26–28).

The German press is listed in *Arndt–Olson* (Vol. 2, p. 293).

Curaçao

The *Bibliografie van de Nederlandse Antilles* (Nederlandse Stichting voor Culturele Samenwerking met Suriname en de Nederlandse Antillen, Amsterdam, n.d. [early 1970s], 271 pp.) is a classified bibliography of material on Curaçao that lists both material published there and works about it published elsewhere. Sections that might be of particular interest are: "Pers (algemeen)—Tijdschriften—Dagbladen—Radio—Televisie" (pp. 15–20), listings for two sports magazines (p. 84), "Letterkunde" (pp. 143–170), "Jeugdlectuur" (pp. 170–172), and "Taalkunde" (pp. 135–143).

The most important bibliography on Papiamento, a Creole language spoken on this island, is that of F. F. Martinus (Arion), *Bibliografie van het papiamentu* (SIICUSA, for the Author, Curaçao and Amsterdam, 1972, xxxiii, 98 pp.).

Dominica

Douglas C. McMurtrie, *The First Printing in Dominica* (Privately printed, 1932, 8 pp.; reprinted from the May 1932 issue of *British and Colonial Printer & Stationer*) would seem to be the only study on Dominica's imprints.

Dominican Republic

Luis Florén Lozano, *Bibliografía de la bibliografía dominicana* (Roques Román, Ciudad Trujillo, 1948, viii, 66 pp.) is the work of a Spanish exile who first lived in the Dominican Republic and later in Colombia. In both countries he played an important role in bibliographic projects.

Marisol Florén R. and Próspero Mella Chavier, "La bibliografía en la República dominicana" (24th SALALM, *Final Report and Working Papers*, 1980, pp. 199–223) is divided into an introduction that discusses the history of Dominican bibliography, important bibliographers, and bibliographic organizations and programs; and a classified annotated bibliography of Dominican bibliographies. Data are provided on 157 bibliographies.

In 1978 the Biblioteca nacional published the *Anuario bibliográfico dominicano* (325 pp.). This title is somewhat deceptive since it describes 3,413 Dominican imprints found in this library. It is arranged according to the Dewey Decimal Classification system, with author and subject indexes.

The Fondo para el avance de las ciencias sociales is sponsoring and will publish a *Bibliografía nacional dominicana* which is being prepared under the direction of Lic. Marisol Florén. The purpose of this bibliography will be to include everything published in and about the Dominican Republic through 1978.

The Oficina de canje y difusión cultural in Ciudad Trujillo (now Santo Domingo, its name before and after Trujillo named the country after himself) published the *Boletín bibliográfico dominicano* (No. 1, July–August 1945), which listed Dominican imprints for 1944, while the second number (September–December 1945) listed those for 1945. The *Anuario bibliográfico dominicano* for 1946–1947 (1947–1948) was first published by the Oficina de canje . . . and then by the Sección de canje y difusión cultural of the Secretaría de estado de educación y bellas artes.

The current bibliographies for the 1950s would seem to be Luis Florén Lozano, "Algunas obras de importancia publicadas en 1951" (*Rev. interamericana de bibliografía*, Vol. 2, 1952, pp. 108–109), and the following bibliographies in the *Anales de la Universidad de Santo Domingo* compiled by Próspero Mella Chavier: "Lista bibliográfica correspondiente al año 1955" (Vol. 21, Nos. 79–80, 1956, pp. i–xxxvi), "Lista . . . año 1956" (Vol. 23, Nos. 85–88, 1958, pp. i–xxxi), and "Lista . . . año 1957" (Vol. 23, Nos. 87–88, 1958, pp. i–xxii). Those by Mella Chavier have a classified arrangement, with an author index. They also provide a list of new periodicals published during the year covered.

Jorge Tena Reyes, "Bibliografía dominicana de 1971" (*Aula,* Vol. 1, April–June 1972, pp. 152–154) and "Bibliografía dominicana de 1972" (*Aula,* Vol. 2, No. 3, July–December 1972, pp. 238–240) provide data on almost 100 books and journals published in these 2 years.

Vetilio Alfau Durán, "100 notículas de bibliografía dominicana" (*An. Universidad de Santo Domingo*, Vol. 20, Nos. 73–76, 1956, pp. 237–255, and Vol. 21, Nos.

77–78, 1956, pp. 21–43) and "Bibliografía dominicana: Hojas sueltas" (ibid., Vol. 19, Nos. 71–72, 1954, pp. i–xxxvii) are also of interest.

Manuel de Jesús Roa Santana is the compiler of the quite useful *Indice de publicaciones periódicas de universidades dominicanas*, Volume 1 (Instituto tecnológico de Santo Domingo, Santo Domingo, 1978, 152 pp.). The appendix to this volume contains a listing of the books and periodicals published by the following Dominican universities: Instituto tecnológico de Santo Domingo (pp. 117–119), Universidad autonoma de Santo Domingo (pp. 121–144), Universidad católica Madre y Maestra (pp. 145–147), Universidad central del Este (p. 149), and Universidad nacional Pedro Henríquez Ureña (pp. 151–152).

The most important works on the history of journalism in the Dominican Republic are: Manuel A. Amiama, *El periodismo en la República Dominicana: Notas para la historia crítico–narrativa del periodismo nacional desde sus origenes a nuestros días* (Talleres la Nación, Santo Domingo, 1933, 97 pp.); Emilio Rodríguez Demorizi, *La imprenta y los primeros periódicos de Santo Domingo*, third edition (Biblioteca nacional, No. 1, Taller de impresiones, Santo Domingo, 1973, 257 pp.); and Marcos Antonio Martínez Paulino, *Publicaciones dominicanas desde la colonia* (Ed. del Caribe, Santo Domingo, 1973, 241 pp.).

Ramón Lugo Lovatón, *Periódicos dominicanos en el Archivo general de la Nación* (Editora Montalvo, Ciudad Trujillo, 1953, 49 pp.) would appear to be the latest attempt at a listing of Dominican newspapers.

The country's first newspaper, *Telégrafo constitucional de Santo Domingo*, was established in 1841 and is the subject of a brief note in *Clio* (Vol. 9, 1941, p. 51).

The following articles deal with Dominican periodicals: Luis Florén Lozano, "Las publicaciones periódicas en la bibliografía trujillista" (*Renovación*, Vol. 1, No. 1, January–March 1953, pp. 138–158), Julio Jaime Julia Guzmán, "Proceso histórico del periodismo en Moca" (*Bol. Archivo general de la Nación* [BAGN], Vol. 18, No. 85, April–June 1955, pp. 124–137), "Periódicos dominicanos en el Archivo general de la Nación" (BAGN, Vol. 7, No. 34, May–August 1944, pp. 209–216), Luis Francisco Thomen, "Revistas filatélicas de la República Dominicana" (BAGN, Vol. 19, No. 90–91, July–December 1956, pp. 256–259), Emilio Rodríguez Demorizi, "La imprenta y los primeros periódicos de Santo Domingo" (*Clio*, Vol. 11, 1943, pp. 98–109, 115–180), and Francois F. Sevez, "El periodismo en la provincia de Samaná" (BAGN, Vol. 16, 1953, pp. 197–202).

German periodicals are listed in *Arndt–Olson* (Vol. 2, p. 295).

Ecuador

Robert E. Norris, *Guía bibliográfica para el estudio de la historia ecuatoriana* (Guides and Bibliographies Series, No. 11, Institute of Latin American Studies, University of Texas, Austin, 1978, viii, 295 pp.) contains "Bibliografías y estudios bibliográficos" (pp. 8–12) and "El periodismo y la imprenta" (pp. 139–143), which are extremely useful.

José Toribio Medina, *La imprenta en Quito (1760–1818): Notas bibliográficas*

(Imprenta Elzeviriana, Santiago de Chile, 1904; N. Israel, Amsterdam, 1964, xxvii, 86 pp.) describes 43 items. This should be supplemented by Alexander Alphonse Marius Stoll, *Historia de la imprenta en el Ecuador de 1755 a 1830* (Casa de la cultura ecuatoriana, Quito, 1953, xv, 261, 26 pp.), which contains "Bibliografía de los impresos ecuatorianos, 1775–1830," "Los periódicos ecuatorianos, 1809–1830," and "Lista cronológica de los periódicos ecuatorianos de 1792–1830; Quito, 1809–1830; Guayaquil, 1821–1830; Cuenca, 1828–1829." This volume describes 264 publications.

At present there exists a gap of more than a century in the Ecuadorean national bibliography.

The Inter-American Book Exchange of Washington, D.C., issued *A General Bibliography of Ecuadorian Publications for 1936 and 1937* (1938; Bibliographical Series, No. 1). Number 4 of this series was the bibliography for 1938 (1939). Ecuador's Biblioteca nacional issued in mimeographed form *Producción bibliográfica ecuatoriana, 1938* (1939). This was reprinted in the *Pan American Book Shelf* (Vol. 2, No. 9, September 1939, pp. 50–60).

Since the late 1960s there have been several attempts at the compilation and publication of a current national bibliography. The *Boletín bibliográfico ecuatoriano* lasted for only two issues (i.e., January–March and April–June 1967). It was to have been a quarterly.

In 1975 the Biblioteca general of the Universidad central del Ecuador began the compilation and publication of the *Bibliografía ecuatoriana* as a bimonthly. In 1976 there appeared a cumulation of the year's issues as *Anuario bibliográfico ecuatoriano 1975 y Bibliografía ecuatoriano no. 6*. Part 1 lists 336 separately published items; items 337–1324 provide an analytical bibliography of material published in journals and in essay collections. The material is alphabetically arranged within the 10 major divisions of the Dewey Decimal system. This cumulated volume is extremely well indexed. With Number 7 (1976) it began the publication of specialized bibliographies, for this issue has extensive bibliographies of Gabriel García Novena and Jorge Icaza.

Broadsides are listed in Leonardo J. Múñoz, *Hojas volantes que se han publicado en las diversas provincias de la República del Ecuador 1790–1920* . . . (Ministerio de Gobierno, Quito, 1941, 16 pp.), which is based on the compiler's collection.

The most important recent studies in Ecuadorean journalism are: Abel Romeo Castillo, *La imprenta de Guayaquil independiente (1821–1822)* (Casa de la cultura ecuatoriana, Guayquil, 1956, 204 pp.), Camilo Destruge, *Historia de la prensa de Guayaquil* (Salerianas, Quito, 1924–1925, 2 vols.), and Carlos A. Rolando, *Crónica del periodismo en el Ecuador (1792–1849)* (Tip. de la Sociedad filantrópica del Guayas, 1947, 145 pp.). Romeo Castillo describes the newspapers and periodicals for this period. Destruge's *Historia* reaches 1920. Rolando provides a chronology of newspapers published through 1849 in Quito, Guayaquil, Cuenca, and Ambato, and official newspapers published in Quito and Guayaquil through 1912.

The following would appear to be the chief lists of newspapers and periodical publications: Cristóbal Gangotena y Jijón, "Ensayo de bibliografía del periodismo en el Ecuador" (*Bol. Biblioteca nacional*, n.s., Vol. 1, December 1925, pp. 46–86), which lists items chronologically from 1792 to 1923; Neptali Casanova Loor, "Cronología del periodismo ecuatoriano desde 1792 hasta 1930," in *El centenario: Homenaje al centenario de la República, 1830–1930* (Imprenta El Tiempo, Guayaquil, 1930, pp. 361–431); Alfonso Andrade Chiriboga, *Hemeroteca azuyaya* (Edit. El Mercurio, Cuenca, 1950, 2 vols.); and Luis F. Madera, *Periódicos ibarreños* (El Comercio, Ibarra, 1927, 34 pp.).

No annual lists of newspapers and periodicals have been published on a regular basis. There are "Diarios, periódicos y revistas" for 1894, published in the Biblioteca municipal de Guayaquil's *Anuario de la prensa ecuatoriana* (Guayaquil, 1895, Vol. 3, pp. 90–105); Dirección general de correos, *Nomina de publicaciones periódicas que se editan en la República al 26 de mayo de 1931* (Quito, 1931); "Principales revistas y publicaciones que se editan en el Ecuador" (*Bol. ínformativo* [Ministerio de relaciones exteriores], Vol. 4, No. 6, February–July 1948, pp. 151–154); and Oscar A. Romero, "Estadística de la prensa nacional: Índice nominativo de las publicaciones periodísticas del Ecuador, que han circulado en 1946, clasificados por provincias, en orden cronológico" (*Trimestre estadística*, Vol. 2, No. 5, January–June 1946, pp. 10–20).

For German-language periodicals, see *Arndt–Olson* (Vol. 2, p. 297).

Falkland Islands

No studies have been located that deal with the history of printing on the Falkland Islands. Spanish studies (the Argentines call this British possession "Las Islas Malvinas") usually are attacks on what papers in the Falkland Islands have published concerning the controversy over whether they should belong to Argentina or to Great Britain.

The Falkland Islands Gazette (Vol. 88, No. 12, November 28, 1979) has been examined. This *Gazette* is "Printed at the Government Printing Office, Stanley, Falkland Islands."

David Colville, editor and publisher of *The Falkland Islands Times*, has supplied some information on current newspapers and journals published in these islands in the 1970s. *The Falkland Islands Times and Monthly Review* was edited by E. Forrester from 1974 to 1976; from 1976 to 1977, by D. Ryan; and from 1977–, by David Colville. In mid-1979 this monthly changed its name to *South Atlantic Free Press* after an argument with the government over the use of the official crest in the paper's masthead, but it reverted in December 1979 to its former title after establishing that there was nothing the government could do to prevent the crest's use. W. Hirtle edited *The Mini Monthly Review* (1976–1977). David Colville in 1979 began publication of *Public Eye* (satire and politics) and *The Blue Suede Shoe* (contemporary music scene in Great Britain and the Falkland Islands). In 1979 G. Bound began *The Penguin News*. In 1898 there existed the *Falkland Islands Church Magazine*.

Guadeloupe

For a history of printing in Guadeloupe, Lenis Blanche, *Contribution à l'histoire de la presse à la Guadeloupe* ([Imprimerie catholique, Basse-Terre, Guadeloupe], 1935, xiv, 55 pp.) would seem to be the fullest study available. The first part of this work deals with the legal aspects of publishing, while the second part deals with printing and newspapers on the island. This study was published under the auspices of the Gouvernement tricentenaire des Antilles. The first book published here was dated 1783.

The Archives de la Guadeloupe possesses an unpublished manuscript by Jules Ballet which contains additional data on printing in Guadeloupe.

Father Oscar Lacroix, "Les mass Média en Guadeloupe: La Presse" (*Eglise de Guadeloupe*, No. 202, 2ème quinzaine de mai 1976, pp. 5–20) is especially valuable for its discussion and list of newspapers and magazines published in Guadeloupe as of 1976.

France-Antilles: Journal de qui? (Document 1, Information Caraibe [ICAR], Centre Gabel, Pointe-à-Pitre, 1974, 16 pp.) discusses the only daily newspaper of the French Antilles.

Guatemala

No Latin American country has a fuller national bibliography than Guatemala. Guatemalean imprints through 1960 are covered by the following volumes in the Colección bibliográfica del 3° centenario de la fundación de la primera imprenta en Centro América: Juan Enrique O'Ryan, *Bibliografía guatemalteca de los siglos xvii y xviii* (Edit. del Ministerio de educación pública "José Ibarra," 1960; earlier edition, Imprenta Elzeviriana, Santiago de Chile, 1897), and eight volumes by Gilberto Valenzuela Reyna, *Bibliografía guatemalteca, y catálogo general de libros, folletos, periódicos, revistas, etc., 1821–1830* (Tipografía nacional, 1961), *Bibliografía . . . 1831–1840* (Edit. del Ministerio de educación pública "José Ibarra," 1961), *Bibliografía . . . 1841–1860* (Tipografía nacional, 1961), *Bibliografía . . . 1861–1900* (1962), *Bibliografía . . . 1901–1930* (1962; i.e., 1963), *Bibliografía . . . 1931–1940* (1963), *Bibliografía . . . 1941–1950* (1963; i.e., 1964), and *Bibliografía . . . 1951–1960* (1964). The volumes that cover the period 1861–1960 were all published by the Tipografía nacional in Guatemala City.

The colonial period was first inventoried by José Toribio Medina, *La imprenta en Guatemala (1660–1821)* (Impreso en casa del autor, Santiago, 1910; 2nd ed., Tipografía nacional, Guatemala, 1960; reprint, N. Israel, Amsterdam, 1964, lxxxv, 696 pp.). The edition published in Guatemala is the second volume of the Colección bibliográfica . . . series. This volume has been supplemented by Gilberto Valenzuela Reyna, *La imprenta en Guatemala: Algunas adiciones a la obra que con este título publicó en Santiago de Chile el ilustre literato José Toribio Medina* (Guatemala, 1933, 62 pp. [Folletín del Diario de Centro América]).

José Luis Reyes Monroy, *Bibliografía de la imprenta en Guatemala (Adiciones de 1769 a 1900)* (Editorial "José de Pineda Ibarra," Ministerio de educación, Guatemala, 1969, 143 pp.) is a supplement to the early volumes published in the Colección bibliográfica del 3° centenario . . . series.

Attempts at a current national bibliography have met with no great success. In May 1932 there began publication of "Obras guatemaltecas ultimamente publicadas," a series in the Biblioteca nacional's *Boletín*. The Inter-American Book Exchange issued *A General Bibliography of Guatemalean Publications for 1938* (Bibliographical Series, No. 3, Washington, D.C., 1939, 8 pp.). The second series of the *Boletín de museos y bibliotecas de Guatemala* in July 1941 began the feature "Publicaciones guatemaltecas recibidas. . . ." The *Indice bibliográfico guatemalteco* was published by the Servicio extensivo of the Biblioteca nacional (1951–1952) and by the Instituto guatemalteco–americano (1958, 1959–1960). The "Anuario bibliográfico guatemalteco 1960 (por autores)" (*Rev. Biblioteca nacional*, 4th ser., Vol. 1, No. 1, 1962, pp. 137–167) would appear to be the last attempt at a current bibliography.

Lourdes Bendfeldt Rojas, *Reseña bibliográfica de las publicaciones periódicas de la Facultad de Humanidades* (Departamento de publicaciones, Universidad de San Carlos, Guatemala, 1971, 76 pp.) is a guide to the serial publications of the Humanities School of this university.

Lists of Guatemalean newspapers and periodicals seem almost nonexistent. The Biblioteca nacional published in its *Boletín* "Lista de prensa del país existente en la Biblioteca nacional de Guatemala" (Vol. 1, No. 2, August 1932, pp. 38–40).

German periodicals are listed in *Arndt–Olson* (Vol. 2, pp. 299–300).

Guyana

Very little seems to have been written concerning printing in British Guiana. James Rodway, "The Press in British Guiana" (*Proc. Am. Antiquarian Soc.*, n.s., Vol. 28, 1918, pp. 274–290) provides a list of "British Guiana Newspapers before 1820" (pp. 288–290).

The *Guyanese National Bibliography* (GNB) (Vol. 1, No. 1–, January–March 1973–) is a subject list of new books printed in the Republic of Guyana and deposited in the National Library under the Publication and Newspapers Act (Chap. 21:01 of the Laws of Guyana, rev. ed., 1973) and of nonbook material. The following types of publications are excluded: (*a*) periodicals (except the first issue of a new periodical, the first issue of a periodical under a new title, and annuals) and (*b*) certain government publications (e.g., gazettes and restricted publications).

The GNB is classified according to the Dewey Decimal Classification (18th ed.) and cataloged according to the British text of the Anglo-American Cataloging Rules (1967) and the requirements of the International Standard Bibliographic Description. It is provided with a full author, title, and series index, and a list of Guyanese publishers. Acts, bills, subsidiary legislation, and parliamentary debates are listed in an appendix. It is published quarterly by the National Library of Guyana. The last quarter is an annual cumulation.

Haiti

Many valuable data are found in Lygia Maria F. C. Ballantyne, *Haitian Publications: An Acquisitions Guide and Bibliography* (Library of Congress, Processing Services, Hispanic Acquisitions Project, Washington, D.C., 1979, 53 pp.) about Haitian publishing and national bibliography. She also provides an annotated list of current Haitian serials (pp. 21–29); a checklist of Haitian monographs, 1970–1979 (pp. 30–46; 311 entries); and a list of books published by Haitians overseas or by foreigners on Haitian subjects (pp. 47–53; 155 entries). It was issued in 1980 as SALALM Bibliography Series, Number 6 (52 pp.).

Ralph T. Esterquest, "L'Imprimerie royale d'Hayti (1817–1819): A Little Known Press of the Western Hemisphere" (*Pap. Bibliographical Soc. America*, Vol. 34, 1940, pp. 171–184) is one of the few studies in English on Haitian imprints. Of special interest are "Complete List of Titles Published at L'Imprimerie royale d'Hayti" (pp. 180–181), which deals with the years 1817–1819; and "Partial List of Works Published Chez P. Roux, imprimeur du roi, Cap-Henry" (pp. 181–184), which deals with publications of the period 1811–1816.

Max Bissainthe is the compiler of *Dictionnaire de bibliographie haitienne* (Scarecrow Press, Washington, D.C., 1951, x, 1052 pp.) and *Dictionnaire . . . premier supplément* (Scarecrow Press, Metuchen, N.J., 1973, viii, 269 pp.). The *Dictionnaire* covers the period 1804 through 1949 and is arranged alphabetically by author. It lists 4,318 works by Haitian authors, and it also provides a list of Haitian periodicals for the period 1764–1949. The supplement has an introduction in both French and English. It has the following parts: Bibliographie haitienne (par année, de 1950 à 1970), Appendice (Liste de publications antérieurs à 1950), Index général (titres, subjet et matière), and Index d'auteurs. The supplement provides data on 1,397 items published during these two decades. The material in the appendix is arranged by author. These two volumes include government documents and are invaluable for the study of works published in Creole.

Bissainthe compiled Haiti's current bibliography in a series published in *Conjonction* (Port-au-Prince) called "Bibliographie haitienne" through 1959; in 1960 its title was changed to "Bibliographie haitienne pour ——." The bibliography for 1950–1951 appeared in Number 81–82 (1961, pp. 61–75); that for 1952, in Number 77–78 (1959, pp. 90–96); that for 1953, in Number 76 (1959, pp. 68–77); that for 1954, in Number 73–74 (1958, pp. 39–50); that for 1955, in Number 72 (1958, pp. 47–57); that for 1956, in Number 67–68 (1957, pp. 50–56); that for 1957, in Number 70–71 (1957, pp. 75–87); that for 1958, in Number 75 (1959, pp. 48–60); that for 1959, in Number 79–80 (1960, pp. 77–84); that for 1960–1961, in Number 94–95 (1964, pp. 67–73); and that for 1962–1964, in Number 98 (1965, pp. 91–104).

Conjonction has published the following bibliographies by Wilfrid Bertrand, "Les livres parus en 1972" (No. 119, 1973, pp. 97–100), "Publications haitiennes des années 1973–5" (No. 126, 1975, pp. 93–103), "Nouvelles publications haitiennes: Une bibliographie" (No. 130, 1972, pp. 83–92), "Nouvelles parutions" (No. 140, 1976, pp. 115–116), "Publications haitiennes (1978)" (No. 141–142, 1979, pp. 102–107), and "Publications haitiennes (1979)" (No. 147, 1979, pp. 85–91).

Optique has published Maurice Lubin, "Publications haitiennes recentes (1950 à

1955)" (Vol. 19, 1955, pp. 31–43), and Milo Marcelin,"Bibliographie haitienne: Romans, récits, nouvelles, chroniques, souvenirs documentaires" (Vol. 35, 1957, pp. 69–79).

A general comprehensive Haitian bibliography listing many Haitian imprints would be Ulrick Duvivier, *Bibliographie générale et méthodique d'Haiti* (Imprimerie de l'Etat, Port-au-Prince, 1941, 2 vols.).

Ira P. Lowenthal and Drexel Woodson, *Catalogue de la collection Mangonés, Pétionville, Haiti* (Occasional Papers, No. 2, Yale University, Antilles Research Program, New Haven, Conn., 1974, xii, 377 pp.), and Lucien Jean Legende, *Catalogue de la bibliothèque de l'Institution Saint Louis de Gonzague* (Port-au-Prince, 1958, 533 pp.) are both based on the largest Haitian collection in Haiti.

Adolphe Cabon, "Un siècle et demi de journalisme en Haïti" (*Proc. Am. Antiquarian Soc.*, n.s., Vol. 49, 1939, pp. 121–205) is reprinted from the weekly *Petite revue hebdomaire* (Port-au-Prince), which ran this study as a serial from April 12 to November 14, 1919. It is the fullest history of Haitian journalism yet written.

Max Manigat, *Haitiana 1971–1975* (Bibliographie haïtienne, Collectif paroles, [La Salle, Québec, © 1979], 1980, 83 pp.) provides data on 418 items arranged alphabetically within each year. It includes works by Haitians on Haiti, the Dominican Republic, and on different subjects as well as works by non-Haitians on this geographical area. The term *Haitian* includes those born in Haiti, those born there but who have had their citizenship revoked, and those Haitians who have become naturalized citizens of some other country. The first appendix (pp. 53–66) provides data on 156 items published between 1950 and 1970 which are not found in the first supplement to the Bissainthe bibliography. The second appendix lists articles on Haiti published in collections between these years. There is an author–subject index. The introduction should be carefully read to determine the compiler's self-imposed limitations as well as the gaps that he indicates he found impossible to fill.

Honduras

The Banco central de Honduras in Tegucigalpa published *Bibliografía hondureña, 1620–1930, 1931–1969* (1971–1972, 2 vols.) and the *Anuario bibliográfico hondureño 1961–1971* (1973, 512 pp.). Both of these titles were compiled by Miguel Angel García, who also compiled *Anuario bibliográfico hondureño, 1961* (Ministerio de educación pública, Tegucigalpa, 1963) and the *Anuario bibliográfico hondureño 1962/1963* (Biblioteca nacional, Tegucigalpa, 1965).

The *Bibliografía hondureña* includes publications by Hondurans published in Honduras as well as material about Honduras or by Hondurans published outside of the country. It also includes government documents. An index to both of these volumes is found at the end of Volume 2.

The *Anuario* provides a classified yearly list of separately published works as well as data on government publications, newspapers, and periodicals. Location symbols occur throughout these three volumes.

Jorge Fidel Durán has published the following articles in *Honduras rotaria:* "Actualidad bibliográfica hondureña" (Vol. 11, No. 126, 1953, pp. 1, 15–16), which lists 1952 imprints; "Los libros y publicaciones hondureñas en 1951" (Vol. 9, No. 107, 1952, pp. 3, 20–23); "Actualidad bibliográfica hondureña" (Vol. 11, No. 126, 1953, pp. 1, 15–16); "Los libros y publicaciones de 1960" (Vol. 18, No. 206, May–June 1961, pp. 14, 31); and "Libros y publicaciones hondureños de 1967" (Vol. 24, No. 239, February–April 1968, pp. 5–11). He also published "Libros y folletos publicados en 1951" (*Rev. interamericana de bibliografía*, Vol. 2, 1952, pp. 103–104), "Los libros y publicaciones hondureñas en 1951" (*Rev. Universidad de Honduras*, Vol. 15, No. 8, January–March 1952, pp. 83–86), and "Las publicaciones hondureñas de 1971" (*Bol. Academia hondureña de la lengua*, Vol. 15, No. 15, November 1972, pp. 7–38).

Little exists on the newspapers and magazines of Honduras. Two studies of interest are: Rafael Heliodoro Valle, "El periodismo en Honduras (notas para su historia)" (*Rev. historia de América*, No. 48, 1959, pp. 517–600), and Carlos Meléndez Ch., "Los primeros años de la imprenta en Honduras" (*An. estudios centro-americanos*, No. 2, 1976, pp. 95–106). Pages 103–104 of the Meléndez article provide a list of the first newspapers published in Honduras, covering those published between 1830 and 1851.

Jamaica

Frank Cundall's following three works are extremely important bibliographies on Jamaica: *Bibliotheca jamaicensis*, subtitled "some account of the principal works on Jamaica in the Library of the Institute . . . Reprinted from *The Handbook of Jamaica for 1895*" (1895, 38 pp.); *Bibliographia jamaicensis*, subtitled "a list of Jamaica books and pamphlets, magazine articles, newspapers and maps, most of which are in the Library of the Institute of Jamaica" (1902, 83 pp.); and *Supplement to Bibliographia jamaicensis* (1908, 38 pp.). They were all published in Kingston by the Institute of Jamaica. These bibliographies have a classified arrangement. Pages 5–28 of the *Bibliotheca jamaicensis* are an annotated bibliographic essay on important works published on Jamaica, with brief sketches on their authors. A brief history of the island is also provided; the rest of this volume is the bibliography and index. *Bibliographia jamaicensis* provides data on approximately 1,200 items, many published on the island. The *Supplement* lists slightly more than 700 entries.

Rae Delattre, *A Guide to Jamaican Reference Material in the West India Reference Library* (Institute of Jamaica, Kingston, 1965, 75 pp.), and Kenneth Ingram, *Sources of Jamaican History*, subtitled "a bibliographical survey with particular reference to manuscript sources" (Inter Documentation, Zug, Switzerland, 1976, 2 vols.), should also prove useful.

Frank Cundall, *A History of Printing in Jamaica from 1717 to 1834*, which carries the description "Reprinted from The Centenary number of the 'Gleaner' 13th September, with biographical and bibliographical notes" (Institute of Jamaica, Kingston, 1935, 63 pp.), is still the standard history of printing for this area. It is divided into the following sections: I. History; II. Printers; and III. Publications; 1. Books, 2. Pamphlets and Broadsheets, 3. Magazines, 4. Legislation and Laws, 5. Book Almanacs, and 6. Newspapers. It contains 19 illustrations. Cundall is also the author of "The Press and Printers of Jamaica prior to 1820" (*Proc. Am. Antiquarian Soc.*, Vol. 24, 1916, pp. 355–356).

Douglas C. McMurtrie published two brief articles on early Jamaican imprints in the *American Book Collector*. They are: "The First Printing on the Island of Jamaica: A Preliminary Report" (Vol. 5, 1934, pp. 218–220) and "The Early Press of Jamaica" (Vol. 5, 1934, pp. 324–325).

More recent studies on printing in Jamaica would include "Early Jamaican Printing: A Selection from the Exhibition Mounted by the Institute of Jamaica at the National Arena for National Heritage Week, 1969, with notes prepared by Judith Richards" (*Jamaica J.*, Vol. 3, No. 4, December 1969, pp. 7–11), Headley Powell Jacobs, "The Jamaican Press 1789–1865" (*Jamaica J.,* Vol. 6, No. 3, September 1972, pp. 3–6), and Rena Reckord, "Jamaican Newspapers of the 18th, Early 19th Centuries" (*Bull. Jamaican Historical Soc.*, Vol. 5, Nos. 14–16, 1972, pp. 189–191).

The Institute of Jamaica has compiled *The Jamaican National Bibliography 1964–1974* (Kraus International Publications, Millwood, N.Y., 1981, viii, 439 pp.), "whose primary purpose . . . is to provide a bibliographical record for material locally published in Jamaica during this ten-year period. . . . This bibliography represents a cumulation of the entries in the 1964–1970 *Jamaican National Bibliography*, which was published in 1973, and the titles of those Jamaican publications acquired and catalogued by the West Indian Reference Library, Institute of Jamaica, between 1971 and 1974" (p. vii). It is further noted that "the scope of this bibliography has also been widened to include Jamaican authors published outside of Jamaica and works about Jamaica published elsewhere" (p. vii). The preface notes that "Books, articles, pamphlets, and microforms are all included in this publication" (p. vii). It states that "certain government publications . . . are not included" (pp. vii–viii).

It includes 3,342 items plus an alphabetical list of Jamaican periodicals and newspapers, a classified list of periodicals, a section devoted to manuscripts, and one devoted to maps.

This bibliography replaces such publications as the *Jamaican National Bibliography*, for 1964–1970, and *Jamaican Accessions. Jamaican National Bibliography* (Vol. 1 –, 1975 –) is a quarterly with an annual cumulation.

Little appears to have been written concerning Jamaican imprints for the first part of the 20th century. Alvona Alleyne, "Literary Publications in the English-Speaking Caribbean" (21st SALALM, 1976, 1978, pp. 238–248) contains "A Preliminary Check List of Literary Works Published in Jamaica 1900–1976."

For serials and newspapers, see Audrey Chambers, "Selected List of Serials Published in Jamaica" (*Jamaica Lib. Assoc. Bull.*, 1975, pp. 35–39), and Audrey Chambers and Alvona Alleyne, "Selected List of Serials Published in Jamaica (1975–1976)" (ibid., 1977, pp. 59–62). These two lists of serials exclude "house journals, publications of government departments, (except those of statutory bodies), programmes, calendars and brochures." Chambers provides data on title, address, and frequency. Chambers and Alleyne note that "where possible, the first date of publication has been included."

Martinique

Jean-Pierre Jardel, Maurice Nicolas, and Claude Relouzat, *Bibliographie de la Martinique* (Cahier special du CERAG, Centre d'études regionales Antilles-Guyane, 3ème trimestre 1969, 231 pp.) is the fullest bibliography yet compiled on Martinique. It includes both material published on this island and material about it published elsewhere. It is a classified bibliography of 3,000 entries. Of special interest would be "Journaux, bulletins, revues" and "Annuaires, almanachs, guides, statistiques et notices d'exposition."

Mexico

Though slightly dated, Luis González, "Estudio preliminar" to *Fuentes de la historia contemporánea de México: Libros y folletos I*, by Luis González with the collaboration of Guadalupe Monroy and Susana Uribe (El Colegio de México, Mexico, 1961, Vol. 1, pp. vii–lxviii), is an excellent history of bibliographic activities in Mexico.

Agustín Millares Carlo and José Ignacio Mantecón compiled *Ensayo de una bibliografía de bibliografías mexicanas* (Biblioteca de la II Feria del libro y exposición nacional del periodismo, Departamento del Distrito federal, Dirección de acción social, Oficina de bibliotecas, Mexico, 1943, xvi, 224 pp.). This and *Ensayo . . . Adiciones I* (III Feria del libro y exposición nacional del periodismo, de cine y radio, issued by the same publisher, 1944, 46 pp.) provide bibliographic data on more than 2,000 items. The *Ensayo* is the work of two outstanding scholars and a model of its kind.

It is unfortunate that the ["Bibliografía de bibliografías mexicanas"] by Leoncio Ortíz González (*Bol. Sociedad mexicana de geografía y estadística*, Vol. 111, 1972, pp. 9–145) is not a compilation of higher caliber; it includes many items that have nothing to do with Mexico, and much of the information included is erroneous.

The *Bibliografía histórica mexicana* (El Colegio de México, Mexico, Vol. 1 –, 1967–; earlier issues appeared as articles in *Memorias de la Academia mexicana de le historia* and *Historia mexicana*) includes material on the history of printing and journalism.

In current usage the term *Mexico* can refer to the country, city, and state. It should be remembered that until 1848 this country included what are today the U.S. states of Texas, New Mexico, Arizona, and California, and parts of Colorado and Utah. During the colonial period this area was referred to as the "Viceroyalty of New Spain." Mexico was the first area in the New World to have printing, which was introduced in 1539 when the first press was established in the city of Mexico.

José Toribio Medina, *La imprenta en México (1539–1821)* (Casa del autor, Santiago de Chile, 1908–1912; N. Israel, Amsterdam, 1965, 8 vols.) is the basic work for the study of the publications of Mexico City for the colonial period. Medina's entries are arranged alphabetically by author within each year. He provides transcriptions of title pages and sometimes quite elaborate notes on the author, printer, or the importance of the work.

Medina's set has been supplemented by Francisco González de Cossio, *La im-*

prenta en México, 1594–1820: Cien adiciones a la obra de Don José Toribio Medina (Antigua librería Robredo, Mexico, 1947, 205 pp.) and *La imprenta en México, 1553–1820: 510 adiciones a la obra de José Toribio Medina en homenaje al primer centenario de su nacimiento* (Universidad nacional de México, Mexico, 1952, xvii, 354 pp.).

The most important bibliographies of the Mexico City presses of the 16th century are: Joaquín García Icazbalceta, *Bibliografía mexicana del siglo xvi*, subtitled Catálogo razonado de libros impresos en México de 1539 a 1600 con biografías de autores . . . (Andrade y Morales, Mexico, 1886, 419 pp.; new edition edited by Agustín Millares Carlo, Fondo de cultura económica, México, 1954, 581 pp.); Angel Ramírez de Arellano, *Apuntes para un catálogo de libros notables impresos en México de 1539 a 1699* (Mexico, 1895, 45 pp.); Emilio Valton, *Impresos mexicanos del siglo xvi* (Incunables americanos; Imprenta universitaria, Mexico, 1935, xixi, 244 pp.); and Henry Raup Wagner, *Nueva bibliografía mexicana del siglo xvi . . .* (Polis, Mexico, 1940 [i.e., 1946], 548 pp.).

Before Medina, Vicente de Paula Andrade published his *Ensayo bibliográfico mexicano del siglo xvii* (Edición de la Sociedad científica Alzate, Mexico, 1894; Imprenta del Museo nacional, Mexico, 1899, 803 pp. [in 1971 Jesús Medina, Mexico City, brought out a facsimile edition]). Paula Andrade seems to have been one of the few individuals to have published concerning 17th-century printing in the Mexican capital. The work contains 1,228 items, and pages 793–803 are a "Bibliografía de Puebla" of 166 items.

Nicolas León, greatest of the early 20th-century Mexican bibliographers, compiled the *Bibliografía mexicana del siglo xviii* (Francisco Diaz de León, Mexico, 1902–1908, 5 vols. in 6); Roberto Valles produced a three-volume index to this work (Vargas Rea, Mexico, 1945–1946). León's set contains elaborate notes and reproduces material published in this century that otherwise would not be as readily available.

Printing during the colonial period spread from Mexico City to other cities in New Spain as well as to Guatemala, so that in order to obtain an overall retrospective bibliography of Mexican imprints, bibliographies for individual states and cities must be consulted. These are listed in León's work in alphabetical order by place of publication.

José Toribio Medina, *La imprenta en Guadalajara de México (1793–1821): Notas bibliográficas* (Imprenta Elzeviriana, Santiago de Chile, 1904; N. Israel, Amsterdam, 1964, 104 pp.) deals with printing in what is now Mexico's second largest city.

Printing was not introduced in Mérida (Yucatán) until the beginning of the independence movement. José Toribio Medina, *La imprenta en Mérida de Yucatán (1813–1821): Notas bibliográficas* (Imprenta Elzeviriana, Santiago de Chile, 1904; N. Israel, Amsterdam, 1964, 32 pp.) was for a half-century the standard study for this city; now one should consult the later edition of this work (E. Suárez, Mérida, 1956, 102 pp.), which contains a prologue and two appendixes by Victor M. Suárez.

Juan B. Iguiniz has been the principal student of the bibliography of Nueva Galicia. Two of his studies are "La imprenta en la Nueva Galicia: 1793–1821 (Apuntes bibliográficos)" (*An. Museo nacional de arqueología, historia y etnología*, Vol. 3,

1911, pp. 253–336) and an article with the same title in *Boletín de la Biblioteca nacional* (Mexico) (Vol. 12, 1920, pp. 58–76).

For Oaxaca there exists José Toribio Medina, *La imprenta en Oaxaca (1720–1820): Notas bibliográficas* (Imprenta Elzeviriana, Santiago de Chile, 1904; N. Israel, Amsterdam, 1964, 29 pp.; and issued in Mexico, 1967, as No. 4 of the series Bibliófilos oaxaqueños).

After Mexico City, Puebla was the most important publishing center in colonial times, and from this city, printing was introduced into what is now Guatemala. José Toribio Medina describes 1,928 titles in his *La imprenta en Puebla de los Angeles (1640–1821)* (Cervantes, Santiago de Chile, 1908; N. Israel, Amsterdam, 1964, 823 pp.). It should be supplemented by Felipe Teixidor, *Adiciones a la imprenta en la Puebla de los Angeles* ([Colección Gavito], Mexico, 1961, 621 pp.).

José Toribio Medina, *La imprenta en Veracruz (1794–1821): Notas bibliográficas* (Imprenta Elzeviriana, Santiago de Chile, 1904; N. Israel, Amsterdam, 1964, 34 pp.) is the outstanding study on this state.

Alberta A. Lamadrid Lusarreta, "Guías de forasteros y calendarios mexicanos de los siglos xviii y xix, existentes en la Biblioteca nacional de México" (*Bol. Instituto de investigaciones bibliográficos*, No. 6, 1971, pp. 9–135), is a useful guide to almanacs printed in Mexico in the 18th and 19th centuries.

The colonial period of Mexican imprints has been well studied in comparison to that of the 19th century. Israel Cavazos Garza, "Algunos impresos jaliscienses del siglo xix existentes en al Archivo general del estado de Nuevo León" (*Bol. Instituto de investigaciones bibliográficas*, No. 4, 1970, pp. 73–83) would seem to be one of the few attempts to describe 19th-century Mexican publications after 1821 and before 1885. There is a tremendous need for a retrospective bibliography that would cover the period between 1821 and 1966, when the *Bibliografía mexicana* began publication.

This last sentence does not mean that nothing exists, but what does exist appeared very sporadically.

Despite the appearance in 1889 of Luis González Obregón, *Anuario bibliográfico nacional*, for 1885 (Oficina tipografía de la Secretaría de fomento, Mexico, 155 pp.), it was only in the 1930s that political conditions, after the Revolution, had sufficiently stabilized for either the government or associations of publishers to consider the publication of a current national bibliography. Indeed, for the period between 1930 and 1966, it would be advisable to consult not only the bibliographies listed in the next several paragraphs but also lists of Mexican books published in such journals as *El libro y pueblo, La torre, Hispanic American Historical Review*, and the *Boletín de la Biblioteca nacional*. Of particular value is "Nueva bibliografía mexicana," which began with the first (1940) issue of Porrúa's *Boletín bibliográfico mexicanó*. It is a classified listing of Mexican current publications, or at least those publications that publishers have sent to this bookdealer for listing. It seems to be much stronger on publications of Mexico City. An annual index would have rendered it much more useful as a bibliographic source.

The Imprenta de la Secretaría de relaciones exteriores published the *Annuario bibliográfico mexicano* for 1931 (1932), 1932 (1933), and 1933 (1934), compiled by Felipe Teixidor.

The years 1938 and 1939 are covered by Francisco Gamoneda's *Bibliografía mexicana, 1938* (Imprenta Cosmes, Mexico, 1938–1939) and his *Bibliografía mexicana, 1939* (S. Turanzas del Valle, Mexico, 1939–1940).

Julian Amó compiled the *Anuario bibliográfico mexicano de 1940* and the *Anuario . . . de 1941 y 1942*, both published by the Talleres gráficós de la nación (Mexico, 1942, 1944).

The Comisión mexicana de cooperación intelectual compiled the *Bibliografía mexicana de 1942* (DAPP, Mexico, 1944).

The *Anuario bibliográfico* volumes for 1958 (1967), 1959 (1968), and 1960 (1970) were published by Mexico's Biblioteca nacional. Those for 1961 (1971), 1962 (1974), and 1963 (1976) were published by the Instituto de investigaciones bibliográficas in Mexico City. They ranged from 663 pages to 804 pages. With the publication of this set of the *Anuario*, Josefina Berroa's *México bibliográfico 1957–1960*, subtitled Catálogo de libros impresos en México (J. Berroa, Mexico, 1961, 189 pp.), became obsolete, though at the time of its publication it was the only available bibliography for this period.

A new period in the history of Mexican current bibliography began in 1967 with the publication of the *Bibliografía mexicana*. This classified bibliography appears six times per year, and the current issues note that it is published under the auspices of the Biblioteca nacional and the Instituto de investigaciones bibliográficas. Each issue is indexed, and a list of publishers and their addresses is a helpful feature.

National bibliography comprises more than the publications of the capital, yet publications issued in areas outside of it often were not included in such attempts at national bibliography as existed before the appearance of *Anuario bibliográfico* (1958–) and *Bibliografía mexicana*. It is for this reason that bibliographies for the individual Mexican states which on examination show that they list the imprints of a particular state are listed alphabetically by state. Most appear in one of two series: Bibliografías mexicanas (BM) or Monografías bibliográficas mexicanas (MBM).

Joaquín Díaz Mercado, *Bibliografía sumaria de la Baja California* (BM, Vol. 2, DAPP, Mexico, 1937, 179 pp.) is a classified bibliography of 957 entries.

Hector Pérez Martínez and Juan de Dios Pérez Galaz compiled *Bibliografía del estado de Campeche* ([Talleres linotip. del Gobierno, Campeche, 1943], xxiv, 377 pp.), which contains 2,000 entries.

Vito Alessio Robles, *Bibliografía de Coahuila, histórica y geográfica* (MBM, Vol. 10, Imprenta de la Secretaría de relaciones exteriores, Mexico, 1927, xxviii, 450 pp.) lists not only books and pamphlets published in Coahuila but also newspapers published in this state, and material that deals in any way with this state as well as topographical, geographical, and orographic maps and manuscripts. It has an alphabetical index.

Unfortunately only the first volume, *A–F*, has appeared of Ramiro Villaseñor, *Bibliografía general de Jalisco* (Publicaciones del gobierno del estado, Guadalajara, 1958, 401 pp.). This bibliography includes works by authors from Jalisco, Jalisco imprints, and works that refer to this state.

The imprints of the state of Mexico have been listed in Mario Colin, *Bibliografía del estado de México* (Biblioteca enciclopedica del estado de México, 3 vols.). The first volume is *Impresos del estado* (1963) and lists 2,291 entries in chronological order. It covers the period from 1821 to 1963. This volume contains two appendixes: The first is a listing of Novaro editores—impresores, S.A., publications for 1955 and 1963; and the second is a listing of the publications during the period 1957–1961 of Editorial Comeval. The annotations for some of these entries are quite extensive, and certain of the broadsides and pamphlets are reproduced in full. Material omitted from this volume is supplemented in Volume 2 (pp. 263–285) and Volume 3 (pp. 519–532). Volume 2 (1964), *Impresos referentes al estado*, contains 1,490 entries; while Volume 3 (1964), *Referencias y autores del estado*, also contains a "Bibliografía del presidente Adolfo López Mateos" (pp. 419–489). This bibliography of 379 items includes much by him that could be classified as government documents.

The Colin set is extremely well indexed. Each volume has several indexes which should lead the user to locate material in it easily.

Jesús Romero Flores, *Apuntes para una bibliografía geográfica e histórica de Michoacán: Archivos, memorias, imprentas, impresores, periódicos, cartas geográficas* (MBM, Vol. 25, Imprenta de la Secretaría de relaciones exteriores, Mexico, 1932, lxxxviii, 325 pp.) is well described by its subtitle. Romero Flores is also the author of *La imprenta en Michoacán* (Publicado como colaboración del Estado a la II Feria del Libro y Exposición Nacional de Periodismo, Mexico, 1943, 135 pp.), which provides a general bibliography for this state from 1821 to 1942, arranged chronologically. It provides data on the state's culture in colonial times and a history of printing in this state from the Independence movement to the present.

Domingo Díez, *Bibliografía del Estado de Morelos* (MBM, Vol. 27, Imprenta de la Secretaría de relaciones exteriores, Mexico, 1933, xxiii, 427 pp.) is a classified bibliography of material published in and on Morelos.

Héctor González and Plinio D. Ordóñez, *Bibliografía del estado de Nuevo León de 1820 a 1945* (Impresora Monterrey, Monterrey, 1946, 208 pp.) leaves much to be desired. It omits pamphlets and provides only the title, author, and date of each volume; and in regard to its list of newspapers and periodicals it omits the dates in which they were published.

Moisés Herrera, *Contribución para una bibliografía de obras referentes al estado de Puebla* (Biblioteca de la II Feria del Libro y Exposición Nacional de Periodismo, Editada por el Gobierno constitucional del estado libre y soberano de puebla, 1943, 112, xv, vii, 20 pp.) is divided into general works, philosophy, religion, and social sciences, with an elaborate index of authors, publishers, printers, presses, etc., as well as one of subjects.

Rafael Ayala Echévarri, *Bibliografía histórica y geográfica de Queretaro* (MBM, 2nd ser., Vol. 2, Secretaría de relaciones exteriores, Departamento de información para el extranjero, Mexico, 1949, xiii, 389 pp.) provides data on 1,288 works either published in or about this state.

Elena Gómez Ugarte and Aurora Pagaza, "Bibliografía del territorio de Quintana Roo," in *Bibliografía sumaria del territorio de Quintana Roo* (BM, Vol. 3, DAPP, Mexico, 1937, pp. 45–111) lists 300 items.

The Universidad de San Luis Potosí has published *Fichas de bibliografía potosina* (San Luis Potosí, 1955, 29 pp.). Rafael Montejano y Aguiñaga published the following bibliographies in *Fichas de bibliografías potosina:* "Bibliografía potosina del año 1952" (Vol. 2, No. 7, January-February, 1953, pp. 12–14), "Bibliografía potosina de 1954" (Vol. 2, Nos. 2–3, March–June 1955, pp. 35–49), "Bibliografía potosina del año 1955" (Vol. 3, No. 2, April–June 1956, pp. 63–78), and "Bibliografía potosina del año 1956" (Vol. 4, Nos. 2–3, April–September 1957, pp. 29–40).

José G. Heredia, *Bibliografía de Sinaloa histórica y geográfica* (MBM, Vol. 6, Imprenta de la Secretaria de relaciones exteriores, Mexico, 1926, viii, 185 pp.) is useful for its "Periódicos oficiales" (pp. 116–122), "Periódicos y revistas de Sinaloa de carácter no oficial" (pp. 122–129), and "Relación de algunas cartas geográficas de Sinaloa o importantes para la geografía sinaloense" (pp. 163–185). Only the barest data are provided concerning newspapers and magazines published in this state. Most of the books listed were published outside of Sinaloa.

E. Y. López, *Bibliografía de Sonora* (Ediciones Fátima, Hermosillo, 1969, 200 pp.) contains 1,631 entries. It lists Sonoran imprints and authors, and works about Sonora.

Francisco Javier Santamaria, *Bibliografía general de Tabasco* (Imprenta de la Secretaría de relaciones exteriores, Mexico, 1930–1946, 3 vols.) and its second edition in one volume (Escritores tabasqueños, No. 37, Gobierno del estado, Villahermosa, 1949, xxxi, 512 pp.) provide this state with a thorough bibliography through the end of the 1940s.

Crisanto Cuellar Abaroa, *Bibliografía de Tlaxcala* ([Tlaxcala], 1960, 98 pp.) was originally compiled by Ramos Cuellar. Earlier, Cuellar Abaroa and Roberto Ramos collaborated on *Bibliografía del estado de Tlaxcala* (Publicaciones de la Dirección de bibliotecas, museos, e investigaciones históricas, Tlaxcala, 1949, 59 pp.).

Joaquín Diaz Mercado, *Bibliografía general del estado de Veracruz* (BM, Vol. 1, DAPP, Mexico, 1937, 715 pp.) is now somewhat dated, as it covers only the years 1794 to 1910. It includes lists of books and newspapers published in Vera Cruz as well as material about this state.

Victor M. Suárez, *Libros yucatecos de 1947* (Mérida, 1948, 38 pp.) lists 67 titles. Felipe Teixidor, *Bibliografía yucateca* (Publicación del Museo arqueológico e histórico de Yucatán, No. 1, Mérida, 1937, 263 pp.) provides data on 238 works on the Mayan language; 1,460 works on history, literature, and science; and 38 manuscripts.

The "Anuario bibliográfico de Yucatán" appeared in *Boletín de bibliografía yucateca* (Nos. 4–5, January–February 1939, pp. 2–17; No. 11, May 15, 1940, pp. 1–15; No. 13, April 1, 1941, pp. 2–20; No. 15, April 1, 1942, pp. 3–14; and No. 17, April–May 1943, pp. 2–14).

Luis Chávez Orozco, *Bibliografía de Zacatecas* (MBM, Vol. 26, Imprenta de la Secretaría de relaciones exteriores, Mexico, 1932, x, 231 pp.) lists 677 items.

Our knowledge of Mexican newspapers and periodicals must be derived from many sources.

Though Millares Carlo and Mantecón (described earlier) list numerous histories of Mexican journalism, it would seem well to mention María del Carmen Ruiz Castañeda, Luis Reed Torres, and Enrique Cordero y Torres, *El periodismo en México: 450 años de historia,* investigación dirigida por Salvador Novo (Editorial tradición, Mexico, 1974, 380 pp.), which is the latest attempt to write a history of journalism in Mexico from its beginnings down to the present day.

The *Boletín del Instituto de investigaciones bibliográficas* published María del Carmen Ruiz y Castañeda, "*La Gaceta de México* de 1722 primer periódico de la Nueva España" (Vol. 1, No. 1, January–June 1969, pp. 39–59), "La segunda *Gazeta de México* (1728–39, 1742)" (Vol. 2, No. 1, January–June 1971, pp. 23–42), and "La tercera *Gaceta de la Nueva España: Gazeta de México* (1784–1809)" (Vol. 3, No. 6, July–December 1971, pp. 137–150); these would seem to be the latest studies on 18th-century Mexican journalism. Page 52 of the first article contains a bibliography of previous studies on this newspaper. Ruth Wold, *El Diario de México: Primer cotidiano de Nueva España* (Gredos, Madrid, 1970, 294 pp.) is more interested in this newspaper's contents than in its history.

Pages 116–117 of Luz María Frutos, "Prensa lozana" (*Historia mexicana*, Vol. 1, 1951, pp. 114–117) present an incomplete list of the newspapers of the provincial capitals during the early part of the Diaz regime. Unfortunately, she provides little more than the name of the capital and its newspapers, with no indication as to when each began and ended.

Jefferson Rea Spell, "Mexican Literary Periodicals of the 19th Century" (*Publ. Modern Language Assoc.*, Vol. 52, March 1937, pp. 272–312) is a study of the history and content of 195 literary periodicals. The bibliography of periodicals appears on pages 295–312. In the same journal, he published "Mexican Literary Periodicals of the Twentieth Century" (Vol. 59, 1939, pp. 835–862), where he describes 156 journals.

Vicente de Paula Andrade, *Noticia de los periódicos que se publican dentro y fuera de la capital* (Tipografía de "El Tiempo," Mexico, 1901, 57 pp.) first appeared as a series in *El Tiempo*.

"Noticia de las publicaciones periódicas existentes en los estados, territorios y distrito federales" (*Diario oficial*, April 13, 1891, pp. 2–4) is apparently the earliest official list of Mexican periodicals.

"Bibliografía mexicana" is reprinted in the *Boletín de la Biblioteca nacional* (2nd ser., Vol. 6, January–March 1955, pp. 38–52) from *La Sociedad* of November 15, 1864. Data on 350 periodicals are provided on pages 42–52.

The Dirección general de correos issued *Noticia de las publicaciones registradas como artículos de segunda clase en las oficinas de correos de la República, hasta junio de 1912* ("El Siglo XIX," Mexico, 1912, 26 pp.).

The Dirección general de correos y telégrafos has published the following lists of periodicals entitled to second-class mailing rates: *Relación general de publicaciones registradas como artículos de segunda clase, vigentes hasta el 30 de abril de 1933 en todas las administraciones de correos y telégrafos de la República, México* (1933, 32 pp.); *Lista general de publicaciones registradas como artículos de segunda clase, vigente hasta el 30 de noviembre de 1935, México* (1936, 49 pp.); *Lista . . . hasta el 31 de diciembre de 1938* (DAPP, Mexico, 1939, 40 pp.); and *Lista . . . hasta el 31 de diciembre de 1940* (DAPP, Mexico, 1941, 31 pp.). As the Dirección general de correos, it issued *Lista publicaciones autorizadas como correspondencia de segunda clase, vigentes en todas las administraciones de la República, hasta el día 31 de julio de 1953* (1953, 53 pp.).

The second series of the *Boletín de la Biblioteca nacional* published a series entitled "Revistas y boletines nacionales recibidos recientemente" (Vol. 1, No. 2, April–June 1950, pp. 50–63; Vol. 1, No. 3, July–September 1950, pp. 62–63; Vol. 2, No. 2, April–June 1951, pp. 57–63; and Vol. 2, No. 3, July–September 1951, pp. 61–63).

The most recent current list of Mexican periodicals is Margarita Mendoza López, *Catálogo de publicaciones periódicas mexicanas* (Centro mexicano de escritores, Mexico, 1959, 262 pp.).

Little seems to have been published on the Mexican political press. Antonio Acevedo Escobedo, "Periódicos socialistas de México" (*El Libro y el pueblo*, Vol. 13, 1935, pp. 3–14) should prove useful.

For data on the Mexican labor press, one should consult Guillermina Bringas and David Mascareño, *La prensa obrera de los obreros mexicanos 1870–1970: Hemerografía comentada* (Universidad nacional autonoma de Mexico, Mexico, 1979, 288 pp.).

Scientific periodicals can be studied through Anita Melville Ker, *A Survey of Mexican Scientific Periodicals, to Which Are Appended Some Notes on Mexican Historical Periodicals* (Publication of the Harvey Bassler Foundation, Printed at the Waverly Press, Baltimore, Md., 1931, 105 pp.), Centro de documentación científica y técnica (México), *Lista de revistas científicas mexicanas* (D.F., Mexico, 1953, 8 pp.), *La prensa médica mexicana* (Mexico, 1963, 64 pp.), and UNESCO, Technical Assistance Mission in Mexico, *Lista de revistas científicas mexicanas* (D.F., Mexico, [1954?], 8 pp.).

The Instituto nacional de bellas artes published in 1963 *Las revistas literarias de México* (Mexico, 254 pp.) and a second series with the same title (Mexico, 209 pp.). Both were published in the Ediciones del Instituto nacional de bellas artes.

Boyd G. Carter, "Mexican Literary Periodicals since 1968" (*Denver Q.*, Vol. 14, No. 1, Spring 1979, pp. 68–81) critically evaluates a variety of Mexican journals.

For data on music journals, see Jesús C. Romero, "El periodismo musical mexicano en el siglo xx" (*Carnet musical*, Vol. 8, No. 3, March 1952, pp. 138–147).

Many more data need to be collected concerning the newspapers and magazines published outside of the capital.

Both newspapers and official government documents are listed in Juan de Dios Pérez Galaz, *Reseña histórica del periodismo en Campeche* (Talleres linotipgráficos del Gobierno del estado, Campeche, 1943, 46 pp.).

For an outstanding study on journalism in Guadalajara, see Juan Bautista Iguniz, "El periodismo en Guadalajara: 1804–1914: Recopilación de datos, históricos, biográficos y bibliográficos" (*An. Museo nacional de arqueología, historia y etnografía*, 4th ser. Vol. 7, 1931, pp. 237–406).

Héctor González, "Periódicos antiguos de Monterrey" (*Bol. Seminario de cultura mexicana*, Vol. 2, No. 4, September 1945, pp. 3–11) discusses newspapers for the period.

Ignaclo Morales, *Breve reseña sobre el periodismo y su influencia moral y económica en el pueblo de Nayarit* (Publicado con ocasión de la II Feria del Libro y exposición nacional del periodismo, [Tepic], 1943, 26 pp.) is a survey of newspapers for this area from 1884 on.

Julio Chacón del Campo, *Reseña histórica de la prensa de Parral y relación de sus fiestas cincuentenarias* (Imprenta "La Democracia," Parral, 1914, 84 pp.) provides a list of newspapers published in this city (pp. 47–52).

Enrique Cordero y Torres studies the history of the Puebla press in his *Historia del periodismo en Puebla, 1820–1945* (Bohemia poblana, Puebla, 1947, 595 pp.).

Rafael Montejano y Aguiñaga, "Cincuenta y tres adiciones a la 'Hemerografía potosina' de Meade" (*Fichas de la bibliografía potosina*, Vol. 3, Nos. 3–4, July–December 1956, pp. 125–149) supplements Joaquín Meade, *Hemerografía potosina: Historia del periodismo en San Luis Potosí* (Bajo del angulo de Letras Potosinas, San Luis Potosí, 1956, 199 pp.).

For Yucatan, consult Miguel Civeira Taboada, "Hemerografía yucateca en la Hemeroteca nacional" (*Mem. Academia mexicana de la historia*, Vol. 19, January–March 1960, pp. 35–103).

Rafael Carrasco Puente, *Hemerografía de Zacatecas, 1825–1950*, subtitled Con datos biográficos de algunos periodistas zacatecanos: Prólogo de José María González de Mendoza (MBM, 2nd ser., No. 4, Secretaría de relaciones exteriores, Departamento de información para el extranjero, Mexico, 1951, 203 pp.) should prove useful for the study of periodicals published in this state.

Little seems to exist on English publications in Mexico. Lota M. Spell, "The Anglo-Saxon Press in Mexico, 1846–1848" (*Am. Historical Rev.*, Vol. 38, October 1932, pp. 19–31) deals with an extremely small period in Mexican history.

Catalogue Five: Americana from the Atlantic to the Pacific (William Reese Company, New Haven, Conn., 1981?, item 252) provides an interesting discussion of *The American Star*, which was published by the U.S. Army in Mexico City from September 30, 1847, until May 30, 1848. There were 207 issues of the paper during this time. This was a bilingual newspaper in English and Spanish.

Even less seems to have been written concerning the French newspapers of Mexico. Bernard Vincent, "El periodismo francés en México" (*Hoy*, Vol. 10, No. 126, July 22, 1939, pp. 16–17, 89) provides the names of journalists and French newspapers in Mexico from 1849 through 1926.

The country's German press has been studied in *Arndt–Olson* (pp. 303–324).

Little has been written on the Hungarian press in Mexico. Attention is called to Györgyi Markovits, "Magyarok a fasizmus ellan Mexikóban a második vilaghaboru idején: A "Szabad Magyarság" (*Az Országos Széchényi Könyvtár érkönyve, 1973*, Budapest, 1976, pp. 313–327), which discusses this journal published in Mexico City.

Monserrat

A list of Monserrat newspapers is found in E. C. Baker, *A Guide to Records in the Leeward Islands* (Basil Blackwell, Oxford, 1965, p. 34).

Nevis

A list of Nevis newspapers is found in E. C. Baker, *A Guide to Records in the Leeward Islands* (Basil Blackwell, Oxford, 1965, p. 45).

Nicaragua

Little was published on Nicaraguan imprints until the early 1970s. However, with the appearance of the *Boletín nicaragüense de bibliografía y documentación* (BNBD; No. 1–, 1974–), edited by the outstanding literary historian, poet, and bibliographer Jorge Eduardo Arellano, one may expect more studies of interest to students of national bibliography.

Jorge Eduardo Arellano, "Los 'incunables' de Nicaragua (1829–1859)" (BNBD, No. 24, 1978, pp. 92–103) is apparently the first attempt to list books for this period.

Arellano and Noel Lacayo Barreto have compiled and published in BNBD (No. 13, September–October 1976, pp. 1–72) "Autores nicaragüenses del siglo xx." It records bibliographic data on 1,500 books by Nicaraguan authors, the vast majority of which were published in Nicaragua.

Jorge Eduardo Arellano, "Bibliografía general de Nicaragua" (*Cuadernos de bibliografía nicaragüense,* No. 1, January–June 1981, pp. 1–88) is subtitled Primera entrega: 1674–1900. This outstanding bibliography is divided into Historia de la bibliografía nicaragüense; Primeras imprentas e impresos; I. Autores coloniales (items 1–50); II. Los "incunables" (1838–1860) (items 51–150); III. Folletos y libros de 1861 a 1900 (items 151–606); IV. Títulos de autores nicaragüenses editados en el extranjero durante el siglo xix (items 609–638); V. Títulos sobre Nicaragua de autores extranjeros editados en el extranjero durante el siglo xix (items 639–728); Suplemento (items 729–767); and Indice de autores. This is the fullest bibliography of Nicaraguan imprints of the 19th century yet compiled. Copies are located and many title pages are photographically reproduced.

The Biblioteca americana in Managua published the *Bibliografía de trabajos publicados en Nicaragua* (title also given in English) for 1943, 1944, and 1945–1947 (Bibliographical Series of the American Library of Nicaragua, Nos. 1, 6, and 7–9).

Arellano has published several annual listings of Nicaraguan books in *La prensa literaria* (Managua). Among these are: "Columna bibliográfica: Los libros nicaragüenses de 1974" (January 19 and 21, 1975) and "Bibliografía nicaragüense del año 1977" (January 7, 1978).

Héctor Vargas, "Libros para la historia: Bibliografía del 81" (*Neuvo amanecer cultural,* año, Vol. 3, No. 93, March 21, 1982, p. 2) indicates that the majority of the works published in Nicaragua during 1981 were political in nature. Several works published outside of Nicaragua but about it are included. The article has no introduction. For each item there are given author, title, imprint data, pagination, and if belles-lettres, genre.

More attention has been given to Nicaraguan newspapers and periodicals than to books.

The Instituto Centroamericano de historia of the Universidad centroamerica in Managua published a *Catálogo de la exposición: Treinta años de periodismo en Nicaragua 1830–1860* (1971, 264 pp.).

The *Revista conservadora del pensamiento centroamericano*, whose title was changed in 1972 to *Revista del pensamiento centro-americano*, has published a series of bibliographies of Nicaraguan periodicals. They are: Carlos Melendez Ch., "Fichero del periodismo antiguo en Nicaragua" (No. 116, 1970, pp. 17–48), which has been corrected and supplemented by Mauricio Pallais Lacayo (No. 127, 1971, pp. 44–56), Andrés Vega Bolaños (No. 133, 1971, pp. 33–41), and Alejandro Montiel Arguello (No. 133, 1971, pp. 53–54). These works and Franco Cerutti's "Apuntes sobre periodismo antiguo en Nicaragua: Otras adiciones al fichero Melendez Chaverri" (No. 127, 1971, pp. 57–64), his 56-page supplement to Number 143 (1972) entitled *Contribución a un fichero de la prensa periódica nicaragüense*, and its second part (No. 153, 1976, pp. 61–62) are indications of a surge in the interest in the study of Nicaraguan newspapers and magazines that began in 1970 and continues.

The BNBD has published the following articles concerning Nicaraguan periodicals: Jimmy Aviles, "Publicaciones periódicas de Granada" (No. 8, 1975, pp. 14–18), Jaime Marenco, "Otros doce periódicos de Rivas" (No. 16, 1977, pp. 36–38), Gabriel Urcuyo Gallegos, "Los periódicos de Rivas" (No. 4, 1975, pp. 27–29), Jaime Marenco, "Revistas y periódicos nicaragüenses de 1947" (No. 5, 1975, pp. 34–37), and Franzella Wilson, "Periódicos conservados en el Instituto historico centroamericano" (No. 5, 1975, pp. 38–49).

Many valuable data can be found in Carlos Tünnermann Bernheim, *La contribución del periodismo a la liberación nacional,* subtitled Lección inaugural del IV congreso de la Unión de periodistas de Nicaragua, marzo 1 de 1981 (Managua, 1981, 262 pp.) concerning the history of printing and journalism in Nicaragua. Pages 197–202 provide a bibliography on the subject.

Panama

The study of Panamanian bibliography should begin with the following works by Juan Antonio Susto: *Introducción a la bibliografía panameña (1619–1945)* (Publicaciones de la Biblioteca nacional, No. 4, Panama, 1946, 35 pp.), an article with this title in *Lotería* (No. 62, July 1946, pp. 19–28), "Panorama de la bibliografía en Panama" (*Rev. interamericana de bibliografía*, Vol. 18, 1968, pp. 3–27), *Panorama de la bibliografía en Panama, 1619–1967* (Editorial universitaria, Panama, 1971, 102 pp.), and "Introducción de la imprenta en América" (*Lotería*, 2a. época, Vol. 31, 1958, pp. 48–55), which provides a brief description of printing in Panama and a partial list of periodicals published there at this time.

The library of the Universidad de Panamá has published *Bibliografía panameña existente en la Biblioteca de la Universidad* (1953, 109 leaves).

The Biblioteca nacional has published *Bibliografía panameña* (Ministerio de educación, Comité nacional Pro-Bibliotecas, Panama, 1954, 66 pp.).

The country's current national bibliography has appeared sporadically. Juan Antonio Susto, *Bibliografía de Panamá en 1938* (Panama, 1939, 15 pp.) also appeared as "National Bibliography of Panama . . . Books Published in Panama in 1938" (*Pan American Book Shelf*, Vol. 2, No. 9, September 1939, pp. 61–70). It lists 96 titles. He is also the compiler of "Bibliografía panameña de 1944" (*Lotería*, No. 41, October 1944, pp. 24–28; and No. 46, March 1945, pp. 24–27), "Publicaciones panameñas en el año de 1947" (*Épocas*, No. 47, January 15, 1948, p. 36), and "Publicaciones panameñas de 1950 (revistas, boletines y periódicos" (*Lotería*, No. 113, October 1950, p. 26).

Ana María Jaén contributed the following compilations to *Lotería:* "Obras panameñas que se encuentran en la Biblioteca nacional de Panamá, años 1939 a 1942" (No. 135, August 1952, pp. 30–31), "Registro bibliográfico de obras panameñas de la Biblioteca nacional de Panama, de 1943 a 1945" (No. 138, November 1952, pp. 18–21), and "Registro bibliográfico (Bibliografía panameña) de 1946–7" (No. 141, February 1953, p. 28).

The University of Panama's library issued *Bibliografía retrospectiva de libros y folletos, 1955–1957* (Oficina de información y publicaciones, Panama, 1958, 63 pp.).

Carmen D. Herrera compiled *Bibliografía panameña de libros y folletos, 1958–1959* (Panama, 1960, 44 pp.), which has been continued by Francisco A. Herrera, "Bibliografía de Panamá de 1960 a 1963" (*Lotería*, 2a. época, No. 118, September 1965, pp. 67–96).

Juan Antonio Susto lists publications for 1960–1961 in these *Lotería* articles: "Bibliografía panameña del 1960: Indice de autores" (2a. ser., No. 63, February 1961, pp. 60–65), which lists 55 titles; "Bibliografía panameña de 1961" (2a. ser., No. 74, January 1962, pp. 85–96), which lists 100 titles; and a contribution in Number 75 (February 1962, p. 82).

For a study of Panamanian newspapers and periodicals, one should consult, in addition to the studies by Susto listed in the first paragraph of this section, the following: Ernesto J. Castillero R., *Origen y desarrollo de la imprenta en Panamá: Primeros periódicos y libros publicados en el Istmo en el siglo diecinueve* (Imprenta nacional, Panama, 1958, 35 pp.), and two volumes by Rodrigo Miró, *La imprenta y el periodismo en Panamá durante el periodo de la Gran Colombia* (Editora Panamá America, Panama, 1963, 30 pp.) and *El periodismo en Panamá durante la década 1831–1841: Los Amigos de País y el aflorar de la conciencia nacional* (Impresora Panamá, Panama, 1966, 32 pp.; reproduced from *Lotería*, No. 122, January 1966, pp. 22–59). Juan Antonio Susto, "Medio siglo de revistas panameñas (1888–1945)" (*Lotería*, No. 60, May 1946, pp. 20–28) should also prove useful.

Paraguay

Little exists concerning Paraguayan publications, and it was only in 1970 that any attempt was made at the publication of a retrospective bibliography of Paraguayan imprints.

Carlos F. S. Fernández-Caballero has compiled or written the following: "Printing, Publishing, and the National Bibliography of Paraguay: A Historical Survey and State of the Art" (Master's thesis, Syracuse University School of Library Science, August 1968, 82 pp.), *Aranduká ha kuatianée paraguai rembia pocué* [The Paraguayan Bibliography: A Retrospective and Enumerative Bibliography of Printed Works of Paraguay Authors] (Paraguay Arandu Books, Asuncion and Washington, 1970, 143 pp.), *Paraguái tai hũme, tove Paraguái arandu taisarambi ko yvy apére* [The Paraguayan Bibliography], Volume 2 (1975, published as No. 3 of the SALALM bibliography series, 221 pp.), and "Paraguayan Bibliographies" (pp. vii–xv of his *Paraguái tai hũme . . .*). With S. Marski and R. Lisboa, he edited *Libros Paraguayos* (Vol. 1, Nos. 1–2, July 1972–March 1973), a recent attempt to compile a current Paraguayan bibliography.

Aranduká ha kuatianée . . . covers books and articles for the period 1724–1969 which either were published in Paraguay or are by Paraguayan authors, regardless of place of publication. The "second volume records additional authors and titles identified and includes works published from the eighteenth century to 1974, by: (1) Paraguayans and non-Paraguayans on the specific subject of Paraguay; and by (2) Paraguayans on any topic" (Prologue to Vol. 2). The set contains 3,786 entries. The title of these two volumes is in Guarani.

Paraguay in colonial times was part of the Viceroyalty of La Plata. Eighteenth-century imprints are described in José Toribio Medina, "Historia y bibliografía de la imprenta en el Paraguay," which is the first part of his *Historia y bibliografía de la imprenta en el antiguo Virreinato del Río de la Plata* (Taller de publicaciones del Museo, La Plata, 1892; reprinted N. Israel, Amsterdam, 1965, xiv, 36 pp.); and Guillermo Furlong Cardiff, "La imprenta en las producciones del Paraguay, 1700–1727," in *Historia y bibliografía de las primeras imprentas rioplatenses, 1700–1850* (Editorial Guaranía, Buenos Aires, 1953, Vol. 1, pp. 45–100). The Jesuit introduction of printing to this area is one of the more interesting chapters in the history of printing in South America.

R. Antonio Ramos, "Una selección de libros, folletos y artículos por autores nacionales publicados en 1950" (*Rev. interamericana de bibliografía*, Vol. 1, 1951, pp. 219–221) lists 24 items by Paraguayans published either in Paraguay or outside this country.

Paraguay's most recent attempt at a current national bibliography would seem to be the *Bibliografía nacional paraguaya* (Universidad Nacional de Asunción, Asunción, 1978), which covered 1971–1977.

Almost nothing would seem to exist on Paraguayan newspapers and periodicals. F. Martínez Barahona, "Reseña histórica del periodismo, 1841–1919" (*La Tribuna* [Asunción], December 31, 1919, and January 1, 1920) is now greatly dated.

German periodicals are listed in *Arndt–Olson* (Vol. 2, pp. 326–328).

Peru

The Catálogo de la Colección peruana de la Biblioteca nacional del Perú (G. K. Hall, Boston, 1979, 6 vols.) is most useful for the study of Peruvian imprints and works about Peru regardless of language. Volumes 1–5 list books, pamphlets, and some music scores; Volume 6 lists periodicals and maps. This set contains data on approximately 94,000 titles.

The first thorough study of colonial Peruvian imprints was the work of José Toribio Medina. He compiled *La imprenta en Lima, 1594–1824* (Impreso y grabado en casa del autor, Santiago de Chile, 1904–1907; N. Israel, Amsterdam, 1965, 4 vols.) and *La imprenta en Arequipa, el Cuzco, Trujillo, y otros pueblos del Perú durante la independencia (1820–1825)* (Imprenta Elzeviriana, Santiago de Chile, 1904; N. Israel, Amsterdam, 1964, 71 pp.). His "Adiciones a *La imprenta en Lima*" appears in *Escritos inéditos de . . .*, Introducción y notas de Alberto Tauro (Ediciones de la Biblioteca nacional, No. 10, Lima, 1954, pp. 25–52). *Fénix* contains not only Medina's "Adiciones inéditas a *La imprenta en Lima, 1594–1810*" (Vol. 8, 1952, pp. 434–461) but also Graciela Araújo Espinoza, "Adiciones a *La imprenta en Lima (1584–1824)*" (Vol. 8, 1952, pp. 466–704; reprinted P. L. Villanueva, Lima, 1954, 238 pp.).

Medina's pioneering imprint survey has now been supplanted by the Jesuit Father Rubén Vargas Ugarte, *Impresos peruanos* (Biblioteca peruana, Nos. 7–12, Lima, 1953–1957, 6 vols.). Volume 7 (1953) covers the period 1584–1650; Volume 8 (1954), 1651–1699; Volume 9 (1956), 1700–1762; Volume 10 (1956), 1763–1805; Volume 11 (1957), 1800–1817; and Volume 12 (1957), 1809–1825. Volume 6 of this set appeared in 1949 and is entitled *Impresos peruanos publicados en el extranjero*.

Vargas Ugarte describes Peruvian imprints through 1825. He notes several times that he completes and perfects Medina's work and that he has added more than 1,600 items to Medina's retrospective bibliography. His volumes contain data on 5,680 items.

He has supplemented the information found in this set in the following articles published in the *Boletín bibliográfico de la Biblioteca central de la Universidad nacional mayor de San Marcos* (BBSM): "Nuevas adiciones a la *Biblioteca peruana*" (Vol. 32, January–June 1962, pp. 105–110; Vol. 35, July–December 1963, pp. 341–349), "Adiciones a la *Biblioteca peruana:* Primera parte: Impresos peruanos publicados en el extranjero" (Vol. 28, 1958, pp. 3–16), "Adiciones . . . Segunda parte: Impresos peruanos publicados en Lima" (Vol. 28, 1958, pp. 16–19), and "Suplemento a la *Biblioteca peruana*" (Vol. 30, December 1960, pp. 3–49). He has also published "Suplemento a la *Biblioteca peruana*" (*Bol. Biblioteca nacional* [BBNL], Vol. 15, No. 21, 1962, pp. 3–32). In 1968 he published a *Suplemento* (Imprenta Gil, Lima, 90 pp.) which was divided into Peruvian imprints published abroad and those published in Peru.

Early 18th-century newssheets are described by M. Bresie, "News-sheets Printed in Lima between 1700 and 1711 by José de Contreras y Alvarado, Royal Printer: A Descriptive Essay and Annotated List" (*New York Public Library Bull.*, Vol. 78, 1974, pp. 7–68).

Luis Agustín Cordero, *Incunables peruanos y estudios bibliográficas* (Universidad nacional mayor de San Marcos, Lima, 1979, 136 pp.) contains a section entitled "Incunables peruanos," with the following parts: 1. Antecedentes conciliares (pp. 9–12), 2. El primer impreso en el Perú (pp. 13–14), 3. El primer libro peruano (pp. 15–25), 4. Incunables del siglo xvi (pp. 26–31), and 5. Relación de incunables del S. XVII (pp. 32–40).

Works on mathematics have been studied in Margarita Kamimoto, "Bibliografía de matemáticas en el Perú durante los siglos XVIII y XIX" (BBNL, Nos. 63–64, 1972, pp. 5–43).

The period from 1826 through the mid-1930s presents a rather large gap in a chronological approach to our knowledge of books and pamphlets published in Peru. The BBSM published between June 1936 and June 1944 a series of articles usually entitled "Bibliografía de libros y folletos peruanos publicados en ——." These are classified, usually annotated lists with author indexes.

Through the volumes for 1953–1954, the *Anuario bibliográfico peruano* (ABP) was divided into three sections: Libros y folletos peruanos o referentes al Perú, Publicaciones periódicas, and Bio-bibliografías de escritores peruanos desaparecidos en ——. Government documents began to be included with the volume for 1955–1957, and with the 1961–1963 volume, it began to list Peruvian theses. Music scores are included under music; maps, under geography.

The *Anuario* volumes for 1943 (1945), 1944 (1945), 1945 (1946), 1946 (1948), 1947 (1949), 1948 (1951), 1949–1950 (1954), 1951–1952 (1957), and 1953–1954 (1959) were prepared under the direction of Alberto Tauro and were issued as Ediciones de la Biblioteca nacional Numbers 1, 2, 4–7, and 9–11. That for 1955–1957 (1961) was compiled under the direction of Cristóbal de Losada y Puga. Lucila Valderrama G. directed the preparation of the volumes for 1958–1960 (1964), 1961–1963 (1966), 1964–1966 (1969), 1967–1969 (1975), and 1970–1972 (1979). The volumes for 1958–1966 do not indicate the director's name on the title pages. The volumes for 1955–1963 are part of the Ediciones de la Biblioteca nacional (Nos. 12–14). The 1964–1966 volume is an unnumbered part of this series. No series note appears on the 1967–1969 and 1970–1972 volumes. As of early 1982, the volume for 1973–1976 was still in press. The volume for 1955–1957 contains a "Suplemento 1951–1954" (pp. 221–287).

Were it not for the rather large time lag, the ABP would certainly be considered one of the outstanding national bibliographies of the Western Hemisphere. Entries are arranged according to the Dewey Decimal Classification system. Each volume is extremely well indexed. The bibliographies of authors who died during the time covered by the *Anuario* are extraordinarily thorough. Each contains a chronology of the author, a list of the author's works regardless of their form, and a list of material about them. Data on newspapers and periodicals are given in a special section.

The BBNL (Vols. 1–29, 1943–1964) published a series with the title "Registro de propiedad intelectual." In the period 1965–1969 (Nos. 33–34 through 45–48), it was called "Certificados de depósito de publicaciones y documentos" and covered the years 1965–1968. In Numbers 51–52 through 73–76 (1970–1976), this section was entitled "Registro nacional de derechos de autor: Certificados de depósitos," for 1969–1976.

The *Boletín de la Biblioteca nacional* has published "Bibliografía nacional en curso, 1977" (Nos. 73–76, 1978, pp. 63–87).

The Biblioteca nacional in 1978 began the publication of *Bibliografía nacional: Libros, artículos de revistas y periódicos*. It should appear 11 times per year, and its compilation is directed by Lucila Valderrama G. The first part of each issue is devoted to new books published in or about Peru. The second part is a classified list of articles published in newspapers and periodicals. Like the *Anuario bibliográfico peruano*, material is arranged by subject headings based on the Dewey Decimal Classification system (i.e., general works, philosophy, religion, etc.). Each issue would seem to index between four and five dozen periodical sources. Each issue has an author and a subject index. Peru's national library is one of the few national libraries in the world which not only issues a current guide to its publications in book form, but also publishes a current index to its most important periodical literature. Its mimeographed form and the small number of copies of each issue produced are drawbacks that may be overcome in the future.

Two studies exist on almanacs. They are: Federico Schwab, "Los almanaques peruanos y guías de forasteros ¿1690-1874" (BBSM, Vol. 18, 1948, pp. 78–125), and the BBNL's "Relación de los 'Conocimientos de los tiempos', 'Guías' y 'Almanaques peruanos' existentes en la Biblioteca Nacional" (No. 27, 1945, pp. 322–328).

Important data on broadsides and pre-Emancipation newspapers are found in Isabel Montoya, "Imprentas volantes en la emancipación" (BBNL, No. 61–62, 1972, pp. 3–12), and Elsa Salas Olivari, "Periódicos de la pre-emancipación (1795–1819)" (BBNL, No. 69–72, 1976, pp. 5–25).

The BBSM has published three studies by Jorge Zevallos Quiñones which deal with printing outside of Lima. They are: "La imprenta en el Norte del Perú: Trujillo, Piura, Huaras, Cajamarca, Chachapopyas (1823–1910)" (Vol. 19, December 1949, pp. 204–283), "La imprenta en Lambayaque" (Vol. 17, June 1947, pp. 1–77), and a supplement to this article in Volume 18 (June 1948, pp. 126–150). For each of these there exists a reprint produced by the Compañía de impresiones y publicidad (Lima).

Tacna imprints (books, periodicals, and newspapers) published between 1834 and 1960 are listed and described in Nancy Gastañeta de Sovero, "La imprenta en Tacna" (BBNL, No. 16, 1962, pp. 32–55).

The following would seem to be the most important histories of Peruvian journalism: Carlos Miró Quesada, *Historia del periodismo peruano* (Librería internacional, Lima, 1957, 320 pp.), Juan Gargurevich, *Introducción a la historia de los medios de comunicacion en el Perú* (Editorial horizonte, Lima, 1977, 217 pp.), and Lope Yupanqui Callejari, *El periodismo en el virreynato peruano* (Impresiones mimeográficas, Lima, 1973, ix, 101 pp.).

The volume by Gargurevich is of interest for its treatment of radio and television as well as of the Peruvian press. Pages 19–96 deal with the history of Peruvian newspapers. The *Historia* by Miró Quesada is the fullest history available. Unfortunately, it is on the popular side, with no footnotes, no bibliography, and no lists that provide pertinent data in tabular form. Lope Yupanqui deals with journalism in colonial Peru.

The first major attempt to list Peruvian newspapers and periodicals would appear to be that of Mariano Felipe Paz Soldán, *Biblioteca peruana* (Lima, 1879, pp. 1–103), which has been supplemented by Evaristo San Cristobal, "Apuntes bibliográficos sobre el periodismo en el Perú" (BBSM, Vol. 3, 1927, pp. 7–12). Paz

Soldán provides data on 842 periodicals published between 1715 and 1879; the San Cristobal supplement lists 43 periodicals published between 1859 and 1877. Paz Soldán's posthumously published "Adiciones y rectificationes . . ." appears in *Mar del sur* (No. 23, 1952, pp. 24–33). Pablo A. Patrón, "Datos bibliográficos" (*El Ateneo*, Vol. 1, 1899, pp. 616–620) is chiefly corrections and additions to Paz Soldán's data on 23 periodicals.

Nineteenth-century periodicals are dealt with in Manuel de Odriozola, "Catálogo de los periódicos nacionales existentes en la Biblioteca nacional" (BBSM, Vol. 1, 1924, pp. 170–179, 234–265), Alejandro Tumba Ortega, "Periódicos nacionales del siglo xix, que existen en la Biblioteca central de la Universidad nacional mayor de San Marcos" (BBSM, Vol. 17, December 1944, pp. 254–301; Vol. 18, 1945, pp. 141–237), and Federico Schwab, "Algunos periódicos desconocidos del Perú, Ecuador y Bolivia" (*Fénix*, Vol. 4, 1946, pp. 894–909).

José Martínez G., "Indice de las revistas peruanos publicadas en 1938" (BBSM, Vol. 12, July 1939, pp. 172–181) and his "Indice . . . en 1939" (BBSM, Vol. 13, June 1940, pp. 134–142) were continued by Alejandro Tumba Ortega, "Indice de las revistas peruanas ingresadas en la biblioteca durante el año 1941 y el primer semestre de 1942" (BBSM, Vol. 12, July 1942, pp. 92–110) and "Revistas peruanas publicadas en el segundo semestre de 1942 y el año 1943" (BBSM, Vol. 13, December 1943, pp. 278–308).

Abigail García de Velezmore, "La producción periodística peruana 1943–1945, periódicos de provincia" (*Fénix*, Vol. 3, 1945, pp. 417–458) deals with periodicals published outside of Lima.

The BBNL has published the following periodical lists: "Publicaciones periódicas del Perú: Nuevas publicaciones aparecidas en Lima y provincias el año de 1944" (No. 5, 1944, pp. 45–46; No. 6, 1945, pp. 199–203), "Nuevas publicaciones aparecidas en el Perú en 1945" (No. 7, 1945, pp. 313–315), "Publicaciones periódicas peruanas a arecidas en el año 1946" (No. 9, 1946, pp. 115–118), "Publicaciones periódicas iniciados en 1947" (No. 10, 1947, pp. 217–220), and "Periódicos peruanos existentes en la Biblioteca Nacional . . . que han dejado de aparecer" (No. 6, 1945, pp. 111–173; No. 7, 1945, pp. 335–380; and No. 9, 1946, pp. 80–114).

The *Anuario bibliográfico peruano* has had a section in each volume listing newspapers and periodicals that were published during the period covered, so that the period 1943–1972 has been covered as of 1979. It does not seem to list books or newspapers in languages which do not use the Latin alphabet. Lima's Japanese newspaper does not seem to be listed, though newspapers and magazines published in English and other Western European languages are listed.

Pedro Mañaricua, "Un siglo de historia del periodismo en Ayacucho" (BBSM, Vol. 14, 1944, pp. 30–69; reprint Compañía de impresiones y publicidad, 1944, 44 pp.) is of value for the newspapers of Ayacucho. César O. Prado, *El periodismo en Ayacucho* ([Imprenta "La Región"], Ayacucho, 1966, 22 pp.) would seem to be the latest account of journalism in Ayacucho.

Lucio Medina Díaz, *Historia del periodismo canchino* (Ed. lit. "La Confianza," Lima, 1965, 44 pp.) is the most recent account of journalism in Cancho.

The early newspapers of Cuzco have been studied in Félix Denigri Luna, "Apuntes para una bibliografía de periódicos cuzqueños (1827–1837)" (*Rev. histórica*, Vol. 26, 1962–1963, pp. 186–235). This article is based on the compiler's personal collection.

César Augusto Arauco Aliaga, *El periodismo en Huancayo* (Ediciones Raiz, Huancayo, [1958], 30 pp.) discusses journalism in Huancayo through 1958.

Antonio Cisneros and Miguel Suarez Osorio, *Historia del periodismo en Junín* (Editorial "Sebastián Lorenta, Huancayo, n.d., [1967?], 127 pp.) provides short essays on the important newspapers and periodicals of this department; it contains the following lists: "Relación de periódicos y otros impresos en Huancayo: Siglo xix y siglo xx" (pp. 44–50), "Relación de periódicos y otros impresos de la provincia de Yauli" (pp. 68–71), "Relación . . . en la provincia de Jauja" (pp. 79–80), "Relación . . . de la provincia de Concepción" (p. 83), "Relación . . . en la provincia de Tarma" (pp. 92 –93), and "Relación . . . del departamento de Pasco" (pp. 102–104). Unfortunately, these are lists with few bibliographic data.

Luis Curie Gallegos, *Periodismo en Parinacochas (1900–1946)* (Compañiá de impresiones y publicidad, Lima, 1946, 68 pp.) has the following parts: Periódicos editados en Parinacochas, Periódicos editados en Lima (por parinacochanos), and Periodistas y escritores parinacochanos fuera de la provincia.

Luis Ginocchio F., *Breve historia del periodismo piurano* ([Piura?], 1957, [8] pp.) deals with the periodicals of Piura from 1842 to 1904.

The country's German press is discussed in *Arndt–Olson* (Vol. 2, pp. 239–335).

Puerto Rico

Puerto Rico was a Spanish colony up to the end of the Spanish–American War, when it became one of the United States. It achieved commonwealth status in 1952. The vast majority of the population speaks Spanish and the majority of its publications are in Spanish. Since no national United States bibliography lists Puerto Rican publications, it is pertinent to have a section that deals with Puerto Rican imprints both before and after 1898.

The following are useful retrospective bibliographies: Manuel María Sama, *Bibliografía puertorriqueña* (Tipografía comercial-Marina, Mayagüez, 1887, 159 pp.), Antonio S. Pedreira, *Bibliografía puertorriqueña (1493–1930)* (Imprenta de Hernando, Madrid, 1932, 707 pp.), and José Géigel y Zenón and Abelardo Morales Ferrer, *Bibliografía puertorriqueña* (Editorial Araluce, Barcelona, 1934, 461 pp.). Sama lists 250 books published in Puerto Rico between 1831 and 1886. The items are annotated and arranged in chronological order. The volume by Géigel y Zenón and Morales Ferrer lists three categories of publications: books written and printed in Puerto Rico, books by Puerto Ricans, and books by foreigners about Puerto Rico.

The *Anuario bibliográfico puertorriqueño*, subtitled Indice alfabetico de libros, folletos, revistas y periódicos publicados en Puerto Rico durante —— (Departamento de instrucción pública, San Juan), is usually several years dated on publication. The first volume, for 1948, was published in 1950; that for 1969–1970 was published in 1978.

Revista del Instituto de cultura puertorriqueña (1958–), *Asomante* (1945–1976), and *La Torre* (1953–1973) often publish (or published) lists of current Puerto Rican books. The lists in the *Revista* are often briefly annotated.

It would seem that almost nothing has appeared concerning newspapers and periodicals. Of value to students of literature would be Juan Martínez Capo, "Las pequeñas revistas literarias (Panorama: 1930–1954)" (*Asomante*, Vol. 11, No. 1, January–March 1955, pp. 102–123).

The date of the introduction of printing into Puerto Rico has been the subject of great discussion. Lidio Cruz Monclova, "La introducción de la imprenta en Puerto Rico y el primer periódico puertorriqueño" (*Rev. Instituto de cultura puertorriqueña*, No. 44, 1969, pp. 4–6) reviews the evidence of the historians who have dealt with this problem and finds that 1806 is the date of the first printing press as well as of the *Gazeta de Puerto Rico*, whose first issue appeared in this year.

Saint Bartholomew

Roderick Cave, "Printing in the Swedish West Indies" (*Libri*, Vol. 28, 1978, pp. 205–214) would seem to be the only study of printing on Saint Bartholomew, which was a Swedish colony from 1784 to 1878. Cave provides a brief history of the *Report of St. Bartholomew*, a newspaper published from April 2, 1804, to October 28, 1819, the date of the last surviving issue.

Saint Christopher

A list of Saint Christopher newspapers appears in E. C. Baker, *A Guide to Records in the Leeward Islands* (Basil Blackwell, Oxford, 1965, pp. 72–75).

Saint Lucia

The Central Library of this island has issued in mimeographed form *A Selective List of Books, Pamphlets and Articles on St. Lucia and by St. Lucians Covering the Period 1844 to Date* [May 1, 1971] (Castries, 1971, 12 pp.). The same library was responsible for *Books, Libraries and St. Lucia: Three Essays in Honour of International Book Year 1972*, by J. H. Pilgrim, Robert Devaux, and Colin Brock (Government Printing Office, Castries, 1972, 15 pp.). It includes Robert J. Devaux, "A Chronological Resumé of St. Lucian Newspapers" (pp. 7–11), which covers the period 1780–1952.

Saint Vincent

A list of Saint Vincent newspapers appears in E. C. Baker, *A Guide to Records in the Windward Islands* (Basil Blackwell, Oxford, 1968, p. 48).

Salvador

In 1953 Salvador's Biblioteca nacional issued *Bibliografía salvadoreña: Lista preliminar por autores* (430 leaves).

The *Revista* of the Biblioteca nacional published "Publicaciones impresas en El Salvador durante los años 1945–" (4th ser., Vol. 1, January–April 1947, pp. 183–195; Vol. 2, May–August 1948, pp. 173–207; and 5th ser., Vol. 4, May–August 1949, pp. 153–184). This set of bibliographies covers the period 1945–1948.

The Biblioteca nacional also published *Bibliografía salvadoreña: Publicaciones impresas en El Salvador durante los años de 1945 y 1946* (San Salvador, 1948, 16 pp.).

Anaquel, a journal published by the Biblioteca nacional, published "Obras impresas en El Salvador durante el año de 1949" (5th ser., Vol. 1, January–April 1951, pp. 149–168), "Anuario bibliográfico salvadoreño, año 1950" (5th ser., Vol. 2, May 1951, pp. 77–100), and "Anuario . . . año 1951" (5th ser., Vol. 3, May 1952–April 1953, pp. 89–107).

The *Anuario bibliográfico salvadoreño* for 1952 appeared as a 39-page supplement to *Anaquel* (5th ser., No. 4, 1954; it also appeared in the form of a separate, San Salvador, Edit. Casa de la cultura, 1954).

Surinam

The *Bibliografie van Suriname* (Nederlandse Stichting voor Culturele Samenwerking met Suriname en de Nederlandse Antillen, Amsterdam, n.d. [early 1970s], 255 pp.) is a classified bibliography that lists material published in Surinam as well as material published elsewhere about it. Pages 15–19, "Tijdschriften—Dagbladen," supply brief data on newspapers and periodicals of the area. Pages 138–144, "Letterkunde," deal with the area's belles-lettres regardless of place of publication. Pages 145–147, "Jeugdlectuur," lists children's literature written in the area.

Trinidad and Tobago

The Central Library has compiled *A West Indian Reference Collection: A Select List of Books, Pamphlets, etc., of Trinidadian Authorship, on Trinidad and Tobago, and Other Material Published in Trinidad and Tobago* (Government Printer, Port-of-Spain, 1966, 21 pp.).

Little seems to exist on the history of printing in this area. Douglas C. McMurtrie, "Notes on the Beginning of Printing on the Island of Trinidad" (*J. National Printing Education*, May 1943) seems to be one of the very few studies on this subject. There exists a four-page reprint of this work.

The Central Library of Trinidad and Tobago issued the *Trinidad and Tobago and West Indian Bibliography* from September 1965 to February 1966.

The Library of the University of the West Indies issued *Recent Acquisitions of Trinidad and Tobago Imprints* (Lists 1–5, 1973–1975).

The *Trinidad and Tobago National Bibliography*, subtitled "a subject list of material published and printed in Trinidad and Tobago" (Vol. 1–, 1975–, Central Library of Trinidad and Tobago, Port-of-Spain; University of the West Indies Library, Saint Augustine), appears quarterly with annual cumulations.

Uruguay

Luis Alberto Musso is the leading Uruguayan expert on bibliographic matters for this country. He is the compiler of *Bibliografía de bibliografías uruguayas con aportes a la historia del periodismo* (Imprenta Castro, Montevideo, 1964, vii, 102 pp.), *Bibliografía bibliotecológica y bibliográfica del Uruguay, 1964–1969* (Centro de estudios del pasado uruguayo, Montevideo, 1970, 49 pp.), *Bibliografía bibliotecológica del Uruguay* (Escuela interamericana de bibliotecología, Bibliografías, No. 20, Editorial universidad de Antiquoia, Medellín, 1964, 199, 11 leaves), *Bibliografía y documentación en el Uruguay* (Montevideo, 1972, 6 pp.), and *Bibliografía uruguaya sobre Brasil*, second edition (Publicaciones del Instituto de cultura uruguayo–brasileño, No. 20, Instituto de cultura uruguayo–brasileño, Montevideo, 1973, 166 pp.).

Guillermo Furlong Cardiff, "La imprenta en Montevideo, 1807–1810," in *Historia y bibliografía de las primeras imprentas rioplatenses, 1700–1850* (Librería de la Plata, Buenos Aires, 1959, Vol. 3, pp. 391–414) is the fullest listing of imprints for this period. Before the appearance of the Furlong bibliography, José Toribio Medina, "En Montevideo (1807–1810)," Part 4 of his *Historia y bibliografía de la imprenta en el antiguo virreinato del Río de la Plata* (Tall. de publicaciones del Museo, La Plata, 1892; N. Israel, Amsterdam, 1965, 16 pp.), had been the most important study.

Dardo Estrada, *Historia y bibliografía de la imprenta en Montevideo, 1810–1865* (Librería Cervantes, Montevideo, 1912, 318 pp.) has been supplemented by Horacio Arredondo, "Bibliografía uruguaya" (*Rev. Instituto histórico y geográfico del Uruguay*, Vol. 6, 1929, pp. 33–610). Arredondo includes material published between 1559 and 1865 in Uruguay and outside of the country concerning it.

José Torre Revello, *Contribución a la historia y bibliografía de la imprenta en Montevideo* (Publicaciones del Instituto de investigaciones históricas, No. 31, Buenos Aires, 1926, 15 pp.) is a brief discussion of its topic.

Guillermo Furlong Cardiff, "La 'imprenta de la Caridad' (1822–1855): Historia," and Enrique Arana (h), "Bibliografía" (*Rev. Instituto histórico y geográfico del Uruguay,* Vol. 9, 1932, pp. 5–61, 161–164) are the major studies of the imprints of this press. Arana lists and describes 162 imprints.

For a study of 19th-century printing, see Benjamin Fernández y Medina, *La imprenta y la prensa en el Uruguay desde 1807 a 1900* (Imprenta de Dormaleche y Reyes, Montevideo, 1900, 87 pp.), a survey that appeared originally in Orestes Araujo, *Diccionario geográfico de Uruguay* (Dornaleche y Reyes, Montevideo,

1900, pp. 924–949). The book is an enlarged version of the article in the *Diccionario*.

Pedro Mascaro compiled the *Anales de la bibliografía uruguaya* (tomo 1, [año 1895], 127 pp.), which was published under the auspices of the Biblioteca nacional.

The Inter-American Book Exchange published *A General Bibliography of Uruguayan Publications for 1938* (Bibliographical Series, No. 2, Washington, D.C., 1939, 15 pp.).

The *Revista nacional* has published the following series based on data provided by the Biblioteca nacional: "La produccion bibliográfica nacional correspondiente al año 1937" (Vol. 1, No. 2, February 1938, pp. 342–352), "La . . . al primer semestre de 1938" (Vol. 1, No. 8, August 1938, pp. 311–330), "La . . . del año 1938" (Vol. 2, No. 16, April 1939, pp. 147–160), "La . . . durante el año 1938" (Vol. 2, No. 17, May 1939, pp. 315–320), "La . . . correspondiente al primer semestre de 1939" (No. 20, August 1939), "La . . . al tercer trimestre de 1939" (Vol. 2, No. 22, October 1939, pp. 155–166, and No. 23, November 1939, pp. 318–320), "La . . . en el cuarto semestre de 1939" (Vol. 3, No. 26, February 1940, pp. 318–320, and No. 27, March 1940, pp. 492–493), and "La . . . durante el año 1940" (Vol. 4, No. 39, March 1941, pp. 374–377, No. 40, April 1941, p. 160, and No. 42, June 1941, pp. 461–477). These are classified lists with pertinent bibliographic data.

The Biblioteca nacional's *Boletín*, Number 1 (1944), lists 1943 imprints.

It began to issue in 1947 an *Anuario bibliográfico uruguayo*, covering 1946–1949 (1947–1951). This set lists data on books and periodicals.

The first volume of the *Bibliografía uruguaya* was for 1962 (1969). The *Bibliografía uruguaya años 1962 a 1968*, inclusive, was compiled by the Biblioteca del poder legislativo (1971) and includes Uruguayan government documents as well as separately published books and pamphlets. The frequency is irregular.

The following would seem to be the most important works concerning Uruguayan journalism: Julio R. Corbacho, *"El Fanal," 1855–1955: Contribución a la historia del periodismo uruguayo* ([Colegio León XIII], Buenos Aires, 1954, 118 pp.); Mario Falcao Espalter, "Bibliografía del periodismo uruguayo" (*Humanidades* (La Plata), Vol. 9, 1924, pp. 271–316; Vol. 10, 1925, pp. 127–164; Vol. 11, 1925, pp. 397–431; and Vol. 12, 1926, pp. 286–313); Washington Lockhart, *Historia del periodismo en Soriano* (Revista histórica de Soriano, Mercedes, 1963, 82 pp.); Oficina de la Prensa, Montevideo, *La prensa del Uruguay* (Bertoni, Montevideo, 1912, 35 pp.); Manuel Olarreaga Leguisamo, *El periodismo en el departamento de Salto* (Salto, 1962, 36 pp.); and Arbelio Ramírez, *Aportes para la historia del periodismo en el departamento de Soriano, 1857–1940* ([LIGU], Montevideo, 1951, 54 pp.).

La Estrella del Sur, Uruguay's first newspaper, was issued by the English occupation forces. It has been studied by Ariosto D. González, who provides a prologue to *The Southern Star, La Estrella del Sur, Montevideo, 1807* (Reproducción facsimilar, Casa A. Barreiro y Ramos, Montevideo, 1942); by Daniel Castellanos, "*La Estrella del Sur* en campo de hipotesis" (*Rev. Instituto histórico y geográfico del Uruguay*, Vol. 18, 1949, pp. 3–28); and by Luis Alberto Musso, who not only has discussed its history but has indexed it in *La Estrella del Sur, The Southern Star: Indices analíticos para su estudio* (Gadi, Florida, 1968, 24 pp.).

The first important attempt to list Uruguayan newspapers and magazines is Antonio Zinny, *Historia de la prensa periódica de la República oriental del Uruguay 1807–1852* (C. Casavalle, Buenos Aires, 1883, 504 pp.). A listing of Uruguayan periodicals from 1807 through 1905 is now provided by Antonio Praderio, *Índice cronológico de la prensa periódica del Uruguay, 1807–1852* (Manuales auxiliares para la investigación histórica, No. 3, Uruguay, Universidad, Instituto de investigaciones históricas, Montevideo, 1962, 126 pp.), and this series of articles by Arturo Scarone published in the *Revista nacional:* "La prensa periódica del Uruguay de los años 1852 a 1865" (Vol. 3, No. 26, February 1940, pp. 213–237), "La prensa . . . 1881 a 1885" (Vol. 3, No. 33, September 1940, pp. 415–444), "La prensa . . . 1886–1890" (Vol. 4, No. 38, February 1941, pp. 239–272), "La prensa . . . 1891–1895" (Vol. 4, No. 42, June 1951, pp. 402–434), "La prensa . . . 1895–1900" (Vol. 5, No. 49, January 1942, pp. 71–99), and "La prensa . . . 1901–1905" (Vol. 5, No. 53, May 1942, pp. 234–254; Vol. 5, No. 60, December 1942, pp. 386–403; Vol. 6, No. 67, July 1943, pp. 104–115; and Vol. 7, No. 74, February 1944, pp. 279–294).

The Biblioteca nacional has issued the following lists (many mimeographed) of Uruguayan periodicals: *Publicaciones periódicas iniciadas, año 1948–1949* (1950, 2 vols., 14, 8 pp.), *Publicaciones periódicas cesadas, año 1948* ([1950], 11 pp.), *Lista de las principales publicaciones periódicas del interior de la República Oriental del Uruguay* ([1949], 3 pp.), *Lista de los principales publicaciones periódicas editadas en Montevideo* ([1949], 4 pp.), *Catálogo de publicaciones periódicas de Montevideo, 1950* (1951, 54 pp.), *Catálogo de publicaciones periódicas; departamentos de interior, 1950* ([n.d.], compiled by José M. Díaz, 19 pp.), *Lista de los principales periódicos del interior* ([1962], 4 pp.), and *Lista de las principales publicaciones periódicas editadas en Montevideo* ([1955], 6 pp.).

The Centro de documentación científica, técnica y económica of the Biblioteca nacional has published the following: *Catálogo de las revistas científicas, técnicas y económicas en curso de publicación en el Uruguay* (1961, 21 pp.), which lists 164 titles; *Catálogo de las revistas científicas, técnicas y económicas publicadas en Uruguay desde 1850* (1954, 29 pp.), compiled by Zulma Pucarull de Pérez Gomar, Marta Nogueira Abella, María Teresa Carballal, and Elena Araujo, which lists 358 titles; *Guía de revistas bibliográficas científicas, técnicas y económicas* (1963, 19 pp.); and *Catálogo de las revistas científicas, técnicas y económicas en curso de publicación en el Uruguay en 1961, con suplemento hasta 1963* (1963, compiled by María Luisa di Vita, 30 pp.).

The Consejo nacional de enseñanza primaria y normal issued an undated *Indice de los periódicos y revistas escolares del Uruguay, años 1949–1950* (Montevideo, 2 pp.).

Julio Bayce, "Revistas en el Uruguay" (*Escritura*, Vol. 5, September 1948, pp. 117–121) deals chiefly with literary magazines published during the years 1947–1948.

A bibliography of the German press of Uruguay can be found in *Arndt–Olson* (Vol. 2, pp. 605–610).

Little has appeared of a bibliographic nature concerning publications in Galician. *Catálogo de la exposición del libro y de la prensa gallegos en el Uruguay*, with the subtitle Organizada por el patronato da cultura gallega y celebrada en la Biblioteca nacional del 23 de octubre al 7 de noviembre de 1974, XIX jornadas de cultura gallega (30 pp.), has a preface that notes that only those books were exhibited which were published in Uruguay or written by Uruguayan authors or Galician immigrants living in Uruguay. This volume attempts to show Galician bibliographic production either published or written in Uruguay. About half of the 99 items listed are in Spanish concerning Galician topics or are in Galician. The classified bibliography (pp. 7–19) is followed by brief biographical sketches of some of the authors exhibited (pp. 20–26). Page 29 provides brief data on five publishers of material by Galicians, about Galicia, or in Galician.

Venezuela

Agustín Millares Carlo, *Ensayo de una bibliografía de la imprenta y el periodismo en Venezuela* (Bibliografías básicas, No. 8, Organization of American States, Washington, D.C., 1971, 91 pp.) is the fullest bibliography yet compiled on the history of printing and journalism of any country in this area. It is chronologically arranged by publication date. Contents are provided for collections of articles. Reprint data are given. Horacio Jorge Becco, *Bibliografía de bibliografías venezolanas: Literatura (1968–1978)* (La Casa de Bello, Caracas, 1979, 62 pp.) provides data on national bibliographies for the decade covered. Pedro Grases, "General Aspects of Bibliographic Activities in Venezuela" (6th SALALM, 1961, Working Paper No. 10, 12 pp.) is an excellent discussion of Venezuelan bibliography as of the beginning of the 1960s. R. J. Lovera de Sola, "Contribución a la bibliografía de bibliografías venezolanas (1971)" (*Bol. histórico*, Vol. 10, No. 33, 1973, pp. 513–552) is also useful. Though now greatly dated, Manuel Segundo Sánchez's "Bibliografía de índices bibliográficos relativos a Venezuela," in *Handbook of Latin American Studies, 1939* (Harvard University Press, Cambridge, Mass., 1940, pp. 428–442; reprinted in his *Obras*, Banco central de Venezuela, Caracas, 1964, Vol. 2, pp. 160–192) is still a most valuable and helpful study with much emphasis on the history of printing and journalism in Venezuela. His scholarly annotations are especially to be commended.

The *Ensayo de un repertorio bibliográfico venezolano (años 1808–1950)*, compiled by Angel Raúl Villasana (Colección cuatricentenario de Caracas, Banco central de Venezuela, Caracas, 1969–1979, 6 vols.) is an attempt to provide a retrospective checklist of Venezuelean books, pamphlets, and broadsides. Unfortunately, it is limited to general works and those in the fields of literature and history. It is a pity that an additional volume of indexes could not have been provided.

Two histories of printing in Venezuela are highly recommended. Pedro Grases, *Historia de la imprenta en Venezuela hasta el fin de la primera república (1812)* (Ediciones de la Presidencia de la República, Caracas, 1967, 247 pp.) has 87 facsimiles in the first part; it also has 112 unpaginated plates, which reproduce title pages, issues of newspapers, etc. Julio Febres Cordero, *Historia de la imprenta y del periodismo en Venezuela 1800–1830* (Colección cuatricentenario de Venezuela, No. 11, Banco central de Venezuela, Caracas, 1974, 262 pp. plus unpaginated plates) continues the history of its subject through 1830, with chapters on printing and journalism in areas outside of Caracas.

José Toribio Medina, *La imprenta en Caracas (1808–1821)* (Imprenta Elzeviriana, Santiago de Chile, 1904; N. Israel, Amsterdam, 1964, ix, 29 pp.) is of value for its detailed descriptions of 26 publications. His *Contribución a la historia de la imprenta en Venezuela*, with an introduction and notes by Pedro Grases (Ediciones del Ministerio de educación, Dirección de cultura y bellas artes, Imprenta nacional, Caracas, 1952, 73 pp.), was issued to commemorate the centennial of Medina's birth. This volume combines his *La imprenta en Caracas* with the Venezuelean parts of *Notas bibliográficas referentes a las primeras producciones de la imprenta en algunas ciudades de la América española . . . 1764–1822)* (Imprenta Elzeviriana, Santiago de Chile, 1904, 116 pp.). Angostura, Maracaibo, Nueva Valencia, Guiaria, and Puerto Cabello are the cities treated. The *Contribución* also appears in *Orígenes de la imprenta en Venezuela y primicias editoriales de Caracas*, compiled, with a prologue and notes, by Pedro Grases (Tip. Vargas, Caracas, 1958, pp. 245–267).

The latest discussion of the publications of Miranda's printing press on the "Leander" in 1806 is that found in Febres Cordero, *Historia de la imprenta . . .* (1974, pp. 30–33), where seven imprints are discussed. It would seem doubtful that several were printed.

For the period through 1812, the standard imprint bibliography is that found in Grases, *Historia de la imprenta en Venezuela . . .* (1967, pp. 167–223), where 112 publications are described in great detail, each accompanied with a plate.

One can only touch upon the numerous studies by Pedro Grases on the early history of Venezuelan printing. However, because they carry the study of Venezuelan imprints a little further into the 19th century, mention is made of his *Facsímiles de Valentín Espinal, 1803–1866* (Fundación Eugenio Mendoza, Caracas, 1966, vii, 100 plates with indexes), and *Domingo Navas Spínola* (Colegio univérsitario Francisco de Miranda, Caracas, 1978, 213 pp.). Pages 16–23 of this volume on Navas describe six of his publications issued between 1823 and 1826. It may be noted that a variety of early books and newspapers have appeared in facsimile editions.

The *Memoria* for 1911 of the Ministerio de fomento (Empresa Guttenberg, Caracas, 1911) includes a section on national bibliography.

The next attempt to provide what could be called a current national bibliography was made in 1917. In this year Manuel Segundo Sánchez (1868–1945), one of the hemisphere's greatest bibliographers, published his *Anuario bibliográfico de Venezuela, 1916* (Litografía del comercio, Caracas, 71 pp.). He divided it into official publications, trade publications, those that were privately printed (publicaciones particulares), and periodicals. It lists 287 books and pamphlets as well as providing a list of periodicals currently received as of 1916 in the Biblioteca nacional.

Segundo Sánchez's "Anuario bibliográfico de Venezuela, 1917" did not appear until 1936, when it was published in the *Boletín de la Biblioteca nacional* (No. 41, pp. 83–95, and No. 42, pp. 181–202). It lists 274 books and pamphlets, along with a list of the "órganos de la prensa nacional." He also compiled "Bibliografía Venezolana: Nomina de los principales libros y folletos venezolanos publicados en los primeros meses de 1918" (*Rev. bibliografía chilena y extranjera*, Vol. 6, 1918, pp. 339–344).

For the next quarter of a century there seemed to be little effort made to produce and publish a current bibliography of the country's imprints. The *Boletín de la Biblioteca nacional* included a section on recent acquisitions in its volumes for 1923–1933, 1936, and 1959–1960.

In 1942 there was created the Oficina de bibliografía, one of whose duties was the publication of the country's national bibliography. Pedro Grases was the head of this office from 1942 to 1945 and from 1947 to 1948. The Tipografía americana published the *Anuario bibliográfico venezolano 1942* (1945), that of 1943 (1945), those of 1944 and 1945 (both in 1947), and that of 1946 (1949). The volume that covered 1947–1948 (1950) was published by Avila gráfica, while that covering 1949–1954 (1960, 2 vols.) was published by Editorial Arte.

The majority of these volumes had the following six sections: bibliographic sources; books, pamphlets, broadsides, etc.; Venezuelan authors who had died during the period covered by the *Anuario;* and dictionary indexes of authors, subjects, and titles.

The mimeographed *Indice bibliográfico de la Biblioteca nacional* (Nos. 1–23, 1956–1965) was a classified acquisitions list.

From 1958 to 1963 the Biblioteca nacional contributed "Obras ingresadas en la Biblioteca nacional" (slight variations occurred in the title) to the *Revista nacional de cultura* (Nos. 126–160, 1958–1963).

The *Boletín bibliográfico venezolano* (Nos. 1–20, 1970–1974) was issued irregularly and included Venezuelan works added to the Biblioteca nacional. The material listed in the *Boletín* was arranged according to the Dewey Decimal Classification system.

The Centro bibliográfico venezolano has issued an *Anuario bibliográfico venezolano* for 1967–1968 (Imprenta del Congreso, Caracas, 1977). A three-volume set will cover the years 1969–1974 (*A–G* was published in 1979), and the volume for 1975 has been issued (Imprenta del Congreso, Caracas, 1977).

Recent years have seen a greater interest in the study, history, and indexing of Venezuelan newspapers and periodicals. No bibliographic source exists that deals with the newspapers and periodicals of the whole country. One must go to a variety of state and city histories of journalism to arrive at an overall view of production in this field.

Pedro Grases compiled, with a prologue and notes, *Materiales para la historia del periodismo en Venezuela durante el siglo xix* (Ediciones de la Escuela de periodismo, Caracas, 1950, xxiii, 595 pp.). This volume has an index of persons, geographical places, titles, and presses. It is referred to here as *Materiales*.

Materiales contains the following articles of a general nature on the history of the press of Venezuela: Manuel Segundo Sánchez, "La prensa periódica en Venezuela" (pp. 5–6), Eloy G. González, "Informe sobre el periodismo en Venezuela" (pp. 8–46; reprinted from *Primer libro venezolano de literatura, ciencias y bellas artes*, 1895, pp. cxiii–cxxiii), Manuel Landaeta Rosales and Víctor M. Ovalles, "Datos generales sobre la imprenta, el periodismo y la litografía en Venezuela" (pp. 47–50; reprinted from *El gran boletiń*, Vol. 2, No. 68, October 25, 1908), Tulio Febres Cordero, "Imprentas libertadoras de Venezuela 1806 a 1821" (pp.

51–58; reprinted from *Arch. historia y variedades*, Vol. 2, pp. 69–71), Tulio Febres Cordero, "Una prensa viajera atraviesa la república fundando el arte tipográfico" (pp. 55–58; reprinted from *Arch. historia y variedades*, Vol. 2, pp. 71–73), Manuel Segundo Sánchez, "La prensa periódica de la revolución emancipadora" (pp. 59–67; reprinted from *Bol. Academia nacional de la historia*), and Tulio Febres Cordero, "La prensa de la Gran Colombia en 1821" (pp. 68–72; reprinted from *Arch. historia y variedades*, Vol. 2, pp. 337–339).

The first Sánchez article is a list of localities and the dates printing was introduced into each. The first newspaper and its date for each locality are also provided. His second article discusses briefly the *Gazeta de Caracas, Semanario de Caracas, El Patriota de Venezuela, Mercurio venezolano, El Publicista de Venezuela*, and *Correo del Orinoco*, which it was expected that the Academia nacional de la historia would issue in facsimile.

In the González article, the third part (pp. 15–36), an alphabetical list of newspapers and periodicals; and the fourth part (pp. 36–42), a list of journalists, are the most valuable sections.

Gran Colombia included the present-day countries of Venezuela, Colombia, and Ecuador. Febres Cordero's third article presents data on eight newspapers published between 1808 and 1821, with the most attention being paid to *La Gaceta de Colombia* (pp. 70–72).

A fairly complete list of Venezuelan newspapers in existence in 1885 could be produced by a study of *Actos del congreso de la Prensa asociado*, subtitled Reunido por vez primera en Venezuela para la aclamacion de Guzmán Blanco . . . (Caracas, October 28, 1885, 71 pp.). Pages 7–8 provide a list of newspapers and their place of publication. Pages 51–53 and 55–57 provide still other lists, which also include the names of each paper's representative, probably its editor or publisher.

The rest of this section is devoted to regional bibliographic studies on the imprints of Venezuelan cities and states.

Adolfo Rodríguez, *Historia del periodismo en Apure* (Biblioteca de autores y temas apureños, No. 3, [Talleres de Italgráfica], San Fernando de Apure, 1978, 178 pp.) is the fullest discussion of periodicals published in this state. The first 104 pages provide much valuable data concerning these publications. Unfortunately, the author omits an index of titles and persons.

For Aragua de Barcelona, see D. Arreaza Monagas, "Periódicos publicados en Aragua y sus redactores," in *Aragua de Barcelona, Apuntaciones históricas* (El Cojo, Caracas, 1911, pp. 53–54; reprinted in *Materiales*, pp. 521–522). This article provides the barest data (sometimes merely the title) on 43 newspapers published here between 1876 and 1910.

For Barcelona, see José Bernardo Gómez, "Crónica del periodismo en Barcelona desde 1834 hasta 1863: Segunda época, de 1863 a 1895" (*Diario de Caracas*, Nos. 465, 467, 468, and 470, April 1, 17, 18, and 22, 1895; reprinted in *Materiales*, pp. 373 –386). Gómez's articles are a history of Barcelona's journalism in the form of a running commentary. Data are provided on title, year in which publication began, publishers, and editors. Unfortunately, the year in which a newspaper ceased publication is not given. Salomón de Lima's brief pamphlet *Historia del periodismo en Barcelona* (Tip. Anzoátegui, Barcelona, 1970, 13 pp.) would seem to be the latest treatment of journalism in this city.

For the state of Barinas, the following studies by Virgilio Tosta are available: *Imprenta y periodismo en Ciudad de Nutrias, Puerto Nutrias y Sabaneta* (Edit. Sucre, Caracas, 1962, 15 pp.), "Imprenta y periodismo en Barinas" (*Siempre Firmes*, Nos. 88–89, November 1962–February 1963, pp. 67–96), *Imprenta y periodismo en Barinas* ([Editorial Sucre], Caracas, 1964, 101 pp.), "Imprenta y periodismo en Barinitas" (*Siempre Firmes*, Nos. 84–85, March–June 1962, pp. 64–93), *Imprenta y periodismo en Libertad de Barinas* (Editorial Sucre, Caracas, 1962, 14 pp.), "La imprenta y el periodismo en Ciudad de Nutrias y Puerto de Nutrias" (*Siempre Firmes*, Nos. 86–87, July–October 1962, pp. 82–112), and "Imprenta y periodismo en Obispos" (*Siempre Firmes*, Nos. 84–85, March–June 1962, pp. 64–93).

Much of the material in *Imprenta y periodismo en Barinas* first appeared in *Siempre Firmes* and in *El Universal*. The first press in this city was introduced during the period 1825–1828, and this work has chapters on individual presses, newspapers, and periodicals. Chapter 15 deals with the periodicals published in this city in the 20th century through 1961.

J. Sáer d'Héguert, "Prensa barquisimetana" (*Materiales*, pp. 340–369) first appeared as *Prensa larense: Lista de algunos periódicos que vieron la luz en Barquisimeto* (1929). It was later enlarged and published under its present title with a prologue by Cecilio Zubillaga (Imprenta Branger, Valencia, 1933, 52 pp.). Printing was introduced to Barquisimeto in 1833, and pages 341–347 deal with the early history of printing in this city. Pages 347–369 provide a chronological list of newspapers published here between 1833 and 1915. For many of the papers, only the barest bibliographic data are given.

Most of the research concerning printing and journalism in the state of Bolívar has centered around the *Correo del Orinoco*. One might recommend for the study of this paper: Corporación venezolana de Guayana (ed.), *Correo del Orinoco, 1818–1822*, which shows the following information, Angostura (Venezuela) 1818–1822: Reprodución facsimilar: Edición de la . . . con motivo del sesquicentenario de la publicación ([Edit. Arte], Caracas, 1968, xv, 262 leaves of facsimiles, 25 leaves of indexes and colophon). For the study of early imprints of Angostura, see Julio Febres Cordero, *Establecimiento de la imprenta en Angostura: Correo del Orinoco* (Universidad central de Venezuela, Facultad de humanidades y educación, Escuela de periodismo, Instituto de investigaciones de prensa, [Imprenta universitaria], Caracas, 1964, 130 pp.), and Pedro Grases, *Impresos de Angostura, 1817–1822: Facsímiles* ([Edit. Arte], Caracas, 1969, 117 pp.). A fuller study for a longer historical period is Lorenzo Vargas Mendoza, *Periódicos de Guayana (1839–1953)* ([Gráfica americana], Caracas, 1968, 188 pp.).

For the state of Carabobo, see Rafael Saturno Guerra, *Apuntes para la historia del periodismo en Carabobo* (Escuela de periodismo de la Universidad central de Venzuela, Edit. universitaria, Caracas, 1949, 58 pp.; reprinted in *Materiales*, pp. 237–267), which is divided into "Prensa oficial," "Periódicos de índole religiosa," "Revista y boletines," "Periódicos humorísticos y satiricos," "Periódicos deportivos," "Periódicos taurinos," and "Prensa periódica y ocasional publicada en Carabobo durante los siglos xix y xx." Unfortunately, only the barest publication details are given. Of particular value for the study of early Valencian imprints are Pedro

Grases, "Boletines del Ejército Libertador de Venezuela en 1813" (*Bol. Academia nacional de la historia*, Vol. 45, 1962, pp. 505–510; reprinted in his *Investigaciones bibliográficas,* Colección vigilia, No. 13, Ministerio de educación, Dirección técnica, Departamento de publicaciones, Caracas, 1968, pp. 187–196), and Agustín Millares Carlo, "Para la historia de la imprenta en Valencia (Venezuela): 1830" (*Bol. Biblioteca general* [Universidad del Zulia], Vol. 4, No. 6, January–July 1964, pp. 69–77).

The following articles published in *Materiales* deal with the newspapers of Caracas: Tulio Febres Cordero, "Notas bibliográficas—Periódicos viejos de Caracas" (pp. 73–77; reprinted from *Arch. historia y variedades*, Vol. 2, pp. 113–115), and José E. Machado, "Lista de algunos periódicos que vieron la luz en Caracas de 1808 a 1900" (pp. 78–111; reprinted from *Bol. Biblioteca nacional*, No. 14, January 1927, pp. 426–429; No. 15, April 1927, pp. 458–465; No. 16, July 1927, pp. 493–498; and No. 17, October 1927, pp. 529–533; also published as a pamphlet by Lit. y tip. Vargas, Caracas, 1929, 74 pp.). These two articles provide data on 143 newspapers; the article by Febres Cordero supplements that by Machado for the period 1830–1857. *Materiales* also published studies on individual important newspapers and periodicals.

For Carora, see Ismael Silva Montáñes, *Imprentas i periódicos caroranos* (Tip. Arte, Carora, 1933, 34 pp.); this is a fuller version of his "La imprenta i el periodismo en Carora," which appeared in the *Boletín de la Biblioteca nacional* (No. 8, July 1925, pp. 240–244). Pages 7–12 deal briefly with the printing establishments from 1875 to 1932 in Carora, and pages 13–34 give an annotated chronological list of newspapers of Carora. The pamphlet has been reprinted in *Materiales* (pp. 493–518).

For Cojedes, see two articles in *El Universal* by Héctor Pedreáñez Trejo, "La cultura en provincia: Introducción al periodismo cojedeño" (December 15, 1964) and "La cultura en provincia: La imprenta en Cojedes" (February 1, 1965).

Cumaná was destroyed by an earthquake in 1853, and its press was transferred to Carúpano. Santos Erminy Arismendi, "La imprenta y el periodismo en Carúpano" (*Bol. Biblioteca nacional*, No. 7, April 1, 1925, pp. 202–206; reprinted in *Materiales*, pp. 451–458) provides data on the history of printing in this city and of its newspapers and magazines through 1923.

The following would seem to be important material on the press of Cumaná: Manuel Segundo Sánchez, "Sobre el periodismo en Cumaná: Algunos de sus órganos iniciales" (*El Universal*, October 21, 1917; reprinted in his *Obras*, pp. 388–391, and in *Materiales*, pp. 335–338), José Silverio González Varela, "Anales del periodismo venozolano: La prensa en Cumaná" (*El Nuevo diario*, October 4, 1917; reprinted in *Materiales*, pp. 329–338), Pedro Grases, "Orígenes de la imprenta en Cumaná" (*El Farol*, Vol. 18, No. 64, June 1956, p. 29; reprinted in his *Orígenes de la imprenta en Venezuela*, pp. 198–204), and Manuel Acereda La Linde, "Periódicos de Cumaná," in *Historia de Aragua de Barcelona del Estado Anzoátegui y de la Nueva Andalucía* (Imprenta nacional, Caracas, 1959, Vol. 1, pp. 242–243). The first two articles deal with the period between 1827 and 1859.

Nothing except extremely specialized studies exists for the history of printing and journalism in Falcón.

For the state of Guárico, the principal studies would appear to be Blas Loreto Loreto, *Historia del periodismo en el Estado Guárico* (Imp. López, Buenos Aires, [1951]), and a work by this author that was published in *El Libro* (Vol. 1, Nos. 1–3, 1929, p. 5). This series was reprinted in *Materiales* (pp. 389–397). P. N. Tablante Garrido, "Periodismo merideño: Desde la sierra (1910–1923) de Emilio Menotti Spsosito" (*Bol. Biblioteca general*, Nos. 9–10, August 1965–July 1966, pp. 135–212) is a detailed study of this newspaper, with brief comments on Menotti's other journalistic ventures. Pedro Godoy lists 199 periodicals in "Estadística bibliográfica de la ciudad de Mérida: Datos para la bibliografía nacional" (*Gaceta de Mérida*, No. 57–58, February 15, 1906, pp. 434–438, and No. 59, March 22, 1906, p. 446). The fullest guide to the newspapers and magazines of Mérida are the compilations by Mauro Dávila: *Arqueo hemerográfico de la Mérida (siglo xix)* (Serie bibliográfico, No. 4, Centro de investigaciones literárias, Universidad de los Andes, Mérida, 1972, vii, 214 pp.) and *Arqueo hemerográfico de la ciudad de Mérida* (Serie bibliográfico, No. 12, Universidad de los Andes, Facultad de humanidades y educación, Instituto de investigaciones literárias "Gonzalo Picón Febres," Mérida, 1977, 161 pp.). The second volume provides data on 259 periodicals published between 1900 and 1950. It also provides a chronological listing of the publications. Lists of directors, editors, and collaborators are given as well as one of the presses that published the periodicals. The press of Ejido has been studied by Augusto Rodríguez A., "Periodismo en Ejido" (*Bol. Archivo histórico de la Provincia de Mérida*, Vol. 5, No. 25, January–February 1947, pp. 3–7). Pedro N. Tablante Garrido has published a series of articles on individual editors, publishers, and periodicals, most of which appeared in newspapers and magazines published in this state.

Unfortunately, Lorenzo Vargas Mendoza, *Prensa petareña* ([Caja de Trabajo penitenciario, Caracas]; cover states "Petare, 1977," 69 pp.) contains no lists of newspapers or magazines published in Petare. It is composed of 11 articles from which a variety of data could be extracted.

Little exists on the state of Portuguesa. Julio Febres Cordero, "La primera imprenta y el primer periódico guarareño" (*El Nacional*, November 25, 1966) would seem to be the only study of importance.

Alí Brett Martínez, *El periodismo y las imprentas de Puerto Cabello, 1806–1945* (Ediciones del Sesquicentenario de la Toma de Puerto Cabello, 1823–1973, [Editado por el Ilustre Concejo Municipal de Puerto Cabello y la Junta Sesquicentenaria, 1973], 309 pp.) is the standard history of printing and journalism for this city.

For Táchira, see Luis F. Briceño, *La imprenta en El Táchira . . .* (Imprenta Bolívar, Caracas, 1883, 16 pp.; reprinted in *Materiales*, pp. 415–448), and Luis Andrés Rugeles, *Primeras imprentas y periodismo del Táchira*, for 1844–1937 (Edit. El Pueblo, Mérida, 1940, 82 pp.; the part that deals with newspapers is reprinted in *Materiales*, pp. 429–448). Briceño provides an interesting table that gives data on 51 periodicals published between 1845 and 1882. It gives the name of the periodical, year it appeared, type, editors, publishers, contributors, and the time it lasted. Rugeles repeats much of the Briceño information and updates it much beyond the late 19th century.

The fullest discussion of journalism in Trujillo is that of Rafael Ramón Castellanos, *Historia del periodismo trujillano en el siglo xix . . .* (Imprenta nacional, Caracas, 1957, 310 pp.). In many respects the volume by Castellanos is one of the better press histories of Venezuela. The arrangement is chronological (i.e., 1864 through 1899), and sometimes several pages are devoted to a single newspaper or periodical. Data are provided concerning the date of its publication, editorial policy, editor, publisher, etc. Among its numerous indexes are: "Nomina de los periódicos trujillanos aparecidos desde 1864 hasta 1900, por orden cronológico" (pp. 201–216), "Nomina de los periodistas que ocuparon cargos directivos en los periódicos trujillanos, desde 1864 hasta 1900" (pp. 225–242), and "Nomina de los periódicos trujillanos aparecidos desde 1864 hasta 1900, por ciudades" (pp. 245–248).

The Castellanos volume now renders obsolete "La imprenta y el periodismo en Valera" (*El Universal*, August 12, 1934; reprinted in *Materiales*, pp. 487–489), which provides data on the newspapers published in Valera from 1872 to 1936; and J. R. Almarza, "Datos históricos sobre la imprenta en Venezuela, Trujillo" (*Materiales*, pp. 475–483), which first appeared as a pamphlet (Imprenta Trujillana, Trujillo, 1906).

Material on the state of Yaracuy is considerably dated. J. T. Martínez, "La Prensa en el Yaracuy" (*El Siglo XX* [San Felipe], No. 44, January 1, 1902) has been enlarged by Federico Quirrón R. and is best accessible in *Materiales* (pp. 461–471).

The Presidencia de la República issued *Materiales para la historia de la imprenta y el periodismo en el Estado Zulia*, compiled by Agustín Millares Carlo and Carlos Sánchez Díaz (Artegrafía, Caracas, 1970, 412 pp.). It is a collection of about two dozen previously published articles that deal with the history of printing and journalism in this state, whose largest and most important city is Maracaibo.

Augusta Faría de Hands, *Los tres primeros periódicos de Maracaibo* (Ed. Universitaria, Maracaibo, 1967, 113 pp. with 169 facsimiles) reproduces *El Correo nacional, Concordia del Zulia*, and *El Posta español*.

José López de Sagredo y Brú, "Indice de periódicos y revistas publicados en el Estado Zulia, desde 1821 hasta 1948" (*Materiales*, pp. 295–325) is part of Chapter 5 of his *Indice de periódicos y periodistas del Estado Zulia (1821–1948)* (Cámara de comercio de Maracaibo, Maracaibo, 1948, 142 pp.). The reprinted part is a chronological list of 19th-century newspapers, so that the title is rather misleading. No 20th-century papers are listed.

For German newspapers in Venezuela, see *Arndt–Olson* (Vol. 2, pp. 611–612). Also of interest is Pedro Grases, "El Boletín bilingüe de la Colonia Tovar (1843–1845)," in *La imprenta en Venezuela y algunas obras de referencia* (Ediciones de la Facultad de humanidades y educación, Caracas, 1979, pp. 104–108), which is a study of the *Boletín de la Colonia Tovar*.

HENSLEY C. WOODBRIDGE
With the research assistance of Jane Larkin

LEIBNIZ, GOTTFRIED WILHELM

The achievements of Gottfried Leibniz (1646–1716) and his enduring reputation as a major philosopher and universal scholar are far too extensive even for brief mention here. Unlike many other scholars and men of letters who held library positions as sinecures, he had a firm grasp on the problems of collection development, cataloging, and administration. He was even meticulously careful in preserving his own manuscripts, some 200 folio volumes and about 15,300 letters, which went to Hannover. The latter collection includes correspondence with some of the major intellectuals of his age.

He studied in philosophy and law in Leipzig, Jena, and the old University of Altdorf. In 1667 he was appointed tutor and librarian at the electoral court in Mainz. He prepared a subject catalog of the library of the minister Count Johann Christian von Boyneburg, "dass dergleichen wohl zuvoren nicht gesehen worden . . . vermöge dessen über alle Materien die davon handelnde Autores zu finden, und ein Traktat oft an mehr als zehn Orten allegirt ist" (*Lexikon des gesamten Buchwesens,* Vol. 3, p. 309). From 1676 until his death he was counselor and personal librarian of Duke Johann Friedrich von Braunschweig-Lüneburg, and after 1690 he was director of the Herzog–August–Bibliothek in Wolfenbüttel. His integrity both as a thinker and as a librarian is illustrated by the fact that in 1688 he declined an attractive offer in the Vatican Library because he doubted the acceptance of uncensored scholarship by the Roman Church.

In 1672 Leibniz was in Paris and had close association with Nicolas Clément (1651–1716) in the Bibliothèque Royale, where he observed the new classification in 23 classes, with a catalog. Clément's bibliographic policies were reflected in Wolfenbüttel. In the period 1690–1696 Leibniz made an author catalog of the library. He proposed luxury taxes as a source of revenue for the library. In 1710 he was able to secure funds for acquiring the 467 manuscripts in the collection of the Danish state counselor Marquard Gude. He established policies for use of the collections that were revolutionary for his day. His *Idea Leibnitizna bibliotecae publicae secundum classes scientiarum ordinendae* includes notions that are viable today.

Leibniz was fully dedicated to every occupation, profession, or intellectual activity which was meaningful for him. Librarianship and information science would have been a century in advance if these disciplines had been his only interest.

BIBLIOGRAPHY

Gurwitsch, Aron, *Leibniz: Philosophie des Panlogismus*, de Gruyter, Berlin, 1974.

Heinemann, Otto von, *Die Herzogliche Bibliothek zu Wolfenbüttel*, J. Zwissler, Wolfenbüttel, 1894.

Lexikon des gesamten Buchwesens (Karl Löffler and Joachim Kirchner, eds.), Karl W. Hiersemann, Leipzig, 1936.

Muller, Kurt, *Leibniz—Bibliographie: Die Literatur über Leibniz*, Veröffentlichungen des Leibniz–Archivs, No. 1, Klostermann, Frankfurt, 1967.

LAWRENCE S. THOMPSON

LESOTHO, LIBRARIES IN

The history of libraries in Lesotho reflects the unique character of the country's geography and history. The Kingdom of Lesotho enjoys the unique distinction of being entirely surrounded by another nation, the Republic of South Africa, and is bounded by three of the latter's four provinces: the Orange Free State on the north and west, Natal on the east, and the Cape Province to the south. Geographically, Lesotho lies between 26° and 31° S and 27° and 30° E, with two distinct physiographic regions comprising its landscape. The eastern three-quarters of Lesotho is occupied by the rugged Maluti Mountains, cut by the valleys of the Senqu (Orange) and Senqunyane Rivers, while the western quarter of the country is formed by the "lowlands," high grass plains at an average elevation of 1 mile. (See Fig. 1.) Lesotho also enjoys the odd privilege of being the only nation in the world with all its land area at more than 3,000 feet above sea level, a circumstance which has earned it the name "the Kingdom in the Sky." In the 19th century the area of the lowlands occupied by the Basotho people extended further west than the present boundaries of the Mohokare (Caledon) and Orange Rivers. It is this area which holds seven of the nine district administrative centers, the best agricultural land, and most of the population: Hence, it is in this area that the birth and growth of libraries and library services in Lesotho has taken place.

Culturally, Lesotho enjoys an advantage over other African nations through possessing one common language, Sesotho, although English is also widely known and used. This linguistic unity reflects the foundation of the Basotho nation by Moshoeshoe I in the early 19th century from an amalgam of refugees whose home villages and clans had been dispersed or destroyed during the terrible *Lifaqane*, a period of internecine warfare occasioned by the irruption of a fleeing vassal of Chaka Zulu, Matiwane, and his people onto the highveld in the early 1820s. From these fragments of refugee peoples, Moshoeshoe forged a unified nation which passed under British colonial administration on March 12, 1868, at his own request. Known as Basutoland until independence on October 4, 1966, the country saw the expansion of mission systems of the Paris Evangelical Mission Society and the Roman Catholic church as well as the establishment of various government service agencies and the evolution of a national advisory council. Upon independence, this last became the National Assembly, with the British administrator being replaced by H.M. Moshoeshoe II under a system of constitutional monarchy. It is against this background that the history of book production and library services in Lesotho must be considered. The most useful approach is to view this development as a gradual growth from several component organizations, each of which contributed significantly to the environment in which the present library and archival centers must function. Accordingly, colonial and postindependence developments in the field are examined separately.

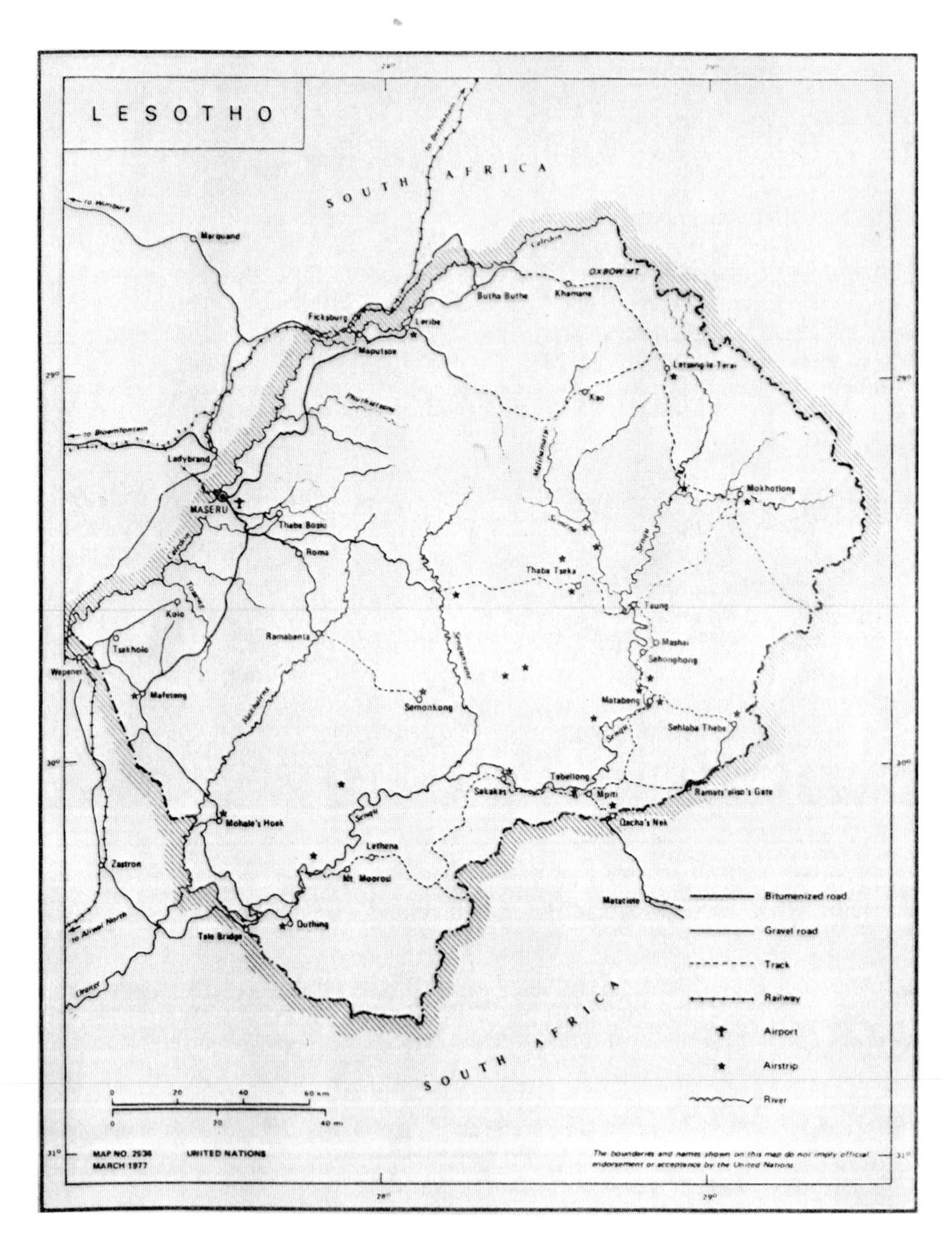

FIGURE 1. *Lesotho*.

Colonial Development (1833–1966)

This period of 103 years witnessed the establishment of centers for book production and translation, the arrival of the missionaries and founding of schools, and the beginnings of the present administrative system under British colonial rule. The major institutions founded during this period were:

Printing Centers
Morija Printing Works: Paris Evangelical Missionary Society, 1863
Mazenod Printing Works: Oblates of Mary Immaculate, 1933

Archives
National Archives, 1868–1869

Libraries
Pius XII/UBBS/UBLS/NUL Library, 1945
Residency Library: Maseru, 1886

In addition to these, several other libraries were extant for brief periods of time in this era, such as the Basutoland Public Library in Maseru, but these made no lasting contribution to library development and were later dissolved.

MORIJA PRINTING WORKS

The history of Morija, the oldest mission station in Lesotho and site of the famous printing works, began in 1833. In that year the first missionaries of the Paris Evangelical Missionary Society (PEMS), Eugene Casalis and Thomas Arbousset, arrived at Thaba Bosiu [Mountain of Night] at the request of Moshoeshoe I. In response to their petition for a place to settle, a tract of land to the southeast was granted them, where the station of Morija (the Sesotho form of "Moriah," the place of Abraham's test of faith) was formally established on July 9 (*1*). In the same period, other PEMS mission stations were also being founded in what is now the eastern portion of the Orange Free State. The most important of these for Lesotho library history was that of Beersheba. It was here that, in October 1841, Rev. Samuel Rolland began operating a printing facility whose products would aid in the evangelization then in progress. This first handpress deserves mention because it was here that the first book to be printed in Sesotho, a Sesotho hymnal (*Lifela tsa Sione*), was produced in 1844 (*2*).

During the period immediately following the establishment of the PEMS missions, one of the primary concerns was the translation of scriptural texts and materials into Sesotho, and the new press did not lack for manuscripts awaiting production. The year 1842 also saw the arrival from Paris of a larger press and with it Joseph Ludorf, a trained printer, to cope with the technical aspects of the new center which required specialized knowledge. Between 1845 and 1858 some 6,000 copies of the New Testament in Sesotho (*Testamente e Ncha*) were produced at Beersheba, a joint translation by Rolland and Eugene Casalis. During the Senekal War in 1858, Beersheba was burned by a Boer commando, and the printing facilities were shifted to the mission of Bethesda for safety. From 1858 to 1862, no printing was done, and although work was resumed at Beersheba in the latter year, renewed hostilities in 1865 (the Sequiti War) led to the expulsion of all PEMS workers from the Orange Free State missions and the expropriation of much of their property. The press was again moved, first to Bethesda and ultimately to the newly founded site of Masitise. This latter move was directed by Rev. Frederic Ellenberger, who had some knowledge of printing techniques. In the course of the journey, the wagon carrying the equipment broke down, scattering bits of type all over the ground, which pieces were subsequently picked up by the Basotho and melted down for bullets (*3*). Masitise remained the center of mission printing for some 8 years (1866–1874); a number of translations were produced in 1871 (Ruth and Kings), 1872, and 1873 (editions of the Books of Genesis, Psalms, and Proverbs). In 1874 it was decided to move the press for a final time to its present site at Morija.

Morija itself enjoyed a unique position with respect to the other PEMS missions for two reasons: It was the oldest, and it possessed (prior to the arrival of the society press from Masitise) the only printing facility within the present boundaries of Lesotho. In 1860 Charles Adolphe Mabille arrived at Morija and set up a small private press similar to the original at Beersheba. Free of the demands placed on the official mission press by the need for religious materials, Morija could explore other avenues of printing, a situation which Mabille exploited with great skill. In November 1863 the first issue of *Leselinyana* [The Little Light] was published. This was the first newspaper in Lesotho and also the first to be issued in any African vernacular in southern Africa (*4*). Originally issued monthly, *Leselinyana* grew into a weekly publication which exerted a great influence on public awareness.

With the formal establishment of the printing center at Morija, book production in Lesotho began a growth and diversification which have not yet ceased. Under Mabille's capable direction, further progress was made in Sesotho linguistics, and the first Sesotho grammar and Sesotho–English dictionary appeared in 1876 and 1878, respectively. In the enforced idleness caused by the border conflicts, the work of translating the Bible (Old Testament) into Sesotho proceeded, with each section being assigned to a different person. These translations were then sent to London and, together with the extant *Testamente e Ncha*, were published by the British and Foreign Bible Society in 1881. Mabille brought the finished editions back to Lesotho in 1882, and subsequent revisions were made as the capabilities of the Morija Printing Works were expanded. This year also saw the appearance of two volumes of Bible stories in Sesotho by Rev. Coillard and Rev. Mabille. Once the primary needs of the mission field had been satisfied, Sesotho printing quickly branched into the production of textbooks for the PEMS schools, a function which Morija continues to perform with a high standard of quality. Readers, geography books, and arithmetic and English texts were among the first items to be published, along with a new edition of the *Lifela tsa Sione* set in tonic sol-fa notation. Amalgamated with a hymnal compiled by Mabille in 1881, these 457 hymns provided a sound base for the growth of Sesotho music and had reached the 19th edition by 1933. By 1894 the only lack evident in the literature was the absence of works (whether religious or not) by Basotho authors. Foreseeing the potential damage such neglect could cause, Mabille charged his colleagues to "write books for the Basotho." With the existence of dictionaries and grammars, the foundation for the later works of such seminal authors as Thomas Mofolo and Azariele Sekese had been laid. It is interesting to note that the products of Morija were also widely used by the Roman Catholic missionaries who arrived in Lesotho in 1862, a development which their authors had definitely not anticipated.

The period from Mabille's death in 1894 until the early 1930s saw the replacement of the old printing equipment with a power-operated press and the appointment of a trained printer both to improve technical aspects of the center and to oversee the training of apprentices. In 1904 Rev. Albert Casalis, who had assumed management of Morija upon Mabille's death, returned from a European tour, bringing with him M. Labarthe of Geneva, and by 1905 the new presses were in full operation. From that time on, the books produced at Morija compared favorably with similar items produced in Europe. The chief importance of this time was that the gap in Sesotho writing which Mabille had bemoaned now began to be filled with the first specimens of modern Sesotho literature: *Buka ea Pokello ea Mekhwa ea Ba-Sotho le Maele, le Litsomo* [The Customs and Proverbs of the Basuto] (1893), by Azariele Sekese; and the famous *Moeti oa Bochabela* [The Pilgrim to the East], by Thomas Mofolo. The latter is renowned for two reasons: its intrinsic value as a moral tale, and because it was here that modern Sesotho fiction came into being. A landmark of literary history was also reached in February 1917, when the 50th anniversary of *Leselinyana* was celebrated.

After 1920, with the arrival of M. Jacques Zurcher to succeed M. Labarthe, the scope and coverage of Morija's activities widened immensely. Until this time, most of the products of the press had been issued for the audience within Lesotho and adjacent portions of southern Africa where Sesotho was also the vernacular. Zurcher altered this traditional focus somewhat by placing large orders abroad for reprints of extant works in Sesotho, rather than issuing them at Morija. This permitted him to offer the facilities to other missions and educational organizations elsewhere in sub-Saharan Africa which required printed material in languages other than Sesotho (5). Pedi, an Nguni language of the northern Transvaal, and Lozi, a Zambian language, were the first of the other African languages in which work was done. Gradually, the area covered grew to include most of modern Swaziland, Botswana, Malawi, Zimbabwe, Mozambique, Tanzania, Namibia, and the Republic of South Africa. During World War II, orders were received from regions as distant as the Cameroons and Zaire, owing to the difficulty of obtaining printed materials from Europe. In addition to these special orders, a large variety of works were produced in such standard languages of southern Africa as Afrikaans, Xhosa, Shona, Sindabele, and English. Mention should also be made of the role played by Morija as the de facto government printing office for the colonial administration of Basutoland, a function it was to hold until 1971 when an official government press was established in Maseru. Thus the libraries of Lesotho may be said to have had their beginnings at Morija, for without the products of this press, the establishment of general literacy and the creation of a public receptive to the ideas of library development would have been greatly delayed.

MAZENOD INSTITUTE

Fr. Joseph Gerard and Bishop Francis Allard of the Oblates of Mary Immaculate (OMI) arrived in Lesotho in 1862 to begin the development of this mission field for the Roman Catholic Church. The first settlement was begun upon a grant of land near Thaba Bosiu which became known as Roma, because the converted Ba-roma, or "people of Rome," lived there. Utilizing the Sesotho linguistic materials already prepared by the PEMS workers, preparation of textual materials was begun shortly afterward. As Mabille's handpress at Morija was insufficient for the volume of printing required, the first book of Catholic literature in Sesotho was printed in Durban in collaboration with the facilities of the *Natal Mercury* newspaper in December 1865. It was a combined catechism and prayerbook and had been prepared by Fr. Gerard with the aid of a Protestant teacher. From this time until 1933, with the establishment of Mazenod Institute, all works for the Catholic church in Lesotho (including such varied materials as the *Imitation of Christ*, school books, and histories of the church) were printed either in Europe or at various locations in South Africa, among them Bloemfontein, Durban, Mariannhill, Ladybrand, and Maritzburg. Funds for this purpose were made available to the church from the Society of Saint Peter Claver.

Efforts at coping with the printing needs of the country were also underway at Roma itself. Between 1872 and 1900 a small handpress produced booklets of various sorts, but not until 1933 was a complete printing center established at Mazenod by Fr. Lebreton, with technical assistance being provided by the main OMI press at Richelieu, Ontario. That year also saw the inauguration of *Moeletsi oa Basotho* [The Basotho Adviser], Lesotho's second newspaper. Some 100 titles had been issued by Mazenod when the entire complex was destroyed by fire on June 19, 1946. Under the direction of Fr. Labrecque, a new press resumed operations on June 30, 1948. To promote the growth of literacy and to stimulate the further development of Sesotho literature, an authors' association was founded at Mazenod in November of 1956. Known as BOSA (Basutoland Organization of Sesotho Authors), it proved instrumental in enhancing public consciousness and pride in the capacities of Sesotho authors. The most successful effort in this direction was the Sesotho Book Exhibition held in Maseru, March 11–13, 1965. In addition to indicating the wide variety of genres comprising Sesotho writing (over 1,000 books including religious tracts and texts, novels, anthropological studies, volumes of poetry, and cookbooks), the exhibition also marked the centenaries of *Leselinyana* and Fr. Gerard's catechism. In conjunction with the extant facilities at Morija, Mazenod thus expanded the variety of material available to the Basotho reading public and also played a seminal role in the development of a national literature through the establishment of a forum of Sesotho writers and playwrights.

NATIONAL ARCHIVES

The history of the Lesotho National Archives begins in 1869 with the founding of Maseru, the police post which was later to become administrative headquarters for the colonial government of Basutoland. The offices of the agent of the British high commissioner were housed in the buildings of a trading store until April 1874, when a 16-day rain caused a portion of them to collapse. Even after reconstruction in stone, these facilities were not thought suitable for their purpose. A scathing description of these earliest Lesotho government offices was provided in 1878 by Col. Griffith, the first resident high commissioner (1871–1881): "The Governor's Agents and Resident Magistrate's offices are in adjoining rooms, which are very small, stuffy and very inadequate. The clerk's offices, two in number, are at a distance in a separate building. The present buildings are entirely unsuitable . . . and quite unworthy of being the head office of government" (*6*). It is these two latter offices which formed the nucleus of the government archives of Lesotho. The town plan of Maseru for 1880 dignified the structures with the title of "Public Offices," and when new quarters were constructed a decade later the name stuck. Colonial Maseru was expanding greatly at this period, and this same construction program also transformed the house of the resident magistrate into the official residence of the British high commissioner. It was in the new extension that the first colonial-period library in Lesotho came into being in 1886. Upon completion of the Secretariat (presently occupied by the offices of the prime minister) in 1912, all archival materials were moved into a specially designated "Records Room." The archives remained there until 1958, when they were moved into their present location in the old Post Office Building on Constitution Avenue, itself likewise a product of the building program of the 1880s.

The *Catalog of the Basutoland Government Archives*, compiled by the first government archivist, Constance Walton, in the late 1950s, provides a fascinating glimpse into the elements of a growing colonial bureaucracy. It details the contents of the Secretariat Records Room and includes such diverse items as the official correspondence of the governor's agents and resident commissioners, census records, diaries, maps, and council proceedings. A second section indicates the expansion of British colonial administration across the lowlands and into the lower mountain regions through reports received from the district commissioners. Each district from Butha-Buthe to Qacha's Nek is represented by files of correspondence, diaries, and registers of local court cases. The entire archives thus provide coverage from 1871 (the beginning of direct colonial administration) to the beginning of World War II. It is to Mrs. Walton that Lesotho owes the very existence of its archives: During her term of office from 1947 to 1960, she made many trips to secure archival records and papers which would otherwise have been destroyed.

Prior to independence, responsibility for the management of the archives rested with the government secretary. With the creation of the Department of Information in 1965, the archives and their accompanying library were transferred to its jurisdiction, and subsequently to the Ministry of Education. The new archivist, Mrs. M. M. Lebotsa, began to arrange the archives in their present form in late 1966. An Interim Committee on Museums and Archives was appointed to oversee these areas and exercised its functions until the end of 1967. That year also saw the passage of the Archives Act, the fundamental piece of Lesotho legislation covering this area. It established the position of chief archivist and provided for a seven-member Archives Commission to replace the Interim Committee. A notable feature of this act is the 35-year statute of limitations placed on access to archival materials, although more recent materials may also be reserved at the discretion of the Ministry of Education, on grounds of potential prejudice to the parties who provided the information in question (7). Supplementary legislation in 1972 clarified the duties of the chief archivist with respect to the destruction and maintenance of archival materials and set forth the rules governing the use of the archives by the Lesotho public. The general period of archival proscription hazily defined in the 1967 Archives Act was explained further, stating that no documents more recent than 30 years may be examined without permission from the Ministry of Education. The Archives Committee was also further limited to a term of 5 years, and all appointees were to serve without pay. These regulations have so far proved sufficient for all legal matters affecting the archives.

In 1970 Mr. M. L. Manyeli succeeded Mrs. Lebotsa as archivist and during his administration conducted a countrywide survey of archival materials. The archives themselves were also augmented at this time by the donation of law reports from the High Court and Law Office and certain documents relating to Lesotho which had been held by the government of Botswana. The creation of the post of assistant archivist in 1973 indicates continuing official interest in this area. Post-1974 developments in the archival field have centered on the issues of preservation and storage space. A proposal was made in 1974 that the archives should be transferred to the library of the National University in Roma, where the terrific overcrowding of their present quarters would be alleviated. In 1976 the Center for South African Studies at the University of York expressed interest in microfilming the entire archival stock, at that time more than 900 letter boxes, 90 files, and 50 box files. Negotiations between the government and the university are continuing, while the latter proposal has not yet been acceded to. Mr. Manyeli retired in 1978 for reasons of health, and the archives were assigned to Mr. A. Sekere. Until such time as larger quarters become available in the projected government building program, it seems probable that the archives will remain in Maseru.

PIUS XII COLLEGE/UBBS/UBLS/NUL

Equally important to the library history of Lesotho was the establishment on April 8, 1945, of a Catholic University College at Roma by the Catholic Hierarchy of South Africa. This was in consequence of a decision taken by the Synod of Catholic Bishops in South Africa to provide African Catholics with education at the postmatriculation level. Originally housed in a temporary school at Roma Mission (the modern Saint Mary's) some 34 kilometers southeast of Maseru, in 1946 the college moved to a 52-acre site deeded to it by Paramount Chief Seeiso Griffith. The period between 1946 and 1964 witnessed a rapid growth and expansion from the original five students to 171, many of them from the other High Commission Territories of Bechuanaland, Swaziland, and Nyasaland. The latter year saw the replacement of Pius XII College by the independent, nondenominational University of Basutoland, Bechuanaland, and Swaziland (UBBS) under a charter granted by H.M. Queen Elizabeth II.

By this time the University Library (which had grown steadily under the able direction of Fr. Ernest A. Ruch) numbered some 40,000 volumes and 400 periodi-

FIGURE 2. *The Bonhomme and Mofolo Library complex, National University of Lesotho, Roma.*

cals, and a new building, funded jointly by the World Council of Churches and the World University Service, was completed in 1966. Upon achievement of independence by the High Commission Territories in 1966, UBBS became the University of Botswana, Lesotho, and Swaziland (UBLS). By 1970 the university librarian, James Hutton, could list the library holdings as some 75,000 items. Depository status had been granted the library by the United Nations, and a similar relationship had also been negotiated with the government of Botswana. A special collection of "all publications, past and present, produced in or relating to Botswana, Lesotho and Swaziland" had been begun and swiftly became an important source of rare Africana on the region. Under the successive direction of Mr. Michael Walpole and Mrs. M. N. Tau, the development continued until in 1979 the collection had reached over 120,000 items. UBLS, however, did not enjoy such a period of smooth growth: The Lesotho National Assembly, by Act 13 of 1975 (the National University Act) transformed the Roma campus of UBLS into the independent National University of Lesotho (NUL). Expansion of the NUL library was badly needed, and through funding from various international sources construction was begun on an extension in 1978. Upon completion, the new complex, comprising the Bonhomme and Thomas Mofolo Libraries, was dedicated by H.M. Moshoeshoe II on September 29, 1979. (See Fig. 2.) The NUL Library thus inherited and passed on the tradition of university-level librarianship begun under Pius XII, and it played a leading role in later developments in the Lesotho professional community.

RESIDENCY LIBRARY

Preindependence Maseru was fortunate in having public library facilities of some sort almost from its foundation. Beginning with the establishment of a library in the high commissioner's residence in 1886, books were subsequently made available by the Basutoland Public Library (an outgrowth of the small collection of the Basutoland Book Club) in the early years of this century. Its 1907 catalog lists some 3,000 volumes covering travel and adventure, sport and games, biography, history, fiction, and "miscellaneous." Among the items included are such memorable titles as *Lady Maud's Mania*, *The Private Life of Marie Antoinette*, and *Dialogues on the Supersensual Life*. Clearly, the colonial public of old Maseru had a varied selection of reading material from which to choose.

The vacuum created by the eventual dissolution of the Basutoland Public Library was filled in 1945 with the donation by a Maseru trading family of their books as a basis for the Maseru Public Library. Due to shortage of staff and general public indifference, this library remained small and played only a minor role in subsequent library history. Public library service was restored to Maseru only upon the establishment of the Lesotho National Library in 1977, although foreign agencies such as the British Council and the United States Information Agency also had small, well-stocked collections open to the public. In concert with the new National Library, they have continued to play a substantial part in coping with the information needs of Maseru's population.

Postindependence Events (1966–1980)

Having reviewed the preindependence status of Lesotho libraries and information services, it remains to consider the role played by the nation's professional community since 1966 in relation to questions of professional development, both within the country and elsewhere in Africa.

At independence, the librarians of Lesotho found themselves facing two problems: a shortage of trained manpower and a climate of public apathy toward the profession in general. Although individuals had been sent for training to various U.K. universities during the colonial period, no scheme for the training of librarians in the countries of the BOLESWA region (Botswana, Lesotho, and Swaziland) had been worked out. The South African universities open to Lesotho nationals did not offer training on librarianship beyond the certificate level in most cases, and so were of limited utility in aiding the search for a solution. The first regional survey of the professional manpower needs was the Benge Report, based upon a survey conducted from January 13 to February 3, 1976, by Professor Benge of the University of Ahmadu Bello, Nigeria. Information services were determined to be required to serve adults, the nonliterate, rural and urban communities, the school population (both primary and secondary), government agencies, and the academic research and scientific sectors. Based upon the recommendations contained in the report with respect to the problem of training, a regional conference of BOLESWA librarians was held in Manzini, Swaziland, on November 23, 1977, to discuss their value and establish priorities for their implementation. It was agreed that a regional training scheme should be adopted along the certificate-diploma-degree lines, although the problems of qualifications for each level were seen to require further clarification. As of 1979 no regional training program had been established, and a projected course in librarianship cosponsored by the National University and the National Teacher Training College (NTTC) remained in the planning stages. It should be noted, however, that prior to the conference, workshops for teacher–librarians from the Lesotho schools had been conducted at NTTC in conjunction with the National University library staff. These workshops have proved both popular and useful, and are now a regular part of the NTTC in-service training program, the latest (July 1979) having as participants some 50 school librarians from every district of Lesotho.

LESOTHO LIBRARY ASSOCIATION (LLA)

The problems of promoting both public awareness of libraries as information centers and the idea of librarianship as a viable career option caused the convening of a meeting of all interested parties in the University Senate chamber at NUL on May 18, 1978. Delegates in attendance came from such varied bodies as the National Manpower Development Survey, the Lesotho National Commission for UNESCO, the British Council, UNDP, and the National Teacher Training College, with the National Library present in observer status. Under the chairmanship of Mrs. M. N. Tau, questions of manpower needs in the various information agencies in Lesotho and the problems of training were addressed. The conference agreed that the proposals put forward at Manzini should be implemented through a joint effort by NTTC and the Faculty of Education at NUL, with the provision that foreign training be continued until such time as a local program could be constructed and implemented: "For the local training to be meaningful it should take place within a clearly defined national manpower and education policy which accords the library profession a clearly recognized career structure" (*8*). A library association was seen to be necessary both to effectively implement the Manzini recommendations and "to negotiate and advise government and all the relevant institutions on matters like grading of librarians, training, etc." (*8*). Mrs. M. M. Lebotsa of NUL agreed to chair a committee to draft a constitution for the proposed association, and a series of subsequent meetings examined sample constitutions of other associations to determine the most effective system for Lesotho. Those examined included the structures of several other African library associations (those of Tanzania, Nigeria, Botswana, and Kenya), in addition to those of Great Britain and the United States. The end product of these meetings was submitted to the assembled membership of the Lesotho Library Association (LLA) on December 16, 1978, at the inaugural general meeting at NTTC in Maseru. Once accepted, elections for the executive committee were next held in May of 1979, which returned Mrs. M. N. Tau to the presidency, an office she assumed at the first annual general meeting on June 30, 1979. The chief activities of the LLA are to be continued involvement with international librarianship through such bodies as IFLA and COMLA, and the development of library awareness in Lesotho and throughout the BOLESWA region. Special attention will be given to the formulation of depository legislation and other legal matters seen to be necessary in the Lesotho information system.

LESOTHO NATIONAL LIBRARY SERVICE (LNLS)

The first efforts at coping with the problem of a national library structure for Lesotho were made in 1965, when the deputy director of the British Council's Book Department visited Lesotho to assess current problems and prospective solutions. A development proposal funded jointly by Lesotho and the British Council was offered to the government; however, due to insufficient local funds, implementation of this offer had to be postponed. Recognition of the need for such a facility remained a part of the new government's plans. The Five-Year Development Plan for 1967–1972 records a repetition of the British offer of funds and the acceptance of such by the Ministry of Education. Subsequent schemes for national development defined the role of this new facility as "to provide pleasure and a means of

FIGURE 3. *Lesotho National Library, Kingsway, Maseru.*

broadening knowledge for the general public and students with its services extended to outlying areas by the use of mobile vans" (*9*). Construction of the new complex began in Maseru in 1976, and the new National Library opened its doors in early 1977. (See Fig. 3.) Prior to this time, however, steps were also being taken to address the problems of staffing: The director of the National Library Service of Swaziland, Mr. Victor Forshaw, was invited to make a survey of the cost of establishing such a service as well as its likely nature and extent. Upon completion of this survey, Forshaw became the first national librarian and exercised that function until late 1979, when he was succeeded by Mr. Andreas Elias. One of the noteworthy features of the new system has been its emphasis on developing school libraries: The fleet of converted Landrovers has brought many isolated schools into the reading public and in several cases has created libraries where none existed before. At the same time, it has restored public library services to Maseru and greatly stimulated interest in literacy.

SPECIAL LIBRARIES AND ARCHIVAL MATERIALS

Special libraries and collections in Lesotho are small in number but extremely varied, ranging from contemporary specialist libraries of various government agencies to historical archives and collections dating from the colonial period. The most important of these collections are the Mazenod and Morija archives, the libraries of the Oblate Scholasticate and Saint Augustine's Seminary in Roma, the Ministry of Agriculture library in Maseru, and the special sections of the Thomas Mofolo Library at NUL.

Mazenod Archives

In addition to functioning as a major printing center, Mazenod also fulfills the role of headquarters for the order of the Oblates of Mary Immaculate in Lesotho. As a part of the traditions of the OMI fathers, someone at each mission was required to keep a record (*codex historicus*) of all events for the aid of later historians and scholars. The quality and depth of codices naturally varied from mission to mission, depending upon the interest shown by the compiler. Until 1969 these records remained dispersed at the various OMI mission stations across Lesotho. In that year, Fr. Albert Langevin retired from active service for reasons of health and was assigned the task of compiling the archives from each mission, as much of the older material was susceptible of destruction through decay and sheer neglect. Accordingly, records from 65 missions (both mountain and lowland) were brought to Mazenod for preservation and storage. The period covered by these materials is chiefly the later 19th and early 20th centuries. These files constitute an important source of information on the expansion of the Roman Catholic Church in Lesotho not available elsewhere; however, they are not accessible without special permission from the bishop of Lesotho or other ecclesiastical authority. A University of Ottawa microfilming project, at work in 1976 on the records of Pius XII College, recognized the value of this archive and accordingly expanded its efforts to include all Mazenod materials, thus further ensuring their preservation.

Morija Archives

Of all the archival sources in Lesotho, the Morija Archives are without a doubt the oldest and most diverse. Their origin lies with the foundation of Morija itself by Arbousset, Casalis, and Gosselin in 1833. Provision for records of the mission was made in the construction of the first church in Lesotho, with a room opening off the sanctuary allocated for this purpose. In 1858 Morija was destroyed by a Boer commando and the church leveled, wiping out a quarter-century of records. Prior to this time, however, the archives had already begun to grow beyond Morija and its activities. This is due chiefly to the special relationship between Moshoeshoe I and Eugene Casalis, who returned to Thaba Bosiu to serve as royal secretary. As a result, copies of Moshoeshoe's correspondence with various authorities of the Cape Province and the Orange Free State found their way to Morija. Casalis was succeeded in this capacity by his brother-in-law, Rev. Dyck, who had taken over the management of the archives from Rev. Arbousset. It was from Morija that G. M. Theal drew much of his primary material during the compilation of the famous *Basutoland Records*. Subsequently, the private collection of the Ellenberger papers was deposited at Morija. Rev. Ellenberger also played an important role by restoring the archives in the early 1900s and gathering together many of the early books and documents relating to PEMS activity in Lesotho. His collection of papers consists of the letters of Frederick Ellenberger of Masitise, his son Rene, and such figures of South African history as Joseph Orpen, Sekhonyana (Nehemiah) Moshoeshoe, and Azariele Sekese. In 1953, with the arrival of Rev. Albert Brutsch, the Morija Archives entered their present phase of development, and acquisition of endangered records became standard policy. Regrettably, it has not yet been possible to adequately house the collection, but various groups within Lesotho have put forward proposals for a properly constructed archival center. When this is established, the accessibility and value of the Morija collection will be more widely recognized.

Saint Augustine's Seminary and the Oblate Scholasticate

The libraries of both major ecclesiastical training centers in Roma are highly specialized in such fields as history of religion and various related areas. The collection at Saint Augustine's is especially noteworthy for its emphasis on patristics, its chief treasure being a complete set of J. P. Migne's *Patrologia Graeca* and *Patrologia Latina*. Begun in 1857 and 1844, respectively, these volumes cover the lives and writings of all major figures in early church history. The Saint Augustine's holdings are one of only three complete sets extant in southern Africa. Many original texts appeared in print in these collections for the first time, thereby stimulating a movement toward more accurate translation and exegesis. The Oblate Scholasticate, while less specialized, also has an extensive collection of highly useful materials on different areas of the religious life and ecclesiastical history.

Government Agency Libraries

Development of departmental special libraries and collections for the various Lesotho government ministries is at present in its earliest phases; however, there are several agencies which have established functioning libraries, such as the Office of Central Planning and the Ministry of Information. The process of resource consolidation and its attendant problems are best illustrated by the new library system of the Ministry of Agriculture. As part of the Lesotho Agricultural Sector Analysis (LASA), a small teaching and research library was established at ministry headquarters in Maseru in 1975–1976. Subsequently, the facility was combined with other collections of ministerial, project, consultant, and international materials in 1978, creating the first unified agricultural information system in Lesotho. Other library collections maintained by the Ministry of Agriculture include those of the Lesotho Agricultural College, the Agricultural Information Service, and the research libraries of the conservation, crops, and livestock divisions. In late 1979 a library specializing in forestry was set up under the direction of Mr. Keith Richardson, a South African attached to the Forestry and Woodlot Project, and this is expanding rapidly. A major expansion of the Research Station library as part of the Farming Systems Research Project was also begun in 1979. Future plans call for the establishment of a central index for relevant agricultural information and further development of connections with the AGRIS and CARIS data bases through the Food and Agriculture Organization of the United Nations.

Special Collections—National University Library

Certain special sections of the NUL Library deserve mention in this context although they do not themselves constitute separate libraries: the BOLESWA and government publications collections, the United Nations depository collections, and the newly established archives and archival library.

The BOLESWA collection was started in 1970 to gather "all publications, past and present, produced in or relating to Botswana, Lesotho and Swaziland." This area now contains several thousand items, including first editions of some early travelers' accounts of the region and recent reports from international aid projects presently underway in Lesotho. Closely connected with this is the collection of government publications which are received from Swaziland and Botswana in depository capacity. The NUL Library was also named the official United Nations depository for the Kingdom of Lesotho in 1968, and the present UN collection has continued to be heavily used since its restoration in 1977. The new Thomas Mofolo Library also permitted the consolidation of the library's collections of historical and archival materials into one archival center. Materials stored include subjects ranging from colonial African missionary archival documents (journals, correspondence, etc.) of the London Missionary Society to the proceedings of the Lesotho National Assembly and legislative publications of areas as disparate as Northern Rhodesia/Zambia, the Transkei, and the original Cape Colony. An archives library has also been established and at present numbers over 700 volumes, many of them rare editions of Africana relating to both Lesotho and southern Africa in general. The chief treasure of the Mofolo Archives is its collection of the *Journal des missions evangeliques*, official publication of the Paris Evangelical Missionary Society. This set, the only one available for research use in southern Africa, contains much primary historical material not only on Lesotho but on the 19th-century mission movement worldwide. Originally, most of the correspondence of such pioneer mission workers as Casalis and Dyck was first issued through this journal, and the time span covered (1826–1952) provides a clear picture of the growth and diversification of mission activities in the southern African region.

The picture of the library world of Lesotho is thus one of constant change and improvement, supported by a tradition of literacy, a lively popular literature, and an energetic professional association. While problems such as supplying books to rural school libraries, public ignorance of librarianship as a distinct profession, and shortages of trained personnel remain, stable foundations for development have been laid, and the future information needs generated by the economic and cultural development of Lesotho will be adequately served.

REFERENCES

1. Ambrose, *Guide to Lesotho*, pp. 145–148.
2. Ellenberger, *A Century of Mission Work,* p. 22.
3. Schmöller, "The Press at Morija," p. 6.
4. Ref. *2*, pp. 92–96.
5. Ref. *3*, p. 10.
6. J. Walton, *Old Maseru*, passim.
7. *Laws of Lesotho*, Vol. 12, pp. 509–514.
8. Minutes of the meeting on May 18, 1978, p. 3.
9. Lesotho National Commission for UNESCO, *Books in National Development*, passim.

BIBLIOGRAPHY

Act 42, 1967 (Archives Act), in *Laws of Lesotho*, Vol. 12, pp. 509–514.

Ambrose, David, *The Guide to Lesotho*, 2nd ed., Winchester Press, Johannesburg, 1976.

Basutoland, 1965, Government Printer, Maseru, 1965.

Benge, Ronald A., *Report on a Visit to Botswana, Lesotho, and Swaziland 13 January–3 February, 1976*, n.p., n.d.

Catalogue of the Basutoland Public Library, Maseru, 1907, Sesuto Book Depot, Morija, 1907.

The Catholic Church in Lesotho at the Hour of Independence, Lesotho Catholic Information Bureau, Maseru, 1966.

Ellenberger, Victor, *A Century of Mission Work in Basutoland, 1833–1933*, Sesuto Book Depot, Morija, 1938.

Ellenberger, Victor, *Landmarks in the Story of the French Protestant Church in Basutoland . . . 1833–1933*, Sesuto Book Depot, Morija, 1933.

Ferragne, Marcel, *A Catalogue of 1,000 Sesotho Books . . .* , Made on the Occasion of the Sesotho Book Exhibition held in Maseru, Lesotho, 11–13 March, 1965, Social Centre, Roma, 1965.

Haliburton, Gordon, *A Historical Dictionary of Lesotho*, Scarecrow Press, Metuchen, N.J., 1977.

Kingdom of Lesotho, *Lesotho Five-Year Development Plan, 1967–1972*, Government Printer, Maseru, 1967.

Kingdom of Lesotho, *Second Five-Year Development Plan, 1975/76–1979/80*, Government Printer, Maseru, 1975.

Legal Notice, No. 28, 1972 (Archives Regulations), in *Laws of Lesotho*, 1972.

Lesotho, Ministry of Education and Culture, *Annual Report*, Government Printer, Maseru, 1966–1973.

Lesotho, Ministry of Information, Maseru, 1966–1972.

Lesotho Library Association, *Chairperson's Report, 1st Annual Meeting*, National Teacher Training College, Maseru, June 3, 1979.

Lesotho National Commission for UNESCO, *Books in National Development*, The Commission, Mazenod/Morija, 1976.

Mohapeloa, J. M., *Government by Proxy*, Sesuto Book Depot, Morija, 1971.

Morija: 30 Years of Service and 30 Languages, 1920–1950, Morija Printing Works, Morija, 1950.

Schmöller, Hans, "The Press at Morija, Basutoland," *South African Lib.*, **25**, 5–11 (1957).

Tylden, G., *Early Days in Maseru*, n.p., Maseru, 1944.

Tylden, G., *The Rise of the Basuto*, Juta, Capetown, 1950.

University of Basutoland, Bechuanaland Protectorate, and Swaziland (UBBS), *Calendar*, 1965.

University of Botswana, Lesotho, and Swaziland, *Official Calendar*, 1967–1975.

University College of Swaziland, *Proceedings of the Conference of BLS University Librarians, Manzini, Swaziland, 22–23 November, 1977.*

Walton, Constance, *Catalogue of the Basutoland Government Archives*, Secretariat, Maseru, n.d.

Walton, James, *Old Maseru*, Morija Printing Works, Morija, 1958.

Witherell, Julian, *Africana Acquisitions: Report of a Publication Survey Trip to Nigeria, Southern Africa and Europe, 1972*, Library of Congress, Washington, D.C., 1973.

R. B. RIDINGER

McKENNA, F. E.

Born in Globe, Arizona, on July 29, 1921, Francis Eugene McKenna grew up in Oakland, California. With the Oakland High School's Symphony Orchestra, McKenna played the violin and was the principal viola performer. In June 1937 he graduated valedictorian of his high school class with awards in science and music as well as the highest scholastic average.

He received a B.S. degree in chemistry from the University of California at Berkeley in 1941 and a Ph.D. in physical chemistry from the University of Washington in 1944. McKenna was 22 years old when he obtained his Ph.D. degree and, at the time, was the youngest person to earn a doctorate in the western states.

His early scientific career included appointments to the research staff of the Manhattan Project and as a research supervisor at the Carbide and Carbon Chemical Corporation. In 1946 McKenna was awarded a postdoctoral research fellowship at the University of Chicago's Institute for Nuclear Studies. At the conclusion of these studies in 1948, he was appointed senior research chemist at the Air Reduc-

Francis E. McKenna (Photo courtesy of Mrs. Vivian D. Hewitt, Librarian, Carnegie Endowment for International Peace).

tion Company, a position he occupied until 1953.

His research interests were in cryoscopy, fluorine and fluorocarbons, physical properties of gases, and chemical reactions in the solid-state phase. His publications include three chapters—"Fluorine and Fluorocarbons"; "Sulfur, Selenium, and Tellurim"; and "Gas Analysis"—in *Analytical Chemistry of the Manhattan Projects* (McGraw-Hill, New York, 1950), three articles in *Nucleonics*, and four articles in the *Journal of the American Chemical Society.*

Dr. McKenna's career interests and activities changed radically in 1953 when he was named senior information specialist at the Air Reduction Company with the specific tasks of organizing information services and the library for the company. Long active in the American Chemical Society, the American Society for Metals, the Electrochemical Society, and many others, McKenna joined the New York Chapter of the Special Libraries Association (SLA) in 1953 and became an active member in the chapters in New York and New Jersey, as well as at the national level. He was elected vice-president of the Special Libraries Association in 1965 and served as president in 1966.

In 1967 McKenna was named editor of *Special Libraries*, the journal of the Special Libraries Association, and manager of the association's Publications Department. He was appointed executive director of the association in 1970. In his new career in librarianship, he continued to write and to receive awards for his endeavors for the SLA and its membership, and for all librarians. He was honored in 1976 when he received the Centennial Citation of the American Library Association, and in 1977 the Special Libraries Association presented him with a Special Citation.

He was especially active in issues surrounding copyright, and after the passage of the new Copyright Law in 1976, he served as chairman of the Copyright Committee of the Council of National Library Associations. McKenna also made many contributions in the area of international library relations.

Francis ("Frank") McKenna was inducted into the Hall of Fame of the Special Library Association in 1979, and the first worldwide conference on special libraries, the 70th Annual Conference of the Special Libraries Association (Honolulu, Hawaii, 1979), was dedicated to his memory.

McKenna's influence on the new copyright law, his interest in and involvement with librarianship on an international level, and his role in propelling the Special Libraries Association to national and international importance, in terms of membership and influence, assure him of an important place in the history of librarianship. Frank McKenna died in his home in New York City on November 10, 1978. He was 57 years old.

In her eulogy of McKenna on November 16, 1978, in Saint Joseph's Church in New York, Mrs. Vivian D. Hewitt, president of the Special Libraries Association, spoke of him as follows:

> Professionally, so many of us have never failed to benefit from his wisdom, his perceptive observations, his logical, deductive mind [and his] flawless memory for detail and keen ability to detect pitfalls to be avoided. His passing is a tragic loss to the library community, special libraries and librarianship nationally and internationally.

JAMES M. MATARAZZO

MOSLEM LIBRARIES (MEDIEVAL)

General

The history of Moslem libraries in the millennium after the Flight is more difficult to reconstruct than that of libraries of Western Europe in the same period (*1*). The major obstacle is the absence of great national and special libraries, comparable to those in Western Europe and North America in terms of current support.

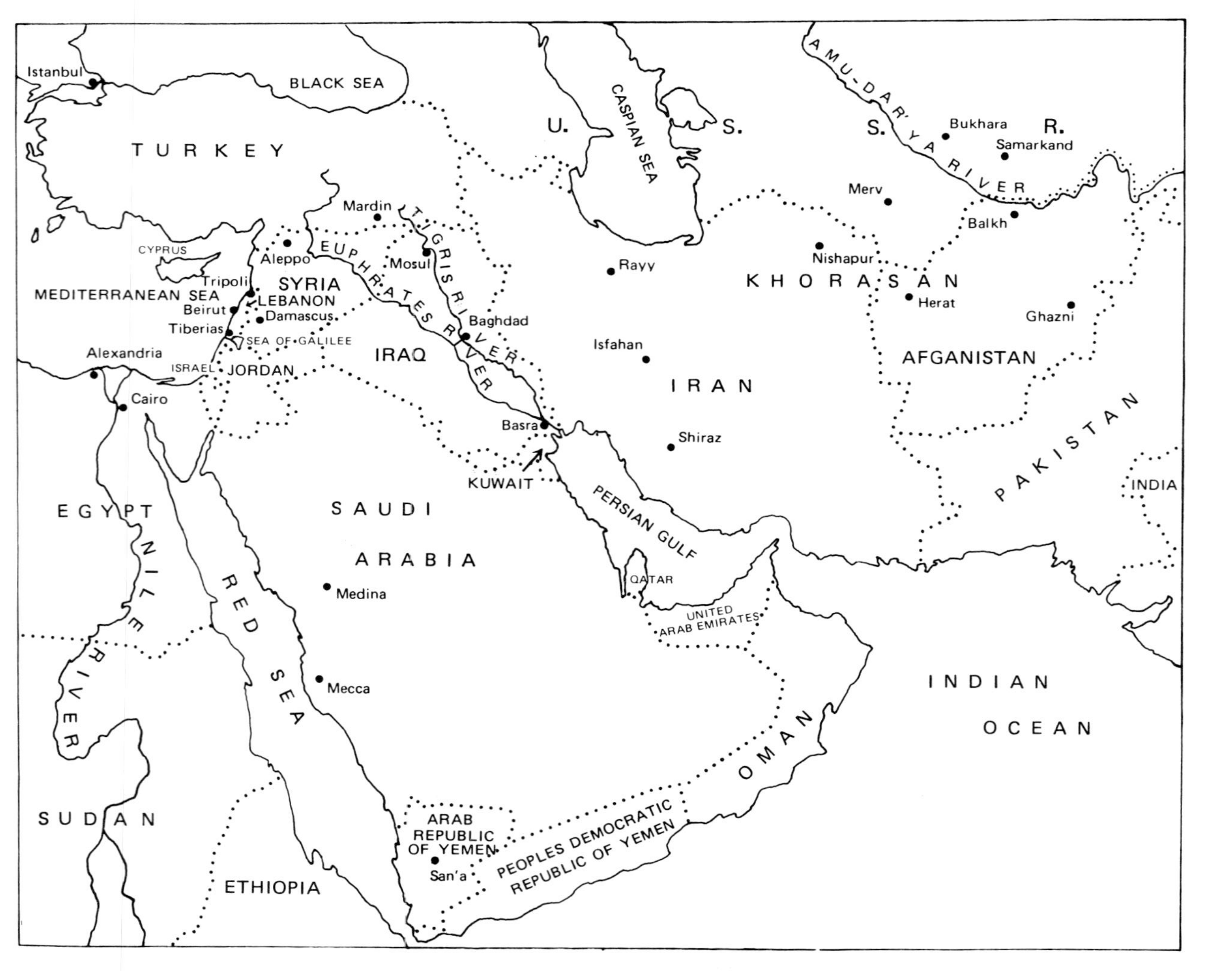

FIGURE 1. *East of the Mediterranean Sea: places where libraries mentioned in the text were located.*

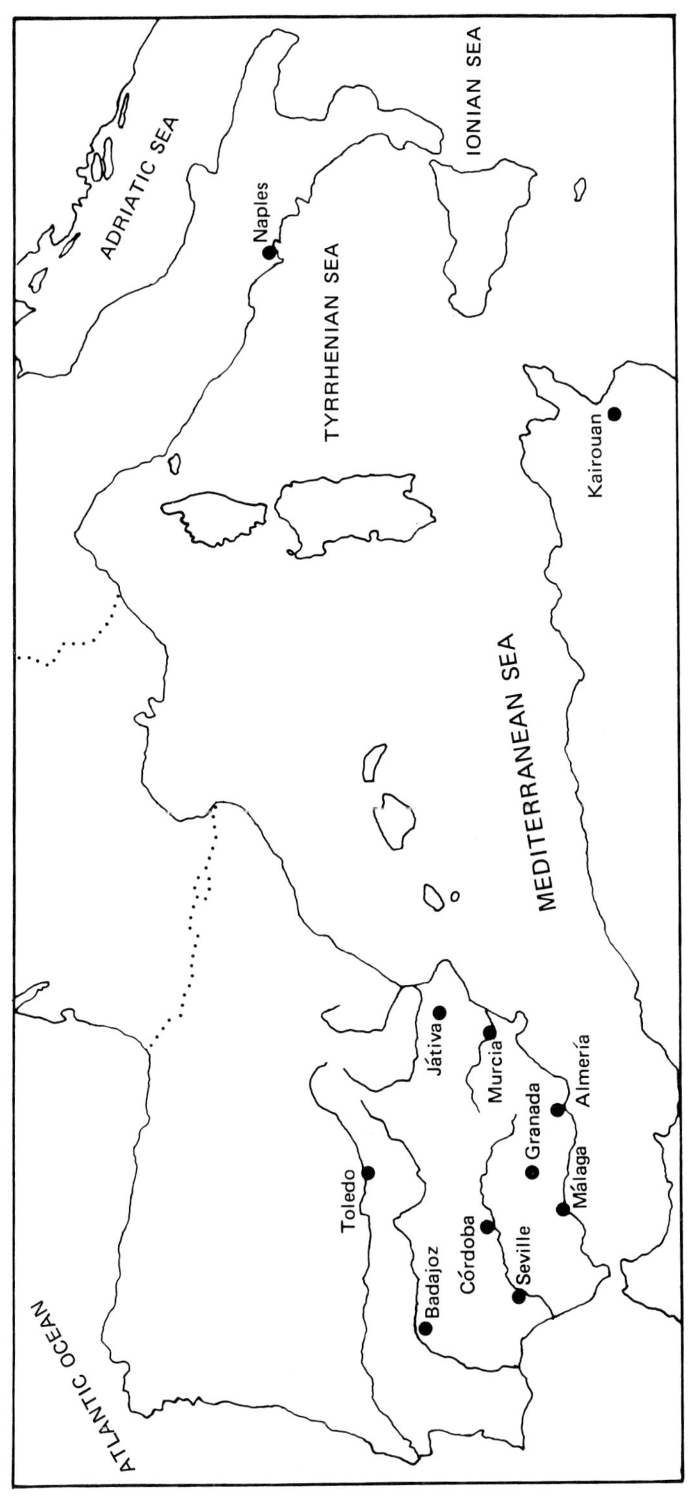

FIGURE 2. *Western Mediterranean area: locations of libraries mentioned in the text.*

There are today noble collections in Istanbul, Cairo, Damascus, and elsewhere in the Moslem world, and much could be learned from them about the history of books and libraries if bibliographic scholarship in those jurisdictions had the same funding that is provided even the smaller countries of Western Europe. Equally as grave an obstacle to research in the history of Islamic books and libraries is the absence in Moslem countries of collectors and antiquarian booksellers remotely resembling those in Western Europe and North America. Just as in Western Europe, tens, probably hundreds of thousands of books were destroyed or dispersed by invasions and political upheavals; and, while scholars in both areas must work from fragments of a once great corpus of medieval books, the orientalist has at this time few of the reference materials and facilities for research that are available to the student of Occidental books and libraries. Since some of the places where medieval Moslem libraries were located are today obscure and not familiar to many readers, maps are provided for the general area.

For centuries the Arabs had been virtually illiterate nomads. Their script, developed from the old Semitic consonantal alphabet possibly as early as the third century, does not appear until the seventh century in Arabic papyri from Egypt in the period of the conquest. In the next 200 years the Arab conquerors of the vast area between India and Andalucia gradually absorbed many elements in the Greco-Oriental, Persian, Syriac, and other cultures, and put significant parts of these literatures into books in their new script. In Persia in particular, the Arabs found a rich corpus of Greek philosophic and scientific thought, much of it translated by Hellenized Syrians in the last century of the Sassanids (*2*). There were always copies of the Koran, and four basic ones existed in the time of Othman, the third Caliph. But only individual books, not libraries, existed in the early Arab imperium (*3*).

The first surviving scraps of the Koran are on papyrus, but most other early Arabic documents are on parchment. Basic for the development of the great collections in later centuries was the access to paper produced in large quantities. Until the ninth century papermaking existed outside China only in Samarkand or its vicinity; the technique probably spread to Damascus, Tiberias, Tripoli, and Egypt in the 10th century, and to Spain perhaps only in the 11th century. But wherever paper was available, more books could be produced than ever before on any other writing surface. Books proliferated everywhere as soon as paper was available.

With the general recognition of Arabic as the official idiom of administrations from India to Spain by the early eighth century, a significant literature in this language developed. A large proportion was in translation from Greek texts, much of it by non-Arabs, or even non-Moslems such as Nestorians, Jacobites, Jews, and Copts. Thus Jabir ibn Hayyan, whose name was associated with *Alchemy* (*4*), was a Sabaean; and Ibn al-Muqaffa, translator of the tales of Bidpai, a Persian (*5*). Within two centuries after the Flight, an impressive corpus of ancient science was available in Arabic, including the Hippocratic writings, Galen, Dioscurides, and, more important, Plato and Aristotle. The great mathematicians, Euclid, Archimedes, Apollonias of Perga, and Ptolemy, became available in Arabic, often through Syriac versions (*6*). Al-Kindi, the only bonafide Arab philosopher of the early period, assembled Greek books in his field and made a compendium. The work of the Persian al-Razi (Rhazes, Rasis, ca. 860–ca. 925), in medicine, was used by Europeans until the 16th century and was among the first scientific books to be printed. The same applies to astronomers and mathematicians such as Abu

Masar (Albumasar, d. 886); al-Farghani (Alfraganus, d. 861); al-Khwarizmi (d. ca. 850, from whom we have *algorism*); and Banu Musa (the three brothers), familiar names to incunabulists. The latter were distinguished as patrons of translators and as bibliophiles. Greek texts were translated and used, but the humanism of classical antiquity was gradually engulfed in Islamic conservatism, of which the theology of al-Ashari (873–935) is a benchmark.

The study of Arab libraries is complicated not only by the lack of strong modern bibliographic scholarship but also by vague, often unreliable and contradictory contemporary sources (in common with classical antiquity and the early European Middle Ages) and by the peculiar position of private and public libraries in Arab jurisdictions. Many were eleemosynary, providing grants—including material for making copies (one modern U.S. library provides unlimited access to electrostatic machines to its grantees)—and often were set up as foundations (*waqf*) (*7*). The *madrasa*, basically a theological school but also concerned with political matters when religion impended on public affairs, had prototypes before we hear of the Sadiriyya, founded 1001 in Damascus. There were equivalents in Baghdad, Nishapur, Balkh, Mosul, Herat, and elsewhere, and libraries were generally associated with them. There were some 150 in Damascus and at least half that many in Cairo (*8*). Related to the traditional madrasa collections were those of the *ribat*, monastic establishments with military responsibilities in addition, many in Iraq (*9*).

By the early 11th century libraries of these various types flourished. We have some notion about their physical appearance from the Hariri-Shefer in the Bibliothèque Nationale, in which there is an illustration of the library of Hulwan, an otherwise unknown place (*10*). With the availability of paper, copies of manuscipts increased in almost geometrical proportions, and there are reports of collections of more than 10,000 (whether titles, volumes, or pieces, we do not know) (*11*). The records are as ambiguous as those on which we must depend for Greco-Roman antiquity. But some authority must be given to a scholar such as the geographer Yaqut al-Hamawi, who had access to 10 libraries in Merv (modern Mary), of which one held 12,000 volumes, and who said that he could borrow some 200 whenever there.

The book trade was well developed in larger centers, and Baghdad is said to have had up to 100 dealers at one time. Just as in medieval Europe they were concentrated in a single quarter of a city. Manuscripts were rented out for copying, and, most important, book lists were prepared; for example, the *Fihrist* of Ibn al-Nadim (d. ca. 915) (*12*). Copyists thrived in Islamic countries into the 20th century, when typographic printing finally took firm hold; and until quite recently manuscript books in Arabic, Persian, and Turkish were as common in the bookstalls of major cities as letterpress products. There was a strongly developed sense of textual accuracy, and autographs and books copied under authorial supervision were held in esteem (*13*). Censorship played as fateful a roll as ever in the Occident under the influence of religious orthodoxy, and there are the sad records of the confiscation of al-Kindi's library in the reign of Caliph al-Mutawakkil (847–861) and that of the materialistic philosopher Ibn Masarra in Spain a little later. Political and religious changes were as serious as the effects of the Protestant reformation and Roman counterreformation in Europe, thus the antagonism of Shiite and Sunnite, the fall of the Fatimids in Egypt and of the Omayyads in Spain, and the Reconquista. Depredations of the Mongols were probably more serious than Viking raids in Europe. And indifference and ignorance, which were often characteristic of the decadent monastic life in Europe in the latter Middle Ages, had their parallels beyond the Bosporus.

The Near East before the Mongol Invasion (1258)

The caliphate of Harun al-Rashid (786–809), most famous of the Abbasid rulers, was marked by flourishing bibliophily. The book-loving Persian Barmecide family helped Harun to power (but fell into his disfavor in 798), and Yahya, best-known member of the clan, is said to have had a collection with at least three manuscripts of each text. The historian Omar al-Waqidi (736–811) is alleged to have owned 20 camel loads of books (*14*). But it was Harun's son, al-Mamun (813–833), who was the real founder of the Abbasid library of Baghdad. He had in his entourage scientific writers and translators of the stature of Ayyub al-Ruhawi (Job of Edessa, ca. 760–845), a Nestorian Syrian; Hunayn ibn Ishaq (809–877), also a Syrian; and al-Razi (supra). al-Mamun's *khizanat al-hikma* ("treasury of wisdom") was established at the beginning of his reign. He brought in substantial collections from places such as Khorasan (100 camel loads, by report) and Ancyra; and while he assembled a great collection, it is hard to accept the figure of a million pieces (*15*). Little is known about the contents or what survived after the Mongol loot of Baghdad in 1258, but we do know that al-Khwarizmi (supra) used the collection (*16*).

In the 11th century there were other bibliophilic caliphs. The Nizamiyya madrasa was founded in 1064 with a significant library in the reign of al-Qaim (1031–1075), heavily used for the next two centuries. The last great library to be established in Baghdad was for the Mustansiriyah madrasa (1223) in the caliphate of al-Mustansir (1226–1242), and it seems to have survived, at least in part, the Mongol sack 25 years after its founding. There is a record of 36 libraries in Baghdad before 1258, including that of the last Abbasid vizier, al-Alqami (d. 1258), which is said to have contained 10,000 volumes. Some of the libraries set up as foundations (*waqf*) may have survived after 1258 (*17*).

There were numerous private collectors, some already noted. Classic in tradition was al-Jahiz (*18*), alleged to have died (869) from having been beaten with his own books. The *cadi* ("judge") Ismail ibn Ishaq (d. 895) was never seen without a book. The vizier al-Fath ibn Khaqan (murdered 861) served under Caliph al-Mutawakkil, and his library is said to have been supported by Ali ibn Yahya (d. 888), astronomer, bibliophile, and patron of scholars (*19*). The collection was in a mansion in Samarra, just north of Baghdad and the Abbasid residence (836–892). There were grants for scholars, and the noted astronomer Abu Masar (supra) was so enthralled by the collection that he could hardly continue his pilgrimage to Mecca. Other Abbasid viziers and scholars had important and, presumably, practical working collections. The historian and poet al-Suli (d. 939) recorded valuable data on libraries he used, based on written sources, not oral tradition (*20*). Most of the scholars' libraries of which we have records were comparable in size and extent with those of many scholar–bibliophiles in our time. The theologian al-Bargani (d. 1053) had 63 hampers and two baskets filled with books. The scientist al-Qazwini (d. 1095) had to load 10 camels with his books. The historian Ghars al-Nima (d.

1087) owned 400 or 1,000 volumes (different sources), which he left as a *waqf* (*21*). The Christian physician Ibn Tilmidh (d. 1165) had 12 camel loads of books. The statistical definitions of modern library holdings are not really improvements on the terms *hampers*, *baskets*, and *camel loads*.

Libraries, public and private, flourished under the Hamdanids in Syria, the Samanids in Bukhara, and the Buwayhids (vice, Buyids) in Shiraz. The absence of catalogs and other substantive information precludes assessment of the quality of these libraries, but it is pertinent to quote Avicenna (Ali ibn Sina, 980–1037), whose *Canon medicinae* was basic for Europeans into the 16th century. Barely 18 years old, he was summoned by Sultan Nuh ibn Mansur to Bukhara, where he used the library effectively and left his impressions:

> One room was allotted to works on Arabic philology and poetry, another to jurisprudence. . . . I inspected the catalogue of ancient Greek authors. . . . I saw in this collection books of which few people have heard even the names and which I myself have never seen either before or since (*22*).

The Buwayhid ruler, Adud al-Daula (d. 982), had a library in his compound, of which there is a detailed account, even with a description of the cabinets and their decoration (*23*). Another prince of the house, Majd al-Daula, was both bibliophile and biblioclast: He is recorded as a zealous reader and copyist, but in the persecution of the Mutazilites he burned many of their books and confiscated others. Muizz al-Daula and his minister, Abd al-Aziz Ibn Hajib al-Numan, had well-known libraries, the latter distinguished for manuscripts with authorial notes (*24*). Baha al-Daula was the master of a library in Shiraz with a 30-volume Koran by the noted calligraphers Ibn Muqla and Ibn al-Bawwab (*25*). The library of the Buwayhid vizier Ibn Shah Mardan in Basra was destroyed by Bedouins in 1090, and that of another Buwayhid vizier, Sahib Ismail Ibn Abhad (d. 995) in Rayy, was burned in 1029. Of the latter there was a 10-volume catalog, and the theological books alone are reported to have amounted to 400 camel loads, although the figure of 114,000 volumes for the entire collection is probably exaggerated (*26*). A later Buwayhid vizier in Baghdad, Sabur ibn Ardashir (d. 1025), had a collection of 10,000 volumes (holdings increased tenfold in some sources) in 991–992, but the Seljuk Turks destroyed much of it in 1058–1059 (*27*). Some of it was rescued by the Seljuk vizier Amid al-Mulk al-Kunduri (d. ca. 1060) for his personal collection. Sabur's library was associated with an academy; it was serviced by important personalities and was used by many other writers and scholars.

Jafar ibn Muhammad (d. 935), a Hamdanid prince, established an academy (*dar al-ilm*) with a substantial library in Mosul, and other members of the dynasty did the same in Tripoli and Aleppo (allegedly with 25,000 volumes, destroyed in 1190 by the crusaders). The vast majority of the crusaders were neither gentle nor intellectual, but at least there were some bookish clergymen among them, and the tradition that they destroyed 3 million books, including 50,000 Korans and 80,000 commentaries, must be viewed with doubt (*28*). In Mardin, Jusam al-Din founded a mosque and a madrasa with a library in the 12th century. Far to the east in Iran there was a library in Ghazni (south of Kabul), where there were remnants of the library that had existed in Rayy as well as of the one founded by the Buwayhid Ala al-Daula in Isfahan after 1033. The Ghazni library was burned in 1155, 2 years after Nishapur, the major center of learning in northern Iran, lost its library when the Ghuzz sacked the city.

In Merv, Yaqut al-Hamawi (supra) was especially gratified by the collection of 12,000 volumes in the Aziziyya, founded by a favorite of the Sultan Sanjar in the 12th century; the Nizamiyya, founded by the Seljuk vizier, Nizam al-Mulk; and the Kamiliyya in the main mosque. Yaqut said that he prowled the libraries of Merv "with the avidity of a glutton" until he had to flee before the Mongols (*29*). The Ayyubids in Syria and Egypt produced no bibliophilic rulers, but there were private collectors. Ibn Matran (d. 1191), personal physician of Salah al-Din (Saladin), had three copyists, and 3,000 of his books were sold after his death. Some were acquired by the Jewish physician Imran (d. 1259) in Damascus (*30*). There is a record of the auction of the collection of Abul-Izz in Palestine from 1225 (*31*). In Aleppo, where the Hamdanids were establishing libraries as early as the 10th century, there was a strong library in the madrasa al-Nuriyya, possibly looted with Saladin's approval. Bibliophilic traditions persisted in Aleppo into the 13th century. At that time Aleppo had two major collectors, the cadi Ibn Saddad (d. 1234), founder of several madrasas and libraries; and the vizier al-Qifti (known also as Cadi Akram, 1172–1248), who commissioned translations from Greek and whose books survived in part in Damascus and later in Baghdad (*32*). There is also evidence of scholarly collections in Mosul and northern Mesopotamia (*33*).

Egypt

The Shiite Fatimid dynasty in Egypt (969–1171) inherited what was once the major center of Hellenistic culture (*34*), but little remained when al-Aziz (caliph, 975–996) established his "house of learning" with subsidies for students (in Cairo, which the Arabs preferred to the Greco-Roman capital in Alexandria) (*35*). The collection may have included as many as 100,000 volumes (the high figure of 600,000 is most questionable), arranged in classified order. The some 2,400 handsomely illuminated Korans were in a separate section. In 1004 much of this collection went into the "house of scholarship" set up by Caliph al-Hakim, and the dedication has been recorded (*36*). al-Hakim made strong efforts to enrich the collections and commissioned agents in many parts of the Moslem world to acquire manuscripts. The annual appropriation in 1012–1013 is recorded as 257 dinars. In 1068 Vizier Abul-Faraj Muhammad ibn Jafar al-Maghribi looted 25 camel loads of books to pay off his recruits. The Turkish guards virtually completed the plunder; fine bindings were sold for shoe leather, and text pages were piled in a dump (*37*). Undaunted by this disaster, the Fatimid rulers again began to collect books. When Saladin took Cairo in 1171, he found a collection said to contain 120,000 volumes, which he gave to his chancellor, al-Qadi al-Fadil Abd al-Rahman ibn Ali.

There are records of several private libraries in the Fatimid period. A prince of the ruling house, Mahmud al-Daula al-Mubassir ibn Fatik, was an enthusiast for ancient science and pulled together a large collection, described in broad terms in Ibn Abi Usaybia's history of Greek and Arabic medicine (*38*). After his death, his wife—neglected for books like the consort of many another bibliophile—dumped the collection in the large water basin with which every mansion in Cairo was equipped. They were in gravely damaged condition when Shaikh Sadid al-Din, a Cairo logician, saw them (*39*). Another private collection recorded by Ibn Abi Usaybia belonged to al-Muarrif, a poet and physician, who wrote a commentary on Aristotle in 1139. It is said to have contained "many thousands" of books in all fields, virtually all with learned scholia (*39*).

During the Fatimid period there was a special and mutually profitable symbiosis between Jews and Moslems, and we hear of several important private collections whose masters were Jews. Although they surely owned Hebrew books, the collections must also be considered as Arabic libraries. An early and noteworthy collection was formed by Yakub ibn Yusuf Ibn Qillis, a financial genius from Baghdad who came to Egypt by way of Syria, became a vizier, and amassed a great fortune in Cairo. He established an academy with a library and employed many copyists, reportedly spending a thousand gold dinars monthly for copyists and binders (*40*). Ephraim, a Jewish physician in Cairo and pupil of the noted Arab doctor Ali ibn Ridwan, owned some 20,000 volumes, the harvest of a life of collecting in the latter part of the 11th century (*41*).

The seven centuries in which the Mamelukes dominated Egypt saw a continuing tradition of book collecting. The *imam* ("spiritual leader") Nur al-din Ali ibn Jabir (d. 1325) owned 6,000 volumes (*42*), and there is the catalog of the collection of the scholar Abd al-Rahim al-Isnawi (1305–1372) (*43*). Various other private collections are known, and 18 volumes from the library of the Mameluke Emir Yashbak (d. 1450) survive in the Topkapi Saray in Istanbul. There were even more madrasa libraries, of which Joseph von Hammer-Purgstall has identified 11 founded from 1263 to 1407 (*44*). Also under the Mamelukes, some of the earliest surviving Arabic manuscripts came to the Occident, mainly Christian and of Coptic provenance. The oldest are in the Vatican, probably sent to Rome about 1441 after the Council of Constance (*45*). There is still a substantial corpus of material of this type in Egypt, in the Coptic Patriarchate in Alexandria, churches, and convents (*46*). The unstable political history of Egypt in the next 600 years did not contribute to the preservation of once great book collections or of individual manuscripts. The centuries of Ottoman influence resulted in the shipment of many books to Istanbul (some resulting in broken sets) by pashas more greedy than bibliophilic; and the last two centuries of Occidental penetration have resulted in the relocation of many important manuscripts in major libraries of the Germanies, France, Britain, and North America. Egypt, perhaps more than any other part of the old Ottoman Empire or points east, has contributed to the rich collections of Arabic manuscripts in libraries from Leningrad to California.

In what is now Saudi Arabia, birthplace of Islam, there was a cultural center in Medina with a library noted for its excellence by Ibn Jubair toward the end of the 12th century. It was probably destroyed by a fire in the main mosque in 1491. Mecca was weaker in book collections, and the deluxe Korans there seem to have been shipped off, in part, to Istanbul during World War I. The Yemeni had close cultural connections with Egypt in the Fatimid and subsequent periods, and books in Cairo must have been copied for Ishmaelite scholars in San'a. About 1300 the library of Malik Muayyad Dawud in San'a was supposed to have contained 100,000 volumes (*47*). Count Landberg and others fetched significant quantities of books from the Yemeni which are now in Munich, Vienna, and New Haven.

Spain, the Maghreb, and Italy

The Vandals, the Visigoths, and other Germanic peoples were on a relatively high cultural level and had absorbed much from Roman and Christian tradition; but, like some other Germanic groups in the migrations, they were too weak numerically to establish an enduring political and cultural hegemony in the Peninsula and North Africa. When the Arabs (and Arabized North Africans) crossed the Straits in 711, it was fairly easy for them to establish a cultural tradition supported by strong libraries at their capital at Córdoba and elsewhere (in all, there may have been 70 libraries in the important cities of Arabic Spain) (*48*). The beginning of the library of the Omayyad rulers at Córdoba goes back to Caliph Muhammad, but the real founder was al-Hakim II (caliph, 961–976), who spent large sums to assemble a collection which was said to hold 400,000 volumes. It was supervised by a eunuch named Talidh, had a catalog in 44 parts, and was supported by a shop with copyists, binders, and illuminators. It is curious that from all this Oriental bibliological splendor there survives only a calendar of Christian feast days given to al-Hakim by Spanish bishops. Even before the disappearance of the dynasty in 1031 the great library suffered. Under the vizier of al-Hakim's successor three *ulema* ("theologians") segregated materialistic and philosophical works for burning, and part of the rest was sold; the palace (Merwan), where the collection was housed, was plundered by Berbers in the beginning of the 11th century; and the city burned in 1013.

Córdoba had a thriving book trade, and this was surely the source of various private libraries of which there is a record (*49*). The productivity of the paper mills in Játiva and Toledo provided material for the busy scriptoria of Córdoba, one of which was said to have kept 170 women busy in copying Korans in Kufic script (*50*). We know of Abu al-Mutrif (d. 1011), a jurist in Córdoba, who lent nothing but employed six copyists to transcribe manuscripts as gifts. After his death the auction of the collection ran over a whole year (*51*). What we don't know about private libraries in Moslem Spain is staggering, but it must be assumed that scholars (many Jews) had personal libraries. There is the great surgeon Abul-Qasim (Albucasis, d. ca. 1013) in the early period. The Jew Hasdai ibn Shaprut, personal physician of al-Hakam II, translated (with the help of one Nicholas, an Orthodox monk) a Dioscurides sent by Constantine VII to the Caliph Abd-al-Rahman III (*52*). Ibn Shaprut was in touch with Johannes of Gorze (a Lotharingian monastery), who had already fetched Greek books to Lorraine from Calabria and who, in 955, brought back a "horse-load" of books to Gorze from Córdoba. Shaprut and his coreligionist Ibn Negdela, a leader of the Jewish community in Granada, are known as bibliophiles and benefactors of the Talmudic academies in Córdoba and Málaga (*53*). An antagonist of Ibn Negdela was the vizier of Almería, Ibn Abbas, himself a collector of distinction. The Spanish Jew Salomon ben Yehuda ibn Gabirol (Avicebron or Avencebrol, 1021–1058 or 1070) was a major personality in the transmission of Islamic philosophy to the Occident and surely a book collector.

The fall of the Omayyads in Spain was followed by a succession of smaller jurisdictions (*reynos de taifa*) with major seats in Badajoz, Toledo, Almería, Murcia, and Seville (*54*). Some of the remnants of the Omayyad library in Córdoba were supposed to have found a home in Toledo, also a leading center of transmissions of Moslem learning to Christendom. Several Englishmen, notably Adelhard of Bath and cousin of Henry I, were among these translators (*55*). Some substantial private libraries may have been at their disposal; for example, that of the vizier Abu Jafar ibn Abbas in Almería, said to have contained 400,000 volumes (*56*).

Despite the religious puritanism of the Almoravids and the succeeding Almohads, these Berber dynasties were not unfavorably disposed to learning and libraries. Ibn al-Jazzar was reported to have owned 25 metric hundredweights of medical books in Kairouan, the sacred city in Tunis (*57*). The Almohad rulers were quite generous to scholars of the stature of Ibn Zuhr (Avenzoar), Ibn Tufayl (d. 1185), and Ibn Rushd (Averroes, 1126–1188). The founder of the Hafsid dynasty in Tunis, Abu Zakariyya I (d. 1249), is said to have owned a collection of 36,000 volumes which lasted into the 14th century, when the scholar Ibn Khaldun went there because of the large book collections (*58*). There were numerous mosques and madrasas known to have contained book collections (*59*).

In Sicily and southern Italy there must have been book collections at the disposal of the numerous translators, but we have few specifics about any libraries or scriptoria. Emperor Frederick II collected Arabic manuscripts at the University of Naples (founded 1224), and he and other Norman and Hohenstaufen rulers encouraged translators such as Michael Scot, Theodore of Antioch, and Admiral Eugenio, who translated Ptolemy's work on optics from Arabic in 1154. Arabic scholars were also welcome here.

The significance of the work of the translators belongs to general cultural history, but they could not have functioned without book collections. By the 13th century the Hippocratic corpus, Galen, and the *Canon of Medicine* by Ibn Sina (Avicenna) were available in Latin; and these texts and other products of the translators were used in Europe into the incunabula period. The best-known translator was Gerard of Cremona (1114–1187), who worked mainly in Toledo and translated over 70 scientific books (*60*). Plato of Tivoli was almost as productive. Gerard was deeply concerned with Aristotle, and it is significant that Averroes and Ibn Tufayl were his contemporaries (*61*). So too was the famous Cordoban Jew Moses ben Maimon (Maimonides, 1135–1204). The profound knowledge of Aristotelianism of these three was to have a decisive effect on Christian philosophy.

It is hazardous to set firm dates for any period in history, and the end of the Middle Ages is an egregious example. We can only go by such dates as thc fall of Constantinople or the completion of the Reconquista at Granada in 1492, for the end of the Byzantine and Moslem Middle Ages, respectively, or at least the beginning of the end. The book burnings, perhaps 80,000 volumes on the Plaza de Bibarrambla in Granada (*62*), were surely the best symbols of the end of the rich Moslem tradition in the Peninsula. With Osmanli power firm in Istanbul, bibliophilic (and often simply acquisitive) pashas in all parts of the far-flung empire began to send books to the metropolis, a large proportion of which survive (*63*). While peace has never come to Islamic countries even for the relatively short periods that Western Europeans have known the area, the violence of the Mongol invasions, internecine war, and sectarian strife has not been repeated on such a large scale in the last five centuries. Thus many manuscript books surviving today in the libraries of the Maghreb, Cairo, Istanbul, Damascus, Beirut, Baghdad, Isfahan, and other centers of Islamic culture have had a longer life than the vast bulk of earlier books written in Arabic script. As Ataturk was quoted by an intimate, the real end of the Islamic

Middle Ages came only in the early 20th century with the firm domination of typographic printing.

REFERENCES AND NOTES

1. The best general work is Kurt Holter, "Der Islam," in *Handbuch der Bibliothekswissenschaft* (Georg Leyh, ed., 2nd ed., Otto Harrassowitz, Wiesbaden, 1955, Vol. 3, pp. 188–242). See also Ruth Stellhorn Mackensen, series of seven articles in *Am. J. Semitic Languages Literatures* (**51–54,** 1935–1937), and "Four Great Libraries of Medieval Baghdad" (*Lib. Q.*, **2,** 279–299, 1932). S. K. Padover, "Muslim Libraries" (in *The Medieval Library*, James Westfall Thompson, ed., University of Chicago Press, Chicago, 1939, pp. 347–372) is a less extensive account than Holter's. For other basic literature, see Holter, pp. 188–190, and his bibliographic footnotes.
2. The importance of the book in Sassanid culture is illustrated by the numerous Middle Persian papyri found in Egypt from the bare decade of Sassanid hegemony there (619–628). See Arthur Emanuel Christensen, *L'Iran sous les Sassanides* (2nd ed., Levin og Munksgaard, Copenhagen, 1944, pp. 416–423).
3. Yahya Ben Khalid (d. 805), of the great Barmecide family, who was vizier of Caliph Mahdi and tutor of Harun al-Rashid, is recorded as a book collector, in Holter, Ref. *1*, p. 196.
4. Paul Kraus, *Jabir ibn Hayyan, contribution à l'histoire des idées scientifiques dans l'Islam*, Impr. de l'Institut François d'Archéologie Orientale, Cairo, 1942–1943, 2 vols., Vol. 1, *Mémoires présentés a l'Institut d'Égypte*, t. 44–45.
5. Aldo Mieli, *La science arabe et son rôle dans l'évolution scientifique mondiale*, E. J. Brill, Leiden, 1938. Kurkis Awwad, *Khaza'in al-kutub al-gadima fi'-l-Iraq mundhu aqdam al-usur hatla sanat nlil-hijra* (Matbaat al-Maarif, Baghdad, 1367 [i.e., 1948], "Collections of Ancient Books in Iraq from the Most Ancient Periods to the Year 1000 A.H.," p. 214) indicates al-Fadl ibn Naubakht, a librarian of Harun al-Rashid, as a translator from Pahlevi.
6. Aldo Mieli, Ref. *5*; and Richard Walzer, "Arabic Transmissions of Greek Thought to Medieval Europe," *Bull. John Rylands Lib.*, **29,** 163 (1946).
7. Carl Heinrich Becker, *Islamstudien, vom Werden und Wesen der islamischen Welt* (Quelle and Meyer, Leipzig, 1924–1932, 2 vols., Vol. 1, p. 269) traces this institution to antiquity.
8. Johannes Pedersen, *Den arabiske Bog*, Fischer, Copenhagen, 1946, p. 128; and S. al-Munajjed, "Bibliographie damasquienne," *Oriens*, **5,** 170–172 (1956).
9. Awwad, Ref. *5*.
10. Adolf Grohmann, "Bibliotheken und Bibliophilen im islamischen Orient," in *Festschrift der Nationalbibliothek in Wien*, Verlag der Österreichischen Staatsdruckerei, Vienna, 1926, p. 433.
11. Ahmet Rufai, *Über die Bibliophilie im älteren Islam nebst Edition und Übersetzung von Ǧahiz' Abhandlung Fi madḥ al-Kutub* [encomium librorum], Diss., Berlin, 1931. As in the case of Greco-Roman antiquity, one cannot be too careful with alleged library holdings. There simply could not have been 3,000,000 books at Tripoli (population 20,000 when sacked by crusaders in 1109). See James Stuart Beddie, "Some Notices of Books in the East in the Period of the Crusades," *Speculum*, **8,** 240–242 (1933).
12. Muhammed ibn Ishaq Ibn al-Nadim, *"Kitab al-Fihrist," mit Anmerkungen hasg. vor Gustav Flügel, nach dessen Tod besorgt von Johannes Roediger und August Müller,* F. C. W. Vogel, Leipzig, 1871–1872, 2 vols.
13. M. Weis, "Das Amt des Mustamli in der arabischen Wissenschaft," *Oriens*, **4,** 27–57 (1951); and Helmut Ritter, "Autographs in Turkish Libraries," *Oriens*, **6,** 63–90 (1953).
14. Grohmann, Ref. *10*, p. 439; and David Samuel Margoliouth, *Lectures* on *Arabic Historians*, University of Calcutta, Calcutta, 1930, p. 192.
15. Rufai, Ref. *11*, p. 22; and Reynold Alleyne Nicholson, *Studies in Islamic Mysticism*, At the University Press, Cambridge, 1921, p. 20 et seq.
16. Mieli, Ref. *5*, p. 82; O. Pinto, "Le biblioteche degli arabi nell'età degli Abbasidi," *La Bibliofilia*, **30,** 15F (1929); Grohmann, Ref. *10*, p. 434; and Pedersen, Ref. *8*, p. 162 et seq.
17. Awwad, Ref. *5*, p. 154 et seq. indicates some such libraries.
18. Adam Mez, *Die Renaissance des Islams*, Carl Winter, Heidelberg, 1922, p. 165. Rufai, Ref. *11*, translates his *Fi madḥ al-kutub* (encomium librorum).

19. Mez, Ref. *18*, p. 165 et seq.; Pinto, Ref. *16*, p. 145; Grohmann, Ref. *10*, p. 437; and O. Pinto, "Al-Fath ibn Khâgân, favorito di al-Mutawakkil," *Revista degli studi orientali*, **13,** 133–149 (1931–1932).

20. Margoliouth, Ref. *14*, p. 45.

21. Awwad, Ref. *5*; Grohmann, Ref. *10*; Mez, Ref. *18*; and Pinto, Ref. *16*, contain material on private libraries in Baghdad and other cities in the area.

22. From Nicholson, Ref. *15*, pp. 265–266. When the library was burned soon thereafter, Avicenna was blamed, implying that he wanted to be the only beneficiary of the accumulation of so much wisdom. See Edward Granville Browne, *Literary History of Persia*, T. F. Unwin, London, 1902–1906, 2 vols., Vol. 2, p. 107.

23. Mez, Ref. *18*, p. 105; Grohmann, Ref. *10*, p. 437; Pinto, Ref. *16*, p. 151; and Alfred von Kremer, *Culturgeschichte des Orients unter den Chalifen*, W. Braumüller, Vienna, 1875–1877, 2 vols., Vol. 2, pp. 483–484.

24. Grohmann, Ref. *10*, p. 439.

25. Pedersen, Ref. *8*, p. FF et seq.

26. M. Quatremère, "Mémoire sur le goût des livres chez les orientaux," *J. asiatique*, ser. 3, **6,** 35–78 (1838).

27. Ruth Stellhorn Mackensen, "Moslem Libraries and Sectarian Propaganda," *Am. J. Semitic Languages Literatures*, **51,** 288–293 (1934–1935); and Philippe de Tarrazi, *Khazáin al-kutub al-arabiya fil-khafigayn*, Ministry of Education and Fine Arts, Beirut, 1947–1951, 4 vols. (cover title: *Histoire des bibliothèques arabes*), Vol. 1, p. 101.

28. Pinto, Ref. *16*, p. 160 et seq.; Tarrazi, Ref. *27*, Vol. 1, p. 139 et seq.; Ibn al-Qalanisi, *The Damascus Chronicle of the Crusades*, Extracted and translated by H. A. R. Gibb, University of London Historical Series, No. 5, Luzac and Company, London, 1932, p. 89; and Beddie, Ref. *11*.

29. Browne, Ref. *22*, Vol. 2, pp. 431–432; and Grohmann, Ref. *10*, p. 439, who mentions another Persian collection described by a contemporary poet in extravagant terms almost equivalent to those used by Richard de Bury for the libraries of Paris.

30. Heinrich Ferdinand Wüstenfeld, *Geschichte der arabischen Ärzte und Naturforscher*, Vandenhoeck und Ruprecht, Göttingen, 1840; and Max Meyerhof, "Über einige Privatbibliotheken im fatimidischen Ägypten," *Rev. degli studi orientali*; **12,** 286–290 (1929–1930).

31. Padover, Ref. *1*, p. 343.

32. Quatremère, Ref. *26*, p. 67; Pinto, Ref. *16*, p. 145; Rufai, Ref. *11*, p. 18; Mieli, Ref. *5*, p. 168; Tarrazi, Ref. *27*, Vol. 1, p. 288 et seq.; and Khuda Bukhsh, "The Islamic Libraries," *Nineteenth Century and After*, **52,** 135 (1902).

33. Kurt Holter, *Die Balen-Handschrift und die Makamen der Hariri der Wiener Nationalbibliothek*, Jahrbuch der Kunsthistorischen Sammlungen in Wien, Sonderheft, No. 104, Vienna, 1937 p. 37; and Bishr Fares, *Une miniature religieuse de l'école de Baghdad, son climat, sa structure et ses motifs, sa relation avec l'iconographie chrétienne d'orient*, Mémoires présentés à l'Institut d'Égypte, t. 51, Impr. de l'Institut Français d'Archéologie Orientale, Le Caire, 1948, p. 6.

34. Whatever the fate of books in Alexandria after capitulation on terms to the Arabs in 642 may have been, they were not destroyed by the conquerors. See Stanley Lane-Poole, *A History of Egypt in the Middle Ages*, Methuen, London, 1901, p. 12.

35. Meyerhof, Ref. *30*. The library served the Azhar Mosque and its theological school, founded in 970 and still surviving.

36. al-Maqrizi, apud Pinto, "The Libraries of the Arabs during the Time of the Abassids," *Islamic Culture*, **3,** 227–228 (1929).

37. Lane-Poole, Ref. *34*, p. 149, for the "hill of books." The allegation that biblioclasts sold fine bindings for shoe leather reappears as political denigration in the Reformation, the French Revolution, the War Between the States, and World War II. See also Pinto, Ref. *16*, p. 162.

38. Ibn Abi Usaybia, *Uyan al-anbafi tabagat al-atibba* (August Müller, ed.), al-Matbaat al-Rahabiyya, Cairo, 1882–1883, 2 vols., and Königsberg, 1884; and sections in Lucien Leclerc, *Histoire de la médecine arabe*, E. Leroux, Paris, 1876, 2 vols., Vol. 1, pp. 583–587.

39. Apud Meyerhof, Ref. *30*, pp. 288–289.

40. Grohmann, Ref. *10*, pp. 437–438.

41. From Ibn Abi Usaybia apud Meyerhof, Ref. *30*, pp. 287–288. The history of Jewish libraries in the Middle Ages has been outlined by Padover in Thompson, *The Medieval Library*, Ref. *1*, pp. 338–346. Many were in Moslem-dominated jurisdictions and also included significant collections in

Arabic. See also Moritz Steinschneider, *Die arabische Literatur der Juden: Ein Beitrag zur Literaturgeschichte der Araber, grossenteils aus handschriftlichen Quellen*, Kauffmann, Frankfurt am Main, 1902.
42. Quatremère, Ref. *26*, p. 62 et seq. also mentions other contemporary collectors.
43. Heinrich Ferdinand Wüstenfeld, *Der Imâm el-Schâfi'í, seine Schüler and Anahänger bis zum Jahre 300 d.h.*, Abhandlungen der Königlichen Gesellschaft der Wissenschaften zu Göttingen, No. 36, Dietrich's Verlag, Göttingen, 1890.
44. "Additions au mémoire de M. Quatremère sur le goût des livres ohez les orientaux," *J. asiatique*, Ser. 4, **11,** 187–198 (1848). See also Tarrazi, Ref. *27*, Vol. 1, p. 184 et seq., carrying the list into later times; and Khuda Buxhsh, "The Renaissance of Islam," *Islamic Culture*, **4,** 297 (1930).
45. Giorgio Levi della Vida, *Ricerche sulla formazione del piú antico fondo dei manoscritti orientali della Biblioteca Vaticana*, Studi e testi, No. 92, Biblioteca Apostolica Vaticana, Vatican City, 1939.
46. Georg Graf, *Catalogue des manuscrits arabes chrétiens conservés au Caire*, Studi e testi, No. 63, Biblioteca Apostolica Vaticana, Vatican City, 1934.
47. Quatremère, Ref. *26*, pp. 69–70; and Rufai, Ref. *11*, p. 19.
48. Rafael Altamira y Crevea, *Historia de la civilización española*, M. Solev, Barcelona, 1900. For schools and libraries in Moslem Spain, see Julián Ribera y Tarragó, *Disertaciones y opúsculos*, Impr. de E. Maestre, Madrid, 1928, 2 vols., Vol. 1, pp. 181–228. See also Hartwig Derenbourg, *Les Manuscrits arabes de l'Escurial*, E. Leroux, Paris, 1884–1903, 2 vols.
49. Reinhart Pieter Anne Dozy, *Histoire des musulmans d'Espagne*, Nouvelle édition par Evariste Levi-Provençal, E. J. Brill, Leiden; 1932, 3 vols., Vol. 2, p. 185; Padover, Ref. *1*, p. 361; Pinto, Ref. *16*, p. 153; Tarrazi, Ref. *27*, Vol. 1, p. 244; and Ribera y Tarragó, Ref. *48*, p. 27.
50. H. Perès, *La poésie andalouse en arabe classique au XI siècle*, Publication de l'Institut d'Études Orientales d'Alger, No. 5, Adrien-Maisonneuve, Paris, 1937, p. 450 et seq.; and Dozy, Ref. *49*, Vol. 2, p. 233. For other private libraries in Omayyad Spain, see Holter, Ref. *1*, p. 222.
51. W. Gottschalk, "Die Bibliotheken der Araber im Zeitalter der Abbasiden," *Zentralblatt für Bibliothekswesen*, **47,** 1–6 (1930); and Grohmann, Ref. *10*, pp. 440–441.
52. Mieli, Ref. *5*, pp. 182 and 6.
53. George Sarton, *Introduction to the History of Science*, Carnegie Institution of Washington Publication, No. 376, Published for the Carnegie Institution of Washington, by Williams and Wilkins, Baltimore, 1953 [ca. 1927–1948], 5 vols., Vol. 2, p. 260; De Lacy Evans O'Leary, *Arabic Thought and Its Place in History*, K. Paul, Trench, Trubner, & Company, London, 1922, p. 241; Abraham Aaron Neuman, *The Jews in Spain, Their Social, Political and Cultural Life during the Middle Ages*, Jewish Publication Society of America, Philadelphia, 1942, 2 vols., Vol. 2, p. 95; and Steinschneider, Ref. *41*, p. xxvii, Note 1.
54. Charles Homer Haskins, *Studies in the History of Medieval Science*, Harvard Historical Studies, No. 27, Harvard University Press, Cambridge, Mass., 1924.
55. Padover, Ref. *1*, pp. 365–366; R. W. Hunt, "English Learning in the Late Twelfth Century," *Trans. Roy. Historical Soc.*, 4th ser., **19,** 24 (1936); and Clemens Baeumker, *Die Stellung des Alfred von Sareshel (Alfredus Anglicus) und seiner Schrift De motu cordis in der Wissenschaft des beginnenden XIII, Jahrhunderts*, Sitzungsberichte der Bayerischen Akademie der Wissenschaften, Philologisch-historische Klasse, 1913, Abhandlung 9, Munich, 1943.
56. Dozy, Ref. *49*, Vol. 3, p. 22 et seq.
57. Meyerhof, Ref. *30*, p. 289.
58. Pinto, Ref. *16*, pp. 147 and 157; and Georges Marçais, *La Berberie musalmane et l'orient au moyen âge*, Éditions Montaigne, Paris, Aubier, 1946, p. 296.
59. Tarrazi, Ref. *27*, Vol. 1, p. 299 et seq.
60. Sarton, Ref. *53*, Vol. 2, p. 338.
61. O'Leary, Ref. *53*, pp. 252 and 290.
62. Mackensen, Ref. *27*, p. 84. It is ironical that Cardinal Francisco Jiménez de Cisneros ordered this terrible biblioclasm but was also the sponsor of the great Complutensian polyglott.
63. Lawrence S. Thompson, "Libraries of Turkey," *Lib. Q.*, **22,** 270–284 (1952).

BIBLIOGRAPHY

Grohmann, Adolf, "Bibliotheken und Bibliophilen im islamischen Orient," in *Festschrift der Nationalbibliothek in Wien*, Verlag der Österreichischen Staatsdruckerei, Vienna, 1926.

Holter, Kurt, "Der Islam," in *Handbuch der Bibliothekswissenschaft* (Georg Leyh, ed.), Otto Harrassowitz, Wiesbaden, 1955, Vol. 3, pp. 188–242.

Mackensen, Ruth Stellhorn, [series of seven articles on Moslem libraries], *Am. J. Semitic Languages Literatures*, **51–54** (1935–1937).

Padover, S. K., "Muslim Libraries," in *The Medieval Library* (James Westfall Thompson, ed.), University of Chicago Press, Chicago, 1939, pp. 347–372.

Pederson, Johannes, *Den arabiske Bog*, Fischer, Copenhagen, 1946.

LAWRENCE S. THOMPSON

NATIONAL COMMISSION ON NEW TECHNOLOGICAL USES OF COPYRIGHTED WORKS (CONTU)*

The temporary National Commission on New Technological Uses of Copyrighted Works (CONTU) was created by Congress as part of the effort to revise comprehensively the copyright laws of the United States. (This revision became PL 94-553 [1976], now codified as 17 USC Sec. 101 et seq.) Early in the congressional hearings on copyright law revision it became apparent that the use of the new technologies of photocopying and computers had effects on the authorship, distribution, and use of copyrighted works, and raised problems that were not dealt with by the pending revision bill. Because of the complexity of these problems, CONTU was created to provide the president and Congress with recommendations concerning those changes in copyright law or procedure needed both to assure public access to copyrighted works used in conjunction with computer and machine duplication systems and to respect the rights of owners of copyrights in such works, while considering the concerns of the general public and the consumer.

The act which created CONTU, approved on December 31, 1974, as Public Law 93-573, gave the commission 3 years to study and compile data and make recommendations on legislation or procedures concerning:

1. The reproduction and use of copyrighted works of authorship:
   a. in conjunction with automatic systems capable of storing, processing, retrieving, and transferring information.
   b. by various forms of machine reproduction, not including reproduction by or at the request of instructors for use in face-to-face teaching activities.
2. The creation of new works by the application or intervention of such automatic systems as machine reproduction.

*A large part of this article is taken from the *Final Report of the National Commission on New Technological Uses of Copyrighted Works*, dated July 31, 1978, and published by the Library of Congress in 1979 (U.S. Government Printing Office, Superintendent of Documents, Washington, D.C. 20402, Stock No. 030-022-00143-8). The author of this article wrote a considerable part of the *Final Report*.

On July 25, 1975, seven months after the bill was enacted, President Ford announced appointment of the following commissioners, according to the criteria set out in the legislation:

1. From authors and other copyright owners:
   John Hersey, president of the Authors League of America, Inc.
   Dan Lacy, senior vice-president, McGraw-Hill, Inc.
   E. Gabriel Perle, vice-president—law, Time, Inc.
   Hershel B. Sarbin, president, Ziff-Davis Publishing Company
2. From copyright users:
   William S. Dix, librarian emeritus, Princeton University (deceased February 22, 1978)
   Arthur R. Miller, professor of law, Harvard Law School
   Robert Wedgeworth, executive director, American Library Association
   Alice E. Wilcox, director, Minnesota Interlibrary Telecommunications Exchange
3. From the public:
   George D. Cary, retired register of copyrights
   Stanley H. Fuld, retired chief judge of the State of New York and the New York Court of Appeals
   Rhoda H. Karpatkin, executive director, Consumers Union
   Melville B. Nimmer, professor of law, University of California at Los Angeles Law School

The librarian of Congress and the register of copyrights were designated ex officio members of the commission; of these two, only the librarian had a vote in commission matters. Stanley H. Fuld and Melville B. Nimmer were designated chairman and vice-chairman of the commission, respectively.

At its initial meeting on October 8, 1975, the commission appointed Arthur J. Levine as executive director and authorized recruitment of a staff. The senior staff members subsequently appointed were Robert W. Frase, assistant executive director and economist; and Michael S. Keplinger, assistant executive director and senior attorney. The final meeting of the commission was held on July 31, 1978, and the commission was then dissolved.

The accomplishments of the commission fall into three categories:

1. Recommendations to the president and the Congress for legislation, and recommendations as to actions to be taken by government agencies and nongovernmental organizations
2. The development of the so-called CONTU Guidelines on Photocopying
3. The information collected in commissioned studies and in public hearings, much of which is summarized and analyzed in the *Final Report*

Recommendations of the Commission

COMPUTER LEGISLATION

Computer Programs

The new copyright law should be amended: (*a*) to make it explicit that computer programs, to the extent that they embody an author's original creation, are proper subject matter of copyright; (*b*) to apply to all computer uses of copyrighted programs, by the deletion of the present Section 117; and (*c*) to ensure that rightful possessors of copies of computer programs may use or adapt these copies for their use. (A bill, HR 6934, to carry out this recommendation was introduced on March 26, 1980, by Representative Robert W. Kastenmeier, chairman of the Subcommittee on Courts, Civil Liberties, and the Administration of Justice, Committee on the Judiciary, United States House of Representatives.)

Commissioner Hersey dissented as follows: The act of 1976 should be amended to make it explicit that copyright protection does not extend to a computer program in the form in which it is capable of being used to control computer operations.

Data Bases

The act of 1976 should be amended to apply to all computer uses of copyrighted data bases and other copyrighted works fixed in computer-sensible media, by the deletion of its present Section 117.

New Works

Works created by the use of computers should be afforded copyright protection if they are original works of authorship within the act of 1976. Consequently, no amendment is needed.

Computer Regulations

The register of copyrights should adopt appropriate regulations regarding the affixation of notice to and the registration and deposit of works of authorship used in conjunction with computers.

Congressional Action Concerning Computers

Any legislation enacted as a result of these recommendations should be subject to a periodic review to determine its adequacy in the light of continuing technological change. This review should especially consider the impact of such legislation on competition and consumer prices in the computer and information industries, and the effect on cultural values of including computer programs within the ambit of copyright.

PHOTOCOPYING LEGISLATION

The act of 1976 should be amended at this time only to provide specific guidance for situations in which photocopying is done by commercial organizations on demand and for profit.

Copyright Office and Photocopying

In conducting the 5-year review of photocopying practices required by Section 108(i) of the act of 1976, the register of copyrights should begin immediately to plan and implement a study of the overall impact of all photo duplication practices on both proprietors' rights and the public's access to published information.

Government and Nongovernment Agencies and Photocopying

Publishers, libraries, and government agencies should cooperate in making information about the copyright status of all published works, both current and older publications, more readily available to the public.

The CONTU Guidelines on Photocopying under Interlibrary Loan Arrangements

The CONTU Guidelines were developed to assist librarians and copyright proprietors in understanding the amount of photocopying for use in interlibrary loan arrangements permitted under the copyright law. In the spring of 1976 there was realistic expectation that a new copyright law, under consideration for nearly 20 years, would be enacted during that session of Congress. It had become apparent that the House subcommittee was giving serious consideration to modifying the language concerning "systematic reproduction" by libraries in Section 108(g)(2) of the Senate-passed bill to permit photocopying under interlibrary arrangements, unless such arrangements resulted in the borrowing libraries obtaining "such aggregate quantities as to substitute for a subscription to or purchase of" copyrighted works (94th Congress, 2nd Session, 1975, Senate Report 22).

At its meeting on April 2, 1976, the commission discussed this proposed amendment to the Senate bill. The commission felt that it might aid the House and Senate subcommittees by offering its good offices in bringing the principal parties together to see whether agreement could be reached on a definition of "such aggregate quantities." This offer was accepted by the House and Senate subcommittees and the interested parties, and much of the summer of 1976 was spent by the commission in working with the parties to secure agreements on "guidelines" interpreting what was to become the proviso in Section 108(g)(2) relating to "systematic reproduction" by libraries. The pertinent parts of that section follow, with the proviso added by the House emphasized:

> (g) The rights of reproduction and distribution under this section extend to the isolated and unrelated reproduction or distribution of a single copy or phonorecord of the same material on separate occasions, but do not extend to cases where the library or archives, or its employee . . .
>
> (2) engages in the systematic reproduction or distribution of single or multiple copies or phonorecords of material described in subsection (d): *Provided, That nothing in this clause prevents a library or archives from participating in inter-library arrangements that do not have, as their purpose or effect, that the library or archives receiving such copies or phonorecords for distribution does so in such aggregate quantities as to substitute for a subscription to or purchase of such work* (PL 94-553 [1976]).

Before enactment of the new copyright law, the principal library, publisher, and author organizations agreed to the following detailed guidelines defining what "aggregate quantities" would constitute the "systematic reproduction" that would exceed the statutory limitations on a library's photocopying activities.

Photocopying—Interlibrary Arrangements

Introduction

Subsection 108(g)(2) of the bill deals, among other things, with limits on interlibrary arrangements for photocopying. It prohibits systematic photocopying of copyrighted materials but permits interlibrary arrangements "that do not have, as their purpose or effect, that the library or archives receiving such copies or phonorecords for distribution does so in such aggregate quantities as to substitute for a subscription to or purchase of such work."

The National Commission on New Technological Uses of Copyrighted Works offered its good offices to the House and Senate subcommittees in bringing the interested parties together to see if agreement could be reached on what a realistic definition would be of "such aggregate quantities." The Commission consulted with the parties and suggested the interpretation which follows, on which there has been substantial agreement by the principal library, publisher, and author organizations. The Commission considers the guidelines which follow to be a workable and fair interpretation of the intent of the proviso portion of subsection 108(g)(2).

These guidelines are intended to provide guidance in the application of section 108 to the most frequently encountered interlibrary case: a library's obtaining from another library, in lieu of interlibrary loan, copies of articles from relatively recent issues of periodicals—those published within five years prior to the date of the request. The guidelines do not specify what aggregate quantity of copies of an article or articles published in a periodical, the issue date of which is more than five years prior to the date when the request for the copy thereof is made, constitutes a substitute for a subscription to such periodical. The meaning of the proviso to subsection 108(g)(2) in such case is left to future interpretation.

The point has been made that the present practice on interlibrary loans and use of photocopies in lieu of loans may be supplemented or even largely replaced by a system in which one or more agencies or institutions, public or private, exist for the specific purpose of providing a central source for photocopies. Of course, these guidelines would not apply to such a situation.

Guidelines for the Proviso of Subsection 108(g)(2)

1. As used in the proviso of subsection 108(g)(2), the words ". . . such aggregate quantities as to substitute for a subscription to or purchase of such work" shall mean:

(a) with respect to any given periodical (as opposed to any given issue of a periodical), filled requests of a library or archives (a "requesting entity") within any calendar year for a total of six or more copies of an article or articles published in such periodical within five years prior to the date of the request. These guidelines specifically shall not apply, directly or indirectly, to any request of a requesting entity for a copy or copies of an article or articles published in any issue of a periodical, the publication date of which is more than five years prior to the date when the request is made. These guidelines do not define the meaning, with respect to such a request, of " . . . such aggregate quantities as to substitute for a subscription to such periodical."

(b) With respect to any other material described in subsection 108(d), (including fiction and poetry), filled requests of a requesting entity within any calendar year for a total of six or more copies or phonorecords of or from any given work (including a collective work) during the entire period when such material shall be protected by copyright.

2. In the event that a requesting entity:

(a) shall have in force or shall have entered an order for a subscription to a periodical, or

(b) has within its collection, or shall have entered an order for, a copy or phonorecord of any other copyrighted work, material from either category of which it desires to obtain by copy from another library or archives (the "supplying entity"), because the material to be copied is not reasonably available for use by the requesting entity itself, then the fulfillment of such request shall be treated as though the requesting entity made such copy from its own collection. A library or archives may request a copy or phonorecord from a supplying entity only under those circumstances where the requesting entity would have been able, under the other provisions of section 108, to supply such copy from materials in its own collection.

3. No request for a copy or phonorecord of any material to which these guidelines apply may be fulfilled by the supplying entity unless such request is accompanied by a representation by the requesting entity that the request was made in conformity with these guidelines.

4. The requesting entity shall maintain records of all requests made by it for copies or phonorecords of any materials to which these guidelines apply and shall maintain records of the fulfillment of such requests, which records shall be retained until the end of the third complete calendar year after the end of the calendar year in which the respective request shall have been made.

5. As part of the review provided for in subsection 108(i), these guidelines shall be reviewed not later than five years from the effective date of this bill.

These guidelines were accepted by the conference committee and were incorporated into its report on the new act (94th Congress, 2nd Session, House Report 1733, pp. 72–73).

The guidelines specifically left the status of periodical articles more than 5 years old to future determination. Moreover, institutions set up for the specific purpose of supplying photocopies of copyrighted material were excluded from coverage by the guidelines.

Commission Hearings and Studies

In the course of its existence the commission held 23 meetings, most of which consisted of public hearings at which witnesses were heard. For the first five meetings, only summaries exist. For the remaining meetings, full transcripts were prepared. The summaries and transcripts for all commission meetings were deposited with the National Technical Information Service (NTIS) of the U.S. Department of Commerce. They are listed in the Bibliography with the NTIS order numbers.

The commission let contracts with outside organizations for six studies. These studies were also deposited with NTIS, and they are listed with order numbers in the Bibliography.

BIBLIOGRAPHY

Final Report of the National Commission on New Technological Uses of Copyrighted Works, U.S. Government Printing Office, Superintendent of Documents, Washington, D.C., 1979.

Commission Meetings

Meetings 1 through 5, 1975, PB 253 757.

Summaries of the first five meetings of CONTU, held on October 17, November 19, and December 18–19, 1975, and February 11–13 and April 1–2, 1976. The first meeting was organizational; the second concerned photocopying, computers and data bases, and related topics; the third, computers, the Australian copyright case, and the economics of the publishing industry; the fourth, information systems, the operations of the National Library of Medicine, and the economics of computerized information storage and retrieval systems; and the fifth, presentations by the Information Industry Association and the New York Times Information Bank, and the results of a study on future alternatives to present-day scientific and technical journals.

Transcript, CONTU Meeting No. 6, May 6–7, 1976, Arlington, Virginia, PB 254 765.
The major subject of the meeting was protection of computer software.

Transcript, CONTU Meeting No. 7, June 9–10, 1976, Arlington, Virginia, PB 254 766.
Verbatim transcript of hearings on protection of computer software and a discussion of photocopying guidelines.

Transcript, CONTU Meeting No. 8, September 16–17, 1976, Los Angeles, California, PB 259 749.
The meeting addressed copyright protection for data bases.

Transcript, CONTU Meeting No. 9, October 21–22, 1976, Arlington, Virginia, PB 261 947.
Transcript of hearings on photocopying, interlibrary loans, and library practices.

Transcript, CONTU Meeting No. 10, November 18–19, 1976, New York City, PB 261 946.
Testimony on the copyrightability of computer software was presented.

Transcript, CONTU Meeting No. 11, January 13–14, 1977, Arlington, Virginia, PB 263 160.
The commission heard testimony on library practices and other aspects of photocopying at the National Agricultural Library and Exxon, the technological capabilities of copying equipment, and a NTIS proposal for supplying authorized photocopies of journal articles. Other witnesses testifying on photocopying were representatives of the Association of American Publishers, the Information Industry Association, and the Authors League of America, Inc.

Transcript, CONTU Meeting No. 12, February 24–25, 1977, New York City, PB 265 765.
Matters under consideration were copyright protection for computer software and automated data bases, and possible approaches to check unauthorized photocopying of copyrighted materials. No testimony was presented at this meeting.

Transcript, CONTU Meeting No. 13, March 31 and April 1, 1977, New York City, PB 266 277.
Testimony included the following subjects: proposal for a copy payment center; the publishing and reprint sales activities of the American Institute of Physics; the sampling, licensing, and payment system of the American Society of Composers, Authors, and Publishers; the licensing, sampling, and payment system of Broadcast Music, Inc.; the problems of newsletter publishers vis-à-vis unauthorized photocopying; and an analysis of computer and photocopying issues from the point of view of the general public.

Transcript, CONTU Meeting No. 14, May 5, 1977, Arlington, Virginia, PB 267 332.
The commission discussed the CONTU subcommittee reports on copyright protection for computer software and automated data bases, made recommendations for amendments to the reports, and agreed to circulate them with dissenting and concurring opinions. The Photocopy Subcommittee discussed a request for additional guidelines to interpret further terms in Section 108 of the Copyright Act, and the commission agreed to offer its good offices to this end.

Transcript, CONTU Meeting No. 15, July 11–12, 1977, Washington, D.C., PB 271 326.
Testimony included the following subjects: the economics of property rights as applied to computer software and data bases; the economics of property rights; an analysis of computer and photocopying copyright issues from the point of view of the general public and ultimate consumer; a survey of publisher practices and present attitudes on authorized journal article copying and licensing; the costs of owning, borrowing, and disposing of periodical publications; and testimony on copyright for computer software and data bases.

Transcript, CONTU Meeting No. 16, September 15–16, 1977, Chicago, Illinois, PB 273 594.
Testimony on the commission subcommittee reports on computer software and data bases with additional comments was presented by the representatives of the computer industry. The commission also heard a report on a study on library photocopying in the United States and its implications for the development of a copyright royalty payment mechanism, and a description of the licensed photocopying activities of University Microfilms.

Transcript, CONTU Meeting No. 17, October 21, 1977, Washington, D.C., PB 275 786.
Testimony on photocopying was presented.

Transcript, CONTU Meeting No. 18, November 17–18, 1977, Cambridge, Massachusetts, PB 278 329.
The first day was a round-table discussion on the technologies which affect the present and future development of the collection, retention, organization, and delivery of information. On the second day, a study sponsored by CONTU, "Legal Protection of Computer Software: An Industrial Survey," was summarized.

Transcript, CONTU Meeting No. 19, January 12–13, 1978, Los Angeles, California, PB 280 052.
A witness testified on copyright protection for computer software; the commissioners heard summaries of current progress on subcommittee reports from members of the staff.

Transcript, CONTU Meeting No. 20, February 16–17, 1978, New York City, PB 283 876.
Witnesses spoke on copyright protection for computer software and the first 6 weeks of operation of the Copyright Clearance Center. The commission also adopted the report of the Data Base Subcommittee, discussed the report of the Software Subcommittee, and discussed a draft report of the Photocopy Subcommittee.

Transcript, CONTU Meeting No. 21, April 20–21, 1978, Washington, D.C., PB 281 710.
The witnesses presented testimony on the draft report of the Photocopy Subcommittee. The commission also discussed the reports of the New Works and Software Subcommittees. The majority of the commissioners voted to accept the report of the Software Subcommittee.

Transcript, CONTU Meeting No. 22, May 8, 1978, New York City.
This meeting transcript, dealing only with procedural matters concerning the printing of the final report, was also deposited with NTIS.

Transcript, CONTU Final Meeting, July 10, 1978, Washington, D.C., PB 284 178.
At this meeting, the commissioners discussed the final report, with the concurring and dissenting opinions, and voted unanimously to submit the report to the president and Congress. The commissioners also voted to have the final report printed for public distribution.

Commission-Sponsored Studies

An Analysis of Computer and Photocopying Issues from the Point of View of the General Public and the Ultimate Consumer, by Marc Breslow, Allen R. Ferguson, and Larry Haverkamp, Prepared under a CONTU contract with the Public Interest Economics Center, PB 283 416.

Costs of Owning, Borrowing, and Disposing of Periodical Publications, by Vernon E. Palmour, Marcia C. Bellassai, and Robert R. V. Wiederkehr, Prepared under a CONTU contract with the Public Research Institute, Center for Naval Analyses, PB 274 821.

Economics of Property Rights as Applied to Computer Software and Data Bases, by Yale M. Braunstein, Dietrich M. Fischer, Janusz A. Ordover, and William J. Baumol, Prepared under a CONTU contract with the New York University Economics Department, PB 268 787.

Legal Protection of Computer Software—An Industrial Survey, by Richard I. Miller, Clarence O'N. Brown, Francis J. Kelley, Deborah C. Notman, and Michael A. Walker, Prepared under a CONTU contract with Harbridge House, Inc., PB 283 876.

Library Photocopying in the United States, with Implications for the Development of a Royalty Payment Mechanism, by Donald W. King et al., Prepared under a CONTU contract with King Research Inc., PB 278 300. (Also available from the Superintendent of Documents, Government Printing Office, Stock No. 052-003-00443-7.)

Survey of Publisher Practices and Current Attitudes on Authorized Journal Article Copying and Licensing, by Bernard M. Fry, Herbert S. White, and Elizabeth L. Johnson, Prepared under a CONTU contract with the Research Center for Library and Information Science, Graduate Library School, Indiana University at Bloomington, PB 271 003.

ROBERT W. FRASE

NOTRE DAME. UNIVERSITY OF NOTRE DAME LIBRARIES

The University and Its History

The University of Notre Dame du Lac was founded in frontier Indiana in 1842 by Rev. Edward Sorin and a small band of brothers of the French religious community of the Congregation of Holy Cross. In 1844 it received a charter from the State of Indiana, authorizing it to confer degrees in the "Liberal Arts and Sciences and in Law and Medicine." During the early years the university had a collegiate program of 6 years in length as well as a manual labor school and an elementary school (the Minems, which was continued until 1929). The first Bachelor of Arts degree was awarded on June 29, 1859. Modeled as it was on the classical French college, or *lycee*, the institution remained largely a university in name only until courses in science, law, and engineering were introduced in 1865, 1869, and 1873, respectively. The administrative structure of the school was refined in 1897 with the establishment of separate units for Arts and Letters, Science, Engineering, and Law, and again in 1905 when those units were formally designated colleges. A fifth college, Commerce, was added in 1920.

Throughout its early history Notre Dame was almost completely an undergraduate institution, although the possibility of some type of graduate study first appeared in announcements as early as 1854–1855. A few Master of Arts degrees were offered, beginning in 1859. However, while it is not possible to distinguish between honorary and earned graduate degrees, most of these appear to have been honorary. Between 1906 and 1919, 34 master's degrees and six doctorates were awarded in a variety of disciplines. While records for this period are most incomplete, the programs were undoubtedly analogous to current graduate degrees in name only. The first real impetus for formal graduate work came with the establishment of the Summer School in 1918. In 1919 the first prescribed programs for graduate degrees were laid out formally in the *University Bulletin*, and in 1920 the Committee on Graduate Study was organized to administer graduate work at the university. Degrees were awarded in many different disciplines in the humanities, social sciences, and sciences, with little regard to the availability of qualified faculty and other necessary resources. The overextended nature of the programs became clear, and in 1932, under a new university director of studies, doctoral programs were cut back drastically to Systematic Botany and Organic Chemistry. That same year a separate Graduate School was founded and clear distinctions between undergraduate and graduate courses were established for the first time. The general tightening of standards which these actions represented signaled the beginning of a steady growth in serious graduate work, slowed but not halted by World War II. Examples of the new emphasis on organized research were the Lobund Institute in germ-free biology, established in 1950, and the Medieval Institute, set up in 1946—both representing institutionalization of long-term research interests of the university. Similarly, while scholarly publishing sponsored by the university began early with the establishment of the *American Midland Naturalist* in 1909, the real drive in this area came in the 1930s with the series *Publications in Medieval Studies* (1936) and the *Review of Politics* (1938), and was continued after the war with the *Texts and Studies in Medieval Education* (1953), *Notre Dame Journal of Formal Logic* (1959–1960), *Natural Law Forum* (1956), and the *Notre Dame English Journal* (1965). The establishment of the University of Notre Dame Press in 1949 and its expansion into a nationally significant outlet for scholarly research in the years after World War II provide another index of the expanded importance attached to the scholarly mission of the university. The driving force behind the development of high standards of scholarship at Notre Dame was the Rev. Philip Moore, C.S.C., who served as secretary of the Committee on Graduate Study (1934) and was later appointed first dean of the Graduate School (1944) and vice-president for academic affairs (1952).

The development and growth of the university's programs, enrollment, and physical plant were especially notable after World War II, though prudent management avoided the rapid overexpansion that characterized many American universities in the late 1940s and again in the '60s. In many respects the development of the university since the '50s has been directed and dominated by its dynamic president, the Rev. Theodore M. Hesburgh, C.S.C., who during his years as president (1952 to the present) both raised academic standards and reinforced the Catholic values of the university. At the same time he laid the groundwork for lay leadership with the formal separation of the university from the Congregation of Holy Cross and the establishment of a lay board of trustees (1967). Under his leadership the university attained national prominence in academic circles outside its traditional football setting.

By 1980 the university had developed solid, and in some cases nationally significant, graduate programs in most disciplines in the humanities, social sciences, natural sciences, and engineering; and had assumed an international leadership role in Catholic learning, teaching, and service. It also developed a first-rate physical plant and a major endowment to support the operations of the university. Throughout this period of achievement, the university remained committed to quality undergraduate education, which continued to be numerically predominant at Notre Dame (6,931 undergraduates in 1979, with 1,837 enrolled in the various professional and graduate programs).

Thus Notre Dame entered the 1980s with a solid academic and fiscal foundation from which to deal with the challenges of inflation, shrinking pools of potential students, changing patterns of outside funding, and pressures from increased faculty and student demands.

The History of the University Libraries

Though the university was established in 1842, apparently no real institutional library was established until 1874. Prior to that time, individual faculty members organized materials as needed and made them available to students in whatever manner they felt appropriate. It appears that there were also several private society libraries on campus, though no records actually remain. When Father Auguste Lemonnier became the fourth president in 1872, he sought to change the institution from a frontier school to a "well equipped college," an essential part of which would be a "circulating library."

Lemonnier called on a layman, James F. Edwards, who had been on the faculty since 1870, to develop the library. Edwards seems to have been an eccentric, with avaricious and wide-ranging collecting interests. In addition to increasing the new College Library holdings to some 10,000 volumes by 1879, he gathered materials on the Catholic Church in America through soliciting individual episcopal archives. He also built a collection of portraits and mementos. Edwards continued this work on both the library and the museum/archives until his death in 1911. However, his earliest efforts received a temporary setback in a disastrous fire on April 23, 1879, which destroyed the main building, including most of the materials Edwards had gathered by that date. The rebuilding of both the building and the collection began at once, and by the start of the school year in the fall, a new main building was completed. (See Fig. 1.) Since funds were extremely tight (the first formal library budget was in 1882, for $500), a large-scale solicitation of gifts was organized to restock the library. Several references exist to the "Lemonnier Library Association" as the vehicle for this effort, but apparently no records of the group survive.

FIGURE 1. *University of Notre Dame Library. A view of the university library about 1895, revealing clearly James F. Edwards's interest in collecting and displaying all types of artifacts and Catholic memorabilia. Photo courtesy of the University Archives.*

In the years following the opening of the new library in late 1879, collections grew sporadically. Total holdings of 700 volumes were reported in 1881; 16,000, in 1882; 25,000, in 1885; 50,000, in 1893; 63,000, in 1913; and 105,000, in 1915. By that time, despite the establishment of a separate Law Library in 1914, the library space allocated in the main building had become severely cramped and many volumes were stored in buildings all across the campus. While records are sketchy, it was apparently during this period that separate departmental collections, particularly in the sciences, developed outside the formal university library system. The need for new quarters had become apparent, and in June 1917 the new 500,000-volume-capacity Lemonnier Library was dedicated. This was the first time the library had space specifically designed for library purposes, and the structure was the first separate library building at any Catholic college in the United States. With the new building the library apparently adopted a subject-oriented approach to the collections and public services, with separate reading rooms for the humanities and the social sciences.

Over the next 40 years the collections continued to grow slowly but steadily, with 128,145 volumes reported in 1924 and reaching 280,903 volumes in 1949. During these years the library became more professional, the staff grew in size (until sometime after 1920 there had been only one librarian and no other regular staff), formal reference and instructional help began during the 1920s, and in 1929 the library adopted its first formal cataloging rules, along with Library of Congress classification and subject headings.

The new emphasis on graduate study and faculty research which began during the 1930s was accelerated after World War II, placing new demands on the library and particularly on its collections, which almost doubled between 1949 and 1959, to 537,510 volumes. This rapid growth put considerable strain on the 30-year-old Lemonnier Library, and in 1963 the university opened the new Memorial Library, 14 stories in height with a capacity for 3,000 seats and over 2,000,000 volumes. The construction and furnishing costs for this were in excess of $8,000,000, more than the combined cost of all other buildings on the campus at the time. This was made possible in good part through the efforts of the Notre Dame Library Association, established in 1959. This group, now known as the Friends of the Library at Notre Dame, has also provided support for the acquisitions programs of the University Libraries through direct contributions and the operation of an annual book sale, and has sponsored for the libraries the publication of several catalogs; for example, *Medieval and Renaissance Manuscripts* (1978), *Incunabula* (1979), and a variety of special exhibition catalogs.

The physical dominance of the campus by the Memorial Library represented in a sense the new importance placed on the library as a support for and center of the university's graduate study and research. Similar reflections of this change appeared in the earlier founding membership of the library in the Midwest Inter-Library Center (now the Center for Research Libraries) in 1953 and in it acceptance into the Association for Research Libraries in 1963.

The Libraries in 1980

Library facilities and services are organized in three major units: the University Libraries system, the Law Library, and the University Archives.

The Law School Library reports directly to the dean of the Law School. Its holdings include some 103,576 volumes, with 635 current serials. While functioning completely outside of the University Libraries system, its holdings are recorded by main entry in the public catalog in the Memorial Library. Otherwise all acquisitions, processing, and services are handled by a staff of five librarians and three support positions. Access to on-line LEXIS service is offered through the Law Library.

The University Archives are located on the sixth floor of the Memorial Library, but they are administratively separate from the University Libraries and report directly to the provost. The collections include both university records and extensive holdings of external personal and organization manuscripts dating back to the pioneer work of James Edwards in gathering personal and episcopal records of the history of American Catholicism. Totaling some 4,500 linear feet of material, the holdings include papers of Orestes Brownson, the Thomas Ewing Family, William Tecumseh Sherman, and the Diocese of Louisiana and the Floridas, all of which were organized and filmed with the support of the National Historical Publications Commission. In recent years particular attention has been paid to the manuscript records of various organizations, and to the rapidly growing collection of photographic materials on the history of the university and of American Catholicism generally. Manuscript materials of other than American Catholic individuals and organizations are collected by the Department of Rare Books Special Collections within the University Libraries system. The staff of the Archives includes four professional archivists and three support positions.

The University Libraries system, with holdings of 1,300,000 volumes and in excess of 700,000 microtext units, is organized in a traditional manner. The director of libraries is appointed by the president and serves at his pleasure, subject to a mandated formal review every 5 years. General library policy is established by the Faculty Committee for University Libraries, which includes six elected faculty members and the director of libraries ex officio. Within the Office of the Director of Libraries there are an associate director and coordinator of service in the Memorial Library, a chief collection development officer, an assistant director for technical services, university librarians for science and engineering, a business manager, and a personnel officer. These individuals—along with the heads of the Reference, Collection Management, Acquisitions, and Cataloging Departments—serve on the Library Administrative Committee, which is responsible for overall library planning, internal operating policies, and budget.

Public services in the Memorial Library consist of two major departments, Reference and Collection Management (which includes units for circulation and stacks, microtexts, reserves, and audio materials), and smaller units for Rare Books–Special Collections, International Studies, and Medieval Studies. The Technical Services Division contains the Cataloging and Acquisitions Departments, with a Preservation Office attached to Acquisitions. The science librarian is responsible for direct service in the Chemistry–Physics Library, coordination of collections and services in the Life Sciences and Mathematics Libraries, and reading rooms for the Radiation Laboratory and the Earth Sciences Department. The engineering librarian is responsible for the Engineering and Architecture Libraries.

Operationally, as well as organizationally, the University Libraries system has been quite traditional. After some tentative experiments with a batch-oriented circulation system in the early 1960s, the libraries returned to a fully manual operation which has continued to date without undo stresses or problems. The Notre Dame Libraries were a founding member of the Indiana Cooperative Library Services Authority (INCOLSA) and have participated in the Ohio College Library Center (OCLC) for cataloging since 1976. Efforts at a computer-based management information system began in the late '60s and were continued until the late '70s, when discrepancies and operational difficulties became evident and the system was dropped. Reference services have been traditional, with little in the way of organized instructional support or machine-based data base services until the late '70s.

Perhaps the major innovative library activity has been the development of the ACQUIS system, a machine-based acquisitions system encompassing ordering, claiming, receipt, and fiscal operations which became operational in 1978. Designed primarily to respond to the difficulties with the libraries' interface with the university's purchasing and accounting offices, the system is in batch mode and not bibliographically oriented or interfaced with OCLC. It has, however, resolved many operational difficulties and significantly improved the efficiency of acquisitions operations. It has also provided the library staff with invaluable experience in planning and operating an automated system.

If there is one area in which the Notre Dame Libraries differ from the mainstream of American academic libraries, it is in the extent to which nonuniversity funds support library operations on an ongoing basis. In recent years the university has been very successful in obtaining outside financial support, particularly in endowment for the university. In the latest "Campaign for Notre Dame," which began in 1977, a goal of $10 million in endowment for the library has been set. By 1979 some 17% of budgeted acquisitions funds were based on endowment income. This is expected to increase substantially as the goal of the campaign is realized. In addition, during the 1970s over $1 million in special nonlibrary funds were utilized to acquire special collections in theology, African studies, Byzantine studies, sports materials, and English literature and history.

Total staffing within the University Libraries system comprises 34 professionals, 85 full-time-equivalent (FTE) support positions, and 25 FTE in student assistants. Support staff and student assistants are administered in accord with policies and procedures established by the University Personnel Office. In recent years major attention has been devoted to upgrading staff salaries and fringe benefits. Professional library staff within the system have been recognized since 1967 as a formal part of the university faculty and as such are represented in the Faculty Senate (where librarians have served as secretary for several years) and the Academic Council, the official internal academic-policy-making body of the university. However, librarians are distinct from the teaching and research faculty in titles and type of contract. There are four ranks for professional librarians: staff, assistant, associate, and full librarian. Staff librarians serve under 1-year contracts, while the three senior ranks each receive 3-year contracts. There is no tenure for librarians at any rank, and all serve 12 months per year, with 20 days of vacation. In all other respects librarians receive the same fringe benefits and perquisites as the teaching and research faculty. They are governed by their own, internally developed, criteria and procedures for appointment and promotion, which are administered by their own, partially elected, Appointments and Promotions Committee. Decisions of this group are subject to final approval by the director of libraries and the provost and president. Full faculty meetings are held at least once every semester, with business conducted through several elected committees.

The physical keystone of the University Libraries system is the Memorial Library, opened in 1963. With some 429,780 square feet, the building was at the time of dedication the largest academic library building in the country, with two large main floors of over 90,000 square feet each, a full basement, and 10 additional tower floors of 17,000 square feet each. The building can comfortably accommodate 3,000 users and 2,000,000 volumes. At the present time, faculty offices occupy much of the basement and two of the tower floors. These are slated to be restored to library use upon completion of a classroom–faculty office building currently in the initial planning stages.

The main floor of the building includes processing offices and the facilities for reference and documents, current periodicals, and circulation. In addition there is a 300-seat auditorium, a large faculty lounge, and the Department of Rare Books–Special Collections, which includes exhibit and reading areas.

The second floor, designated as the College Library, contains a microforms area, 10 group study rooms, and the Audio-Learning Center with 76 listening stations. Each of the tower floors currently devoted to library purposes includes several seminar rooms and a number of private, enclosed study carrels for the use of students working on dissertations. The Medieval Institute and the Area Studies programs have special reading rooms on the seventh and twelfth floors, respectively, and the University Archives is quartered in a part of the sixth floor.

Originally the building was designed to function on a subject-divisional basis, with use of the tower limited to graduate students and faculty. However, because of costs and a variety of service problems, operations reverted to a more traditional mode with open stacks and a single general reference department in the early 1970s.

Despite the growth of the collections and the restructuring of services since opening, the building has stood the test of time well. Moreover, unlike most major library buildings, generous initial planning will probably permit the building to serve adequately for many years to come, provided that space currently devoted to nonlibrary use can be recovered.

If the physical facilities of the Memorial Library are very good, those of the other units in the University Libraries system range from modest to disastrous. The Architecture Library is housed in a reading room in the old Lemonnier Library in quarters that are both attractive and reasonably able to accommodate its collections. The libraries for Mathematics and Life Sciences are also in relatively new quarters, being opened in 1962 and 1970, respectively. However, in both cases, planning was inadequate: The Mathematics collection is currently very crowded, with almost no room in currently assigned space for collection growth, while the Life Sciences Library can house the journal literature for the last 10 years only. To make matters worse, in the case of the Life Sciences Library, expansion of currently assigned space would be very difficult, even with new construction (which is unlikely in the foreseeable future). The Chemistry–Physics Library dates back to 1953 and is similarly crowded, although modest relief from overcrowding is possible. The Engineering Library is a special case. For nearly 40 years it was housed in one room in the Cushing Hall of Engineering. Additional adjacent space was acquired in 1973, but by 1979 the total assigned space was literally jammed, with 18-inch aisles between stacks and only 34 seats for a faculty of 80 and 1,023 students in the College of Engineering. Fortunately, a major addition to the Engineering building will permit the assignment of over 5,000 square feet in the existing building for a new library. This new facility, through the combination of standard and compact shelving, will provide 100 seats and shelving for over 40,000 volumes, which, with a new microform project for serials, should adequately handle growth for the next 10 years at least.

Facilities for the other specialized reading rooms are generally adequate, with the Radiation Laboratory Library in a relatively new building (1963) and the Earth Sciences Reading Room in facilities that are being remodeled. This last unit was formerly a full library, but because of space and other problems, only current journals and selected reference works are being retained, primarily for faculty use.

The Collections

A primary purpose of a university library is, of course, to develop collections to support the functions of the institution. Prior to World War II Notre Dame was basically an undergraduate institution, and its collections in general reflected this fact. Reasonably strong research-oriented collections existed in a very limited number of areas, reflecting specific faculty interests.

By the late 1920s a very strong collection in biology had been developed, aided by extensive exchange agreements with the *American Midland Naturalist* and the acquisition in 1915 of the Edward L. Greene Collection of 4,000 volumes of 19th-century and earlier botany. Research interest in chemistry—centered around the work of Rev. Julius A. Nieuwland, C.S.C., a biologist and pioneer in the chemistry of synthetic rubber—resulted in an unusually strong collection at a relatively early date. The rapid proliferation of journals and skyrocketing inflation rates in recent years have seriously affected the early comprehensiveness of the collections in these two areas. Less affected by these factors have been the holdings in Mathematics, which developed rapidly from the late 1930s into a solid collection of both journals and monographic literature in pure mathematics totaling some 25,780 volumes. In recent years the Mathematics Library was significantly bolstered by the gift of the private library of Marston Morse, a nationally prominent mathematician associated with the Institute of Advanced Studies at Princeton.

The early interest of James Edwards, the first librarian, in collecting the records of the history of the Catholic church in America was renewed with the establishment of the Center for the Study of American Catholicism (1976). Particularly significant was the development of a collection of microfilms of American Catholic newspapers and the intensive collecting of ephemeral materials, including popular and homiletic pamphlets, prayer books, and histories of individual parishes. Related to and occasionally overlapping these collecting interests was the work of the University Archives in gathering the papers of prominent Catholic individuals and organizations.

In the 1930s Father Philip Moore, then secretary of the Committee on Graduate Studies, stimulated research and library collecting in the area of medieval studies. Further impetus in this area came with the establishment of the Medieval Institute in 1946. In the years since, an outstanding collection has been developed in this area, highlighted by the purchase of the library of Anson Phelps Stokes in 1954 and the acquisition of the Frank M. Folsom Ambrosiana Microfilm and Photographic Collection, a project of the Samuel H. Kress Foundation which contains microfilms, slides, and photographs of the entire medieval and renaissance manuscript holdings of the Ambrosiana Library in Milan. A long-term program to catalog all the manuscripts is currently underway with support from the Mellon Foundation and the National Endowment for the Humanities. Overall, the University Libraries' holdings are particularly rich in materials on medieval intellectual life, including philosophy and theology, and the history of medieval education. Included in the latter area are originals and microfilms of manuscript lists of students, curricula, and financial statements. In recent years materials in paleography have become of increasing interest and collections in this area have been greatly enriched.

Separate from but intimately related to medieval studies is the John A. Zahm Dante Collection of over 5,000 volumes of primary and secondary materials on Dante. Begun by the Rev. John A. Zahm, C.S.C., as a private collection, it came to the university in 1921, and despite periods of neglect it has been, and remains, one of the outstanding collections in the country, particularly in terms of early editions of Dante texts.

Somewhat surprisingly, the systematic development of a research collection in theology has been a rather recent development, having come about largely since the 1950s. Aiding in this progress has been the purchase of large collections from France, England, and the United States, including the private library of the French medievalist Canon Eugene Jarry (15,000 volumes); that of Douglas Woodruff, long-time editor of the English Catholic journal, *The Tablet* (12,000 volumes); and a large portion of the William Bacon Stevens Collection from the Philadelphia Divinity School (30,000 volumes). Particularly strong collections have been built in recent years in patristics, liturgy, and canon law. Perhaps the most outstanding single area of strength is Byzantine theology and culture, as represented in the recently acquired Milton V. Anastos Collection (40,000 volumes).

The most recent area of collecting interest centers on sports and games in their various ramifications. Activity in this area began in the early 1960s, based largely on gifts. In the 1970s collecting became more aggressive, with the purchase of a very large dealer's stock and several other smaller, more specialized collections. Organized as the International Sports and Games Research Collection, the collection is, not unexpectedly, particularly strong in nonprint material relating to the history of athletics at Notre Dame, but there are also rich holdings in a number of areas, including the history of the Olympic Games, golf, and billiards. All told the collection exceeds 500,000 pieces in books, journals, programs, guidebooks, photographs, films, scrapbooks, and manuscript items.

Other special collections of note include the previously mentioned Greene Collection of Botany, the Robert H. Gore, Sr., Collection of Orchidiana (300 volumes), the John Bennett Shaw Collection of English and American Literature (20,000 volumes), the Elias V. Denissoff Collection on Descartes (600 volumes), the Jeremiah D. M. Ford Collection on Romance Languages and Literature (3,000 volumes), the Lester W. Olson Collection on Franklin Delano Roosevelt (2,000 volumes), the Robert H. Gore, Jr., Collection of Numismatics (6,000 coins and pieces of currency), the Arnold C. Hackenbruch Collection of Historical Newspapers (3,000 original issues of American newspapers from 1684 to 1871), and the Ervin C. Kleiderer Collection on Horology (1,500 volumes).

In more recent years the university's teaching and research programs have expanded. At the same time, the volume of scholarly publishing has increased dramatically, as have the costs of such material. These concurrent developments have presented the Notre Dame Libraries with increasing difficulties in both supporting traditional areas of interest and meeting demands in new areas. Moreover, as the academic standards of the university rose, the nature and volume of faculty research also increased. When the faculty turned to the library for support for their work, they too often encountered collections which lacked the depth required for research, particularly in new areas of interest. The receipt of a $400,000 NEH Challenge Grant has enabled the libraries to attack some of the most glaring problem areas, and the prospect of significantly increased support from endowment income may in the years ahead enable a more balanced, overall development of the collection.

In part as a result of the recognition of shortcomings in collections as well as services, the libraries in 1978 initiated a long-range planning process involving library faculty and staff, the Faculty Committee for University Libraries, and the external Advisory Council for University Libraries. A 5-year development program was presented to the university in early 1980. The plan highlighted the ways in which the libraries could deal constructively with the variety of challenges in the areas of bibliographic access, preservation, services, space, and collection development, and the fiscal resources required to do this most effectively.

During the years of retrenchment in the 1970s the libraries at Notre Dame did not suffer any actual cutbacks in funding for either staffing or acquisitions, as many other libraries did. On the other hand, they had never experienced the earlier affluence of the '60s. This tradition of cautious but steady fiscal support, together with a solid planning framework, should put the libraries in a better state, psychologically as well as financially, to face the inevitable fiscal and other challenges of the 1980s.

ROBERT C. MILLER

THE PHILIPPINES, LIBRARIES IN

Introduction

In the story of ancient libraries told by many writers, it has been repeatedly expressed that libraries were invariably found in the great seats of civilization. The Assyrian libraries in Nineveh, with thousands of well-organized tablets; the library of the Ptolemies of Egypt, to which scholars flocked; the library at Pergamon in Asia Minor; and the Greek and Roman libraries that were established as the countries rose to glory and grandeur—all were evidence of the truth of this statement.

On the other hand, scholars are agreed on the high level of the equally ancient civilization of the Orient. China had large imperial libraries established and enriched continuously during the Chou dynasty (1122–256 B.C.). Masterpieces of Chinese literature, the work of Confucius, and other works on Chinese philosophy and learning were to be found in well-organized libraries in the years even after the end of the said dynasty. India, which was the center of Aryan civilization, is another country that is rich in prehistoric culture. It developed a literature that was unbroken for 3,000 years, consisting of epics, hymns, dramas, fables, and lyric poetry.

These two countries, China and India, had great cultural influence on the early people of the Philippines. The system of writing of the early Filipinos, in fact, had Sanskrit characters. And a great number of Filipino words were derived from the Chinese vocabulary. If these two countries had libraries, it would not be irrelevant to presume that the ancestors of the settlers of the Philippines could have been recipients of the benefits of those libraries. The early Filipinos had their own system of writing, and they had their own literature and their own codes of laws when the Spaniards arrived in the early 16th century. And yet no extant record stands to give evidence of the existence of libraries when the Spaniards came to the islands.

This account of the libraries in the Philippines, therefore, begins with the establishment of libraries by the Spanish colonizers as the situation demanded. Three hundred years of Spanish rule, however, produced libraries that were not centers of learning but were institutions to support the religious conversion of the natives. The American occupation established American libraries on Philippine soil and made them a medium in instilling the tenets of democracy. At present the Philippines is still in the midst of a dilemma and is still searching for the identity of the real Philippine library.

The Philippines, a country of 7,100 islands and islets with an approximate land area of 116,000 square miles, is one of the countries belonging to the Southeast Asia region. Its population of 42.5 million is concentrated mainly in urban areas. The people, primarily of Malayan stock, speak a variety of dialects. Tagalog, as one of the major dialects, was made the base of the national language called *Pilipino language*. English, however, is the language of government, education, and the majority of the mass media and the means of communication.

The country is politically divided into three parts: Luzon, Visayas, and Mindanao. The subpolitical organization consists of 74 provinces grouped into 13 regions. There are 61 chartered cities, 1,439 municipalities, 21 municipal districts, and 33,776 barrios (*1*).

The Spanish Contribution

THE DISCOVERY OF THE PHILIPPINES

The Philippines, a tiny speck on the world map, has a very significant role in the history of civilization in that its discovery led to the first circumnavigation of the earth. The fleet headed by Ferdinand Magellan which left Spain on September 20, 1519, and sailed westward reached the Philippines on March 16, 1521. The return voyage of the rest of the fleet, under the command of Juan Sebastian Elcano, continued the westward direction, and it finally reached Spain on September 16, 1522, after crossing the Indian Ocean, going around the Cape of Good Hope at the lower tip of Africa, and up the Atlantic Ocean.

It might seem inconceivable that spices could lead to the discovery of the Philippines, but it was in fact the quest for new trade routes that brought European explorers to the Pacific. The crusades that lasted for hundreds of years enabled people from different parts of Europe to meet people from different parts of the Orient, with the result that the people of Europe developed a liking for Oriental goods, particularly spices, fruits, silks, and other luxuries. Spain, England, Portugal, France, and Holland had a race for trade with the Eastern countries, using several trade routes from the West to the East. The trade with China, India, and other countries of the East was a flourishing one, but two well-established trade routes to the East were closed due to the conquest of Constantinople by the Turks in 1453.

In Spain's effort to blaze a new trail to the East, for the much desired Oriental goods, a fleet of five ships started the voyage and reached the East after almost 18 months. The search for food for the crew of the fleet led Ferdinand Magellan to stop at different tiny islands in the Pacific until he reached the vicinity of Samar on March 16, 1521, and landed in Homonhon the following day. Still in search of food and a comfortable place to rest, Magellan continued to move to other places—Limasawa, Cebu, and then to the historic island of Mactan.

RELIGIOUS CONVERSION AS A MOTIVE OF SPAIN

The discovery of the Philippines opened for Spain bright prospects of an extremely lucrative trade and included the amazing discovery of an assemblage of humanity that was easily made ready to be converted into the Catholic religion. The economic motive, which was foremost in the efforts of Spain in sending Magellan and his crew to the East, was in a way gradually dimmed by the religious motive. Several expeditions were sent by Spain to the Philippines after the discovery made by Magellan, but for a considerable time no permanent settlement was made due to the natives' protests and hostility. It was Manuel Lopez de Legaspi who in 1565 succeeded in establishing a permanent settlement in Cebu. It is of interest to us that Legaspi had with him Fr. Andres de Urdaneta, an Augustinian friar, obviously to carry out the religious phase of the expedition. In the settlement made in Manila in 1571, among the first buildings to be constructed were a church and a convent for the Augustinian friars. By 1590, besides the Augustinians, there were the Franciscan, Jesuit, and Dominican orders; these, according to Robertson, had by that time already established their libraries (*2*), which later developed in size and importance. European countries at that time were all well aware of the importance of libraries and the use of libraries to support religious and moral instruction. At that time the religious orders in the Philippines were doubling their efforts in their mission of religious conversion. They were apprehensively conscious of the faltering religious stability of the Catholic Church due to the Lutheran movement in Europe. It appeared that Martin Luther was using the library as an instrument of religious enlightenment in the controversy with the Catholic Church.

In like manner, the religious orders in the Philippines used the convent libraries with real diligence for effective religious conversion of the natives. The enrichment and development of these libraries depended on the assistance coming from the mother country, and these convent libraries were fortunate in this regard because King Philip II of Spain was a library enthusiast (*3*). He was known to have established a superb monastery library with his own 2,000 volumes as the nucleus, which grew due to the addition of items collected from different countries. The fate of many of these early convent libraries in the Philippines, however, is difficult to trace from the 16th century, when they were founded, as there are no records to go by, but it may be said that they still existed in the middle of the 18th century. The account by James A. Robertson states that in 1762 the British looted the libraries in Manila and burned many books, while some books were brought to the British Museum (*2*).

THE LIBRARIES ESTABLISHED BY SPAIN

Also religious in nature were the school and college libraries that were organized, since education then was in the hands of the religious orders. The earliest among these was the University of Santo Tomas library, which opened its facilities in 1611 (*4*). The founder of the school was Fr. Miguel de Benavides, who was a member of the group of Dominican fathers that arrived in Manila on July 25, 1578. On April 15, 1602, he became the archbishop of Manila, and on July 24, 1605, he laid the foundation of the "Colegio Seminario," the forerunner of the University of Santo Tomas. In 1610 work on the establishment of the university was started. The initial library collection was composed of donations of books from Fr. Benavides and Fr. Diego de Soria, another Dominican father. The activities of the two donors were recorded as follows:

> His Excellency the Archbishop of Manila, Señor Benavides, a Dominican, projected the foundation of the college of Santo Tomas, aided by his Excellency Don Fray Diego de Soria of the same order, a bishop of Segovia. With the one thousand pesos fuertes donated by Señor Benavides and the four thousand by Señor Soria, and the acquisition of the libraries of both, the works were commenced in the year 1610 (*5*).

The libraries that were established after 1611 were mostly "college libraries" (as they were called) which in reality were only of secondary level and not of college level. The College of San Felipe de Austria was founded (1640–1641) by Sebastian Hurtado de Corcuera (*6*), and it was later annexed to the College of San Jose in Manila. The library was open only 4 hours a day, 2 hours in the morning and 2 hours in the afternoon. Between 1761 and 1769 a description by Murillo Velarde made known the existence of another college library, the College of San Ignacio library. The description made by Velarde was cited in Guilaume le Gentil's *Voyages dans les mers del'Inde*, where it was said that "the library has no equal in the islands, in either the number or the select quality of the books, which include all branches of learning" (*7*). Such a high evaluation of a college library in 1769 revealed the early recognition of the important role of the library in education. At the same time, it was further made known that the educator and/or the librarian had the skill and specialized knowledge needed in selecting books for the collection.

Similar to colleges, but more specialized in functions, were the seminaries. There were seminaries in Manila, Cebu, Jaro, Nueva Caceres, and Nueva Segovia, all of which were furnished with libraries (*8*).

About the last quarter of the 18th century, libraries for nonreligious purposes began to be established by Spain in the Philippines. The Real Sociedad Economica de Amigos del Pais, to which was attached a library, was created by a royal decree of August 27, 1780 (*9*). An archivist–librarian (*archivero–bibliotecario*) was appointed to take care of the library (*10*). Another nonreligious library was the Biblioteca Militar de Manila established by a royal decree of 1846, obviously for the use of the members of the armed forces stationed in the Philippines (*11*).

So far, the libraries that were being established were school and special libraries. There were libraries for students in *colegios*, for seminarians, for the religious orders, for the development of "science, art, industry, and commerce of the archipelago" (as stated in the objectives of the Real Sociedad Economica de Amigos del Pais), and for the military group. The government of Spain evidently was already aware of the pent-up feelings for nationalism of the Filipinos that were raging beneath the calm prevailing between the fragmentary insurrections. As a prudent and cautious move, Spain shared with the Philippines in its nationalist feeling and made a policy of encouragement rather than repression. An evidence of the decision was the royal decree of August 12, 1887, for the establishment of the Museo–Biblioteca de Filipinas (in essence, a national library of the Philippines), the actual establishment taking place in 1891. The library was temporarily housed in No. 12 Gunao Street, Quiapo; it was free to the public and open every day from 8 to 12 A.M. and from 2 to 5 P.M. (*12*). The staff was composed of the following: director, Pedro Alejandro Paterno; secretary, Eugenio Ochagavia; librarian, Manuel Pineyro y Merino; and collector, Jose de Jesus y Rosario (*13*). Paterno, who had lived in Spain for 18 years, was known for his literary interest and industry. When he decided to return to his native Philippines, the Spanish government took the opportunity to appoint him as director of the newly established Museo–Biblioteca de Filipinas, believing in his qualification for the position. He arrived in the middle of 1894. His first project in his capacity as director of the Museo–Biblioteca de Filipinas was the publication of the *Boletin* as the official organ of the Museo–Biblioteca. This was a monthly publication, and the first issue was published on January 15, 1895 (*14*).

The fact that it took 4 years before the decree was implemented shows that there was some hesitancy on the part of the local officials of the Spanish government to give encouragement to and facilities for the growth of the nationalistic movement. But Spain should be credited for extending to the Philippines liberal ideas about the use of libraries.

The Public Library Idea

THE BEGINNING OF LIBRARIES FOR THE PEOPLE

Accounts of the development of libraries in different countries are clear on the concept that the early libraries were for kings, priests, and the nobility. The library of the Ptolemies of Egypt and the library of the Attalids of Pergamon were both libraries of the ruling houses; the libraries of the different Roman emperors were really spoils of war and were kept as private properties and were even presented as gifts to kings and emperors. The libraries of the Middle Ages, which developed with the universities of Europe, were for scholars and not for the people.

It was only after the birth of democracy, with the recognition of human dignity and the natural right to equal opportunities for individuals, that public education was introduced. The revolutions of the late 18th century that brought forth the concepts of liberty, fraternity, and equality also had an impact on the philosophy of library service. European libraries that were formerly exclusive opened their doors to the public and thereby started the popular library movement (*15*). Spain must have been in the path of the movement and must have accepted and believed in the new concept of library practice. Records show that the Philippines in a small way benefited from Spain's newly acquired principle of extending library facilities to the public. The Real Sociedad Economica de Amigos del Pais created by a royal decree of August 27, 1780, made a report of its activities in 1823, among which was "free distribution of one thousand three hundred twenty copies of [books of] grammar, orthography, and reading lessons for popular use" (*16*).

Whether the distribution indicated in the preceding quotation was a distribution of books in a library to its readers, or distribution of books (textbooks) by the school to the school population, is not clear. However, whatever it was, the fact is that there was a distribution of materials for "popular use," which portended the beginning of allowing the public equal opportunities in the use of materials of learning. This was not an isolated case, as there is a record of an 1871 royal order that mentioned directly the formation of popular libraries, as given in the following:

> Royal order of the ministry of colonies, asking the superior civil government of these islands for the names of teachers who distinguished themselves by zeal for the good of teaching, their intelligence and power to work, in order to inform the Ministry of Public Works [Fomento] so that, if it deems it advisable, it may reward them as those of the Peninsula, by sending them collections of books for the formation of popular libraries (*17*).

There are indications that the trend for liberalizing the use of libraries was meant to be continued and perhaps to be developed by the Spanish government as an extension of the popular library movement in Europe. After the establishment of the Superior Normal School in Manila in 1892, a reference to "public libraries" was noted in one of the regulations for the school in the matter of supply of books for the pupils. The regulation was stated as follows:

> Since the economic conditions of the pupils of this center will not permit them to acquire a certain class of books, which would be necessary for them to know, the governor general shall assign the said center a copy of the books, which have application to the school which these regulations treat, and the ministry of colonies shall send them for the encouragement of the public libraries (*18*).

It is quite surprising, though heartening, to find the term *public libraries* used with reference to book service in the Philippines in a statement made in 1892. It would require a great deal of digging into historical documents to know whether the term should be accepted at its face value. The term could be something that does not conform with what we now know as *public library*. But it is also true that Spain was making efforts to maintain its hold on its colonies, and the method employed was the liberalization of its policies, which leaned toward more democratic relations with the natives.

The Philippine Census of 1903 also used the term *public libraries* in its report, stating that "there were only twelve public libraries in the Philippine Islands when the census was taken, in all of which only 4,019 books were contained" (*19*). These, presumably, were the "public libraries" referred to as those being encouraged by the Ministry of Colonies in 1892 and the "popular libraries" that were the objects of the royal order of 1871.

AMERICAN CONTRIBUTION TO THE MOVEMENT

The people who established colonies in America came from the Old World, where the principle of democracy was beginning to be conceived. The settlers found in America a very appropriate place where the newly conceived ideas could thrive. Individuals were free to organize themselves; for example, for the purpose of providing themselves with reading facilities. Membership fees or subscription fees were used to maintain the collection of books, which grew in size as the yearly support continued. Also in the same category as these *subscription libraries* were the *society libraries;* in this case a society made up of some special group of people of the same interests would establish a library for the use of the members of the society. The society might have been made up of a religious group, or a group of people interested in legal matters, or a group interested in the study of philosophy, etc. Libraries of this sort usually could not be maintained indefinitely, hence the common recourse was to turn the library over to the government.

As long as the library was supported by the members of a private group and operated exclusively for the use of the members of the group, the library was a private library and not for popular use, unless the private group that owned the library opened it to the public. The moment the library was turned over to the government it became a public institution, and therefore it was operated for the public. And thus was started the so-called popular library idea.

The *public library*, established for the people and supported by the people, is genuinely an American idea. The early national leaders, imbued with the spirit of nationalism and with the enthusiasm for good government, knew very well that education was the means by which they could realize their goal. Besides public schools, public libraries were used as instruments of public education. After the dwindling of the early forms of libraries—subscription libraries, society libraries, mercantile libraries, mechanics libraries, etc.—the tax-supported library emerged, with the library of Peterborough, established in 1833, as the first one in the said category. Most of the subscription and society libraries were gradually turned over to the care of the government.

Such mode of operation in the establishment of public libraries was brought to the Philippines when the Americans occupied our country. In the first place, the American colonial policy was based on the belief that education would be a powerful weapon in the pacification of the people and would also be the surest way to successful government. Hence, 3 weeks after the American triumph in the battle of Manila Bay on August 13, 1898, the schools in Manila were reopened, and additional ones were established during the following months. On January 21, 1901, Act 74 of the U.S. Philippine Commission was passed creating the Department of Instruction, thereby establishing a system of public education in the Philippines. English was used as the medium of instruction and English books that were shipped from the United States were the main materials of instruction. As the teaching of the English language would require the use of books, or "readers," it was clear that classroom collections were a necessary tool in the teaching process. These collections were, in fact, collections of supplementary readers, and not books for recreational or reference use such as we have in our libraries today; also, the books were not organized in the same way as the collections in centralized libraries of today. Yet, in a strict sense, it may be stated that these were the first libraries established in the Philippines by the Americans.

THE AMERICAN CIRCULATING LIBRARY

Not to be outranked in the introduction of library facilities in the Philippines was the American Circulating Library that was turned over to the Philippine government in 1901 (*20*). In 1900 an association called the American Circulating Library Association was formed in Manila through the initiative of Mrs. Charles R. Greenleaf, who solicited donations of books and money from wives of army officers in Manila and from individuals and organizations in the United States. The objective of the association was to provide recreational and informational materials to the American sailors, soldiers, and civilian residents in Manila, and to serve as a memorial to those naval and military men who died in the war of occupation. To maintain the service, a subscription fee of 50 centavos a month, or 5 pesos a year, was collected from readers who borrowed books for home use. Nonmembers were not allowed free use of the reading room.

The librarian of this subscription library was Nelly Young Egbert, the widow of General H. C. Egbert, who died during the war in the Philippines. Mrs. Greenleaf, who was appointed director of the library, continued to augment the collection by increased efforts in soliciting materials from friends, societies, libraries, and other organizations in the United States, such that by 1901 the library already had a collection of 10,000 volumes.

Following the pattern of the U.S. public library beginnings—where the private library, whether subscription or society, etc., was turned over to the government to continue the service to the public—the American Circulating Library was turned over to the Philippine government in 1901. The terms of acceptance of the gift by the government were stated in Act No. 96 enacted by the U.S. Philippine Commission on March 5, 1901. Part of Section 1 of the act states that the gift was "to be administered under the legislative control of the Military Government, or its successor, the Civil Government of the Philippine Islands, on condition that suitable appropriations, within the discretion of the Government of these Islands, shall be made for the proper housing of the books and their circulation in accordance with the purposes of the original gifts, and that the name shall remain unchanged, that the memorial feature shall be perpetuated, and that the magazines and such books as can be spared shall be sent as promptly as possible to the outlying districts of the archipelago." The act was making sure that the services would be continued and that the resources would be made available to the other parts of the country, which was in effect foreseeing the extension of library services over wider areas to include the whole Philippines. Also, the inclusion of the statement that "the establishment of a source of instruction and profitable entertainment for all residents of Manila, whether permanent or transient, and of whatever race or nationality" confirmed the motive of the association that the library was intended to be a public library—a library for everybody in the Philippines. Hence, the general idea is that the transfer of the American Circulating Library to the Philippine government marked the start of the public library movement in our country. Still adhering to the American pattern of public library administration, the library was placed under a Board of Trustees. The collection increased to about 21,000 books, and traveling libraries were sent to different parts of the Philippines in the effort to extend library services to the soldiers and to more and more people.

Mrs. Egbert, who remained as librarian up to 1912, was responsible for the growth of the library. With the increasing activities, an assistant librarian, Mrs. Emma O. Elmer, was appointed in 1904. When Mrs. Egbert went on leave in 1905, Mrs. Elmer was designated as acting librarian, but unfortunately she was taken ill. Miss Bessie Dwyer, a law clerk in the Bureau of Forestry who had 10 years' experience as an associate librarian in the Library of Congress, had to take her place. It was at this time that the library had to be moved from Calle Rosario to the Oriente Building. As the collection increased, a cataloger, Miss Syrenna McKee, was recruited by the Bureau of Insular Affairs from among the U.S. Civil Service successful examinees. In addition to cataloging work, she undertook many other library tasks including the improvement of the loan system.

But as a public library to give service to Filipinos, we may say that this library was a premature gesture. A library that presumptuously tried to provide recreational and informational books in English to Filipinos who were not at all familiar with the language was bound to fail. In 1905, under Section 2 of Act 1407, the library was transferred to the Bureau of Education where it became the Division of the American Circulating Library. The Board of Trustees was removed and the library was to function under the supervision and control of the director of the Bureau of Education.

The transfer of the administration of the American Circulating Library into the hands of the director of the Bureau of Education implied that the function of the library was within the sphere of the task of the Bureau of Education, and that this educational function could find better fulfillment if the library was placed close to the area that would benefit from it. As a division of the Bureau of Education, the library became the "laboratory" not only of the staff of the bureau but of the teachers in the field, whose great need for instructional materials and professional reading was certainly obvious. A portion of Section 4 of Act 74 says that American soldiers were asked to teach in schools while there were no trained teachers available. Surely the 10,000 books in this library provided ample "teacher training" materials which those American soldiers endeavored to utilize. Some of those soldiers stayed and remained in the teaching profession until their retirement, and it can be said that their contribution to educational development in the Philippines should be credited partly to the service that the library extended to them.

Teachers and school officials in the provinces could also utilize the facilities of the library as a result of the provision of Act 96 that library materials that could be spared were to be sent to the different parts of the country. If books and magazines were to be sent to the provinces, the most logical places to send them were the offices of the superintendents of school divisions. The materials of instruction and materials for professional growth were then brought closer to school officials, teachers, and pupils. It is possible, therefore, that one of the purposes of the turnover of the American Circulating Library to the Philippine government was to support the educational system that was then being established all over the country.

The director of the Bureau of Education at the time was David P. Barrows, who was interested in libraries. Through his initiative, a Filipiniana collection was started, and with this was consolidated the collection of the Museo–Biblioteca de Filipinas. Also, the endeavors of Director Barrows to enrich the collection of the library included the purchase of Spanish books. Five years later the American Circulating Library Division of the Bureau of Education was transferred to be a part of the Philippine Library, as provided by Act 1935; this was enacted May 20, 1909, although the transfer actually took place on June 30, 1910. The portion of the collection consisting of Philippine materials and the Museo–Biblioteca de Filipinas became the nucleus of the Filipiniana Division of the said Philippine Library, and the American Circulating Library itself became a part of the Circulating Division.

From 1910 to 1955 the Circulating Division, with its rich collection of standard classics and popular novels, supplied the readers of metropolitan Manila with recreational reading and information materials. The reading public by that time was at home with the English language and patronized the collection with genuine interest. The American Circulating Library (whose collection dominated that of the Circulating Division of the Philippine Library, of which it was a part) was functioning finally as a public library. In 1955 the Circulating Division was abolished as the City of Manila (which was the main recipient of its services) had by that time already established a system of public libraries that provided branches in the different districts of the city.

School Libraries

THE CLASSROOM LIBRARIES

The pattern of development of school libraries in many countries shows that it was the university that first incorporated the library as one of its integral parts. The idea spread down to the secondary school, and the last to include the library as a unit in the school organization was the elementary school. But this type of development was not true in the case of the Philippines. This statement, of course, does not take into consideration the existence of the University of Santo Tomas Library and the libraries of schools of secondary level that were organized by the religious orders in the Philippines; rather, this statement refers to the American government's efforts in establishing the educational system in the Philippines. The unusual objective of the public schools that were established early—that is, to teach the English language to all the pupils—required the presence of many books to be read. Hence, school libraries, on the elementary level, were the first to be organized.

Classroom libraries proved to be useful as far as supplying supplementary readers to the pupils was concerned. But the advantages and benefits to be gained from a centralized library serving the whole school were not availed of by the pupils. The centralized library acts as an agency that coordinates major activities of the school, especially where the trend for integration of content is given considerable stress. In this case, the child does not acquire particular or individual facts but is concerned with a whole body of knowledge gained from a variety of sources. This trend in education, which can be supported by a library with a rich collection, was recognized early in the Philippines, though in an extremely limited way.

THE EARLY HIGH SCHOOL LIBRARIES

The first library that was organized to function as a coordinating agency and to serve the whole school population was the Pampanga High School Library. The credit for the organization of this library goes to Mrs. Lois Stewart Osborn, an

American teacher in the said school. Because of the need for an organized library for her English composition and literature classes, Mrs. Osborn campaigned very seriously for books to start the library. She succeeded in making the teachers and pupils of the school interested in the campaign, and subsequently even the town officials heeded with enthusiasm the call for cooperation. The division superintendent, Mr. G. N. Anderson, was greatly helpful in spreading the interest and was instrumental in making the fund campaign a success. All sorts of programs were used to raise money for the initial collection and for the maintenance of the library, such as benefit dances, benefit stage shows, and voluntary contributions. At the end of 2 years the library had 950 volumes in its collection.

Inspired by the success of the Pampanga High School Library campaign and the evident necessity of the library as a tool in teaching, other provinces followed suit. Tayabas (now Quezon Province) and Bulacan undertook similar campaigns, and both were able to start their high school libraries with enough books to support the courses offered in their schools. In Manila, by 1913 the Manila High School had almost 4,000 volumes, and the Philippine Normal School had 2,000 volumes.

MATRICULATION FEES

At this point the matter of financial support from the government should be considered. Up to 1916 no specific provision in any official act made any reference to financial support of school libraries, in spite of the interest and encouragement shown by the Bureau of Education. Donations and voluntary contributions could not be a perpetual source of money for the purchase of books and continued maintenance of library service in public schools. The government had to provide for regular financial support if the public schools were to be equipped with libraries. The Bureau of Education resorted, therefore, to the collection of matriculation fees, a move that became necessary when the director of the Bureau of Education campaigned for the purchase of more books for school libraries. A fee of 2 pesos each was collected from pupils of the intermediate grades; and four pesos each, from pupils of secondary schools. In 1922 General Instruction Number 14 of the Bureau of Education specified that 40% of the total sum collected in each school was to be used for the purchase of books, magazines, library supplies, and school library equipment. In 1925, because of the insufficiency of the 40% allocated to the library, the amount was raised to 60%. In spite of the increased support, the school library book collections and other facilities were never sufficient to enable the libraries to render satisfactory service. Through the years the same amount was collected from each pupil, notwithstanding the fact that prices of books and other materials needed in the library continued to go up. Yet in 1964 (by R.A. No. 4092) the matriculation fee—the only source of regular funds for the support of the school libraries—was abolished, in line with the policy of providing free education to everybody.

PROBLEMS FACED BY THE PUBLIC SCHOOL LIBRARIES

It appears that, up to this point, building the book collection was the main problem being tackled by the pioneers of the library idea for Philippine public schools. The raising of funds, of course, was the first step taken preliminary to the purchase of books, but the facilities for book buying were almost nil; there were no bookstores from which to buy books, and above all, no book selection aids were available. Considering the emergency nature of the need for books to push through with haste the public education venture, it would be realistic to take note of the difficulty of depending for supplies and equipment on sources thousands of miles beyond the seas, and to remember the sluggish rate of movement of the ships of those times. In the matter of book selection aids, if the American educators could get lists from U.S. sources, these would, of course, be selection aids for books for American pupils.

But even during the first decade of the public education system and the accompanying libraries, suitability of books for Filipino pupils was already recognized as a huge problem being faced by the early educators. Mrs. Lois Stewart Osborn's interest in libraries led her to request an interview with the director of education, Mr. Frank White. The result of the interview, or conference, was the creation in 1911 of a committee composed of Mr. Chester A. Buckner as chairman and Mrs. Lois Stewart Osborn, Mrs. Silva Beckner, Mrs. Neva S. Beckner, and Mr. Charles Storms as members. The committee at once set to work and soon put out Bulletin 44, "Libraries for Philippine Public Schools." This was a classified list of books from which schools could select books for their libraries. In 1915 Director of Education W. W. Marquardt asked Mrs. Osborn to review the list to limit it to titles that would be of interest to Filipino boys and girls (*21*).

Another problem that faced teachers and school administrators was the lack of organization of the book collections of school libraries. Educators and teachers even then were agreed that a book collection will be of little use if not organized. Because of the absence of librarians trained in school library work, the book collections of the early school libraries were not organized according to standard classification schemes. Libraries were organized according to local schemes constructed by the person in charge of each library. Hence there was no uniform method of classifying and cataloging the school library collections. Mrs. Osborn, who had no library training, developed her own device to enable her to locate books when they were needed.

The 1911 committee made efforts to help the people in charge of school libraries, at least in the arrangement of their collections. In the Bulletin 44 list of books that was issued in 1912, one of the members of the committee, Mr. Storms, arranged the list according to the Library of Congress (LC) Classification system. Thus the list served as an aid in the classification of the books.

INTRODUCTION OF PROFESSIONAL TRAINING FOR LIBRARIANS

It is clear that the main factor in good library service is the librarian. It is also clear that for several decades in the existence of school libraries, the care of the library was given to schoolteachers without library training. In many cases clerical workers in the school were assigned to take charge of the school library.

Again it was Mrs. Osborn who first insisted that only a librarian with special training in school library methods could enable the library to give satisfactory service to the school program. In 1914, when Mrs. Osborn was transferred to the Philippine Normal School (now Philippine Normal College), she worked for the inclusion of a library methods course in the curriculum, not only for those teachers who would be assigned to work in the school libraries but for all teachers who were interested in the course. Surely, all the teachers would find it beneficial and profitable for their classroom teaching if they gained familiarity with the various sources of information and became acquainted with the ways the library could be used by their pupils.

Apparently it took some time before a course on library methods became a full-fledged normal school course. The report of the director of education in 1917 was disappointing with regard to the training in library methods given in the Philippine Normal School. The report said that a few students were being given some training in school library work, but that no well-organized course of study was in existence (*22*).

In the following year the report of the director of education cited a more definite course in library work, but it appears that the course was directed toward a different group of trainees. The report stated that an elementary course in library practice from the standpoint of the public school was given to those enrolled in the class for supervisors and principals at the Philippine Normal School (*23*). The implication of this statement was, perhaps, that supervisory work in schools should include supervising the work of the librarian. Equipped with knowledge of library economy, the supervisor would be in a better position to help the librarian. But it would seem impractical to train supervisors and principals and leave out the very people who needed the training. Problems would be encountered if supervisors and principals were to supervise librarians who did not have any knowledge of the rudiments of library management, and rate them on what they did not know. On the other hand, viewed from another angle, the system might have been devised as a way of spreading knowledge of library economy. This may be gleaned from Mrs. Osborn's remarks regarding the said course offered in the Philippine Normal School. In 1929 she wrote an article where she noted her reminiscence, a part of which said:

> Library training was placed in the curriculum at the Philippine Normal School, and from the Normal School classes, some knowledge was carried to the provincial schools (*24*).

In present in-service training parlance, the activity is called "training trainers," and this could have been the objective of giving the course to supervisors and principals. However, the succeeding reports of the Bureau of Education were silent on any activity of supervisors and principals in the training of school librarians. Another probable argument for giving the library methods course to supervisors and principals was to prepare them and to enable them to guide teachers in their classroom instruction. The teachers needed guidance and advice on how to explore and exploit all available aids to teaching.

At the time that Mrs. Osborn was working for the inclusion of a library methods course in the Philippine Normal School curriculum (in 1914), the University of the Philippines was already starting a library science course as a regular specialization in the College of Liberal Arts. Through the efforts of Dr. James A. Robertson, then director of the Philippine Library, and Miss Mary Polk, librarian of the Bureau of Science, the University of the Philippines agreed to offer courses for the training of the library assistants in the Philippine Library and in the Bureau of Science Library. With the development of the courses, the enrollment increased, such that in the years that followed the University of the Philippines was the only agency that supplied trained librarians to the public schools.

THE BUREAU OF EDUCATION'S CONCERN IN THE IMPROVEMENT OF SCHOOL LIBRARIES

In 1919 Miss Dorothy Rogers was assigned as supervisor of school libraries. Miss Rogers, who had received library science training in the United States, saw that the Library of Congress scheme would be too cumbersome for school libraries and replaced the LC Classification system with the Dewey Decimal Classification scheme. Miss Rogers assisted school librarians in the use of the Dewey Decimal System and in the cataloging of the books in their libraries. She gave suggestions for the improvement of library service and helped the school librarians in planning activities to make the libraries vital tools in the educative process.

It must have been through the efforts of Miss Rogers that the first in-service training for school librarians was conducted by the Bureau of Education. In 1920 the bureau gave a course in library practice during the Teachers Vacation Assembly in Manila. The 1921 report of the director of education states the following:

> To train personnel for the administration of school libraries and for work with the Dewey Decimal Classification, a course in library practice was offered last year to teachers attending the Teachers Vacation Assembly in Manila. The enrolment in the course was very representative, the teachers who chose to take the work having come from nearly all parts of the islands (*25*).

The assembly was later referred to as the Teachers' Institute, which took care of the orientation of teachers before the school year started. Teachers were then lacking in both training and experience; hence, 2 or 3 weeks before the start of classes the teachers were required to attend the institute to prepare them for the work for the coming school year. It was fortunate for the school libraries that in 1920 training in library work was included as an institute activity.

Meanwhile printed instructions were being issued by the Bureau of Education to help and guide school library workers in operating their libraries. The list of approved books put out in 1912 by the 1911 committee was revised and updated in 1923. In 1928 another revision came out, with a list of 4,000 approved books. The list was Part II of the publication. Part I contained the instructions to school librarians and touched on accessioning, cataloging, classifying, and other techniques used in the processing of books. The old *Service Manual* (*26*), which contained the rules governing the Bureau of Education, had specific sections pertaining to the book-ordering routine to be followed by the school library. Sections 262, 298, and 299 contained instructions as to the procedure in the selection and buying of books. Item (b) of Section 262 said in part:

> Books so ordered must be chosen from the lists of books approved by the Bureau of Education for primary, intermediate, and professional libraries (*27*).

In subsequent years the bureau continued to release bulletins that guided and instructed librarians in the field, such as:

Academic Bulletin No. 7, 1934: *Cataloging of Magazine Articles*
Academic Bulletin No. 10, 1934: *Record Card for Periodicals, B.E. Form 4 and 27*
Academic Bulletin No. 11, 1934: *Pamphlets in the School Library*
Academic Bulletin No. 25, 1934: *Index to Local Magazines*
Bulletin No. 3, 1935: *Filing Newspaper Clippings*
Bulletin No. 9, 1935: *Mounting, Filing, and Cataloging Pictures*

In 1927 another in-service training course was conducted at the General Office in Manila from December 21 to 24. The course was specifically for high school librarians, emphasizing accessioning, classification, cataloging, and book selection. The course was authorized by the Bureau of Education's Memorandum Number 58 of 1927, which entitled each school division to send one representative to take the course.

In the year following this in-service training course, emphasis remained on the training of librarians. Suggestions were given by the bureau that library training be included among the courses offered in Normal Institutes. In Memorandum Number 5, issued on January 23, 1928, and entitled "1928 Division Normal Institutes," Paragraph 16 listed the special courses suggested. Among the special courses was Library Science or Library Methods, which was described as "a library training course to include (1) accessioning, (2) classifying, (3) cataloging, (4) book repair, (5) book selection." Although the usual length of a Normal Institute was only 6 weeks, these courses could be quite helpful, especially if due emphasis was given to proper segments of the training course.

In conducting the 1929 Division Normal Institutes, the same suggestion was made by the Bureau of Education regarding special courses for teachers. That memorandum stated that "courses in measurements and statistics, library training, health, character, and thrift education are suggested" (*28*). Since no report or account of the Division Normal Institutes is available, it is not known whether the suggestions were carried out. In the following years the memoranda of the bureau carried the same suggestion regarding the offering of library training courses. In 1933 a report of the Bureau of Education tabulated the courses completed in vacation normal schools and trade schools for 1929, 1930, 1931, and 1932 (*29*). For Library Methods, the column for 1932 in the table indicated that 14 high school graduates completed the library training course. It is understood that the Normal Institutes were conducted to give training to teachers who did not have any professional preparation, especially to those with only high school attainment.

THE LIBRARY METHODS COURSE IN THE PHILIPPINE NORMAL SCHOOL

In the Philippine Normal School, the scope of the course in Library Methods was widened in 1923, and it was made a general elective although still with some restrictions, as shown by the following passage from a Bureau of Education report:

> The work in library practice that was sometime ago required at the Philippine Normal School of all students enrolled in the first year of the supervising teachers and principals course has recently been made elective. It may now be chosen in place of any half year academic subject in the third and fourth year of any course offered at the Philippine Normal School, but only one student from each province is allowed each year to take it, such students being designated the work by the Division Superintendent of his or her province or by the Superintendent of the Philippine Normal School if the Division Superintendent so desires (*30*).

Later the restriction of "only one student from each province" disappeared, and by the early 1930s any student from any province might elect Library Methods. And although the course was still a one-semester course, it was by that time already a more solid and stable one. More rigorous study of classification and cataloging was required, and more practice in cataloging elementary school books was given, as well as practice in the selection of books from the Bureau of Education Approved Library List.

In spite of continuous strengthening of the course, dissatisfactions were still expressed regarding the adequacy of a one-semester course in the preparation of elementary school librarians. There was a need for more training in reading guidance, selection of books for children, and most of all, in the philosophy of library service for children.

In 1934 Library Methods was offered in the Baguio Summer School as a professional subject for principals and supervisors. From then on up to the outbreak of the war in 1941, the course was offered every year. The subject was equivalent to a one-semester normal school course.

The demand for library training became more felt, and the Philippine Normal School started offering the course in its summer session in Manila in 1938. Instead of giving the course to principals and supervisors, as had always been done in the Baguio Summer School, the subject offered in the Philippine Normal School was open to schoolteachers and school librarians. The course was the same as the one offered during the regular school year in the said school and consisted of a general survey of the different phases of the subject field. But the summer courses had due emphasis on library management, which those already taking care of school libraries needed.

In 1945, after the Philippine Normal College had reorganized its curriculum, the one-semester Library Methods course was again offered. Up to 1955 this three-unit course was offered as an elective that could be taken in lieu of any one-semester subject. In 1955 the Philippine Normal College library science offering was increased to two subjects. Again in 1957 the school changed its library science curriculum and approved a library education curriculum of 18 units. The completion of the 18 units entitled the student to a Certificate of Library Service, which qualified the holder to be a teacher–librarian. In later years the Philippine Normal College continued to revise and update its library science curriculum. Today the school offers the B.S.E. major in Library Science; the B.S.L.S., or Bachelor of Science in Library Science; and the M.A. in Education with specialization in library science.

SCHOOL LIBRARY SUPERVISION

For some time after Miss Rogers left after 2 years' service, the school libraries were again deprived of technical assistance. But about the middle of the 1920s, the chief of the Academic Division of the Bureau of Education, Mr. J. Scott McCormick, and the general office librarian of the Bureau of Education, Mr. Prudencio Lim, resumed the work that Miss Rogers started. The two officials of the bureau traveled to different school divisions to give on-the-spot assistance to librarians, such as in the cataloging of books, the filing of cards, maintenance of the shelflist, the accessioning of books, etc. Mr. Lim, the librarian, took charge of such practical instructions, while Mr. McCormick attended to the use of the library in conjunction with classroom assignments and activities.

In the matter of actual visits to the school libraries in the different school divisions, the supervisory work done before the war was resumed as soon as the general office librarian, Mrs. Estanislawa C. Manzo, could take up her supervisory duties over the school libraries. By that time several in-service education sessions were already being conducted for school library work. The supervision being done by the Bureau of Public Schools (formerly the Bureau of Education) general office librarian, who was also functioning as the supervising librarian of the Bureau of Public Schools, was similar to the supervising routine of subject or grade supervisors. Observations of actual conditions and library work were done, followed by a conference with the librarian visited. Then suggestions were given, and other aids were offered. Actual cataloging of the books for the school librarian, arranging the books on the shelves according to the classification scheme, filing the catalog cards, etc., which formerly had been done by the early supervisors to demonstrate the right library procedures, were not done anymore, unless the library being visited really needed such detailed assistance.

RELATIONSHIP OF THE PUBLIC LIBRARY AND THE SCHOOL LIBRARY

It has been said that the early library laws of the Philippines were patterned after American library laws. Obviously Section 4 of Act Number 1935 of the Philippine legislature, passed in 1909, was modeled on United States practice regarding what the American librarians called public library–school library cooperation. In the United States up to about 1940, a predominant feature of school library progress was due to the close attention given by the public library to library service to schools. In a survey of school library service in the United States completed in 1939, this cooperative arrangement was among the characteristics studied in a group of cities that used such a system. The following observation was made regarding the situation:

> Twelve cities particularly Grand Rapids, Minneapolis, and Oklahoma City, report somewhat extensive use of public library branches in school buildings. Cooperative agreements in Oklahoma City, for example, call for the organization of school libraries as public library branches whenever conditions permit (*31*).

It should follow that administrative control would also be based on a cooperative arrangement, but the survey revealed that the public library had a bigger share of administrative control, as stated in the following:

> While cooperative arrangements are based upon joint agreements and the cost of service is shared, general administrative control, to a large extent, is left in the hands of the public library (*31*).

Section 4 of Act Number 1935 contains traces or evidences of the U.S. idea of the public library helping the school in the provision of library service to the school population. The particular section states:

> Said Library Board shall give particular attention to making available of said Library, in all its parts, for the use of teachers and students of either public or private schools by the establishment of suitable reading rooms, and the opening of said library and reading rooms, for such use and for the use of the public under proper regulations, at all times, including holidays and evenings, and the said Board is empowered to make all rules and regulations for the use of said library. Such Board shall also make a provision for the temporary placing of books in the high school and in other public schools, or with Bureaus which may desire to use certain books at certain times.

This provision was incorporated in the Philippine Administrative Code of 1917 as Section 1698 under Article II of Chapter 44.

In later years it was seen that the extension of reading facilities to schools by the public library was not implemented, at least not in the same way as the U.S. public libraries extend library service to schools. The Circulating Division of the National Library, which extended public library service to the people of Manila for many years, gave special privileges to teachers in the number of books that could be borrowed. As to the "temporary placing of books in the high school and in other public schools," the Philippine Library perhaps did place some books in the high school. The City of Manila had at the time only one high school, the Manila High School (later the Manila South High School, and much later the Araullo High School). In the 1930s there were a few books in the library of the said high school that had the stamp of the Philippine Library, an evidence that those books were placed there by the latter library. The books were never returned to the Philippine Library (as would have been in accordance with the provision for the "temporary" placing of books in the high school), for the books were already accessioned as properties of the high school.

It has already been stated that school libraries were organized almost simultaneously with the opening of schools because of their use in the teaching of the English language. These libraries therefore grew with the schools, and in many instances they were richer than the public libraries. Furthermore, the public libraries were slow in their extension work, such that by 1927 there were only 10 provincial branches of the Philippine Library and Museum. The schools did not depend on the public libraries for the necessary book service. The situation in the Philippines was the opposite of that in the United States in that the school libraries were the ones helping the public libraries.

The 1918 *Annual Report of the Director of the Bureau of Education* recorded the use of the school library by the public in the following:

> The number of outsiders availing themselves of the use of school libraries increased to some extent. The development of the school library as a library serving the entire community, is bound to be slow, but it is an important function because the school library must pave the way for the public library that will come in the future.

The idea embodied in this statement hinted at two views on the introduction of public libraries. First, the school, in teaching the children how to read, was in fact producing the future users of the public library. Second, the people must be made to know the benefits that the library can give so that when they already have the library habit, they will be the ones who will clamor for libraries. The second view must have been the objective of the director of education when he said that "the school library must pave the way for the public library that will come in the future." The 1918 report had high hopes for the coming of the public library, but the "future" proved to be quite far away. The public continued to use the school library, and the demand seems to have increased in volume such that in 1928 the Bureau of Education made a clear policy of opening school libraries to the public:

> School libraries should be made available for use during vacation. For convenience, certain hours in which books can be borrowed or returned should be announced. Some teachers can always be found who will be glad to take charge of the library for that time. Library books should not be called in during the short vacation.
>
> It is highly desirable that the school library should be open to the public as soon as there are books to warrant it. Pupils who leave school should be encouraged to come back and get books to read (*32*).

A confirmation of the policy was made by the late J. Scott McCormick, who was chief of the Academic Division of the Bureau of Education and who belonged to the policy-making body of the bureau. In 1934 he wrote a paper for the First National Book Week and the 1934 Librarians' Convention, where he stated the following:

> The public school library in the Philippines has the dual purpose of serving the school and the community as well. There are at present but fifteen branches of the National Library in the entire Philippines for the 1,178 municipalities and municipal districts and their thousands of fair-sized barrios. The school libraries of which there were 5,065 in December 1933, must play a tremendous, if silent, part in the education of the Philippine citizenry (*33*).

The preceding statements show a major modification of policy for the school library. Starting as a classroom library in 1901 to aid in the teaching of the English language, after barely 30 years the library assumed a position that was not at all expected. As early as the period between 1918 and 1934, we can already recognize the sowing of the seeds of the community school, a new direction of elementary education that reached its height in the 1950s. At the same time, it was confirmed that the library was the earliest means of education to reach the public directly.

The National Library and Public Libraries in the Philippines

EARLY LIBRARY LEGISLATION

The first library established in the Philippines during the American occupation was the American Circulating Library that was acquired in 1901 by the Philippine government from the American Circulating Library Association. It was clearly a public library, "a source of instruction and profitable entertainment for all residents of Manila. . . ." Another provision was that "the magazines and such books as can be spared shall be sent as promptly as possible to the outlying districts of the Archipelago" (*34*). Eight years later, on June 3, 1908, Act Number 1849 was passed by the Philippine Legislature. The public library idea introduced by the American Circulating Library must have inspired this legislation. This act, entitled "An Act Providing for the Establishment of a Public Library to Be Known as 'The Philippine Public Library' Making Suitable Appropriations Therefore, and for Other Purposes," was clear on the purpose of the law, the establishment of a public library. But Section 2 of this act stated the following:

> A Public Library Committee shall be appointed by the Governor General and the Speaker of the Assembly, and shall collect, select, for purchase and purchase out of the funds appropriated by this Act, such books, papers, documents, and periodicals relating to the Philippines and to the history thereof, and such other books, papers, documents, and periodicals as the said committee may deem proper for the establishment and uses and purposes of the Philippine Public Library. It shall be the duty of said committee to make a careful investigation of all books, papers, documents and periodicals now in the hands of the Government relating to the Philippines and to the history thereof, and to make due report of its investigations to the Governor General, who upon the recommendation of said committee may direct the transfer of all said books, papers, documents, and periodicals not required for official purposes, to the Philippine Public Library upon the appointment of the librarian provided for by this Act.

The provisions of this section of Act Number 1849 have elements of the establishment of a national library; that is, collection of documents and other materials relating to the Philippines and its history. Furthermore, the collection of this library was to be composed of such materials as those that were then in the different government agencies and would be turned over to the new library. The library to be established was, therefore, a "public" library in name only.

This act was never implemented. The following year Act Number 1935 was passed, an act whose provisions included some parts of Act Number 1849 that appeared to constitute the fundamental distinction of a national library. The collection of the library was to be made up of the collections of the libraries of all government departments, bureaus, and other offices; and the library was to "procure and preserve from time to time all books, papers, documents, and periodicals of every kind or class which related to the history of the Philippine Islands or to the Filipino people." The act was entitled "An Act Providing for the Consolidation of All Libraries Belonging to Any Branch of the Philippine Insular Government for the Creation of the Philippine Library and for the Maintenance and Regulation of the Same, and for Other Purposes." Why the word *public* was removed from the title was not explained; its elimination may mean that the objective of the legislation was the establishment of a national library.

But this act also had public library provisions; this can be seen in Section 4, which says that the Library Board of the library shall give particular attention to "the opening of said Library and reading rooms for such use and for the use of the public under regulations, at all times."

Several acts were passed after this that continued to change the name of the library with no apparent purpose of giving it national library standing. On February 4, 1916, the name was changed to Philippine Library and Museum, as provided by Act Number 2572. The act was another move to consolidate further the libraries of the different agencies of the government. The title of the act was "An Act to Authorize in the Interest of Efficiency and Uniformity of the Public Service, the Consolidation of the Philippine Library, the Division of Archives, Patents, Copyrights, and Trademarks of the Executive Bureau, and the Law and Library Division of the Philippine Assembly, to Form an Organization to Be Known as 'Philippine Library and Museum,' Under the Administrative Control of the Secretary of Public Instruction." On December 7, 1928, Act Number 3477 was passed for the purpose of creating the National Museum of the Philippine Islands, thus separating the Museum from the Library. Without the Museum, the Library was given the name National Library. As in previous library legislation, the law was silent on the reason for naming it the National Library. But Professor Gabriel A. Bernardo deduced that the status of the library at the time was such that it had attained a national character. In summarizing the accomplishment of the Library and Museum, Professor Bernardo wrote the following:

> It must be stated, however, that the entire life-cycle of the Philippine Library and Museum was not altogether barren of constructive work and projects. Deposit and branch libraries were established in Manila and in the provinces; the library's services to the Legislature, through the work of its Legislative Research Office, are largely responsible for many of the laws now embodied in the Philippine statute books; its function as the official archives of the government in charge of the custody and preservation of more than five million documents of administrative, historical, and political character covering three centuries of Spanish administration, and its being the depository not only of the United States and other foreign government documents, but also of all printed works copyrighted in the Philippines or published by the Bureau of Printing, in addition to having accumulated what is now considered as the most comprehensive collection of Philipiniana in the world, have given it the double status of a public and national library. The recognition of its character as a national institution led the Philippine Legislature to change its name to "National Library" in 1928, although its scope was somewhat narrowed by the conversion of its museum branch into an independent "National Museum" (*35*).

In the reorganization made in 1947 by Executive Order Number 94, the National Library was given the name Bureau of Public Libraries, again without stating any reason for doing so. The functions relating to patents, trademarks, and copyrights that were incorporated with the functions of the library by Act Number 2572 were transferred to the Patent Office. The Copyright Office was later returned to the Bureau of Public Libraries as provided in Section 28 of Executive Order Number 392, issued on December 31, 1950. Finally in 1964 R.A. Number 3873 changed the name of the Bureau of Public Libraries to the National Library.

The laws were unclear not only as to the nature of the library being created but also in regard to the administrative control under which the library was to operate. Mr. Severino Velasco's narration gives the different controlling bodies of the library as it underwent the changes provided by the different legislations:

> On June 3, 1908, the Philippine Assembly passed Act No. 1849 which merely contemplated the creation of a public library to be known as the Philippine Public Library, by consolidating all government libraries. In the following year, Act 1935 was passed, which provided for the creation of the Philippine Library that was planned in the previous year. A Library Board was then created which was given "general management authority" over the said library that was thereby removed from the administrative control and supervision of the Bureau of Education. Almost 7 years later or on February 4, 1916, the Library Board was abolished and the Library was placed under the administrative control and supervision of the Secretary of Public Instruction, now Secretary of Education. Again, on December 18 of the same year, mainly as a result of the passage of the Jones Law that called for accelerated filipinization of the government, the Library was transferred to the administrative supervision of the Secretary of Justice. It might be mentioned in this connection that the Jones Law specifically provided that among the departments that should remain in the hands of the Americans was the Department of Public Instruction. For this reason, if for no other, the Philippine Legislature transferred the library to the Department of Justice which was then placed in the hands of Filipinos. For 12 years the library remained under the Department of Justice. In 1928, it was transferred under the administrative control and supervision of the Philippine Legislature. Subsequently, on August 23, 1936, it was returned once more under the administrative control of the Department of Public Instruction, where it has remained up to the present time. From the standpoint of administrative control and supervision, therefore, there are ample indications that our responsible government authorities have not been quite certain as to the real nature of the library or its basic functions, otherwise, they would not have placed it under various branches of the government, such as the Department of Education, Department of Justice, Philippine Legislature, not to mention the Library Board and the Board of Trustees (*36*).

Whether purposely done or not, the laws regarding the National Library contain a combination of provisions for both a national library and a public library. Professor Bernardo observed this when he said that the many constructive works and projects carried out by the Philippine Library and Museum "have given it the double status of a public and national library." And Mr. Velasco rejoined that our National Library is performing dual major functions, namely those of a national library and a public library.

CREATION OF THE PHILIPPINE LIBRARY

It was Act Number 1935, passed in 1909, that set the library on a firm course toward becoming a library of the Philippines, with the double function of a public library and a national library. Called the Philippine Library, it was placed under the administrative control of a library board, called the Philippine Library Board and composed of five members, the secretary of public instruction, the secretary of finance, the secretary of justice, and two other members to be appointed by the governor-general. For the operation of the library, the activities were divided into divisions: Division for Processing Materials, Filipiniana Division, Law Division, Scientific Division, and Circulation Division. As early as the year of its establishment, the library was required by law to compile "a complete catalog of all books and publications belonging to the Philippine Library and each of its divisions." The phrase "all books and publications belonging to the Philippine Library" should be interpreted to be the books and publications contained in the different libraries in the offices of the Philippine insular government. The Filipiniana Division that was created was to have as its nucleus the materials salvaged from the Museo–Biblioteca de Filipinas and those Philippine titles acquired by Director of Education David Borrows when the American Circulating Library was under the Bureau of Education. The Circulation Division was to have as its nucleus the collection of the American Circulating Library. The Scientific Division was placed in the Bureau of Science, and the Law Division was placed in the Supreme Court. Other divisions were added as the need for them arose; for example, the Documents Division, the Philippine Assembly Division, the Periodicals Division, etc.

STEPS TAKEN IN THE DEVELOPMENT OF THE PHILIPPINE LIBRARY

On February 20, 1910, Dr. James A. Robertson was appointed to head the library with the title bibliographical expert, which was changed to librarian on May 20 of the same year by a resolution of the Philippine Library Board (*37*). Some of the American pioneers in the staff of the American Circulating Library continued to work with Dr. Robertson. Mrs. Elmer became the head of the Documents Division, and Miss Dwyer became the head of the Periodical Division.

Immediately after assuming the directorship of the library, Dr. Robertson instituted what he called the round table conferences, where plans for the library were discussed. For the first conference, set for March 4, 1910, he invited all the library workers of government libraries in Manila, among whom were: Miss Syrenna McKee, cataloger; Mrs. Osgood Brooks, cataloger of the Bureau of Science Library; Mr. Manuel Ortigas, curator of the Filipiniana Division; Mrs. Nelly Young Egbert, head of the Circulating Division; Miss Bessie Dwyer, head of the Periodicals Division; Miss Mary Polk, librarian of the Bureau of Science; and Miss Hayes of the Bureau of Agriculture. Among the topics taken up were: (*a*) the consolidation of the various collections and how it was to be undertaken, (*b*) the making of a general catalog, (*c*) the binding and preservation of books, and (*d*) the advisability of establishing a library school.

Improving reference services was the topic discussed in another round table conference that took place some 4 years later. Among those invited by Dr. Robertson to the conference were: Frank W. Carpenter, executive secretary; Major George P. Ahern of the Bureau of Forestry; President Murray Butler of the University of the Philippines; Jose Escaler, who became the first Filipino assistant director of education; Ponciano Reyes, who was the secretary of the Department of Mindanao and Sulu; Jose Abad Santos, associate justice of the Supreme Court; attorney Juan Sumulong, member of the Philippine Commission; Conrado Benitez, later director of the School of Commerce and Business Administration, University of the Philippines; and Teodoro M. Kalaw, secretary of the Philippine Assembly. It is heartening to take note of the impressive lineup of people who at that early date in the development of libraries in the Philippines were ready to help Dr. Robertson in determining ways and means of providing efficient reference service to government researchers, more especially to the legislators. The result was the organization of the Legislative Reference Division. The collection was made up of the materials in the former Philippine Assembly Library and the materials in the Documents Division of the Philippine Library. With improved research facilities—for example, the maintenance of a file of bills with the necessary indexes—both houses of the Legislature made use of this library in preparing bills, in searching for information and data, and in examining sources for the interpretation of laws. Such a service was in great demand at a time when numerous laws were being enacted, a number of laws were being repealed, and a growing number of Supreme Court decisions were being studied in interpreting the laws.

In describing the use of the Philippine Library and its divisions, Dr. Robertson mentioned the status of the collection of these divisions in his article "Growth of the Library Instinct among Filipinos," published in *Philippine Education* (Vol. 11, December 1914, pp. 233–235). He gave the following statement:

> The books in all divisions, bureaus, and offices outside the main building are designed especially for the work of that government division where they are located, but their use is not restricted in practice. Such outside book resources are in round numbers about as follows: Scientific Division, 45,000; Law Division, 20,000; Philippine Assembly Division, 12,000 and others, 20,000. The books of the main building exist only for the use of the public and are in number approximately as follows: Circulating Division, 30,000; Filipiniana Division, 20,000; Public Documents Division, 100,000. In addition, there are a few thousands of manuscripts, the chief of which are the original manuscripts of Rizal's *Noli Me Tangere* and his *Ultimo Adios*, 3 old Visayan manuscripts written in the old native characters, many copied from originals in Spanish archives; and the provincial papers which contain much valuable local history. The Filipiniana and Public Documents Divisions are for reference, and their books may be used freely only in the library (*38*).

The growth of the Filipiniana Division was due to the purchase of several private collections, among which were the collections of James A. Leroy, Clemente J. Zulueta, Dr. T. H. Pardo de Tavera, the Compania General de Tabacos de Filipinas, and Jose Rizal. In 1914 the contents of the Filipiniana Division were considered the finest collection of Filipiniana in the world.

READERS SERVICES

In the space of 14 years, from the turnover of the American Circulating Library in 1901 to 1914, the public education system obviously had succeeded in its "English-language venture," so that by 1914 the Filipinos could be called an English-language-reading people. There was a notable increase in reading room attendance in the Circulating Division and in the Periodical Division. Incentives given to attract readers were the removal on July 1, 1914, of the membership fees collected from readers and the opening of the reading rooms on Sundays and holidays. Other facilities were offered to the public, such as the publication of a bulletin that gave the readers information as to the resources and other library activities that might benefit the public.

FILIPINO LIBRARY WORKERS

From the start Dr. Robertson had Filipino apprentices in addition to the American staff members in the library. He saw at once the need for the young Filipinos working with him and working in other libraries to be taught at least the rudiments of library economy. He had in mind that these young Filipino apprentices should be prepared to take over the management of these libraries when the American library pioneers pulled out of the scene. That was why the agenda of the first round table conference included the matter of establishing a school for the training of librarians. But since the University of the Philippines already existed, the idea of having the said university provide the training appeared to be the solution. With the help of Miss Mary Polk, the librarian of the Bureau of Science, Dr. Robertson succeeded in convincing the College of Liberal Arts of the University of the Philippines to offer library science courses. As planned, the Filipino apprentices in the National Library and in other government libraries were the first enrollees.

To make sure that the training would develop to such an extent as to enable the students to take care, in turn, of the training of librarians in the years to come, further training of the Filipino librarians who took the course in the University of the Philippines was proposed that necessitated attendance in American library schools. Miss Mary Polk and Mrs. Lois Stewart Osborn, who was active in the promotion of school libraries in the Bureau of Education, obtained the cooperation of their co-members in the Women's Club of Manila in working for a bill for sending Filipino *pensionados*, or government fellows, to the United States to take up the study of library science. The Legislature passed the bill sponsored by Tomas Alonso of Cebu in February 1918 as Act 2746. This provided that the secretary of justice, under whose office the Philippine Library operated, was authorized to send four students to the United States to study library science and bibliography. Another provision of the act was that the students should be those who had finished the library science courses in the University of the Philippines.

The American library pioneers, who succeeded in having the College of Liberal Arts give library science courses, were apprehensive as to the training that the initial group of students could acquire beyond what was offered in the University of the Philippines. The volunteer group of American teachers was not, in the strict sense, prepared to teach or to impart professional library training to prospective librarians. Furthermore, the volunteer group was intended only for training the apprentices, as they were merely on temporary assignment in the Philippines. The fact is that by 1918 Miss Polk was left alone to continue the work started in 1914.

In the same year that the law was passed, four library assistants (three from the Philippine Library and one from the Bureau of Science Library) who completed the library science courses in the University of the Philippines were sent as government fellows to the University of Wisconsin. These were Eulogio B. Rodriguez, Jose Munda, and Gabriel A. Bernardo, all assistant catalogers in the Philippine Library; and Cirilo B. Perez, junior assistant in the Bureau of Science Library. In 1919 a fifth student, Ismael V. Mallari, who took Library Methods in the Philippine Normal School under Mrs. Osborn, was sent to the University of Wisconsin to take up college work in English and library science. In 1920 two more were sent to the United States: Isidoro Saniel, assistant in the Bureau of Science Library, was sent to the New York State Library School in Albany, New York; and the other, Isaac V. Lucero, another assistant in the library, was sent to the Library School of Pratt Institute. The latter continued the following year in the Library School of the University of Illinois.

THE PERIOD FROM 1916 TO 1939

It may appear that efforts did not immediately fulfill the objectives of sending government fellows to the United States to train Filipinos to take over the leadership in librarianship in the Philippines and to occupy responsible positions when the American librarians left. After Dr. Robertson left, Filipino scholars who occupied the position of head of the library included the following: Teodoro M. Kalaw, March 31, 1916–January 14, 1917; Macario Adriatico, July 1, 1917–April 14, 1919; Enrique Filamor, April 25, 1919–November 25, 1920; Jose Zurbito, acting assistant, November 16, 1920–December 20, 1921; Trinidad H. Pardo de Tavera, January 23, 1923–March 25, 1925; Jaime C. de Veyra, acting assistant, March 25, 1925–June 14, 1925; Epifanio de los Santos, May 16, 1925–April 18, 1928; and Teodoro M. Kalaw, February 16, 1929–December 1939. As scholars these directors gave the national library functions more emphasis. The senior members of the staff, or the middle administrators, however, were professionally trained and were rich in experience in library service.

THE PERIOD AFTER 1940

Eulogio B. Rodriguez was the first director who had professional library training. He belonged to the first group of government fellows sent to the University of Wisconsin to study library science and bibliography. In 1920, after finishing his studies, he returned and resumed work in the Philippine Library. He rose from the ranks and became director in 1940. In 1948, after the preliminary work of putting the library in shape after the ravages of war, he sent a circular to all libraries in the Philippines asking their cooperation in the compilation of a Union Catalog of all books in the possession of all government libraries in the Philippines. The compilation of a union catalog is one of the provisions of the Administrative Code of the Philippines. But Director Rodriguez died without succeeding in his project.

After the death of Eulogio Rodriguez, Assistant Director Luis Montilla took over the directorship of the library. Unfortunately, he did not stay long enough to be able to implement fully the program set for the library. Upon the retirement of Montilla, the administration of the library fell into the hands of nonlibrarians. The unfortunate coincidence of this situation was that the period was clouded by vague notions as to the real function of the library and by the equally confused goals set for the library. There was a mad rush for rehabilitation, but nobody seemed to have asked "Rehabilitation for what purpose?"

Chapter 44 of the Philippine Administrative Code of 1917 refers to the National Library, providing, among other things, for the chief officials of the library, the powers and functions of the library, the scope of the library, and maintenance of a union catalog, and also requiring that documents and publications of the different government agencies be sent free to the library.

The powers and functions of the library as provided by the Administrative Code are:

1. The preservation of all books, libraries, and library material or equipment belonging to the institution or confided to its custody.
2. The acquisition, by purchase, loan, or gift, of additional books, libraries, or other material contributory to its ends and purposes.
3. The supplying of adequate reading facilities to the public in the City of Manila, and so far as practicable, the extension of such facilities into the provinces, in response to the needs and increasing advancement of the people of the Philippines.
4. The supervision over the use of the facilities of the institution by the public at large, with a view to the most advantageous utilization of the means of study and culture supplied by it.
5. The organization, preservation, equipment and maintenance of a special administrative and legislative reference library, to be of aid to the several departments of the Government, and especially to the Congress, their committees or members, in the consideration, preparation, and drafting of bills.
6. The acquisition, organization, preservation, administration, and increase, as the resources of the library may allow, of a museum containing pictures, portraits, paintings, sculptures, photographs, maps, geographical charts, and all objects which, by reason of their archeological, artistic, scientific, or as a memento of, and out of veneration for the great men of the country, as a testimony of the national history and culture, or for the benefit of culture in general.
7. The preparation, printing and publication of prints, pamphlets, bibliographic catalogues, manuscripts, monographs, or any literary or scientific work deserving to be published in the interest of the Government, or the public welfare, of the history of the Philippines or of science and art in general.
8. The exercise of the powers and duties pertaining to the division of archives (patents, copyrights, trade marks and corporations).
9. The organization of a system of filing, distributing and exchanging publications and objects of art and natural history with foreign countries or institutions which may desire to reciprocate in such exchanges.

THE PUBLIC LIBRARIES

It appears that in spite of the repeated provisions in all the library laws passed from 1901 to 1941 regarding the supplying of reading facilities to the public and the extension of library services to the provinces, the public library function of the National Library was neglected. Perhaps, as was mentioned before, the directors were more inclined to develop the library as a national library. Up to 1928 there were only 10 provincial libraries, or branches as they were called. In 1931 there were 15 provincial and city libraries, and just before the war, in 1941, there were 18 provincial and city libraries all over the Philippines. Also, in 1928 the City of Manila made a move to include in its budget an appropriation to help in the support of three Manila branches of the National Library. And finally, in 1946, the National Library gave up its Manila branches to the City of Manila, which decided to organize its own library system, independent of the National Library.

As a result of the war, the Filipiniana Collection was almost entirely wiped out. More than 96% of the collection was lost (*39*). With this unfortunate circumstance the "national library phase" of the National Library was thought to have ceased, with the "public library phase" surviving. The term *survival* does not mean that the public library collection remained undamaged. Only 5% of the public libraries' collections were salvaged (*39*). But with the reestablishment of the Commonwealth of the Philippines, donations flowed in, with the United States giving generous shares. The U.S. Army surplus started the rebuilding of the collections of the different National Library branches, and later on the books from the American Book Center filled the shelves of the libraries.

A sad fact about these donations was that the books were not at all the books that would have filled the needs of the readers, nor were they books that could satisfy the interest of the readers. Discarded American textbooks, old books containing antiquated descriptions of machines, boats, prairie life, etc., were extremely far from the understanding and concern of the public, especially the rural or provincial readers. Such was the condition of the libraries in the Philippines during the first decade after the end of the war.

The Filipiniana Collection was not augmented by donations. Only government appropriations could have replenished the collection to a certain extent, of course, but government appropriations at the time were extremely limited. Furthermore, a great many of the lost works were irreplaceable, such as the manuscripts pertaining to the Philippine Revolution in 1898, the Rizal collection, and many other valuable materials pertaining to Philippine culture and history. With the national library function hindered and with little hope of reactivation in the next few years, attention was then focused on the public library function.

The war, in a way, performed an amazing transformation of the rural areas. The former complacency and conformity were replaced by aggressiveness and eagerness for self-realization. Such transformation was due to several factors. There were elements in Philippine society who sincerely believed in the democratic way of life and who had the conviction that the poor should be given the opportunity to enjoy the facilities and advantages enjoyed by the more affluent and the more favored groups. After the war, these people became more vocal and articulate in demanding from the government a better deal for the peasants in the rural areas. Dr. Jose Abueva, who analyzed postwar rural problems, stated that the evacuation of city residents to the provinces during the war resulted in more sympathetic understanding of the lot of the barrio people, as shown in the following account:

> The Japanese occupation drove thousands of urban residents to the hinterlands. In their forced habitat, they experienced the hard life of their rural countrymen. Moreover, many barrio folks shared their food and shelter with the urban evacuees. When the latter returned to the *poblaciones* and cities, many carried with them a better and more sympathetic understanding of conditions in the barrios. The resulting official and civic attitudes, conditioned by a new realism and gratitude, favored the extension of governmental services to the rural areas and the adoption of other measures calculated to improve rural life. There were those, of course, who were sympathetic with the underprivileged people due to *noblesse oblige*.
>
> On their part, many barrio people began to realize needs and personal qualities which they had in common with their wartime neighbors. This reduced somewhat their feelings of inferiority and encouraged them to be more assertive of their rights (*40*).

The interest of the government that was aroused by different elements clamoring for rural reforms reached its peak during the Magsaysay administration. President Ramon Magsaysay, whose administration was identified with efforts to uplift the poor, mobilized all resources and set up the Presidential Assistant on Community Development (PACD). Everybody is familiar with the achievements of the PACD: the construction of feeder roads so that farmers can easily transport their products, the stimulation of home industries, provision of facilities for the improvement of the health of the people, etc. Other community improvement organizations existing before the creation of the PACD were reactivated and new ones were organized.

The rural people received with understanding and effective action the benefits extended to them by the improvements in social, economic, political, and educational aspects of their life. As has been said previously, they became more articulate and more assertive of their rights. The social and economic problems brought by the war were taken up as a challenge, seeking ways and means of solving their problems. More knowledge, more information, and more facts were sought by the people. The situation was one more reason why the public library function was given more concentrated attention by the National Library.

THE BUREAU OF PUBLIC LIBRARIES

After the termination of the war, when the members of the National Library staff were called to pick up the pieces and start work over again, the prewar organization was resumed, adopting modifications as needs arose. The National Library, whose name was changed to Bureau of Public Libraries, remained under the Department of Education, and it was headed by a director and an assistant director, both of whom were appointed by the president of the Philippines. The different divisions through which the functions of the bureau were executed were the Administrative Division, the Filipiniana Division, the Circulating Division, the General Reference Division, the Research and Bibliography Division, the Catalog Division, the Extension Division, the Archives Division, the Copyright Office, and the Office for Registration of Priests and Ministers. The Archives Division was later transferred to the Records Division of the Department of General Services, but the Office for Registration of Priests and Ministers, which was clearly a nonlibrary function, was retained. The Circulating Division, which had been the mainstay of the public library function of the National Library from its very earliest days, was abolished on June 30, 1955. The presence of several Manila public libraries at that time made the services of the Circulating Division of the Bureau of Public Libraries a duplication of the services being offered to the people of Manila.

The extension of library services to the provinces then became the most important function of the Bureau of Public Libraries. The Extension Division was, in 1941, only a section in the Administrative Division. In 1945 the Extension and Traveling Libraries Division was established, to be followed in 1947 by the creation of the Municipal Libraries Division. The Extension Division was given charge of establishing, administering, and supervising the provincial, city, and barrio libraries; while the Municipal Libraries Division was in charge of establishing, administering, and supervising municipal libraries. Clearly there was an overlapping of functions, for the establishment, administration, and supervision of municipal libraries was also extension work and should have belonged to the Extension Division. It did not take long, however, for the two divisions to merge into one, operating under one head.

Meant to be an upward shove to the movement for library development in the rural areas was the enactment of R.A. Number 411 in 1949, known as the Municipal Libraries Act and also as the Pecson Bill (*41*). The act provided for the establishment of 1,000 municipal libraries in the Philippines over a period of 5 years, with an appropriation of P300,000 a year for the establishment of 200 libraries in each year. The act was never fully implemented since the Legislature failed in subsequent years to appropriate the necessary funds that were called for in the law. Twenty-seven years afterward, in 1976, there were only 291 municipal libraries, which included the municipal libraries existing before the passage of the law in 1949.

Before the enactment of this law, the only legal basis for the establishment of libraries outside Manila was Paragraph (c) of Section 1689 of the Revised Administrative Code of the Philippines; this included the statement calling for "the supplying of adequate reading facilities to the public of the City of Manila, and in so far as practicable, the extension of such facilities into the provinces, in response to the need and increasing advancement of the people of the Philippines." There is need for the creation of a bureau separate from the present National Library that will concentrate its services on the improvement and development of public libraries in provinces, cities, municipalities, and barrios of the Philippines. Such an agency could be the hope for the rural folk, not only providing them the enjoyment of recreational reading but bringing within their reach resources for their growth—social, economic, cultural, and educational.

THE EXTENSION DIVISION

The function of the National Library as far as public library services are concerned is handled by the Extension Division. This means the establishment, organization, and maintenance of public libraries in cities, provinces, municipalities, and barrios throughout the country. In the 5-year development plan of the National Library (1973–1978) the following objectives of the division are stated:

1. To make the library service in our provincial and far-flung regions responsive to their particular needs;
2. To build within each library an information center about the community—its resources, its history, its people, its customs and traditions, etc.;
3. To organize eleven (11) regional libraries to take care of the existing branch libraries as well as those to be established in the future and to serve as reference centers;
4. To organize children's collections in each of these regional libraries to draw children to the treasures found in books and develop future readership;
5. To train the field librarians (*42*).

Due to the perennial shortage of funds, the Extension Division is continuously faced with problems in its efforts to implement its impressive objectives. In fiscal year 1975–1976 the 444 branch libraries that served 3,384,909 readers had an allocation of only P2,954,250 (*43*), a sum that is extremely far below the standard for satisfactory service.

Even in the establishment of public libraries, the Extension Division has not been able to go far. In 1976 the 444 public libraries actually operating consisted of: 33 provincial libraries, 21 city libraries, 291 municipal libraries, 50 barrio libraries, 18 deposit stations, and 31 district libraries (*44*). Since there are 74 provinces, 61 cities, 1,439 municipalities, and some 33,776 barrios (*45*), it is obvious that only a very small percentage of these local units have library facilities.

REORGANIZATION OF THE NATIONAL LIBRARY

The emerging national library service was an expected result of the increasing activities in research, especially in the social science field. The socioeconomic problems that faced the country during the last few decades compelled the intellectuals to dig into records, documents, and literature in the effort to bring out the facts that can help solve our national problems. In trying to meet the demands of such tasks, the National Library tried to strengthen and enrich its collection and accelerate the production of research tools such as indexes and bibliographies.

The development plan that the National Library drew up in 1967 projected nationwide activities. Although limited budgets prevented the implementation of the recommendations in the plan, it can be said that the National Library now has a clearer direction for its goals and a more definite understanding of the activities to be performed.

As the Bureau of Public Libraries, the functions were discharged by eight divisions, including the Archives Division, plus the Copyright Office and the Office for Registration of Priests and Ministers. With the expansion of activities and with the changes in organizational arrangement, the Archives Division was moved to another executive department, and 11 divisions resulted from the reorganization of 1967, namely: Accounting Division, Administrative Division, Budget and Fiscal Division, Book Selection Division, Catalog Division, Filipiniana Division, General Reference Division, Public Documents Exchange and Gifts Division, Bibliography Division, Publication Division, and Extension Division.

At the head of these divisions are the director and assistant director of the National Library. The Administrative Division provides those services ordinarily performed by government administrative offices, such as accounting, personnel administration, supply, management, etc. The Acquisition Division takes charge of the selection, ordering, and accessioning of all books and other publications to be added to the collection. The Bibliography Division is responsible, among other things, for maintenance of a union catalog, preparation of the country's national bibliography, preparation of subject bibliographies and indexes, and coordination of the bibliographic activities of the country. The Catalog Division is in charge of classifying, cataloging, and other processing routines for all materials possessed by the National Library, including those of the branches. The Extension Division, whose activities and importance have been discussed previously, performs the public library function of the National Library. The Public Documents Division is responsible for the acquisition of materials through exchange and gifts, and the organization and processing of said materials. The division provides a reading room for reference service. As to the resources of the division, the following report was given:

> . . . the Public Documents Division has in its collection some 3,891 titles received from 219 agencies of the Executive, Judicial, and Legislative branches of the Philippine government; 6,310 titles from 139 United States federal agencies; 1,879 titles from institutions in 38 American states; 871 titles from 38 foreign countries except Asia, and 2,405 titles from the United Nations and its specialized agencies and other inter-governmental organizations.

The Publication Division is one of the means of the National Library in performing the function of disseminating knowledge. Paragraph (g) of Section 1969 of the Revised Administrative Code (1951) provides the legal basis for this function, which is stated in the following:

> The preparation, printing and publication of prints, pamphlets, bibliographic catalogues, manuscripts, monographs, or any literary or scientific work deserving to be published in the interest of the Government, of the public welfare, of the history of the Philippines or of science and art in general.

The Reference Division provides facilities to readers who are in need of information. With the use of the resources of the library and the resources outside the library, the Reference Division assists researchers in their investigations, whether as directly requested by the library patrons, or by letters, or through telephone calls.

The Filipiniana and Asia Division maintains a collection of Philippine materials and a collection of publications about the other countries in the Asian region. The Filipiniana Section has the function of collecting and preserving for posterity all manuscripts, maps, pictures, and printed works about the Philippines whether by

Filipinos or by foreign writers. It maintains a reading room to serve researchers, scholars, professionals, and college students.

The efforts of the National Library to be truly a repository of treasures on Philippine culture and history have been a continuing endeavor. In a 1970 report on the National Library resources, the following statement was given:

> The Filipiniana Division has a collection of 49,950 volumes of books plus an undetermined number of materials included in the 21 special collections of the National Library acquired from private individuals, and the Quezoniana collection. The entire collection is organized into: (a) a general reference collection; (b) rare book collection; (c) periodical collection; (d) map collection; (e) a manuscript collection; (f) a picture collection; (g) microcopy collection (*46*).

The Asia Collection consists of around 3,500 volumes written in Western and Asian languages. Though still in its initial stage of organization, the collection covers all subject fields and also different types of publications, such as monographs, directories, catalogs, annuals, etc.

THE STAFF OF THE NATIONAL LIBRARY AND ITS BRANCHES

To broaden their background in library service and to update professional techniques, senior staff members of the National Library were sent to different training schools. The National Library took advantage of scholarship grants from UNESCO and the Colombo Plan and also from the University of the Philippines.

For the junior members of the staff, the in-service training sessions include: orientation for new employees, lectures on the functions of the different divisions, lectures on employee behavior and attitude, training for staff members handling Filipiniana and Asian materials, and refresher courses in cataloging, indexing, abstracting, etc.

For the personnel assigned to the branches all over the Philippines, the Extension Division has been conducting in-service training sessions since 1955. The 1955 in-service training program was organized in Manila from April 18 to May 28. It was attended by provincial, city, and municipal librarians from all over the Philippines. The program was divided into two parts: (*a*) familiarizing the trainees with the organizational setup of the National Library, the mother institution, with lectures on the functions and activities of the different divisions; and (*b*) lectures on general principles in the management of a library. Discussion, practical exercises, and trips to different libraries in the city were parts of the training program. This was one of the most extensive programs ever held for library workers, as will be noted from the following summary of the lectures alone, excluding the other activities:

1. The major policies of the National Library, especially on the acquisition of materials, appointments, and promotions; relation of the National Library with provincial, city, and municipal officials and groups
2. The functions of the Reference Division, Catalog Division, Filipiniana Division, Circulating Division, Extension Division, etc.
3. The meaning of librarianship and its philosophy

4. The librarian, his training and necessary qualities
5. Methods of preparing library exhibits and displays
6. Public relations in libraries
7. Audiovisual aids in libraries
8. Library service to children
9. Cooperation between school libraries and public libraries

After this general in-service training program, the National Library sponsored regional workshops in cooperation with other agencies. A chronological listing of these workshops follows, with a brief description of each:

1957—Visayas and Mindanao Librarians' Regional Conference Workshop held in Bacolod City, May 13–18: The conference workshop aimed to instill in the trainees the responsibilities of public library service, to bring them up to date in library techniques and practices, and to develop the necessary skills required in library work.

1959—Regional Conference Workshop of Librarians, held in Tarlac City, Tarlac, April 27–May 2: With emphasis on closer community cooperation, the objectives underscored the important role played by public officials, civic groups, and citizens in maintaining the public libraries. Another objective was to keep libraries abreast of progressive techniques in library administration and organization.

1963—Regional Conference Workshop for Librarians of Central and Southern Luzon, held in Marikina, Rizal, March 25–April 1: The provinces and cities included in the conference workshop were Pangasinan, Tarlac, Zambales, Bataan, Nueva Ecija, Pampanga, Bulacan, Quezon, Batangas, Rizal, Cavite, Laguna, Mindoro Oriental, Marinduque, Cabanatuan City, Quezon City, Pasay City, Lipa City, Naga City, and Dagupan City. The theme of the conference workshop was "The Role of the Public Library in the Social and Economic Advancement of the Community."

1964—Conference Workshop for Librarians of Mindanao and Sulu, held in Cagayan de Oro City, February 24–28: Delegates who attended the conference represented Agusan, Bukidnon, Cotabato, Davao, Lanao del Norte, Lanao del Sur, Misamiz Oriental, Misamiz Occidental, Sulu, Surigao del Norte, Surigao del Sur, Zamboanga del Norte, Zamboanga del Sur, Butuan City, Cagayan de Oro City, Cotabato City, Davao City, Gingoog City, Marawi City, Zamboanga City, and Ozamis City. The general theme was "The Improvement of Library Resources and Services in Mindanao and Sulu."

1964—Regional Conference Workshop for Librarians of Southern Luzon and the Eastern Visayas, held in Legaspi City, December 6–13: With the general theme "Reaching Readers: The Library's Responsibility and Opportunity," the conference workshop tackled problems of adult education through the public library and library service to children.

1966—Conference Workshop for Librarians at Cabanatuan City, January 31–February 5.

1969—Librarians' Seminar Workshop, Laoag City, April 13–16.

1971—Public Librarians Association sponsored the Librarians Workshop on Upgrading Technical Services in the Library: Held in the Rizal Provincial Library, Pasig, Rizal, December 1–3.

1972—First Training Program for Librarians Handling Filipiniana and Southeast Asian Materials: Manila, April 11–14.

1972—10th Librarians' Conference Workshop: Baguio City, April 24–29.

EARLY PROVINCIAL LIBRARIES

Many times in the foregoing account, the terms *provincial library* and *city library* have been used. It is relevant at this point to call to mind the establishment of the first provincial public library. As early as 1904 the government made a move to establish a public library in the province of Albay by enacting a law for the purpose (Act 1175). But the law was never implemented as no funds were provided for the operation of the library (*47*).

The provincial library that is considered to be the first one established is the Iloilo Provincial Library. The formal opening of the library took place on October 29, 1916. The Province of Iloilo provided the building with all the necessary furnishings, and the National Library provided 13 cases of books. The gesture elicited further support from Ilongo leaders and the public at large, with the result that the growth was greatly accelerated. Before the war the library had the distinction of having the richest Filipiniana collection among all the provincial branches. Unfortunately, the collection was totally burned during the war. But the people of Iloilo had the magnificent stamina to rebuild their library, with the full-hearted support of the Iloilo provincial government. At the time of the celebration of its golden anniversary in 1966 the library had 13,286 volumes and 4,550 registered borrowers (*48*).

Baguio, the summer capital of the Philippines, received library facilities from the National Library even earlier than Iloilo. But Baguio did not become a regular branch upon the receipt of collections of books from the National Library, as explained in the following:

> We might say, therefore, that the first public library service in the Philippines outside the City of Manila actually began in March 1910 when the Philippine Library "sent a part of its personnel and approximately 1,000 books from the Circulating Division (American Circulating Library) to Baguio. The books were largely fiction, history, and travel but all classes were included. At the close of the season the books were returned to Manila, and books in larger numbers each succeeding year were sent to the branch for the official seasons of 1911, 1912, and 1913." It might be noted, however, that the Baguio Branch Library did not become a regular branch library until much later (*49*).

THE MANILA CITY LIBRARIES

Regarding the City of Manila, it is known that when the American Circulating Library was turned over to the Philippine government in 1901, the City of Manila was the main area where its services were to be rendered. Hence, the people of Manila enjoyed the facilities of the National Library from that early period up to 1946, when the city government decided to establish its own public library system. But even long before 1946 the City of Manila had already provided funds for the establishment, in 1930, of four Manila branches of the National Library. The Manila Business Library (now the Santa Cruz Branch), Tondo Branch, Paco Branch (now the Manila–Sacramento Friendship Library), and the Sampaloc Branch were operated out of city funds but under the stewardship of the National Library.

Then, on October 28, 1946, Ordinance Number 2982 was passed by the City

Council, which provided that the Manila City Library and all its branches shall be controlled, managed, and administered by a superintendent who shall be under the general supervision of the city mayor (*50*). Today there are 16 branch libraries located in the different districts of Manila, all under the administration and supervision of the superintendent.

The Manila City Libraries' *Annual Report* for 1976–1977 gives the following data: a total book collection of 79,498 volumes, 408,106 registered borrowers, 124,782 volumes circulated, and 1,783,304 books and periodicals consulted in the reading rooms. It is quite a sad fact that the 79,498-volume collection is much too small to provide satisfactory service to the approximately 3 million residents of Manila.

College and University Libraries in the Philippines

In the Philippines, colleges and universities may be divided into state institutions and private institutions. State institutions are supported by taxes for their establishment and maintenance. Private institutions are the responsibilities of the individual(s) or corporation(s) that established them. The schools depend upon the fees paid by the students, and in some cases they depend upon other funds provided by foundations or upon assistance from the religious orders or missions which founded the schools. Both private and state institutions are governed and supervised by the Bureau of Higher Education (*51*), which functions under the Department of Education and Culture.

At present there are 558 private colleges and universities and 39 state colleges and universities (*52*). Out of the 558 private institutions, 40 are universities, and out of the 39 chartered state institutions, 7 are universities.

A grouping of the 47 universities based on the year of establishment shows that 3 were established between 1611 and 1899, 10 were established between 1900 and 1919, 6 were established between 1920 and 1941, and 28 were established between 1945 and 1977. Of the 19 schools established before 1941, only the University of the Philippines was established purposely to provide higher education. The rest began by offering only elementary and high school courses, acquiring university status after due expansion of their courses. The 28 universities established after the war were likewise started as elementary schools and high schools, or as institutes offering collegiate courses. University status was granted to them by the Bureau of Higher Education upon fulfillment of the requirements imposed by the bureau.

In a survey of private colleges and universities made by the Fund for Assistance to Private Education in 1977, the answers to the questionnaire returned by 31 private universities revealed a range of enrollment from 547 to 55,328; and in library collection, a range of 640 to 223,704 volumes.

An estimate of the total collegiate enrollment for 1977 has been given as 750,000, an increase of 15% from the enrollment 5 years previously (*52*).

Due to the requirements imposed by today's socioeconomic and cultural conditions, the universities have instituted some curricular innovations that have changed the trends in Philippine education. Higher education not only gives training for high-level professions to provide leadership for the nation, but also gives courses to meet new manpower needs such as hotel management, tourism, etc.

LIBRARIES IN COLLEGES AND UNIVERSITIES

In a state college or in a state university the library functions under the direct administrative control of the president of the university, who usually delegates said administrative authority to the academic vice-president if there is one. The legal basis for the establishment of a state college or state university is the charter granted to it. However, an examination of the charters of the different state institutions revealed that there were no provisions for the organization of a library as a unit within these institutions. But when the different units of a university or college are organized, the library is always included in the organization plan. A state university is governed by a Board of Regents, the members of which are appointed by the president of the Philippines. The president of the university is appointed by the president of the Philippines upon the recommendation of the Board of Regents. The librarian is appointed by the Board of Regents upon the recommendation of the president of the university.

THE UNIVERSITY OF THE PHILIPPINES LIBRARY*

The University of the Philippines (UP) is widely referred to as the premier state institution of higher learning in the Philippines. This reputation for excellence has sprung from the UP Library's continuing commitment to scholarship. Through the constant support of the administration and additional financial aid from external foundations, the total collection of the UP Library has more than doubled since 1961. The present library holdings comprise 823,384 volumes, 19,234 serial titles (of which 4,029 are paid subscriptions), 13,526 microforms, 12,001 music scores, 2,808 phonodisks, and 2,616 maps. The collection primarily supports the teaching, research, and extension needs of the university. However, the various specialized collections also serve the needs of government departments and agencies, industrial firms, and graduate students and researchers from local and foreign institutions.

Library holdings are now located for maximum use in a network of libraries comprising the Main Library and 36 unit libraries. These are spread out over seven campuses of the University of the Philippines.

The UP Library is under centralized administration, making it possible to integrate and coordinate staffing, acquisitions, and organization of library materials. A union catalog for the entire collection is located in the main lobby of the Main Library Building, which is also the headquarters for library administration.

To process the library collection, manage it for the use of its clientele, and perform other specialized services, the UP Library has 71 full-time librarians, 49 re-

*From a paper read by the University of the Philippines university librarian, Marina G. Dayrit, at the Seminar on Quality Libraries and Information Systems held at Silliman University, December 13–15, 1976.

search personnel, and 89 library assistants, library aids, bookbinders, utility men, etc.

The bulk of the collection in the social sciences, the humanities, and the natural sciences, which is housed in the Main Library, primarily serves the undergraduates and graduate programs, and research in the arts and sciences. The resources of the Main Library are also strong in reference and bibliography, and in government publications.

The richness of the Filipiniana research collection in the Main Library is well known to local and foreign researchers. This collection at present comprises 36,000 volumes on Philippine literature, history, political science, bibliography, and other subjects, as well as extensive runs of Philippine newspapers and periodicals.

Being responsive to the academic interests of the faculty and students, the UP Library continues to acquire increasingly sophisticated tools of scholarship. Among these is an air-conditioned microfilm room that houses a growing collection of microforms, microform readers, microfilm machines, and a film processor and other duplicating machines.

During the period January–December 1977, the recorded use of the library collection totaled more than 2,850,000 items, broken down as follows:

Circulation	635,744 volumes
Filipiniana	150,021 volumes
Reference	199,652 volumes
Reserve	943,087 volumes
Periodicals	381,538 pieces
Newspapers	291,710 pieces
Microforms	2,298 pieces
Other materials	241,897 pieces
Borrowed on intralibrary loans	1,877 volumes
Lent on intralibrary loans	3,352 volumes

The maintenance of widely scattered unit libraries in the various campuses of the university has had a profound effect on the development of the collections of the University Library. Except for the libraries of the regional units and UP College Manila, all the unit libraries have developed as special libraries, with collections geared toward the curricular research needs of the colleges or institutes they serve. Highly specialized book and periodical collections pertinent to their respective subject fields are found in all of these libraries.

Among the major strengths of the UP Library are its serial and document collections. The serial collection, numbering 18,510 titles, consists of periodicals, continuations, proceedings, transactions of societies, and memoirs, all indispensable for scholarly research.

Selected U.S. federal and state documents, Philippine government documents, and publications of other international bodies and foreign governments constitute the document collection. The UP Library has also been a depository of UN documents since 1950, which are distributed among the various unit libraries according to subject. Accessibility to the contents of its serial and document collections is provided by the UP Library through subscriptions to foreign abstracting and indexing services covering all fields.

One of the special collections of the UP Library is its microform materials, which include more than 12,000 reels of microfilm. The collection has grown since the library started generating its own microfilm. In addition, microfilm copies of theses and dissertations and other Filipiniana research materials have been purchased from foreign repositories. A good number of the microfilm holdings are donations from the national archives of Mexico and the United States.

The UP Library receives one copy each of all theses and dissertations submitted to the UP Graduate School. Copies of these are available in the Filipiniana Reading Room and in the libraries of individual colleges and institutes. These are bibliographically controlled through the *U.P. Theses and Dissertation Index.* Theses from foreign institutions are also received in the Main Library and are also made available to researchers.

Of interest to scholars are the rare materials, manuscripts, and personal papers in the Rare Book Collection, including valuable retrospective and current Filipiniana materials. The UP Library has a strong collection of literary materials written in the major Philippine languages. Works of vernacular writers in Cebuano, Hiligaynon, Tagalog, Pampango, Bikol, and Ilokano are part of the special materials.

Extensive microfilming activities have become a regular part of the operation of the UP Library. The library has one 35-mm microfilm machine and two 16-mm microfilmers. A microfilm-processing laboratory is being used to produce negative and positive microfilms. All the publications of the university and also special collections, manuscripts, and vernacular materials in the Main Library and unit libraries are microfilmed for preservation. In addition, important materials from some government offices are borrowed and microfilmed.

Owners of special private collections and some libraries and museums have also cooperated with the UP Library by lending some of their materials for microfilming. Among these, to cite only a few, are the Lopez Memorial Museum and the University of Nueva Caceres in Naga City. The Solicitor-General's Office has also allowed the UP Library to microfilm the records of the People's Court and other important materials.

One of the important functions of the UP Library in support of research is its involvement in bibliographic activities. It has pioneered in national bibliographic control with the publication, in five issues, of the *Philippine Bibliography;* this lists Filipiniana books, pamphlets, and serials published in the country during the 10-year period 1963–1972.

Another bibliographic activity of national importance is the *Index to Philippine Periodicals.* Formerly published by the Interdepartmental Reference Service of the UP College of Public Administration, the publication of the *Index* has been taken over by the UP Library.

PRIVATE UNIVERSITIES

Private universities may be divided into sectarian and nonsectarian schools. At the head of a Catholic university is the rector or president, who is responsible to the head of the religious organization to which he and the school belong. The library is usually under a library prefect, who is a member of the religious organization in control of the university. His function is mainly advisory. The technical and the professional services are done by a staff of library workers. In some Catholic universities and colleges, however, the religious official in charge of the library is professionally trained in library work and has, therefore, full responsibility in directing all the activities of the library. In the case of Protestant universities, the president is responsible to the religious mission, whether Presbyterian, Baptist, etc., that established the school. The librarian is directly responsible to the president of the university. The government of a nonsectarian private university is vested in a Board of Directors headed by a president. In large schools the president is assisted by one, two, or even more vice-presidents, each one handling a different phase or set of administrative functions such as academic affairs, research and development, etc. The library may be placed under the supervision of the vice-president for academic affairs or the vice-president for research and development, or under the supervision of any vice-president whose sphere of administrative functions relevantly covers the library's activities. In small universities where there are no vice-presidents, the librarian is directly responsible to the president of the university.

The government has strict rules regarding the establishment of private schools. Before a college or a university can be authorized or can be recognized by the government, certain requirements issued by the Bureau of Private Schools (now the Bureau of Higher Education) have to be met. Among the specific requirements for recognition and for granting permits are those that pertain to library facilities. The requirements as given in the *Manual of Regulations* state the following:

> The library must have an adequate and well-distributed and up to date book collection and publications of high quality and well equipped and professionally administered library necessary for strong general education, professional courses and graduate study and research. At least ten percent of the collection shall constitute a Filipiniana collection (*53*).

Regarding the maintenance of the library, the Bureau *Manual* issued the following:

> Schools should have a continuous library development program. The library fees should be spent exclusively for this purpose but in no case shall the yearly appropriation for library development, exclusive of salaries of the library personnel, be less than 5% of the annual operating expenses of the institution (*54*).

Besides government attention, continuing efforts to improve private education in the Philippines are being carried on by accrediting associations such as the Philippine Association of Colleges and Universities, the Catholic Educational Association of the Philippines, and the Association of Christian Schools and Colleges. Another means of improving private education is by financial assistance. In 1968 the Fund for Assistance to Private Education (FAPE) was organized; this was the result of an agreement between the governments of the Philippines and the United States creating a fund of $6,154,000 representing the unpaid balance from the War Damage Fund from the United States, which was labeled as a fund for assistance to private education. The fund is kept intact; only the earnings are spent for this assistance program (*55*).

In establishing priorities for assistance, the following was stated:

> Areas billed to received immediate assistance were faculty fellowships, graduate development programs, guidance and testing, educational research, textbook production, laboratory equipment, school administration programs, college library assistance programs, educational television and technology, and honors programs (*55*).

The college and university library assistance program consisted of aid to 47 schools in 1970–1971. Basic reference books, book selection aids, and professional books for librarians worth half a million pesos were distributed to the said schools (*56*).

SAN BEDA COLLEGE LIBRARY*

San Beda College is an educational institution for boys and young men conducted by the Benedictine Fathers, who came to Manila on September 13, 1895. The school was founded on June 17, 1901, and was located at 226 Arlegui Street, Quiapo, Manila. The first courses offered were Primera and Segunda Ensananza, Perito Mercantil, and Bachillerato.

The college, named after the Benedictine saint and scholar Bede, was moved to its present site on Mendiola Street and was inaugurated on June 13, 1926. The monastery was completed in May 1930, and other buildings were constructed later on: Saint Benedict's Hall, the Clinic, and Saint Anselm Hall, a four-storey building costing P1.5 million.

With the birth of the college came the organization of the library on June 19, 1901. Assigned to occupy a room in the building on Arlegui Street, the library was organized with the private collections of the Fathers forming the initial library collection. The books were mostly in Spanish. When the school was transferred to the present site on Mendiola Street, the library was given a larger place occupying two rooms adjacent to the church. By 1941 there were more than 6,000 volumes in the library collection.

The end of World War II brought many changes, not only an increase in enrollment but changes in the facilities that were promptly provided. At present the library that provides service to almost 3,000 students occupies the second floor of the Saint Anselm building, which is fully air conditioned and can accommodate 320 students at one time. The collections are now called the San Beda College Concon Libraries, named after their donor alumnus, Gregorio Concon.

The goals of the San Beda College library are precisely those of the college itself, namely to impart to the students a Christian education and to develop in them both academic excellence and social responsibility. The library, which is geared primarily toward the needs of the students and faculty members, includes books, magazines, newspapers, pamphlets, clippings, maps, and other informational materials. All materials are chosen for purposes of both general and specialized study.

The Technical Processing Section is housed in the mezzanine floor, where books

*From a report prepared by the San Beda College director of services, Fr. Paul de Vera, and the college librarian, Fe Guanzon.

are accessioned, classified, cataloged, labeled, and prepared for loan to borrowers. It should be mentioned at this point that since July 1977, the International Standard Bibliographic Description has been used, replacing the old cataloging form. This section also takes care of the selection and ordering of books, prepares reports, compiles bibliographies, sets up displays, and takes care of correspondence.

The Concon Libraries have three main divisions, namely the College of Arts and Science Library, the Law Library, and the Periodical Library. The College of Arts and Sciences Library has around 36,640 volumes. The Law Library has approximately 6,300 volumes consisting mostly of *Philippine Reports*, bound volumes of *Official Gazette*, and bound law periodicals. The Periodical Library is located on the mezzanine floor. The collection consists of 3,000 bound periodicals made up of 120 subscriptions and 60 foreign and local publications acquired through gifts and exchange.

Adjacent to the College of Arts and Sciences Library is the Discussion Room, which can accommodate 35 students at one time. And nearby is a typing booth accessible for the use of students. The Law Library also has a Discussion Room, a typing booth, and a faculty section where the professors have privacy to study, do research, or do other paper work related to their teaching.

Among the special facilities offered to the library clientele are the map collection, which has been cataloged and made easily available to researchers; and the readers advisory service, which takes care of the location of information necessary for any particular research and compiles bibliographies needed by researchers. A duplicating machine has been provided to enable students and researchers to copy articles from periodicals and other documents in a matter of seconds. There are also regular showings of educational films and sound slides for students and faculty members. Piped-in music is provided in the reference sections of both the College of Arts and Sciences Library and the College of Law Library.

CENTRO ESCOLAR UNIVERSITY LIBRARY*

The Centro Escolar University (CEU) was founded in June 1907 by a group of civic-spirited women headed by Librada Avelino, a pioneer in educational leadership. The school was named Centro Escolar de Señoritas, as the school was intended to provide education only for women. Kindergarten, elementary, general high school, music, and home arts courses were the first studies offered by the school.

In the course of 50 years, a number of courses and colleges (including the Graduate School) were organized: College of Pharmacy, College of Liberal Arts (now College of Arts and Sciences), College of Eudcation, College of Dentistry, College of Law, the Graduate School, College of Commerce and Business Administration, College of Optometry, Conservatory of Music, College of Foods and Nutrition, College of Social Work, and College of Medical Technology. Recently, the College of Nursing was added.

The Centro Escolar University, although started as a girls' school, now admits

*From a report prepared by the university librarian, Concordia Sanchez.

male students. After World War II male students were admitted in the College of Optometry, College of Medical Technology, College of Dentistry, College of Arts and Sciences, and the Graduate School.

From the start a library has always been in existence, even if at times it consisted of a table, a few chairs, and books in bookcases set aside for the use of the students. At present the library consists of the Main Library for the undergraduate students, the graduate students, and the faculty members; and two separate branches on the main campus, one for the High School and one for the Elementary School. Off campus there are two other branches, one in Generosa de Leon Memorial College in Parañaque, south of Manila, and one for the CEU Malolos Branch in Bulacan Province, north of Manila.

The Main Library occupies the first and second floors and the mezzanine floor of a new building called the Carmen de Luna Building, which is located in the south quadrangle fronting Mendiola street. With a total area of 1,990 square meters, it provides five reading rooms with a total seating capacity of 590, space for carrels and individual study tables, and bookstacks. The General Circulation Section, the bookstacks, the Graduate Reading Room, and the Reserve Book Room are on the second floor. The Filipiniana–Asian Reading Room and the Reference–Periodical Reading Room are on the first floor.

The northern end of the second floor is occupied by the workroom for Technical Services and the Office of the University Librarian. The sections making up the Technical Services Division are the ones that prepare library materials for the use of the whole university clientele, including all the branches. These are the Acquisition Section and the Cataloging Section, both of which handle the "behind the scenes" services. The Acquisition Section takes care of the selection (done cooperatively with the deans and heads of departments of the colleges in the university), purchase, and accessioning of the books that are added to the collection. The Cataloging Section takes care of the classifying and cataloging of the materials, steps vital in the organization of the resources of the library. Another service rendered by this division is the care given to the repair and binding of books and magazines. The bindery occupies the rear space of the Filipiniana–Asian Section on the first floor.

At present the collection consists of 84,600 volumes, more than 6,700 of which are Filipiniana and Asian books, and 4,516 bound periodicals. Several thousand pamphlets are filed in vertical files and pamphlet boxes. No audiovisual materials are kept in the library as there is a separate department taking care of such materials and the apparatus and equipment for their use.

The Readers Services Division is organized into sections, each of which takes charge of some specific functions. The Reserve Section contains the books which instructors have assigned their students to read. Books in this section are in multiple copies and may be borrowed for use in the reading room only. The Circulation Section is the unit that takes care of lending books for home use. This is the section that lends the main bulk of the library collection. Most of the books are of the recreational type, such as fiction, plays, poems, and biography. But there are also numerous nonfiction books, such as books on philosophy, social sciences, natural science, technology, history, etc., that may be borrowed for 1 or 2 weeks.

The Reference–Periodical Section provides sources of information that answer inquiries in connection with class assignments, or with extracurricular activities, or simply with the borrowers' personal interests or hobbies. Unlike the Reserve Section and the Circulation Section, where books are borrowed across the counter or charging desk, this section is operated on the open-shelf basis. Readers are allowed to browse and to select the books that they want from the shelves. A vertical file, or an information file service, is maintained by this section. Pamphlets, clippings, pictures, maps, and other materials are organized in steel cabinets for use as reference sources.

The CEU subscribes to 300 different periodicals, which are on display in the Reference–Periodical Section. Also filed in this section are the bound volumes of periodicals and the collection of bibliographies and periodical indexes useful in research work.

The Filipiniana–Asian Section is the place where all books and other materials about the Philippines and Asia are concentrated. The subject coverage extends to all fields: language, education, economics, history, literature, etc. This is also an open-shelf area where readers are free to select the books they want from the shelves.

The Readers Services Division is open from 7 A.M. to 7 P.M. from Monday to Saturday. Library attendance in the Main Library during the school year 1976–1977 recorded 350,000 readers, while book loans totaled 540,000 volumes.

UNIVERSITY OF SANTO TOMAS LIBRARY*

The University of Santo Tomas was founded in 1611 in Manila by the archbishop of Manila, Rev. Fr. Miguel de Benavidez. Originally named the College of Our Lady of the Rosary, 5 years later the name was changed to College of Santo Tomas. In 1645 the college was transformed into a university by Pope Innocent X acceding to a petition of Philip IV.

The expansion of the university, however, began in 1734 with the establishment of the Faculty of Canon Law and the Faculty of Civil Law. The establishment of other faculties and colleges followed: Faculty of Medicine, Faculty of Pharmacy, Faculty of Philosophy and Letters, Faculty of Engineering, College of Liberal Arts, College of Education, College of Architecture and Fine Arts, College of Commerce and Business Administration, etc.

The university library, which functions under the administrative control of the vice-rector, consists of the Main Library and 10 branch libraries. The main library, which occupies the first floor of the main building, has 11 reading rooms: Asian Library, Audio-Visual Room, Filipiniana Section, General Periodicals, General Reference, Humanities, Spanish Books Reading Room, Rare Books, Religion, Science and Technology, and Social Sciences. The branch libraries consist of the Commerce Library; Ecclesiastical Faculties; Education Library; Elementary School Library; High School Library; Education High School Library; Engineer-

*This section is taken from a report prepared by the university librarian, Juana Abello.

ing, Architecture, and Fine Arts Library; Law Library; Medicine Library; and Music Library.

The Main Library occupies a space of 2,924 square meters, and the branch libraries altogether occupy a total area of 2,984 square meters. The Stackroom of the main library has an area of 1,980 square meters.

At present the collection consists of 394,577 volumes, 488 titles of periodical subscriptions, 12,000 rare books, and 5,900 pieces of film and other microforms. Loan statistics for 1976–1977 recorded 256,000 books, 75,000 periodicals, and 1,165 pieces of audiovisual materials.

The Rare Books Section occupies Rooms 111, 113, and 115 in the Main Library, located on the ground floor of the Main Building of the university. (This description of the Rare Books Section was obtained from the brochure *357th U.S.T. Anniversary 1611–1968*, Manila, 1968.) The section represents the best collection of rare books in the Philippines. Some of the volumes are those formerly kept in the university's Ecclesiastical Faculties Library, and some were donations from Dominican priests and private individuals, plus gifts from missionaries who worked in the Philippines. Part of the big collection of rare books is a group of some 500 volumes printed from 1500 to 1599, in Antwerp, Lyons, Nice, Paris, Naples, Venice, Padua, Genoa, Frankfort, Oxford, Seville, Cadiz, Alcala, Madrid, etc. Represented are famous printers like Aldo, Platinus, Jean Petit, Robertus Stephanus, etc. The books treat of different subjects like theology, law, philosophy, medicine, history, music, geography, etc. To show the rarity of the books in this section, some titles are given here:

1. *Opus Regale*, Lugdumi, 1521 (2 vols.), Vivaldus de Monte Regale, Joan Lug., O.P.: A Gothic book that contains a series of philosophical and theological treatises.
2. *Opera Omnia*, Compluti, 1572, Ed. Ambrosius de Morales, Eulogius Cordubensis, Sanctus: Contains the works of the famous martyr and bishop of Cordoba (Spain) St. Eulogius, illustrating one of the interesting periods in the history of Spanish Christianity when the Christians were subjected to the first Mohammedan invaders.
3. *Naturalis Historiae Libri XXVLL*, Basileae, 1535, Ed. Joannes Frobenius, Secundud, Plinus: One of the most important sources of study for scholars of the Middle Ages.
4. *Adagiorum Chilliades*, Basileae, 1536, Erasmus Rotterdamus, Desiderius: Contains a collection of Greek and Latin proverbs with explanations and some related historical and scholarly comments.
5. *Olympia Pythia—Nemaea—Isthmia*, Frankfort, 1552, Ed. Petrus Bubrachius, Pindarus: The collected works of the prince of Greek lyric poetry characterized by a knowledge of classical antiquity that nurtured the spirit of the Renaissance.
6. *Collection Operum Classicorum Latinitatis*, Parisios, 1561, Ed. Thomas Brumennius, Cicero, Aulus, Persius, Publius, Ovidus, Naso, Horatius, Flaccus: A pedagical edition of classical authors.
7. *Elementa—Phaenomerna—Specularia—Perspectiva—Data Bartholomeo Zamberto Veneto Interprete*, Venetiis, 1558, Megarensis, Euclides: The works of the most famous mathematician of classical times which were translated into Latin during the Renaissance.
8. *De Materia Medica*, Coloniae, 1529, Ed. Joannes Soterius, Dioscorides Anazarbaeus, Pedacius: The most famous book that contributed much to the development of modern medicine, which was edited in Greek with a corresponding translation and commentaries in Latin.

Another section of interest to researchers is the Filipiniana Section, which occupies Rooms 114, 116, 118, and 120 on the ground floor of the Main Building. (Information on this section was obtained from *Pamana Filipiniana*, published for an exhibit in connection with National Book Week, 1968, by the UST Library, Manila, 1968.)

The collection consists of 10,500 bound books, plus a number of maps, atlases, documents, manuscripts, etc. The books deal with various aspects of Philippine studies: history, literature, government, economics, and other sciences, written in Spanish, English, French, and in several local dialects. Of the 10,500 volumes, some 2,354 are rare books printed in the 16th to the early 19th centuries.

Some titles held by the Filipiniana Section are:

1. *Guia official de las Islas Filipinas*: An annual publication containing facts and figures about the country during the later periods of Spanish colonization. The collection in the University Library includes issues from 1879 to 1898.
2. *Vocabulario de la lengua Tagala*, Higino Roldan, Valladolid, Spain, 1832, Fathers Juan de Noceda, S.J. and Pedro de Sanlucar, S.J.: It took 30 years to finish this work. Fr. Francisco de San Jose started the work. Two Dominican priests continued it up to letter *O*, and the two Jesuit fathers made the necessary corrections, improvement, and preparation of the materials for publication.
3. *Suma de una Junta que se hizo a manera de concilio el año 1582* (MS): This manuscript is an 18th-century copy of the call for the First Synod of Manila summoned by the first bishop of the Philippines, Domingo Salazar, O.P. in 1582.
4. *Libro de asiento de los grados y claustros de la Real y Pontifica Universidad de Santo Tomas* (MS): This is the first of several volumes recording the examination proceedings for the degrees granted by the University of Santo Tomas. It contains all the degrees conferred from 1663 to 1713, to a total of 193 graduates with the titles of *bachiller, maestro*, and *doctor* in the three faculties at the time: Arts, Philosophy, and Theology.
5. *Gaceta de Manila*: A daily four-page publication which first came out on February 26, 1861. The large part of the newspaper carried articles about the government and official decrees, orders, and similar information. The library has a complete set of all issues until August 8, 1898.
6. *Cedulario de la insigne muy noble y siempre leal Ciudad de Manila*, D. Jose Dayot, 1836: A collection of *cedulas* and *ordenes reales*, or royal orders, from Spain on the administration of the City of Manila. The first royal order was dated June 21, 1574, and the last was issued on March 5, 1832.
7. *Catalogo sistematico de toda fauna de Filipinas*, University of Santo Press, 1895 (3 vols.), Fray Casto de Elera, O.P. (Director, Museum of the Dominican Fathers, and Professor, Natural History): Written for the Philippine Regional Exposition. The three volumes contain 12,900 names of zoological species.

Special Libraries

SPECIAL LIBRARIES DURING THE SPANISH REGIME

In the previous discussions it has been stated that convent libraries were the first ones to be established by the religious organizations that accompanied the first Spanish settlers in the Philippines. Later on seminary libraries were established and were in existence as early as 1862. Earlier still than the seminary libraries were two nonreligious special libraries. In 1781 the Real Sociedad Economica de Amigos del Pais was organized, and a library of over 500 volumes was an adjunct of this society. In 1846 a royal decree created the Biblioteca Militar, placed under the charge of retired Spanish army captains.

All of these were special libraries in the sense that the collection of each one of them covered a special field and each offered services to a special clientele. The convent libraries, the seminary libraries, and even the college libraries during Spanish rule in the Philippines were all focused on the religious conquest that dominated the colonial policy of Spain in the Philippines. The convent libraries were used by the clergy, the very special clientele that formed the group responsible for disseminating religious doctrines. The libraries were not for the people who were the objects of religious teachings.

For hundreds of years the Filipino industries—shipbuilding, lumber, metal works, etc.—were controlled by the ruling country. Trade and commerce likewise suffered restrictions. But toward the end of the 18th century there were evidences of interest in economic advancement and better commercial policy. In the endeavor to develop the natural resources of the Philippines, Spain organized the Sociedad Economica de Amigos del Pais in 1781 and the Real Compania de Filipinas in 1785, the first to develop industry and commerce and the second to advance trade relations of the Philippines with Spain and with the other Spanish colonies. The Library of the Sociedad Economica was organized to support the search for information regarding means of stimulating and subsequently exploiting the economic potentials of the Philippines.

SPECIAL LIBRARIES DURING THE AMERICAN OCCUPATION

A similar motive prodded the early American government in the Philippines to establish research institutions to develop the natural resources of the Philippines. At the same time, the new government believed that training the Filipinos for self-government necessitated, first, the establishment of good government. A representative form of government with executive departments made up of bureaus and offices was organized: The two targets with high priorities, the development of natural resources and the advancement of the democratic form of government, were the focus of interests and activities. And these interests and activities were reflected in the libraries that were formed.

Each executive department, each bureau, and each agency or commission was equipped with a library, whether purposely organized to serve the office or simply an outgrowth of the accumulation of publications relating to the work of the agency. A few of the government agencies had useful collections, while the majority had merely a thin aggregation of materials. The activities of an office are determined by the purpose or purposes of the particular office. Hence, the subject coverage of the collection and facilities offered by the library of a government office are geared to the sphere of the functions of the agency—thus making the library services *special;* that is, tailored to fit the special demands of the office.

At the start of the American occupation a few libraries were promptly organized, as the work of the government necessitated background knowledge and guidance in the serious business of establishing the particular form of government in a country so different from the United States. There was also the necessity of knowing the country more deeply, especially its natural resources. Among these libraries were the Bureau of Science Library, the Supreme Court Library, the Legislative Reference Service, and the City Fiscal's Office Library. There were other technical offices besides the Bureau of Science—such as the Bureau of Forestry and the Weather Bureau—at the start of the American occupation, but the Bureau of Science was the one that concentrated fully on science and technology. This was the bureau that very early had a well-developed library.

THE BUREAU OF SCIENCE LIBRARY

This library, which is now the Division of Documentation of the National Institute of Science and Technology, has a very impressive, almost exciting history. In the establishment of government agencies by the American occupation forces in 1901, the Bureau of Government Laboratories was among those given top priority. Dean C. Worcester, who was then the secretary of the Department of the Interior and a member of the Philippine Commission, was responsible for the approval on July 1, 1901, of Act Number 156 for the creation of the Bureau of Government Laboratories, which in 1905 was changed to Bureau of Science. Secretary Worcester strongly pushed through its creation because he believed that having one laboratory for all the technical offices in the Philippine government would result in efficiency and economy. Among the provisions of the act that created the said bureau was the organization of a reference library for the use of its staff. It was Dr. Paul C. Freer, the first director of the Bureau of Government Laboratories, who strongly advocated the organization of the library to support the scientific researches to be done by the bureau. Although the original intention was to limit the clientele to the staff of the bureau and other researchers of other government offices, the general public was later allowed to use the facilities of the library. And the original plan of limiting the use of the library as a reference library was later liberalized to include limited circulation.

In 1909 Act Number 1935, which consolidated all libraries of the insular offices of the Philippine government, resulted in the Bureau of Science Library becoming the Scientific Division of the Philippine Library. The provision of the act, however, specified that "the scientific division shall be housed in the building of the Bureau of Science," and that "when a division is located in another place than at the place of the main library, property responsibility for the custody of the books shall rest upon the Bureau or Office in which it is located, and the employees occupied in cataloguing and caring for the books shall be employees of such Bureau or Office."

The actual establishment of the library took place in 1902 when 50 books in the Board of Health were transferred to the bureau, along with the board's subscriptions to scientific periodicals. A recounting of the rapid growth of the collection from the nucleus of 50 books would sound like describing "a library in a hurry." Through sheer hard work the librarian, Miss Mary Polk, was able to secure more funds, to solicit donations, and even to reach as far as Europe where she was able to secure the back volumes of several important scientific journals. In 1904 the collection rose to 11,021 volumes, in 1914 the figure rose to 30,860, and in 1924 there were 85,485 volumes, parts (individual unbound serial issues), and pamphlets. In 1935 there were 149,360 bound volumes, parts, and pamphlets; and in 1941, at the outbreak of the war, the library had 357,000 volumes, pamphlets, and unbound issues of serials.

The collection was especially rich in scientific serials (which formed 85% of the whole collection), a good part of which were acquired through exchange. Its exchange publication, the *Philippine Journal of Science*, started in 1906 and has been continued up to the present. The collection covered all branches of science and applied science, with a small portion consisting of publications on social science, bibliography, and library science.

From the very start the librarian made efforts to organize the collection so that the researchers could make good use of the resources. The collection was accessioned, classified according to the Dewey Decimal Classification, and provided with author cards and a shelflist record, but no subject entries were made. When a regular cataloger was assigned in 1908, the collection was reclassified using the Library of Congress Classification as this scheme was better suited to a special collection, especially a collection that was rapidly growing. A dictionary card catalog was provided with numerous analytical entries.

As the collection continued to grow and the borrowers increased in number and became more varied, the charging routine gradually was made more systematic: The memorandum receipt system was changed to a card charging system with provision for a personal record file. A trained reference librarian was assigned to help researchers manipulate the research tools and thereby utilize to the fullest the rich scientific resources of the library.

In his article "The Status of the Popular Library Movement in the Philippines," Professor Bernardo spoke highly of the Bureau of Science Library, attributing its excellent service to the staff of the said library. He expressed his admiration when he said that "the wisdom and foresight of its founders have been so faithfully translated into effective service by its executive and staff" (*57*). The credit for the start and rapid growth of the Bureau of Science Library is given to Miss Mary Polk, who showed great capability as an administrator. When the Bureau of Government Laboratories was organized, she occupied the position of stenographer to the director of the bureau. Upon passing an examination given by the Civil Service Board, she was appointed librarian of the bureau. She held this position from the date of her appointment in 1903 to the time of her death on April 12, 1924. Her great endeavor to make the library a truly competent aid in scientific research was almost an obsession. Starting with one clerk as a helper, she had 17 in her staff at the time of her death in 1924.

The cataloger, Mrs. Brooks, had 13 years of experience in the Catalog Division of the Library of Congress before she came to the Philippines. She was the one who undertook the task of changing the classification scheme from the Dewey Decimal Classification to the Library of Congress scheme, and she made complete sets of cards for each title, instead of providing only the author card and the shelflist card. She also organized the loan procedure, adopting a method similar to the Newark charging system.

Miss Emma E. Keinne was appointed assistant librarian on February 3, 1911. She continued the work of Mrs. Brooks in cataloging and classifying the collection. When Miss Keinne left in 1914, Mr. Luis Montilla, a cataloging assistant since March 1910 in the Bureau of Science Library, took her place. He resigned in 1917 to become the cataloger of the Philippine Library and Museum. Miss Catalina Sucgang, who had studied library science with Mr. Montilla and other Filipino library apprentices in the initial library science courses at the University of the Philippines, took over the cataloging work, a position she held up to her retirement in 1959.

Holding a major position among the Filipino library assistants in the Bureau of Science Library was Mr. Cirilo B. Perez, who took library science courses at the University of the Philippines. His training in library science was intensified in the United States when he was sent as a government fellow for further training in bibliography and library science. He returned in 1910 to become the assistant librarian in the Bureau of Science Library, and he finally became the librarian in 1924 when Miss Polk died. Another assistant at the Bureau of Science Library who was sent to the United States (in 1920) for advanced training in library science was Isidoro Saniel, who upon his return became the reference librarian.

In the 1930s the library underwent certain administrative changes. The Reorganization Act of 1932 fused the Bureau of Science Library with the libraries of the Bureau of Plant Industry, Bureau of Commerce, Bureau of Forestry, and the Weather Bureau; and the combined facilities became the Scientific Library, forming one of the divisions under the direct executive supervision of the secretary of the Department of Agriculture and Commerce. On August 14, 1934, the library was returned to the Bureau of Science and was again placed under the direct jurisdiction of the said bureau.

The total destruction of this library in 1945 during the war of liberation has been repeatedly described. Suffice it to say that from the heaps of ashes and debris, the Bureau of Science Library had to be rebuilt, and great efforts had to be mounted to push against insurmountable difficulties. The Reorganization Law of 1947 converted the Bureau of Science into the Institute of Science and Technology, and the library became its Scientific Library Division. Rehabilitation work was a continuous begging for funds and requests for aid to build the collection, to provide for quarters, and to recruit suitable staff members. Up to the 1950s rehabilitation work was proceeding at a turtle's pace, but the working staff through hard and persistent effort gave what service it could to the research program that was already being undertaken by the institute.

In 1958 another reorganization of the Philippine government took place. The Institute of Science and Technology became the National Institute of Science and Technology by R.A. Number 2067. The act made the Scientific Library Division into the Division of Documentation. This change was due to a UNESCO project to install a scientific documentation center in the Philippines, to be attached to and incorporated with the Library of the National Institute of Science and Technology. Today this Division of Documentation, now called the Scientific Library and Documentation Division, is directly under the administrative control of the National Science Development Board, and it has assumed a position as the national scientific library of the Philippines that coordinates all science and technology libraries existing in the different government agencies.

SCIENTIFIC LIBRARY AND DOCUMENTATION DIVISION OF THE NATIONAL SCIENCE DEVELOPMENT BOARD*

The National Science Development Board (NSDB), whose chairman has cabinet rank, is in charge of science and technology development in the Philippines. It is located in Bicutan, some 20 kilometers south of Manila. Its library, which gives service to the Philippine scientific and technological community, has over the years evolved from several sources: the old Bureau of Government Laboratories established in 1901; the Bureau of Science Library, before World War II; the Institute of Science and Technology Library, after the war; and in the reorganization of the government in 1958, the Division of Documentation of the National Institute of Science and Technology (NIST). In May 1975 the NIST Division of Documentation, the NSDB Reference and Exchange Library, and the Scientific Library and Documentation Center Project of the NSDB were merged to become the Scientific Library and Documentation Division (SLDD), directly under the NSDB's Education and Public Affairs Service. Part of the NIST Division of Documentation collection was brought to Bicutan to form the nucleus of the SLDD collection; however, the division itself is still in Manila giving service to the staff of the National Institute of Science and Technology and to the Manila science community.

One wing of the ground floor of the NSDB building in Bicutan is occupied by the SLDD. In this area of 408 square meters are the reading room, the bookstacks, the Acquisition Unit, the Cataloging–Classification Unit, the Special Projects Group, and the offices of the chief and assistant chief of the division. The Abstracting Unit and the Indexing–Bibliography Unit are in the basement of the Science Display Center building in the NSDB Bicutan compound, occupying an area of 111 square meters.

The book collection consists of 25,624 volumes (of which only 7,680 are in Bicutan; the rest are in the NIST Division of Documentation in Manila). The periodical collection consists of 454 titles acquired by subscription, 1,600 titles acquired through exchange, and 950 titles acquired as gifts.

The collection is available to the general public for reading room use only. But NSDB personnel may borrow books for a period of 2 weeks, subject to recall when needed by other borrowers. Reference inquiries are received directly at the desk, by letter, by telephone, or by radio message from the NSDB's regional offices.

Current issues of periodicals are displayed in the reading room and are frequented by researchers and the general library users who browse through them for the latest developments in their subjects of interest.

To provide current awareness devices, abstracting, indexing, and bibliography compilation are done on a continuing basis. Tables of contents of current journals are reproduced and circulated to the different division staffs.

*From a paper read by Delia Torrijos, acting chief of the Scientific Library and Documentation Division of the National Science Development Board, at the Seminar on Quality Libraries and Information Systems held at Silliman University, December 13–15, 1976.

The program calls for acquisition of materials in science and technology in cooperation with the NSDB's implementing agencies and other research institutions, both within the government and in private sectors. The SLDD has put out a union list of serials with nationwide coverage and is about ready to launch a union catalog of nonserials. Once the inventory of holdings is finished, a meaningful cooperative acquisition program can be fully implemented, and this network can then begin to serve its "publics" all over the country.

The SLDD is actively updating the very useful projects started in 1960 by the NIST Division of Documentation, namely:

1. *Philippine Abstracts:* Published quarterly, this gives summaries/abstracts of all current publications on science and technology.
2. *Philippine Science Index:* Issued bimonthly, this indexes current scientific and technological publications. It serves as the national bibliography on science and technology.
3. Series of specialized bibliographies: These provide retrospective comprehensive lists of references on specific topics, based on anticipated needs or on request.

The SLDD is charged with the following responsibilities: (*a*) to coordinate and centralize library and information services for science and technology—not only for the NSDB and its agencies but including other institutions, government and private—with already existing significant resources and capabilities; and (*b*) to maintain linkages with existing and planned relevant information systems on science and technology, including international and regional systems.

While the SLDD gradually works toward organizing itself and increasing its capabilities and resources, it does not lose sight of developments in information and library services in other national organizations and private and academic institutions, especially those relevant to science and technology. Thus, the SLDD keeps itself informed of developments in other areas. On the regional level—that is, Asia and the Pacific, but more specially Southeast Asia—the SLDD is fortunate to have made contacts with a number of organizations. The SLDD is now involved in the planning and implementation of regional projects in library and information services, such as in ASEAN, ASCA, SEARCA/AIBA, the former ASPAC, and other regional activities of UNESCO and UNDP.

THE LEGISLATIVE REFERENCE SERVICE LIBRARY

Another special library of distinct importance is the Legislative Reference Service Library of the House of Representatives of the Congress of the Philippines. The real beginning of this library may be traced as far back as 1916 when the Philippine Library and Museum was created and placed under the directorship of Teodoro M. Kalaw. In describing the library he was handling—which was quite different from its predecessors, the Philippine Public Library and the Philippine Library—Director Kalaw stated that the library's functions had increased both in scope and in intensity. Regarding the services of the library to legislative research, he enumerated the activites in the following:

> We are in charge of the Legislative Research Office for the members of the Legislature and Officials of the executive departments, the work of which consists in compilation of correct, complete, and condensed information on any subject of legislation available on short notice; preparation of briefs showing facts, opinions, and arguments upon any public question; furnishing and citing of documents and authorities to support both sides of the question; drafting of bills, resolutions, and memoranda; making researches and studies on matters of public importance (*58*).

In 1939 Commonwealth Act Number 451 created the Legislative Service Office of the National Assembly of the Commonwealth of the Philippines, and this office maintained a library called the Legislative Reference Service Library. This was the Legislative Research Office cited by Director Kalaw. The transfer of the Legislative Research Office from the National Library to the National Assembly (later the House of Representatives) was prompted by the propriety of having the Legislative Reference Service under the National Assembly instead of under the National Library, which was functioning under the Department of Public Instruction, one of the agencies of the executive branch of the government.

The library has always been intended primarily for the members of the House of Representatives, but all who need materials on Philippine legislative matters are allowed to use its resources. The functions described by Director Kalaw have, of course, widened in later years to support the increasingly complicated legislative activities. Always wide-awake, the library supplies information at a moment's notice, and when Congress is in session it has to stay open until the end of the daily session, whatever time it may be. As to its collection, one librarian has given the following information:

> Reflecting closely the interests and work of Congress, the collection of the Legislative Reference Library distinguishes itself with the preponderance of its collection of bills and acts not only of the Philippines but also of places or countries whose current interests are similar. Unlike the collections of its counterparts in the various states of the United States and the Legislative Reference Service of the U.S. Library of Congress, our library is forced by circumstances to keep a very extensive law collection. Every effort is made to secure the most important publication on legislation and governmental problems and other significant problems which may confront Congress at any given time (*59*).

THE EXECUTIVE OFFICES

It should be stated here that as soon as civil government was organized, the necessary departments, bureaus, commissions, and offices were created. The operation of these agencies involved functions that generally required studies and investigations, and this necessitated the consultation of records and other sources of information. It may be said that almost all government agencies had some kind of working collection, and these appeared to be duplicating one another in many instances. Such a situation, perhaps, prompted the passage of Act Number 1935 in 1909, which called for the consolidation of all libraries in insular offices, to form the Philippine Library. Some agencies had libraries directly organized for their purposes, but the majority of the agencies simply found themselves furnished with a collection of materials that had accumulated over time. For example, the Department of Labor and the Bureau of Education were very early provided with libraries. The Bureau of Education, by the very nature of its functions, clearly needed a library. Called the General Office Library, the facilities were utilized by the General Office staff; but soon the library had to extend its services to the field, especially during summer vacations when the field staff made intensive use of the collection. The Department of Labor Library had, likewise, a very early beginning, as the following narration shows:

> Ever since the creation of this office [Department of Labor], first as a mere bureau under the then Department of Commerce and Police in 1908, and later as a Department in 1933, it had a library collection. This was because from the start, the Division of Labor Statistics, an office then under the Bureau of Labor, had to collect, compile, systematize and make use of all available materials pertinent to labor, both local and foreign (*60*).

Among all the government agency libraries, the Weather Bureau Library had the most unusual beginning. It was, in fact, the library of the Manila Observatory that the Jesuit Fathers of Ateneo de Manila started in 1865. The official creation, however, took place on June 14, 1881, when the Observatorio Meteorologico de Manila was established by a royal decree (*61*). The office continued to operate as a private institution, and the library services were handled by priests until 1901, when it was transformed into a government bureau by Act Number 131 of the Philippine Commission (*62*). In 1932 the Reorganization Act placed the library under the administrative control of the Department of Agriculture and Commerce, with other government agency libraries, but it was placed under the Bureau of Science in 1954. By the time the Pacific War broke out, the library had 10,000 volumes, all of which perished during the battle waged by the liberation forces in Manila. In 1947 Executive Order Number 94 created the Department of Commerce and Industry, under which the Weather Bureau was placed.

BUSINESS LIBRARIES

In a different category of government agency was the Philippine School of Commerce (now the Philippine College of Commerce). This was the first school established for the training of young people in the field of business. Organized in 1904, it grew in prestige and developed into an excellent school of business which through the years turned out graduates to fill positions of executive level in large business and industrial firms. From the start there was a library to support the school instruction, although the library service was handled by nonlibrarians. It was only in 1929 that the library was placed under the care of a professional librarian (*63*).

It appears that business libraries were not far behind science and technology libraries and legislative libraries in the matter of priority of establishment. Even the private sector was very early desirous of industrial and business progress. The Chamber of Commerce of the Philippines, for example, in its effort to expand Philippine trade and commerce, had to seek information from a variety of sources to acquire knowledge and gain acquaintance with trade conditions in different parts of the world. Hence a library was, from the beginning of the Chamber's existence, a working tool that helped in its operation. "Since its organization in 1903, the Chamber of Commerce of the Philippines had been the recipient of trade publications from all over the world. Before the outbreak of World War II, the Chamber could boast of a sizeable collection of trade literature" (*64*).

The City of Manila also evidently felt the need for a business library. In 1937 the Manila Business Library was established (*65*). However, it did not flourish as a business library, as was intended. The need for public libraries overshadowed the need for a business library, or perhaps there were already business libraries that were accessible to Manila businessmen. Hence, the library was converted into a public library and was called the Santa Cruz Branch Library of the Manila City Library.

Such was the state of our special libraries when the Pacific War broke out. Once again it should be stated that the majority of what may be called *special libraries* were libraries of Philippine government bureaus and offices, with which may be mentioned the Military Information Division Library of the U.S. Army (*66*). As has been repeated many times before, these libraries were devastated during the war.

GOVERNMENT AGENCY LIBRARIES

Postwar rehabilitation work was faced with gigantic problems, such that it took some time before definite plans could be laid out. As usual, the libraries were among the last organizations to receive the blessings of attention. In the case of special libraries, some fortunate circumstances occurred together that resulted in reviving government agency libraries. The flow of foreign aid to the Philippines during the rehabilitation years included both financial and technical assistance. With the sums of money appropriated through the ECA (now the U.S. Agency for International Development) came technical staff to study and determine the full measure of the necessary rehabilitation work. To channel the U.S. aid to the right direction, the Philippine Council for U.S. Aid (PHILCUSA) was established with Dr. Amando Dalisay as the executive officer. Men in the technical assistance staff were assigned to the different sectors needing aid and development: medical, agricultural, educational, labor, banking, statistics, etc. Technicians and advisers had to study the background, analyze the problems, and determine the structure of the projects on which U.S. financial aid was to be spent. The American labor statistician Dr. Meredith Givens, who came in late 1951 to work on a program of statistics for the Philippines, then held an office in the Department of Labor, and he found the library of the department to be too disordered to be of any help in his work. The condition in other government agency libraries, he found to be the same. The materials that accumulated for over 5 years after the termination of the war in 1945 had been left uncared for. So it was not so much the dearth of research materials but the lack of proper organization and lack of bibliographic aids in the said libraries that formed the barriers to research work. Valuable documents and source materials had been dumped in dark corners of government offices and could not be put to use because of the absence of any index or any subject guide. Sets of documents, reprints, foreign agency series, etc., were piled in storerooms because nobody took care of the continuous flow of publications distributed by foreign and local agencies.

The labor statistics expert found the situation to be a factor that was holding back the progress of rehabilitation projects. He requested that the Department of Labor assign a member of the department staff to take care of the library. Then he asked the ECA to provide an American library consultant, who was to map out the plan of work in organizing the library. The U.S. Information Service librarian in Bangkok at the time was sent to the Philippines in response to the request of the labor statistician. The library consultant not only attended to the problems of the Department of Labor Library but made a survey of library conditions in the government departments, bureaus, and offices in Manila. The three memoranda prepared by the consultant show the scope of the work she did:

1. Notes on the conditions of Philippine government libraries
2. Proposal for installation of a technical reference facility in the Department of Labor
3. Proposed Interdepartmental Reference Service in social science and government

The memoranda were dated February 13, 1952, February 14, 1952, and February 20, 1952, respectively. The cooperative reference project was the one that appeared to be the most appropriate to fill the need of the moment. A portion of the said memorandum stated the following:

> In this field, there are a number of government agencies with partially overlapping interests. By organizing some cooperative reference service, a great deal of duplication and consequent unnecessary expenditure will be avoided.
>
> A cooperative project can be started by the following agencies which others can join at any time on expression of interest and agreement to meet the conditions. This first group should consist of the National Economic Council, the Department of Commerce and Industry, the Bureau of the Census and Statistics, the Department of Labor, the Department of Agriculture, the Central Bank, and the University of the Philippines.

The labor statistician succeeded in convincing the Philippine Council for U.S. Aid to finance at least the initial stage of the project. For the purpose, PHILCUSA retained the services of an American special librarian to begin on March 10, 1952. This was part of the recommendation of the USIS library specialist who had been detailed to the Philippines for a few days to survey and map out plans to develop government agency libraries.

THE INTERDEPARTMENTAL REFERENCE SERVICE

On March 17, 1952, a conference was held in the office of the executive secretary of PHILCUSA to discuss the proposed interdepartmental reference service. Besides the executive secretary of the PHILCUSA, the labor statistician, the University of the Philippines librarian, and the special library consultant, at the meeting there were representatives from the Department of Agriculture and Natural Resources, the Department of Commerce and Industry, the Department of Labor, the Bureau of the Census and Statistics, the National Economic Council, the Central Bank of the Philippines, and the Philippine National Bank, all agencies which were interested in the said proposal. Two committees were formed: a committee of librarians of the previously mentioned agencies and a policy committee composed of division heads under whose direction the libraries in their respective agencies operated. The committee composed of librarians of the cooperating agencies was to meet regularly once a week under the chairmanship of the special library consultant to discuss the library problems encountered in their respective libraries and work toward a solution to the problems, and to find ways and means to improve the services of their respective libraries. The policy committee was the body that drafted the recommendations for the implementation of the project. The recommendations were presented to PHILCUSA, which in turn submitted the project to the MSA with a request for assistance. On April 30, 1952, an agreement was signed between PHILCUSA and the MSA providing a budget to launch the undertaking, to be known as Project Number 23.

It was clear that individually the libraries were ineffectual due to untrained personnel and poor resources. Combined resources, especially under the guidance of experienced librarians, would yield better results. The labor statistics expert, in his memorandum on March 21, 1952, to the head of the Special Technical and Economic Mission, emphasized the value of the project, as seen in the following:

> I am convinced that a cooperative technical reference base within the government departments concerned with economic problems and related activities will aid fundamentally in providing a needed foundation for needed fact finding . . . in these fields in the Philippines. Pooled resources and cooperative efforts are the right approach to the strengthening of the weak links and in the stimulation of effective use of collective facilities.

As a project under PHILCUSA, the Interdepartmental Reference Service Project was headed by a library coordinator who took the place of the special library consultant. The activities outlined for the project were the following:

1. Meetings of the librarians of the cooperating libraries for instructions on immediate tasks, and for orientation on specific functions of special libraries.
2. Actual help in organizing and cataloging of the holdings of the libraries.
3. Compilation of a union catalog and a union list of serials held by government agency libraries.
4. Publication of *Current Acquisitions* and *Instructions to Librarians*. The *Current Acquisitions* was to be a monthly listing of the combined acquisitions of the libraries of the participating agencies, to serve as an information guide to patrons and other libraries. The *Instructions* contained simple directions on the provision of facilities to the library clientele.
5. Make contacts with other government agency libraries for cooperation with the project, especially in the compilation of the union catalog and the union list of serials.

Cooperation and comprehension of the purpose of the project were evident in the interest shown in the development of libraries in the participating agencies. The cooperating libraries therefore expressed their desire to have the project placed on a permanent basis. To be an ongoing project, the Interdepartmental Reference Service had to be placed within an agency with permanent status. PHILCUSA negotiated with the University of the Philippines regarding the possibility of maintaining and operating the said project as a unit of the UP Institute of Public Administration. On October 16, 1952, an agreement was signed by PHILCUSA and the University of the Philippines giving the UP Institute of Public Administration the responsibility of maintaining, operating, and supervising the Interdepartmental Reference Service.

The Interdepartmental Reference Service (IDRS) was then permanently absorbed by the College of Public Administration of the university (formerly the Institute of Public Administration), but it is now under the administration of the University of the Philippines Library. The former activity of directly helping the cooperating libraries and coordinating their services and resources has been given up as most of the libraries now are headed by librarians with professional training. The compilation of the Union Catalog and the Union List of Serials has gradually become secondary activity. The IDRS's main service now appears to be the indexing of local serials. The project therefore was transferred to the UP Main Library, and it is now a regular unit of the library.

This account of the history of the IDRS has been given liberal space in this work because its creation spearheaded the development of special libraries in the Philippines. Under the sponsorship of the IDRS, the Association of Special Libraries of the Philippines (ASLP) was formed in 1954. From the 40 members that attended the inauguration ceremonies in 1954, the ASLP membership has grown to over 300, representing both government and private libraries. Services in these libraries cover different fields, such as medicine, economics, law, education, science and technology, agriculture, banking, labor, commerce and trade, history, mining, public administration, engineering, the different industries, etc. As if by sudden inspiration, in less than 10 years from 1954, special libraries put themselves boldly and insistently to the front as a distinct type of library that promised to do its part in the development of the Philippines toward economic, social, political, scientific, and technological advancement. There were, of course, several factors that prodded such an awakening. The government's attempt to modernize public administration and public service, thereby instituting a variety of in-service training programs, seminars, conferences, forums, and group discussions that necessitated studies and research; the government's industrialization programs that required keen and in-depth investigations; the inflow of foreign aid that took care of the rehabilitation of libraries and the training of librarians—all these, with the stimulation rendered by the IDRS and the ASLP, were the contributing elements that hastened the growth and development of special libraries. Some of these libraries are small and still suffer from insufficient financial support and inadequate professional competence of their librarians, but the general situation shows great improvement, especially among the major special libraries.

In addition to the government agency libraries already mentioned and briefly described, there are quite a number, many of them of postwar vintage, that have been making the best of the impoverished condition of their respective mother agencies and have been making progress in improving their services. Almost all the executive departments and their subsidiary offices are provided with libraries; the same is true of the offices under the Office of the President, such as the Budget Commission, the Civil Service Commission, and the National Economic Council (now the National Economic Development Authority). The judicial branch of the government has also established libraries to provide for the reference and research demands arising from its functions. The Supreme Court Library, which provides legal materials to its research staff, has already been mentioned as the law library division of the Philippine Library created by Act Number 1935 in 1909. Also, a considerable number of private agencies, especially industrial firms, have established libraries.

THE SYCIP, GORRES, VELAYO, AND COMPANY LIBRARY*

In more ways than one, the growth of a firm may be gauged by the growth of its library. In the case of Sycip, Gorres, Velayo, and Company (SGV), a professional services firm, this has proven true. As SGV progressed from an accounting firm with only two staff members, Messrs. Sycip and Velayo, to one with a present workforce of more than 2,000, its library evolved from a small, unorganized handful of books located in different divisions of the firm to an organized collection that now has more than 17,500 volumes.

Today the Sycip, Gorres, Velayo, and Company Group maintains a network of 19 library units scattered throughout its different offices in Southeast Asia. There are nine units in the Philippines: two in the Makati office and seven in the local branches. Indonesia maintains four units. The rest are found singly in Hong Kong, Korea, Malaysia, Singapore, Taiwan, and Thailand.

Individually most of these units are small, informal collections of books and journals. However, when consolidated as the SGV Group Libraries, the entire aggregation becomes a formidable storehouse of information on accounting and auditing as well as on other phases of business.

The heart of the collection is in the SGV Makati Library, which is composed of the Main and Tax Libraries. The Main Library is located on the third floor of the newly constructed SGV Development Center at 105 Dela Rosa Street, Legaspi Village. Covering an area of 200 square meters, it accommodates 20 readers and 7 library staff members. Its features include a processing room where library materials are accessioned and cataloged, a chief librarian's room, and five carrels. The library presents a striking and attractive picture in an orange–cream–blue color scheme. The Tax Library, on the other hand, is located at the center of the Tax Division, the 10th floor of the SGV Building, 6760 Ayala Avenue, Makati. Occupying a space of 63.84 square meters, the rectangularly shaped room has a vibrant atmosphere through the combination of the warm colors of carmine and peach. It can accommodate 16 readers.

The SGV Library has a collection of business information sources that is extensive in its coverage and in subject expertise. The Tax Library houses a special collection of in-depth sources on law and taxation in the Philippines, the United States, and other foreign countries. Special emphasis is currently being given to law and taxation in Southeast Asia, where the SGV Group has its scope of operations. The Main Library, on the other hand, houses a more general collection of information sources on business and allied fields. Understandably, accounting and auditing receive special emphasis in the acquisition of materials.

Four distinct types of information materials are found in the SGV Library.

*From a report prepared by Celia Samson, librarian of Sycip, Gorres, Velayo, and Company.

These are: (*a*) books, (*b*) periodicals, (*c*) annual reports, and (*d*) pamphlets and clippings in vertical files. To effectively bring out the usefulness of these materials, the library has devised a system of organization especially adapted to the firm's information needs; for example, books and periodicals are interfiled together in subject areas.

The collection is divided into the regular Filipiniana, Reserve, Reference, and Circulation Sections. In addition, the following collections were also set up:

1. Industry Reference Collection: This is an aggregation of books, periodicals, and pamphlets on the different industries. The materials are classified by industry and are shelved in specially designated sections.
2. Asia Collection: This is a country-by-country grouping of information sources on the different Asian nations. Emphasis is given to Southeast Asia.
3. Philippine Accounting Section: This is a special section of the Filipiniana Collection which includes all materials on auditing theory and practice in the Philippines. Publications of the Philippine Institute of Certified Public Accountants and publications of the National Association of Accountants form the nucleus of this section.
4. Corporate Data Files: Initially composed of Philippine and foreign corporate annual reports and financial statements, the Corporate Data Files now include brochures, prospectuses, special supplements, news clippings, and company publications.
5. Business Information File: This is the library's most handy source of ready information on business and related topics.

The SGV Library pursues a very active yet highly selective acquisition policy. The members of the different divisions of the SGV recommend books and periodical titles needed in their job engagements. These recommendations are, however, subject to the screening and approval of the Library Committee. An average of 150 volumes are acquired each month.

To provide for the leisure reading of the SGV staff, the library also acquires nontechnical reading materials such as best-selling fiction and nonfiction books. The latest editions of encyclopedias, handbooks, almanacs, and manuals are available in the library, as well as a collection of books on art, philosophy, and social sciences.

To adapt to the needs of the SGV clientele, the library utilizes a special classification scheme which was devised by a partner in the firm. The scheme incorporates the applicable elements in the different standard classification schemes, such as the Dewey Decimal Classification system, the Library of Congress scheme, and the Baker Library scheme. The following is the general framework of the special classification scheme:

100: Accounting
200: Auditing
300: Banking and Finance
400: Economics
500: Statistics
600: Management
700: Insurance
800: Law and Taxation
900: Marketing
1000: Office Management

1100: Personnel and Industrial Relations
1200: Production Management
1300: General Works
1400: General Reference
1500: Industry

Subject headings are formed in consonance with the needs of the library users. As much as possible, direct and specific keywords are utilized to effect simple and easy retrieval. The Sears List of Subject Headings, the Accountants Index, and the Business Periodicals Index are used as tools in assigning subject headings.

The library has set up various indexes and guides, and has compiled bibliographies, the more important of which have been printed for the use of the staff. Periodicals are scanned and are routed to the different staff members to call their attention to the articles of interest to them.

In the monthly acquisition list that is distributed to the staff, books are annotated to help the staff in selecting the desired materials. The library also maintains a collection of miscellaneous materials such as bank letters, newsletters, and government and quasi-government agency publications which provide up-to-date statistics on and insight into the developments in special sectors of the business world.

The SGV Library is staffed by eight professionally trained librarians, consisting of the chief librarian, four senior librarians, and three junior librarians. One junior librarian is assigned to the Tax Library while the rest are with the Main Library.

Library staff members are included in the firm's training program. Recently, four of the staff members underwent training in topics such as Business and Accounting Fundamentals, Technical Report Writing, and Industrial Engineering. The purpose of this is to familiarize the librarians with the activities and priorities of the different divisions and thus enable them to anticipate the company's needs and understand the terminology used.

THE LIBRARY OF THE FUND FOR ASSISTANCE TO PRIVATE EDUCATION*

The Fund for Assistance to Private Education (FAPE) is a nonprofit organization created by an executive order of the president of the Philippines in 1968. From the start, FAPE has been concentrating the bulk of its assistance programs at the college and university level, aiming at improved education and academic excellence.

In April 1970 a library was organized to meet the research needs of educational administrators and educational planners, the FAPE personnel, graduate students, and scholars. The collection was built to serve this special clientele. At present there are 5,500 volumes, some 800 pamphlets, and 860 bound volumes of periodicals. There are 160 subscriptions to periodicals and 87 publications received as gifts. The collection includes a number of special materials such as maps, government publications, films, filmstrips, microfilms, microfiche, dissertations on microfilm, and tape cassettes.

*From a report prepared by Corazon Nera, librarian of the Fund for Assistance to Private Education.

There are now 2,265 registered borrowers. In 1976–1977 library attendance totaled 3,500 readers using 8,680 books, more than 3,000 periodicals, and a number of microfiche, tapes, and films.

Designed originally for educators, the library is now used by a variety of borrowers since it was opened to the public; however, the majority are educators and people whose occupations are related to education. On record for 1976–1977 were readers from 74 schools and 26 offices. Some of the subjects of inquiry are communication systems, adolescence, behavior research, drug addiction, curriculum, environmental education, guidance and counseling, job evaluation, population, mental hygiene, sex education, underachievers, systems analysis, etc.

Some ongoing projects are being undertaken by the library. Special efforts are being made to maintain as comprehensive as possible a collection of materials on Philippine educational matters. Since most of the materials are already out of print, photocopies are being acquired.

The "information for management" project consists of analyzing publications for information needed by management. The library staff is therefore presently involved in intensive and extensive indexing and bibliography compilation.

THE RAMON MAGSAYSAY AWARD FOUNDATION ASIAN LIBRARY*

The Asian Library of the Ramon Magsaysay Award Foundation is the only private library on contemporary Asia open to the general public. It was started in 1958 primarily to meet the reference needs of the Board of Trustees in making selections for the annual awards. As the collection grew and became known, scholars, journalists, and government officials concerned with Asian affairs came to use the materials. In response to their requests, the library was formally opened as a public service in December 1963.

With the completion of the Ramon Magsaysay Center in 1968, the reading room was named the Wilkinson Reading Room, in memory of Gerald Hugh Wilkinson, an English friend and admirer of Ramon Magsaysay who made his home in the Philippines for over three decades. For the Wilkinson Memorial Fund, set up in 1966, his widow solicited contributions totaling $100,000 from family, associates, and friends. With this fund, the reading room, the stackroom, and office (occupying a total area of 308 square meters) were finished, furnished, and equipped. Five carrels in the stackroom were also provided for serious study and research.

For assistance in broadening the basic reference materials, and for ongoing additions to the Wilkinson Memorial Fund, the library is indebted to the Rockefeller Foundation for two grants totaling $25,000.

The collection, as of December 31, 1977, consisted of over 11,000 books and pamphlets, and 378 periodical titles and other publications. Through subscriptions the library receives 73 titles, while 305 titles are complimentary subscriptions from generous agencies and friends of the library here and abroad.

*From a report prepared by Gelacio Anglo, librarian, Asian Library of the Ramon Magsaysay Award Foundation.

The library also maintains a vertical file on organizations, personalities, and other topics pertinent to the award program and related activities of the library.

A special collection consists of the Magsaysay Papers, about 300,000 items of papers and documents of the late President Magsaysay. The papers are presently being processed under a special fund derived entirely from local contributions.

The library's collection of Asian educational films and slides is made available to schools in Metro Manila. Also presently being organized is the collection of maps of Asian countries. And for information on and requirements of the new society, the Presidential Decree Collection is being maintained.

On special shelves for use by recipients of the Magsaysay Award are articles, books, and other materials containing information about the lives and achievements of the awardees.

The library is open from 8 A.M. to 5 P.M., Monday to Friday, and from 8 A.M. to 1 P.M. on Saturdays. College students from over 30 colleges and universities in Metro Manila comprise about 50% of the library's patrons, high school students comprise about 40%, and professionals comprise about 10%. Records show an average of 1,300 readers a month. Library card holders entitled to check out books for home use for 10 days total 670. Borrowing privileges are extended to library users upon application, with recommendation from a responsible person known to the Ramon Magsaysay Award Foundation and upon payment of a P30 deposit. Borrowers are responsible for loss or defacement of books loaned to them.

To further enhance the usefulness of the collection, an interlibrary loan arrangement has been extended to 17 government and private libraries. Special requests for the loan of books are granted to agencies and associations sponsoring seminars and conferences. Library privileges are likewise extended to visiting scholars from foreign countries working on contemporary Asian history. These scholars come from the United States, Thailand, Korea, India, and Japan, to mention a few.

The library publishes its annotated list of acquisitions of books and pamphlets, entitled *A Guide to the Collection of the Asia Library*, which is sent to over 300 libraries here and abroad.

INTERNATIONAL RICE RESEARCH INSTITUTE LIBRARY*

Aware that the world's annual supply of rice falls short of global needs, and knowing the seriousness of the problem, the Ford and Rockefeller Foundations in 1959, with the cooperation of the Philippine government, established a world center for the study of rice. Formally inaugurated on February 7, 1962, the International Rice Research Institute (IRRI) is situated at Los Baños, Laguna, 40 miles south of Manila. One of the objectives of the institute is "to conduct basic research on the rice plant and on all phases of rice production, management, distribution, and utilization, for the nutritive and economic benefits of the people of Asia and other rice-growing areas through the improvement in the quality and quantity of rice production."

Consistent with this main objective and the rest of the objectives set forth in the

*From a report compiled by Lina Vergara, librarian of the International Rice Research Institute.

Memorandum of Agreement with the Philippine government, the IRRI established a library and documentation center to make available to scientists and scholars everywhere a collection of the world's literature on rice.

Considering the comprehensive coverage of the science disciplines as applied to rice, the library prepared an exhaustive acquisition program on the subject of rice and its ramifications. Everything that is written in the field for which it is responsible is included: books, pamphlets, periodicals, abstracting and reviewing media, government publications, loose-leaf systems, doctoral dissertations, translations from other languages into English, institutional reports, leaflets, etc., in all languages and in all editions.

The first measure undertaken was the compilation of the *International Bibliography of Rice Research*, which covered the years 1951–1960. This became the basis for the initial collection of literature, both for monographic and for periodical titles. With the continuing compilation of annual supplements for the period 1961–1972, practical completeness of the acquisition program was assured. Every item indexed and picked up for inclusion in the compilation is acquired, prior to publication of the bibliography, in whatever form it is available—printed or microform, mimeographed or typewritten. As long as the material has direct bearing on the rice crop, the material is added to the collection. However, the collection also includes books and periodicals in the supporting sciences.

The collection includes all the important works, as well as the latest and the best editions in the widely used languages, in all of the cognate agricultural disciplines of soil science, organic and physical chemistry, cereal chemistry, soil microbiology, agricultural economics, agricultural engineering, plant pathology, agronomy, entomology, plant physiology, plant genetics, plant breeding, statistics, extension, and sociology. A collection of basic reference tools is also acquired, such as language dictionaries, encyclopedias, bibliographies, periodical indexes, abstracting services, directories, handbooks and manuals, gazetteers, atlases, and maps, in the latest and best editions.

The Library of Congress Classification system is used. However, because only one number is used for rice, SB191.R5, a scheme was devised by the library to classify rice literature and IRRI publications. Taking the numbers SB194–SB305 of the LC scheme, a detailed expansion of the system was made without breaking down the whole classification system.

Standard cataloging rules and principles are adapted, considering, of course, local needs. The collection, the type of library, and the needs of the clientele are the deciding factors in the recording of cataloging information and classification. Simplified cataloging is used for all titles. Analytics are made for all numbers in important series. Reprints, translations, microfilms, maps, and phonorecords are numbered consecutively, with additional marks to distinguish one form from the other. Journals are arranged alphabetically on the shelves under title or corporate entry. Serial holdings are recorded in the Kardex File. All author, subject, and added entry cards are arranged in one general alphabetical sequence in the dictionary catalog according to the rules given in the *ALA Rules for Filing Catalog Cards*.

English is the official language in the IRRI.

The major purpose in developing the book and periodical collection and the special files of unique materials, all cataloged and indexed with meticulous attention, is to provide the group of persons for whom the service is planned—in this case, rice scientists everywhere—with these sources of information to use when needed. This use is administered through procedures that are adapted to the convenience of the clientele insofar as possible. Routine procedures controlling the lending–borrowing transaction are established on the basic principle of keeping them as simple as experience allows. All interests are served impartially, though the requirements of the institute's scientists and scholars are given priority.

As a policy, and because of the fact that the library is being built on single copies, the collection does not circulate outside of the institute. However, the general public is welcome to make use of the entire collection within the library premises only. Loans between libraries within the Los Baños area, however, may be arranged.

Rice scientists and scholars may request literature from the IRRI Library directly. The institute recognizes that some scientists making rice studies may not always have access to funds or appropriate foreign exchange to purchase reference materials needed to advance significant research. The institute encourages scientists in such situations to request literature needed. Within its capabilities, the institute may wish to finance such distribution.

At the IRRI, the library's immediate clientele is provided with a "current awareness" service. It involves reviewing all publications immediately upon receipt, and selecting information from periodicals, books, pamphlets, patents, and reports—in fact, from anything of serious content that is pertinent to the program of the institute. The information is then brought to the attention of the scientists and the departments concerned by duplicating the table of contents (with the items duly marked) if a periodical, or by sending a duplicate order slip if a monograph. When the need for the information is urgent, personal telephone notifications are made.

The table of contents duplication has been extended to include arrangements with the Bangladesh Rice Research Institute, the All-India Coordinated Rice Improvement Project, and the Lembaga Penelitian Pertanian Maros in Indonesia.

Every month the library issues its *New Acquisition List* of monographs, new serial titles, and translations. This gives, in addition to date of issue, the classification number, other pertinent location symbols, and the form of the material; if in a language other than English, it specifies the language in which it is written and notes the presence of English summaries or abstracts.

At least 23 languages are used in reporting scientific investigations of this one cereal group. A huge percentage of these works are in languages other than English, with Japanese taking the lead. Despite the fact that abstracting services are available, and despite the fact that most journals now include summaries and abstracts in English, it is common knowledge that the information given by abstracts and summaries does not suffice. A scientist gains knowledge of the way in which one piece of research suggests another, of the method of attacking a problem, and of the experimental methods and details from reading the article itself. In other words, the greater part of what is published is inaccessible to most of those who could otherwise benefit from it.

To meet the problem, the IRRI established a branch of its library in Tokyo. All requests for translations of Japanese literature into English are being channeled through this office, which is staffed by a Japanese rice expert and two librarians. It is through this office that competent translators are located: These may be proficient in the English language only to a certain extent but are recognized technical experts in the rice research field. Translations from other languages into English are also being done by special arrangement with the JCRR in Taiwan and other commercial translation services.

THE AGRICULTURAL INFORMATION BANK FOR ASIA*

The most recent project on research intended to cover as wide a region as possible is the Agricultural Bank for Asia (AIBA), based in Los Baños, Laguna, Philippines. The AIBA is a project of the Southeast Asian Regional Center for Graduate Study and Research in Agriculture (SEARCA).

AIBA was conceived because of the need for an effective information system in efforts to improve the research capability of the countries in this region and because of the utility value of the research output. It serves as a catalyst for the improvement of national information systems in agriculture and as the channel through which national agricultural information in this region flows into the international systems and back to individual nations, making possible the free flow of information generated anywhere in the world.

Officially approved by the Agricultural Government Board of SEARCA as a project in October 1973, AIBA started actual operations almost a year later, in July 1974, when IDRC/Ottawa agreed to fund its activities for a developmental year. This financial support was then extended through 1976.

Specifically AIBA's objectives are:

1. To serve the research needs of Asian countries in the field of agriculture and allied disciplines
2. To promote new and better techniques for handling and disseminating agricultural information
3. To serve as the input/output center in Southeast Asia and other Asian countries for FAO's worldwide project, the International Information System for the Agricultural Sciences and Technology (AGRIS)

Added to these objectives were the formation of the Agricultural Information Society for Asia (AISA) and promotion of interaction between AIBA and other regional agencies and the international networks.

AIBA proceeds from a regional stance, concerning itself—within one area of information, agriculture—with the development of national information in this area and linkages with other regional systems and with the world's agricultural system, AGRIS.

At present five SEAMEO (Southeast Asian Ministers of Education Organization) and four non-SEAMEO countries in Asia are participating in the AIBA net-

*From a report prepared by Filomena M. Tann, project manager of the Agricultural Information Bank for Asia.

work. In each of these centers there is a government-designated AGRIS center acting as agricultural information pool for that country. Through it, the country's agricultural literature enters into the international system through the regional center, AIBA. These government or national centers are: (*a*) Bibliotheca Bogoriensis in Indonesia; (*b*) Perpustakaan Negara Malaysia in Malaysia; (*c*) Thai National Documentation Center in Thailand; (*d*) Nanyang University in Singapore; (*e*) University of the Philippines at Los Baños in the Philippines; (*f*) Bangladesh National Scientific and Technical Documentation Center in Bangladesh; (*g*) Korea Scientific and Technological Information Center in Korea; (*h*) Department of Agriculture, Research Division, in Sri Lanka; and (*i*) Ministry of Agriculture and Fisheries in Hong Kong.

There are other centers in this part of the world that are still outside the agricultural global information system. There is a strong possibility for the future participation of the states of Brunei, New Guinea, Cambodia (Khmer), Vietnam, and Burma, through the initiative of the FAO AGRIS Coordinating Center.

The AGRIS-participating centers cover the agricultural literature produced in their country or region by all types of institutions and individuals in the following main subject areas: general agriculture; geography and history; education, extension, and advisory work; administrative and legislative; economic development and rural sociology; plant production; protection of plants and stored products; forestry; animal production; aquatic sciences and fisheries; machinery and buildings; natural resources; food science; human nutrition; and pollution and auxiliary disciplines. The scope is further defined in one of the AGRIS reference tools, *Subject Categories;* and the criteria for the selection of documents are given in another tool, *Guidelines for Bibliographic Description*. Each center selects the materials for inclusion in AGRIS on the basis of the criteria provided. With the application of such criteria and guidelines, the adoption of international standards in documentation is being achieved.

AGRIS has two tangible products: the AGRINDEX and the AGRIS output tape for computer retrieval of information. AGRINDEX is a hard-copy output that can be used as is for manual searching, and the output tape is used for computer searching. As these products store the world's total output of agricultural information, it has become necessary to cull from them any topic or topics relevant to a specific research project, to a product or an area, or to any point of access provided for in its storage.

In the utilization of the AGRIS output, AIBA culls from it all the literature relevant to Asian agriculture and adds to it the extension materials that the member countries, through their national centers, have deemed important to be recorded. This result is AGRIASIA. The impact of AGRIASIA has been encouraging. National centers have found it a valuable addition to their reference and bibliographic tools. An index "compiled by the region for the region," it has become a medium of Asian agricultural literature not only for Asia but also for all other parts of the world.

The output tapes of AGRIS will also be used to prepare computer-generated national agricultural bibliographies. The Philippine national agricultural bibliography has been used as a test. It will be made available soon in hard-copy form. On-line to follow the Philippine national agricultural bibliography are those of Indonesia, Thailand, Malaysia, Singapore, Korea, Sri Lanka, Bangladesh, and Hong Kong.

Again, the AGRIS output tape is put to use for the retrieval of information in response to queries received at AIBA. The more recent of those that come to mind were on rattan and agrarian reform.

The ultimate end of all the indexing and bibliographic activities of any information system is to provide the information or the source of the information to the user. As a well-known information scientist puts it: "It is in the retrieval of a useful citation where the importance of resource sharing looms very large. It is here where libraries, data base services and information centers are allies fully dependent on each other" (*67*). With this in view, AIBA has been utilizing the libraries in the region and the member libraries of the AGRINET system in retrieving information sources.

This method may work for conventional materials such as journal articles and published documents, but it has been found to be problematical especially in the provision of copies of nonconventional materials. A proposal for providing microfiches for this type of material is under study: "Each network country provides a micro record of its non-conventional literature including theses for submission to AIBA where a regional file will gradually be built up. Each centre in return will receive a copy of the file" (*67*).

AIBA, as the information arm of SEARCA, is providing the literature support for its research programs. Some current projects of AIBA under SEARCA support include abstract bibliographies on the following: (*a*) tropical vegetables—soybeans, mungbeans, cowpeas, chinese cabbage, groundnuts, sweet potatoes, and winged beans; (*b*) tropical fruits such as avocado, sweetsop, bananas, durian, guavas, mangoes, papayas, rambutan, chicos, and citrus fruits; and (*c*) such other crops as cassava, mushrooms, garlic, ginger, onions, and ipil-ipil (*Leucaena leucocephala*).

It has completed the following bibliographic and reference tools: (*a*) Small Farm Development Bibliography, (*b*) Livestock Production in the Tropics, (*c*) Sugarcane Production in Asia and the Pacific, (*d*) List of Southeast Asian Serials in Agriculture and Allied Sciences, (*e*) List of Asian Corporate Names, (*f*) AIBA/AGRIS Authority List of Corporate Names, and (*g*) List of Philippine Scientific Periodicals in Agriculture and Allied Sciences.

AIBA has other commitments which demand just as much of its staff's time and energies. One such obligation is the continuous training of staff at the national as well as at the regional centers. It has conducted two seminar/workshops. The first was the Training Program on the AGRIS Methodology held on February 16–27, 1976, and the second was a short-term training course on Information Systems and AGRIS held on June 1–21, 1977. The staff of AIBA has also traveled to the national centers in Indonesia, Malaysia, Thailand, Korea, and Bangladesh to train their AGRIS inputting staff. Recently, a staff member from Hong Kong trained at Los Baños from April 11 to 28, 1978.

Along this line, AIBA attempts to maintain a personal dialogue with its national participants in the region to sustain active collaborative efforts. It has further attempted and has achieved some degree of success in the advancement of the formal education of its own regional staff as well as of those in the national centers. It has cooperated in this area with institutions in the Philippines—such as the Institute of Library Science of the University of the Philippines, the University of the Philippines Library System, the National Science Development Board Documentation Center, the National Library, and other Philippine special libraries in agriculture and technology—and with institutions abroad such as the Royal Tropical Research Institute; the University of Wales; the Commonwealth Agricultural Bureaux in England; the Inter-American Agricultural Documentation and Information Center in Costa Rica; the College of Tropical Agriculture of the University of Hawaii; the System Development Center in Santa Monica, California; the University of California in Davis, California; Lockheed Information Systems in Palo Alto, California; and other world information systems.

It has established relations with other information networks and documentation centers in both developed and developing countries. It is exploring the possibility of venturing into collaborative work with other information centers like the Tropical Products Institute, the Commonwealth Agricultural Bureaux, and the Centre for Agricultural Publishing and Documentation. In recognition of its potential and capability, AIBA is being considered as the international documentation center for one agricultural commodity. It has made inroads in the area of users' training by collaborating with other institutes such as the Tropical Products Institute, London, and the Philippine Council for Agriculture and Resources Research in the first training program for processors and users held for 3 weeks in Los Baños in 1973.

The human factor, an unstable variable in many human endeavors, is the most delicate of all elements in any man-made system. In the case of AIBA "a great deal of effort has been poured into creating a vibrant interpersonal network of contacts which, hopefully, are capable of mutual progress based on the principles of cooperation" (*67*). This link is consolidated, reinforced, and strengthened through the Agricultural Information Society for Asia (AISA), which aims for personal and professional contacts among all in the region engaged in agricultural library and documentation work. AISA also aims to bring information processors and specialists working in both great and small libraries in contact with their colleagues in the region as well as in the world agricultural information services. It seeks to help build up agricultural library associations such as the ALAP (Agricultural Libraries Association of the Philippines) and to link them regionally and internationally with the International Association of Agricultural Librarians and Documentalists (IAALD).

The Sixth Congress of IAALD was held in Manila in 1980. It may be that the congress has acted as an accelerator in efforts to bring about the interlinkage of all agricultural libraries in this region with those in other parts of the world.

AIBA has indeed come a long way, not only in point of time but also in point of accomplishments. It has reached the stage where its initial projects have been accomplished or are on the verge of being accomplished. It has reached a stage where it is called upon for active involvement in the international area of agricultural librarianship and information work. It has reached a stage where enhancement of its future development requires the meeting of many minds. To this end, a Consultative Committee composed of the National Center heads of the SEAMEO countries was created. Its main functions are:

1. To act as the advisory body to SEARCA on matters relevant to the purposes and objects of AIBA
2. To assist AIBA in planning projects to meet the needs for agricultural information in this region
3. To meet regularly on the dates and at the places decided upon by the committee

The first formal meeting of the committee was held May 10–13, 1973, at Los Baños, Laguna, Philippines, with the senior adviser of AIBA and the project manager in attendance. After 5 days of fruitful sessions, it submitted its recommendations and resolutions to the director of SEARCA.

Through the Consultative Committee, AIBA staff members feel that they have gained more vigorous and intensive support for their efforts. They feel further that they can look to this committee for the regional "pulse" in agricultural information needs, and that it will serve to convey and satisfy these needs through mutual assistance.

SPECIAL LIBRARIES ESTABLISHED BY THE AMERICAN GOVERNMENT

Not to be left out in the discussion of special libraries in the Philippines are the libraries established here by the American government or under the sponsorship of American associations. One has been mentioned previously: the Military Information Division Library of the U.S. Army, which was established mainly for the members of the U.S. Army, Navy, and Marine Corps, and the Philippine Constabulary. Also to be mentioned are the U.S. Agency for International Development Central Resources Library and the United States Information Service (USIS) Film Loan Section. But the one that is familiar to many people is the library known for many years as the USIS Library. In September 1945 the Office of War Information (later the U.S. Information Service and now the U.S. International Communications Agency) established a library in Manila that was formally opened in the Soriano Building, Plaza Cervantes, Manila. Miss Hazel Ferguson of the USIS was in charge of the administration and operation of the library, with the assistance of three staff members detailed temporarily from the University of the Philippines Library. The library was intended to provide information and recreational reading to the American soldiers stationed in Manila, but it soon opened its doors to the public. Branches were established in several parts of the Philippines such as Davao, Baguio, Pangasinan, Legaspi City, etc. After 2 years the Manila Library moved to the old Heacock Building on the Escolta, where it stayed for over 10 years. In 1960 the library moved to a building at the corner of Apolinario Mabini and Padre Faura Streets, and in 1963 it moved again to new quarters on Ramon Magsaysay Boulevard. By that time the name of the library was no longer USIS Library. Due to the need for better understanding of American life and ideals, the cultural promotion goals of the agency were given priority. The name was then changed to Thomas Jefferson Cultural Center in 1962. After 7 years in Ramon Magsaysay Boulevard, the center moved to its own building on Araneta Avenue. The building has a music section with tapes, records, and music scores. It has an auditorium and several conference rooms. The library, situated on the first floor, has 10,000 volumes, 140 periodical titles, and over 1,000 reference books in the Reference Section. Mainly for information about American life, the special collection is limited to materials on this particular area.

Another library of American sponsorship is the American Historical Collection established by the American Association. Located in the Chancellery of the American Embassy on Roxas Boulevard, this library, "mainly a research library covering, though not exclusively, the American period in Philippine history, has become one of the leading libraries in its field in both the Philippines and the U.S." (*68*). It was American Ambassador Myron Melvin Cowen who started the movement for this library and requested the American Association to make arrangements for its establishment. The American Association formed a committee for the acquisition of materials. In a few months a collection was built through requests, donations, gifts, and purchase. In August 1950 Professor William Solheim was appointed librarian and curator. In February 1952 the library was officially inaugurated and opened its doors to the public. Of great interest to researchers, the rich Perkins collection known as the E. A. Perkins Memorial Library was donated in 1961 to the American Historical Collection by his heirs. The collection has 3,500 titles which were brought from Baguio to Manila.

PRIVATE COLLECTIONS

Finally, as sources of information of a specialized nature, the personal collections of scholars, collectors, and specialists constitute a wealth of Philippine research materials. The Quezonian collection now in the Filipiniana Division of the National Library and the other private collections acquired by the National Library by purchase form a valuable source on Philippine history and culture. The Magsaysay Papers housed in the Ramon Magsaysay Award Foundation provide rich resources on the Philippine democratic form of government, the birth of the land reform movement, and community development. Not to be overlooked are the private collections in the provinces. Batangas, for example, is proud to inform the public that it has the Laurel Library and Museum, Leviste Law Library, Noble–Caniza Library and Museum in Taal, and the Doña Aurelia Malvar Leviste Library and Museum in Santo Tomas (*69*).

REFERENCES AND NOTES

1. *Philippine Yearbook 1975*, National Economic Development Authority, National Census and Statistics Office, Manila, pp. 1–2.

2. James A. Robertson, "Collections of Religious Corporations in Manila," *Bull. Philippine Lib.*, **1**(6), 63 (February 1913).(Cited by Gabriel A. Bernardo in his "Development of Libraries in the Philippines," 1962.)

3. Jean Kay Gates, *Introduction to Librarianship*, McGraw-Hill, New York, 1968, p. 51.

4. Candida C. Agcaoili, "Special Materials in the U.S.T. Library," *ASLP Bull.*, **3**(1/2), 12 (June 1957).

5. Emma Helen Blair and James A. Robertson, *The Philippine Islands, 1493 to 1889*, Arthur H. Clark, Cleveland, Ohio, 1904, Vol. 46, pp. 340–341.

6. Ref. *5*, Vol. 45, pp. 177–178.
7. Ref. *5*, Vol. 28, pp. 201–202.
8. Ref. *5*, Vol. 45, p. 230.
9. Ref. *5*, Vol. 52, p. 309.
10. *Guia Oficial de las Islas Filipinas para 1898*, Manila, 1898, p. 340.
11. Gabriel A. Bernardo, "Libraries in the Philippines," in *Program of the Silver Jubilee Anniversary Celebration of the Philippine Library Association, November 1948–August 1949 Biennial Conference*, Manila, 1949, p. 37.
12. *Guia Oficial*, Ref. *10*, p. 343.
13. Ref. *10*, p. 765.
14. W. E. Retana, *Aparato Bibliografico de la Historia General de Filipinas*, Imprenta de la Sucesora de Minuesa de los Rios, Madrid, 1906, Vol. 3, pp. 1733–1734.
15. "Libraries. Modern Foreign Libraries. The Popular Library (Volksbucherei) in the 19th and 20th Centuries (up to 1945)," in *Encyclopedia Americana*, Americana Corporation, New York, 1955, Vol. 17, p. 331.
16. Blair and Robertson, Ref. *5*, Vol. 52, p. 309.
17. Ref. *5*, Vol. 46, p. 244.
18. Ref. *5*, Vol. 46, pp. 169–170.
19. U.S. Bureau of the Census, *Census of the Philippine Islands Taken under the Direction of the Philippine Commission in 1903*, Washington, D.C., 1905, Vol. 4, p. 407.
20. Isidoro Saniel, "Modernizing the Libraries in the Philippines," Manila, 1952, pp. 2–6 (Typewritten).
21. Ref. *20*, p. 24.
22. Philippine Islands, Bureau of Education, *Eighteenth Annual Report of the Director of Education, January 1, 1917 to December 31, 1917*, Bureau of Printing, Manila, 1918, p. 38.
23. Philippine Islands, Bureau of Education, *Nineteenth Annual Report of the Director of Education*, Bureau of Printing, Manila, 1919, p. 65.
24. Lois S. Osborn, "An Adventure in Dreams," *Lib. Mirror*, **1**, 32 (July 1929).
25. Philippine Islands, Bureau of Education, *Twenty-Second Annual Report of the Director of Education, January 1, 1921 to December 31, 1921*, Bureau of Printing, Manila, 1922, p. 46.
26. Philippine Islands, Bureau of Education, *Service Manual*, Bureau of Printing, Manila, 1927, pp. 93, 106–107.
27. Ref. *26*, p. 93.
28. Philippine Islands, Bureau of Education, "Memorandum No. 96, s 1928. 1929 Division Normal Institutes," Manila, 1928.
29. Philippine Islands, Bureau of Education, *Twenty-Third Annual Report of the Director of Education for the Calendar Year 1922*, Bureau of Printing, Manila, 1923, p. 59.
30. Philippine Islands, Bureau of Education, *Twenty-Fourth Annual Report of the Director of Education*, Bureau of Printing, Manila, 1924, p. 38.
31. Henry L. Cecil and Willard A. Heaps, *School Library Service in the United States*, H. W. Wilson, New York, 1940, pp. 238–239.
32. Philippine Islands, Bureau of Education, *Approved Library List: Bulletin 44*, Bureau of Printing, Manila, 1928, p. 34.
33. J. Scott McCormick, "School Libraries in the Philippines," in *Philippine Library Association: Proceedings of the First National Book Week and the 1934 Librarians Convention*, Manila, 1935, p. 59.
34. Section 1 of Act 96 of the U.S. Philippine Commission.
35. Gabriel A. Bernardo, "The Status of the Popular Library Movement in the Philippines," University of the Philippines, Manila, 1932, pp. 9–10 (Typewritten).
36. Severino I. Velasco, "The National Library," Manila, 1964, p. 1 (Mimeographed).
37. Saniel, Ref. *20*, p. 6.
38. Cited by Saniel, Ref. *20*, p. 7.
39. Severino I. Velasco, "Public Libraries in the Philippines Today," Manila, 1955, p. 39 (Typewritten).
40. Jose V. Abueva, *Focus on the Barrio*, Institute of Public Administration, University of the Philippines, Manila, 1959, p. 13.

41. The bill was sponsored by Senator Geronima Pecson.
42. The National Library, *The National Library Five-Year Development Plan (1973–1978)*, Manila, 1975, p. 20.
43. The National Library, *Annual Report, July 1, 1975–June 30, 1976*, Manila, 1976.
44. The National Library, Extension Division, *Annual Report, 1975–1976*, Manila, 1976.
45. *Philippine Yearbook 1975*, Ref. 1, p. 2.
46. Jose J. Ferrer, "Libraries in the Context of Philippine Culture," *Bull. Philippine Lib. Assoc.*, n.s., **5**(1/4), 9 (1970).
47. Severino I. Velasco, "The National Library," in The National Library, *Focus on the National Library*, Manila, 1964, p. 11 (Mimeographed).
48. Hermenegildo G. Peñaranda, "History of the Iloilo Provincial Library," in *First National Conference Workshop of Librarians in Conjunction with the Golden Anniversary of the Iloilo Provincial Library, October 24, 1966: Souvenir Brochure*.
49. Velasco, Ref. *47*, p. 12.
50. "The Manila City Library: Its Genesis and Growth," in *20th Anniversary, Kamaynilaan*, Manila City Library, Manila, October 28, 1966.
51. All the duties and functions of the defunct Bureau of Private Schools pertaining to colleges and universities have been assumed by the newly organized Bureau of Higher Education.
52. "Tertiary Education Becomes a Necessity," *Philippines Today*, No. 5, 1977, p. 29.
53. Philippines, Bureau of Private Schools, *Manual of Regulations for Private Schools*, 7th ed., Manila, 1970, p. 27.
54. Ref. *53*, p. 45.
55. Antonio Isidro and Maximo D. Ramos, *Private Colleges and Universities in the Philippines*, Alemar–Phoenix Publishing House, Manila, 1973, p. 150.
56. Remedios Viloria, "A Special Library for Educators," *ASLP Bull.*, **17**(1/2), 68 (March–June 1971).
57. Bernardo, Ref. *35*, p. 14.
58. Teodoro M. Kalaw, "The National Library: Its Present Organization," *Lib. Mirror*, **2**(2), 63 (December 1931).
59. Gerarda S. Llave, "The Legislative Reference Library," *ASLP Bull.*, **2**(4), 234 (December 1956).
60. Cecilia R. Paraiso, "The Department of Labor Library," *ASLP Bull.*, **1**(3), 60 (March 1954).
61. Anastacio R. Flores and Jose A. Parilla, "The Weather Bureau Library," *ASLP Bull.*, **1**(8/9), 162 (August–September 1954).
62. Philippines (Republic) Office of the President, Office of Public Information, *Government Manual*, Bureau of Printing, Manila, 1950, p. 465.
63. Dolores A. Teotico, "The Philippine College of Commerce Library," *ASLP Bull.*, **2**(2), 100 (June 1956).
64. Adriana C. Flandez, "Chamber of Commerce of the Philippines Library," *ASLP Bull.*, **2**(2), 95 (June 1956).
65. Angela P. Liongson, "The Sta Cruz Library," in *20th Anniversary, Kamaynilaan*, Manila City Library, Manila, 1966.
66. Augustus Jacumin, "Military Information Division Library," *Bull. Philippine Lib.*, **1**, 100 (March 1913). (Cited by Bernardo, Ref. *35*, p. 13.)
67. Filomena Tann, *Annual Report,* Agricultural Information Bank for Asia, 1975–1979.
68. A. V. H. Hartendorf, "The American Historical Committee, 1949–1972," *Bull. American Historical Collection*, **1**(1), 1 (June 1972).
69. Lourdes M. Curata, "Situation Report—Southern Tagalog Area," Paper read during the Phillippine Library Association Biennial Conference, April 27–28, 1973.

CONCORDIA SANCHEZ

PIETSCH, ERICH

Erich Pietsch, retired director of the Gmelin Institute of Inorganic Chemistry, Frankfurt, West Germany, died on April 9, 1979, at the age of 77 after a brief illness. Dr. Pietsch was one of the early pioneers of chemical documentation in West Germany.

Erich Pietsch.

Erich Pietsch received his Ph.D. degree in 1926 at the famous Bodenstein Institute for Physical Chemistry of the University of Berlin with a thesis on reaction kinetics. During his early career he engaged in a wide range of research—from the complex field of heterogeneous catalysis to corrosion and passivity of metals—the results of which were published in numerous papers. This work was done mostly at night; during the day Dr. Pietsch was one of the editors of *The Gmelin Handbook of Inorganic Chemistry*, the eighth edition of which had just been started under the auspices of the German Chemical Society.

In the following years Dr. Pietsch became more and more captivated by the work on the *Handbook*. Appointed as director of the Gmelin group, he managed to hold together a nucleus of the organization through the war years. In 1946, with the help of the British and American military authorities (particularly Roger Adams, who was science adviser to the U.S. Military Government), the Gmelin group was evacuated from Berlin to West Germany. Shortly thereafter, it was reconstituted as an institute of the Max-Planck-Society for the Advancement of Science.

In addition to his work on *The Gmelin Handbook*, Dr. Pietsch developed a consuming interest in scientific documentation. He developed new methods for storage and retrieval of scientific literature. His first paper on mechanized documentation in chemistry using punched cards was presented in 1948 before the fall meeting of the American Chemical Society in Washington, D.C. In the following years his research results appeared in many scientific journals.

As the leading expert in the field, Dr. Pietsch was requested in 1963 by the West German government to organize a documentation center for nuclear energy, and this grew into the present National Information Center for Energy, Physics, and Mathematics in Karlsruhe. In recognition of his accomplishments in science documentation, Dr. Pietsch was appointed a professor at the University of Frankfurt, where he lectured on chemical literature and organized special study courses for information scientists.

Erich Pietsch was a rare individual with far-ranging interests, combining unbounded energy and enthusiasm with personal modesty and kindness. He will be sorely missed.

He leaves his wife, Dr. Gisela Pietsch, and two married daughters and four grandchildren.

DIMITRI R. STEIN

PUBLIC LIBRARY SYSTEMS

Public library systems have grown very rapidly in recent years and play an increasingly important role in development and improvement of library services to people of all ages.

A public library system consists of an association of public libraries which are formally organized for the purpose of promoting better library services through sharing of resources, both library materials and personnel. Some systems cover less than one county while others serve large areas consisting of a number of counties. Population served also ranges widely, with some systems serving a fairly small number of people while a few serve several million. Most systems serve at least about 100,000 people since a population at least that large is needed to provide the necessary financial resources for adequate library services.

Public library systems differ from all other types of library systems and networks in that they are composed solely or primarily of public libraries. It should be remembered, however, that there is a growing trend for public library systems to include other types of libraries in their membership. Other types of libraries are generally associate rather than full members, and they participate only in certain programs which are most beneficial to them; for example, school libraries often join public library systems in order to receive interlibrary loan. Also, public library systems often belong to multitype library organizations and participate in programs beneficial to them, such as on-line cataloging service.

Types of Public Library Systems

Public library systems are classified in two major ways: (*a*) whether they are special-purpose or general-purpose and (*b*) according to their type of governance.

A special-purpose system is one which offers one or two selected services to member libraries but less than the full range of basic services. One example is an area reference and interlibrary loan system which assists local libraries in providing answers to reference questions and specific books and other materials through interlibrary loan. Other examples are film centers, processing centers, and storage centers for little-used materials.

A number of special-purpose systems have developed into general-purpose systems. During the late 1950s and 1960s many special-purpose systems were established with the assistance of federal funding available under the Library Services Act and its successor, the Library Services and Construction Act. After member libraries saw the value of the services provided, these systems often developed into full general-purpose systems. For example, in 1960 Library Services Act funds from the California State Library were used to initiate the San Joaquin Valley Information Service. The new program, with headquarters in the Fresno County Free Library, provided answers for difficult reference questions to public libraries throughout the San Joaquin Valley, a large, mainly rural area in central California. Several years later the general-purpose San Joaquin Valley Library System was inaugurated, and additional services were made available to the members.

When classified by governance, systems can be divided into the following four types:

1. Single-jurisdiction system
2. Multijurisdiction system

3. Cooperative system
4. Statewide hierarchical system or network

SINGLE-JURISDICTION SYSTEMS

A single-jurisdiction library system is one which provides service to one jurisdiction, such as a city or county; is responsible to the one jurisdiction; and receives funding from it.

These systems are consolidated in that they operate under one policy-making body, such as a library board or city management office, and have one central library administration which is responsible for management of all units of the library system, including the central library, branches, deposit stations, and bookmobiles.

The city library system is the most common type of single-jurisdiction system. The Chicago Public Library, which has a structure fairly typical of large city library systems, operates under a board of trustees which appoints the system's executive director, in this case called the commissioner. The board has policy-making responsibility for the entire system, which has approximately 80 library outlets throughout the city.

The Prince George's County Memorial Library is a consolidated single-county library system located in northern Maryland. The system operates 18 buildings and several bookmobiles which serve a total population of more than 600,000, and it is governed by an elected board of trustees.

MULTIJURISDICTION SYSTEMS

A multijurisdiction library system provides service to two or more neighboring communities such as cities, towns, counties, or villages; and it receives funding from the governmental units which it serves. The city–county library is one example of such a system. Usually the city library, in addition to providing library service to the city, also administers services for the surrounding county. This is so in the case of the Memphis/Shelby County Library and Information Center in Tennessee. Library service is administered by the city, with the county paying a flat percentage of the total operating cost. While most funding is derived from the city or county, the system also receives regular funding from the state. Five incorporated places, in addition to the City of Memphis, are served by the system.

Multicounty libraries are another type of multijurisdiction system. Usually in these systems each county contributes funding to the system and is represented on a system board.

Minnesota has a number of consolidated regional library systems, each of which serves a number of counties. The East Central Regional Library, for example, serves six counties and receives funding from the counties and from the state.

As with single-jurisdiction systems, multijurisdiction systems are also usually consolidated; there is one central authority such as a library board and one central administration responsible for the various units of the system, and the library outlets are branches of the system rather than independent libraries.

COOPERATIVE SYSTEMS

A cooperative library system is made up of independent libraries which voluntarily join together to provide cooperative and centralized library services. In a cooperative system each member library remains autonomous, retains its own governing board, hires its own staff, and usually receives most of its funding from local government. Generally the system is governed by a board, representative of the member libraries.

Cooperative systems have grown very rapidly in recent years for several reasons, one being that, as noted earlier, member libraries may retain their independence. In an area in which there are many existing local libraries prior to the establishment of a system, it is very difficult to persuade local library authorities to give up their independence and turn their libraries over to the system as branches. Moreover, once favorable state legislation is enacted, cooperative systems can be formed relatively easily by action of local library boards which wish to participate. Early efforts to establish multicounty or regional library systems often failed because of the difficulty of persuading governmental bodies, such as county boards, to approve establishment of such a system and contribute to its support. Also, system services in cooperative systems are often funded fully or mainly from state sources, thus removing a major obstacle to system development—the necessity for localities to pay an annual assessment for system services. The library community in several states has been quite successful in securing favorable state legislation and funding for cooperative systems: for example, Illinois, New York, Minnesota, and Michigan.

The Nassau Library System in New York State is a good example of a large cooperative system. It is made up of 54 independent member libraries which serve the total county population of approximately 1½ million. It is governed by a nine-member board, each board member representative of a particular geographic area of the county. Funding for the system programs is derived almost entirely from the state, which makes annual grants to each of New York's public library systems. Nassau County also usually makes a relatively small annual appropriation for system services.

STATEWIDE HIERARCHICAL SYSTEMS

Statewide hierarchical systems, administered or coordinated by the state library agencies, provide a structure which makes it possible for residents of all areas of a state to have access to a wide range of library information and materials located throughout the state. These systems are now often called *networks* since they generally include library systems and different types of libraries in their membership and serve a relatively large area; that is, a state. (Public library systems serve only a part of a state.)

Statewide systems or networks must have at least two levels—local and state—yet most states include at least three levels—local libraries, library systems, and state programs. In some states there are a number of levels: local, county, district, region, and state. The number of levels is related to various characteristics of the state, such as geography, size and density of population, and number, size, and distribution of library facilities. In many states the various levels of the network—local, regional, etc.—receive significant amounts of state and federal funding through the state library agency.

States such as New York, Illinois, California, and Minnesota have a number of public library systems and a number of levels in the statewide network. In New York independent local libraries belong to cooperative public library systems. (In some areas independent municipal libraries belong to county systems which in turn are members of a cooperative system covering two or more counties.) The public library systems participate in the 3Rs (Reference, Research, and Resources) Systems; these generally cover an area served by two or more public library systems, include academic and special libraries as well as public in their membership, and provide specialized materials and services to libraries in their areas. If needed materials are not available within the area of a given 3Rs System, requests may be sent to the next level, which consists of a few large research libraries that have been designated as statewide resource centers. The entire network is coordinated by the state library agency, which provides state aid for operation of various network services.

In some smaller or less populous states such as Vermont, New Hampshire, and Tennessee, the state has set up regional centers. The Vermont network, for example, is coordinated by the State Department of Libraries, which has a central headquarters in the state capital and administers the five regional libraries situated in convenient locations throughout the state. Local public libraries, of which there are almost 200, receive some services from the regional libraries and others from the state agency's central headquarters. School, academic, and special libraries are also eligible for such services as interlibrary loan of books and films, supplementary book collections, reference service, and continuing-education programs.

In Pennsylvania, New Jersey, and Massachusetts, area library centers are funded but not operated by the state library agency. Pennsylvania has district library centers located throughout the state, most of them being large or medium-sized public libraries which are paid by the state to provide specified services to independent local libraries in their areas. Two large city libraries, one university library, and the state library have been designated as resource centers for specialized or hard-to-obtain materials. The state library agency is responsible for providing funding and for overall supervision of the network.

Services of Library Systems

Special-purpose library systems provide selected services, such as reference, interlibrary loan of books or films, or processing, as already noted. General-purpose library systems provide a variety of services for libraries and library users. System services can be grouped into the categories in the following list. Most general-purpose systems offer some services in most of the areas listed, the depth of such services being dependent on area needs and funding, and staff available.

1. Direct user access to collections
2. Interlibrary loan and reference service
3. Supplementary collections of books or other materials for member libraries
4. Professional assistance to local library staffs and boards
5. Services to special groups
6. Centralized technical service
7. Administrative services

DIRECT USER ACCESS

Perhaps the greatest contribution of public library systems is that they have made possible much greater direct user access to library collections, both to basic collections and to strong, in-depth collections. This improved access has been achieved in two ways. First of all, the creation of county and regional library systems has resulted in extending public library services to large areas of many states which were previously unserved or inadequately served. Second, many systems have organized reciprocal borrowing programs so that everyone residing in the system area may freely borrow books and other materials from any member library, thus giving residents of large geographic areas the same type of access which users of city libraries have traditionally enjoyed. In many systems, users may also return materials to whichever library is most convenient, with interlibrary delivery systems providing for return to the library which owns the materials.

Many area systems have also designated headquarters libraries or other strong libraries as resource centers, somewhat as the large central library of a city library system serves as a resource center for the city. System resource libraries often receive special financial assistance to pay for free access for all system area residents.

INTERLIBRARY LOAN AND INTERLIBRARY REFERENCE SERVICE

Interlibrary loan and reference services are very popular with member libraries and are often cited as major reasons for joining or remaining in systems. The popularity of these services with users is readily apparent from statistics from some systems which indicate dramatic increases in the number of interlibrary loan and reference requests once an effective program is initiated.

Interlibrary loan has existed for many years, but traditionally it was quite restricted until liberal arrangements were worked out by library systems and until funds were provided to pay resource libraries which provide a high proportion of loans to system members. Interlibrary reference was very minimal or nonexistent in most areas until the establishment of system reference programs.

In many states there is a statewide interlibrary loan and reference service which is part of the state's hierarchical network. When a local library cannot fill a request, it contacts the system for the needed book or information. Most such requests can be filled within the system. However, even in well-developed systems a significant proportion of requests cannot be filled and must be forwarded to the next level in the hierarchy, usually the state library or a large public or university library designated as a statewide resource center.

Many systems also maintain strong central film collections for loan to member libraries and sometimes directly to community groups or individuals. Central film collections are very useful for local libraries since films are very popular with library users, yet most libraries cannot afford to purchase more than a very small collection because films are so expensive. It is much more cost-effective to have a central collection shared by member libraries, rather than to expect each library to try to build up its own collection.

SUPPLEMENTARY COLLECTIONS

Many systems provide supplementary collections of books or other library materials to their member libraries. One collection of this type is called a *rotating collection;* that is, a collection of books is assembled by the system for rotation from one member library to another. Each library keeps the collection for a stated period, often about 3 months, and circulates the books to local users. At the end of that period the books are sent on to another library.

Another type of supplementary collection is that assembled by a local library representative. Usually the local librarian visits a central system "book pool" and picks out any books he or she would like to borrow for the local collection. Sometimes bookmobiles visit local libraries and librarians choose books from the bookmobile collection. In some systems, libraries which are not system members, such as school libraries, may also borrow system supplementary collections. While the most common type of supplementary collection consists of books, some systems also lend collections of films or phonograph records to local libraries.

These kinds of collections have been provided by systems for many years, and in areas in which systems are not organized they are often provided by state library agencies. They are especially valuable for small libraries since they contain useful materials which local libraries could not afford, including specialized and expensive materials.

PROFESSIONAL ASSISTANCE

Systems offer various types of professional assistance to member libraries, including:

1. Individualized advisory help
2. Workshops and other group educational programs
3. Prepared materials and program suggestions for local library activities

Individualized Advisory Help

In many systems, especially those in sparsely populated areas, relatively few local libraries have fully trained professional librarians. Therefore, system staff assist member libraries on a wide variety of matters, ranging from routine tasks, such as weeding collections, to complex problems in services and administration. In systems in which most local libraries have one or more professionals, system staff concentrate their efforts on the more complex and specialized problems which arise in local libraries.

Systems include on their staffs specialist consultants in such areas as children's, young adult, and adult services; technical processing; reference and information service; and special services for such groups as the blind, the physically and mentally handicapped, the institutionalized, and the homebound. These consultants provide help in their areas of expertise to member libraries throughout the system, and they often organize group educational programs for local librarians. In addition, other system staff will often provide advisory help to local libraries when needed. For example, a system director may assist local libraries in areas with which he or she is familiar, such as budgeting, work with a library board, or physical facilities problems.

Typically, system consultants will visit a local library as a result of a special request or as a regular visit made at a particular time interval, such as once or twice a year. An increasing amount of consulting is done by telephone or letter since many matters can be effectively settled in those ways and also because small travel budgets, increasing costs of travel, and shortages of system staff sometimes make frequent visits to member libraries difficult.

In many states, state library agencies have designated system headquarters to assist local libraries in making applications for funds administered by the state and for monitoring the use of those funds (i.e., state aid and federal Library Services and Construction Act funds). Thus system staff will assist local librarians in filling out application forms and in developing proposals for new or innovative programs, and will assist them with problems which might arise once programs have been funded.

Group Educational Programs

Since many local librarians have limited professional education and since the knowledge and skills required of all librarians, including those with a professional degree, are constantly growing, in-service training and continuing education are extremely important.

In systems in which a significant proportion of local librarians have little professional education, system staff offer in-service training workshops on the fundamentals of such topics as materials selection, reference, cataloging, and storytelling. In systems in which a fairly large proportion of member libraries have professional staffs, system educational programs generally emphasize new trends in library services and administration which provide member library staffs with opportunities for updating their knowledge.

System group meetings have another distinct advantage for local library staffs. Both educational programs and system business meetings facilitate the association of peers, which can lead to many improvements in library services throughout a system. For example, many system children's consultants organize regular meetings for local librarians who work with children. Since many local libraries have only one staff member who works with children, system meetings are often the only regular opportunity for these librarians to interact with their peers and to discuss common concerns.

Prepared Materials and Program Suggestions

Many systems prepare or purchase program or public relations materials which are distributed to local libraries, such as reading lists, brochures, exhibits, posters, and sample news releases. Themes for local library programs are often developed under system auspices. For example, a system children's consultant will often coordinate development of a theme for a summer reading program in cooperation with local children's librarians. Once a theme is decided on, the consultant may then take responsibility for development of materials to be used by local libraries in their own programs—exhibits, posters, certificates for children participating in the programs, etc.

SPECIAL SERVICES

Systems are playing an increasingly important role in providing services to adults and children who have difficulty using regular library materials and services, such as the blind and handicapped, the institutionalized, and the homebound. Special clientele often are relatively few in number, are scattered over a large geographic area, and have need of very specialized and costly types of library materials and services. Therefore it is usually most economically feasible to organize such services on the system, rather than the local, level.

In many systems one large library is designated as a regional or subregional library for the blind and physically handicapped in the national network coordinated by the Library of Congress. As such, that library maintains a collection of talking books which are mailed upon request to eligible blind and handicapped users throughout the system. Braille collections are usually housed in only one or two large regional libraries in a given state because of the high cost of maintaining such collections and because they are used by only a minority of the blind.

In most states, state library agencies coordinate library services in state-operated institutions while library systems and local libraries serve county and municipal jails, hospitals, and group homes. In many areas system staff visit institutions on a regular basis to pick up and deliver books, to provide reading guidance to residents, and to offer group programs, such as film showings and discussion sessions. Some systems assign library staff or volunteers to take books to those who are homebound. This service has been very successful in most areas where it has been provided; however, only a relatively few libraries provide it because it is so costly.

Books-by-mail programs have proven to be tremendously successful and popular in almost any area in which they have been initiated. Unlike visiting librarian service, books-by-mail is an economical service which can reach many potential users who could not visit a library, such as the handicapped, the institutionalized, and the homebound of all ages. In most of these programs a catalog listing the books available for mailing is distributed to potential users. People send their requests through the mail, and the materials are subsequently mailed out by the library. In some books-by-mail programs, users may write or call a library and request that any circulating book in the collection be sent to them. Books-by-mail programs have been established by many library systems since the late 1960s, and they have increased library use in many areas in that they reach a new group of users—people who previously rarely or never used a public library because of some handicap or because they live in remote areas distant from a library. Some systems will provide books-by-mail service to any user who requests it. In most areas, however, the priority for such service is given to special clientele.

CENTRALIZED TECHNICAL SERVICES

Centralized ordering, cataloging, and physical preparation of materials have been very important and popular services of library systems. The processing center was one of the first widespread types of cooperative projects which made public libraries aware of tangible values of library systems since centralized processing freed local librarians from the rigors of technical processing and gave them more time to work with the public. Some systems can trace their beginnings to processing centers which began in the 1950s and 1960s and received Library Services and Construction Act grants from state library agencies to assist in their support.

In recent years some library systems have discontinued centralized technical services because of the cost and have contracted with larger library systems or with commercial agencies for such service. This trend may be accentuated in the future. Only those agencies which deal in a very large volume of materials will be able to provide cost-effective technical service which utilizes modern processing methods, including the automated system with on-line cataloging data provided by the OCLC.

ADMINISTRATIVE SERVICES

Some library systems offer a variety of administrative services for local libraries. Many of these are activities which a system can carry out efficiently and effectively while most local suburban or rural libraries would find them very costly. Following are some of the administrative services which may be provided by a system for member libraries:

1. Central personnel services, such as recordkeeping, issuing of payroll checks, coordination of advertising, and interviewing of prospective candidates for positions in local libraries
2. Printing of booklists, brochures, posters, etc.
3. Development and printing or microfilming of catalogs which list the holdings of member libraries
4. Purchase of furniture, equipment, and supplies at greater discounts than an individual local library would generally receive
5. Purchase of automated circulation systems which may be used by member libraries
6. Coordination of legislative activity aimed at securing legislation favorable to member libraries, including authorization of state and federal funding for library services

The Role of State Library Agencies

For many years state library agencies have played a critical role in development of library systems, and it is undoubtedly true that relatively few systems would be in existence today if the states had not given priority to system development.

In the early days of public library development, independent public libraries were established throughout the United States by municipalities. Since most cities, towns, and villages were, and still are, very small, most of the libraries established were inadequately supported because their service areas had such small populations. According to recent census figures, there are more than 18,500 municipalities nationally, and only 178 have more than 100,000 population. Thus, beginning early in the 20th century, library leaders took steps to organize public libraries by "larger units of service"; that is, libraries which served more than one municipality and usually at least one entire county.

The state library agency inevitably played a major role in the organization of these larger units. In California, for example, under the leadership of the state librarian, James B. Gillis, 37 county libraries were organized between 1911 and 1917. Other states followed suit as the years went on. State agency staff spent much of their time meeting with local officials and community leaders, giving them advice on how to establish systems. In the early years the state agencies concentrated on establishment of county libraries. From the 1920s on, however, efforts in many states were focused on beginning multicounty and regional libraries since the county was much too small to provide the resources for adequate library services in many areas.

In addition to providing advisory services, many state library agencies also provided grants of money for establishment of library systems. Although state funds for this purpose were usually minimal, these funds nonetheless provided great incentive for system development, psychological as well as financial.

The effect of the Library Services and Construction Act (LSCA) on development of library systems cannot be overemphasized. First passed by Congress as the Library Services Act (LSA) in 1956, the law requires that the program be administered by the state library agency in each state and that the funds be used for development of public library services throughout each state. Since the beginning of the program many of the states have used substantial portions of these funds for development of public library systems on the theory that the best way to extend adequate library service throughout a state is usually through systems. Thus, in vast areas previously unserved or inadequately served, LSA (and later LSCA) funds were granted by the states to begin systems, as already noted. In many areas special-purpose systems such as processing centers were started at first, and later these grew into full general-purpose systems.

At the present time many of the states are now fully or largely covered by public library systems. Therefore, a number of state library agencies are focusing major attention on development of systems involving different types of libraries. Usually this involves bringing academic, special, and school libraries into cooperative ventures with public library systems. The organization of state library agency heads known as COSLA (Chief Officers of State Library Agencies) is playing a major leadership role in this activity, including development of legislation to provide funding for establishment and continuing support of intertype library systems and networks.

Library Systems in Other Countries

While the United States has pioneered development of public library systems, a number of other countries have also developed systems, and often for reasons similar to such development in the United States. In various countries many small, inadequate local public libraries were established in cities, towns, and villages; and systems were begun in order to provide a mechanism for resource sharing and also to extend services to unserved areas.

The type of system developed relates to characteristics of a particular country. In small, compact nations the library system or network is often highly centralized in the nation's capital. In countries which are made up of fairly autonomous states, provinces, or republics, library services are often the responsibility of those governments and they play a major role in library system activities.

More advanced countries often have fairly well-developed library systems and networks. The situation in developing nations varies greatly from one country to another. In a number of those countries the central government is working toward development of a centralized library network covering the entire country.

CANADA

Public library systems began many years ago in Canada, and at the present time they serve a large portion of the country. Provincial library agencies are responsible for public library service within the respective provinces, and the systems which have developed vary considerably from one province to another.

A landmark experiment in development of large public library units began in 1930 with the establishment of the Fraser Valley Regional Library in British Columbia. Various governmental units joined together to provide library service—cities, district municipalities, school districts, and villages. The success of this experiment provided impetus for development of regional library services throughout Canada.

Regional library systems exist throughout the Atlantic provinces, with branches and bookmobiles serving remote areas. Central services are provided by the provincial library agencies.

Traditionally, public library service had been less well developed in Quebec than in most areas of Canada. The recent systematic development of Quebec public library services dates from the establishment of the Direction of Public Libraries of the province in 1960. Also in 1960, a survey of the public library situation in Quebec resulted in the findings that public libraries and book collections were very inadequately developed and that there was a shortage of professional librarians. Various steps were taken to improve the situation, one of the most far-reaching being development of a plan for regional library services. These plans include establishment of 23 regional library systems, several processing centers, and a central provincial library.

Beginning in the late 19th century, many small public libraries were established in the towns and villages of Ontario, and by 1957 there were over 800 individual public libraries in the province. It was clear that most of those libraries were very inadequate. During the 1960s a great reorganization of Ontario public libraries into 18 multicounty regional library systems took place, the 18 regions serving the entire province. The Provincial Library Service provides considerable financial and other types of support to the regional libraries.

In recent years, regional systems have been established that now serve much of the population of the prairie provinces (e.g., Manitoba and Saskatchewan) and also those of Alberta and the Northwest Territories.

Since the establishment of the Fraser Valley Regional Library in British Columbia, much progress has been made in development of library systems in that province. As the result of a 1966 study, the province was divided into 13 library service regions. The Provincial Library Development Commission is responsible for the supervision of the regions.

GREAT BRITAIN

Since 1974 the number of local authorities providing public library services in Britain has been substantially reduced, and the size of population served by the average library authority has increased dramatically. Improvement in the library situation in Britain stems from the Public Libraries and Museums Act of 1964. That act had two far-reaching provisions: (*a*) public library service was placed on a statutory basis, and (*b*) the secretary of state for education and science was given responsibility to supervise and promote the development of library services provided at the local level in England and Wales. Thus every local authority was required to upgrade library service, and the secretary had responsibility to see that library service was adequately funded.

One major problem remained. Many of the local library authorities served very small populations and therefore did not have the resources to provide adequate service. For example, in England outside London, there were a total of 314 authorities, a number of which served fewer than 30,000 people and only 10 of which served more than ¼ million.

This situation was remedied by the Local Government Act of 1972, which provided for the creation of 75 local library authorities in England outside Greater London (rather than the existing 314) and 8 authorities in Wales (compared with the existing 37). Most of these new authorities have a population of at least 100,000, and 56 of those in England outside Greater London serve more than ¼ million.

Under the new legislation the library authorities are coterminous with the authorities for education, health, and social services. This situation greatly facilitates the development of efficient, cost-effective library support services for schools and for health and social service agencies.

Since 1974 Scotland and Northern Ireland have also substantially reduced the number of local library authorities and thus increased the size of each remaining authority.

AUSTRALIA

The state library board of each Australian state is responsible for development of library services throughout the state. Since the country is so vast, and since most local authorities do not have populations large enough to support adequate library services, the state library boards (which were established between 1939 and 1951) have fostered the development of coordinated library systems. The boards are also responsible for the state libraries, which provide direct services to users and reference and bibliographic services to libraries within the states.

Types of services developed may be divided into two categories. Western Australia, South Australia, and Tasmania have developed highly centralized library systems under the control of the library board of the respective state. The boards provide a variety of services to local libraries, including centralized purchasing of books, centralized cataloging and processing, and reference and bibliographic service.

New South Wales, Victoria, and Queensland have less centralized systems. The library boards of those states have fostered the development of regional systems and joint systems in which several local authorities cooperate. Substantial state subsidies are granted to those agencies for their operation.

In Victoria, for example, regional systems are well developed throughout the state. A state plan for library development was adopted in 1969. Its principal recommendations called for further development of regional systems, increased subsidies to the regions, and capital grants for buildings and materials.

THE SOVIET UNION

Control of Soviet libraries begins in the U.S.S.R. Ministry of Culture and descends through corresponding ministries in each of the 15 republics on down to smaller administrative areas such as provinces, regions, districts, cities, and towns.

The Ministry of Culture coordinates planning for library development nationally, and each of the republics and smaller units draws up plans which consider particular area needs as well as national priorities. Recent plans call for the formation of centralized library systems under unified administration in which the resources of libraries in particular areas can be pooled in order to provide improved services to users.

Libraries are grouped into networks consisting of one type of library. The public library network is made up of more than 130,000 libraries which serve all areas of the Soviet Union. The national, republic, and regional libraries serve the entire population and also give bibliographic and methodological assistance to libraries. Central district or town libraries serve as links between main regional libraries and smaller town and rural libraries and provide assistance to the smaller libraries.

The origin of modern Soviet library service can be traced as far back as Lenin, who believed it was necessary to create a national library system which could provide equal access to all despite the huge size of the nation and wide variations in such factors as climate and geography.

A major advantage of such a highly centralized system is that it assures at least a minimum level of service in almost all areas. Disadvantages are that local libraries tend to be very similar in bookstock, and little discretion is left to the local librarian in such matters as collection development.

DEVELOPING NATIONS

Many developing countries in Africa, Asia, Latin America, and elsewhere are establishing nationwide library networks, often with the assistance of UNESCO. In most cases a national library agency is responsible for development of such networks. Indonesia, for example, has been working on such development since the early 1970s. The Center for Library Development of the Indonesian Ministry of Culture, which is responsible for library development throughout the country, initiated an experiment in public library development in 1975. The center offered to supply local governments with books, equipment, and furniture on the condition that villages would provide a building and staff. Each collection of about 2,000 volumes is to be exchanged regularly between libraries. Thus money will be used most effectively, and local users will have access to more books than a local library could generally afford.

Conclusion

In recent years the amount of publishing has increased at a tremendous rate and the needs of readers have grown enormously. Even the largest research libraries have difficulty providing for those needs, and small community libraries cannot possibly do so. Therefore, library systems and networks have been established throughout the United States and much of the world. By sharing of resources libraries can meet the full needs of their users, and only by sharing can they do so.

As we approach the 21st century the necessity of library systems and networks becomes more and more apparent. Therefore public library systems and networks consisting of more than one type of library will continue to grow.

BIBLIOGRAPHY

American Library Association, Standards Committee and Subcommittees, *Minimum Standards for Public Library Systems, 1966*, The Association, Chicago, 1967.

Association of State Library Agencies Interlibrary Cooperation Committee, *The ASLA Report on Interlibrary Cooperation*, The Association, Chicago, 1976.

Balnaves, John, *Australian Libraries*, 2nd ed., Linnet Books, Hamden, Conn., 1975.

Bowker Annual of Library and Book Trade Information, Bowker, New York, various editions.

Bowler, Roberta, ed., *Local Public Library Administration*, International City Managers Association, Chicago, 1964.

California Public Library Systems: A Comprehensive Review with Guidelines for the Next Decade, Peat, Marwick, Mitchell, and Company, New York, 1975.

Campbell, H. C., *Canadian Libraries*, 2nd ed., Linnet Books, Hamden, Conn., 1971.

Canadian Library Systems and Networks, Canadian Library Association, Ottawa, 1974.

Casey, Genevieve M., "Administration of State and Federal Funds for Library Development," *Lib. Trends*, **27,** 145–163 (Fall 1978).

Casey, Genevieve, *The Public Library in the Network Mode: A Preliminary Investigation*, Commissioned Papers Project No. 8, Teachers College, Columbia University, New York, May 1974.

Chandler, George, *Libraries, Documentation, and Bibliography in the USSR, 1917–1971*, Seminar Press, London, 1972.

Coughlin, Violet L., *Larger Units of Public Library Service in Canada*, Scarecrow Press, Metuchen, N.J., 1968.

Garceau, Oliver, *The Public Library in the Political Process*, Columbia University, New York, 1949.

Gates, Jean Key, *Introduction to Librarianship*, McGraw-Hill, New York, 1976.

Gregory, Ruth W., and Lester Stoffel, *Public Libraries in Cooperative Systems*, American Library Association, Chicago, 1971.

Ladenson, Alex, ed., *American Library Laws*, 4th ed., American Library Association, Chicago, 1973.

McCrossan, John A., "Planning and Evaluation of Library Programs throughout the States," *Lib. Trends*, **27,** 127–143 (Fall 1978).

"A Mission Statement for Public Libraries: Guidelines for Service. Part I," *Am. Lib.*, **8,** 615–620 (December 1977).

Molz, Kathleen R., *Federal Policy and Library Support*, MIT Press, Cambridge, Mass., 1976.

Nelson Associates, *Public Library Systems in the United States*, American Library Association, Chicago, 1969.

Prentice, Ann E., *Public Library Finance*, American Library Association, Chicago, 1977.

Schenk, Gretchen K., *County and Regional Library Development*, American Library Association, Chicago, 1954.

Shubert, Joseph F., "The Impact of the Federal Library Services and Construction Act," *Lib. Trends*, **24,** 27–44 (July 1975).

Smith, Hannis, ed., "Regional Public Library Systems," *Lib. Trends*, **13**(3), (January 1965).

Wellish, Jean B., Ruth J. Patrick, and Donald V. Black, *The Public Library and Federal Policy*, Greenwood Press, Westport, Conn., 1974.

JOHN A. MCCROSSAN

PUBLISHING DIVISION, SPECIAL LIBRARIES ASSOCIATION

Historical Background

The Special Libraries Association (SLA) is an international organization of professional librarians and information experts. In January 1982 it had approximately 12 thousand members. Special librarians serve industry, business, research, educational and technical institutions, government, special departments of public and university libraries, newspapers, museums, and other organizations that provide specialized information. The association is organized into 44 regional chapters and 29 subject divisions, one of which is the Publishing Division. SLA was founded in 1909 and for many years librarians of publishing houses were members of the Newspaper Division. Then in 1947, recognizing a need for a specific division of their own, they broke away and formed the Publishing Division.

Since its inception, the division has been an active part of the association, fulfilling the needs of fellow publishing librarians and acting as a source of help and information for other librarians. The division has sponsored very active programs at the SLA annual conferences. Much planning has gone into making these programs of interest and value to members of the division as well as to other librarians. Some highlights of recent years' programs include: University of Hawaii Press sponsorship of a meeting on the contributions of the press in improving East–West understanding; "Aspects of Multinational Publishing"; "Selection Criteria"; "Canadian Publishing: Problems and Perspectives"; "Copyright: Partisanship or Partnership?"; and "Standardization in the Publishing Industry," with discussions on International Standard Book Numbers (ISBN), International Standard Serial Numbers (ISSN), and Cataloging in Publication (CIP).

The Publishing Division has been instrumental in cosponsoring, along with the association's Library–Publisher Relations Committee, periodic meetings at annual conferences between librarians, publishing representatives, and jobbers. These meetings develop a dialogue that enables each group to be aware of the others' problems. They also provide an open forum for discussion between what some might view as antagonist groups (e.g., publishers and librarians). As an example of the type of meetings planned, the 1980 Washington, D.C., Conference had a meeting sponsored by the Publishing Division and the Library–Publisher Relations Committee entitled "Cost Concerns of Publishers and Librarians." The meeting centered around the cost of producing books and periodicals (with representatives from each industry), and the rising cost of buying books and periodicals (with two representative librarians). The purpose of the meeting was to give all groups an awareness and better understanding of the others' problems.

Over the years the Publishing Division has also sponsored a popular event, the Book and Author Luncheon, which has included such speakers as Studs Turkel, John Tebbel, S. I. Hayakawa, Paul Wasserman, Ben Bova, Margaret Atwood, and Edgar Tafel.

"Profiles of Publishing Libraries" Series

The official publication of the Publishing Division, its *Bulletin*, has an ongoing series entitled "Profiles of Publishing Libraries." This series was begun in 1968. While all libraries are basically the same, each has a specific function or goal that makes it unique and "special." The series is the best (and perhaps only) recorded description of what makes these libraries in the publishing industry similar and dissimilar at the same time. To date the libraries featured include: Scott, Foresman; Field Enterprises; Encyclopedia Britannica; American Heritage; Newsweek; Houghton-Mifflin; Standard Education Corporation; R. R. Bowker Company; R. R. Donnelly and Sons Company; American Chiropractic Association; American Education Publication; Harcourt Brace Jovanovich, Inc.; McGraw-Hill; Playboy Enterprises; Scholastic Magazine; Book Arts Press; Consumers Union; Macmillan; National Geographic; Johnson Publishing Company; Harper and Row; Addison-Wesley; Magazine Publishers Association; United Methodist Publishing House; Silver Burderr; Addison Wesley (California); Commerce Clearing House; Sociological Abstracts; Gale Research; and Minority Business Information Institute. The librarians of these companies have written detailed descriptions of their libraries with information concerning their purpose, holdings, clientele, and unique features. Some libraries are large and some are small, in both staff and the number of books they hold and journals to which they subscribe. Each has a different function.

"Topics in Publishing" Series

Beginning in the fall of 1980 a new series was introduced in the *Bulletin:* "Topics in Publishing." The purpose and intent of the series was to introduce to the *Bulletin*'s wide audience of readers (most of whom are librarians interested in the many phases of publishing, not necessarily librarians in publishing houses) the many aspects and topics involved in the publishing industry. So far "Topics" have included: "Acronyms and Initialism in Publishing," "The American Printing History Association," "Consultants and the Library Information Department of Pergamon Press," "American National Standards Committee: Z39," and "Publishers Requiring Cash with Order." A Special Issue compiled by students at the University of Hawaii Graduate School of Library Studies, entitled "International Flow of Information: Publishing in National Information Infrastructures," included separate articles by the students about publishing information in Algeria, the Ivory Coast, the Republic of Korea, and the South Pacific. Further articles in the "Topics" series have concerned indexing, marketing techniques, sales, reprints, reference book publishing, book binding, and product development.

Publishing Libraries in the New York Metropolitan Area

In an attempt to discover (*a*) what publishing libraries exist in the New York area, (*b*) what services they provide, and (*c*) how publishing companies without libraries obtain their information, a survey was conducted in 1973. This was carried out by the Publishing Group (a unit of the New York Chapter) and a large nucleus of the division members—through Ron Coplen (librarian, Harcourt Brace Jovanovich, Inc.), Carol Nemeyer (Association of American Publishers), and Jean Peters (librarian, R. R. Bowker). A questionnaire was designed and sent to almost 150 publishing companies in the New York area, including those with and without libraries. Almost 70% of the companies replied. The results of the survey were published in *Special Libraries* (Vol. 65, No. 10/11, October–November 1974). Since the findings are indicative of the publishing industry and the work of a unit of SLA, the results of the survey are reported in this article as a microcosm of the industry.

No clear picture of a "typical" publishing company library emerges from the responses of the 19 companies with libraries. Each company appears to have designed some features of special library service to meet its particular needs. This finding reinforces the frequently made observation that publishers are individualistic, with each house following its own path to achieve its goals.

It was known that not all publishing houses had libraries, but it was surprising to find that while 19 of responding companies did have libraries, 81 did not. Those with a library had either archival collections or research collections. It seems incredible that most publishing houses have not kept archival or retrospective collections of their published works, but for the most part they have not. If a hypothetical library could emerge from all the data accumulated, the library would probably include the following components:

1. Staff:
   a. 2 professional librarians
   b. 2–5 clerical personnel
2. Collection:
   a. books: 15,000
   b. journal subscriptions: 500
   c. vertical files/clipping files: 1,000
3. Services offered:
   a. maintain a collection of competitive publishers' books
   b. general reference work for editorial staff
   c. picture research
   d. maintain company archives
   e. indexing and abstracting
   f. maintain a business or legal collection for various internal departments
   g. maintain a collection of annual reports

Once again it must be emphasized that each collection is unique within the parent organization. The degree of support is also inconsistent and ranges from tepid to complete corporate support.

Other information obtained in the survey included more detailed discussion of a number of topics: who the users are, specific services provided, the specific collection, intercompany communications about the presence of the library, book selection, whether or not the library has a written policy statement, background of the librarian, and the library's place within the corporate hierarchical structure. Most companies without libraries indicated that they probably had "some books" around but would not call the collection a library. Internal service in houses without a library is erratic. Most obtained needed information from either the New York Public Library or one of the many university libraries in the area.

The Future of Libraries in Publishing Houses

While support of the existing libraries is at best inconsistent, what the future holds is probably even more perplexing. As more and more small publishing houses are swallowed up by conglomerates and more in-house services are consolidated, the future seems to be doubtful. At least two of the libraries featured in the "Profiles" series have ceased to exist, with perhaps one or two more in doubt.

There is hope, however. Some of the remaining libraries have solid corporate support and will continue to grow. As more and more alternative publishers emerge on the West Coast, some will see the need for a central resource center. Many libraries (full of books) will begin to be incorporated into information services (full of computers), and it seems likely that the future publishing library will offer services such as computer information, searches, and retrieval of information. Word-processing equipment will be a part of the library function. The future holds much hope and potential, and promises to offer exciting and fulfilling jobs for the publishing librarian.

In 1979–1980 the Publishing Division, cognizant of the "endangered species" of publishing house librarian, refocused its goals and announced to the library and publishing world that the division would in the future be concerned with topics of interest to people who are interested in all phases of book and magazine publishing. This obviously gives the division a wider scope and audience. The response has been rewarding, with new members joining, new "Topics" suggested for the *Bulletin*, and a renewed interest in the division.

RON COPLEN

RENAISSANCE LIBRARIES

To define the Renaissance in broadly acceptable terms or to set limits for its beginning and end, and its geographical scope is all but impossible (*1*). One aspect, perhaps the central one, is beyond any dispute: The book—its collecting, preservation, reproduction, and exploitation for new ideas—was the key to the break with medieval tradition. While there are early and late manifestations of the spirit of the

Renaissance, the role of books and libraries in the revival of learning begins, roughly, in the mid-14th century and may be said to continue into the latter 16th century when classical scholarship began to take full advantage of the revival of ancient learning and its application to contemporary culture. The library of the 17th century is in a direct continuum from those of the previous two centuries; and, as far as modern libraries are concerned, the institutions we know today took shape in the 17th and 18th centuries.

The humanists found in the book something permanent, over and above its specific service in perpetuating the traditions of classical antiquity (*2*). Thus they viewed libraries, the basic tool for preserving books, as the most important servants of scholarship. When Cardinal Bessarion gave 746 manuscripts to the Venetian Republic in 1468, the origin of the Marciana, it was "ad communem hominum utilitatem" (*3*). Time and again we have expressions of confidence in libraries as the one indispensable tool of scholarship (*4*). A legend was created which endures today, sometimes to the detriment of scholarship in the reverence for the printed book, much as the respect for the manuscript affected the acceptance of the printed book in the 15th century.

Italy

Francesco Petrarca (Petrarch; 1304–1374) stands at the head of the roll of Italian humanists (*5*). He must have been an impassioned bibliophile at an early age. In 1337 he prepared a list of "libri mei," and he was well on his way to developing the first great humanistic library. He copied Cicero's letters, discovered in the Verona Cathedral library in 1345; and after he found a manuscript of Vergil, now in the Ambrosian Library in Milan, he always took it on his extensive travels despite its size. In 1362 Petrarch left Milan on account of an epidemic; he went to Padua and then to Venice, where he made an arrangement to deposit his books in Saint Mark's. He was in Venice for 5 years, must have left some books there (a sorry remainder was discovered two and a half centuries later), and then went to Arquà (near Padua), with whose master, Francesco da Carrara, he was acquainted. Petrarch's will of 1370 does not mention his library, and it has been assumed that most went to Carrara. The latter's library was seized by the Visconti of Pavia in 1388, and in 1500 it was taken by Louis XII with other bibliological booty and shipped to Blois, then removed in 1544 to Fontainebleau. Twenty-six manuscripts from Petrarch's library are in the Bibliothèque Nationale today, a few others in other places. While Petrarch's library did not survive intact, it was the prototype of the Renaissance book collection, in the method of acquisition, in content, and in its intended use. His notion about a library in Venice for scholars was an enduring one among later humanists.

If Petrarch or his friend Giovanni Boccaccio had never contributed a line to creative literature, they would still be major personalities of the Italian Renaissance on account of their dedication to collecting books for the revival of learnings (*6*). Boccaccio, unlike Petrarch, had limited means and copied most of the manuscripts he found. His most famous discovery was the Tacitus (*Annales*, XI–XVI, and

Historiae, I–V) at Monte Cassino, whose library he described in some detail for the neglect it had suffered—possibly an excuse to justify removal of the manuscript (*7*). The Tacitus manuscript fell into the hands of Niccolò dei Niccoli (1363–1437; infra), who allowed Poggio Bracciolini ("Florentinus," 1380–1459; infra) to copy it; and it ended in the Marciana after Niccoli's death. In 1374 Boccaccio wrote a will bequeathing his collection of over 200 volumes to his confessor, the Augustinian Martino da Signa, after whose death it went to the monastery of San Spirito in Florence with the understanding that it be generally available. Niccoli heard about the neglected books and had a cabinet made for them, but after the remodeling of the monastery in 1560 most were lost. Fortunately, we do know titles from an inventory of 107 items preserved in Ashburnham 1897 of the Laurentian Library (*8*). Of these, 10 have been found in the Laurentian and the Riccardiana in Florence, of which two were copied in whole or in part by Boccaccio. A third has notes in his hand.

Coluccio Salutati (1331–1406) did not attain the literary renown of Petrarch and Boccaccio, but his services as a manuscript collector are no less significant (*9*). He held high civil office in Florence, and his position enabled him to identify and acquire many valuable manuscripts, notably Cicero's *Epistolae ad familiares* (now in the Laurentian) and Cato's *De agricultura*. He had a copy made of the Catullus manuscript in Verona (Petrarch had done it earlier), and he also possessed a Tibullus manuscript (Ambros. R 26 sup.). Salutati did not plan to found a library, but the purchase of his books by Giovanni de' Medici had the same effect.

Petrarch, Boccaccio, Niccoli, and Salutati placed much heavier emphasis on Latin than on Greek literature; but when Antonio Corbinelli (ca. 1370 to 1375–1425) left his collection to the Abbey of Santa Maria in Florence, it included 194 Latin and 79 Greek manuscripts, with 105 Latin and 65 Greek authors (*10*). Many of the latter were not known by the humanists of the time, and there were basic things such as an 11th-century Thucydides, a manuscript of Sophocles and Euripides (now Cod. Laur. C.S.71), and an *Odyssey* (Cod. Laur. C.S.52).

The most famous of all manuscript collectors of the Renaissance was Poggio, prototype of the book hunter down to the age of Lyman Copeland Draper and Herbert Hoover (*11*). Salutati took Poggio into his service when the latter was barely 20 years old and introduced him to his circle, which included Niccoli. In 1403 Salutati arranged for Poggio to secure a position in the Roman Curia, where he was able to intensify his work in copying manuscripts. His great opportunity came when he went to the Council of Constance as a secretary (1414–1418), even though he lost his job when the first John XXIII lost his. He probably spent much of his time poking around monasteries looking for manuscripts, and he was as shocked by the condition of their collections as Boccaccio was by the situation at Monte Cassino. His most significant discovery was the first known complete text of Quintilian's *Institutio oratoria*. Subsequently he found other texts, lost up to that time, in monastic libraries of Switzerland, Germany, and France: notably three and a half books of Valerius Flaccus's *Argonautica*, Asconius Pedanius's commentary on five speeches of Cicero, Lucretius, Silius Italicus, Ammianus Marcellinus, Tacitus, Plautus, Columella, Tertullian, and others. Poggio collected more for others than for himself, since only 95 manuscripts appeared in the inventory taken after his death. His sons and nephew inherited them, but today there are only five in the Laurentian, one in the Vatican, and one in the Riccardiana. But Poggio's service to scholarship in locating, copying, and preserving classical manuscripts will be remembered long after schoolboys stop snickering over his amusing but naughty *Facetiae*.

The concentration of early humanists in Florence and presence of the wealthy and influential family of Medici (*12*) were decisive elements in making Florence a major cultural center with incomparable art collections and libraries. Cosimo the Elder (1389–1464) established a firm position and a fortune for his family after he became the acknowledged head of the Florentine state in 1434. He established a Platonic academy headed by Marsilio Ficino (*13*), but directly pertinent here is that Niccolò dei Niccoli was his adviser in matters relating to books (*14*). Niccoli collected some 800 volumes which he wanted to be available to scholars in the Camaldolese monastery of Santa Maria degli Angioli in Florence; but, on account of his debts, he changed this decision shortly before his death and left the disposition of his collection to a committee of 16 fellow humanists. Happily, Cosimo assumed responsibility for these liabilities and acquired 200 manuscripts for his personal collection (*la Medicea privata*); he also placed some 400 in the Dominican monastery of San Marco in 1441 in the handsome hall designed by Michelozzo and still basically intact, the first public library in Italy (*la Medicea pubblica*). The librarian, Giuliano Lapaccini, was allowed to draw on the Medici bank for new acquisitions.

Cosimo also rehabilitated the library of the Abbey of Fiesole (the Badia) and provided it with a corps of copyists under the supervision of Vespasiano da Bisticci (1421–1498), who produced some 200 manuscripts in less than 2 years. Along with the collection placed in San Marco, it is the oldest part of the modern Medicea–Laurenziana. The *Medicea privata* was housed in San Lorenzo and was rather modest until Cosimo's grandson, Lorenzo il Magnifico (1449–1492) (*15*) assumed leadership of the family and of Florence in 1469. Especially constructive was his concern for the acquisition of Greek manuscripts and the effective support of his agent, Andreas Janos Laskaris (ca. 1445–1535), in the Levant (*16*). The library was used by such humanists as Politian, Pico della Mirandola, and Marsilio Ficino. From the expulsion of the Medici in 1494 the library was subject to many vicissitudes (and losses), taken to Rome by Lorenzo's youngest son (Leo X after 1513), and finally returned to Florence by Clement VII (Giulio de' Medici) in 1532. Clement had commissioned Michelangelo in 1525 to design and construct a library building in the upper cloisters of the basilica of San Lorenzo, but it was not finally opened until 1571, 7 years after Michelangelo's death. The magnificent structure is recognized generally as the finest of all Renaissance library buildings (*17*). The collection in San Marco (the Marciana) was combined with the Laurenziana in 1808 when monastic property was secularized. The Medicea–Laurenziana has survived wars and political changes, but of its subsequent history we may note only the acquisition of 1,903 Ashburnham manuscripts in 1885.

When Petrarch left Milan on account of the plague in 1362, he went to Venice, where he gave part of his collection to San Marco in return for personal housing in the Palazzo di Due Torri; but, as we have noted, it did not develop into the public library for scholars that Petrarch probably envisioned. It remained for Basilios

Bessarion (1395–1472) of Trebizond—bishop of Nicea and later a Roman cardinal (1439) in the movement for reconciliation—to establish a scholarly library in Venice (*18*). In Italy with the authority of a cardinal he collected and copied zealously, and after the fall of Constantinople (1453) he made a special effort to protect remnants of Greek culture by acquiring manuscripts. His young associate, Niccolò Perotti, who traveled as far as Trebizond, was particularly successful (*19*). Further, his connections with Giovanni Aurispa and Francesco Filelfo, two prominent humanists who had been in Constantinople and acquired manuscripts there, must have been productive (*20*). In 1423 Aurispa brought back 238 volumes of Greek classics, including the basic collective volume with the plays of Aeschylus and Sophocles and the *Argonautica* of Apollonius Rhodius.

On May 31, 1468, Bessarion presented his library of 482 Greek and 264 Latin manuscripts to the Republic of Venice (*21*). In the humanistic tradition he expressed in the document of transmission his concept of books as the best companions of the scholar. The collection was originally destined for the Benedictine monastery of San Giorgio Maggiore, but San Marco was substituted on May 14, 1468. The library was not adequately housed, and consequently it was not used to full advantage in the beginning. Finally, in the period 1536–1553, Jacopo Sansovino constructed the magnificent quarters for the library long admired as one of the great architectural achievements of Renaissance Italy (*22*). Over the last five centuries the library has had various homes and made important acquisitions (*23*), but most significant are the tradition of Bessarion and his contributions to the preservation of ancient Greek culture.

Outside of Florence and Venice there were other collections in princely residences. The Visconti and the Sforza had an impressive library in Pavia, in which 988 manuscripts were recorded in 1426 (*24*), when the Medici and Niccoli had no comparable collections. But, unlike the Medici, the Visconti and the Sforza and their courtiers had no passion for learning comparable to that of the Medici. Florence and, somewhat later, Venice had stature and influence in Renaissance Italy that grew from men who knew how to use books as well as how to collect them.

In Ferrara the house of Este owned a library which had origins at least in the 14th century (*25*). A catalog of 1436 recorded 279 manuscripts, mostly Latin but with some Italian and French, and in 1495 there was a record of 512 manuscripts, with only two Greek titles. After Clement VIII claimed Ferrara as a papal fief in 1597, Duke Caesar took the library to Modena in 1598, where it survives today in association with the university (founded 1772). There are remarkable illuminations, bindings (*26*), and vernacular works (Dante, Tasso, Provençal, among others), in all some 9,000 manuscripts in addition to important printed works acquired during the librarianships of Muratori, Tiraboschi, and other competent bookmen.

The Aragonese kings of Naples were diligent bibliophiles and patrons of scholarship, in particular Alfonso V, who assumed power in 1435. He was not only deeply concerned for the development of his library but also entertained such brilliant personalities as Lorenzo Valla (*27*). His son, Ferdinand, had less personal interest but continued to add to the collection, particularly with confiscated collections, until his death in 1494. A decade later Naples became a viceroyalty of the Spanish crown, and the noble library was broken up, part going to France and another part to Valladolid. Much of both portions survives.

Perhaps most famous of all the libraries in the smaller residences was that of Federigo da Montefeltro (1410 or 1411–1482), duke of Urbino. Primarily a politician and an effective condottieri chieftan, Federigo nevertheless made strong and successful efforts to furnish his seat with books and works of art. He was not well informed about literature but he was wise enough to entrust Vespasiano da Bisticci with his buying. He kept a corps of some 30–40 copyists busy in Urbino. An inventory taken after Federigo's death recorded 1,120 volumes (*28*). In 1658 Alexander VII bought the collection and turned over the manuscripts (1,767 Latin and Italian, 165 Greek, and 128 Oriental) to the Vatican Library, but he gave the printed books to the library he had recently established for the University of Rome (henceforth called the "Biblioteca Alessandrina").

The Gonzaga family assumed power in Mantua in 1328. During the next century Gianfranco and Lodovico III were personally concerned about the development of their book collections. In 1407 there were some 300 volumes, including some important Greek manuscripts (*29*).

The Vatican Library

The Vatican Library was destined to be the most important of all Renaissance libraries and to hold a leading position through the centuries (*30*). From very early periods there had been archives in the Holy See, and there were major collections in the 14th century at Avignon, now partially surviving in the Bibliothèque Nationale in Paris and in the Borghese Collection which finally came into the possession of the Holy See in 1902. The real founder of the modern Vatican Library was Tommaso Parentucelli (1397–1455), who held the pontificate as Nicholas V for the last 8 years of his life (*31*). As a young man he established a respected position for himself among the Florentine humanists and was an eager collector. Bisticci recorded him as a bibliophile whose appetite for books excelled his means (*32*). When Cosimo was developing the library of San Marco, he entrusted Parentucelli with the chore of drawing up a list of desiderata (*33*).

The modest collection of some 350 manuscripts which Nicholas inherited from his predecessor, Eugene IV, was increased by every possible means through agents in Constantinople and book centers in Italy. He accepted only the best copies in fine bindings. His librarian, Giovanni Tortelli, a competent humanist in his own right, did much to promote Nicholas's objective to make the papal library the world's greatest scholarly collection. In 1455 there were some 1,200 important manuscripts, of which about 800 were in Latin. At Nicholas's death it was the largest library of its time.

Calixtus III (1455–1458) was not a bibliophile and scholar of the same stamp, and it was only in the papacy of Sixtus IV (1471–1484), of the della Rovere family, that the library began to thrive again. In 1481 there is a record of 3,499 volumes. Sixtus's first librarian was Giovanni Andrea dei Bussi (*34*), succeeded at his death in 1475 by another distinguished humanist, Bartolomeo Platina. In the same year a budget was provided for the library, and it was increased in 1477. Adequate housing was provided in handsomely decorated quarters, executed by Domenico, David Ghirlandaio, and Melozzo da Forli. The standards of service in the Vatican Library were superior for the age.

Two Medici popes whom we have already encounted, Leo X and Clement VII, were active patrons of the library. Under Paul III a new catalog of manuscripts was prepared by Cardinals Marcello Cervini and Jacopo Sadoleto. During the sack of Rome by imperial forces in 1527 the library, now with over 4,000 manuscripts, was probably saved because Philibert of Orange had headquarters in the papal palace, a situation which probably made it immune to looting. It cannot be overlooked that the Vatican itself was the beneficiary of two of the greatest loots of libraries of all time, first, when Tilly captured Heidelberg in 1622 and Duke Maximilian of Bavaria gave the great collection of the Palatina to Gregory XV; and second, when the apostate queen of Sweden, Christina, took to Rome the handsome collection made up largely of the spoils from her father's campaigns in Poland and the Germanies. The latter was bought by Alexander VII in 1690. The subsequent history of the Vatican Library and some of its great acquisitions belongs to the world history of scholarship, but the policies of Nicholas V have had an abiding influence.

France

It is ironical that France benefited enormously from the productive activities of Italian collectors and scholars, and yet there were few counterparts of the Italian Renaissance bibliophiles. The remnants of some of the great princely collections such as those in Pavia and Naples found a home in Paris, and rulers of the land promoted the Bibliothèque du Roi. While France produced a collector of the stature of Jean Grolier de Servin (1479–1565), private book collecting in France did not reach the proportions it had attained in Italy in the quattrocento until the age of Richelieu.

There had been a royal library in the Louvre, but as the Hundred Years' War waned about 1430, a new collection began to take shape in Blois (*35*). Here the collections brought from Naples by Charles VIII and from Pavia by Louis XII found a home. The first French monarch to perform bibliologically in the style of the Medici was Francis I (1494–1547). He founded a library in Fontainebleau (*36*) which included the family collection of his own house (Angoulême), and in 1544 he combined the Bibliothèque du Roi in Blois with it. After Laskaris acquired important Greek manuscripts for Lorenzo il Magnifico, he rendered the same service to Francis. Francis invested Guillaume Budé (1467–1540) with the office of *maître de librarie*, and this great humanist was lifelong adviser to the king (*37*). Although Francis preferred the manuscript to the printed book, he initiated legal deposit when, in 1536, he gave the librarian at Blois, Mellin de Saint-Gelais, the right to claim a copy of every book printed in France (*38*). Henri II (1547–1559) was an aficionado of fine bindings (as was Francis), and his monograms were an *H* combined with a *D* (his mistress, Diane de Poitiers; 1499–1566) or a *C* (his wife, Catherine de Médicis; 1519–1589).

Catherine was completely imbued with the bibliophilic tradition of her family (*39*). She had a library of some 4,000–5,000 ancient and modern texts in the Château of Saint Maur, supervised by her confessor, Benciveni, abbé de Bellebranche. It was the collection of a great *femme bibliophile* as well as of an avid reader. Her most noteworthy acquisition was the collection of some 800 manuscripts held by Marshal Pietro Strozzi after he fell at Thionville in 1558. She claimed it as Medici property. After her death her creditors claimed the Strozzi collection, but it was saved by J.-A. de Thou for only 5,400 écus put up by Henri IV, and most of the collection is in the Bibliothèque Nationale today. The beautiful Diane's collection remained in the Château d'Anet until it was auctioned in 1724 after the death of Anna of Bavaria, who had inherited the castle in 1718 (*40*). J. B. Guyon de Sardière bought most of the books, and they ultimately went with his collection to the Duc de La Vallière (*41*).

Eastern Europe, England, and Spain

In the Germanies, the late arrival of humanism was to coincide with the early proliferation of printing and, later, with the Reformation, and to lend a peculiarly national character to the development of libraries and of private and princely collections. Elsewhere the Renaissance collector appeared sporadically although occasionally in brilliant instances. Most famous was the great collection of King Matthias Corvinus (Hunyadi; 1458–1490) of Hungary (*42*). His chancellor, John Vitéz, had studied in Italy, knew the humanists of his day, and was a zealous collector of manuscripts; and his nephew, John Pannonius, followed in his steps. The Hunyadi had had relations with the Visconti and the Sforza, and in 1476 Matthias married Beatrice of Aragon, daughter of King Ferdinand of Naples. With the help of Bisticci and others, he put together a library in Buda that any Italian prince might have envied. His preference was for handsomely decorated manuscripts from Italian artists, and he was not greatly concerned with the importance of texts. The fame of the Corviniana created exaggerated rumors about its quantity, but there may well have been up to 3,000 titles. His early death, Beatrice's return to Italy, and the indifference of Matthias's successors hastened the dispersion of the collection. After the crushing defeat of the Hungarians at Mohácz in 1526 the Turks took what had survived (finally restored in part to the University of Budapest by the Osmanli sultan in 1877). There are other remnants all over the Western Hemisphere (*43*).

Hungary's northern neighbor, Poland, had a major intellectual center in Cracow, where the university had been founded in 1364 and was to acquire distinction, particularly in mathematics and astronomy, culminating in the work of Italian-trained Copernicus a century and a half later. Gregory Sanok, a *magister* at Cracow, was a zealous humanist and book collector, and the Jagiellonian University owes much to him (*44*).

Humanism found its way to England by the end of the 15th century with scholars of the stature of William Grocyn and Thomas Linacre, but neither they nor others were collectors in the tradition of the Italians. Thomas Wotton (1521–1587), a sort of an English Grolier who inscribed his Italianate bindings "Thomas Wottoni et amicorum," was the closest to a Renaissance collector that England had (*45*). Sir William Pickering (1516–1575) had similar tastes. His daughter married Sir Edward Wotton, Thomas's son. The combined library came to the Stanhope (Chesterfield) family, and the collection survived until 1920 when it was sold at Sotheby's.

Spain had a distinguished collector in the son of the admiral, Don Fernando Colón (1488–1539), who assembled an important library of some 12,000 volumes and deposited it in the Dominican monastery of San Pablo in Seville, but it was neglected and plundered (*46*). The library of San Lorenzo del Escorial was a commitment by Philip II after the battle of Saint Quentin in 1557, established formally in 1565 (*47*). Both contained rich collections on Renaissance culture from the beginning, but neither were collected or administered in the same spirit, or for the same purpose as were the libraries of the Medici or of the Holy See of Nicholas V.

The Germanies

Humanism first touched German-speaking territories when Cola di Rienzi, friend and confidant of Petrarch, pleaded with Charles IV in Prague for regeneration of the church. Petrarch himself corresponded with the imperial court. But humanism came north slowly. In 1417 and 1418 Poggio was actively engaged in his constructive carpetbagging in German-speaking areas. Poggio rescued many a basic manuscript; but another brilliant contemporary, Enea Silvio Piccolomini (1405–1464), Pius II after 1458, was the most effective representative of humanism north of the Alps when he served as secretary in the chancellery of Friedrich III (*48*). Thus in the University of Vienna, and later in other institutions, interest in classical studies began to expand slowly. There is only slight evidence of the acquisition of classical manuscripts by the existing collections in universities, city halls, and monasteries. Most important were private collectors whose inventories reflected the penetration of the new learning. Nikolaus von Cues, Albrecht von Eyb, Hartmann Schedel, and the Fuggers were among the prominent early collectors inspired by Italian humanism.

Nikolaus von Cues (1401–1464), latinized as Cusa or Cusanus, cardinal after 1448, had become a doctor of both laws in Padua and was influenced not only by German mysticism but also by Neoplatonism and humanism (*49*). He recognized significant classical manuscripts in Fulda and probably took a basic Plautus manuscript (now Vat. Lat. 3870) from there to Rome. He also discovered Tacitus manuscripts and may have been the first German in modern times to know the *Germania*. He read Greek and had the opportunity to collect in Constantinople. A significant fact is that in 1459 his long-time friend Enea Silvio appointed him papal vicar-general. Cues willed his property, including philosophical apparatus and books, to a hospital in his home town of Bernkastel–Kues on the Mosel, and 314 manuscripts (270 from his own collection) are still there, although much has been removed over the centuries (e.g., more than 30 now in the British Library).

Albrecht von Eyb (1420–1475), Franconian baron, spent 13 years in the south and was a zealous collector (*50*). He translated Plautus, and two of his manuscripts of this author are in Augsburg today. His library, including printed books, went to the Eichstätt Cathedral, but it was dispersed without any accurate record. About 20 pieces have been identified in modern German libraries.

Hermann Schedel (1410–1485) and his cousin Hartmann Schedel (1440–1514) both studied medicine in Padua and brought humanism to their native Nuremberg (*51*). Hermann's library was inherited by Hartmann, famous for his *Weltchronik*. The latter had studied Greek as well as medicine in Padua. While he owned important manuscripts, he also collected printed books. The catalog shows 632 titles. The collection was sold in 1552 to Hans Jakob Fugger, and it contained some 400 collective manuscript volumes and 700 printed books. It was acquired in 1571 by Duke Albrecht V of Bavaria, the founder of the Munich Hofbibliothek (now Bayerische Staatsbibliothek). About 360 manuscripts belonging to Hartmann Schedel have been identified in the modern collections.

Johann von Dalberg (1455–1503) spent most of his productive life in Heidelberg, where he was chancellor of the university from 1480 to 1497 (*52*). He was closely associated with humanists of the stature of Rudolf Agricola, Johannes Reuchlin, and Dietrich von Plenningen, and he also collected a significant library. He bought manscripts in Italy and, back home, commissioned the Strassburg printer and bookseller Adolf Rusch to buy classical texts at the Frankfurt Fair. His librarian, Johannes Vigilius, professor of law, also bought for him at the fair. After Dalberg fell out with the Palatine elector in 1497, he retired to Worms where he was bishop. Presumably his collection remained in the episcopal see but was gravely neglected. Fewer than 20 titles from this once great collection can be identified today, mainly in various German libraries.

Maximilian I, emperor from 1493 to 1519, had a library as archduke and acquired a vastly greater treasure of books in the dowry of Marie of Burgundy (*53*). He was a romantic ("the last knight") but may well have listened to Enea Silvio in Vienna. Certainly his confidence in Konrad Celtis (1459–1508) indicated his inclination to humanism (*54*). Celtis was entrusted with the custody of part of Maximilian's collection, inherited from his father, Friedrich III, and left in the residence of Wiener Neustadt (the more valuable part was moved to Castle Ambros near Innsbruck). In 1497 Celtis was appointed by Maximilian to the chair of poetry and eloquence at the University of Vienna, and it became an important center of humanistic activity with men such as Celtis, the versatile Joachim von Watt (Vadianus; infra), and the historian Johannes Cuspinianus. The latter built a handsome collection which was acquired in 1530 by the Vienna bishop Johannes Faber (died 1541), whose collection of 2,162 items passed to the University Library. The collections in Innsbruck were not always given the best care, but ultimately most of these (with subsequent additions) and the material in Wiener Neustadt found a home in the Austrian National Library.

One of the most spectacular events in Celtis's career was the discovery of a map of Roman military roads, 34 centimeters by 7 meters in length, in Worms. It was to have been edited by Konrad Peutinger (1455–1547), but it disappeared until 1714 when Prince Eugene of Savoy discovered it and later willed it to the Hofbibliothek in Vienna. The *Tabula Peutingeriana* is famous enough (*55*), but the role of Peutinger, an Augsburg patrician, in German humanism is even more important (*56*). Today his collection of over 2,000 works, a good proportion reflecting Peutinger's humanistic interests, has been scattered, with less than 100 items identified (happily, 36 went to the Augsburg Stadtbibliothek in 1810). Peutinger did compile two catalogs, a rich source for our knowledge of humanistic book collecting in Germany.

In Nuremberg the patrician Willibald Pirckheimer (1470–1550) was the central figure in the humanistic movement (*57*). After study in Pavia and Padua, he assumed a respected position in his native city. He was a friend not only of Celtis but also of Reuchlin and Erasmus. An indefatigable collector, he boasted in 1504 in a letter to Celtis that he owned every Greek book printed in Italy. Pirckheimer's library remained in the family for over a century after his death and was sold to Thomas Howard, earl of Arundel, in 1636. It was donated by Henry Howard to the Royal Society in 1667, and in 1831 the manuscripts (except the Oriental ones) were sold to the British Museum.

Schlettstadt in Alsatia produced two major humanists, Jakob Wimpheling (1450–1528) (*58*) and Beatus Rhenanus (1485–1547) (*59*). We know almost nothing about Wimpheling's library, although he gave books regularly to the church library there. Today the rich old Stadtbibliothek of Schlettstadt has two manuscripts and three printed books that once belonged to Wimpheling. His literary production is well known, but his interest in book collecting is equally meaningful. In 1496 he and Johannes Vigilius (supra) visited Johannes Trithemius (or Tritheim; 1462–1516), abbot of the Benedictine monastery in Sponheim (*60*). Trithemius's collection of over 2,000 works included many Greek works and others of obvious humanistic interest. It was a victim of secularization in 1564, and only about 30 pieces are identifiable in various repositories today. Rhenanus, a competent historian, critic, and philologist, was associated with the great Basel printers Amerbach and Froben (Erasmus's intimate) and had a collection of over 900 volumes which he willed to his native city. Neglected for centuries, it was finally given a suitable home in 1889.

Ulrich von Hutten (1488–1523), famous for his participation in the second part of the *Epistolae obscurorum vivorum* (1515–1517) in defense of Reuchlin's cause, led too turbulent and itinerant a life to have gathered a substantial library (*61*). Yet he did have a collection probably useful at least for reference. It was with his friend Franz von Sickingen on the Ebernburg when the latter fell at the end of the Knights' War in 1523 and was captured and sold in Heidelberg by the imperial forces. Most curious about Hutten's bibliological interests is the rather strong evidence that he stole books from Fulda (*62*).

In Münster the canon Rudolf von Langen (ca. 1438–1519) had traveled in Italy in 1466 and most probably acquired books (*63*). The cathedral library received them as a legacy, but virtually all were destroyed in the Anabaptist disturbances of 1534. More important was a protégé of Langen and a friend of Hutten and Reuchlin, Hermann von dem Busche, or Pasiphilus (1468–1534), best known for his *Vallum humanitatis* (1518). Langen urged him to travel in Italy, and he was later at various German universities, always defending Lutheran principles. He collected a small but choice library which he willed to the Münster Cathedral; but a friend,

Rotger Schmising, himself the master of a library, took the books to protect them from the violence of the Anabaptists. The latter carried out his friend's wishes and willed them to the cathedral upon his death in 1547. Most passed about 1589 to the Jesuits, whose library became the basis of the University of Münster Library. Some 20 books, mostly Venetian editions of Greek and Roman authors, have been identified as Busche's original property.

The greatest of the German humanists, Johannes Reuchlin (1455–1522), was also one of the most zealous book collectors of his age (*64*). He began to collect books as a student in Paris under his famous master, Johannes Heynlin vom Stein (*65*), and he constantly acquired books during his Italian trips of 1482, 1490, and 1498. He knew Aldus Manutius and corresponded with him about book acquisitions. Latin, Greek, and Hebrew books fell within the scope of his interest. Active in a troubled era and the central figure of all sorts of political issues and controversies about church policy, Reuchlin left an enduring legacy to subsequent ages in his dedication to seeking historical accuracy through sound texts. When the converted Jew Johann Pfefferkorn proposed the destruction of all books in Hebrew, Reuchlin replied that only books which were antagonistic to Christendom should be removed from the shelves, and that the Jews should be compelled to furnish books for the universities and set up chairs of Hebrew in all of them. Reuchlin was vigorously supported by the humanists, above all in the *Epistolae obscurorum vivorum* (supra; first part most probably largely by Crotus Rubianus and the second most probably largely by Ulrich von Hutten), a satire in purposely bad Latin reinforcing the *Epistolae clarorum vivorum* (1514) issued by Reuchlin's friends. Toward the end of his life he encountered grave problems about the disposition of his books. The larger part of his collection went first to the church in Pforzheim and ultimately to the Landesbibliothek in Karlsruhe, but there are also a few in other major libraries of Western Europe (*66*).

Desiderius Erasmus (1466 or 1469–1536) was the most influential of the humanists, north or south; and it was inevitable that his prestige, his intimacy with Aldus Manutius, his position as an authoritative consultant of Johannes Froben, and his stature in the world of learning resulted in a major private collection (*67*). In the years 1524–1526 a young Polish nobleman, Johannes Laski, lived with Erasmus in Basel. The latter, feeling the need of funds to live in the style he desired, sold his books to Laski on the condition that he keep them and have the use of them in his lifetime. At the time of Erasmus's death there was a sketchy checklist of 413 titles. The new owner, who had held a high position in the church in his native Poland, forsook his old faith in 1538 and dedicated himself to promotion of Protestantism in North Germany, Denmark, the Low Countries, and England. He sold the books piecemeal, and today only 15 can be identified, scattered from England to Cracow.

Reformation Libraries

A major emphasis of the Reformation leaders—above all of Luther himself and of Philipp Melanchthon (1497–1560), the "Preceptor Germaniae" and great-nephew of Reuchlin—was on the utility of books and libraries for the new faith and for popular culture in general (*68*). An immediate result was the incorporation of policies for church libraries in the organizational documents of individual congregations. The oldest (1528) and one of the most important policy statements is that of Johannes Bugenhagen for the church of Saint Andreas in Braunschweig, but the collection of 336 volumes willed to the church in 1495 by Gerwin von Hameln was reported in 1587 to have been sadly neglected (*69*). Bugenhagen drew up similar policy statements for churches in Hamburg, Lübeck, and his native Pommerania, where he visited all libraries and archives in the province on the order of Duke Bogislaus X. We know something about at least nine newly founded church libraries at Melanchthon's death in 1560.

The libraries depended on gifts and secularization of Roman establishments for their growth. Just as in England, they would have been vastly richer had not biblioclasm accompanied the dissolution of monasteries. A ducal order in Pommerania in 1552 directed that unsuitable (i.e., "popish") books from monasteries be sold for scrap. More serious was the violence in the Peasants' War of 1524–1526 (*70*). In Thuringia alone, 70 monasteries and their contents were destroyed, and reports from other places are staggering. Libraries of secular nobility and high church officials also suffered.

Luther's insistence on the development of education resulted in a number of new schools with libraries. Some 40 such institutions which had libraries survived into the 20th century, and one might guess that in the 16th century there were probably as many more for which we have no firm evidence of the presence of libraries. Even more significant was the effect of the Reformation on the universities, both the older ones and those founded at this time (Marburg, Königsberg, and Jena).

In Leipzig there was no general university library, only faculty collections, until 1543 (*71*). Thanks to the secularization of three monasteries in Leipzig and seven others in Saxony, the university library was enriched by about 1,500 manuscripts and 4,000 printed books. The real founder of the library, Kaspar Börner, left his collection to it upon his death in 1547. Melanchthon's friend Joachim Camerarius was librarian until his death in 1574. After 1550 the library was open for 2 hours every week.

In Basel the puny university library received a major impulse forward in 1535 when the rector, Bonifatius Amerbach, persuaded all shops in this major center of printing to deliver one copy of each book to the university (*72*). In 1559 the university acquired the holdings of the Dominican monastery and of the cathedral. The catalog of Heinrich Pantaleon, the librarian, shows a *bibliotheca antiqua* (to 1583: 150 manuscripts and 243 printed books) and a *bibliotheca nova* (810 volumes, excluding 190 works donated by Professor Martin Borrhus in 1564).

In Tübingen there was provision for a library in 1477 when the university was founded (*73*). There were faculty libraries and also a Bibliotheca Publica as early as 1501, but the latter was most likely destroyed with the burning of the *Sapienzhaus*. It was just about the same time that the Reformation reached Tübingen, and a new general library was put together and housed in a recently constructed university building, where it remained until 1819.

Elector Frederick ("the Wise"; 1486–1525) founded the University of Wittenberg in 1502, where humanism was welcomed from the beginning; and in less than two decades the Reformation was to find there an intellectual stronghold (*74*). The first sure evidence of the founding of a library at Wittenberg is from December 1512 when the elector wrote to Aldus Manutius asking him for a list of available titles, most probably on the advice of his secretary, the humanist and reformer Georg Spalatin (born Burckhardt; 1484–1545). A catalog of Spalatin's personal library in the Gotha Landesbibliothek also contains invoices for other books purchased on behalf of the elector. Under Elector John Frederick ("the Magnanimous"; 1532–1547), Spalatin again became librarian and had an annual appropriation of 100 guilders after 1534. We know a good deal about Spalatin's administration of the Electoral Library (*75*), and we know that the library served the faculty and that Luther and Melanchthon used it (*76*). Some pieces from Luther's personal library can be identified (*77*), but of Melanchthon's collection we know only a volume in the Halle University Library and perhaps one in the Vatican (*78*).

Margrave Phillip I ("the Generous"; 1509–1567) of Hessia founded the University of Marburg in 1527, and its library was established on the basis of secularized monasteries (*79*). About 1532 the library was moved from the castle to the Discalced monastery, but it grew slowly despite a regular appropriation. We know a good deal about the administration of the library. Medieval traditions (e.g., chaining of books in the 1564 regulations) persisted. The professor of logic, Heidericus Theophilus Leonicerus, supervised the library from 1564 to 1581, and he prepared a catalog (not preserved) in 1578. The collections were increased substantially in 1605 with about 650 volumes from the collection of Count Christoph Ernest zu Diez, but the library did not thrive for two centuries, what with the division of holdings with Giessen in 1650. A major impulse forward came in 1748 when Marburg acquired the collection of the lawyer Johann Georg Estor.

Elector John Frederick I of Saxony ("the Magnanimous") was finally defeated in the Schmalkaldic War at Mühlberg in 1547, and the gymnasium founded at Jena in 1548 received his library, the "Electoralis." A decade later the school became the University of Jena (*80*). The "Electoralis" was extraordinarily rich in manuscripts and printed books, altogether about 3,100 pieces, relating to the Reformation, and it remains today one of the major resources for the study of the origin and early development of Lutheranism.

There was a library in the University of Heidelberg soon after its founding in 1386 (*81*), but it was the incomparable Palatina which served the university for three-quarters of a century until it was sent to Rome by Duke Maximilian of Bavaria (supra) (*82*). It was actually founded by Elector Philipp ("the Honest"; 1476–1508), patron of Chancellor Johann von Dalberg (supra), but it was developed by Ottheinrich (1502–1559; elector 1556–1559). He not only promoted the Reformation vigorously but also had the laudable ambition to develop a library comparable to those of the Italian Renaissance princes. He purchased books from all over Europe, incorporated into his collection that of the famous old monastery at Lorsch, and conveniently forgot to return manuscripts borrowed from the Mainz Cathedral. The library from his seat at Neuburg and the Electoral Library were housed with a collection in the Church of the Holy Spirit, and it is clear from various sources that Ottheinrich meant for the collection to be used by the members of the university along with other books that had been at their disposal. One of the most noteworthy additions came to the library in 1584 upon the death of Ulrich Fugger, the only Protestant in this distinguished Augsburg patrician family. He left his collection to the Palatina in gratitude for the hospitality of Elector Frederick III (1553–1576). As we have noted in connection with the Vatican Library, the catastrophe came in 1622 when Tilly directed the greatest bibliological loot in history. Except for the partial restoration of 1816, the modern University of Heidelberg Library dates from 1706.

The situation was somewhat similar in Königsberg, where there was a court library (Schlossbibliothek) available to the university and also a university library (*83*). The last grand master of the Teutonic Order, Albrecht von Brandenburg, became a Protestant in 1525 and made the old lands of the order a hereditary duchy of Prussia. He soon began to acquire books with Lukas Cranach and his own secretary, Crotus Rubianus (supra), as his agents. After Crotus left Königsberg, a Dutchman, the ex-Carthusian Felix König, became Albrecht's librarian and conducted his office vigorously (*84*), as did Heinrich Zell, librarian from 1557 to 1564. Over the years the library was reasonably well cataloged and available to scholars. When Albrecht founded the university in 1544 he provided it with its own library, and ultimately, in 1827, the Schlossbibliothek and the University Library were combined as the Königliche (Staats-) und Universitätsbibliothek, a great library which disappeared in 1945. Albrecht had his private collection, famous for the 20 volumes of his "Silver Library" books bound in finely wrought silver covers, most executed in Königsberg, as were the more conventional bindings (*85*).

There were princely libraries elsewhere in Germany (notably in Dresden, Wolfenbüttel, Dessau, and Kassel) that were significant into our own times, but these generally pushed beyond the immediate objectives of Renaissance and Reformation. In Switzerland the university libraries in Bern, Lausanne, and Geneva (originally based in part on Calvin's collection) have roots in the Reformation. A particularly noteworthy monument of the period is the collection of Joachim von Watt, or Vadianus (1483 or 1484–1551; supra), humanist and reformer of Saint Gall, now in the local municipal library (Stadtbibliothek) (*86*).

Perhaps with the founding of the University of Leiden in 1575, Renaissance, humanism, and Reformation had run their destined courses, and libraries began to serve scholars in a gradually evolving tradition of analytical scholarship with meticulous attention to detail. The resources had been provided by the great collectors of the previous two centuries; the methods and standards, by scholars with the insight and discipline of Erasmus and Reuchlin.

NOTES AND REFERENCES

1. Jakob Burckhardt, *Die Cultur der Renaissance in Italien: Ein Versuch*, Durchgearbeite Auflage von Ludwig Geiger, 7, E. A. Seemann, Leipzig, 1899, 2 vols. (translated by S. G. C. Middlemore, *The Civilization of the Renaissance in Italy*, Allen and Unwin, London, 1937); and John Addington Symonds, *Renaissance in Italy*, Modern Library, New York, 1935, 2 vols. Both works have appeared in other editions.

2. See Poggio Bracciolini, *Opera*, Strassburg, 1513, Preface.

3. Ludwig Mohler, *Kardinal Bessarion als Theologe, Humanist und Staatsmann*, Quellen und Forschungen aus dem Gebiete der Geschichte, 20, 22, and 24, F. Schoningh, Paderborn, 1923–1942, 3 vols., Vol. 1, pp. 408–415.

4. Aloys Bömer, "Von der Renaissance bis zum Beginn der Aufklärung," Revised by Hans Widmann, in *Handbuch der Bibliothekswissenschaft* (Georg Leyh, ed.), 2nd ed., Otto Harrassowitz, Wiesbaden, 1952–1957, 3 vols., Vol. 3, Part 1, pp. 502–503. The motivations and the genius of Italian Renaissance book collectors are effectively summarized in Gustav Adolf Erich Bogeng, *Die grossen Bibliophilen: Geschichte der Büchersammler und ihrer Sammlungen,* E. A. Seemann, Leipzig, 1922, 3 vols., Vol. 1, pp. 39–86, covering Italy.
5. Of the extensive Petrarch bibliography, only the following may be noted here: Berthold Louis Ullman, "Petrarch's Favorite Books," *Transactions and Proceedings of the American Philological Association*, **54,** 25–38 (1923); E. H. R. Tatham, "The Library of Petrarch," *Fortnightly Review*, n.s., **79,** 1056–1067 (1908); Heinrich Morf, "Die Bibliothek Petrarcas," in his *Aus Dichtung und Sprache der Romanen*, K. J. Trübner, Strassburg, 1903–1922, 3 vols., Vol. 1, pp. 172–184; K. Schneider, "Die Bibliothek Petrarcas und ihre Schicksale," *Zeitschrift für Bücherfreunde*, n.s., **1,** 157–160 (1909/1910); Hanns Wilhelm Eppelsheimer, "Petrarca und seine Bücher," *Jahrbuch deutscher Bibliophilen*, **12/13,** 9–16 (1925–1926); Luigi Arrigoni, *Notice historique et bibliographique sur vingt-cinq manuscrits . . . ayant fait partie de la bibliothèque de François Pétrarque*, [Firenze, Tipografia dell'arte della stampa], Milan, 1883; and Pierre de Nolhac, *Petrarch and the Ancient World*, Merrymount Press, Boston, 1907, Part 2, "Petrarch's Library."
6. Oskar Hecker, "Die Schicksale der Bibliothek Boccaccios," *Zeitschrift für Bücherfreunde*, **1,** 183–186 (1897–1898); id., *Boccaccio-Funde, Stücke aus der bislang verschollenen Bibliothek des Dichters*, G. Westermann, Braunschweig, 1902; Enrico Rostagno, "La libreria del Boccaccio," *Rivista delle biblioteche*, **14,** 93–94 (1905); and Bogeng, Ref. *4,* Vol. 1, pp. 47–50.
7. Now Laurentianus 68, II. It also contained the *Agricola*, perhaps more, when the monk Petrus Diaconus used it for his life of Saint Severus about 1135. See H. Bloch, "A Manuscript of Tacitus' Agricola," *Classical Philology*, **36,** 183–187 (1941); and Ludwig Pralle, *Die Wiederentdeckung des Tacitus: Ein Beitrag zur Geistesgeschichte Fuldas und zur Biographie des jungen Cusanus*, Quellen und Abhandlungen zur Geschichte der Abtei und der Diözese Fulda, 17, Verlag Parzeller, Fulda, 1952.
8. A. Goldmann, "Drei italienische Handschriftenkataloge," *Zentralblatt für Bibliothekswesen*, **4,** 137–155 (1887).
9. Alfred Wilhelm Otto von Martin, *Coluccio Salutati und das humanistische Lebensideal*, Beiträge zur Kulturgeschichte des Mittelalters und der Renaissance, No. 23, B. G. Teubner, Leipzig, 1916; Berthold Louis Ullmann, *The Humanism of Coluccio Salutati*, Medievo e umanesimo, 4, Editrice Antenore, Padua, 1963; and Armando Petrucci, *Coluccio Salutati*, Bibliotheca biographica, No. 7, Istituto della Enciclopedia Italiana, Rome, 1972.
10. Rudolf Blum, *La biblioteca della Badia Fiorentina e i codici di Antonio Corbinelli*, Studi e testi, 155, Biblioteca Apostolica Vaticana, The Vatican, 1951.
11. Ernest Walser, *Poggius Florentinus, Leben und Werke*, Beiträge zur Kultur des Mittelalters und der Renaissance, No. 14, B. G. Teubner, Leipzig, 1914.
12. Albert Castelnau, *Les Médicis*, Calmann Lévy, Paris, 1879, 2 vols.; George Frederic Young, *The Medici*, J. Murray, London, 1909, 2 vols.; Lacy Collison-Morley, *The Early Medici*, G. Routledge, London, 1935; Ferdinand Schevill, *The Medici*, Harcourt, Brace, New York, 1949; Edoardo Bizzari, *Il Magnifico Lorenzo*, Mondadori, Milan, 1950; and Harold Mario Mitchell Acton, *The Last Medici*, rev. ed., St. Martin's Press, New York, 1959.
13. Paul Oskar Kristaller, *The Philosophy of Marsilio Ficino*, Columbia Studies in Philosophy, 6, Columbia University Press, New York, 1943.
14. Giuseppe Zippel, *Niccolò Niccoli, contributo alla storia dell' umanesimo*, Florence, 1890.
15. Luisa Gervasio Macina (Luigi di San Giusto, pseud.), *La vita e l'opera di Lorenzo il Magnifico*, Felice Le Monnier, Florence, 1927; Roberto Palmarocchi, *Lorenzo de' Medici*, Grandi italiani, collana di biografie, 5, Unione Tipografico-Editrice Torinese, Turin, 1941; and Bizzari, Ref. *12.*
16. Karl Konrad Müller, "Neue Mittheilungen über Janos Laskaris und die Mediceische Bibliothek," *Zentralblatt für Bibliothekswesen*, **1,** 333–412 (1884).
17. The libraries and library rooms of the Renaissance in Venice (the Marciana), Siena (in the cathedral), Urbino (in the castle), and elsewhere are noteworthy more for their architectural significance than for any advances in coordinating physical facilities with readers' needs. See Carl Martin von Stegmann and Heinrich von Geymüller, *Die Architektur der Renaissance in Toscana*, F. Bruck-

mann, Munich, 1885–1908, 11 vols., Vol. 2, passim.
18. Ref. *3,* Vol. 1, pp. 408–415.
19. Giovanni Mercati, *Per la cronologia della vita e degli scritti di Niccolò Perotti, arcivesco di Siponta,* Studi e testi, 44, Biblioteca Apostolica Vaticana, Rome, 1925.
20. Remigio Sabbadini, *Biografia documentata di Giovanni Aurispa,* F. Zammit, Noto, 1890, and his edition of *Carteggio di Giovanni Aurispa,* Fonti per la storia d'Italia: Epistolari, Secolo XV, 70, Tipografia del Senato, Rome, 1931; and Aristide Calderini, "Ricerche intorno alla biblioteca e alla cultura greca di Francesco Filelfo," *Studi italiani della filologia classica,* **20,** 204 et seq. (1913).
21. Henri Auguste Omont, "Inventaire des manuscrits grecs et latines donnés à Saint Marc de Venise par le Cardinal Bessarion en 1468," *Revue des bibliothèques,* **4,** 129–187 (1894). See also Mohler, Ref. *3.*
22. G. Lorenzetti, "La libreria Sansoviniana di Venezia," *Accademie e biblioteche,* **2,** 75–98 (1929), and **3,** 22–36 (1929–1930).
23. Laura Pittoni, *La Libreria di San Marco, cenni storici,* Tipo-lito di G. Flori, Pistoia, 1903.
24. Gerolamo d'Adda, *Indagini storiche, artistiche e bibliografiche sulla libreria Visconteo-Sforzesca del castello di Pavia, I,* G. Brigola, Milan, 1875, and *Appendice,* 1879; and Otto Eduard Schmidt, "Die Visconti und ihre Bibliothek zu Pavia," *Zeitschrift für Geschichte und Politik,* **5,** 444 et seq. (1888).
25. A. Capelli, "La Biblioteca Estense nella prima metà del secolo XV," *Giornale storico della letteratura italiana,* **14,** 1–30 (1889); Giulio Bertoni, *La Biblioteca Estense e la coltura ferrarese ai tempi del duca Ercole I (1471–1505),* E. Loescher, Turin, 1903; and Domenico Fava, *La Biblioteca Estense nel suo sviluppo storico,* G. T. Vincenzi e Nipoti di D. Cavallotti, Modena, 1925.
26. Giuseppe Fumagalli, *L'arte della legatura alle corte degli Estensi a Ferrara e a Modena dal secolo XV al XIX, col catalogo delle legature pregevoli della Biblioteca Estense di Modena,* Tammaro de Marinis, Florence, 1913.
27. Giuseppe Mazzatinti, *La biblioteca dei re d'Aragona in Napoli,* L. Capelli, Rocca S. Casciano, 1897; Tammaro de Marinis, *Per la storia della biblioteca dei re d'Aragona in Napoli,* Stab. tip. Aldino, Florence, 1909; id., *La biblioteca napoletana dei re d'Aragona,* Hoepli, Milan, 1947–1952, 4 vols.; and Henri Auguste Omont, "Inventaire de la bibliothèque de Ferdinand I d'Aragone, roi de Naples (1418)," *Bibliothèque de l'École des Chartes,* **70,** 456–470 (1909).
28. Cosimo Stornajolo, *Codices Urbanates graeci Bibliothecae Vaticanae I,* ex Typographeo Vaticano, Rome, 1895, containing a substantial proportion of the original collection. See also Walter Bombe, "La biblioteca di Federigo da Montefeltro," *Rassegna marchigiana,* **8,** 235–246 (1929–1930); and Cesare Guasti, "Inventario della libreria Urbinate compilato nel secolo XV da Federigo Veterano," *Giornale storico degli archivi toscani,* **6,** 134–147 (1862), and **7,** 45–55, 130–154 (1863).
29. P. Girotta, "La biblioteca di Francesco Gonzaga secondo l'inventario del 1407," *Atti e memorie della R. Accademia Virgiliana di Mantova,* n.s., **14–16,** 60–72 (1921–1923).
30. Eugène Müntz and Paul Fabre, *La bibliothèque du Vatican au xv*[e] *siècle, d'après des documents inédits,* Bibliothèque des écoles françaises d'Athènes et de Rome, 48, E. Thorin, Paris, 1887.
31. Ludwig Pastor, *Geschichte der Päpste seit dem Ausgang des Mittelalters,* Herder, Freiburg im Breisgau, 1866–1938, 21 vols., Vol. 1, pp. 562–570.
32. Armin Lucchesi, "Der Buchhändler des Cosimo de' Medici: Aus den Erinnerungen des Vespasiano da Bisticci," *Philobiblon,* **11,** 292–305 (1939).
33. Giovanni Sforza, *La patria, la famiglia e la giovinezza di Papa Niccolò v, ricerche storiche,* Giusti, Lucca, 1884, pp. 359–384.
34. O. Hartlich, "Giovanni Andrea dei Bussi, der erste Bibliothekar der Vaticana," *Philologische Wochenschrift,* **59,** 327–336, 364–368, 395–399 (1939); and Konrad Haebler, *Die deutschen Buchdrucker des XV. Jahrhunderts im Auslande,* J. Rosenthal, Munich, 1924, p. 13 et seq.
35. Of the extensive literature on the origins and history of the Bibliothèque Nationale, see Leon Vallée, *La Bibliothèque Nationale: Choix de documents pour servir à l'histoire de l'établissement et de ses collections,* É. Terquem, Paris, 1894; Alfred Franklin, *Précis de l'histoire de la Bibliothèque du Roi,* 2nd ed., L. Willem, Paris, 1875; Arundell J. K. Esdaile, *National Libraries of the World,* Grafton, London, 1934, pp. 61–92; and Cornelia Serrurier, *Bibliothèques de France,* M. Nijhoff, La Haye, 1946.
36. Ernest Quentin-Bauchart, *La bibliothèque de Fontainebleau et les livres des derniers Valois à la Bibliothèque Nationale (1515–1589),* L. Huard et Guillemin, Paris, 1891; Théophile Lhuillier, *La bibli-*

othèque et les bibliothécaires du château de Fontainebleau, Meaux, 1878; Henri Victor Michelant, *Catalogue de la bibliothèque de François Ier à Blois en 1518*, Franck, Paris, 1863; and Henri Auguste Omont, *Catalogues des manuscrits grecs de Fontainebleau sous François Ier et Henri II*, Imprimerie Nationale, Paris, 1889.

37. F. Hamel, "The Libraries of the Royal Library at Fontainebleau," *Library*, ser. 1, **3**, 190–199 (1903).
38. Henri Lamaître, *Histoire du dépôt légal: I. France*, A. Picard et fils, Paris, 1910.
39. Antoine Jean Victor Le Roux de Lincy, *Notice sur la bibliothèque de Cathérine de Médicis avec des extraits de l'inventaire de cette bibliothèque*, Extrait du Bulletin du bibliophile, mai 1858, 13e serie, J. Techener, Paris, 1858.
40. Bogeng, Ref. *4*, Vol. 1, pp. 93–94.
41. For the subsequent history of the La Vallière and other important collections mentioned here see Bogeng, Ref. *4*, Vol. 1, p. 135 et seq.; and Lawrence S. Thompson, "Private Libraries," in *Encyclopedia of Library and Information Science* (A. Kent, H. Lancour, and J. E. Daily, eds.), Dekker, New York, 1978, Vol. 24, pp. 125–192. The history of many of the great libraries of our time is inextricably tied to the story of great private collections of the Renaissance.
42. Pál Gulyás, *Matyás Király Könyvtára*, Franklin-társulat, Budapest, 1916; André de Hevesy, *La bibliothèque du roi Matthias Corvinus*, Pour les membres de la Société Française de Reproductions de Manuscrits à Peintures, Paris, 1923; L. Karl, "Le roi Matthias de Hunyad, mécène et bibliophile," *La Bibliofilia*, **36**, 370–382 (1934); Wilhelm Weinberger, *Beiträge zur Handschriftenkunde: I. Die Biblioteca Corvina*, Sitzungsberichte der Akademie der Wissenschaften in Wien, Philosophisch-historische Klasse, 159, 1908, Abh. 6, A. Hölder, Vienna, 1908; and József Fitz and Klára Zolnai, *Bibliographia bibliothecae regis Mathiae Corvini*, Az országos Széchényi könyvtar kiadvanyai, No. 10, Budapest, 1942.
43. Karl Löffler and Paul Ruf, "Allgemeine Handschriftenkunde," in *Handbuch der Bibliothekswissenschaft* (Georg Leyh, ed.), Ref. *4*, Vol. 1, pp. 120–123, provides an adequate résumé of the dissipation of the Corviniana and present whereabouts of the pitiful remnants.
44. Henry K. Barycz, *Historja Uniwersitetu Jagiellońskiego w epoce humanizmu*, Nakl. Uniwersytetu Jagiellońskiego, Krakow, 1935, pp. 659–712.
45. Edward Gordon Duff, "The Bindings of Thomas Wotton," *Library*, 3rd ser., **1**, 337–350 (1910).
46. Henri Harrisse, *Grandeur et décadence de la Colombine*, 2nd ed., Chez tous les marchands de nouveautés [Macon, Impr. Protat Frères], Paris, 1885. The Colombina issued a *Catálogo de sus libros impresos, bajo la inmediata dirección de su bibliotecario Servando Arboli y Faraudo, con notas bibliográficas del Dr. D. Simón de la Rosa y López*, Impr. de E. Rasco, Seville, 1888–1948, 7 vols. See also *Catalogue of the Library of Ferdinand Columbus: Reproduced in Facsimile from the Unique Manuscript in the Columbine Library of Seville*, Archer M. Huntington, New York, 1905.
47. Guillermo Antolin, *La Real Biblioteca de El Escorial*, Impr. del Real Monasterio del Escorial, Escorial (?), 1921(?). A number of catalogs of the Escorial manuscripts have been printed, notably the Latin (1910–1916), Greek (1936), Spanish (1924–1929), Catalan (1932), and French and Provençal (1933), all recorded and described under Escorial, Biblioteca, in the *National Union Catalog*.
48. Thea Buyken, *Enea Silvio Piccolomini: Sein Leben und Werden bis zum Episkopat*, L. Röhrscheid, Bonn, 1931 (part of a Cologne dissertation).
49. Karl Heinz Volkmann-Schluck, *Nicolaus Cusanus: Die Philosophie im Übergang vom Mittelalter zur Neuzeit*, V. Klostermann, Frankfurt am Main, 1957; Erich Meuthen, *Die letzten Jahre des Nikolaus von Kues*, Wissenschaftliche Abhandlungen der Arbeitsgemeinschaft für Forschung des Landes Nordrhein-Westfalen, 3, Westdeutscher Verlag, Cologne, 1958; Paolo Rotta, "La biblioteca del Cusano," *Rivista di filosofia neo-scolastica*, **19**, 22–47 (1927); and Pralle, Ref. *7*.
50. Max Herrmann, *Albrecht von Eyb und die Frühzeit des deutschen Humanismus*, Weidmann, Berlin, 1893; and Lawrence S. Thompson, "German Translations of the Classics between 1450 and 1550," *Journal of English and Germanic Philology*, **42**, 343–363 (1943).
51. Karl Schottenloher, "Hartmann Schedel (1440–1514): Ein Gedenkblatt zum 400. [i.e., 500] Geburtstag des Nürnberger Humanisten," *Philobiblon*, **12**, 279–291 (1940); and Richard Stauber, *Die Schedelsche Bibliothek*, Hrsg. von Otto Hartig, Studien und Darstellungen aus dem Gebiete der Geschichte, 6, Heft 2–3, Herder, Freiburg im Breisgau, 1908.

52. Karl Morneweg, *Johann von Dalberg, ein deutscher Humanist und Bischof*, C. Winter, Heidelberg, 1887.
53. Heinrich Ulmann, *Kaiser Maximilian I auf urkundlicher Grundlage dargestellt*, J. G. Cotta, Stuttgart, 1884–1891, 2 vols.; and Theodor Gottlieb, *Die Büchersammlung Kaiser Maximilian I: Mit einer Einleitung über älteren Bücherbesitz im Hause Habsburg*, Die Ambraser Handschriften, Beitrag zur Geschichte der Wiener Hofbibliothek, 1, M. Spirgatis, Leipzig, 1900.
54. Bogeng, Ref. *4*, Vol. 1, p. 237. Celtis's personal collection went to the Hofbibliothek at his death.
55. Konrad Miller, *Die Konrad Peutinger'sche Tafel oder Weltkarte des Castorius*, 2nd ed., Strecker und Schröder, Stuttgart, 1929.
56. Erich König, *Peutingerstudien*, Studien und Darstellungen aus dem Gebiete der Geschichte, 9, Heft 1–2, Herder, Freiburg im Breisgau, 1914.
57. Emil Reicke, *Willibald Pirckheimer: Leben, Familie und Persönlichkeit*, Deutsche Volkheit, 75, E. Diederichs, Jena, 1930 (?); E. Offenbacher, "La bibliothèque de Willibald Pirckheimer," *La Bibliofilia*, **40,** 241–265 (1938); and Bogeng, Ref. *4*, Vol. 1, p. 234.
58. Joseph Knepper, *Jakob Wimpheling (1450–1528): Sein Leben und seine Werke*, Erläuterungen und Ergänzungen zu Janssens Geschichte des deutschen Volkes, 3, Heft 2–4, Herder, Freiburg im Breisgau, 1902; and Richard Newald, *Elsässische Charakterköpfe aus dem Zeitalter des Humanismus*, Alsatia Verlag, Kolmar, 1944.
59. Gustav Carl Knod, *Aus der Bibliothek des Beatus Rhenanus: Ein Beitrag zur Geschichte des Humanismus*, O. Harrassowitz, Leipzig, 1889.
60. Wilhelm Schneegans, *Abt Johannes Trithemius und das Kloster Sponheim*, R. Schmithals, Kreuznach, 1882; J. Fischer, "Der Nachlass des Abtes Johannes Tritheims," *Archiv des Historischen Vereins von Unterfranken*, **67,** 41 et seq. (1928); and Paul Lehmann, *Johannes Sichardus und die von ihm benutzten Bibliotheken und Handschriften*, Quellen und Untersuchungen zur lateinischen Philologie des Mittelalters, 4, Heft 1, pp. 176–179, C. H. Beck, Munich, 1911. This latter work deals with Johannes Sichardus (1499–1552), who studied church and monastic libraries; in 1526–1530 he published 24 different texts he found in Fulda and Lorsch.
61. David Friedrich Strauss, *Ulrich von Hutten: His Life and Times*, Daldy, Isbister, and Company, London, 1874; and Josef Benzing, *Ulrich von Hutten und seine Drucker*, Beiträge zum Buch- und Bibliothekswesen, 6, O. Harrassowitz, Wiesbaden, 1956.
62. Otto Clemen, "Ulrich von Hutten—ein Bücherdieb?" *Archiv für Reformationsgeschichte*, **23,** 150–155 (1926); and Paul Kalkoff, "Huttens Bücherraub," ibid., pp. 300–306.
63. Heinrich Detmer, "Zur Geschichte der Münsterschen Dombibliothek," *Westdeutsche Zeitschrift*, **14,** 203–229 (1895).
64. Heinz Otto Burger, *Renaissance, Humanismus, Reformation: Deutsche Literatur im europäischen Kontext*, Frankfurter Beiträge zur Germanistik, 7, Gehlen, Bad Homburg, 1969; Max Brod, *Johannes Reuchlin und sein Kampf*, Kohlhammer, Stuttgart, 1965; François Secret, *Les kabbalistes chrétiens de la renaissance*, Collection Sigma, 5, Dunod, Paris, 1964; Johannes Reuchlin, *Briefwechsel*, Hrsg. von Ludwig Geiger, Bibliothek des Litterarischen Vereins in Stuttgart, No. 126, Litterarischer Verien in Stuttgart, Tübingen, 1875 (reprinted, Olms, Hildesheim, 1962); *Festschrift der Stadt Pforzheim zur Erinnerung an den 400. Todestag Johannes Reuchlins*, Sonderdruck aus der Zeitschrift für die Geschichte des Oberrheins, n.s., 37, Heft 3, O. Riecker, Pforzheim, 1922; and Johannes Willms, *Bücherfreunde, Büchernarren, Entwurf zur Archäogie einer Leidenschaft*, Eine deutsche Humanistenbibliothek—Die Bibliotheca Reuchliniana, Harrassowitz, Wiesbaden, 1978, pp. 61–77.
65. Heynlin died in the Carthusian monastery in Basel and left his collection to this institution. The books have been in the University of Basel Library since the Reformation. See Andreas Heusler (1834–1921), *Geschichte der öffentlichen Bibliothek der Universität Basel*, Universitätsbuchdruckerei von F. Reinart, Basel, 1896.
66. Bömer, Ref. *4*, pp. 554–553; Wilhelm Brambach, *Die Grossherzogliche Hof- und Landesbibliothek in Karlsruhe*, A Spaarmann, Oberhausen, 1875; and Karl Christ, *Die Bibliothek Reuchlins in Pforzheim*, Beiheft zum Zentralblatt für Bibliothekswesen, 52, O. Harrassowitz, Leipzig, 1924.
67. Of the voluminous Erasmus literature, one might start with Preserved Smith, *Erasmus: A Study of His Life, Ideals, and Place in History*, Harper, New York, 1923; Karl Heinz Oelrich, *Der späte Erasmus und die Reformation*, Reformationsgeschichtliche Studien und Texte, 86, Aschendorf,

Münster, 1961; Ernst Wilhelm Kohls, *Die Theologie des Erasmus*, Theologische Zeitschrift, "Sonderband," No. 1, F. Reinhardt, Basel, 1966, 2 vols.; Percy Stafford Allen, ed., *Opus epistularum Desiderii Erasmi*, In typographeo Clarendoniano, Oxonii, 1906–1947, 12 vols.; Fritz Husner, "Die Bibliothek des Erasmus," in *Gedenkschrift zum 400. Todestage des Erasmus von Rotterdam*, Braus-Riggenbach, Basel, 1936, pp. 228–259; J. H. ter Horst, "Nog enkele aantekeningen over de bibliotheek van Erasmus," *Het Boek*, **24,** 229 et seq. (1937); and Bömer, Ref. *4,* pp. 269 et seq.

68. Otto Radlach, "Bibliothekswesen," *Realencyklopädie für protestantische Theologie und Kirche*, 3rd ed., Hinrichs, Leipzig, 1896–1913, 24 vols., Vol. 3, pp. 187–192; Gustav Kohfeldt, "Zur Geschichte der Büchersammlungen und des Bücherbesitzes in Deutschland," *Zeitschrift für Kulturgeschichte*, **7,** 354–375 (1900); and Bömer, Ref. *4*, pp. 559–584.
69. Hermann Hering, *Doctor Pomeranus, Johannes Bugenhagen*, Schriften des Vereins für Reformationsgeschichte, 6, Stück 1, Nr. 22, Verein für Reformationsgeschichte, Halle, 1888; and Hermann Herbst, "Die Bibliothek der St. Andreaskirche zu Braunschweig," *Zentralblatt für Bibliothekswesen*, **58,** 301–338 (1941).
70. Karl Schottenloher, "Schicksale von Büchern und Bibliotheken im Bauernkrieg," *Zeitschrift für Bücherfreunde*, **11,** 396–408 (1908–1909).
71. Emil Albert Friedberg, *Die Universität Leipzig in Vergangenheit und Gegenwart*, Veit and Company, Leipzig, 1898, pp. 29 et seq. and 54 et seq.
72. Heusler, Ref. *65*.
73. Karl August Klüpfel, *Die Universität Tübingen in ihrer Vergangenheit und Gegenwart*, Fues's Verlag [R. Reisland], Leipzig, 1877; and L. Zoepf, "Aus der Geschichte der Tübinger Universitätsbibliothek (1477–1607)," *Zentralblatt für Bibliothekswesen*, **52,** 471–485 (1935).
74. Max Steinmetz, "Die Universität Wittenberg und der Humanismus (1502–1521)," in *450 Jahre Martin Luther-Universität Halle–Wittenberg*, Martin Luther-Universität, Halle, 1952, 3 vols., Vol. 1, pp. 103–139; Bernhard Weissenborn, "Die Wittenberger Universitätsbibliothek (1547–1817)," ibid., pp. 355–376; and E. Hildebrandt, "Die kurfürstliche Schloss- und Universitätsbibliothek zu Wittenberg 1512–1547: Beiträge zu ihrer Geschichte," *Zeitschrift für Bücherkunde*, **2,** 34–42, 109–129, 157–188 (1925).
75. Georg Buchwald, "Zu Spalatins Reisen insbesondere nach Wittenberg in Angelegenheit der Kurfürstlichen Bibliothek," *Archiv für Bibliographie, Buch- und Bibliothekswesen*, **2,** 92 et seq. (1928–1929).
76. C. G. Brandis, "Luther und Melanchthon als Benutzer der Wittenberger Bibliothek," *Theologische Studien und Kritiken*, **90,** 206–221 (1917).
77. Johannes Luther, "Review of Max Herrmann, *Ein feste Burg ist unser Gott*," *Zentralblatt für Bibliothekswesen*, **23,** 128 et seq. (1906).
78. Willi Göber, "Aus Melanchthons Bibliothek," *Zentralblatt für Bibliothekswesen*, **45,** 297–302 (1928).
79. Gottfried Zedler, *Geschichte der Universitätsbibliothek zu Marburg von 1527–1887*, N. G. Elwert, Marburg, 1896.
80. Karl Konrad Müller, "Geschichte der Universitätsbibliothek Jena," *Zentralblatt für Bibliothekswesen*, **19,** 380–384 (1902); Bernhard Willkomm, "Die Bedeutung der Jenaer Universitätsbibliothek für die reformationsgeschichtliche Forschung," ibid., **30,** 245–261 (1915); and Herbert Koch, "Die 'Electoralis'," ibid., **66,** 345–358 (1952).
81. See Lawrence S. Thompson, "University Libraries, Medieval," in *Encyclopedia of Library and Information Science* (A. Kent, H. Lancour, and J. E. Daily, eds.), Dekker, New York, 1981, Vol. 32, p. 169.
82. Friedrich Wilken, *Geschichte der Bildung, Beraubung und Vernichtung der alten heidelbergischen Büchersammlungen: Ein Beitrag zur Literärgeschichte vornehmlich des fünfzehnten und sechszehnten Jahrhunderts; nebst einem meist beschreibenden Verzeichnis der im Jahre 1816 von dem Pabst Pius VII. der Universität Heidelberg zurückgegebenen Handschriften, und einigen Schriftproben*, A. Oswald, Heidelberg, 1817; Jakob Wille, "Aus alter und neuer Zeit der Heidelberger Bibliothek," *Neue Heidelberger Jahrbücher*, **14,** (1906); and Karl Schottenloher, *Pfalzgraf Ottheinrich und das Buch: Ein Beitrag zur Geschichte der evangelischen Publizistik*, Reformationsgeschichtliche Studien und Texte, 50, 51, Aschendorf, Münster, 1927.
83. Ernst Kuhnert, *Die Königliche und Universitätsbibliothek zu Königsburg in Preussen*, Hartungsche

Buchdruckerei, Königsberg, 1901, and *Geschichte der Staats- und Universitätsbibliothek zu Königsberg*, K. W. Hiersemann, Leipzig, 1926, Band 1, "Von ihrer Begründung bis zum Jahre 1810."

84. Joseph Förstemann, "Felix König (Rex), erster Bibliothekar des Herzogs Albrecht von Preussen," *Zentralblatt für Bibliothekswesen*, **16,** 306–314 (1899).

85. Paul Schwenke and Konrad von Lange, *Die Silberbibliothek Herzog Albrechts von Preussen und seiner Gemahlin Anna Maria*, K. W. Hiersemann, Leipzig, 1894; and Alfred Rohde, *Die Silberbibliothek des Herzogs Albrecht in Königsberg*, Bilderhefte des deutschen Ostens, 4, Gräfe und Unzer, Königsberg, 1928.

86. A. Ruland, "Die Vadianische Bibliothek in St. Gallen," *Serapeum*, **26,** 1–12, 17–23 (1865); and Werner Näf, *Vadian und seine Stadt St. Gallen: I. Bis 1518. Humanist in Wien*, Fehr'sche Buchhandlung, St. Gallen, 1944–1957, 2 vols., and *Vadianische Analekten*, Vadian-Studien: Untersuchungen und Texte, 1, Fehr'sche Buchhandlung, St. Gallen, 1945.

BIBLIOGRAPHY

Bogeng, Gustav Adolf Erich, *Die grossen Bibliophilen: Geschichte der Büchersammler und ihrer Sammlungen*, E. A. Seemann, Leipzig, 1922, 3 vols.

Bömer, Aloys, "Von der Renaissance bis zum Beginn der Aufklärung," revised by Hans Widmann, in *Handbuch der Bibliothekswissenschaft* (Georg Leyh, ed.), 2nd ed., Otto Harrassowitz, Wiesbaden, 1952–1957, 3 vols., Vol. 3, Pt. 1, pp. 499–584.

Burckhardt, Jakob, *Die Cultur der Reniassance in Italien: Ein Versuch*, 7. durchgearbeitete Aufl. von Ludwig Geiger, E. A. Seemann, Leipzig, 1899, 2 vols.; Translated by S. G. C. Middlemore, *The Civilization of the Renaissance in Italy,*, Allen and Unwin, London, 1937. (Both the English and German have appeared in several other editions.)

Esdaile, Arundell J. K., *National Libraries of the World*, Grafton, London, 1934.

Löffler, Karl, and Joachim Kirchner, eds., *Lexikon des gesamten Buchwesens*, Hiersemann, Leipzig, 1935–1937, 3 vols. (New edition is in preparation.)

LAWRENCE S. THOMPSON

SWITZERLAND, LIBRARIES IN

The libraries of every country have been shaped by their national history. The course of Swiss history can be traced as follows: At the beginning there were a number of rural and urban communities; these first formed a conglomerate of loose alliances, then a confederation, and in the end, our modern federal state. Given the diversity of its parts, federalism was the only possibility. This process took place in a steady, unspectacular way, without a break in tradition and without any war, at least not within the last 100 years. The advantage of federalism and the qualities of prudence and conservatism have deeply influenced the thinking of the Swiss citizen. The Swiss librarian must be sensitive to this particular basic attitude of his fellow citizens. It is a conservative attitude which has political motives, and the librarian must allow for it in his plans and actions. Love of tradition and continuous development may certainly be commendable in a librarian, but in a dynamic epoch like that of the 1960s and 1970s, it can easily lead to dangerous backwardness. Federalism promotes the initiatives of separate groups, and it provides responses to immediate needs and favors the execution of work of many kinds, but it also often prevents a rational organization of labor and efficient collaboration.

By the will of the Swiss nation (i.e., its federal constitution), the 26 cantons and more than 3,000 municipalities are responsible for policy in the areas of culture, science, and education, and accordingly for the administration of the libraries. This makes national coordination of otherwise excellent library work more difficult. The explosive increase in book publication poses serious obstacles to orderly and efficient work in the sectors of bibliography, acquisitions, and cataloging.

As already mentioned, the explanation for the present situation of Swiss librarianship will be found in the history and political constitution of the country. Besides, the evolution of Swiss libraries followed the trends of European library development until the 19th century, first that of German libraries and library types. This influence is still apparent in many professional and technical organizations of Swiss libraries. Later, in the 20th century, the model of the public libraries of Great Britain and the United States gained increasing influence on Swiss public libraries; and from the 1960s onward, also the example of Danish public libraries.

In Switzerland, as in other countries, medieval book culture was fostered by the monasteries. We shall only mention some of the best-known library foundations of that time: Saint Gall (founded around 720), Einsiedeln, and Engelberg. To the age of humanism, one important library owes its existence: the University Library of Basel (founded 1460). In the Protestant cantons, the Reformation gave birth to a series of theological school libraries, which soon became municipal libraries (Stadt- und Universitätsbibliothek Bern, Bibliothèque cantonale et universitaire de Lausanne, and Bibliothèque publique et universitaire de Genève). The Counter-Reformation created the ecclesiastical libraries of the Jesuits and the Capuchins, which were subsequently incorporated into public libraries (Bibliothèque cantonale et universitaire de Fribourg, Zentralbibliothek Luzern, Biblioteca cantonale di Lugano, Bibliothèque cantonale Sion, and Bibliothèque de l'Ecole cantonale de Porrentruy). In the 17th and 18th centuries numerous libraries were established, not by powerful patrons, as was the case in neighboring monarchies, but by the upper-middle classes and their love of cultural values. They were intended as civic and city libraries (Zentralbibliothek Zürich, founded 1629; Stadtbibliothek Winterthur and Stadtbibliothek Zofingen; Bibliothèque de la Ville de Neuchâtel). In the course of the 19th century many of them became committed to the ideals of democracy and were consequently changed into regional libraries, addressing themselves either to the whole population of the old cantons (Zentralbibliothek Zürich, Zentralbibliothek Luzern, Bibliothèque cantonale et universitaire de Fribourg, and Bibliothèque cantonale Sion) or to the inhabitants of the new cantons brought forth by the revolution (Kantonsbibliothek Aarau, Thurgauische Kantonsbibliothek Frauenfeld, and Biblioteca cantonale di Lugano). The new federal state of 1848 retained its federalist structure and therefore produced only a few important libraries (Eidgenössische Parlaments- und Zentralbibliothek, ETH-Bibliothek Zürich, the library of the Ecole polytechnique fédérale de Lausanne, and the Schweizerische Landesbibliothek—the Swiss National Library). The turn of the 20th century at last marked the beginning of a great many special libraries of all kinds and was the starting point for the rapid evolution of a handful of elaborate metropolitan systems of public libraries.

Today Switzerland has about 6,000 libraries. This number is surprisingly high for a population of 6.3 million inhabitants. However, most of these libraries are so small that they can hardly satisfy the needs of modern readers or the demands made on a modern library in general. Moreover, the collaboration between individual libraries and between various types of libraries (as well as documentation centers) is not quite satisfactory yet; it should be organized more efficiently.

The most substantial bookstocks are found in the central university libraries: about 2 million volumes in the two largest ones, the University Library of Basel and the Zentralbibliothek Zürich, and between 800,000 and 1½ million in the university libraries of Geneva, Berne, Fribourg, and Lausanne. These central university libraries have the additional functions of regional libraries; that is, they provide educational material for the population of a whole canton. The University of Neuchâtel is an exception in not having a central library; it has separate libraries for the various institutes, whose interaction a coordinator is trying to integrate. Since the 1950s the six large general university libraries have not had at their disposal sufficient funds to meet the needs of science and research. At present, moreover, they lack an appropriate number of specialists to cope with the steadily growing tide of publications. More or less successfully, they have tried to solve the problem of library collaboration in the university community as a whole. At present there are, in addition to the central university libraries, about 100 faculty or seminar libraries of greater or lesser importance. They are mostly run by unskilled staff members. There is as little coordination between them as there is with the central university library. The administrative control of the faculty libraries often differs from that of the central university library, an independence which the faculty libraries maintain successfully. The central university library tries to create effective cooperation with regard to acquisitions and analysis of literature, mainly in the field of periodicals. Certain limits are set to these efforts regarding personnel and financial resources. In their function as cantonal libraries (Kantonsbibliotheken), the university libraries also have to provide literature for the public of the whole region. The closest cooperation between a central university library and faculty libraries has been attained by the Bibliothèques cantonales et universitaires of Fribourg and Lausanne.

A special committee has been formed by the libraries concerned mainly with adult education. They consist, first, of those cantonal libraries not affiliated with a university and, second, the municipal libraries founded before 1900. They vary in size and importance: The libraries of Lucerne and Neuchâtel have a staff of 20 to 24 full-time employees each, and the smallest of them must be content with only two employees. They formerly served a small elite class of readers; since World War II some of them have successfully opened their stocks to the population of the whole region (Bibliothèque de la Ville de La Chaux-de-Fonds and the city libraries of Biel, Baden, and Zofingen). In deliberate contrast to the more recent general public libraries, they furnish their reading rooms with scientific and bibliographic reference works; they also systematically collect and classify regional and local publications, and continue to hoard and preserve their previously acquired stocks.

The general public libraries have received a strong impulse from, and modeled their outward structure after the public libraries of the Anglo-Saxon countries and Denmark. Their expansion set in after World War II, particularly in the mid-1950s. In the big cities, whole library systems have come into being, supplying the population with open-access shelves furnished with books for their information, education, and entertainment. The Bibliothèques Municipales in Geneva produced the first modern network of public libraries, and at present the Pestalozzigesellschaft in Zürich operates the widest library system. The Berner Volksbücherei has undergone an extraordinary evolution since the 1960s.

In some towns and regions of French-speaking Switzerland, the dissemination of literature has been intensified by the services of bookmobiles (Geneva, Lausanne, Vevey, Canton of Neuchâtel, and Canton of Jura). Unfortunately, public libraries have not developed accordingly in the rural areas.

Library policy is practiced differently from canton to canton. The best-organized network of libraries is to be found in the Canton of Zürich, with a library in almost every community and several district libraries entrusted with extensive charges. The Canton of Berne has far-reaching plans to increase the efficiency of its libraries, especially those in rural areas. The Canton of Lucerne has produced a number of modern grammar school libraries. (They also provide books for people in nonurban areas.) The school libraries often play a substantial part in cantonal plans. They are seen as centers of information where the students become acquainted with information media, which may lead to continuing self-education and a lifelong contact with and use of libraries. One of the main objects of Swiss librarianship will be to smooth out national and regional differences in the propagation of literature and information. This object has been reached only in a few parts of the country; for example, in the Cantons of Zürich and Geneva.

Three national institutions are at present striving for this common purpose: the Schweizerische Volksbibliothek (SVB), the cooperative society Schweizer Bibliotheksdienst (SBD), and the Schweizerische Arbeitsgemeinschaft für allgemeine öffentliche Bibliotheken (SAB), a group within the Association of Swiss Librarians.

The SVB works for the most part in the poorer regions. It supplies large bookstocks as long-term loans for the foundation of new libraries and completes the collections of smaller libraries with selected groups of publications (foreign-language literature for foreign workers or specialized literature). Its main concern is to counterbalance the enormous disparity in the supply of literature between the different regions. The SBD is a cooperative society which delivers books already equipped for library use (with catalog cards and classification) to school libraries and municipal libraries, sells library materials, and gives advice on library installation and building projects. The SAB is an association of all public librarians which provides training and assistance mainly for nonprofessional librarians in smaller libraries. It has issued the handbook *Arbeitstechnik für Schul- und Gemeindebibliotheken* (Bern, 1975).

A governmental committee of experts has pointed out the importance of public libraries for the democratization of culture in its final report, *Beiträge für eine Kulturpolitik in der Schweiz* (August 1973). This would require more effective support of the three previously mentioned institutions. The Swiss government is not as yet able to satisfy this demand. The policy of economy imposed on it by the voters is one of the main reasons.

At all times special libraries have played a considerable part in the exchange of information: Today they are still increasing in number and significance. Having no association of their own, they have partly joined the Schweizerische Vereinigung für Dokumentation (SVD, constituted in 1939); and partly, the Vereinigung Schweizerischer Bibliothekare (VSB). Their aims, prevalent type of collection, size and kind of administration present an astonishing variety.

There are several great government libraries of the Swiss Federal State (Library of the Parliament and Federal Administration; Library of the Swiss Federal Military Department; Library of the Swiss Federal Institute for Gymnastics and Sports; and the libraries of the Swiss Federal Railroads, the Swiss Post Office, and the Federal Office of Statistics), which to a limited extent also supply information to a larger public. Other than these, we mention here just two special libraries which work on a cooperative basis and are subsidized by the Swiss government for the national character of their activities: Schweizerisches Sozialarchiv and Schweizerische Osteuropabibliothek. The international libraries with facilities in Geneva (the library of the United Nations Organization, the library of the International Labor Office, and the library of the World Health Organization) hold rich specialized stocks, and they participate in the Swiss interlibrary loan system if a required work is not available in Swiss libraries. Two special libraries of an entirely different kind enjoy a high international reputation: the Stiftsbibliothek St. Gallen, the oldest and richest collection of medieval manuscripts in our country, and the Bibliotheca Bodmeriana, originally a famous private collection of the Swiss bibliophile Martin Bodmer in Cologny near Geneva.

Swiss industrial libraries have become more and more indispensable for supplying special information. In Switzerland, two-thirds of all expenses for research are paid by private industries. Industrial libraries take part in national interlibrary lending without any substantial restrictions and create worldwide connections with international documentation centers. Moreover, the new techniques which they use (electronic data processing) have paved the way for library automation. These libraries associate in groups of specialists, in order to coordinate their activities.

The leading professional groups in this respect are those representing the two most important branches of industry: the chemical and the machine-building industries. The concentration of important chemical firms in Basel provides an excellent basis for cooperation, particularly with regard to a common analysis of patents and periodical literature; for this purpose the "codeless scanning" method was developed by Roche and Sandoz in the 1960s. Today the problem is preeminently a matter of the availability of buyable machine-readable data. The working group for documentation of the Verein Schweizerischer Maschinenindustrieller (VSM) tries to gain access for its members to the important automatic documentation services of the world. The Swiss aluminum industry is an integrated and active member in international information work, whereas the Swiss PTT services (post, telephone, and telegraph) play a prominent part in the collaboration with European PTT libraries and documentation centers. For medicine, the documentation service DOKDI of the Swiss Academy of Medical Science has been the on-line connection to the data bases in the United States and Europe since 1971. As to technical publications, this task is accomplished—apart from the library of the Eidgenössische Technische Hochschule in Zürich—by the Swiss Institute for Technical Information (SITI), which was founded in 1979. The centers for retrospective research and for selective dissemination of information are located in the same place in Berne.

Unfortunately, collaboration in a wider sense—concerning interdisciplinary research work—has not yet reached the standard required. However, efforts in this respect are made by the Bundesamt für Bildung und Wissenschaft, an office established by the Swiss government with a view to coordination. For the IFLA meeting of 1976 in Lausanne, it sponsored the publication of the fourth edition of a useful guide to Swiss libraries, archives, and documentation centers, *Archive, Bibliotheken und Dokumentationsstellen der Schweiz.* This volume offers a comprehensive survey of Swiss research libraries and their collections and activities. It is the result of close cooperation between the three professional associations that represent the essential modes of information: the Vereinigung Schweizerischer Bibliothekare (VSB), the Vereinigung für Dokumentation (SVD), and the Vereinigung Schweizerischer Archivare (VSA). Two of them, the VSB and the SVD, publish a professional journal, *Nachrichten VSB/SVD*, demonstrating thereby their will to solve with joint efforts future problems in the field of information.

Finally we mention the two greatest special libraries in our country: the library of the Swiss Polytechnic School in Zürich (Eidgenössische Technische Hochschule, or ETH), which, owing to its extensive holdings of technological literature, is one of the largest special libraries of Europe; and second, the Swiss National Library (Schweizerische Landesbibliothek).

The ETH Library in Zürich (founded in 1855) has undergone the strongest development of all research libraries. Originally intended as a school library, it now fulfills the functions of the central technical library of the country. Since the mid-1960s its holdings have grown in number from ½ million to 2½ million. The Swiss National Library (founded in 1895) is really a special library covering the geography, history, literatures, and institutions of Switzerland. Its statutory functions are confined to collecting, analyzing, and lending *Helvetica;* that is, works written by Swiss authors or relating to Switzerland, and especially works published in Switzerland. The Swiss National Library compiles the Swiss National Bibliography and various national subject bibliographies. For the use of all Swiss research libraries, the National Library has set up a checklist of foreign periodicals and serials in Swiss libraries, and it is also in charge of the Swiss Union Catalog, the general information center for foreign monographs in the research libraries of our country. The Swiss Union Catalog (begun in 1928 by the Association of Swiss Librarians) and the Interlibrary Loan Service (which is directed by the Swiss National Library) are the two strongest links between the various libraries and documentation services of Switzerland. Local and national interlibrary lending within Switzerland works in a quite satisfactory manner. On the international scale the Interlibrary Loan Service tries to achieve three main objects in the transfer of information: liberality, speed, and low costs. Recently, the number of orders has grown rapidly as a result of more frequent use of on-line documentation services, and this has produced new problems regarding acquisition and exchange of publications. At present various measures by which these difficulties might be overcome are being explored.

There is still a great deal of important work to do. First of all, the inequalities in the national supply of literature must be removed. For this purpose an efficient national network of general public libraries should be developed. A direct democracy such as Switzerland needs a smoothly functioning network of general public libraries in order to maintain a productive scientific system of libraries and information centers. More stress should be laid on the national aspect than has hitherto been the case. But this presupposes a central national organization including both specialists trained in information science and users. This alone could ensure the continuity of information policy and would reward extraordinary efforts, exceeding the limited requirements of a particular city or region. The legal basis for such measures does not yet exist.

Two recommendations to this effect were made in the early 1970s by a governmental commission (called Kommission Sydler, after its president, the director of the ETH Library) for the coordination of scientific information work:

1. The setting up of a permanent national commission for scientific information to be in charge of developing and carrying out a national policy in this field
2. Promulgation of a federal law on the promotion of scientific information

A third recommendation of the commission concerns the foundation of an institute of information science, where its application could be studied and specialists in information science could be trained (*Rapport de la Commission d'experts chargée des questions de documentation scientifique*, Zürich and Bern, 1972).

A second commission of experts (called Kommission Schneider, after its president, the director of the Board of Education of the Canton of Basel-Stadt) was established in 1977 in order to realize the recommendations of its predecessor with all due efficiency. This commission deals with the practical aspect of acquisitions, the development of cooperative acquisition programs (following the example of the Sondersammelgebiete of the Federal Republic of Germany), the improvement of international loan by means of electronic data processing, affiliation with international information services and centers, the creation of specialized working groups, and finally, the realization of pilot schemes. This work led to the formation of two committees: one for documentation in the social sciences and another for biomedical documentation. Their work resulted in publication of the computer-generated periodicals register *Répertoire des périodiques bio-médicaux suisses et étrangers déposés dans les bibliothèques en Suisse* (Bibliothèque cantonale et universitaire, Lausanne, 1979). A final joint report of the committees is planned.

It is only gradually and hesitantly that public libraries begin to use modern information techniques, in particular electronic data processing. In contrast, special libraries and documentation services have introduced computer devices since 1960 onward: the chemical industry (Roche and Sandoz's "codeless scanning"), the machine-building firm Sulzer ("Sulis"), and the International Labor Office in Geneva ("Isis").

To date, only three of the great public research libraries have put into effect their plans for automation. At the BCU in Lausanne, the system "Sibil" is applied to cataloging, to the lending department, and to the utilization of "intermarc tapes." On-line access to the catalogs is planned for the 1980s. The ETH Library in Zürich has adopted automation in cataloging, periodicals, and lending. Its microfiche catalogs will soon be replaced by direct interrogation of the screen, and the electronic documentation and information system "Edis" will permit future literature searching by on-line access, even for orders placed by libraries in other cities. The Zentralbibliothek in Zürich uses electronic data processing for acquisitions and for publication of periodical acquisition and accession lists, which renders possible better coordination of acquisition policy within the university community. Further automation projects have been developed for the faculty library of bioscience and earth sciences at the University of Berne and for the University Library in Basel.

The reserve of the great general research libraries toward these advanced technologies is not surprising, considering that there is still no provision in Switzerland for a university education or special high school training in information science or librarianship. What is still needed are academically trained staff members familiar with modern library techniques. A suitable college curriculum for them does not yet exist. For the nonacademic librarian with a diploma from the Association of Swiss Librarians or the Ecole bibliothécaire de Genève, study programs and practical training must be oriented more toward modern techniques, especially automation.

As to library construction in Switzerland, there were two buildings which were regarded as models of library architecture in Europe before World War II: the Zentralbibliothek in Zürich, dating from 1917, and the Swiss National Library, dating from 1930. Switzerland having been spared in World War II, several new library buildings have been erected since then (the BC Lugano, the ZB Lucerne, the KB Aarau, and the ZB Solothurn), and others have been enlarged or renovated (the UB Basle, the Stadt- und UB Berne, and the ETH Library in Zürich)—but all of them follow conventional lines. Only the BCU in Lausanne and the Bibliothèque de l'Ecole polytechnique fédérale in Lausanne have been provided with totally modern buildings, mostly because of their relocation to the outskirts of the city. Many libraries, particularly the Zentralbibliothek in Zürich and the Swiss National Library (both situated in the center of the city), suffer from lack of space. Portions of the bookstocks of these two libraries have been transferred to the suburbs.

The main objects of Swiss librarianship for the last decades of our century would have to be, we feel, to bring about a better balance in the national supply of basic educational literature; to advance the availability and purchase of relevant scientific literature for research, education, business, and administration (the general research libraries and the special libraries will have to cooperate in concerted efforts toward this aim); to improve (particularly to accelerate) the exchange of publications by means of technical devices; and above all, to provide efficient training of information specialists and librarians, and also a user education program that should begin at the earliest possible age. Besides, many Swiss librarians are convinced that after the present stage of national planning and national collaboration, an international collaboration (i.e., a worldwide division of labor) will gain in significance. A start has been made in this respect with the treatment of information materials according to subject matter; international cooperation in acquiring and collecting information will follow, but accessibility will always play a major role. The basis for a satisfactory utilization of these resources can only be the willingness to place one's own stock of information unselfishly and unrestrictedly at the disposal of the interested partner.

BIBLIOGRAPHY

Alliance culturelle romande, *La lecture et les cités du livre*, Cahier No. 20, November 1974, Chêne-Bourg/Geneva, 1974.

Archive, Bibliotheken und Dokumentationsstellen der Schweiz, Amt für Wissenschaft und Forschung, Führer durch die schweizerische Dokumentation, 4th ed., Eidg. Drucksachen- und Materialzentrale, Bern, 1976.

Beck, Marcel, "Die schweizerischen Bibliotheken: Eine historische Skizze," *Atlantis*, **18,** 153–156 (1946).

Bibliotheken in der Schweiz—Bibliothèques en Suisse—Biblioteche in Svizzera—Bibliotecas in Svizra, Vereinigung Schweizerischer Bibliothekare, Bern, 1976.

Buser, Hermann, "Das Büchereiwesen in der Schweiz," in *Handbuch des Büchereiwesens*, Hrsg. von Johannes Langfeldt, 2nd Halbband, Otto Harrassowitz, Wiesbaden, 1965, pp. 757–767.

Les Fiches professionnelles romandes, *Bibliothécaire*, Grop/Asosp, Lausanne, 1977.

Fünfzig Jahre Schweizerische Landesbibliothek 1895–1945, Bern, 1945.

Leitfaden des interbibliothekarischen Leihverkehrs—Guide du prêt interbibliothèques, 1979, Schweizerischer Gesamtkatalog, Bern, 1979.

Nachrichten—Nouvelles—Notizie VSB/SVD, Vereinigung Schweizerischer Bibliothekare, 1925– (6 times a year).

Rapport final de la Commission d'experts chargée des questions de documentation scientifique, Zürich and Bern, 1972.

Schweizerische Bibliotheken—Bibliothèques Suisses (for 1950), Eidgenössisches Statistisches Amt, Bern, 1951 (annual).

FRANZ GEORG MAIER
Translated from the German by Elisabeth Hess

UNITED STATES AND CANADIAN NATIONAL BIBLIOGRAPHY: FOREIGN LANGUAGES

This article deals with the sources for the study of non-English-language imprints of the United States and the non-English- and non-French-language imprints of Canada.

It must be noted that in the case of the United States, foreign-language, or non-English-language, imprints do not appear in what might be considered the nation's national bibliography. Thus, the *Cumulative Book Index* lists only material published in English; *Books in Print* is compiled from data taken from publishers, the majority of whose works are in English. The *Canadian National Bibliography* lists all publications regardless of language that were published in Canada during the period covered.

This article draws a distinction between non-English imprints and ethnic publications, and thus does not deal in any way with groups who use English as their chief means of communication. No mention is made, therefore, of books, newspapers, and serials produced by Blacks, Irish (unless they are in Gaelic), American Indians, etc., if they are in English.

The focus of this article, then, is on a linguistic rather than a geographical or cultural distinction.

Up to this point, it appears that no one has tried to provide an overall discussion of materials that exist for the study of this type of U.S. and Canadian imprints.

The most obvious methods for the study of this type of imprint do not seem to function in this case. For example, with the existence of G. Thomas Tanselle, *Guide to the Study of U.S. Imprints* (Harvard University Press, Cambridge, Mass., 1971, 2 vols.), one would assume that there would be no need for such a study. Yet a thorough study of the Tanselle bibliography, excellent though it is, shows the omission of numerous books and articles published in periodicals and newspapers. For the study of newspapers and serials, one would have the expectation that bibliographies of United States journalism would consider the non-English press as part of the United States journalism scene and would include references to it. The standard journalism bibliographies are woefully lacking in dealing with the non-English-language press. Indeed, of those examined, only Carl L. Cannon, *Journalism: A Bibliography* (New York Public Library, 1924; reprinted Gale Research Co., Detroit, 1967) had a section dealing with it (pp. 94–99).

Many useful bibliographic references are found in "Ethnic Newspapers in the United States," an unpublished paper by Rosanne Singer, presented to the Minorities and Communication Division of the Association for Education in Journalism annual convention (Seattle, Wash., August 1978).

In the period since World War II more and more studies have appeared concerning cultural diversity in the United States and Canada, and when individuals write of the contributions of the Swedes, Spanish, Germans, etc., to the cultural development of these two countries, references are given to what members of these groups have published. Studies and publications of these different cultural groups have often resulted in them being the chief source for the study of their imprints. It has also been discovered that certain college and university libraries were founded by immigrant groups and have developed highly specialized collections of the publications of such groups. The Augustana College Library collection of Swedish-American material comes to mind. These libraries have sometimes published catalogs or lists of their holdings. This has been especially true in the case of newspapers held in such collections.

One can only express a certain dismay over the fact that the Library of Congress apparently has never had a method for collecting such material if it was never copyrighted. For countless imprints of the non-English-language press, no copies have survived.

The arrangement of the material in this article is a simple one. After a section that lists works that deal with more than one language, material is then arranged alphabetically by language. Within each language there is first a listing of sources for the study of books in this language, then a listing of sources for the study of newspapers and periodicals in this language; material may also be subdivided by state or province. Each language section concludes with sources for the study of this language's imprints in Canada. As French is one of Canada's two national languages, it is not dealt with under the section that deals with the French language. Material on the history of the non-English-language press is sometimes also included.

Multilanguage Sources

James Constantine Pilling compiled numerous bibliographies of the American Indian languages during the 1880s and 1890s. These were published by the U.S. Government Printing Office as bulletins of the Bureau of Ethnology. He listed material in about 300 Indian languages. Most of the publications in these languages were religious in nature and were, usually, the work of missionaries rather than works by the Indians. These bibliographies are: *Bibliography of the Eskimo Language* (1887, v, 116 pp., Bull. No. 1), which includes material in and on the Eskimo languages of Alaska, Canada, and Greenland; *Bibliography of the Siouxan Languages* (1887, v, 87 pp., Bull. No. 5); *Bibliography of the Iroquoian Languages* (1888, vi, 208 pp., Bull. No. 6); *Bibliography of the Athapascan Languages* (1892, xii, 125 pp., Bull. No. 14); *Bibliography of the Chinookan Languages* (including the Chinook jargon) (1893, xiii, 81 pp., Bull. No. 15); *Bibliography of the Salishan Languages* (1893, xi, 86 pp., Bull. No. 16); *Bibliography of the Wakashan Languages* (1894, x, 70 pp., Bull. No. 19); *Bibliography of the Algonquian Languages* (1891, x, 614 pp., Bull. No. 13); and *Bibliography of the Muskhogian Languages* (1889, v, 114 pp., Bull. No. 9).

Material published in the Indian languages of Arizona and New Mexico would seem to be almost all of a religious nature and the product of missionaries. James H. Fraser, "Indian Mission Printing in Arizona: An Historical Sketch and Bibliography," in *Journal of Arizona History* (Vol. 10, 1969, pp. 67–102), and his "Indian Mission Printing in New Mexico: A Bibliography," in *New Mexico Historical Review* (Vol. 43, October 1968, pp. 311–318), would appear to be the discussion of this subject. The first article lists material in Apache (8 items), Cocopa (1), Hopi (13), Navajo (32), Pai (1), and Pima (6). The second article lists 17 items in Keresan, Tewa, and Zuni.

Jane McGary's fascinating *Bibliography of Educational Publications for Alaska Native Languages* (2nd ed., under the sponsorship of the Alaska State Department of Education, bilingual-bicultural program, Juneau, Alaska, 1979, vi, 168 pp.; 1st ed., 1978, vi, 145 pp.) provides data on educational publications in Tlingit, Haida, Tsimshian, Ahtna Athabaskan, Han Athabaskan, Holikachuk Athabaskan, Ingalik Athabaskan, Koyukon Athabaskan, Kutchin Athabaskan, Tanacross Athabaskan, Tanaina Athabaskan, Tanana Athabaskan, Upper Kuskokwim Athabaskan,

Upper Tanana Athabaskan, and the following Eskimo Aleut languages: Aleut, Alutiiq, Central Yupik Eskimo, Siberian Yupik Eskimo, Inupiaq Eskimo, and Inupiaq. Pages 150–168 are a "1979 Supplement." The bibliography for each language is usually divided into general, reference, and educational materials.

The introduction by Michael Krauss notes that religious works in various Alaskan languages had been published between 1834 and 1904, but that from 1910 through 1960, "there was a tragic period in the Alaska schools of neglect and suppression of Native Languages, during which virtually no more books were printed in any of them, as education was imposed strictly in English, in the name of assimilation" (p. 1).

Phyllis J. Kimura Hayashibara, "A Guide to Bilingual Instructional Materials for Speakers of Asian and Pacific Island Languages," in *Amerasia Journal* (Vol. 5, 1978, pp. 101–114), is an excellent annotated bibliography of bibliographies of bilingual instructional materials. Of special interest is the "selected bibliography of bilingual instructional materials for Asian and Pacific Island languages [which] has been assembled by the author. It is confined to 494 titles which had been available in the U.S. since no earlier than 1970" (p. 107). This bibliography is described in pages 107–108 and lists material in Cambodian, Chamorro, Chinese, Japanese, Korean, Laotian, Samoan, Tagalog, Thai, and Vietnamese. The bibliography, rather than the guide, provides such data as "source, author, grade level applicability, language content, and media type (e.g., book, film, cassette)" (p. 111). "Selected sources" (pp. 111–114) gives addresses of organizations that have produced bilingual material in Asian and Pacific languages.

Slavic-American Imprints, subtitled A Classified Catalog of the Collection at Lovejoy Library, Southern Illinois University at Edwardsville (edited by Stanley B. Kimball, cataloged by Rudolph Wierer and Milton Moore, Bibliographic Contributions No. 7, The Libraries, Southern Illinois University, Carbondale and Edwardsville, 242 pp.) is a bibliography of this library's holdings in Czech (pp. 1–103), Bulgaro-Macedonian (pp. 104–110), Croat (pp. 111–116), Slovak (pp. 117–147), Polish (pp. 148–189), Russian (pp. 190–191), Serbian (pp. 192–194), Slovene (pp. 195–213), and Ukrainian (pp. 214–117), as well as the following non-Slavic languages: Hungarian (pp. 226–228), Romanian (p. 229), and Lithuanian (pp. 230–232). Listed are 1,867 items (books, periodicals, newspapers, almanacs). Supplement I, by the same editor and catalogers, appeared in 1979. It was issued by the Southern Illinois University at Edwardsville.

The Immigration History Research Center of the University of Minnesota has issued *The Baltic American Collection* (Estonian, Latvian, and Lithuanian; IHRC Ethnic Collections Series No. 1, compiled by Joseph D. Dwyer, 1976, 10 pp.) and *South Slavic American Collections* (Croatian, Macedonian, Serbian, and Slovenian, 2nd ed., IHRC Ethnic Collections Series No. 8, compiled by Joseph D. Dwyer, revised by Lynn Schweitzer Toscano, 1979, 16 pp.). Both describe the center's collection of books, manuscripts, and newspapers of the area covered.

The Church of the Latter-Day Saints has published a large number of works in foreign languages which have been used in their attempts to explain the tenets of their faith. Chad J. Flake has edited *A Mormon Bibliography: 1830–1930* (University of Utah Press, Salt Lake City, 1978, xxxi, 825 pp.). The arrangement is alphabetical by author and the only index is a chronological one. A survey of the first 2,000 items reveals publications issued in the United States and Hawaii in the following languages: Danish (items 96, 546, 1751–1752), Hawaiian (items 728–730, 1941, 1989–1991), Italian (item 732), Maori (item 113), Samoan (items 500–501, 736, 1137, 1850–1851), Spanish (items 737–741, 1853), Swedish (items 452, 517, 1274), Tahitian (items 744–745), and Tongan (item 1870).

John Miska has compiled *A Bibliography of Ethnic and Native Canadian Literature 1850–1979*, subtitled A Bibliography of Primary and Secondary Materials (Microform Biblios, Lethbridge, Alberta, 1980, 7 microfiches). According to page i, "Authors of ethnic Canadian literature are considered to be persons who have published collections of poetry, fiction, or drama, in any language, whose mother tongues are other than English or French, and who have spent their formative years in Canada or settled in this country as adults." It has the following ethnic divisions: Austrian, Bulgarian, Byelorussian, Ceylonese, Chilean, Croatian, Czech, Danish, East Indian, Estonian, Finnish, Gaelic, German, Haitian, Hungarian, Icelandic, Iraqi, Italian, North American Indian, Inuit, Jewish, Latvian, Lithuanian, Norwegian, Pakistani, Polish, Serbian, Slovak, Spanish, Swedish, and Ukranian. It contains 2,968 entries. There are author and chronological indexes as well as a list of periodicals and their abbreviations. Each ethnic group's section begins with bibliographies concerning this group's imprints, literature, and periodicals. Many of the Canadian references in this article have been taken from this extraordinarily useful bibliography.

The earliest attempt at compiling a list of United States newspapers would seem to be that of Isaiah Thomas, *The History of Printing in America and an Account of Newspapers* (from the press of Isaiah Thomas, Worcester, Mass., 1810; 2nd ed., J. Munsell, Albany, N.Y., 1874; 2nd ed. reprinted Burt Franklin, New York, 1964, 2 vols.). Volume 2 (pp. 294–302) contains an appendix entitled "List of Newspapers, Published in the Colonies, Now the United States, at the Commencement of the Revolutionary War, in 1775, and Those Published at the Beginning of the Year 1810." This appendix lists titles in German, Spanish, and French.

This was followed by Daniel Hewett's "List of Newspapers and Periodicals in the United States in 1828," which was first published in *The Traveller and Monthly Gazetteer* for June 1828; it was reprinted with an introduction by Clarence S. Bingham (introduction signed C.S.B.) in the *Proceedings of the American Antiquarian Society* (n.s., Vol. 44, 1934, pp. 365–396). Bingham has provided indexes to this list, which provides data on papers in German, French, and Cherokee.

J. C. G. Kennedy compiled "Catalogue of the Newspapers and Periodicals Published in the United States," which was published in *Livingston's Law Register* for 1852 (56 pp. at the end of the volume).

In 1861 there appeared Daniel J. Kenny, *The American Newspaper Directory and Record of the Press*. Subtitled Containing an Accurate List of All the Newspapers, Magazines, Reviews, Periodicals, etc., in the United States and British Provinces of North America, it includes material in French, German, Italian, Spanish, and Welsh (Watson, New York, 123 pp.).

The Annotated and Enlarged Edition of Ernst Steiger's Precentennial Bibliography: The Periodical Literature of the United States of America, by Karl J. R. Arndt

(Kraus International Publications, Millwood, N.Y., 1979, 228 pp.) lists newspapers published in the 1870s in the United States in Cherokee, Chinese, Czech, Danish–Norwegian, Dutch, French, German, Italian, Pennsylvania Dutch, Polish, Portuguese, Russian, Spanish, Swedish, and Welsh. These languages are indexed in "A List of Periodicals Printed Wholly or in Part in Languages Other Than English" (pp. 184–185).

This bibliography provides data on 8,081 newspapers, and the Arndt edition of this work originally published by Steiger in 1873 provides a variety of annotations on numerous entries. Arndt describes Steiger's work in his Introduction as "the earliest, complete bibliography of American periodical literature as it existed in the 1870's."

Simon Newton Dexter North, *History and Press Condition of the Newspaper and Periodical Press of the United States, with a Catalog of the Census Year* (Government Printing Office, Washington, 1884, 446 pp.; U.S. Census Office, 10th Census, Vol. 8) discusses German-American newspapers (pp. 126–128), the French-American press (pp. 128–129), the Welsh-American press (pp. 129–130), and the American press in other languages (pp. 130–131). Table IX (p. 184) is "Statistics of Newspapers and Periodicals Published in Foreign Languages, Other Than German, in the United States." "Appendix B, Catalogue of Periodical Publications" (pp. 199–355) includes data on non-English-language periodicals.

George P. Rowell, *The American Newspaper Directory* (1869–1908) was absorbed in 1910 by *N. W. Ayer and Son's Directory of Newspapers and Periodicals* (1880–). The majority of the annuals published by N. W. Ayer contain a list of non-English-language newspapers and journals arranged by language. Scholars in this field have noted publications omitted from this compilation and items that have been poorly classified. It does provide data that can probably be used for comparative purposes. As it covers a century, one can in a relative way trace numerically the rise and fall of the non-English-language press.

Wayne Charles Miller (with Faye Nell Vowell et al.), *A Comprehensive Bibliography for the Study of American Minorities* (i.e., ethnic) (New York University Press, New York, 1976, 2 vols.) provides a brief bibliography that deals with the history and lists the newspapers and periodicals of the following groups: Blacks, Arabs, French, Germans, Spanish, Portuguese, Spanish-Americans, Italians, Jews, Greeks, Swedes, Norwegians, Danes, Icelanders, Finns, Poles, Czechs, Slovaks, Yugoslavs, Slovenians, Croatians, Serbians, Bulgaro-Macedonians, Ukrainians, Russians, Romanians, Lithuanians, Latvians, Albanians, Hungarians, Chinese, Japanese, Filipinos, Puerto Ricans, Cubans, American Indians, and the Mexican-Americans in the United States. Though the title speaks of this being a comprehensive bibliography, if the section on periodicals can be judged as representative, then it is best described as a selective bibliography, for much is omitted, especially material in non-English languages.

Lybomy R. and Anna T. Wynar, *Encyclopedic Directory of Ethnic Newspapers and Periodicals in the United States* (2nd ed., Libraries Unlimited, Littleton, Colo., 1976, 248 pp.) provides current data on the Albanian, Arabic, Armenian, Assyrian, Basque, Bulgarian, Byelorussian, Carpatho-Ruthenian, Chinese, Cossack, Croatian, Czech, Danish, Dutch, Estonian, Filipino, Finnish, French, Georgian,

German, Greek, Hebrew and Yiddish, Hungarian, Iranian, Italian, Japanese, Korean, Latvian, Lithuanian, Norwegian, Polish, Portuguese, Romanian, Swedish, Serbian, Slovak, Slovene, Spanish, Turkish, Ukrainian, and Welsh press in the United States.

"The Ethnic Press: Many Voices," in *Spectrum* (Vol. 3, No. 2, March 1980, pp. 1–12), describes some of the holdings of the Immigration History Research Center under the following sections: Czech and Slovak (pp. 2–4), Finnish (pp. 4–5), Italian (pp. 5–7), Polish (pp. 8–10), South Slavic (pp. 10–11), and Ukrainian (pp. 11–12).

Stefan R. Rodney, "Foreign Language Papers Fire the U.S. Melting Pot," in *Editor and Publisher* (Vol. 92, No. 33, August 15, 1959, pp. 15, 60–62), contains a table, "Circulation of Foreign-Language Daily Newspapers in United States," which is arranged by language and provides data on title, city, and circulation.

Spyridon Granitsas, "Ethnic Press Alive & Well: 440 Published in the United States," in *Editor and Publisher* (Vol. 103, No. 48, November 28, 1970, pp. 12, 23), is the introduction to a six-part series on the ethnic press in the United States.

Neva S. Ledhe-White, Sharon M. Murphy, and James E. Murphy, *Directory of American Indian Print and Broadcast Media* (1978, 29 pp.; available from Native American Student Movement, University of Wisconsin–Milwaukee, Box 67, Milwaukee, Wis.) provides data on title, address, and frequency of publication of more than 400 newspapers and magazines in 39 states as well as over 100 radio and television stations in 23 states. Some of the Alaskan publications probably contain sections in one of the native languages. Otherwise, most of these papers are in English.

James E. and Sharon M. Murphy, *Let My People Know: American Indian Journalism, 1828–1978* (University of Oklahoma Press, Norman, 1981, xxi, 230 pp.) is the fullest and most up-to-date history of American Indian journalism yet published. Its bibliography (pp. 215–222) should be carefully examined by all interested in this topic. Pages 177–194 are Appendix C: American Indian Media—A Directory, Newspapers and Magazines. One would assume that most of these publications are in English as there are no indications that any are bilingual or entirely in the Indian language.

Maureen E. Hady and James P. Danky have compiled *Asian American Periodicals and Newspapers*, subtitled A Union List of Holdings in the Library of the State Historical Society of Wisconsin, and the Libraries of the University of Wisconsin–Madison (State Historical Society of Wisconsin, Madison, 1979, 53 pp.), which provides data on 104 periodicals and newspapers published in the United States in Chinese, Japanese, Korean, Vietnamese, Laotian, Cambodian, Urdu, and Filipino as well as English. It has the following indexes: geographic, name, subject, and chronological.

David H. Crowe, Jr., "The Contemporary Baltic Press in the Non-Soviet World," in *Lituanus* (Vol. 24, No. 2, 1978, pp. 57–61), is useful for its discussion of Estonian, Latvian, and Lithuanian periodicals published not only in the United States and Canada but also in Europe, Australia, and Latin America.

Ethnic Serials: At Selected University of California Libraries (Asian American Studies Center, University of California, Los Angeles, 1977, 368 pp.) is described as "a union list compiled by the ethnic material librarians from most of the campuses of the University of California. Includes over 1,800 periodicals from Afro-American, American Indian, Asian American, and Chicano Studies collections." Many of the Chicano journals are either in Spanish or in Spanish and English.

Neil E. Strache and James P. Danky have compiled *Hispanic Americans in the United States*, subtitled A Union List of Periodicals and Newspapers Held by the Library of the State Historical Society of Wisconsin and the Libraries of the University of Wisconsin–Madison (State Historical Society of Wisconsin, Madison, 1979, 76 pp.), which provides data on 129 titles in Spanish, English, and Portuguese. It has the following indexes: geographic, name, subject, and chronological.

In 1937 the H. W. Wilson Company published Winifred Gregory, *American Newspapers, 1821–1936* (xvi, 791 pp.). This union list gives titles and locations for newspapers published in the United States regardless of language. It is arranged by state, then alphabetically by title within the city of publication. An index of titles by language would have been most helpful to the student of the non-English-language press.

Since 1937 there have been published several union lists of the newspapers of individual states. Among these are: *Louisiana Newspapers 1794–1961*, edited by T. N. McMullan (Louisiana State University Library, Baton Rouge, 1965, x, 281 pp.); *Guide to Ohio Newspapers 1793–1973*, subtitled Union Bibliography of Ohio Newspapers Available in Ohio Libraries, edited by Stephen Gutgesell (Ohio Historical Society, Columbus, 1974, 412 pp.); *Guide to Colorado Newspapers 1858–1963*, compiled by Donald E. Oehlerts (Bibliographical Center for Research, Rocky Mountain Region, Inc., Denver, 1964, 184 pp.); and *New Mexico Newspapers . . .*, edited by Pearce S. Grove, Becky J. Barnett, and Sandra S. Hanson . . . (University of New Mexico Press, Albuquerque . . . , 1975, 641 pp.).

A study of the Louisiana compilation (there is no index by language) reveals that it lists newspapers in German, French, and Spanish published in this state.

The Ohio list contains a language index which shows that it lists newspapers published in Czech, German, Hungarian, Italian, Lithuanian, Polish, Serbian, and Slovenian.

Oehlerts's volume is arranged by county, then alphabetically by title within each city. There is a title index. It provides data on 105 papers in German, Spanish, Italian, Swedish, Japanese, Slovenian, and Serbian.

New Mexico Newspapers has the same arrangement as the Colorado volume. It has three indexes and lists newspapers in Spanish and Italian.

Bibliographies exist of the press, including that in foreign languages, of several cities of the United States.

For the press of Buffalo, New York, one should consult Fr. H. Severance, *Periodical Press in Buffalo* (Historical Society, Buffalo, 1915, 392 pp.).

For Chicago, there should be consulted the Chicago Public Library Omnibus Project—apparently a subdivision of the Federal Works Agency, Works Projects Administration—which issued in Chicago in 1942 *Bibliography of Foreign Language Newspapers and Periodicals Published in Chicago* (150 leaves) and *The Chicago Foreign Language Press Survey*, subtitled A General Description of Its Contents (20 leaves).

Alex Ladenson, in the Preface to the latter, states that "In listing the publication the attempt was made to include the following information: title, translation of title, frequency of issue, type of publication (newspaper or periodical), editorial policy, date of establishment, date of expiration, name of editor, name and address of publisher, and library location symbols designating holdings." Material is listed in the following languages: Albanian, Arabic, Bulgarian, Chinese, Croatian, Czech, Danish, Dutch, Finnish, French, German, Greek, Hebrew, Hindustani, Hungarian, Italian, Lettish, Lithuanian, Norwegian, Persian, Polish, Romanian, Russian, Slovak, Serbian, Slovenian, Spanish, Swedish, Syriac, Ukrainian, and Yiddish.

The *Survey* describes the contents of the 100,000 pages of translation from the Chicago foreign-language press and lists the papers from which the translations were made.

Michael J. O'Malley, "Foreign Language Newspapers of Chicago," in *Chamberlin's* (May 1916, pp. 27–28), notes the publication of 169 newspapers in Albanian, Assyrian, Bohemian, Bulgarian, Croatian, Danish, Dutch, French, German, Greek, Hebrew, Hungarian, Italian, Japanese, Lithuanian, Norwegian, Persian, Polish, Romanian, Russian, Serbian, Slovenian, and Swedish. They are then divided into daily, semiweekly, weekly, biweekly, semimonthly, monthly, bimonthly, and quarterly.

The *History of Foreign Journalism in San Francisco*, supervised by Emerson Daggett (WPA Project 10008, O.P. 665-08-3-12; San Francisco, March 15, 1939, iv, 95 leaves) provides data on French, Italian, Swiss, German, Jewish, Hindustani (according to p. 40, *The Hindustan Gadar* "printed editions in Punjabi, Urdu, Gujarati, Afghan, and Gurkha"), Japanese, Korean, Chinese, Spanish, Portuguese, Scandinavian, Slavonian, Russian, Hungarian, Greek, and Croatian newspapers. The introduction notes that "the present study is limited to a survey of the founding, merger, suspension and resumption date of the city's foreign language press, with circulation records wherever available" (p. i).

Dirk Hoerder, "Bibliography and Archival Preservation of Non-English Language Labor and Radical Newspapers and Periodicals in North America, 1845 to 1976," in *International Labor and Working Class History* (Vol. 16, Fall 1979, pp. 46–50), and *Immigration History Newsletter* (Vol. 13, No. 1, May 1981, pp. 11–12), is an outline for the development of this project of compiling a bibliography of and preserving non-English-language labor and radical serials published in North America.

James H. Fraser presents interesting data on "Foreign Language Publishing for Children in the United States: A Comment on Yiddish, Estonian, Ukrainian, and Armenian Materials," in *Society & Children's Literature*, edited by James H. Fraser (David R. Godine, publisher, in association with the American Library Association, 1978, pp. 77–92).

Those interested in works published in the native languages of Canada should consult Joyce M. Banks, *Books in Native Languages in the Collection of the Rare Books and Manuscripts Division of the National Library of Canada* (National Library of Canada, Ottawa, 1980, xiii, 93 pp.).

Several issues of *Polyphony*, the Bulletin of the Multicultural History Society of Ontario, have been examined and in them are found the following articles of interest: "Church Records and Publications," which is divided into "Church Almanacs and Parish Jubilee Volumes" (Vol. 1, No. 2, Summer 1978, pp. 11–18) and "Pamphlets from St. Vladimir's Ukrainian Greek Orthodox Cathedral" (Vol. 1, No. 2, Summer 1978, pp. 18–20); and "The Religious Press in Ethnic Communities." The latter has the following divisions: Jung-Gun Kim, "The Toronto Korean United Church and the Toronto Korean Presbyterian Church" (Vol. 1 No. 2, Summer 1978, pp. 37–38), Benedykt Heydenkorn, "Gazeta Katolicka" (ibid., pp. 38–39), Eleoussa Polyzoi, "The St. George Greek Orthodox Church in Toronto: Early Parish Publications" (ibid., p. 40), and Mark Boekelman, "Pioneer: Christian Monthly—An Immigrant Journal" (ibid, pp. 41–42), which deals with a publication that was begun in Dutch, *Wally Mraz* (see "The Ethnic Press," Vol. 2, No. 1, Winter 1978, p. 78).

Duncan McLaren is the compiler of *Ontario Ethno-Cultural Newspapers 1835–1972: An Annotated Checklist* (University of Toronto Press, Toronto, 1973, 234 pp.), which provides data on newspapers published in Ontario in Armenian, Byelorussian, Bulgarian, Chinese, Croatian, Czech, Danish, Dutch, East Indian, Eskimo, Estonian, Filipino, Finnish, German, Greek, Hungarian, Italian, Japanese, Korean, Latvian, Lithuanian, Macedonian, Maltese, Norwegian, Polish, Portuguese, Romanian, Russian, Serbian, Slovak, Slovenian, Spanish, Swedish, Ukranian, and Yugoslav.

In 1981 the National Library of Canada's Newspaper Division, Public Services Branch issued *Checklist of Canadian Ethnic Serials* (viii, 381 pp.). It was compiled by Ruth Bogusis and edited by Liba Blazek under the editorial direction of Sabine Sonnemann: ". . . it contains approximately 3,000 entries of newspapers, periodicals, church bulletins, directories, almanacs, yearbook and conference proceedings of about 60 cultural groups. Embassy periodicals, commercial publications and political publications are not included. Neither are Inuit and Indian publications a part of this list" (p. vi).

This union list includes publications in the following languages: Arabic, Armenian, Bulgarian, Byelorussian, Chinese, Croatian, Czech, Danish, Dutch, Estonian, Farsi, Finnish, Flemish, German, Greek, Hebrew, Hungarian, Icelandic, Italian, Japanese, Korean, Latvian, Lithuanian, Macedonian, Maltese, Norwegian, Polish, Portuguese, Romanian, Russian, Serbian, Slovak, Slovenian, Spanish, Swedish, Talagok, Ukrainian, Vietnamese, and Yiddish. Pages 377–381 are a list of sources consulted.

Stephen J. Jaworsky, "Newspapers and Periodicals of Slavic Groups in Canada (during the period of 1965–1969)" (M.A. thesis in Slavic Studies, University of Ottawa, 1971, ix, 123 leaves), describes 74 Canadian newspapers and periodicals published in Bulgarian, Byelorussian, Croatian, Czech, Macedonian, Polish, Russian, Serbian, Slovak, Slovenian, Ukrainian, and Yugoslav. It also discusses 37 serials published abroad and circulated in Canada.

Single-Language Sources

ARABIC

George Dimitri Selim, *Arab-World Newspapers in the Library of Congress* (Near East Series, Library of Congress, Washington, D.C., 1980) provides data on Arabic-language newspapers published in Brazil (p. 4) and Venezuela (p. 35) which exist, usually in a sample copy, in the Library of Congress.

Spyridon Granitsas, "Arab Papers Believe in Freedom of Press," in *Editor and Publisher* (Vol. 103, No. 50, December 12, 1970, pp. 18, 20), provides a list of Arab newspapers which were then published. The majority are in Arabic; a few are in English.

Vivian Doche, *Cedars by the Mississippi* (R & E Research Association, San Francisco 1978, pp. 27, 35) provides brief data on the Arabic-American press.

Beverlee Turner Mehedi, compiler and editor, "Table 4: The Press of the American Arabic-Speaking Community," in *Arabs in America 1492–1977: A Chronology and Fact Book* (Oceana Publications, Dobbs Ferry, N.Y., 1978, pp. 140–142) includes Canadian newspapers as well as radio stations that broadcast in Arabic in the United States.

ARMENIAN

The Armenian newspapers of California are discussed in Charles Mahakian, *History of the Armenians in California* (R. & E. Research Associates, Los Angeles, 1974, pp. 70–73, 79–80). He notes that "most of them have been and are organs of Armenian organizations or parties, because the publication of a newspaper as a business venture among comparatively few people is a difficult, if not, an impossible task" (p. 70). This is a reprint of Mahakian's 1935 thesis.

Spyridon Granitsas, "Press Is a Vital Force in Armenians' Identity," in *Editor and Publisher* (Vol. 104, No. 1, January 2, 1971, p. 28), provides a list of Armenian newspapers by state.

J. H. Fraser discusses "Armenian Language Maintenance in the United States and Literature for Children," in *Phaedrus* (Vol. 6, No. 1, 1979, pp. 79–81).

Edward Gulbekian has edited the *Armenian Press Directory* (Harq Publications, London, 1st ed., 1967; 2nd ed., 1971). The first edition had 286 titles, while the second (74 pp.) provides data on "some 400 titles." "Alphabetical List I of Newspapers, Periodicals and Journals Published in Armenia and by the Armenian Communities Abroad" (pp. 7–47) and "Alphabetical List II of Annual and Less Frequent Periodicals Published in Armenia and by the Armenian Communities Abroad" (pp. 48–58) are followed by a classified index, a bibliography, and a list with addresses of Armenian publishers. Unfortunately, there is no geographical index. Armenian publications of the Western Hemisphere are included. The bibliography of material on the Armenian press should be of special interest to those who read this language.

BASQUE

Basque-language publications have been little studied. William A. Douglass and Jon Bilbao, "Literature and Communication," in *Amerikanuak: Basques in the New World* (University of Nevada Press, Reno, Nevada, 1975, pp. 367–370) would seem to be the fullest general discussion of Basque newspapers in the United States. This volume contains other references to Basque newspapers scattered throughout the section that deals with the Basque in this country.

Jon Bilbao, "Publicaciones periódicas vascas aparecidas en América entre 1936–1946," in *Ikuska* (Sare) (Vol. 1, Nos. 4–5, 1947, p. 164), should also be consulted.

BULGARIAN

Little seems to exist concerning Bulgarian-American imprints. For Canadian imprints, see Marianne Raduloff, "Bulgarian-Canadian Periodical Publications: A Preliminary Check List," in *Canadian Ethnic Studies* (Vol. 2, 1970, pp. 1–3), where data are provided on 11 periodicals.

BYELORUSSIAN

Volume 2 (1970) of *Canadian Ethnic Studies* has published Alex A. Hrycuk and Alexander Malycky, "Byelorussian-Canadian Periodical Publications: A Preliminary Check List" (pp. 5–7), which lists a dozen titles; and Alex A. Hrycuk, "Byelorussian-Canadian Imprints, 1945–1970: A Preliminary Check List" (pp. 9–12), where 16 entries include "(1) Byelorussian language titles published on any subject in Canada, (2) titles published in any language by Canadians of Byelorussian origin, (3) titles dealing in any language with the Byelorussian-Canadians, (4) titles published in any language by Byelorussian-Canadian publishers and dealing with matters of concern to the Byelorussian-Canadians" (p. 9).

CHAMORRO

Apparently no bibliography exists of works in Chamorro, the language of the natives of Guam. The chief source for the study of Guamian material is the Micronesian Area Research Center on the University of Guam campus. Much of the material in Chamorro is religious in nature—translations of the Bible, hymns, and Bible stories for children. The Department of Education, Bilingual-Bicultural Program, Agana, Guam, has produced small-format elementary textbooks.

Jim Richstad and Michael McMillan, *Mass Communication and Journalism in the Pacific Islands: A Bibliography* (published for the East–West Center by the University Press of Hawaii, Honolulu, 1978) provides a list of newspapers and periodicals published on Guam (pp. 84–86). It identifies only one paper as being in both English and Chamorro.

CHEROKEE

The fullest treatment of the Cherokee press, whether Cherokee or Cherokee and English, is the University of Minnesota doctoral dissertation by Cullen Joe Holland, "The Cherokee Indian Newspapers, 1828–1906: The Tribal Voice of a People in Transition" (1956, iv, 606 leaves; *Diss. Abstr.*, Vol. 17, 1957, pp. 2592–2593).

George E. Foster, "Journalism among the Cherokee Indians," in *Magazine of American History* (Vol. 18, 1887, pp. 65–70), is a brief history of the press of the Cherokee Indians both in Georgia and in what is now the state of Oklahoma. This article is apparently one of the first in English to deal with this subject. The author's attitude is one of great admiration for the Indians and their accomplishments, especially Sequoyah's invention of the Cherokee syllabary.

For Oklahoma imprints in Cherokee, see Carolyn Thomas Foreman, *Oklahoma Imprints: 1835–1907* (University of Oklahoma Press, Norman, 1936), pages 5–21 and 27–39, and "Newspapers of the Cherokee Nation" (pp. 55–101). Most of the newspapers are in English.

Sam G. Riley, "The *Cherokee Phoenix:* The Short Unhappy Life of the First American Indian Newspaper," in *Journalism Quarterly* (Vol. 53, 1976, pp. 666–671), discusses the history of this paper, which first appeared on February 21, 1828, and whose last issue is dated May 31, 1834. Several footnotes present brief data on other 19th-century Indian papers.

CHICKASAW

For Oklahoma imprints in Chickasaw, see Carolyn Thomas Foreman, *Oklahoma Imprints: 1835–1907* (University of Oklahoma Press, Norman, 1936), pages 39–40.

CHINESE

Material on Chinese-American imprints other than newspapers has not been studied.

Karl Lo and H. M. Lai have compiled *Chinese Newspapers Published in North America, 1854–1975* (Bibliographical Series No. 16, Center for Chinese Research Materials, Association of Research Libraries, Washington, D.C., 1977, xiii, 138 pp.), which is valuable not only for its union list of Chinese newspapers, arranged alphabetically by city of publication, but for Lai's "A Short History of Chinese Journalism in the U.S. and Canada" (pp. 1–15) and its bibliography of references on this subject in both English and Chinese (pp. 137–138).

Lo and Lai call attention to Yuk Ow's unpublished manuscript in the Bancroft Library, "A Selected List of Published and Unpublished Materials Written by the California Chinese . . . ," (1960); Ednah Robinson, "Chinese Journalism in California," in *Outwest* (Vol. 16, No. 1, January 1902, pp. 33–42); and Louis J. Stellman, "Yellow Journals," in *Sunset* (Vol. 24, No. 2, February 1910, pp. 197–201). Lo is also the author of "Kim Shan Jit San Luk," in *Bulletin of the Chinese Histori-*

cal Society of America (Vol. 6, No. 8, October 1971, pp. [1–4]), which deals with the *Golden Hills News* (title translated from the Chinese), San Francisco's first commercial Chinese newspaper.

Lim P. Lee, "Chinese Journalism on the West Coast," in *Chinese Digest* (Vol. 2, No. 46, November 13, 1936, pp. 16–17), is divided into two parts. The first section of this article deals with the history of the Chinese press in San Francisco, while its second part discusses the *Chinese Digest*.

The following three M.A. theses deal with the Chinese press in the United States: Tung-chen Chin, "Chinese-Language Daily Newspapers in the United States" (Indiana University, 1949, 78 leaves); Shao-huang King, "A Study of the Chinese-Language Press and the Chinese Community in the United States" (Southern Illinois University, Carbondale, 1965, iv, 163 leaves); and James En-wei Wang, "Chinese Newspapers in the United States" (University of Missouri, 1968, 143 leaves).

The thesis by Tung-chen Chin devotes leaves 3–12 to "General Remarks and History." She states that of the "eleven Chinese dailies in this country, five are in New York, five in San Francisco, and one in Chicago" and discusses each briefly (leaf 3). She notes the paucity of material on this subject, and her bibliography includes the Works Progress Administration publication *Chinese Journalism in San Francisco* (WPA Project 10008, O.P. 665-08-3-12; San Francisco, 1939), and Carl Glick, "The Dragon Goes to Press," in *Coronet* (Vol. 12, No. 6, October 1942, pp. 79–83).

Chapter four of the King thesis is "Historical Sketches of Individual Newspapers." It discusses Chinese newspapers published in San Francisco, New York, Chicago, Los Angeles, and Hawaii.

Leaves 139–143 of the Wang thesis provide "A List of Present Chinese Newspapers in the United States."

He notes that the following have been written at the University of Missouri: Paul Po-chi Fung, "The Chinese Press in the United States" (M.A., 1925); James Cheng-Yee Shen, "Liang Chi-Chao and His Times" (Ph.D., 1953); and Paul H. C. Wang, "A Historical Study of the Chinese Press of 3,000 Years" (M.A., 1955).

Among Wang's sources are: "Chinese Newspapers," in *The Inland Printer* (Vol. 3, 1886, p. 738); "How News Is Furnished by the Press of Chinatown (ibid., Vol. 9, 1892, p. 968); Morrisson Pixley, "A Chinese Newspaper in America," in *World's Work* (Vol. 3, 1902, pp. 1951–1952); and Nat Wood, "The Chinatown Press: A Mysterious Revolution," in *The Quill* (Vol. 54, No. 8, August 1966, pp. 27–28).

Elliott S. Parker, *Chinese Newspapers in the United States: Background Notes and Descriptive Analysis* (ERIC Documentation Reproduction Service, Arlington, Va., 1978, ED 165 178, 31 pp.) is the text of a 1977 paper which provides data on the "background and current status of Chinese newspapers in the United States" (*ERIC*, Vol. 14, No. 6, June 1979, p. 7).

Andy McCue, "Evolving Chinese Language Dailies Serve Immigrants in New York City," in *Journalism Quarterly* (Vol. 52, 1975, pp. 272–276), notes that "the Chinese language press is experiencing a period of rebirth and change. Two newspapers have been started in the past year and a half, raising the number of Chinese dailies to seven" (p. 272).

Hawaiian-Chinese newspapers are briefly discussed in Lun Chock, "Chinese Newspapers in Hawaii," in *Pan Pacific* (Vol. 1, No. 3, 1937, pp. 54–55). Chock finds that the first Chinese newspaper was published in Hawaii in 1883 and that as of 1937 three Chinese papers were being published in Honolulu. Also of value is Yuan Su, "Chinese Newspapers in Hawaii," in *Overseas Chinese Affairs Monthly* (No. 84, June 30, 1959, pp. 11–12).

Pages 134–135 of Jim Richstad and Michael McMillan, *Mass Communication and Journalism in the Pacific Islands: A Bibliography* provide a listing of material in both English and Chinese that deals with the Chinese press in Hawaii. There are also several additional entries that deal with individual newspapers.

Canada. Julian L. Laychuk, "Chinese-Canadian Periodical Publications: A Preliminary Check List," in *Canadian Ethnic Studies* (Vol. 2, 1970, pp. 15–20), provides data on 20 periodicals.

CHOCTAW

For Oklahoma Choctaw imprints, see Carolyn Thomas Foreman, *Oklahoma Imprints, 1835–1907* (University of Oklahomas Press, Norman, 1936), pages 21–25 and 40–44; see also "Newspapers of the Choctaw Nation," pages 136–173 in the same work.

CREEK, OR MUSKOGEE

For Oklahoma Creek, or Muskogee, imprints, see Carolyn Thomas Foreman, *Oklahoma Imprints, 1835–1907* (University of Oklahoma Press, Norman, 1936), pages 1–3, 25–26, and 44–47. "Newspapers of the Creek Nation" appears on pages 174–223.

CROATIAN AND SERBIAN

George J. Prpic, *The Croatian Publications Abroad After 1939: A Bibliography* (The Author and the Institute for Soviet and East European Studies [of] John Carroll University, 1969, 66 pp.) should be useful for the study of Croatian publications of the United States and Canada.

Almost nothing would seem to exist concerning publications in these languages in the United States.

Nada (Kasterianek) Vujica, "Publication of Croatian Newspapers in the United States and Canada" (Marywood College, Dept. of Librarianship, Master's thesis, 1952, 39 leaves) has two parts of interest. They are: III. Croatian Newspapers, Magazines, and Calendars in the United States and Canada (leaves 11–14) and IV. Croatian Publications (leaves 15–35).

For Canada, see the following: Večéslav Holjevac, "Histori krvatskih iseljenika u Kanadi," in his *Hrvati izvan domovine* (Matica hrvatska, Zagreb, 1967, pp. 178–179; a slightly expanded edition with the same imprint appeared in 1968); Zelimir B. Juričić and Alexander Malycky, "Croatian-Canadian Periodical Publications: A Preliminary List," in *Canadian Ethnic Studies* (Vol. 2, 1970, pp. 21–25);

Juričić and Malycky, "Serbian-Canadian Periodical Publications: A Preliminary Check List," in *Canadian Ethnic Studies* (Vol. 2, 1970, pp. 187-189); Zelimir B. Juričić, "Croatian-Canadian Creative Literature: A Preliminary Check List," in *Canadian Ethnic Studies* (Vol. 5, 1973, pp. 27–29); Vladimir Markotić, "Croatian Imprints of Canada: A Preliminary Check List," in *Canadian Ethnic Studies* (Vol. 5, 1973, pp. 19–26); and Vladimir Markotić, compiler and editor, *Biographical Directory of Americans and Canadians of Croatian Descent with . . . and Periodicals* (4th rev. and enl. ed., Occasional Monographs No. 1, Research Centre for Canadian Ethnic Studies, Calgary, 1973, xiii, 204 pp.).

The first *Canadian Ethnic Studies* compilation provides data on 24 periodicals; the second, on 9 in Serbian, Croatian, Slovenian, Macedonian, and English.

Robert P. Gakovich and Milan M. Radovich compiled the quite useful *Serbs in the United States and Canada: A Comprehensive Bibliography* (IHRC Ethnic Bibliography No. 1, Immigration History Center, Minneapolis, 1976, xii, 129 pp.).

CZECH AND SLOVAK

The most important study of Czech and Slovak imprints is that of Esther Jerabek, *Czechs and Slovaks in North America: A Bibliography* (Czechoslovak Society of Arts and Sciences in America, New York, and Czechoslovak National Council of America, Chicago, 1976, 448 pp.). This is a classified bibliography of 7,609 items, the majority of which are in either Czech or Slovak. Of special interest are Bibliography of Journalism and the Press (pp. 113–116), Literature (pp. 128–169), and Periodicals and Newspapers (pp. 314–364).

Vojtěch N. Duben, *Czech and Slovak Press Outside Czechoslovakia: Its Status in 1978*, with Preface by Rudolf Sturm (SVU Publications, Occasional Paper No. 4, Czechoslovak Society of Arts and Sciences in America, Washington, D.C., 1978, 62 pp.) is the latest revision of Duben's *Czech and Slovak Press Outside Czechoslovakia: Its History and Status as of January 1962* (SVU, Washington, D.C., 1962; revised editions published in 1964 and 1968). This work includes the following parts: "Czech Periodicals" (pp. 14–30), "Slovak Periodicals" (pp. 31–39), "Periodicals in Other Languages" (pp. 40–46), "Geographical Index" (pp. 48–58), and "Selected Bibliography and Notes: Addenda" (pp. 60–62).

Page 10 of Duben's bibliography notes that the University of Chicago's Archives of Czechs and Slovaks abroad "contains entries identifying 750 periodicals published during the past 125 years of Czech and Slovak in the United States."

The Immigration History Research Center in 1980 issued the second edition of its *Czech and Slovak American Collections*, compiled by Joseph D. Dwyer and revised by Lynn Schweitzer Toscano (IHRC Ethnic Collections Series No. 2, University of Minnesota, 14 pp.).

Though dated, Thomas Čapek's "Journalism and Literature," in *The Čechs (Bohemians) in America* (Houghton Mifflin, Boston, 1920, pp. 164–221), may still be useful for the period it covers.

Vlasta Vráz, *Three Stages in the Development of the Czech Press in the United States* (7 pp., mimeographed, n.d.) is a brief history of the Czech press; it is the text of a presentation at the Czechoslovak Society of Arts and Sciences Congress in Cleveland in 1978.

Oklahoma. Karel D. Bicha, *The Czechs in Oklahoma* (University of Oklahoma Press, Norman, 1980, pp. 34–37) provides a short sketch of the Czech press in this state. Footnote 4 on pages 78–79 discusses his sources for this brief survey.

For the Slovak press in the United States, the following will be found useful: George Leo Yashur, "A Preliminary History of the Slovak Press in America" (M.S.L.S., Catholic University of America, 1950, 75 leaves); and Konštantín Čulen, *Slovenské časopisy v Amerika* (Prva Katolícka slovinská jednota, Cleveland, 1970, 192 pp.).

Čulen lists in alphabetical order data on 230 Slovak periodicals. Though useful, Čulen fails to mention many periodicals, particularly those of more liberal persuasion.

The thesis by Yashur provides a series of important tables that allow the user to determine without much effort the status of the Slovak press at different periods of the 20th century. They are: Table V: Slovak Publications in 1900, Table VIII: Slavonic Publications in 1900 as Shown in Dauchy's Newspaper Catalog, Table IX: Slavic and Slovenic Newspapers in 1901 as Shown in Ayer's Directory, Table X: Slovak Publications in 1910, Table XI: Slovak Publications in 1915, Table XII: Defunct Slovak Publications Up to 1920, Table XIII: Slovak Publications in 1920, Table XVII: Slovak Publications in U.S. in 1924, Table XVIII: Slovak Publications in 1938, Table XIX: Slovak Publications Arranged According to Frequency of Publication, Table XX: Slovak Publications in 1938 Arranged According to State, Table XXI: Slovak Publications in 1938 Arranged According to City, Table XXII: Slovak Publications in 1948, Table XXIII: Slovak Catholic Publications in 1949, and Table XXIV: The Catholic Almanac List of Slovak Catholic Publications in 1949.

Draga Pauco, "Slovak American Journalism," in Joseph C. Krajsa, *Slovaks in America: A Bicentennial Study* (Slovak League of America, Middletown, Pa., 1978, pp. 66–78), includes a listing of Slovak newspapers and periodicals published in America (pp. 73–78). This work would seem to be the most recent study of Slovak journalism in the United States.

Other studies on the Czech and Slovak press outside of Czechoslovakia would include Thomas Čapek, *Padesát let českého tisku v Americe* (Bank of Europe, New York, 1911, viii, 273 pp.), and Fratišek Stědronský, *Zahraniční krajanské noviny, časopisy a kalendáře* (Národni knihovna, Prague, 1958, 166 pp.).

Pavol Halaša and Samuel Chorvat, *Provizorný súpis americkej krajanskej tlače: 1886–1947: Knihy, Brožúry, Kalendáře* (Matica slovenska, Martin, 1969, 313 pp.) should also prove helpful.

Canada. For Canada, see Joseph M. Kirschbaum, "The Slovak Press in Canada," in *Slovakia* (Vol. 18, 1968, pp. 78–108); George J. Škvor, "Czech-Canadian Periodical Literature: A Preliminary Check List," in *Canadian Ethnic Studies* (Vol. 1, 1969, p. 3); Joseph M. Kirschbaum, "Slovak-Canadian Periodical Publications," in *Canadian Ethnic Studies* (Vol. 1, 1969, pp. 65–68); and G. A. Zekulin, "Czech-Canadian Periodical Publications: First Supplement," in *Canadian Ethnic Studies* (Vol. 5, 1973, pp. 31–34).

The first part of Kirschbaum's article is a history of the Canadian Slovak press (pp. 78–94). Pages 94–100 deal with almanacs and religious and cultural periodicals, and pages 100–104 are entitled "Slovak-Czech Relations in the Slovak Press in Canada." Slovak-language press in Canada (pp. 107–108) is divided into newspapers, almanacs and periodicals, and religious publications.

DANISH

Enok Mortensen, *Danish-American Life and Letters: A Bibliography* (Scandinavians in America series, Committee on Publications of the Danish Evangelical Lutheran Church in America, Des Moines, Iowa, 1945; Arno Press, New York, 1979, 91 pp.) is a classified bibliography that lists material published in the United States in both Danish and English as well as published material about the Danish-Americans published in Denmark.

The history of Danish-American newspapers is dealt with in Svend Thorsen, "Den danske-amerikanse presse," in *Den danske Dagspress* (Danske Selslab, i kommission hos G.E.C. Gad, Copenhagen, 1947–1951, 2 vols., Vol. 1, pp. 152–157).

Marion Marzolf has written the most concerning the Danish press in the United States. Her dissertation is "The Danish-Language Press in America" (University of Michigan, 1972, 276 leaves; *Diss. Abstr.*, Vol. 33, 1973, p. 6295; published with the same title in the series Scandinavians in America by Arno Press, New York, 1980, 276 pp.). She is the author of an article with this title in *Norwegian-American Studies* (Vol. 28, 1979, pp. 274–289; reprinted in *The Bridge* [journal of the Danish American Heritage Society], Vol. 4, No. 2, September 1981, pp. 20–30), and of "The Pioneer Danish Press in Midwest America, 1870–1900," in *Scandinavian Studies* (Vol. 48, 1976, pp. 426–440).

Of particular value in the dissertation are the following chapters: III. A Cooperative Beginning: The Dano-Norwegian press, IV: The Emergence of a Danish-American Press: 1870–1899, V. A Flourishing Press, 1900–1919, and VI. The Decisive Twenties and Beyond. The dissertation's appendix contains a "Publications List" (pp. 222–228) divided into Dano-Norwegian and Scandinavian newspapers, Danish-language newspapers, English-language publications (for Danes, Norwegians, and Scandinavians), Danish-language magazines, Danish community newspapers in English, Christmas yearbooks and annuals, and religious publications. Pages 271–273 of the bibliography list material on the Danish, Norwegian, and Swedish immigrant press as well as general works on the U.S. and Danish press.

Canada. Karlo Jensen, "Danish-Canadian Periodical Publications: A Preliminary Check List," in *Canadian Ethnic Studies* (Vol. 2, 1970, pp. 27–29), provides data on nine periodicals.

DUTCH

The best overall bibliography of the Dutch in the United States is Linda Pegman Doezema, *Dutch Americans: A Guide to Information Sources* (Gale Research Co., Detroit, 1979, 314 pp.). This volume contains a section, "Newspapers and Periodicals" (pp. 259–266), which is the fullest available listing of the Dutch-American press.

Hendrik Edelman, *Dutch-American Bibliography 1693–1794*, subtitled A Descriptive Catalog of Dutch-Language Books, Pamphlets, and Almanacs Printed in America (B. de Graaef, Nieuwkoop, 1974, 125 pp.), provides bibliographic data on 100 items.

Doezema notes two articles in Dutch on Dutch-American journals. They are: Henry Beets, "Hollandsche Couranten en Tijdschriften in de Ver. Staten," in *Gereformeede Amerikaan* (Vol. 20, December 1916, pp. 514–522); and Theo De-Veer, "Hollandsche Journaliek in Amerika," in *Elseviers' Geillustreerd Maandschkrift* (Vol. 19, February 1909, pp. 107–114).

Beets provides data on publication dates and editors, while DeVeer's article has a geographical arrangement and provides circulation statistics. Neither article provides sources. DeVeer was a Dutch journalist.

Iowa. The Dutch press of Iowa has been studied in Jacob Van der Zee, "The Dutch Press in Iowa," in *The Hollanders of Iowa* (State Historical Society of Iowa, Iowa City, Iowa, 1912, pp. 245–255). About three-fourths of this chapter deals with the Dutch press of Pella.

Michigan. The fullest discussion of the Michigan Dutch press is Harry Boonstra, "Dutch-American Newspapers and Periodicals in Michigan, 1850–1915" (M.A. thesis, University of Chicago, 1967, 109 leaves). An appendix lists Dutch titles published in Michigan.

Henry Beets, "Dutch Journalism in Michigan," in *Michigan History Magazine* (Vol. 6, 1922, pp. 435–441), presents rather incomplete data on Dutch papers in Grand Rapids, Holland, Kalamazoo, Battle Creek, and Muskegon.

Canada. René Brengelmans, "Netherlandic-Canadian Periodical Publications: A Preliminary Check List," in *Canadian Ethnic Studies* (Vol. 1, 1969, p. 56), lists 15 titles in Dutch and English.

ESTONIAN

The number of Estonians in the United States and Canada has never been large in comparison with West European national groups. The largest number of Estonians came to the North American continent between 1949 and 1952, when annual arrivals numbered 1,000–2,000.

The first Estonian newspaper in the United States was the *Eesti Ameerika Postimees* [Estonian American Courier], which was established in 1897 and continued through July 1911. Juhan Sepp's *Dollarite maalt* (1899) was the first Estonian book published in the United States. In the same year E. Melldorf in New York published his *Luhike Ingliskeeleopetus ja sonaraamat* [A Short Course in English and a Dictionary]. The standard bibliography for Estonian publications published by Estonians in exile is Bernard Kangro, *Eestiraamat vabas maailmas: Bibliograafiline ulevaade 1944–1970* (Eesti kirjanike kooperatiiv, Lund, 1971, 44 pp.). This volume provides bibliographic data on an estimated 1,770 imprints; that is, separately published books and pamphlets of more than 16 pages. Though the title page does not say so, this is considered by the compiler to be a fourth amended edition. Early editions had appeared in 1957, 1960, and 1966. Approximately 400 of the listed items were published in Canada (chiefly Toronto, with Orto as a major publisher of Estonian works), and almost 135 U.S. Estonian imprints are listed for this period.

Riita M. Viise, "Estonian Children's Literature in the Diaspora," in *Phaedrus* (Vol. 6, No. 1, 1979, pp. 64–70), deals with recent children's literature published outside of Estonia.

Canada. Jaan Olvet, "Estonian-Canadian Periodical Publications: A Preliminary Check List," in *Canadian Ethnic Studies* (Vol. 2, 1970, pp. 35–40), provides data on 44 periodicals.

FINNISH

Little seems to exist on Finnish books published in the United States and Canada. Most of the imprint studies deal with newspapers and periodicals.

John Ilmari Kolehmainen is the author of *The Finns in America: A Bibliographical Guide to Their History* (Finnish American Historical Library, Suomi College, Hancock, Mich., 1947, 141 pp.), "Finnish Newspapers in Ohio," in *Ohio State Archaeological and Historical Quarterly* (Vol. 47, 1938, pp. 123–138), "Finnish Newspapers and Periodicals in Michigan," in *Michigan History Magazine* (Vol. 24, 1940, pp. 119–127), and *Sow the Golden Seed* (Raivaaja Publishing Company, Fitchburg, Mass., 1955; reprinted Arno Press, New York, 1979, 150 pp.).

Not only is *Sow the Golden Seed* valuable as a history of the Finnish newspaper *Raivaaja*, but it also contains "The Current Roster of Finnish-Language Newspapers" (pp. 122–123), an extremely valuable "Bibliographical Note" (pp. 135–139) in which the majority of the items are in Finnish, and "A Catalogue of *Raivaaja* Publications" (i.e., books for 1905–1954 and periodicals, pp. 143–150).

Finns in America's eighth chapter, "Newspapers and Periodicals" (pp. 73–97), is divided into: A. Material Relating to the History of the Finnish Language Press (pp. 75–79), B. Agricultural Journals (p. 79), C. Humorous and Satirical Journals (pp. 79–80), D. General Independent Newspapers (pp. 80–84), E. Literary Journals (pp. 84–85), F. Newspapers and Periodicals with a Religious Emphasis (pp. 85–89), G. Temperance Newspapers and Periodicals (pp. 90–91), H. Women's Newspapers and Periodicals (p. 91), I. Workingclass Newspapers and Periodicals (pp. 91–94), and J. Miscellaneous Publications (pp. 95–97). D. T. Haltrola states that this source is "a nearly complete listing of American-Finnish language newspapers and periodicals, including the church press" (p. 87).

The article in *Michigan History Magazine* comments briefly on the Finnish press of Michigan. The periodicals are arranged according to the date of publication.

D. T. Haltrola, "Finnish Language Newspapers in the United States," in *The Finns in North America: A Social Symposium* (published by Michigan State University Press for Suomi College, Hancock, Michigan, 1969, pp. 73–90) notes that many Finnish papers were sponsored by religious organizations.

Michael G. Karni is the compiler of *The Finnish American Collection* (2nd ed., IHRC Ethnic Collections Series No. 4, Immigration History Research Center, University of Minnesota, 1978, 14 pp.).

Henry P. Schofer, *Urban and Rural Finnish Communities in California 1860–1960* (R & E Research Associates, 1975, pp. 89–90) provides the title and type of 12 periodicals, chiefly newspapers, that might be found in Finnish-American homes.

Material on the Finnish-American press in Finnish would include: F. V. Kava, "Amerikan Suomettaren Historia," in *Amerikan Suometar, 1899–1919* (Hancock, Mich., 1919, pp. 11–44); F. Tolonen, "Muutamia historia-tietoja Amerikan Suomalaisista Sanomaleldista" (ibid., pp. 78–92); S. Ilmonen, *Amerikan Suomislasten Sisstyshistoria* (Hancock, Mich., 1930, Vol. 1, pp. 189–190); F. J. Syrala, *Historia-aileita Amerikan Suomslacaesta työväen-lükeestä* (Fitchburg, Mass., n.d., pp. 30–32); and Kalle H. Masserkopi, *Asktabula Harborin Betania Seurakunnan 25 Vuotes Julkaisu, 1891–1916* (Hancock, Mich., 1916, pp. 45–48).

Canada. For Canada, see W. D. Bohm, "Finnish-Canadian Periodical Publications: A Preliminary Check List," in *Canadian Ethnic Studies* (Vol. 1, 1969, pp. 5–6), which lists nine titles in Finnish and English; and Aino Korvela, "Finnish-Canadian Periodical Publications: First Supplement" (ibid., Vol. 5, 1973, pp. 59–62).

FRENCH

French-speaking groups appear chiefly in Louisiana and New England.

For the United States as a whole, one should consult French Institute in the United States, *Publications contemporaines de langue française aux Etats-Unis et au Canada* (Exposition, New York, 1942, 45 pp.); K. I. Jamieson, *American (U.S.A.) Authors in French Translation and Americans Who Have Written in French (1690–1961): A Bibliography with Notes and Plates* (Princeton Microfilm Co., Princeton, 1970, 2876 leaves); James Comly McCoy, *Canadiana and French Americana in the Library of J. C. McCoy: A Hand-list of Printed Books* (Grasse, 1931, 87 pp.); and Union Saint Jean Baptiste d'Amérique, Bibliothèque, *Catalogue: Collection Mallet* (2nd ed., Woonsocket, R.I., 1935, xiii, 302 pp.).

Louisiana. For this state, see Ruby Van Allen Caulfield, *The French Literature of Louisiana* (Institute of French Studies, Columbia University, New York, 1929, 282 pp.), with bibliography (pp. 190–277); Edward Larocque Tinker, *Les écrits de langue française en Louisiane au xixème siècle: Essais biographiques et bibliographiques* (Kraus Reprint, Nendeln, 1970, 502 pp.); two articles by Alcee Fortier in *Modern Language Notes*, "The French Literature of Louisiana in 1887 and 1888" (Vol. 4, 1889, pp. 97–101, 228–233) and "The French of Louisiana in 1889 and 1890" (Vol. 5, 1890, pp. 165–169, 349–352); and Douglas C. McMurtrie, *Early Printing in New Orleans, 1794–1810*, with a bibliography of the issues of the Louisiana Press (Searcy and Pfaff, New Orleans, 1929, 151 pp.).

New England. For works published in French in New England, see Mary Carmel Therriault, "Bibliographie," in *La littérature française de Nouvelle-Angleterre* (Fides, Montreal, 1946, pp. 287–314); and Laurent André Houle, "A Preliminary Checklist of Franco-American Imprints in New England, 1780–1925" (M.A. thesis, Catholic University of America, 1955, 166 leaves).

Houle writes that "our efforts have been directed toward listing and locating whenever possible all books, pamphlets, albums, newspapers, periodicals, and other unpublished material written in French and published in New England, or originally written in another language but translated into French and printed in this same region" (p. 1). He provides data on 285 books and pamphlets, and 309 newspapers and periodicals.

There seems to be no one single source for the study or listing of French newspapers in the United States. Most commentators on this subject have found great fault with Alexander Belisle, *Histoire de la presse franco-américaine* (Ateliers typographiques de L'Opinion publique, Worcester, Mass., 1911, 434 pp.), which contains an "Inventaire chronologique des journaux et revues publiés en langue française aux Etats-Unis pour les Canadiens-français émigrés, de 1838 jusqu'á 1911, et qui n'existent plus aujourd'hui" (pp. 27–38).

South Carolina. James F. Shearer, "French and Spanish Works Published in Charleston, South Carolina," in *Papers of the Bibliographical Society of America* (Vol. 34, 1940, pp. 137–140), covers the period 1765–1886. It lists 68 items. However, it is slightly misnamed, for many of these items are English translations from either French or Spanish.

The fullest discussion of 18th- and early 19th-century French newspapers is that found in S. J. Marino, "The French Refugee Newspapers and Periodicals in the United States, 1789–1825" (Ph.D. dissertation, University of Michigan, 1962, ix, 385 leaves).

In the late 1970s Georges J. Joyaux was the individual most interested in the French press of this period. He published the following articles in *French-American Review:* "French Periodicals in Early America: I. *Le petit censeur*" (Vol. 1, Winter 1976, pp. 96–98), "French . . . : II. *L'Hémisphère*" (Vol. 1, Spring 1977, pp. 163–165), and "French . . . : III. *Le journal des dames*" (Vol. 1, 1977, pp. 249–251).

Part 2 of Volume 14 (1920) of the *Papers of the Bibliographical Society of America* is devoted to the French press of this period. It contains: Augustus H. Shearer, "*Le Courier de l'Amérique*, Philadelphia, 1784" (pp. 44–55) and "*Le Courrier-New Orléans*, 1785–6" (p. 56); George Parker Winship, "Two or Three Boston Papers" (pp. 57–81), which deals with *Courier de Boston* (1789), *Courier de l'Univers* (1792), and *Courier des deux mondes* (1794?); George Parker Winship, "French Newspapers in the United States from 1790 to 1800" (pp. 82–91) and "The Philadelphia Papers" (pp. 92–126), which presents data on six newspapers; and William Beer, "*Moniteur de la Louisiane*" (pp. 127–131), "*Le patriote français*, Charleston, 1794 (?)–1795" (pp. 132–133), and "The New York Paper" (pp. 134–147), which discusses the *Gazette française et américaine* and the *Gazette française*.

Albert Krebs, "Régis de Trobriand et *Le Courrier des Etats-Unis, journal français de New York* (1841–1865)," in *Revue d'histoire moderne contemporaine* (Vol. 18, October–December 1971, pp. 574–588), is a biographical sketch of Trobriand as well as a history of this paper for this period.

California. Clifford H. Bissell, "The French Language Press in California," in *California Historical Society Quarterly* (Vol. 39, 1960, pp. 1–18, 141–173, 219–262, 311–353), concludes with a union list of surviving files of the French newspapers of this state.

Etienne Derbec "operated a French–Spanish newspaper in San Francisco from 1852 to 1865," according to item 52 of *Catalogue 5: Americana from the Atlantic to the Pacific* (William Reese Company, New Haven, 1981). Most bilingual newspapers published in the United States have been in English and another language.

Illinois. Louis-Philippe Cormier, "La presse française de l'Illinois," in *Revue d'histoire de l'Amérique française* (Vol. 11, No. 3, 1957, pp. 361–392), is a short history of French newspapers published in Illinois between 1857 and 1931. The bibliography (pp. 386–392) is a union list of these newspapers arranged chronologically. The author has been able to locate files in Canadian libraries with these newspapers which were not listed in Gregory's *American Newspapers, 1821–1936.*

Louisiana. Edward Larocque Tinker, "Bibliography of French Newspapers and Periodicals of Louisiana," in *Proceedings of the American Antiquarian Society* (Vol. 42, October 1932, pp. 24–370), has the following parts of special interest concerning the history of the Louisiana French press: "Bibliography of French Newspapers and Periodicals Published in New Orleans" (pp. 283–331), which provides data on 139 titles; "Bibliography of French Newspapers and Periodicals Published in the Parishes of Louisiana" (pp. 332–358), which provides data on 107 titles; "Chronological Lists of Newspapers and Periodicals Published Wholly or Partly in French in Louisiana Outside of New Orleans" (pp. 359–361); "Alphabetical Index of Newspapers and Periodicals of the Parishes" (pp. 363–364); and "Index of Parish Newspapers of Louisiana by Towns Where Published" (pp. 365–367). He is also the author of a brief note, "Les 'français de France et le journalisme Creole," in *Français-Amérique* (Vol. 27, 1937, pp. 128–132), which deals with French journalism from 1794 to the end of the 19th century.

Earlier studies on the French press of Louisiana would include John S. Kandall, "Early New Orleans Newspapers," in *Louisiana Historical Quarterly* (Vol. 10, July 1927, pp. 383–401), and his "The Foreign Language Press of New Orleans" (ibid., Vol. 12, July 1929, pp. 363–380); and J. G. de Baroncelli, "Journaux français: Nouvelles-Orléans et campagnes 1794–1900," in *Une colonie française en Louisiane* (G. Muller, New Orleans, 1909, pp. 106–108).

Samuel J. Marino, "Early French Language Newspapers in New Orleans," in *Louisiana History* (Vol. 7, February 1966, pp. 301–322), describes *Moniteur de la Louisiane, Le Télégraphe, Courrier de la Louisiane, L'ami des lois*, and *Louisiana Gazette.*

Michigan. George J. Joyaux, "French Press in Michigan: A Bibliography," in *Michigan History* (Vol. 36, 1952, pp. 260–278), brings together from a variety of sources such data as can be discovered concerning approximately 30 French papers published in this state.

Missouri. Many valuable data concerning the French press of Missouri are found in the footnotes to John Francis McDermott, "Louis Richard Cortambert and the First French Newspapers in St. Louis, 1809–1854," in *Papers of the Bibliographical Society of America* (Vol. 34, 1940, pp. 221–253). It is briefly discussed in Alexander Nicolas DeMenil, "French Newspapers," in William Hyde and Howard L. Conrad, *Encyclopedia of the History of St. Louis* (Southern Historical Society, St. Louis, 1899, Vol. 2, pp. 836–837).

New England. An important study on the French press of the area is Maximilienne Tetrault, *Le rôle de la presse dans l'évolution du peuple franco-américain de la Nouvelle-Angleterre*, with the subtitle Avec une liste chronologique des journaux publiés dans les états de l'Illinois, Michigan, Minnesota, New York et de la Nouvelle Angleterre (Imprimerie Ferran, Marseille, 1935, 135 pp.).

GAELIC

Gaelic publications of the United States do not seem to have been studied. For Canada, see Donald McLean Sinclair, "Gaelic Newspapers and Prose Writings in Nova Scotia," in *Collections of the Nova Scotia Historical Society* (Vol. 27, 1945, pp. 105–113).

GERMAN

Oswald Seidensticker, *The First Century of German Printing in America, 1728–1830* (Schafer and Koradi, Philadelphia, 1893; Kraus, New York, 1966, 253 pp.) was for a long time the standard work on German printing in the United States. He is also the author of "Die deutsch-amerikanischen Incunabeln," in *Der deutsche Pionier* (Vol. 8, February 1877, pp. 475–484). His work has been supplemented by Ammon Stapleton, "Researches in the First Century of German Printing in America," in *The Pennsylvania-German* (Vol. 5, 1904, pp. 81–89, 183, and Vol. 6, 1905, pp. 262–263); and Gerhard Friederich, "A New Supplement to Seidensticker's American–German bibliography," in *Pennsylvania History* (Vol. 7, October 1940, pp. 213 224), which is a check list of 53 books, 30 almanacs, and 4 broadsides not listed by Seidensticker.

German Catholic publishing in the United States is discussed in the following master's theses written at the Catholic University of America: Sister M. Justina Grothe, "German Catholic Publishing and Book Distribution within the United States from 1865 to 1880" (1950, v, 164 leaves); Charles Fehrenbach, "German Literary Activities of the Redemptorists in the United States, 1837–1838" (1937, 68 leaves); M. Thomas Johannemann, "Max Oertel, Convert and Journalist" (1939, 82 leaves); and Anthony L. Saletel, "Damian Litz and the Catholic German–American press 1870–1903" (1939, 134 leaves).

Of value are the following parts of Sister Grothe's thesis: Chapter II. The German Catholic Publishing Houses in the United States during the Period of 1865–1880; Chapter III. The Production of German Catholic Literature in the United States during the Period of 1865–1880: German Catholic Newspapers and Periodicals, German Catholic Calendars, German Catholic Books and Pamphlets; and Chapter VI. Appendix: Table of German Catholic Newspapers and Periodicals Founded during the Period from 1865–1880, Table of German Catholic Calendars Founded during the Period from 1865–1880, and List of German Catholic Books and Pamphlets Published. . . .

Maryland. Felix Reichmann, "German Printing in Maryland: A Checklist, 1786–1950," in *Report of the Society for the History of the Germans in Maryland* (Vol. 27, 1950, pp. 9–70), provides a historical sketch of German printing in Maryland. The checklist is divided into: Maryland German almanacs, summary of

Maryland German newspapers and magazines, and German books printed in Maryland. Reichmann records 812 books either in German or concerning German culture.

Pennsylvania. Wilbur H. Oda has published the following imprint lists in *The Pennsylvania Dutchman:* "German-Language Imprints of Allentown, Pennsylvania" (Vol. 4, No. 1, May 1952, pp. 12–14), "German-Language Imprints of Carlisle, Pennsylvania" (Vol. 4, No. 2, June 1952, pp. 12–14), "German-Language Imprints of Chambersburg, Pennsylvania" (Vol. 4, No. 3, July 1952, pp. 12–14), "Easton German-Language Imprints" (Vol. 4, No. 5, September 1952, pp. 6–7, 13), "Economy German Imprints" (Vol. 4, No. 6, October 1952, p. 7), "Ephrata German Language Imprints" (Vol. 4, No. 8, December 1952, pp. 12–13, and Vol. 4, No. 9, January 1, 1953, pp. 10–12—which supplements Eugene H. Doll and Anneliese M. Funke, *The Ephrata Cloisters: An Annotated Bibliography*, Carl Schurz Memorial Foundation, Philadelphia, 1944, 136 pp.), "Gettysburg German Imprints" (Vol. 4, No. 10, January 15, 1953, p. 13), "Greensburg German Imprints" (Vol. 4, No. 11, February 1, 1953, p. 14), "Hanover German Imprints" (Vol. 4, No. 12, February 15, 1953, pp. 14–15), "German Language Imprints of Harrisburg" (Vol. 4, No. 14, April 1953, pp. 12–14), and "New Berlin German Imprints" (Vol. 4, No. 13, March 1, 1953, pp. 13, 15).

Oda provides pertinent bibliographic and historical data concerning the imprints and locates copies. Most of these imprint studies go through the year 1830 and start with whatever year first saw the publication of a German-language imprint.

Alfred L. Shoemaker has published "A Check List of Imprints of the German Press of Leheigh County, Pennsylvania, 1807–1900 with Biographies of the Printers," in *Proceedings of the Leheigh County Historical Society* (Vol. 16, 1947, pp. 1–240), and "A Check List of the German Press of Northampton County, Pennsylvania, 1766–1905 with Biographies of the Printers," in *Publications of the Northampton County Historical and Genealogical Society* (Vol. 4, 1943, pp. 1–162). Also of value is Frank Reid Piffenderffer, "Early German Printers of Lancaster and the Issues of their Presses," in *Papers Read Before the Lancaster County Historical Society* (Vol. 8, 1904, pp. 53–93; reprinted from *New Era*).

The Leheigh County study is divided into: I. German Press of Leheigh County 1807–1900, II. Check List of Dated Imprints, III. Undated Imprints, IV. List of Imprints, V. List of Publishers, VI. List of German Newspapers and Periodicals, VII. Taufscheine, and VIII. Biographies of the Publishers.

The Northampton County study is divided into: I. Historical Sketch of the German Press in Northampton County, II. Check List of Dated Imprints, 1766–1905, III. Undated Imprints, IV. Undated Broadsides, V. List of German Newspapers and Location of Presses, and VI. Biographies of Printers.

Both studies conclude with a bibliography.

Virginia. For German imprints in Virginia, see Klaus G. Wust, "German Printing in Virginia: A Check List, 1789–1934," in *Report of the Society for the History of the Germans in Maryland* (Vol. 28, 1953, pp. 54–66); and Lester Jesse Cappon and Ira V. Brown, editors, *New Market, Virginia Imprints, 1806–1876: A Check-list* (Alderman Library, Charlottesville, Va., 1942, 36 pp.). The latter volume contains "Appendix: New Market (Va.) Newspapers, 1807–1876" (pp.

33–34).

Wust provides a list of Virginia German newspapers followed by a section entitled "German Books and Broadsides Printed in Virginia 1804–1834," which lists 97 items.

Horst Dippel, *Americana Germanica, 1770–1800: Bibliographie deutscher Amerikaliteratur* (Amerikastudien No. 42, J. B. Metzler, Stuttgart, 1976, 214 pp.), is the most recent bibliography of German-American literature. It provides data on 836 items arranged chronologically. It has a combined author and title index.

J. R. Arndt and May E. Olson, *The German Press of the Americas, 1732–1968: History and Bibliography* (Part I, Johnson Reprint Corp., New York, 1965, 810 pp.; and Part II, Verlag Dokumentation, Munich, 1973, pp. 237–603) is an extremely comprehensive and thorough listing of all kinds of German newspapers and periodicals including those issued by German prisoners of war interned in the United States. Especially valuable is the "Selected Bibliography of Works Consulted and Used" (Part I, pp. 783–795; Part II, pp. 613–688).

The earliest attempt at a complete listing of German newspapers of Canada and the United States would seem to be *Tobias Brothers' German Newspaper Directory*, which carries the description "containing a carefully prepared complete list of all German newspapers published in the United States, territories and Dominion of Canada (omitting those not inserting advertisements) with valuable information regarding their circulations, issue, date of establishment; also separate list of religious newspapers" (Tobias Brothers, German Newspaper Advertising Agents, 1890).

According to Sister Grothe, the *Literarischer Handweiser* published the following articles on the German Catholic press: Johannes N. Enzlberger, "Die katholische Presse in den Vereinigten Staaten Nordamerikas" (Vol. 12, No. 140, 1873, pp. 363–364); Johannes N. Enzlberger and Elias F. Schauer, "Neues über die katholische Presse in den Vereinigten Staaten" (Vol. 13, No. 149, 1874, pp. 71–74); and J. B. Müller, "Das katholische Zeitungswesen in den Vereinigten Staaten Nordamerikas" (Vol. 8, No. 77, March 20, 1869, pp. 108–113).

The most recent history of the German-language press is Carl Frederick Wittke, *The German-Language Press of America* (University Press of Kentucky, Lexington, 1957; Haskell House Publishers, New York, 1973, 311 pp.).

Much can be learned of the periodicals of the German exiles of the Hitler era by consulting Lieselotte Maas, *Handbuch der deutschen Exilpresse 1933–1945* (Carl Hanser Verlag, Munich, 1976–1978, 2 vols.). The arrangement is alphabetical by title. A place of publication index would have been quite helpful.

Spyridon Granitsas, "Dim Future Is Seen for German Papers," in *Editor and Publisher* (Vol. 104, No. 3, January 16, 1971, pp. 34–36), provides a list by state and province of the German papers published in the United States and Canada. A letter by Gerald R. Kainz (ibid., Vol. 104, No. 5, January 30, 1971, p. 5) added data on a paper omitted from the earlier list.

California. T. L. Broadbent, "The German-Language Press in California: Record of a German Immigration," in *Journal of the West* (Vol. 10, October 1971, pp. 637–661), provides not only a history of the German press in this state but "Appendix: German Language Newspapers of California: Chronologically by

Date of Origin" (pp. 660–661), which adds several titles not found in *Arndt–Olson.*

District of Columbia. Klaus German Wust, "German Immigrants and Their Newspapers in the District of Columbia 1789–1959," in *Report of the Society for the History of Germans in Maryland* (Vol. 30, 1959, pp. 36–66), includes a list of newspapers for the period 1843–1959.

Hawaii. Bernhard Hörmann, "The Germans in Hawaii" (M.A. thesis, University of Hawaii, 1931, 162 pp.) discusses the German press of Hawaii briefly on pages 98 and 122.

Illinois. The Illinois German press has been discussed in Heinrich Bornmann, "Deutsche Zeitungswesen in Quincy," in *Deutsch-amerikanische Geschichtsblätter* (Vol. 6, 1906, pp. 32–36); Emil Mannhardt, "Eine Illinois Staatszeitung aus dem Jahre 1852" (ibid., Vol. 7, 1907, pp. 42–47); Arthur Lorenz, "Chicago's deutsche Presse im Kriegsjahr," in *Jahrbuch der Deutschen in Chicago für das Jahr 1916* (Chicago, 1916, pp. 165–173); and Peter Gross, "*Volksfront* and *Abendpost:* A Study of Two Chicago German-Language Newpapers (1933–1945)" (M.A. thesis, University of Iowa, 1977, ii, 121 leaves).

Indiana. Anton Eickhoff, "Die deutsche Press," in *In der neuen Heimath* (E. Steiger, New York, 1884, pp. 303–304), is a brief discussion of the German press in Ohio and Indiana. Oscar L. Bockstahler, "The German Press in Indiana," in *Indiana Magazine of History* (Vol. 48, 1956, pp. 161–168), provides a history and list of the German newspapers of this state.

Iowa. Little seems to have been published on the Iowa German press; see "Rudolph Reichman, ein Pionier der deutschen Presse in Iowa," in *Deutsch-amerikanische Geschichtsblätter* (Vol. 8, 1908, pp. 99–101).

Kentucky. Leonard Koester, "German Newspapers Published in Louisville," in *American-German Review* (Vol. 20, No. 5, June–July 1954, pp. 24–27), notes that 22 German newspapers were published in almost a century.

Louisiana. John Hanno Deiler, *Geschichte der New Orleanser deutschen Presse* (The Author, New Orleans, 1901, 40 pp.) would seem to be one of the few studies on the German press in this state. He provides histories of about three dozen German Louisiana newspapers.

Minnesota. The most important studies on the German-American press in this state would appear to be Hermann E. Rothfuss, "Westward with the News," in *American-German Review* (Vol. 20, February–March 1954, pp. 22–25); and Donald Tolzmann, "The German Language Press in Minnesota, 1855 to 1955," in *German-American Studies* (Vol. 5, 1972, pp. 169–178).

Missouri. The fullest account of the German press in Missouri would seem to be Friedrich Schnake, "Geschichte der deutschen Bevölkerung und der deutschen Presse von St. Louis and Umgegend," in *Der deutsche Pionier* (Vol. 3, September 1871–February 1872, pp. 209–212, 229–234, 272–277, 299–305, 333–338, 378–382; Vol. 4, March–May and September 1872, pp. 4–6, 46–49, 85–87, 233–235; Vol. 5, June and August 1873, January–February 1874, pp. 100–110, 181–186, 230–235, 378–382).

The Saint Louis *Westliche Post* has been studied by Harvey Saalberg in his University of Missouri Ph.D. dissertation, "The *Westliche Post* of St. Louis . . . 1857–1938" (1967, 430 pp.); "The *Westliche Post* of St. Louis: German Language

Daily, 1857–1938," in *Journalism Quarterly* (Vol. 45, 1968, pp. 452–456, 472); and "Dr. Emil Preetorius, editor-in-chief of the *Westliche Post* 1864-1905," in *Bulletin of the Missouri Historical Society* (Vol. 24, No. 2, 1967, pp. 103–112).

Alvis Avelino Dunson, "A Checklist of German Newspapers in Missouri up to 1940" (Ph.D. dissertation, Ohio State University, 1954, 134 leaves; *Diss. Abstr.*, Vol. 20, August 1959, pp. 657–659) states that "the present work was undertaken to ascertain a chronological list of all German newspapers and periodicals published, dating from 1835 up to 1940" (p. 657). The abstract also notes that "the writer has endeavored to give dates of establishment, suspension, change of name or political party, mergence, discontinuation, and in most cases, the causes for suspension and discontinuation" (p. 658). This dissertation presents data on 187 titles.

North and South Dakota. The fullest general discussion of the German press in the Dakotas is that of Anton H. Richter, "'Gebt ihr den Vorzug': The German-Language Press of North and South Dakota," in *South Dakota History* (Vol. 10, Summer 1980, pp. 189–209).

The *Dakota Freie Presse* was an outstanding German-language paper for many years and has been the subject of two articles by La Vern J. Rippley in the *North Dakota Historical Society of Germans from Russia Heritage Review*. They are: "A History of the *Dakota Freie Presse*" (Vol. 7, 1973, pp. 9–17) and "The *Dakota Freie Presse:* Its Brightest and Its Darkest Hour" (Vol. 9, 1974, pp. 15–20).

It should be noted that many of the German-speaking individuals who immigrated to the Dakotas were originally from Russia.

Hanno R. E. Hardt, "*Der Staats-Anzeiger*—Wilson Stutze in Nord Dakota," in *Publizistik* (Vol. 12, Nos. 1–2, 1967, pp. 140–147), notes that this paper backed Wilson in World War I.

Ohio. Ohio's newspapers have been studied in Henry J. Groen, "Notes on the German-American Newspapers of Cincinnati before 1860," in *Festschrift für M. Blakemore Evans* (Ohio State University Press, Columbus, Ohio, 1945, pp. 67–71); Groen, "A History of the German-American Newspapers of Cincinnati before 1860" (Ph.D. dissertation, Ohio State University, 1944, 224 leaves); and Carl Frederick Wittke, *German-Americans and the World War (with Special Emphasis on Ohio's German Language Press* (Ohio Historical Collections No. 5, Ohio State Archeological and Historical Society, Columbus, Ohio, 1936, 223 pp.)

The article by Groen notes that "before 1860 no fewer than fifty-two German-American newspapers and periodicals of all descriptions were founded in Cincinnati. Of these, twenty-five were political, fifteen were religious, four belletristic, and eight of them belonged to no particular classification" (p. 68).

Oklahoma. The German press in Oklahoma is briefly discussed in Rochard C. Rohrs, *The Germans in Oklahoma* (University of Oklahoma Press, Norman, Oklahoma, 1980, pp. 24–26).

Pennsylvania. Alfred Lewis Shoemaker has published the following articles in the *Pennsylvania Dutchman:* "German-Language Agricultural Periodicals in Pennsylvania" (Vol. 3, No. 11, November 1, 1951, p. 4), "Adams County German Newspapers" (Vol. 4, No. 10, January 15, 1953, p. 14), "Checklist of German-Language Newspapers of Berks County" (Vol. 3, No. 18, February 15, 1952, pp. 3–5), "German-Language Press of Milford Square and Quakerstown" (Vol. 3, No.

16, January 15, 1952, p. 4), "Checklist of Carbon County German-Language Newspapers" (Vol. 3, No. 13, December 1, 1951, p. 4), "Carlisle German-Language Newspapers" (Vol. 4, No. 2, June 1952, p. 14), "Chambersburg German Newspapers" (Vol. 4, No. 3, July 1952, pp. 13–14), "Central Pennsylvania (Columbus and Lycoming Counties)" (Vol. 5, No. 13, March 1, 1954, p. 14), "Checklist of German-Language Newspapers of Dauphin County" (Vol. 3, No. 21, April 1, 1952, pp. 4, 7), "Checklist of German-Language Newspapers of Doylestown" (Vol. 3, No. 15, January 1, 1952, p. 4), "German-Language Newspapers of Easton, Pennsylvania" (Vol. 4, No. 4, August 1952, pp. 12–13), "Hanover Newspapers" (Vol. 4, No. 12, February 15, 1953, p. 15), "German Newspapers of the Coal Regions (Lackawanna, Lucerne and Wayne Counties)" (Vol. 3, No. 14, March 15, 1954, p. 10), "Checklist of the German-Language Newspapers of Lancaster County" (Vol. 3, No. 22, April 15, 1952, pp. 4, 8), "Checklist of German-Language Newspapers of Lebanon County" (Vol. 3, No. 20, March 15, 1952, pp. 4, 7), "German-Language Papers of Monroe County" (Vol. 3, No. 14, December 15, 1951, p. 4), "German-Language Newspapers of Montgomery County" (Vol. 3, No. 17, February 1, 1952, pp. 4–5), "Northampton County German Newspapers" (Vol. 4, No. 5, September 1952, p. 13), "German Newspapers of Central Penna" (Vol. 5, No. 12, February 1954, p. 10), "Checklist of the German Language Newspapers of Schuykill County" (Vol. 3, No. 19, March 1, 1952, p. 4), "Union County German Newspapers" (Vol. 4, No. 13, March 1, 1953, pp. 12, 14), "Westmoreland County German Papers" (Vol. 4, No. 11, February 1, 1953, p. 15), and "York County Checklist" (Vol. 5, No. 11, February 1, 1954, p. 10).

The vast majority of these lists and bibliographies cover the period 1821–1875.

The following articles deal with the *Philadelphische Zeitung:* "The First German Newspaper Published in America," in *Pennsylvania Magazine of History and Biography* (Vol. 24, No. 3, October 1900, pp. 306–307); F. C. Huch, "Die erste deutsche Zeitung in Amerika," in *Deutscher Pionier-Verein von Philadelphia: Mitteilungen* (Vol. 8, 1908, pp. 29–32); F. C. Huch, "Die erste deutsche Zeitung in Philadelphia" (ibid., Vol. 7, 1907, pp. 20–27); "*Philadelphische Zeitung*, the First German Newspaper Published in America" (ibid., Vol. 26, 1902, p. 91); and Juluis Friedrich Sachse, "The First German Newspaper Published in America," in *Proceedings and Addresses of the Pennsylvania-German Society* (Vol. 10, 1900, pp. 41–46).

Daniel Miller is the author of "The German Newspapers of Berks County (Pa.)," in *Berks County Historical Society, Transactions* (Vol. 3, 1912, pp. 4–22); "Early German American Newspapers," in *Proceedings and Addresses of the Pennsylvania-German Society* (Vol. 19, 1908, pp. 5–107); and "The German Newspapers of Lebanon County," in *Lebanon County Historical Society* (Vol. 5, 1909–1911, pp. 131–150).

The first Miller study traces the development of the Berks County German press from the late 18th century through the late 19th century. His second study is an essay on the development of German-American newspapers primarily in Pennsylvania. It has the following chapters: 1. General Discussion, 2. German Press in Philadelphia, 3. Germantown, 4. Lancaster County, 5. Berks County, 6. Northampton County, 7. Dauphin County, 8. York County, 9. Montgomery County, 10. Lebanon County, 11. Leheigh County, 12. Bucks County, 13. Schuylkill County, 14. Central and Western Pennsylvania, 15. Maryland, 16. New York, 17. The South, and 18. German Newspapers in the United States.

Texas. For German newspapers published in Texas, see Gilbert Giddings Benjamin, "Newspapers," in *The Germans in Texas* (Americana Germanica, n.s.v. No. 11, Publications of the University of Pennsylvania Press, Philadelphia, 1909, pp. 114–116); T. Herbert Etzler, "German-American Newspapers in Texas with Special References to the *Texas Volksblatt*, 1887–1889," in *Southwestern Historical Quarterly* (Vol. 57, 1954, pp. 423–431); and Hugo Müller, "Deutsche Zeitungen in Texas," in the *Freie Presse für Texas* (San Antonio) (May 12, 1915, pp. 5, 8). A German newspaper published in Giddings is discussed in Frank Daniel Starr, "The Giddings *Deutsches Volksblatt*, 1899–1917" (M.A. thesis, University of Texas, 1967, vi, 136 leaves).

Wisconsin. Emil Baensch's brief comment "Die deutsche Presse in Wisconsin," in *Deutsch-amerikanische Geschichtsblätter* (Vol. 7, 1907, pp. 136–138), would seem to be one of the few published studies concerning the press in this state.

Albert Strobl, "German Newspaper Publishing in Milwaukee" (University of Illinois, 1951) is listed in *Arndt–Olson* but in mid-1980 was not available for examination.

German-American children's books have been studied in two *Phaedrus* articles: Howell J. Heaney, "A Century of Early American Children's Books in German, 1738–1838" (Vol. 6, No. 1, 1979, pp. 22–26); and Sibylle Fraser, "German Language Children's and Youth Periodicals in North America: A Checklist" (Vol. 6, No. 1, 1979, pp. 27–31); as well as in Walter Kleinefelter, "The ABC Books of the Pennsylvania Germans," in *Publications of the Pennsylvania German Society* (Vol. 7, 1973, pp. 1–104).

Fraser describes 78 titles published in the United States, 15 published in South America (Argentina, Brazil, and Chile), and 2 published in Canada. The arrangement is by country and alphabetically within each country. Pertinent bibliographic data for each title are given.

Canada. Canadian Ethnic Studies has published the following: Rolf E. S. Windthorst, "German-Canadian Creative Literature: A Preliminary Check List of Imprints" (Vol. 2, 1970, pp. 55–62); Clive H. Cardinal, "A Preliminary Check List of Studies on German-Canadian Creative Literature: Part I. General Studies" (Vol. 1, 1969, pp. 38–39), and "A Preliminary . . . Part II. Specific Studies" (Vol. 2, 1970, pp. 63–69); and W. R. Gilby, "Imprints of German-Canadian Creative Literature: First Supplement" (Vol. 5, 1973, pp. 87–90). These and Hartmut Froeschle, "Deutsch-kanadische Bibliographie: Eine Auswahl," in *Deutschkanadische Jahrbuch* (Historical Society of Mecklenburg Upper Canada, Toronto, 1973, Vol. 1, pp. 327–344), would appear to be the chief sources for the listing of German-Canadian creative literature and for critical studies on it. This must be considered a fraction of what must exist in the way of German-Canadian imprints. One would assume that there must exist, for example, a number of imprints that deal with religious topics.

Besides *Arndt–Olson* (Vol. 2, pp. 223–262), one should consult Alexander Malycky and Clive H. Cardinal, "German-Canadian Periodical Publications: A Preliminary Check List," in *Canadian Ethnic Studies* (Vol. 1, 1969, pp. 13–30); its "first supplement" (ibid., Vol. 2, 1970, pp. 47–54); and Alexander Malycky and R. O. W. Goertz, "German-Canadian Periodical Publications: Second Supplement" (ibid., Vol. 5, 1973, pp. 64–86). The *Canadian Ethnic Studies* bibliographies provide data on slightly more than 400 periodicals in English, Low German, Pennsylvania German, and German.

Important studies of both a historical and bibliographic nature of the German-Canadian press would include Herbert Karl Kalbfleisch, *The History of the Pioneer German Language Press of Ontario, 1835–1918* (University of Toronto Press, Toronto, 1968, 133 pp.); Heinz Kloss, "Materialien zur Geschichte der deutschkanadischen Presse," in *Der Auslanddeutsche* (Stuttgart) (Vol. 11, 1928, pp. 382–384); Heinz Lehmann, "Die deutsche Presse," in *Das Deutschtum in West-kanada* (Junker und Dunnhaupt Verlag, Berlin, 1939, pp. 319–325); and Heinz Lehmann, "Deutsche Zeitung für Canada: Zur Geschichte der deutschkanadischen Presse," in *Deutsche Arbeit* (Berlin) (Vol. 35, 1935, pp. 482–487).

GREEK

Michael N. Cutsumbis, *A Bibliographic Guide to Materials on Greeks in the United States, 1890–1968* (Center for Immigration Studies, Staten Island, N.Y., 1970, 100 pp.) lists, among other types of material: publications of church and parish groups, fraternal works, parish and archdiocesan materials, and Greek-American serials currently published and those suspended.

Emmanuel Hatziemmanuel is the editor of the *Yearbook 1970* of the Greek Orthodox Archdioceses of North and South America (n.p., n.d.), which contains "Newspapers and Magazines (in Greek)" (pp. 213–214).

Helen Kakabelaki, "Greek-Canadian Periodical Publications: A Preliminary Check List," in *Canadian Ethnic Studies* (Vol. 2, 1970, pp. 71–74), lists 20 periodicals.

HAITIAN CREOLE

Pages 31–34 of Jean-Baptiste, *Haitians in Canada* (Minister of Supply and Services Canada, Hall, Quebec, 1979) provide a list of Haitian authors and their books of poetry and prose published in Canada.

HAWAIIAN

Several important bibliographies exist for the study of Hawaii as a whole. In 1963 the G. K. Hall Company of Boston published *Dictionary Catalog of the Hawaiian Collection* (i.e., of the University of Hawaii Library, 4 vols.); David Kittelson, "A Bibliography of Hawaiian Bibliographies Held by the Hawaiian Collection of the University of Hawaii at Manoa Library" is a 10-page, 160-item typescript. For material published in or about Hawaii, one should consult *Current Hawaiiana*, a quarterly published since 1944 by the Hawaiian Collection.

For the study of Hawaiian imprints and material in this language, the following works should be consulted: Howard M. Ballou and George Carter, "The History of the Hawaiian Mission Press, with a Bibliography of the Earlier Publications," in *Papers of the Hawaiian Historical Society* (No. 15, 1928, pp. 9–44); Bernice Judd, Janet E. Bell, and Clare G. Murdoch, *Hawaiian Language Imprints, 1822–1899: A Bibliography* (The Hawaiian Mission Children's Society and University Press of Hawaii, Honolulu, 1978, 274 pp.); Esther Mookini, *The Hawaiian Newspapers* (Topgallant Publishing Co., Honolulu, 1974, xxxx, 55 pp.); Nancy Morris, *Bibliography of Hawaiian Language Materials at the University of Hawaii, Manoa Campus* (University of Hawaii, Manoa Campus, University of Hawaii Pacific Islands Program, 1974, 60 pp.); and Newberry Library, *Edward E. Ayer Collection, Hawaiian Language* (Chicago, 1941, 33 pp.).

Ruth Lapham Butler, in the "Foreword" to the Newberry catalog, notes that "of the 301 items, the most numerous are, naturally, translations of the Bible, doctrinal tracts and hymnals, but non-religious subjects are well represented."

Ballou and Carter provide data on 75 Hawaiian imprints produced between 1822 and 1834.

The Judd–Bell–Murdoch bibliography is an extremely well-presented bibliography of material (with the exception of government documents) published in the Hawaiian language regardless of place of publication. The majority of the items were published in the Hawaiian Islands. Copies are located in almost three dozen libraries. Hawaiian titles are translated into English. The vast majority of the works listed in this bibliography are religious in nature.

Many valuable bibliographic data on the press and history of printing in Hawaii, Guam, American Samoa, and other areas in the Pacific controlled by the United States are found in Jim Richstad and Michael McMillan, *Mass Communication and Journalism in the Pacific Islands: A Bibliography* (data provided in the Chamorro section); pages 97–110 of this volume provide a listing of newspapers and periodicals of Hawaii published in Hawaiian, Portuguese, Chinese, Japanese, and Korean as well as English.

Pages 162–166 of the Richstad and McMillan bibliography are a bibliography concerning printing in Hawaii and its history.

C. Willowdean Handy compiled "Newspapers Published in Hawaii: A Survey of the Holdings of the Historical Society and Other Honolulu Libraries" (1953, 52 pp., mimeographed).

"Hawaiian Periodicals Published in Several Languages," in *Hawaiian Historical Society Report* (1902, pp. 32–37), provides brief data on 140 periodicals published in this state.

HEBREW AND YIDDISH

Though not the same language, they are treated together since both are or have been used by those of the Jewish faith; for this reason Hebrew and Yiddish publications are often discussed together. Ladino, or Judeo-Español, is discussed under Ladino.

The fullest bibliography of bibliographies of things Jewish is that of Shlomo Shumani, *Bibliography of Jewish Bibliographies* (Magnes Press, The Hebrew University, Jerusalem, 1965), and its supplement published under the same imprint in 1975. Pages 102–106 and page 19 of the supplement list bibliographies of the Jewish press of the United States and Canada. These entries are in English, Hebrew, and Yiddish.

The standard bibliography for books published in Hebrew in the United States is *Koheleth America: Catalogue of Hebrew Books Printed in America from 1735–1925*, compiled by Ephraim Deinard (Minnesota Printing Co., St. Louis, Mo., 1926, 2 vols. in 1). The title is given in both Hebrew and English.

For Jewish Americana, regardless of language, before 1851, the most important studies are: A. S. W. Rosenbach, "An American Jewish Bibliography: Being a List of Books and Pamphlets by Jews or Relating to Them, Printed in the United States from the Establishment of the Press in the Colonies until 1850," in *Publications of the American Jewish Historical Society* (Vol. 30, 1926, pp. iii–xvii, 1–486); Jacob R. Marcus, *Jewish Americana . . . a Supplement to A. S. W. Rosenbach's . . .*, compiled by Fanny Berg (Monographs of the American Jewish Archives No. 1, American Jewish Archives, Cincinnati, 1954, ix, 115 pp.); Edwin Wolf 2nd, "Some Unrecorded American Judaica Printed before 1851," in *Essays in American Jewish History* (American Jewish Archives Publications No. 4, Hebrew Union College, Cincinnati, 1959, pp. 187–245); and Nathan M. Kaganoff, "Supplement III: Judaica Americana Printed before 1851," in *Studies in Jewish Bibliography, History and Literature in Honor of I. Edward Kiev* (KATV, New York, 1971, pp. 177–209).

Rosenbach provides data on 687 titles, Marcus lists 227 items, Wolf lists 239 titles, and Kaganoff gives data on 199 items. The vast majority of this material is in English, with only a small number of items being in other languages.

Bernard Drachman, "Neo-Hebraic Literature in America: A Hitherto Unnoticed Side of the Intellectual Activity of the Jewish People," in *Proceedings of the Jewish Theological Seminary Association* (7th Annual Convention, 1900, pp. 57–91), is divided into: The Early Period, Poetic Writings, Philosophic Writings, Exegetical Writings, Halachic Writings, Controversial Writings, Historical Writings, Satirical Writings, Lexicographical and Encyclopaedic Writings, Zionistic Writings, and Periodical Literature.

George Alexander Kohut, "Early Jewish Literature in America," in *Publications of the American Jewish Historical Society* (Vol. 3, 1895, pp. 103–147), lists works in Hebrew. It deals more with the Jews of Brazil, Surinam, and Curaçao than with the United States.

Ellen M. Oldham, "Early Jewish Books Printed in America," in the *Boston Public Library Quarterly* (Vol. 5, 1953, pp. 83–96), discusses "an exhibit of early Jewish books printed in America" arranged "in the Treasure Room of the Boston Public Library" (p. 83) in mid-February 1953. Some of these titles are in Hebrew.

David Persky compiled "American Hebrew Books," which was published in Volumes 11–19 (1952–1960) of *Jewish Book Annual;* while D. Abramowicz compiled "American Yiddish Books" for 1950–1972, which was published in Volumes 10–30 of the *Annual*. Theodore Wiener continued Persky's works in Volumes 20–30 (1961–1973), which covered the period 1961–1972.

American Jewish Newspapers and Periodicals on Microfilm: Available at the American Jewish Periodical Center (Cincinnati, 1957, 56 pp.) has been continued by Herbert C. Zafren, who compiled its first supplement (Cincinnati, 1960, 32 pp.).

Fannie M. Brody, "The Hebrew Periodical Press in America, 1871–1931: A Bibliographical Survey," in *Publications of the American Jewish Historical Society* (Vol. 33, 1934, pp. 127–170), is based on the New York Public Library collection. Pages 131–134 are a "General Bibliography" which lists the sources for the numerous notes that conclude each bibliographic entry.

Michael Gary Brown, "All, All Alone: The Hebrew Press in America from 1914 to 1924," in *American Jewish Historical Quarterly* (Vol. 59, 1969–1970, pp. 139–178), contains the appendix "List of American Hebrew Periodicals, 1914–1924" (pp. 175–177).

Joseph Chaikin, *Yidishe bleter in Amerike* (The Author, New York, 1946, 424 pp.) has the following on the verso of its title page: Yiddish leaves in America: A contribution to the history of the Yiddish press in the United States and Canada from 1870 to 1945.

Hermann Eliassof, "Journals Printed in the Hebrew Language," in *The Reform Advocate* (Vol. 51, May 27, 1916, pp. 524–534), is part of his series Main Currents of American Jewish Journalism.

Joseph Esterman, "The American Jewish Press," in *American Weekly Jewish News* (Vol. 1, June 14, 1918, pp. 262, 275), is a discussion of the Jewish press regardless of language. The linguistic and political orientations of the various newspapers are presented.

In 1945 the Yiddish Writers' Union issued *Finf un zibetsik yor Yiddishe Presse in Amerike, 1870–1945* (the title on the added title page reads *75 Years Yiddish Press in the United States of America [1870–1945]*) (New York, 196 pp.). This volume includes a listing of Yiddish newspapers and magazines.

The American Jewish Yearbook publishes in each volume a listing of Jewish periodicals. The first such list was that of Abraham Solomon Freidus, "A List of Jewish Periodicals Published in the United States" (Vol. 1, 1899, pp. 271–282). Recently the title has been changed to "Jewish Periodicals: United States (Canada)." These lists include periodicals in English, Hebrew, Yiddish, and Ladino.

The Joseph Jacobs Directory of the Jewish Press in America, issued in New York by the Joseph Jacobs Organization, has appeared in two editions. The first was published in 1970 (140 pp); the second, in 1972 (144 pp.). Both list Jewish periodicals published in the United States and Canada.

Illinois. The Yiddish press of Chicago has been briefly discussed in Moses Heskuni, "The Yiddish Press of Chicago, 1877–1907," in *The Chicago Pinkas*, edited by Simon Rawidowicz (College of Jewish Studies, Chicago, 1952, pp. lxix-lxxviii).

Michigan. Irving I. Katz, "The Jewish Press in Detroit," in *Michigan Jewish History* (Vol. 14, No. 1, January 1974, pp. 18–22), contains an introduction and sections entitled "English–Jewish Newspapers," "Yiddish Newspapers," and "Hebrew Periodicals."

New York. Mordecai Soltes, "A. List of Yiddish Dailies Published in New York City (1885–1923)" and "B. Yiddish Daily Periodicals Appearing in New

York City in 1923," in *The Yiddish Press, an Americanizing Agency* (Columbia University Teachers College, New York, 1925; reprinted in 1950 and distributed by Bloch Publishing Co., New York, pp. 182–184), provides data on the Yiddish press through July 1924.

Joseph Margoshes, "A List of Jewish Periodicals Published in New York City Previous to 1917," in *The Jewish Communal Register of New York City, 1917–1918*, second edition, edited by the Kehillah (New York, 1918, pp. 619–628), is divided into English, German, English journals with German supplements, Hebrew, Judeo-Spanish, and Yiddish. This is continued by "A List of Jewish Periodicals Appearing in New York City during 1917" (pp. 628–633). This part is divided into dailies, weekly family journals, weekly party organs, monthly organs, professional and trade journals, trade union papers, recreational and cultural agencies, general business papers, organization bulletins, neighborhood journals, juvenile periodicals, humorous papers, and annuals.

Western U.S. For this area, see Suzanne Nemiroff, *Catalog of Western Jewish Periodicals 1849–1945 at the Western Jewish History Center and Guide to the Resources at Other Depositories* (Western Jewish History Center, Berkeley, 1976, 15 leaves).

Canada. Golda Cukier has compiled *Canadian Jewish Periodicals: A Revised Listing* (Jewish Public Library, Montreal, 1978, 38 leaves). This is a later edition of her *Canadian Jewish Periodicals: A Preliminary Listing* (Jewish Public Library, Montreal, 1969, 30 leaves). The compiler provides data on periodicals in English, French, Yiddish, Hebrew, and Hungarian. The preface to the 1978 edition notes that "The present listing includes independently published serials, as well as institutional organs published currently and also those which have ceased publication. Synagogue bulletins are not included." David Rome has compiled *A Selected Bibliography of Jewish Canadiana* (Canadian Jewish Congress and the Jewish Public Library, Montreal, 1959). This is a collection of classified lists on the Jew in Canada. Each list has its separate pagination. Material is included in Hebrew and Yiddish. These lists were issued "On the bicentenary of the settlement of the Jews in Canada (1759–1959)." Cukier's list has a bibliography of seven items.

Pinches, "Di Yidishe Prese in Kanada," in the *Jewish Eagle* (August 8, 1915); and Abram Rhinewine, *Der Yid in Kanade* (Farlag Canada, Toronto, 1925) would seem to be especially pertinent for the study of the Yiddish press in Canada.

Rowena Pearlman and Alexander Malycky published two works in the *Canadian Ethnic Studies:* "Jewish Canadian Periodical Publications: A Preliminary Check List" (Vol. 1, 1969, pp. 44–49), which lists 38 items, and "Jewish . . . First Supplement" (Vol. 2, 1970, pp. 131–149).

Critical comments on Canadian writers who use Yiddish are found in Eugene V. Ornstein's *University of Toronto Quarterly* articles: "Publications in Other Languages" (Vol. 47, 1978, pp. 501–503), on the works of R. Korn, M. M. Shaffer, and S. Shtern; and "Publications in Yiddish" (Vol. 46, 1976–1977, pp. 500–506).

HUNGARIAN

Joseph Széplaki, *Hungarians in the United States and Canada: A Bibliography*, holdings of the Immigration History Research Center of the University of Minnesota (IHR Ethnic Bibliography No. 2, Immigration History Center, Minneapolis, 1977, 113 pp.) should be the starting point for the study of this ethnic group.

Joseph D. Dwyer has compiled *Hungarian American Collection* (IHRC Ethnic Collections Series No. 4, Immigration History Research Center, University of Minnesota, 1976, 9 pp.)

Newspapers and periodicals from the United States and Canada are found in Koloman Mildschutz, *Bibliographie der Ungarischen Exilpresse (1945–1975)* . . . (Studia Hungaria No. 12, Rudolf Trofenik, Munich, 1977, xi, 149 pp.).

Hungarian-American literature has been studied by Z. Czorba, *Adalekok as amerikai magyar irodalom tortenetehez* (Pecs, 1930); and Leslie Könnyü, *A History of American-Hungarian Literature* ([Cooperative of American Hungarian Authors, St. Louis, 1962], 124 pp.).

David Aaron Souders, "List of Magyar Publications in the United States," in *The Magyars in America* (George H. Doran, New York, 1922, pp. 138–142), is divided into secular and religious publications.

Otto Arpad Taborsky, "The Hungarian Press in America" (M.A. thesis, Catholic University of America, 1955, v, 117 leaves) is divided into Part 1. Background, Part 2. Papers and Periodicals, Part 3. Book Publication, Conclusion, and Appendix: Tables and Bibliography.

Taborsky has brought together much information concerning Hungarian publications, both books and serials, in the United States. Tables VII–XIV should prove of interest to students of Hungarian journalism in the United States. These are: Decennial Lists of Hungarian Papers from Ayer's Directories, 1180–1953; Date of Origin of Oldest Existing Foreign Language Dailies; Number of Hungarian Papers in the United States, 1884–1920; Papers Listed in Sequence of Their Appearance in 1910; Papers Existing in 1910; Magyar Secular Papers in the United States in 1922; Distribution of Hungarian Papers in 1930; and Papers Published in Chicago in 1942.

Canada. For Hungarian-Canadian imprints, see: Leslie Duska and Alexander Malycky, "Hungarian-Canadian Periodical Publications: A Preliminary Check List," in *Canadian Ethnic Studies* (Vol. 2, 1970, pp. 75–81), which provides data on 50 periodicals; John M. Miska, "Hungarian-Canadian Creative Literature: A Preliminary Check List of Imprints" (ibid., Vol. 5, 1973, pp. 131–137); and Jenó Ruzsa, "A kanadai magyar sajtó," in *A kanadai magyarság története* ([Toronto], 1940, pp. 362–369).

ICELANDIC

No one seems to have attempted a bibliography of Icelandic imprints published in the United States. Cornell University Library's *Catalogue of the Icelandic Collection* (1914, 1927, 1943, 3 vols.) records only four such items.

Canada. Walter J. Lindel, "Icelandic-Canadian Periodical Publications: A

Preliminary Check List," in *Canadian Ethnic Studies* (Vol. 2, 1970, pp. 85–90), provides data on 54 periodicals.

Margarét Sigvaldatóttir-Geppert compiled "Icelandic-Canadian Creative Literature: A Preliminary Check List," published in *Canadian Ethnic Studies* (Vol. 5, 1973, pp. 139–151).

ITALIAN

Lynn A. Schweitzer compiled *The Italian American Collection* (2nd ed., IHRC Ethnic Collections Series No. 5, Immigration History Research Center, University of Minnesota, 1977, 21 pp.).

Part VI, "Newspapers and Periodicals" (pp. 165–173) of Francesco Cordasco, *Italian Americans: A Guide to Information Sources* (Gale Research Co., Detroit, 1978) would seem to be one of the few lists of Italian-American newspapers.

Canada. For Italian-Canadian periodicals, see Luciano Bianchini and Alexander Malycky, "Italian-Canadian Periodical Publications: A Preliminary Check List," in *Canadian Ethnic Studies* (Vol. 2, 1970, pp. 121–126) and "Italian-Canadian . . . First Supplement" (ibid., Vol. 5, 1973, pp. 197–204).

JAPANESE

The Social Science Research Institute of the University of Hawaii in Honolulu has published two bibliographic studies compiled by Mitsuga Matsuda. They are *The Japanese in Hawaii, 1868–1967: A Bibliography of the First Hundred Years* (1968) and *The Japanese in Hawaii: An Annotated Bibliography of Japanese Americans . . .*, revised by Dennis M. Ogawa and Jerry Y. Fujioka (1975). The first of these contains the section "Japanese Materials" (pp. 1–94); the majority of the items listed are in Japanese and published in Hawaii. Pages 183–291 of the second volume should also be of value to the student of Japanese imprints in Hawaii.

Y. Soga, "The Japanese Press in Hawaii," in *Mid-Pacific Monthly* (Vol. 23, January 1922, pp. 39–41), is an early article now greatly dated.

KOREAN

Taehan Min'guk Kukhoe Tosogwan, *Han'guk sinnun chapchi ch'ong mongnok: 1883–1945* (Seoul, 1966, 230 pp.) provides data on early Korean-language publications in Hawaii.

LADINO

The Ladino press of the Western Hemisphere is included in Moshe David Gaon, *ha'Itouit be-Ladino* (Beni-Zvi Institute for Research on Jewish Communities in the Middle East, The Hebrew University, Jerusalem, 1965, 143 pp.). The title on the English title page is *A Bibliography of the Judeo-Spanish (Ladino) Press*.

This volume has four indexes: (*a*) by first date of publication, (*b*) by place of publication, (*c*) personal name index (including editors, publishers, and printers in

Hebrew characters), and (*d*) personal name index in the Roman alphabet (for journals with double title pages or double titles).

LATVIAN

The best bibliographies of Latvian publications issued outside of Latvia are the three volumes compiled by Benjaminš Jegers and published in Stockholm by Daugava: *Latviešu trimdas izdevumu bibliografi ja 1940–1960: 1. Gramatas un brošuras* [Bibliography of Latvian Publications Published Outside Latvia 1940–1960: 1. Books and Pamphlets] (1968, 338 pp.), *Latviešu trimdas izdevumu bibliografi ja 1940–1960: 2. Periodika, notis, kartes, programmas un katalogi* [. . . 2. Serials, Music, Maps, Programs and Catalogs] (1972, 407 pp.), and *Latviešu trimdas izdevumu bibliografija 1961–1970* (1977, 461 pp.).

Volume 3 includes books, pamphlets, serials, music, maps, programs, and catalogs, and can be considered typical of the set. It has five indexes: 1. Subjects, 2. Places of Publication, 3. Publishers, Institutions, and Organizations, 4. Persons, and 5. Titles.

An examination of the place of publication index leads one immediately to several types of materials: publications of all kinds published in the United States in Latvian, English translations of Latvian works, and works by Latvians written originally in English.

These volumes deal with Latvian material published outside of Latvia between 1940 and 1970 and are an excellent guide to Latvian exile publications.

Edide Franklina, with an introduction by Rasma Simáte, "Latvian Children's Literature in Exile: A Bibliography of Children's Books and Periodicals Published Outside Latvia from 1945–1979," in *Phaedrus* (Vol. 6, No. 1, 1979, pp. 44–63), contains more than 400 items published in the United States and Europe.

Canada. For Canada, see Osvalds Akmentinš, "Latvian-Canadian Periodical Publications: A Preliminary Check List," in *Canadian Ethnic Studies* (Vol. 5, 1973, pp. 213–220).

LITHUANIAN

The fullest study of Lithuanian-American imprints is an unpublished study by Vaelovas Birziska in the Library of Congress manuscript collection. To date only its introduction has been published: "The American Lithuanian Publications, 1875–1910," in *Journal of Central European Affairs* (Vol. 18, 1959, pp. 396–408). According to Birziska, 1,350 books and pamphlets were published in Lithuanian in the United States between 1875 and 1910.

The earliest bibliography of Lithuanian-American imprints is Jonas Zilinskas Zilius (published under the pseudonym of Jr. Jonas), *Suskaita arba statistika visu Lietuviszku Knygu Atspaustu Amerikoj nuo Pradzios Lietuvisz kos Amerikon Emigracijos ligi 1900 metu* (Plymouth, Pa., 1900, 35 pp.), which had been prepared for the Paris World's Fair of 1900.

Many of items 2335–2424 of Adam and Filomena Kantautas, *A Lithuanian Bibliography* (University of Alberta Press, Edmonton, 1975) were published in the

United States; most of these are in Lithuanian. One should also consult the Kantautas' *Supplement to a Lithuanian Bibliography*, subtitled A Further Check List of Books and Articles Held by the Major Libraries of Canada and the United States (University of Alberta Press, 1979, xxviii, 316 pp.). Items 449–539 list serials, some of which are published in the United States or Canada. Many other sections list items published in North America.

B. Jonaitis has compiled "Lithuanian Books and Books on Lithuanian Affairs Published Abroad in 1964," published in *Lituanistikos darbai* (Vol. 1, 1966, pp. 191–203) and "Lithuanian . . . in 1965" (ibid., Vol. 1, 1966, pp. 204–217). Aleksandras Ruzancovas, "Lietuviu knyga tremtyje: 1945–1949," in *Naujienos* (published serially in Nos. 50, 133, 174, 192, 227, and 292 for 1959; and Nos. 31 and 67 for 1960), and "Lietuviu iseiviu 1958 metu bibliografija," in *Knygu lentyna* (No. 2, March–April 1960, pp. 29–40) deal with Lithuanian books published in exile between 1945 and 1949 and in 1958. Ruzancovas and Bronius Kuiklys, "Lietuvos iseiviu 1959 . . .," in *Knygu lentyna* (No. 1, 1960, pp. 2–14; No. 2, 1960, pp. 25–28), list books published in exile by Lithuanians in 1959. For the listing of Lithuanian publications published outside of Lithuania in 1967, see *Uzsienio lietuviu spaudos metrastis . . . 1967*, compiled by Z. Asoklis et al. (JAV LB Kulturos fondas, Chicago, 1968, 64 pp.).

Nijole Julia Abraitis, "An Annotated Bibliography of Lithuanian Books Published Outside of Lithuania since 1944" (Master's project, Western Reserve University, 1958, 49 leaves), is arranged alphabetically by author. Based on the collection of the Cleveland Library, the 267 books were published chiefly in Germany and the United States. The appendix (pp. 48–49) is a classified index.

Susivienijimo Lietuviu Amerikoja Kalendorius (New York, 1916) gives names, addresses, type of publication, frequency of appearance, and subscription rate (pp. 181–182).

Kovos Metai del savosios spaudos, edited by Vytautas Bagdanavicius (Lithuanian Community of Chicago Area and the Lithuanian Book Club, Chicago, 1957) contains two articles of interest: Juozas Prunskis, "Amerikiniai lietuviu laikrasciai" (pp. 297–314), and Vytautas Sirvydas, "Amerikos lietuviu knygos" (pp. 239–296); the later article is based on the Birziska manuscript.

Lithuanian publications of the United States are treated under their titles in both the *Encyclopedia Lituanica* (1970–1978, 6 vols.) and *Lietuviu Enciklopedija* (1953–1969, 36 vols.). Both of these sets are published in South Boston, Massachusetts, by the Lithuanian Encyclopedia Publishing Company.

The most recent study of the Lithuanian press is J. P. Balys, "The American Lithuanian Press," in *Lituanus* (Vol. 22, 1976, pp. 42–58), which provides data on 12 newspapers and 42 journals that were being published in the 1970s. Both newspapers and magazines are listed in *Amerikos lietuviu laikrasciai, 1879–1955* (F. Lavinskas, Long Island, N.Y., 1956, 191 pp.).

There are two M.A. theses that deal with the Lithuanian press in the United States, both accepted in 1961. These are: Enata Skrupskelis, "The Lithuanian Emigrant Press in the United States after World War II" (University of Chicago, 90 leaves), and Danute-Dana J. Taulvilas, "The Lithuanian Press in America" (Catholic University of America, 127 leaves).

Skrupskelis notes that "the over-all picture of the Lithuanian immigrant publishing in the United States between 1950 and 1959 is as follows: There were published during this time a total of 1,062 items, distributed between 499 books and 562 pamphlets" (leaf 82). Part 3 is "Lithuanian Publishing Activities in the U.S.," and Part 4 is "Lithuanian Publishers in the U.S."

The author gives no listing of the slightly more than 1,000 items covered. Instead, she provides a content analysis of the publications by noting how many titles would be classified into each of the 10 main divisions of the Dewey Decimal System.

Part 2 of the Taulvilas thesis deals with "Lithuanian Newspapers and Periodicals" (leaves 38–66), and the most important portions are "First Steps 1874–1904," "Lithuanian Press between 1905–1945," and "Growth of Lithuanian Press in Postwar Period." Part 3 devotes Chapter 8 to "Selected Popular Books and Pamphlets" (leaves 68–81).

Table 6, Lithuanian Newspapers and Periodicals in Sequence of Their Appearance in the U.S.A. 1879–1959 (leaves 94–102), lists 186 titles. Table 9 lists 58 Lithuanian newspapers and periodicals published in the United States between 1959 and 1960 (leaves 110–113). Leaf 119, Table 13, lists 9 Lithuanian book publishers in the United States.

Other articles on the Lithuanian newspapers and periodicals are: Juozas Lingis, "The Lithuanian Emigrant Press," in *Baltic Review* (Vol. 1, No. 6, 1946, pp. 299–303); "The Lithuanian American Press," in *Lithuanian Bulletin* (Vol. 8, Nos. 7–12, 1950, pp. 19–20), which provides a list of 49 newspapers and periodicals; and *Lithuanian Publications in the United States* (Common Council for American Unity, New York, [1959], 5 leaves unpaged [lists of foreign-language publications in the United States]), which provides such data, on 36 publications, as title with translation, owner or publisher, editor and address, character, periodicity, and circulation.

[Jonas Sliupas], *Lietuviszkeijie rasztai ir rasztininkai* (Tilsit, 1890, pp. 206–218) comments on Rev. Alexander Burba, a journalist; and on *Unija* and *Lietuviszkas Balsas*, Lithuanian-American newspapers.

William Wolkovich-Valkavicius, "The Impact of a Catholic Newspaper on an Ethnic Community: The Lithuanian Weekly *Rytas*, 1896–98, Waterbury, Connecticut," in *Lituanus* (Vol. 24, No. 3, Fall 1978, pp. 42–54), presents a history of this newspaper and comments on other Lithuanian newspapers published during this same time.

M. G. Slavemas, "Lithuanian Children's Literature in Exile, 1945–1978," in *Phaedrus* (Vol. 6, No. 1, 1979, pp. 32–40), "traces development, trends, present status of Lithuanian children's literature in exile against its sociohistorical background, [and] attempts to include all authors who have distinguished themselves in this field during this period by at least mentioning one or two of their most successful works; excluded are translations, compilations, readers, anthologies, textbooks and other school related materials" (p. 32).

Canada. Pranas Guida and Peter Baltgailis, "Lithuanian-Canadian Periodical Publications: A Preliminary Check List," in *Canadian Ethnic Studies* (Vol. 2, 1970, pp. 151–155), provides data on 37 periodicals.

NORWEGIAN

Apparently no published bibliography exists of Norwegian-American books and pamphlets. Thor Andersen of Norway has worked for years on such a project, and a committee has been organized to see it through publication. Lloyd Hustvedt, secretary of the Norwegian-American Historical Association, estimates that this association's collection contains 6,000 American imprints in Norwegian.

The fullest bibliography of the Norwegian press is that compiled by Johanna Bartsaal and published by the Library of the University of Oslo: *Litteratur om utvandingen fra Nord-Amerika* . . . (1975, 205 pp.). "Presse" (pp. 155–158) is divided in sections on bibliography, general studies, and studies on the following individual newspapers: *Decorah-Posten, Emigranten og Faedrelander, Nordisk Tidende, Nordlyset, Normannen, Skandinaven, Skandinavia, Vinland*, and *Washington Posten*.

Luther College of Decorah, Iowa, has a complete card file of all "Decorah Imprints" that includes items published by the Amundsen Publishing Company and by the Old Lutheran Publishing House, which was the publishing house of the Norwegian Synod. This synod existed until 1917, and up to at least 1910 most of the synod's publications were in Norwegian.

Olaf Morgan Norlie, *Norwegian-American Papers, 1847–1946* (Northfield, Minn., 1946, mimeographed, 37 unnumbered leaves); and Olvind M. Hovde and Martha E. Henzler, *Norwegian-American Newspapers in Luther College Library* (Luther College Press, Decorah, Iowa, 1975, 82 pp.) are the chief bibliographies of newspapers.

Norlie includes both newspapers and other types of periodical literature. It is unfortunate that copies are not located in U.S. or Norwegian libraries.

Hovde and Henzler, in a brief prefatory note, state that "entries are arranged alphabetically by title and include as much information as can be gathered from the very limited resources available in this area and from the newspapers themselves." Pages 81–82, "Index to Places of Publication," would allow a geographical approach to the study of Norwegian-American newspapers. Pages 76–80 list the library's Danish-American papers, and page 80 lists one Norwegian-English paper.

Jacob Hodnefield, "Norwegian-American Bygdelags and Their Publications," in *Norwegian-American Studies and Reports* (Vol. 18, 1954, pp. 163–222), is a useful discussion and a listing of the publications of *bygdelags*. According to the author, "a *bygdelag*, in Norwegian speech, is a society where members are of one community" (p. 163).

Odd Sverre Løvoll, *A Folk Epic: The Bygdelag in America* was published for the Norwegian American Historical Association by Twayne Publishers (Boston, 1975); pages 301–306 provide a list of *bygdelag* publications.

Vinland (Vol. 16, Nos. 32–33, September 6, 1973) contains Bertram Jensenius, "Dedicated to the Memory of the Norwegian-American Press" (pp. 1, 15) and "1847 Norwegian-American Newspapers 1973 Updated and Listed Both Alphabetically and Chronologically" (pp. 5–13), which provides brief data on more than 560 newspapers.

The following would appear to be the most important overall discussions of the

Norwegian-American press: Albert O. Barton, "The Beginnings of the Norwegian Press in America" in *Proceedings of the State Historical Society of Wisconsin* (1916, pp. 186–212); Theodore C. Blegen, "The Early Norwegian Press in America," in *Minnesota History Bulletin* (Vol. 3, November 1920, pp. 506–518); John Sabert Johnson, "Den norsk-amerikanski presse," in *Minnesota . . .* (McGill-Warner Co., St. Paul, [1914], pp. 114–121); Julius E. Olson, "Literature and the Press," in Harry Sundby-Hansen, *Norwegian Immigrant Contributions to America's Making* (The International Press, New York, 1921, pp. 125–138); Olaf Holmer Spetland, "Den norsk-amerikanske presse," in *Syn og segn* (Vol. 80, No. 1, 1974, pp. 35–38); two sections of *Norsk-amerikanernes festskrift 1914* (Symra Co., Decorah, Iowa, 1914): Carl Hansen, "Den norsk-amerikansk press: I. Pressen til borgerkrigens slutning" (pp. 9–40), and Johannes B. Wist, "Den norsk-amerikanske press: II. Pressen efter borgerkrigen" (pp. 41–203); and Juul Dieserud, "Den norske press i Amerika: En historisk Oversigt," in *Normands-Forbundet* (Vol. 5, April 1912, pp. 153–176). Carl Hansen is the author of "Den norsk-amerikanske press for borgerkrigen," in *Symra* (Vol. 4, 1908, pp. 25–44) and of "Et stykke Norsk-amerikanske press historie," in *Kvartalskrift* (Vol. 1, No. 3, January 1907, pp. 14–28).

Hansen's section in the *Festskrift 1914* deals with the Norwegian press to the end of the Civil War. Wist's material in this work takes this history from the end of the Civil War through the early 20th century. Barton provides data on "the first book published by a Norwegian in this country"; biographical sketches concerning important 19th-century Norwegian-American printers, publishers, and editors; and a state-by-state account of the Norwegian-American press. Blegen's article must have been extremely valuable at the time that it was published, for his first footnote is an exceedingly helpful bibliography of the Norwegian-American press, and he has made an attempt to locate files of the most important of the newspapers that he discusses. His article deals with the Norwegian-American press from the late 1840s through the late 1860s.

Martin Ulvestad, *Nordmaendene i Amerika* (History Book Company's forlag, Minneapolis, 1907, pp. 431–444) provides a list of Norwegian-language newspapers published in the United States.

Arlow William Andersen, *The Immigrant Takes His Stand*, subtitled The Norwegian-American Press and Public Affairs, 1847–1872 (Norwegian-American Historical Association, 1953), "deals with editorial opinion on public affairs in the first quarter of the Norwegian-American press . . . " (p. v). Pages 12–13 are a table of the 21 papers published between 1847 and 1873. This table gives each paper's title, place of publication, time, editors, and political affiliation.

Two Norwegian-American newspapers studied in *Norwegian American Studies* are: Jean Skogerboe Hansen, "*Skandinaven* and the John Anderson Publishing Company" (Vol. 28, 1970, pp. 35–68), which notes that this firm published about 400 titles in Norwegian; and Odd S. Løvoll, "*Decorah-Posten*, the Story of an Immigrant Newspaper" (Vol. 27, 1977, pp. 77–100), which provides important data on this important long-lasting newspaper. *Symra*, a Norwegian-American periodical, is discussed by Einar Haugen, "Symra: A Memoir," in *Norwegian-American Studies* (Vol. 27, 1977, pp. 107–110).

Haldor L. Hove, "Five Norwegian Newspapers, 1870–1890: Purveyors of Literary Taste and Culture" (Ph.D. dissertation, University of Chicago, 1962, x, 470 leaves) deals with the following newspapers: *Budstikken, Decorah-Posten, Norden, Skandinaven*, and *Faedrelandet og emigranten*. Hove writes that "it is the purpose of this dissertation, therefore, to examine the five leading secular Norwegian immigrant weekly newspapers published in the Midwest from 1870 to 1890 for their literary context and to trace their editorial activity with respect to the publication of literature and the fostering of literary culture among the Norwegian immigrants" (leaf iii).

New York and New England. For the Norwegian-American press of this area one should consult A. N. Rygg, "Newspapers," in *Norwegians in New York 1825–1925* (Norwegian News Co., Brooklyn, 1941, pp. 133–136); and Sigurd Daasband, "The Norwegian-American Press in the East," in *They Came from Norway*, edited by Erik J. Friis (Norwegian Immigration Sesquicentennial Commission, New York, 1975, pp. 59–63). More than half of the Daasband article is devoted to the *Nordisk Tidende*, which the author edits. There is a history of this paper by Karsten Roedder, *Av en utvandreravis' saga—Nordisk Tidende i New York gjennon 75 år* (Norwegian News–Norway Printers, Brooklyn, 1966–1968 2 vols.), which appeared to celebrate this paper's 75th anniversary.

North Dakota. Odd Sverre Løvoll, "The Norwegian Press in North Dakota," in *Norwegian-American Studies* (Vol. 24, 1970, pp. 78–102), is based on his M.A. thesis, "History of Norwegian-Language Publications in North Dakota" (University of North Dakota, 1969, 72 leaves). The major portion of this article is a history of Norwegian newspapers in this state. The last two pages are a listing of the Norwegian newspapers, dates of the files, and locations of the newspapers studied.

J. H. Fraser, "A Comment on Norwegian-American Children's Literature and Language Maintenance," in *Phaedrus* (Vol. 6, No. 1, 1979, pp. 41–43), briefly discusses outstanding Norwegian-American writers and their works from the 19th to the early 20th century. It also provides data on periodicals.

Canada. For Norwegian-Canadian newspapers, see data in Alexander Malycky, "Norwegian-Canadian Periodical Publications: A Preliminary Check List," in *Canadian Ethnic Studies* (Vol. 2, 1970, pp. 159–161); and P. K. With, "Norwegian-Canadian . . . First Supplement" (ibid., Vol. 5, 1973, pp. 235–238).

POLISH

Much of what follows in this section is based on Wladyslaw Chojnacki and Walter M. Drzewieniecki, "Towards a Bibliography of American Polonia," in *Polish American Studies* (Vol. 35, No. 1–2, 1978, pp. 54–77). This is an extremely valuable bibliographic essay on Polish-American imprints and collections in the United States and Canada.

Frank Renkiewicz compiled *Polish American Collection* (2nd ed., IHRC Ethnic Collection Series No. 7, Immigration History Research Center, University of Minnesota, 1977, 18 pp.), which discusses the IHRC Polish-American materials.

Another Polish-American collection is described in Gene Baranouski, "Polish Americana, 1873–1890," in *Polish American Studies* (Vol. 16, No. 1–2, 1959, pp.

34–44), which lists "Polish language publications that have appeared in the United States . . . and are still to be found in the Polonica Americana Collection of the Alumni Memorial Library at Orchard Lake, Michigan" (p. 35).

M. Liguori Pakowska, "The First Polish Book Printed in the United States," in *Polish American Studies* (Vol. 5, No. 1–2, 1948, pp. 1–7), studies this volume published in 1834 in Philadelphia.

Alphonse S. Wolanin has compiled *Polonica Americana: Annotated Catalogue* (Polish Roman Catholic Union of America, Chicago, 1950, 295 pp.).

Artur Leonard Waldo provides a list of literary works in both Polish and English of Polish-American authors in his *Zarys historii literatury polskiej w Ameryce szkic bibliograficzny*, Biblioteca Pisarzy Polonii (Nakl. Dziennika Zjednoczenia, Chicago, 1938, 48 pp.). Many of the works in Polish were published in the United States.

Data about Polish imprints can be found in the following articles about Polish-American printing published in *Polish American Studies:* Helena Chrzanowska, "Polish Book Publishing in Chicago" (Vol. 4, No. 1–2, 1947, pp. 37–39); M. Ancilla Samsel, "Catholic Polish Books Published in United States, 1871–1900" (Vol. 16, No. 1–2, 1959, pp. 1–11); Richard Śnieżyk, "Polish Editions of Sienkiewicz Published in America" (Vol. 15, No. 3–4, 1958, pp. 67–69); and Casmir Stec, "Pioneer Polish-American Publisher" (Vol. 18, No. 2, 1961, pp. 65–83).

Sister M. Ancilla Samsel's article is based on her master's thesis: "Catholic Polish Book Publishing in the United States . . . 1871–1900" (Catholic University of America, 1957, iv, 130 leaves), which provides data on about 400 items.

Jacek Przygoda, "Szkic historyczny polskiej katolickiej literatury homiletycznej w Stanach Zjednoczonych," in *Sacrum Polonial Millennium* (Vol. 4, 1957, pp. 559–566), includes Polish-American homiletic literature.

Jan Kowalik is the compiler of the four-volume *World Index of Polish Periodicals Published Outside of Poland Since September 1939* (American Polish Documentation Studio, Sunnyvale, Calif., 1972–1974), which is arranged alphabetically by title and has a place of publication index.

The following would appear to be the most important studies in English on the Polish press in the United States: Edmund G. Olszyk, *The Polish Press in America* (Marquette University Press, Milwaukee, 1940, 95 pp., originally a master's thesis); Jan Kowalik, *The Polish Press in America* (R. & E. Research Associates, San Francisco, 1976, iv, 76 pp.); Benjamin Chapinski, "Ethnics and Their Media: A Specific Documentation of Polonia in the United States," in *Gazette* (Vol. 25, 1979, pp. 87–95); and Eugene Obidinski, "The Polish American Press: Survival Through Adaptation," in *Polish American Studies* (Vol. 34, No. 2, 1971, pp. 38–55).

Part 3 of Olszyk's study provides a historical sketch of important Polish-American newspapers (pp. 50–62), and Part 6 (pp. 76–91) provides a chronological "listing of all the known Polish-American publications beginning with the first newspaper in 1863 to Jan. 1, 1939" (p. 76).

Kowalik's work is divided into: Definitions, Historical Outline, The Contemporary Press, Polish and Other Ethnic Publications, General Evaluation, The Purpose and Attitudes of the Polish-American Press, The Role of the Polish-American Press in the Integration Process, Appendix I: References, Appendix II:

Alphabetical Checklist of the Polish-American Press 1974, Appendix III: Geographical Distribution of the Polish-American Press 1974, Maps and Diagrams, and Name Plates of Publications.

Chapinski presents interesting historical and statistical data on the Polonian press.

Obidinski had access to two unpublished manuscripts by Waclaw S. Flisinski: "Prassa Polonija w Ameryce, 1842–1972" and "Polish American Periodical Publications, July 1977." His article is divided into: Dimensions of the Polish American Press, Functions of the Polonian Press, Adaptations and Survival, Classification of Press Contents, Content of Polonian Papers: Findings, Polish American Press: Interpretations and Conclusions, and Summary and Conclusions.

The earliest history of the Polish press in the United States is that of Henryk Nagiel, *Dziennikarstwo polskie w Ameryce i jego 30-letnie dzieje* (Nakladem Kom. centr. obeslavia wystwy lwowskiej przez polonie amerykanska, Chicago, 1894, 130 pp.).

Waclaw Kruszka, "Gazeciarstwo polskie w Ameryce," in *Historia polska w Ameryce* (Kuryer Polski Publishing Co., Milwaukee, 1905–1908; Vol. 4, pp. 83–123, and Vol. 5, pp. 1–84), provides not only a history of the Polish-American press but also a chronological list of the newspapers that appeared between 1863 and 1905. Kruszka discusses 129 titles.

W. Koniuszewski, "Dziennikarstwo polskie w Ameryce," in *Sprawa polska w Ameryce Polnocnej* (Chicago, 1912), is a short account of the Polish-American press.

Stanisław Osada, *Prasa i publicystyka polska w Ameryce* ("Pittsburczanin," Pittsburgh, Pa., 1930, 96 pp.) lists 354 publications and provides biographical data about publishers and editors.

The following list Polish-American newspapers: "Czasopisma wydane w Ameryce w r. 1903," in *Przeglad bibliograficzny* (Vol. 27, No. 10, 1904, pp. 202–203, 257–258); "Spis gazet polskich w Ameryce," in *Kalendarz i przewodnik amerykańsko-polski na rok 1909* (A. A. Paryski, Toledo, 1908, pp. 221–226); *Wykaz prasy polskiej* ("Hygieia" Publishers, Berlin, 1911, pp. 87–91); "Pisma polskie w Ameryce Północenej i Południowej," in *Rocznik Towarzystwa Polskiego Literacko-Artystycznego w Paryżu* (Vol. 1, 1911–1912, pp. 44–46); S[tanislaw] J[urkowiski], "Prasa polska Ameryki Północnej w r. 1921," in *Książka* (Vol. 15, No. 5, 1922, pp. 242–247); and Mieczysław Szalewiski, *Wychodźstwo polskie w Stanach Zjednoczonych Ameryki* (Lwow, 1924, pp. 156–158), which gives 107 titles for 1923.

Michigan. R. Jarzabowska, "History of the Polish Press in Detroit," in *Poles in Michigan*, edited by Benjamin C. Stanczyk et al. (Poles in Michigan Associates, Detroit, 1955, Vol. 1, pp. 77–81), is a brief treatment of its subject.

New York. The Polish press of Buffalo has been studied in Kazimierz Smogorzewski, "Prasa Polska w Buffalo," in *Wychodźca* (Vol. 6, No. 13, 1927, pp. 4–5), and his "Prasa polska w Stanach Zjednoczonych" (ibid., Vol. 8, No. 35, 1929, pp. 2–3); Mierczysław Haiman, "*Polak w Ameryce* i prasa polska w Buffalo," in *Księga pamiątkowa zlotego jubileuszu osady polskiej i parafii Św. Stanisława, Buffalo, New York, 1873–1923* (The Publishing Committee, Buffalo, 1923, pp. 93–103); Walter M. Drzewieniecki, *Polonica buffalonensis*, subtitled Annotated

Bibliography of Source and Printed Materials Dealing with the Polish-American Community in the Buffalo, New York, Area (Buffalo and Erie County Historical Society with a grant from the Polish Cultural Foundation, Buffalo, 1976, xi, 148 pp.); Henry M. Senft, "The Pole in America: Study of Pioneer Newspapers of Buffalo, N.Y., 1887–1920" (M.A. thesis, Canisius College, 1950, v, 196 leaves); and Sister Mary [Somińska] Donata, "Polish-American Press in Buffalo," in the *Am-Pol Eagle* (Buffalo) (May 3, 1973).

Drzewieniecki's bibliography provides data on numerous books and pamphlets published in Polish in Buffalo and its surrounding area, and Part V, "Newspapers and Magazines" (pp. 138–144), provides pertinent data such as names of editors, addresses, and location of files or microfilms on 50 titles.

The Senft thesis deals with *Polak w Ameryce*, a leading Buffalo Polish newspaper.

The Buffalo and Erie County Historical Society has a folder, "Polish American Press in Buffalo, 1885–1975," which according to Drzewieniecki's *Polonica buffalonensis* (p. 16) is "an annotated list of forty-eight Polish American papers published in Buffalo area in Polish and English."

Wisconsin. Samuel Bonikowski, "The Polish Press in Wisconsin," in *Polish American Studies* (Vol. 2, No. 1–2, 1945, pp. 12–23), is a bibliographic essay concerning the Polish press from 1880 to the mid-1940s.

For the bibliographic control of Polish-American serials, see Jan Wepsiec, *Polish American Serial Publications, 1842–1966: An Annotated Bibliography* (Privately printed, Chicago, 1968, 191 pp.); Eugene P. Willging and Herta Hatzfeld, the compilers of two bibliographies published in *Polish American Studies:* "Nineteenth Century Polish Catholic Periodical Publications in the U.S." (Vol. 12, No. 3–4, 1955, pp. 88–100; Vol. 13, No. 1–2, 1956, pp. 19–35, and No. 3–4, pp. 89–101), and "A List of Nineteenth Century Polish Catholic Periodical Publications in the United States" (Vol. 14, No. 1–2, 1957, pp. 37–40); and Zofia Grzybowska, "A Contribution to Polish American History: Nineteenth Century Catholic Serials in the United States," in *Polish American Studies* (Vol. 12, No. 3–4, 1955, pp. 84–87). These list Catholic serials either in Polish or issued with Polish-Americans particularly in mind.

Canada. Victor Turek is the compiler of *Polonica Canadiana: A Bibliographical List of Canadian Polish Imprints, 1848–1957* (Instytut Polski w Kanadsie, Prace, Studies No. 2, Polish Alliance Press, Toronto, 1958, 38 pp.) and "Canadian Polish Imprints, 1848–1957: Additional Entries," in *The Polish Past in Canada*, edited by Victor Turek (Polish Research Institute in Canada, Studies No. 3, Polish Alliance Press, Toronto, 1960, pp. 123–131).

Vincent Zolobka, *Polonica Canadiana: A Bibliographical List of the Canadian Polish Imprints, 1958–1970*, with Foreword by Dr. B. B. Budurowycz (Canadian-Polish Research Institute, Studies No. 13, Polish Alliance Press, Toronto, 1978, 414 pp.) also includes a cumulative supplement to Victor Turek's *Polonica Canadiana, 1848–1957.*

Also useful is V. Zolobka, "Polonica Canadiana," in *Przesclość i Teraźniejszość*, edited by Benedykt Heydenkom (Canadian Research Institute, Toronto, 1975, pp. 143–192).

William Boleslaus Makowski, *History and Integration of Poles in Canada* (Canadian Polish Congress, Niagara Peninsula, Lindsay, Ontario, 1967), according to Stephen J. Jaworsky, "provides a list of Polish newspapers and periodicals based mainly on Victor Turek's work . . ." (p. 109).

Victor Turek, *The Polish Language Press in Canada* (Canadian Polish Congress and the Polish Research Institute in Canada, Toronto, 1962, 248 pp.) would seem to be the fullest treatment of its subject.

Benedykt Heydenkom provides a detailed history of *Zwiazkowiec* in his *Monografia pisma Polonijnego* (Polish Alliance Press, Toronto, 1963, 151 pp.).

PORTUGUESE

Portuguese immigrants settled chiefly in New England, California, and Hawaii.

The standard bibliography on Portuguese-Americans is Leo Pap, *The Portuguese in the United States: A Bibliography* (Center for Migration Studies, [Staten Island], 1976), which has the following sections of interest: 2A. Portuguese Immigrant Newspapers and Magazines (pp. 10–11), 3A. New England . . . Portuguese Immigrant Newspapers (pp. 17–18), 5A. California: Portuguese Immigrant Newspapers and Magazines (pp. 34–35), and 6A. Hawaii: Portuguese Immigrant Newspapers (p. 45).

Manoel da Silveira Cardozo has compiled and edited *The Portuguese in America 590 B.C.–1974, a Chronology and Fact Book* (Oceana Publications, Dobbs Ferry, N.Y., 1976), which contains scattered references to data on Portuguese newspapers in its chronology section.

California. Pages 244–245 of Frederick G. Bohme, "The Portuguese in California," in *California Historical Society Quarterly* (Vol. 35, 1956, pp. 233–252), discuss briefly the Portuguese-language press in California.

Alberto Corrêa, "Jornais portugueses publicados na California," in *Jornal português* (October 1958, n.p.), should also be useful.

"A imprensa portuguesa na California," in *Jornal português* (special ed., September 1938, n.p.), provides a brief note on 22 Portuguese newspapers.

The *Jornal português* (November 22, 1979) contains Manuel C. Rodrigues, "Velho mas sempre jovem" (pp. 1, 5); and Fernando M. S. Silva, "91° aniversario: O 'Jornal português' e o rodar da historía luso-californiana" (pp. 1, 16).

August Mark Vaz, "The Portuguese Press in California," in *The Portuguese in California* (I.D.E.S. Supreme Council, Oakland, Calif., 1965, pp. 139–140), would seem to be the fullest discussion of this topic in English. The volume would have been more useful had its sources been cited and had it been provided with a bibliography.

Hawaii. Edgar C. Knowlton, Jr., "The Portuguese Language Press in Hawaii," in *Social Process in Hawaii* (Vol. 24, 1960, pp. 89–99), would seem to be the longest study on the Portuguese-American press in English. I find nothing on this topic in John Henry Felix and Peter F. Senecal, *The Portuguese in Hawaii* (The Authors, Honolulu, Hawaii, 1978, 182 pp.).

PUNJABI

G. S. Basran lists material in both English and Punjabi in "East-Indian-Canadian Periodical Publications: A Preliminary Check List," in *Canadian Ethnic Studies* (Vol. 5, 1973, pp. 43–45).

ROMANIAN

Joseph D. Dwyer compiled *Romanian American Collection* (IHRC Ethnic Collection Series No. 7, Immigration History Research Center, University of Minnesota, 1976, 6 pp.).

RUSSIAN

Valerian Lada-Mocarski, "Earliest Russian Printing in the United States," in *Homage to a Bookman . . .* , edited by Hellmut Lehmann-Haupt (G. Mann, Berlin, 1967, pp. 231–233), is one of the few articles on Russian-language imprints in the United States.

David Shur, "The Russian Press in the United States," in *Russian Review* (Vol. 3, No. 1, Autumn 1943, pp. 120–128), is a brief history of the Russian press, chiefly in Alaska, California, and New York.

Vladimir Wertsman, "Russian American Periodicals," in *The Russians in America 1727–1970* (Oceana Publishers, Dobbs Ferry, N.Y., 1977, p. 133), lists periodicals in Russian and English as of the end of the 1970s.

Attention is also called to Elin Schoen, "The Russians Are Coming! The Russians Are Here!" in the *New York Times Book Review* (September 7, 1980, pp. 11, 20, 22–23).

Little seems to have been written concerning the Russian imprints of the United States. The most important work in this field would appear to be that of Robert Anthony Karlowich, "The Russian-Language Periodical Press in New York City from 1889 to 1914" (D.L.S., Columbia University, 1981, 537 pp.).

Canada. For Russian-Canadian imprints, see: Roman Piontkovsky, "Russian-Canadian Imprints: A Preliminary Check List," in *Canadian Ethnic Studies* (Vol. 2, 1970, pp. 177–185); Serge A. Sauer, "Russian-Canadian Periodical Publications: A Preliminary Check List" (ibid., Vol. 1, 1969, pp. 61–64); and Sauer, "Russian-Canadian . . . First Supplement" (ibid., Vol. 5, 1973, pp. 253–257).

SERBIAN

See Croatian and Serbian.

SHAWNEE

Almost nothing has been published concerning publications in the Shawnee language. There is Douglas C. McMurtrie, "The Shawnee Sun: The First Indian-Language Periodical Published in the United States," in *Kansas Historical Quarterly*

(Vol. 2, 1933, pp. 338–342). Page 338 reproduces the first page of the issue for November 1841. The newspaper there appears as *Siwinowe Kesibwi.*

SLOVENIAN

Rudolf Cuyes, "Slovenian-Canadian Periodical Publications: A Preliminary Check List," in *Canadian Ethnic Studies* (Vol. 1, 1969, pp. 70–71), provides data on nine titles in Slovenian and Serbo-Croatian.

SPANISH

Spanish is spoken by many people in Texas, New Mexico, Arizona, California, and parts of Utah and Colorado. These individuals are descendants of persons who lived in the area when it was annexed to the United States in 1848, or they have immigrated from Mexico. Puerto Ricans live chiefly in the New York–New England area, while those of Cuban origin have settled chiefly in Florida.

No bibliography of Spanish publications in the United States, either retrospective or current, exists. There is a need for such a bibliography. Miami has become a center for publishing material in Spanish, yet there is no current method for determining what is being published there.

Robert F. Brand, "A General View of the Regular Spanish Language Press in the United States," in *Modern Language Journal* (Vol. 33, May 1949, pp. 363–370), hopes to provide an "overall view of the main features of the Spanish press in this country" (p. 370). It is more historical and descriptive than bibliographic in nature.

Roberto Cabello-Argandoña, Juan Gómez-Quiñones, and William Tamayo, "Library Services and Chicano Periodicals: A Critical Look at Librarianship," in *Aztlán* (Vol. 2, 1971, pp. 151–172), provides data on Chicano newspapers and magazines, some in Spanish, some in English, and some bilingual.

Anne Jordan, "Mexican American Publishing Guide," in *Journal of Mexican American History* (Vol. 3, 1973, pp. 190–208), is divided into "Book Publishers," "Periodicals," "Addendum," and "Distributors."

Guadalupe Castillo and Herminio Ríos, "Toward a True Chicano Bibliography: Mexican-American Newspapers, 1848–1942," in *El Grito* (Vol. 3, 1970, pp. 17–24), provides brief data on 193 newspapers. Ríos, "Toward a True Chicano Bibliography," in *El Grito* (Vol. 5, 1972, pp. 40–47), provides brief data on 185 Mexican-American newspapers published between 1881 and 1958.

Volume 4 (No. 2, Summer 1977) of *Journalism History* is its "Spanish Language Media Issue." It contains the following articles on the Spanish-language press: Félix Gutiérrez, "Spanish-Language Media in America: Background/Resources, History" (pp. 34–41, 65–67); Ricard Griswold del Castillo, "The Mexican Revolution and the Spanish-Language Press in the Borderlands" (pp. 42–47); Ramón D. Chacón, "The Chicano Immigrant Press in Los Angeles: The Case of *El Heraldo de México*, 1916–1920" (pp. 48–50, 62–64); Juan Gonzales, "Forgotten Pages: Spanish-Language Newspapers in the Southwest" (pp. 50–51); and Félix Gutiérrez and Jorge Reina Schement, "Chicanos and the Media: A Bibliography of Selected Materials" (pp. 53–55). Pages 52–53 of the last article reproduce the first page of "Mas de cuatrocientos periódicos en español se han editado en los Estados Unidos," published in a 1938 issue of *La prensa* (San Antonio). Four hundred and fifty-one Spanish-language periodicals are listed in this special issue.

Sharon Murphy, *Other Voices: Black, Chicano and American Indian Press* (Pflaum/Standard, Dayton, Ohio, 1974, pp. 92–95) provides a list by state of "Chicano papers."

Guillermo Rojas, "Chicano/Raza Newspaper and Periodical Serials Listing," in *Hispania* (Vol. 58, 1975, pp. 851–863), provides data on approximately 150 newspapers and periodicals, the majority of which are in Spanish or in Spanish and English.

La Palabra (Vol. 2, No. 1, 1980) contains two articles of great interest. They are: Ernestina Eger, "Hacia una nueva bibliografía de revistas y periódicos chicanos" (pp. 67–75); and Yvonne Yarbro-Bejarano, "Reseña de revistas chicanas: problemas y tendencias" (pp. 76–85). Eger's notes occupy pages 72–75 and are quite comprehensive; they should be consulted by anyone interested in the Chicano press. Yarbro-Bejarano begins a discussion of Chicano periodicals. In this article she describes at length *Fuego de Aztlán, Vértice, Prisma, Maize*, and *Mango*.

Iliana L. Sonntag, Appendix 1: Selected and Annotated List of Chicano Periodicals, in the paper "Chicano Studies: Building a Core Collection" (Submitted for the Joint LASA–ALAS meeting, Indiana University, Bloomington, Ind., October 17–19, 1980, pp. 23–28 [LASA Panel S 122]), provides useful data on 27 periodicals published either in English, Spanish, or Spanish and English.

The introductory material to Francine Medeiros, "*La Opinión*, a Mexican Exile Newspaper: A Content Analysis of the First Years, 1926–1929," in *Aztlán* (Vol. 11, No. 1, 1980, pp. 65–87), provides interesting historical data concerning the Mexican-American press in the United States.

In two periods of the history of the United States there have arrived a great number of individuals from Cuba. During the 19th century many Cubans who desired to work toward Cuban independence from Spain went into exile either in Florida or New York. "Relación de periódicos cubanos editados en los Estados Unidos en el siglo xix existentes en la Biblioteca nacional," in *Revista de la Biblioteca nacional* (Vol. 1, No. 2, February 1950, pp. 51–58), lists 68 titles. *Impresos relativos a Cuba editados en los Estados Unidos de Norteamérica* (Publicaciones de la Biblioteca nacional, 1950, 350 pp.) provides data on 75 Cuban newspapers published in the United States. It includes works by Cubans in Spanish published in the United States. Both of these were published in Havana.

As a result of the overthrow of the Batista government by Fidel Castro, much of Cuba's upper and middle class went into exile. Those who came to the United States settled chiefly in Florida, New York, and New Jersey. Several publishing firms were established by Cuban emigrés in Miami. Among the bibliographies that deal with 20th-century Cuban-American publications are: Yara González and Matías Montes Huidobro, "Bibliografía de la poesia cubana en el exterior, 1959–1974," in *Final Report and Working Papers of the Twentieth Seminar on the Acquisition of Latin American Library Materials* (Austin, 1978, pp. 416–422); and Rosa Abella, "Bibliografía de la novela publicada en Cuba, y en el extranjero por cubanos, desde 1959 haste 1965," in *Revista iberoamericana* (Vol. 33, 1966, pp. 313–338).

California. Among the studies on early California imprints the following would be useful: Robert E. Cowan, *A Bibliography of the Spanish Press of California, 1833–1845* (San Francisco, 1919, 31 pp.); Robert E. Cowan, "The Spanish Press of California (1833–1844)," in *California Historic–Genealogical Society* (Publication No. 3, [1902], pp. 10–20); George L. Harding, "A Census of California Spanish Imprints, 1833–1845," in *California Historical Society Quarterly* (Vol. 12, 1933, pp. 125–136); Herbert Fahey, *Early Printing in California, from Its Beginning in the Mexican Territory to Statehood, Sept. 9, 1850* (Book Club of California, San Francisco, 1956, ix, 142 pp.); Robert Greenwood, *California Imprints, 1833–1862: A Bibliography*, compiled by Seiko June Suzuki and Marjorie Pulliam and the Historical Records Survey (Talisman Press, Los Gatos, 1961, xxxvi, 524 pp.); and Millicent Lawrence, *A Check List of California Non-Documentary Imprints, 1833–1855*, with Preface by Thelma Ziemer (American Imprints Inventory No. 31, Historical Records Survey, San Francisco, 1942, xvii, 109 leaves).

Florida. There are numerous individuals of Cuban origin in Florida, yet little seems to be available either about their publishing companies or their periodicals. The appearance of *El Miami-Herald* has been discussed in "*El Miami-Herald* Gets Big Welcome," in *Editor and Publisher* (Vol. 109, No. 32, August 7, 1976, p. 28).

Guam. Jim Richstad and Michael McMillan, *Mass Communication and Journalism in the Pacific Islands: A Bibliography* (p. 85) notes that the *Guam News Letter* appeared in both English and Spanish from 1909 to August 1911.

Louisiana. Raymond R. MacCurdy, "A Tentative Bibliography of the Spanish-Language Press in Louisiana," in *Americas* (Vol. 10, 1953–1954, pp. 307–339) and his *A History and Bibliography of Spanish-Language Newspapers and Magazines in Louisiana, 1808–1949* (University of New Mexico Press, Albuquerque, 1951, 43 pp.) are the chief sources for Spanish serials of Louisiana. The book lists "only commercial newspapers and magazines" (p. 7). Pages 7–33 provide a brief history of these newspapers and magazines, pages 34–40 are a bibliography of these publications, and pages 41–43 are the "Bibliography of Works Consulted."

New Mexico. The various bibliographies of New Mexican printing, while not, for the most part, specifically dealing with Spanish publications, do list them. The following studies are useful: Lester D. Condit, *Check List of New Mexico Imprints and Publications, 1784–1876*, Foreword by Sargent B. Child (American Imprints Inventory No. 25, Historical Records Survey, Lansing, Michigan, 1942, xiii, 115 pp.); Douglass C. McMurtrie, "The History of Early Printing in New Mexico, with a Bibliography of the Known Issues of the New Mexican Press, 1834–1860," in *New Mexico Historical Review* (Vol. 4, 1929, pp. 372–410) and his "Some Supplementary New Mexican Imprints, 1850–1860" (ibid., Vol. 7, 1932, pp. 165–175); Henry R. Wagner, "New Mexico Spanish Press" (ibid., Vol. 12, 1937, pp. 107–110); and Annabelle M. Oczon, "Bilingual and Spanish Language Newspapers in Territorial New Mexico" (ibid., Vol. 54, 1979, pp. 45–52).

McMurtrie's two articles describe 121 items, many of which are in Spanish.

Wagner describes 27 items published between 1834 and 1845.

Oczon provides valuable data of a historical nature concerning the territorial press in this state.

Pennsylvania. María Luisa Colón, "Impresos en español publicados en Filadelfia durante los años 1800 a 1835" (M.A. thesis, Catholic University of America, 1951, 74 leaves) lists and describes 133 publications. Its title is slightly misleading, for besides listing books and newspapers published in Spanish, it lists works translated from the Spanish into English and works in English that deal with Spain and Spanish America. Most of the "Preambulo histórico" (leaves 4–13) is an analysis of the types of material published in Philadelphia during this period.

South Carolina. James F. Shearer's "French and Spanish Works Published in Charleston, South Carolina" has already been commented upon (see the French section of this article).

Texas. Little seems to exist on Spanish imprints of Texas. Kathryn Garrett discusses "The First Newspaper of Texas: *Gaceta de Texas*," in *Southwestern Historical Quarterly* (Vol. 40, 1937, pp. 200–215; Vol. 41, 1938, pp. 21–27).

Joe Colunga III, "A Content Study of Spanish-Language Newspapers in Texas" (M.A. thesis, East Texas State, 1977, vii, 72 leaves) would seem to be the only study of any kind on the Spanish-language press in Texas.

SWEDISH

The earliest Swedish-American imprints were published in either 1700 or 1701. Andrew Rudman's hymnals, *Twenne Andelige Wisor* (Reiner Jansen, Philadelphia) and *Några Andeliga Wisor* (probably Reiner Jansen, n.p., n.d.), have been discussed in A. B. Carlson, "En svensk-amerikanisk raritet i Uppsala universitetsbibliotek," in *Nordisk tidskrift för bok-och biblioteksväsen* (Vol. 15, 1928, pp. 56–57); Ragner Dalberg, "Rara svensk-amerikanska tryckalster i Helsingfors universitetsbibliotek" (ibid., Vol. 1, 1914, pp. 41–43); and Arthur G. Renstrom, "The Earliest Swedish Imprints in the United States," in *Papers of the Bibliographical Society of America* (Vol. 39, 1945, pp. 181–191).

The fullest listing of Swedish-language publications of the United States is O. Fritiof Ander, *The Culture Heritage of the Swedish Immigrant: Selected References* (Augustana Library Publications No. 27, Augustana Book Concern, Rock Island, Ill., 1956, 191 pp.). It has 10 chapters. Those of most interest are: 1. Bibliography of Bibliographies; 5. Swedish Immigrants in American Life: General Contributions; 6. Church and Education; 7. Religion and Secular Literature; 8. Art, Music, and the Theater; and 9. Newspapers, Periodicals, and Annuals: Religious and Secular. Material may appear that is either in Swedish or English, published either in the United States or in Sweden. An index would have greatly improved the volume's usefulness. The bibliography of bibliographies contains references to studies on the Swedish-American press and Swedish-American literature.

Swedes in America, 1638–1938, edited by Adolph B. Benson and Naboth Hedin (Published for the Swedish American Tercentenary Association, Yale University Press, New Haven, 1938; reprinted Haskell House Publishers, New York, 1969) contains the following chapters of interest: Oliver A. Linder, "Newspapers" (pp. 181–190), "American Publications in Swedish, 1938" (pp. 189–190), and "Canadian Publications in Swedish" (p. 190); Joseph E. A. Alexis, "Writers in Swedish" (pp. 191–205); and Adolph B. Benson, "Magazines" (pp. 206–208).

The first bibliography of the Swedish-American press is Bernhard Lundstedt, *Svenska tidningar och tidskrifter utgifna inom och Nord-Amerikas Förenta Stater: Bibliografisk öfversight* (Kungliga biblioteket, Kongl. bibliotekets handlingar: 1885 No. 8, P. A. Norstedt & Söner, Stockholm, 1886, iv, 58 pp.), which lists 174 Swedish-American newspapers and magazines and 14 periodicals.

Augustana College of Rock Island, Illinois, has the finest collection in the United States of Swedish-American newspapers and periodicals. The following articles describe this collection and its microfilming: Ira O. Nothstein, "The Swedish-American Newspaper Collection at Augustana College, Rock Island, Illinois," in *The Swedish Pioneer Historical Quarterly* (Vol. 3, 1952, pp. 45–55); Ingrid Bergom Larsson, "Microfilming the Swedish American Press" (ibid., Vol. 19, 1968, pp. 32–36); and Lilly Setterdahl's "The Microfilming of Swedish-American Newspapers by the Augustana College Library" (ibid., Vol. 29, 1978, pp. 217–218).

Nothstein notes that as of 1952 this collection included 404 Swedish-American periodicals, 425 Swedish-American parish papers, etc., and "some 215 Scandinavian (mainly Swedish) covering the religious background, culture, and economic condition of the immigrants" (p. 55).

Larsson states that ". . . about 1910, it is estimated that 1,500 newspapers and different kinds of tracts were published in the Swedish language. Swedish newspapers were issued in thirty of the American states. . . . In 1938 the number had dwindled to thirty and today there are only seven left" (p. 32).

Hemlandet (Chicago) for May 19, 1897, celebrated its 2,000th weekly edition by publishing its own history, with a list of 61 Swedish papers and periodicals published between 1870 and 1897 that were no longer published.

J. Oscar Backlund, *A Century of the Swedish American Press* (Swedish American Newspaper Co., Chicago, 1952, 132 pp.) is a sometimes amusing account of the history of the Swedish newspapers and periodicals in the United States. This volume has sections on the religious and atheistic press as well as socialist, fraternal, and literary journals. Backlund devotes a brief chapter to women's publications and Swedish-American women journalists. Prior to publication in book form it appeared serially in the *American Swedish Monthly*. Gustavus Nelson Swan, *Swedish-American Literary Periodicals* (Augustana Historical Society Publication No. 6, Augustana Historical Society, Rock Island, 1936, 91 pp.) discusses the history and importance of two dozen literary periodicals.

E. Walfred Erickson, *Swedish-American Periodicals: A Selective and Descriptive Bibliography* (Scandinavians in America Series, Arno Press, New York, 1979, xiv, 144 pp.) provides subtitle, dates, publisher, editor, frequency, format, price, contents note, and library locations for 132 Swedish-American periodicals. An appendix gives briefer data on 175 periodicals.

Alfred Sönderström, "Svenska tigningar och tidskrifter utgifna Nord-Amerikas Forenta Stater och Canada," in *Blixter pa Tidnings Horisonten* (The Author, Warroad, Minn., 1910, pp. 16–53), is a brief history and a listing of Swedish-language periodicals and newspapers arranged by state and city.

The Swedish Pioneer Historical Quarterly has published Franklin D. Scott, "Literature of Periodicals of Protest of Swedish-America" (Vol. 16, 1965, pp. 193–215); and Michael Brook, "Radical Literature in Swedish America: A Narrative Survey" (Vol. 20, 1969, pp. 111–132).

Scott mentions many radical periodicals published in the United States and discusses several in great detail.

Brook notes that "The literature . . . described in this article is restricted almost entirely to books, pamphlets, newspapers and periodicals in Swedish, produced by individuals and organizations preaching the various kinds of anti-capitalist gospel to the Swedish-American and Swedish-Canadian public" (p. 11).

As of the mid-1970s H. Arnold Barton reported in his edition of *Letters from the Promised Land: Swedes in America, 1840–1914* (Published by the University of Minnesota Press, Minneapolis, for the Swedish Pioneer Historical Society, 1975, p. 324), that there were nine newspapers being published in Swedish in the United States and Canada. Barton provides title and place of publication.

Other studies on the Swedish-American press would include O. Fritiof Ander, *Swedish-American Political Newspapers*, subtitled A Guide to the Collection in the Royal Library, Stockholm, and the Augustana College Library, Rock Island (Almquist & Wiksell, Stockholm–Uppsala, 1936, 29 pp.); Gustav Andreen, "Den nuvarande svensk-amerikanska pressen," in *Prärieblomman* (Vol. 5, 1905, pp. 165–184); Oliver A. Linder, "Newspapers," in *Swedes in America*, compiled by Adolph B. Benson and Naboth Hedin (Yale University Press, New Haven, 1938, pp. 180–191); Ernst Teofil Skarstedt, "Den svensk-amerikanska pressen, literaturen och konsten," in his *Svensk-amerikanska folket i helg och söcken* (Björck & Börjesson, Stockholm, 1917, pp. 148 218); "Swedish American Press," in *American Swedish Handbook* ([Vol. 1], 1943, pp. 82–85; Vol. 2, 1945, pp. 105–109; Vol. 3, 1948, pp. 126–130); C. F. Peterson, "Bok- och tidnings pressen," in *Sverige i Amerika* (Royal Star Co., Chicago, 1898, pp. 94–144); Nicolay Grevstad, "The Scandinavian-American Press," in *The Minneapolis Tribune* (October 2, 1887, p. 17); and Edgar Swenson, "The Swedish American Press," in *American Swedish Monthly* (Vol. 42, No. 8, August 1948, pp. 6–7, 28–29).

Illinois. Illinois Swedish imprints have been studied by Henriette C. K. Naeseth, *The Swedish Theatre of Chicago 1868–1950* (Augustana Historical Publications No. 12, Augustana Historical Society and Augustana College Library, Rock Island, 1951, 390 pp.); Ernst Wilhelm Olson, in collaboration with Anders Schön and Martin J. Engbert, "Press and Literature," in *History of the Swedes in Illinois* (Engberg–Holmberg Publishing Co., Chicago, 1908; also Scandinavians in America Series, Arno, New York, 1979, pp. 760–842); and Ulf Beijbom, "A Swedish American Press Is Founded," in *Swedes in Chicago: A Demographic and Social Study of the 1846–1880 Immigration*, Translated from the Swedish by Donald Brown (Studia Historica Upsaliensia No. 38, Laromedelsforlaget, Stockholm, 1971, pp. 288–301).

Naeseth provides a useful bibliography of Chicago and Moline Swedish newspapers consulted as well as a helpful list of U.S. Swedish imprints, chiefly Swedish plays published in Chicago (pp. 345–358).

Much valuable information can be gleaned from Olson. He mentions and provides the history of various firms in Chicago that published books, pamphlets, tracts, magazines, and newspapers in Swedish.

Beijbom has written a bibliographic essay on the Swedish press in Chicago and nearby communities from 1846 to 1880. It contains a list of 22 papers published in Chicago from 1858 to 1880. Some are classified as church affiliated, others as "liberal." Table 81 is Swedish Newspapers in Chicago 1858–1880 (pp. 292–293).

Minnesota. The latest discussion of the Swedish press in Minnesota is Janet Nyberg, "The Swedish Immigrant Press in Minnesota" (M.A. thesis, University of Missouri, 1975, 112 leaves), which provides data on about 110 Swedish-language papers published in this state. She notes that it "examines the Swedish language newspapers established in Minnesota" (p. viii) and that its emphasis "is on the Swedish language newspapers in Minnesota—their number, their duration, their characteristics, and their demise" (p. xii).

Besides an introduction and bibliography, it is divided into: I. Swedish Emigration, II The Press, III. Religion and Political Influences before World War I, IV. Wartime Influences, and V. The Decline of Swedish Language Newspapers. Pages 104–112 are an appendix entitled "Swedish Language Newspapers in Minnesota."

Her "Swedish Language Newspapers in Minnesota," in *Perspectives on Swedish Immigration*, edited by Nils Hasselmo (Swedish Pioneer Historical Society, Chicago, and University of Minnesota, Duluth, 1978, pp. 244–255), is based on her master's thesis.

An earlier study is that of A. E. Strand, "The Swedish-American Press of Minnesota," in *A History of the Swedish-Americans of Minnesota* (Lewis Publishing Co., Chicago, 1910, Vol. 1, pp. 299–316).

"The Swedish-American Press," in *Viking* (Fremont, Neb.) (Vol. 1, No. 7, January 1907, pp. 4–5; No. 8, February 1907, pp. 2–3; No. 9, March 1907, pp. 1–4), deals with the Minneapolis Swedish press.

New York. Vilhelm Berger, *Svenska Tidningar i New York* (The Author, New York, 1929, 24 pp.) is a brief account of the New York Swedish press.

Pacific Coast. Sverre Arested is the author of two articles published in the *Pacific Northwest Quarterly*. They are: "Scandinavian-Language Newspapers" (Vol. 34, 1943, pp. 305–308) and "Bibliography on the Scandinavians of the Pacific Coast" (Vol. 36, 1945, pp. 269–279). The first article is a union list of Danish, Norwegian, and Swedish newspapers published on the west coast of the United States and Canada. The second article lists Scandinavian newspapers not included in the 1943 listing. He lists the files of Norwegian papers reported by Pacific Lutheran College, Norwegian newspapers listed in Martin Ulvestad's *Normandene i Amerika* not in the first article, and (p. 278) Swedish newspapers taken from studies on the Swedes in California and Washington which had been omitted from his earlier list.

Wisconsin. Tell G. Dahllöf, "Swedish Language Newspaper [sic] in Wisconsin," in *Swedish Pioneer History Quarterly* (Vol. 31, 1980, pp. 134–135), corrects several errors found in earlier treatments of the Swedish press in Wisconsin.

Margareta Hamrin, "A Study of Swedish Immigrant Children's Literature Published in the United States 1850–1920," in *Phaedrus* (Vol. 6, No. 1, 1979, pp. 71–78), examines "the role of literature for Swedish-American children and young adults in at first maintaining the native language and then later failing to maintain it."

Canada. Little work seems to have been done concerning Swedish publications in Canada. Attention is called to Ann Mari Borys, "Swedish-Canadian Periodical Publications: A Preliminary Check List," in *Canadian Ethnic Studies* (Vol. 2, 1970, pp. 191–192); and M. Brook and Alexander Malycky, "Swedish-Canadian Periodical Publications: First Supplement" (ibid., Vol. 5, 1973, pp. 263–267).

There are scattered references to the Swedish press of Vancouver in Irene Howard, *Vancouver's Svenskar* (Occasional Paper No. 1, Vancouver Historical Society, Vancouver, 1970, 127 pp.).

TAGALOG

Tagalog is the national language of the Philippines. However, most of the Filipino-American newspapers and periodicals are in English.

The earliest article on the Filipino press would seem to be that of Emory S. Bogardus, "The Filipino Press in the United States," in *Sociology and Social Research* (Vol. 18, 1934, pp. 582–585), which is partly based on Benicio Catapusan's M.A. thesis, "The Filipinos in Los Angeles" (University of Southern California, 1934).

Page 82 of Philip B. Whitney, "Forgotten Minority Filipinos in the United States," in *Bulletin of Bibliography and Magazine Notes* (Vol. 29, No. 3, 1972, pp. 73–83), is the fullest list of the Filipino press. This bibliography lists 52 items.

Donn U. Hart, "The Filipino-American Press in the United States: A Neglected Resource," in *Journalism Quarterly* (Vol. 54, 1977, pp. 135–139), discovered that as of 1976 there were 28 Filipino-American and Filipino-Canadian publications. He states that "all these publications are in English but a few have Tagalog . . . features" (p. 136). This article is a content analysis of the current Filipino press in the United States and Canada, rather than a bibliography. Hart notes that Northern Illinois University is collecting such publications and will provide a list of its holdings in this field on request.

Hart is also the author of "American Filipiniana: Current Filipino-American Serial Publications in the United States," in *Southeast Asia* (Vol. 2, 1972, pp. 531–533).

Shiro Saito, "Appendix D: Filipino Newspapers and Periodicals Published in Hawaii Located in the Hawaiian Collection, University of Hawaii Library," in *Filipinos Overseas: A Bibliography* (Center for Migration Studies, [Staten Island, N.Y.], 1977, pp. 139–141), unfortunately does not indicate the language of the almost two dozen titles listed.

THAI

Almost nothing seems to have been written on the Thai-language press in the United States. "California Editor Stable after Shooting," in *Editor and Publisher* (Vol. 114, No. 7, February 14, 1981, p. 28), mentions *Sereechan* as "Southern California's largest Thai-language newspaper."

No Thai-language newspapers are listed in *'80 Ayer Directory of Publications.*

TONGAN

"Tri-Lingual Newspapers," in *Pacific Islands Communications Newsletter* (Vol. 4, No. 1, August 1973, p. 4), is a brief article on the *Samoa News* which began publishing articles in Tongan in February 1973.

UKRAINIAN

The best current guide to Ukrainian serial publications in the United States and Canada is compiled by Alexander Fedynskyj and published in Cleveland by the Ukrainian Museum Archives in Cleveland, Inc. The title page is in Ukrainian. The English titles are taken from the copyright pages. Volumes 11–14 and 18–19 of the series, which has the same name as the publisher, are as follows: *Bibliographical Index of Ukrainian Periodicals Outside Ukraine for 1966* (1967, 76 pp.), *Bibliographic Index . . . for 1967* (1968, 56 pp.), *Bibliographical Index . . . for 1968–1969* (1970, 64 pp.), *Bibliographical Index . . . for 1970–1971* (1972, 80 pp.), *Bibliographical Index . . . for 1972–1974* (1975, 84 pp.), and *Bibliographical Index . . . for 1975–1978* (1979, 88 pp.).

Wolodymyr Doroshenko, "Ukrainian Press in the U.S.A.," in *Guide to Ukrainian-American Institutions, Professionals and Business*, compiled and edited by Vasyl Weresh (Carpathian Star Publishing Co., New York, 1955, pp. 181–190), provides a classified list of the Ukrainian-American press as of the early 1950s. Data are provided on 160 titles: 116 in Ukrainian and 44 in English. Of these, 83 were printed and 77 mimeographed.

An early history of the Ukrainian press in the United States is found in Chapter VIII, "The Press," in Wasyl Halich, *Ukrainians in the United States* (University of Chicago Press, Chicago, 1937, pp. 111–124). It notes that many papers which were no longer published as of the late 1930s are discussed in Julian Batchinsky, *Ukrainska Immigracia* (Lwow, 1914, pp. 443–461).

The Ukrainian Bibliographical–Reference Center of Chicago has published two works by Roman Weres: *Directory of Ukrainian Publishing Houses, Periodicals, Bookstores, Libraries and Library Collections of Ukrainica in Diaspora* (Ukrainian Reference Series No. 2, 1976, 56 pp.) and *Bibliography of the Ukrainica Diaspori-ana Published in Years 1973, 1974, 1975* (Ukrainian Reference Series No. 3, 1977, 63 pp.). The title of the later appears also in Ukrainian on the title page.

Halyna Myroniuk and Maria Samilo compiled *Ukrainian American Collection* (IHRC Ethnic Collection No. 9, Immigration History Research Center, University of Minnesota, 1976, 13 pp.).

Canada. *Canadian Ethnic Studies* has published seven bibliographies of interest for the study of Ukrainian-Canadian publications. They are: Alexander Malycky's "Ukrainian-Canadian Periodical Publications: A Preliminary Check List" (Vol. 1, 1969, pp. 77–142), "Ukrainian-Canadian . . . First Supplement" (Vol. 2, 1970, pp. 195–203), and "Ukrainian-Canadian . . . Second Supplement" (Vol. 5, 1973, pp. 275–292); Elaine Verchomin Haraymiw and Alexander Malycky, "Ukrainian-Canadian Creative Literature: Part I. General Studies" (Vol. 1, 1969, pp. 161–163); Malycky and Haraymiw, "A Preliminary . . . Part II. Specific Studies" (Vol. 2, 1970, pp. 229–244); Malycky, "Studies in Ukrainian-Canadian Creative Literature: Part II. General Studies: First Supplement" (Vol. 5, 1973, pp. 279–386); and O. L. Prokopiw and Malycky, "Imprints of Ukrainian-Canadian Creative Literature: First Supplement" (Vol. 5, 1973, pp. 365–378).

The *Canadian Ethnic Studies* has also published Alexander Royick, "Ukrainian Imprints of British Columbia: A Preliminary Checklist" (Vol. 5, No. 1–2, 1973, pp. 293–301); and Celestin N. Suchowersky, "Ukrainian Imprints of Edmonton, Alberta: A Preliminary Check List (Vol. 5, No. 1–2, 1973, pp. 303–340).

Also of value is Yar Slavutych, "Ukrainian Textbooks Published in Canada," in *Slavs in Canada* (Toronto) (Vol. 3, 1971, pp. 209–215).

J. B. Rudnyckyj is the compiler of two bibliographies published in the *Papers of the Bibliographical Society of Canada:* "Ukrainian Canadian Bibliography" (Vol. 1, 1962, pp. 44–48) and "A Bibliography of Ukrainian-Canadian Press Surveys" (Vol. 2, 1963, pp. 74–78).

The first article provides data on the history of Ukrainian-Canadian bibliography. Pages 46–47 provide a discussion of *Ukrainica Canadiana* for the period 1953 through 1961. Page 47 discusses some desiderata in the field.

The student of the Ukrainian-Canadian press will be particularly helped by the bibliographic sources for its study provided by the second article. It is divided into Surveys in English and Surveys in Ukrainian.

Studies of Ukrainian-Canadian press and literature are found in M. H. Marunchak, "The Press," in *The Ukrainian-Canadians: A History* (Ukrainian Free Academy of Sciences, Winnipeg, 1970, pp. 238–296, 470–498, 632–653); Paul Yuzyk, "The Press" and "Ukrainian Literature," in *The Ukrainian in Manitoba* (issued under the auspices of the Historical and Scientific Society of Manitoba by the University of Toronto Press, Toronto, 1953, pp. 113–126, 137–143); and Panylo Lobay, "Ukrainian Press in Canada," translated and revised by Olenka Negrych in Ol'ha Woycenko, *The Ukrainians in Canada* (Canada Ethnica No. 4, Trident Press, Ottawa and Winnipeg, 1967, pp. 223–238).

Lobay lists 205 titles published between 1910 and the mid-1960s. It is an update of Lobay's bibliography published in the *Jubilee Almanac to Commemorate the Fiftieth Anniversary of Ukrainian Voice, 1910–1960* (Winnipeg, 1960, pp. 130–140).

The Faculty of Arts of the University of Ottawa has accepted the following M.A. theses on the Ukrainian-Canadian press: Mykhailo Borowyk, "The Ukrainian Press in Eastern Canada" (1960, 174 leaves); and Brother Isidore, F.S.C., "The Ukrainian Catholic Press in Canada" (1959, 126 leaves).

Christine L. Wymar, "Ukrainian Children's Literature in North America," in *Phaedrus* (Vol. 6, No. 1, 1979, pp. 6–21), "attempts to describe current status of Ukrainian children's literature in North America in its broadest terms and to describe its origins. Included are Ukrainian language fiction, stories, poems, legends, and national tales and non-fiction books for children to about age 14" (p. 6). Language instruction material is also included.

VIETNAMESE

The Vietnamese in the United States have established numerous newspapers, periodicals, and newsletters published in Vietnamese or Vietnamese–English. To date, few individuals have tried to list these publications. Ten items are listed in the *Standard Education Almanac 1977–1978* (Marquis Academic Media, Chicago, 1979, p. 387).

"Vietnamese Refugees Start a Daily with Gannett Aid," in *Editor and Publisher* (Vol. 108, No. 21, May 24, 1975, p. 20), notes the establishment of the bilingual *Chan Troi Moi*.

WELSH

Edward George Hartman, "Welsh-American Journalism and Printing," in *Americans from Wales* (Christopher Publishing House, Boston, 1967, pp. 137–138), is based on Bob Owen, "Welsh American Newspapers and Periodicals," in *Journal of the National Library of Wales* (Vol. 6, 1949–1950, pp. 373–384); Idewal Lewis, "Welsh Newspapers and Journals in the United States" (ibid., Vol. 2, Summer 1942, pp. 124–130); Henry Blackwell, "Printers of Books in Welsh in the United States," in *Cambrian Gleanings* (Vol. 1, May 1914, pp. 65–69); and Richard H. Costa,"Utica Is Home of Only Welsh Language Paper," in *Y Drych* (Vol. 105, December 15, 1956, pp. 9, 15).

Henry Blackwell, *A Bibliography of Welsh Americana* (2nd ed., National Library of Wales, Aberystwyth, 1977, ix, 126 pp.) is a revision of a work with the same title, by the same author and publisher (Supplement Series 3, No. 1, 1942, vii, 92 pp.).

Lewis provides many pertinent data on 33 journals and 11 newspapers published either in Welsh or by the Welsh in the United States. He provides information concerning each item's full title, place of publication, publisher, and editor as well as its publication history. The majority of the Welsh journals were religious in nature.

Owen provides brief historical sketches of 56 newspapers and periodicals.

Conclusion

Much has been done to catalog and describe the many non-English-language imprints of the United States and the non-English- and non-French-language imprints of Canada. Much still needs to be done, and it is to be hoped that scholars interested in bibliography, journalism, and ethnic groups will be constantly working to fill the numerous gaps in our knowledge. The longer such projects are delayed, the more impossible their completion becomes.

HENSLEY C. WOODBRIDGE
With the research assistance of Jane Larkin